The Lost World of the Impressionists

The Lost World of the Impressionists

Alice Bellony-Rewald

Photographic Consultant and Documentator
Robert Gordon

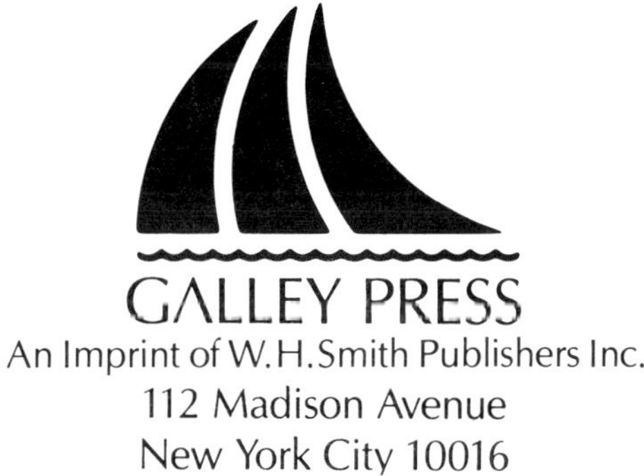

GALLEY PRESS
An Imprint of W. H. Smith Publishers Inc.
112 Madison Avenue
New York City 10016

Published by Galley Press
An imprint of W.H. Smith Publishers Inc.
112 Madison Avenue
New York, New York 10016

Manufactured in Hong Kong
Printed and bound by Mandarin Publishers Ltd
Edited by Esther Jagger
Designed by Gerald Cinamon
1 2 3 4 5 6 7 8 9 10

ISBN 0-8317-9521-2

Contents

I would like to express my thanks to Mr François Daulte, Mr and Mrs Denis Rouart, Mr Robert Schmit, Mr Rodolphe Walter and Mr Daniel Wildenstein for giving me information and documents; to Mr Peter Graham for his translation; and to Mr Michael Peppiatt for his invaluable assistance at all stages in the preparation of this book.

Introduction

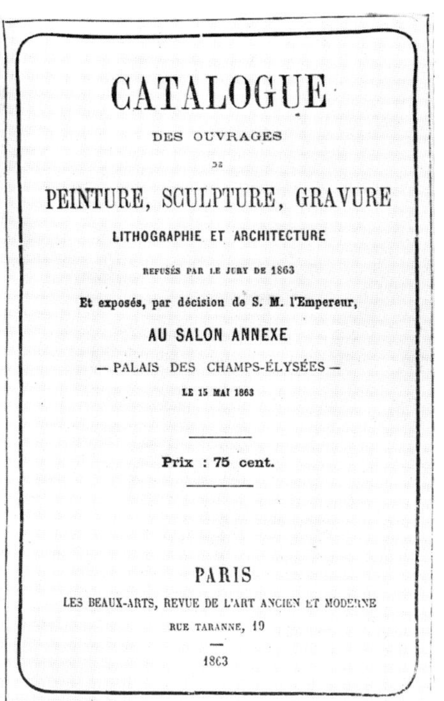
CATALOGUE
DES OUVRAGES
DE
PEINTURE, SCULPTURE, GRAVURE
LITHOGRAPHIE ET ARCHITECTURE
REFUSÉS PAR LE JURY DE 1863
Et exposés, par décision de S. M. l'Empereur,
AU SALON ANNEXE
— PALAIS DES CHAMPS-ÉLYSÉES —
LE 15 MAI 1863

Prix : 75 cent.

PARIS
LES BEAUX-ARTS, REVUE DE L'ART ANCIEN ET MODERNE
RUE TARANNE, 19
—
1863

In 1863, Emperor Napoleon III authorized the artists rejected by the jury of the Salon to show their works in a special room next to the official exhibition. This so-called Salon des Refusés met with public scorn and mockery.

On 15 April 1874, a body of artists sonorously entitled the Société Anonyme des Artistes Peintres, Sculpteurs et Graveurs held its first exhibition in Paris, at 35 Boulevard des Capucines, in the premises that the famous photographer Nadar had previously used as a studio. The pictures on show, by Pissarro, Degas, Cézanne, Sisley, Monet, Morisot, Renoir and a few guest artists, caused the public to react with appalled dismay.

A painting by Claude Monet entitled *Impression, Sunrise* gave Louis Leroy, a facetious critic, the idea of coining the word 'impressionist' to describe the group's new technique. The group, who were in search of their own identity, promptly adopted the term and thenceforth called themselves the 'Impressionists'. The extraordinary history of the movement, which marked the beginning of modern art, covers the twelve years that preceded, and the twelve that followed, this decisive exhibition; it also coincides with a particularly intense period in the history of France and of the world.

The stars in the Impressionist galaxy – Pissarro, Degas, Cézanne, Sisley, Monet, Berthe Morisot, Renoir, Manet and Bazille – who were all born between 1830 and 1841, spent their early childhood in a royalist, religious and rural France still heady with the last lingering emanations of Romanticism. Their adolescence was doubtless galvanized by the magic of new scientific inventions, such as the railways and photography. The enormous hopes pinned on such mechanical discoveries coincided wonderfully with the Impressionists' own prodigious vitality. And the important changes brought in by the Empire prepared them for all that was new and unusual.

The Impressionists, who identified so perfectly with their times, appear to modern eyes as the last of the great landscape painters. Scarcely had they had time to immortalize, with a few dashes of colour, the vision of Normandy's bracing beaches and their crinolines, the spotless sails of boats bobbing on the Seine, the vineyards of Argenteuil, and the open-air dancing in the centre of Paris, where horsedrawn traffic was still the rule, before that whole world vanished for ever. The landscape the Impressionists captured in their paintings was on the threshold of upheavals that were to change its appearance completely. A certain kind of undisturbed rural life was about to disappear, just as life in the capital was to become centred on the new notions of technological progress that were bringing about thoroughgoing changes at every level of the country's economic, social and cultural framework.

In 1862, when the youngest Impressionists were beginning their careers, art was in the hands of the state. According to an age-old tradition, the government regarded painting as an important element in the country's glory, and a reflection of national moral values. The Académie des Beaux-Arts (a section of the Institut de France) and the Comte de Nieuwerkerke,

Intendant aux Beaux-Arts (who was in charge of the national museums), made sure, through a subtle system of rewards and censorship, that French painting did not overstep certain narrow ethical and aesthetic bounds.

The Salon, a huge annual exhibition that provided painters with their only chance of making themselves known to the public, was characterized by a particular ritual aimed at protecting the cultural and moral tenets of the bourgeoisie. In April each year, France's 200,000 or so professional painters were invited to submit three of their works to a jury made up equally of Academicians chosen by the Intendant aux Beaux-Arts and of individuals elected by artists who had already exhibited at the Salon. This jury had to pick the works they thought worthy to be hung in the Palais de l'Industrie. Their already difficult task was complicated by pressures from all quarters: being accepted by the Salon was immensely important to every artist, and represented his only chance of communication, confirmation and, last but not least, the much hoped for commissions.

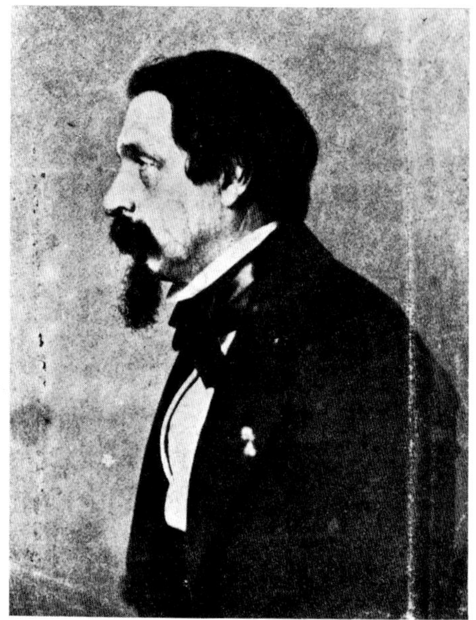

One of the earliest portraits of Prince Louis-Napoleon, when he was still only President of the Republic. The novel and still controversial technique of photography attracted members of high society into the sumptuous studios of the first famous photographers.

The jury's severity varied, depending on the year and on the political atmosphere. In 1863, so many artists were refused that the Emperor Napoleon III decided, as an exception, to arrange for their rejected works to be shown in a special room – called the Salon des Refusés – near the official gallery. It was there, in an atmosphere of scorn and sarcasm on the part of the general public, that Monet, Renoir, Sisley and Bazille, who were still too young to exhibit, saw works by Pissarro, Jongkind, Guillaumin and Cézanne, as well as Manet's *Le Déjeuner sur l'Herbe*, which caused a sensation.

The Salon was a highly fashionable event in the social calendar, and provided a perfect occasion for Parisian ladies and gentlemen to vie with each other in wit and elegance. Visitors to the show, who sometimes numbered more than 30,000, would shuffle slowly past the clutter of paintings that covered every inch of wall, the more serious amateurs among them attempting to detect a hint of the 'ideal beauty' sought after by the artists. Keenest interest was shown in historical subjects; then came religious or classical genre paintings, portraits, and lastly landscapes, which were long considered to form a minor branch of art.

Like all craftsmen at that time, the artists responsible for works shown at the Salon had undergone a long period of apprenticeship. They learnt their skills either at the Ecole des Beaux-Arts (like Renoir), where, according to Delacroix, teachers from the Institut taught 'beauty as though it were algebra', or else at the private studios of famous and influential painters: Degas chose Louis Lamothe, and Manet studied for six years with Thomas Couture, while Monet, Bazille, Renoir and Sisley were taught by Charles Gleyre, who enjoyed the reputation of a liberal.

A handful of very independent-minded artists preferred to eschew such opportunities and work without tuition: they copied works of their choice by the great masters in the Louvre, and practised their art at the Académie Charles Suisse, where in return for a modest fee they could obtain the models and equipment they needed. Pissarro and Cézanne, for instance, preferred this system. Berthe Morisot was fortunate enough to come into direct contact with the master of her choice, Corot, who provided her with a grounding in the art of painting. An already famous artist not only passed on his technical knowhow but was often in a position to influence his fellow members of the jury and get his pupils accepted at the Salon.

Artists at that time were forced to make a name for themselves without the benefit of financial and moral support from dealers. Private galleries were very thin on the ground, and only the father of Paul Durand-Ruel took an active interest in the painters who had gone out to Barbizon, near Fontainebleau, to paint landscapes. Shortly before the Franco-Prussian War,

In a society that was still rural and largely illiterate at the beginning of the nineteenth century, caricature was an ideal medium for communicating with and entertaining the French people as a whole.

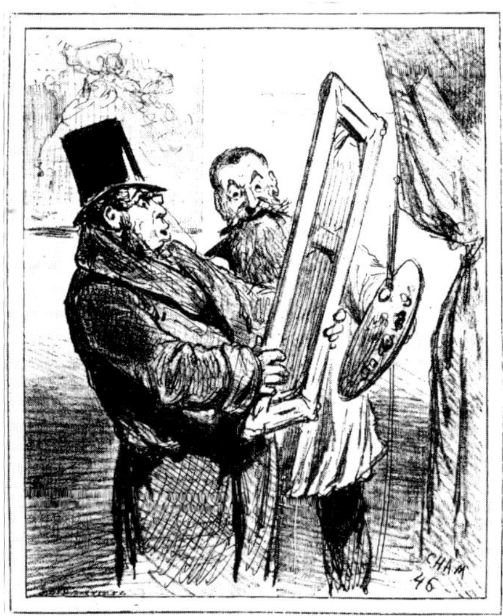

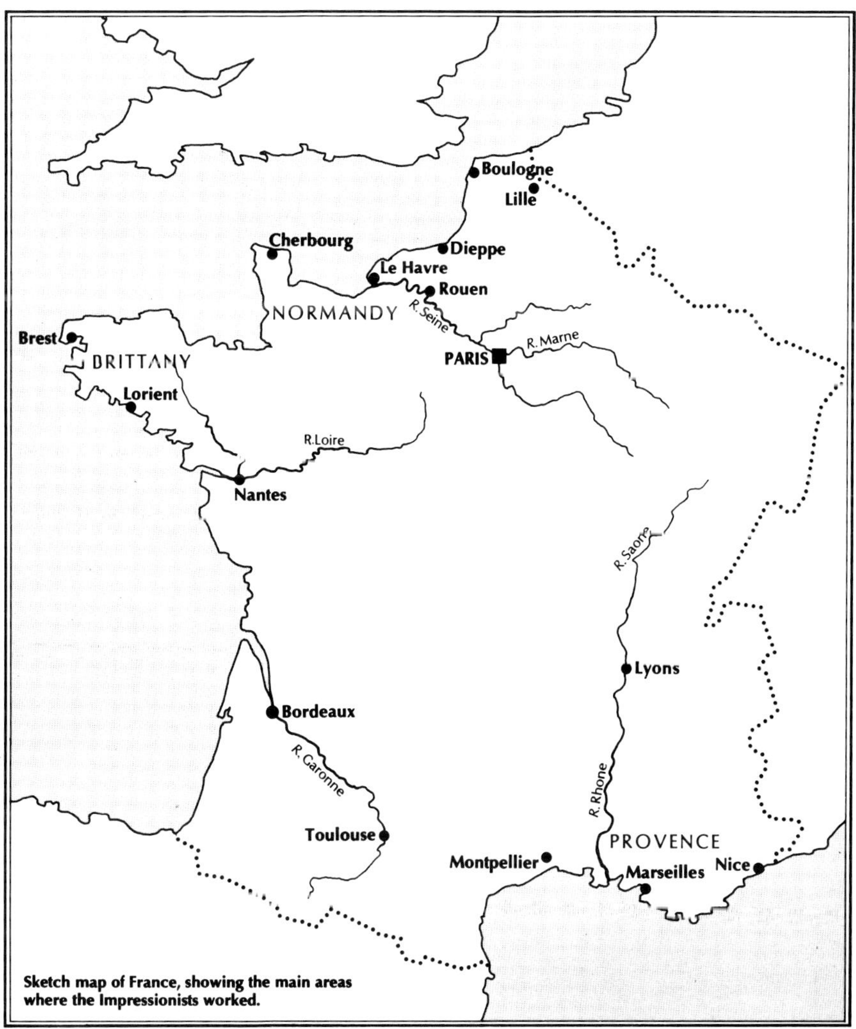

Sketch map of France, showing the main areas where the Impressionists worked.

Paul Durand-Ruel had begun to be attracted by the independents. But it was only during his exile in London that he made the acquaintance of Monet and Pissarro, and first bought their paintings. On his return to Paris Durand-Ruel became the Impressionists' regular dealer, supporter and friend.

Outside such official nurseries of talent, the budding painter could familiarize himself with the aesthetic preoccupations of the time in certain cafés much frequented by artists, who would meet over a glass of beer when it had become too dark to continue working in their studios. They never tired of debating the merits of great masters such as Ingres and Delacroix, whose influence was still strongly felt. At the Brasserie des Martyrs, in Montmartre, the *enfant terrible* of painting, Courbet, although still a noisy and staunch defender of realism, was beginning to be eased out by the representatives of the new wave of painters. The young independents were only too delighted to frequent writers such as Emile Zola, Duranty and occasionally the Goncourt brothers, and poets such as Baudelaire and Théophile Gautier, who supported their endeavours. The Café Guerbois on the Avenue de Clichy, and later the Nouvelle-Athènes, were also favourite haunts of the Impressionists and their entourage.

Within the space of a quarter-century, between 1862 and 1886, which had the Impressionists' first joint show as its pivot, not only was the course of art changed, but a certain world was lost forever. It is difficult nowadays to walk through one of the great collections of Impressionist paintings without feeling a certain envy of the robust love of life which they radiate. Their world was in very many ways more openly hard and unjust than ours. Yet time and again in their paintings comes the feeling that their attitudes to life and their quite exceptional vigour allowed them to respond above all to the pleasure that it brought.

This lost world of the Impressionists is also, of course, a geographical one. No one might suspect today that the Montmartre of their time was made up of leafy lanes, gardens and even farms – a whole universe away from the bright, bustling capital of which it is now part. Similarly, a present-day visitor to the gloomy suburb of Argenteuil would see no trace of its former glory as a centre for early vegetables and a delectable little white wine. It is this elusive world, at once so familiar and so far from our own, that this book sets out to recreate.

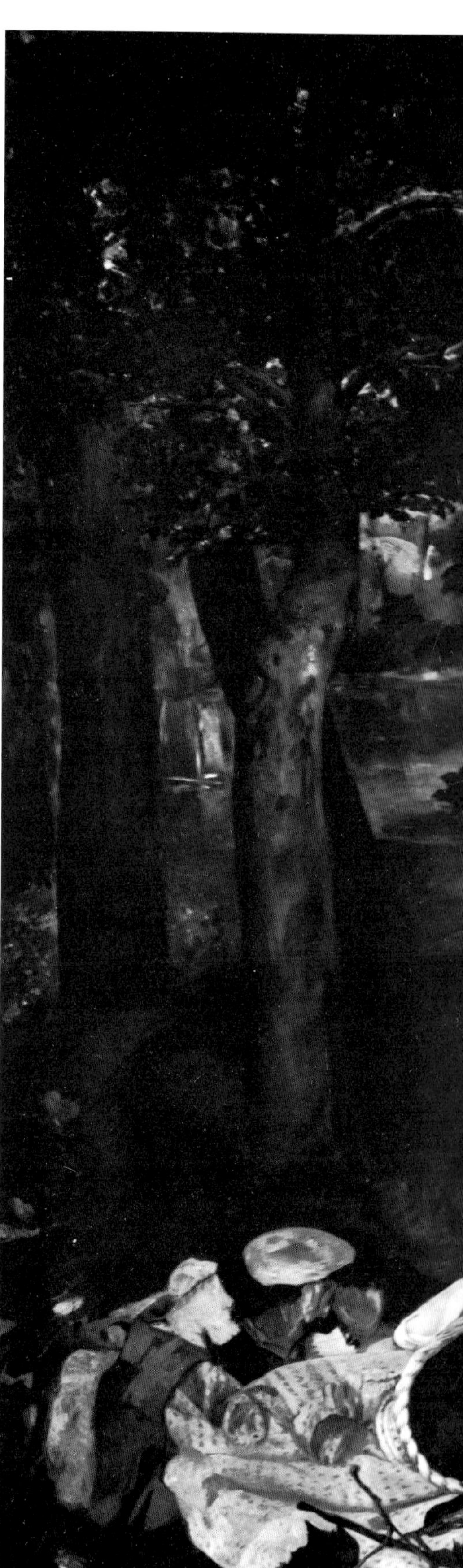

Edouard Manet: *Le Déjeuner sur l'Herbe*, 1863 (Musée du Louvre, Paris). This painting caused a scandal at the Salon des Refusés. 'With instinctive boldness, M. Manet has entered the domain of the impossible. I utterly refuse to follow him there'—Paul Mantz, a contemporary critic.

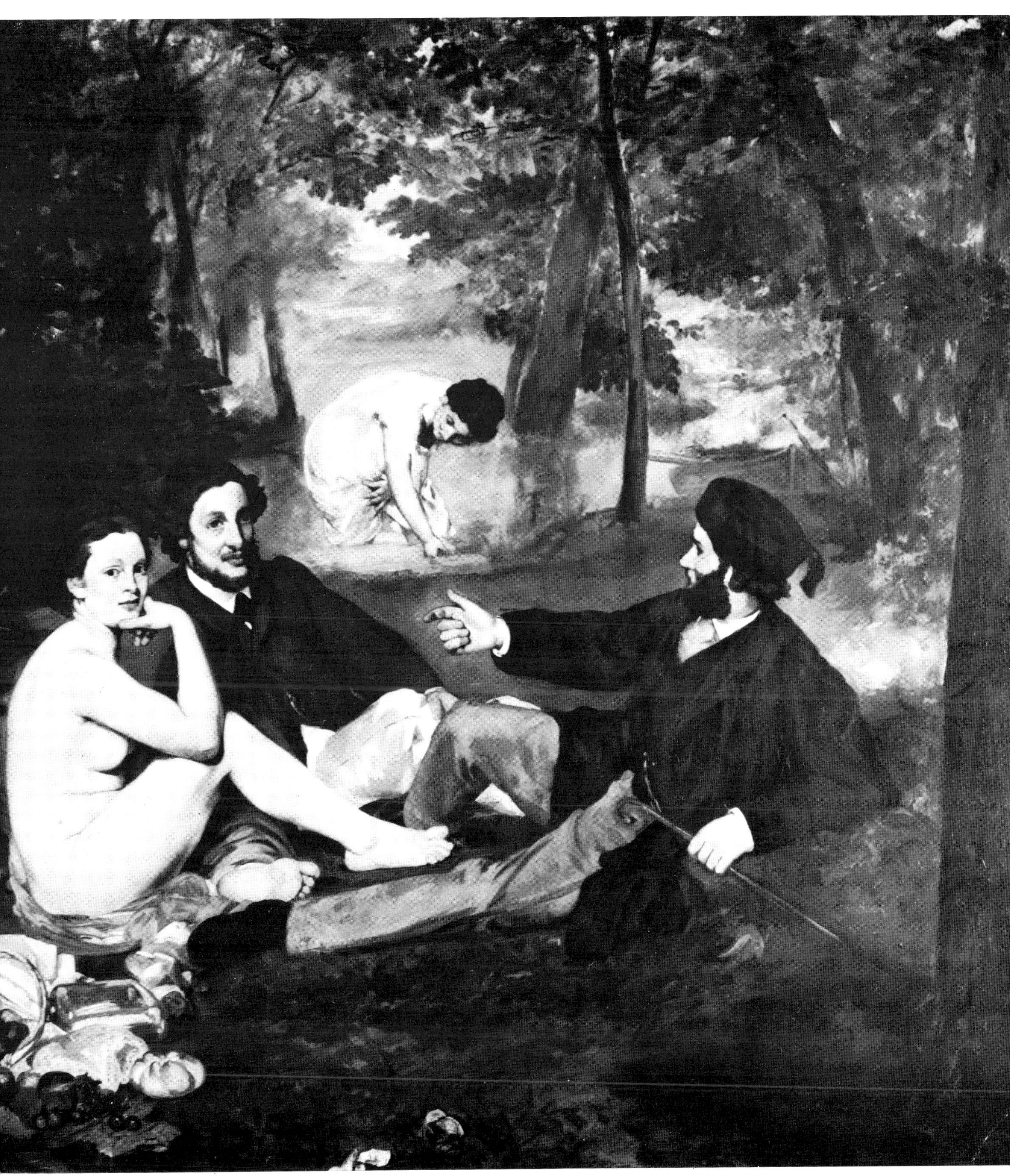

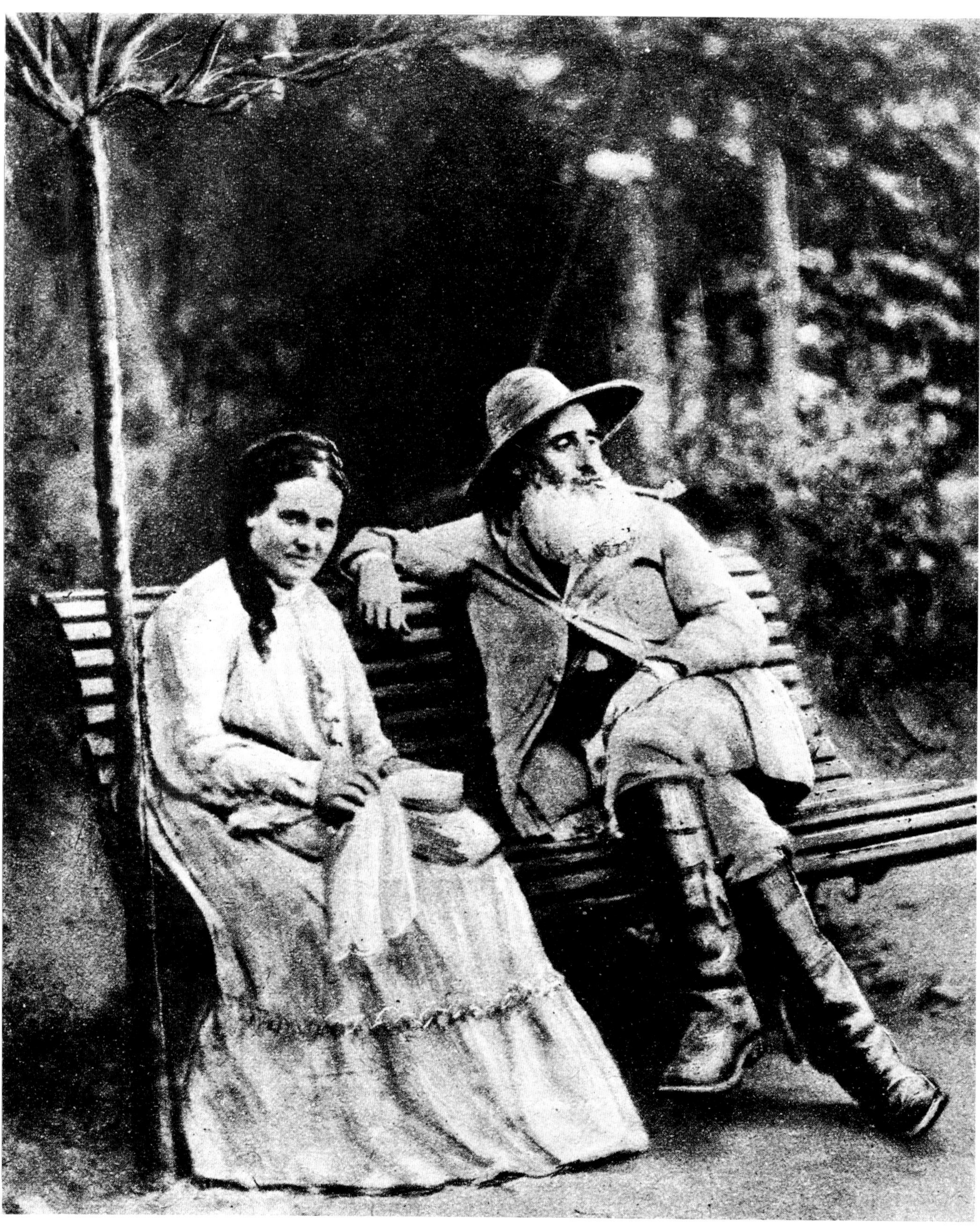

1 Beginnings and First Encounters

If the time had not been so ripe for revolt, it is unlikely that artists of such different temperaments and backgrounds as Degas and Renoir, or Cézanne and Manet, would ever have been able to join under a single banner. But the conditions imposed by the annual Salon were so oppressive and so hostile to any spark of real originality that the newness of their interests and their discontent with the existing situation turned out to be a persuasive rallying point.

But although they all shared an overriding desire to let some fresh light into the sombre conventionalism of officially acclaimed art, they clearly remained a group of determined individualists. Many of the reasons why they remained so essentially themselves even within the group are to be found, of course, in the conditions surrounding their birth and upbringing.

Camille Pissarro, who was in many ways the staunchest member of the Impressionist group, was born on 10 July 1830, at Charlotte-Amalie, the capital of Saint-Thomas, a small island forming part of the Danish Antilles. His father, Abraham Gabriel Pissarro, a Jew born in Bordeaux, and his mother, Rachel Manzano-Pomié, who was of Spanish origin, were provided with a very comfortable living by their export–import business. Abraham Pissarro wanted his son to have a French education, and accordingly sent him, at the age of twelve, to a boarding school near Paris. After leaving school at the age of seventeen, Pissarro went back to Saint-Thomas, already passionately interested in art. He worked conscientiously in the family business for five years, but spent all his spare time drawing and painting around the harbour and in the exotic surroundings of Charlotte-Amalie. Then one day he decided he had to make a break; he left his family an explanatory note of farewell and sailed for Venezuela with a Danish painter, Fritz Melbye, whom he had got to know down by the harbour.

After staying several months in Caracas, Camille Pissarro obtained his father's permission to devote himself entirely to painting, and returned to Paris in 1855. He arrived there in time to see the works of the English landscape painters, among them Bonington and Constable, which were being shown at the Paris World's Fair. Pissarro spent the next four years trying desperately to find some way of furthering his artistic education beyond what he had learnt at school and from Fritz Melbye. But he was completely put off by the few contacts he had with traditional teaching in the studios of Couture and Picot. He preferred to work on his own at the Académie Charles Suisse, the open studio by the Seine on the Quai des Orfèvres, and attempt to express his personal feelings as directly as he could. His natural inclinations and the strong impression that had been left on him by the English landscapists made him admire painters such as Daubigny, Courbet, Millet and Corot, who were still not officially recognized.

Painting was all that counted for Pissarro, who left his hard-working, thrifty and rather forbidding wife to deal with the problems of daily life.

Pissarro decided to follow the landscape painters he admired, and worked alone from nature. Early in the morning, he would leave the studio he shared with a friend in the Batignolles quarter of Paris, go through the Clichy gate and a few minutes later be in the village of Montmartre. He walked past fields and silent leafy gardens up to the top of the hill, where there was a view as far as the distant villages of Pontoise and Argenteuil. Pissarro would spend the day sketching and painting in the narrow, pretty streets of Montmartre. The young artist possessed an innate sense of observation and a natural gift for finding the outlines that would reflect his way of seeing things in the most direct manner possible. He occasionally ventured as far as the suburbs of Montmorency, or the lakes of Ville-d'Avray, where Corot lived. Pissarro made rapid progress, and in 1859 one of his works was accepted by the jury of the Salon.

The same year his parents settled in Paris and he was able, for a time, to enjoy a life of relative luxury with his family. But in 1863, it became inescapably clear that he was having an affair with their young maid, Julie Vellay, who was expecting his child. The 'misalliance' infuriated Gabriel Pissarro, who sent the couple packing and cut off his son without a penny. From then on, Camille and his mistress had great difficulty in making their way. The young couple settled at La Varenne-Saint-Hilaire, a village on the River Marne not far from Paris, where it was cheaper to live, and where there was an abundance of subjects. Pissarro continued to work alone on his painting without a teacher, although he stayed in touch with artistic circles in Paris.

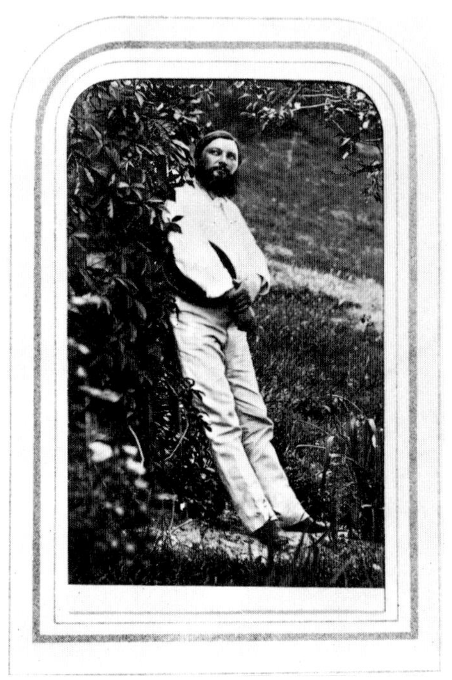

Gustave Courbet, *enfant terrible* of painting and champion of realism, was enthusiastic about photography from its very beginnings.

Edouard Manet had the very enviable distinction of being the first of the Impressionists to gain public recognition. He was born on 25 January 1832, in the smart Rue Bonaparte, beside Saint-Germain-des-Prés. His father was an unbending, punctilious and scrupulously honest man who had an important job in the Ministry of Justice. His mother, née Eugénie Fournier, was the god-daughter of Prince Napoleon, who was to become Emperor of France. She was a charming society woman who adored receptions and concerts. The Manets belonged to that class of senior civil servants who rose to the top of the social scale under the Second Empire and ended up by outshining the old nobility of the Faubourg Saint-Germain.

At school, the young Edouard was an absent-minded and frivolous pupil, who far preferred gymnastics and drawing to mathematics or Latin. Colonel Fournier, his uncle on his mother's side, encouraged his liking for art: he organized and financed drawing lessons for the young Manet and took him to see the royal collections on show in the Louvre. The paintings of Goya, El Greco, Velasquez and Zurbaran left a deep impression on the boy, who was to remain particularly fond of Spanish painting all his life.

In spite of his poor academic showing, Edouard was urged by his father Auguste (as were his younger brothers Eugène and Gustave) to take up a respectable career. To please him, he prepared to enter a naval college, but failed his first examination. He then served as a naval apprentice on a boat before retaking the examination. The boat, the *Le Havre et Guadeloupe*, took him and its cargo of Dutch cheeses to Rio de Janeiro.

After an uneventful crossing, Edouard Manet, then a charming and fun-loving seventeen-year-old, proved tremendously successful with the beautiful Brazilian women (if his companions are to be believed). The trip was not without its mishaps, however. During a walk in the jungle, he was bitten on the leg by a snake – an incident that was later to be partly responsible for his death.

On his return to Paris after the Revolution of 1848, the young man announced to his father that he intended to become a painter. Edouard Manet had spent much of his time drawing during the voyage (the boat's commanding officer had even called upon his talents as a colourist to touch up the rinds of the cheeses, which had faded as a result of too long a spell in the hold), and he was now quite convinced of his vocation. His father's anger and despair failed to make him change his mind.

Instead of entering the Beaux-Arts school, as his father suggested, Manet became a pupil of the famous official painter Thomas Couture, who was also an excellent teacher. He was to spend six stormy years in Couture's studio: the respect he felt for his teacher did not stop him flouting the preposterously old-fashioned traditions whereby professional models had to assume grotesquely unnatural poses. One day, for instance, Manet infuriated Couture and set all his fellow pupils laughing when he paid a nude model to put on modern clothes.

Corot painting outdoors.

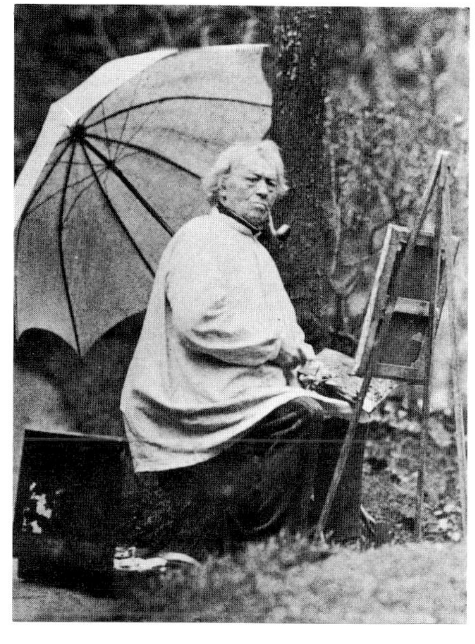

During his years of apprenticeship, Manet continued to live with his parents. In his mother's salon, he met not only his father's colleagues (highly-placed civil servants of the Empire), but the artists and musicians whose company his mother preferred. Two or three times a week, Manet attended the music lessons his mother was given by a young violinist, Suzanne Leenhoff, with whom he fell in love. They kept their liaison secret, and to avoid embarrassment Suzanne Leenhoff gave her mother's maiden name, Koëlla, to Léon, the son she bore Manet. When his father died in 1862, Manet married Suzanne and set up house with her, his mother and Léon on the Rue de Saint-Pétersbourg in the Europe area of Paris.

Edouard Manet exhibited two paintings at the Salon of 1861, *Portrait of His Parents* and *Spaniard Playing the Guitar*. The very personal, lively and contrasted style of the latter work, combined with its piquant and modern subject matter, produced an enthusiastic response both from young artists and from the most rigorous critics. The influential poet Théophile Gautier

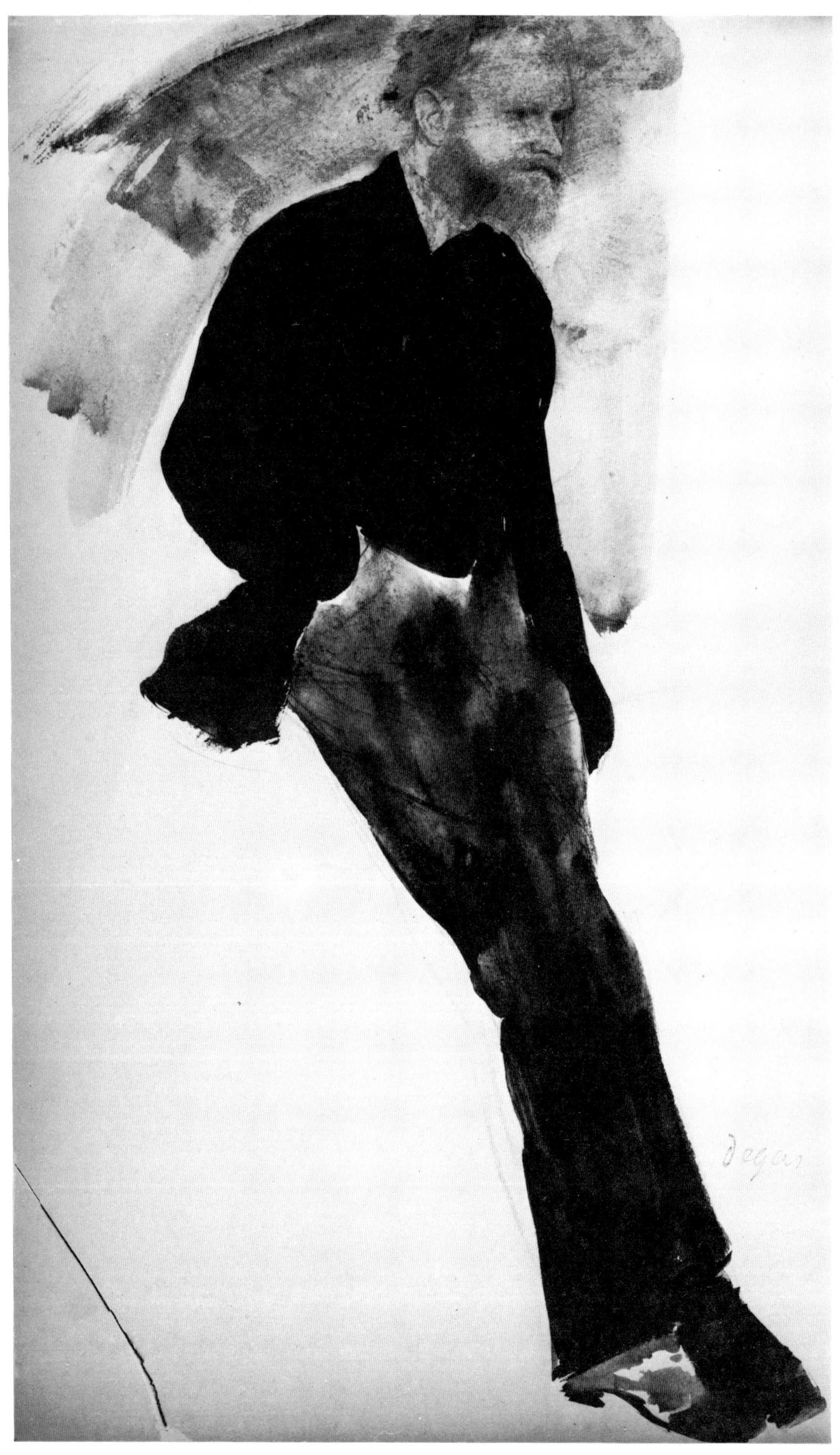
Degas

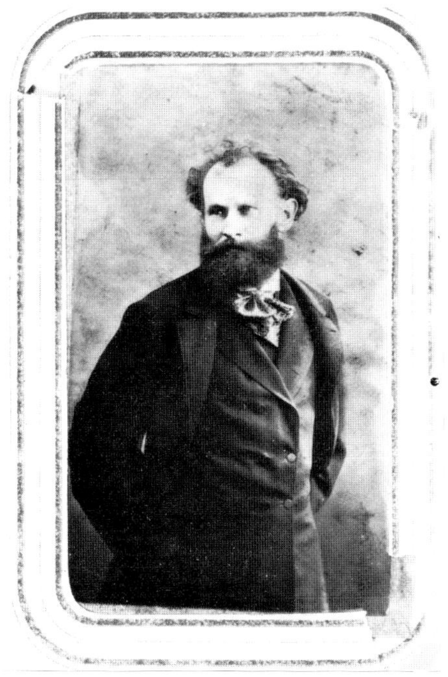

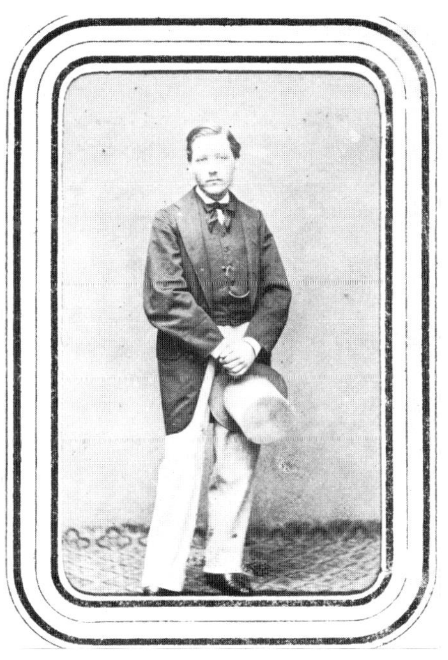

Degas and Manet, both of whom moved in fashionable Parisian circles, were close friends as young men. OPPOSITE Pencil and wash portrait of Manet by Degas (Rouart Collection, Paris). Photographs of Manet (ABOVE), and Degas (BELOW), both from their respective personal albums.

wrote of it: 'There is much talent in this natural figure, which is painted with a full, bold brush and very true colours.' When the Salon was over, Manet was visited by a delegation of young painters, who came to congratulate him at his studio. At the age of twenty-nine, he was considered to be the leader of the new school of realist painting.

By then, Manet had left Couture and was working alone in his studio or in the Louvre, where he spent much time studying the old masters. Henceforth he divided his time between painting and the demands of high society, which greatly appreciated his elegance and wit.

Both socially and artistically, Manet found his peer in Edgar Germain Hilaire Degas. Born in Paris on 19 July 1834, Degas' background was both noble and exotic. His father, Auguste de Gas, a banker in Naples and Paris, was descended from the Seigneurs de Bagnols, an old Languedoc family whose origins went back to the thirteenth century. His mother, Marie-Célestine, daughter of an important businessman, Germain Musson, was born in New Orleans.

As was only to be expected, Edgar Degas, the eldest of five children, was given an excellent and expensive education by his parents, who were cultured, sophisticated and very much aware of their social status. He was deeply affected, at the age of thirteen, by the death of his mother; at the time he was attending the Lycée Louis-le-Grand, the school where most members of the upper classes sent their sons. After his baccalauréat he began to read law, while at the same time satisfying his keen interest in art. He was taught engraving by a friend of the family, Prince Soutzo.

Shortly afterwards he decided to devote himself completely to art. In 1856, he entered the Beaux-Arts, where he decided to work under Louis Lamothe, himself a pupil of Ingres, whom Degas admired so much. He went on a trip to Italy, where he had relatives, and was much taken by the painters of the quattrocento. While staying in Florence with his aunt, Baroness Bellelli, he painted *Portrait of the Bellelli Family*, a work which, although clearly influenced by Ingres, reveals a remarkable gift for composition and colour. Degas spent much of his time drawing; he did numerous portraits of his father and brothers, and worked on some large historical canvases with a view to showing them at the Salon. *Young Spartans Practising Combat* was accepted by the jury in 1860, and *Semiramis Founding a City* the following year.

Like most artists of that period, Degas devoted a good deal of his time to copying masterpieces in the Louvre. One day, while he was engraving a copy directly on to a copper plate, he caught the attention of Manet, who introduced himself and congratulated him on his dexterity. The two artists quickly discovered that they had an enormous amount in common: they both loved the old masters, adored Parisian life, frequented the same salons and were interested in the same subjects. Manet, however, was more adventurous and already better known. He took Degas to the races and introduced him to his friends, young bohemian painters who used to meet in the cafés of Les Batignolles.

The most enigmatic and self-divided member of the future group was undoubtedly Paul Cézanne, born on 6 January 1839, in the Rue de l'Opéra in Aix-en-Provence. The bigoted bourgeois citizens of that sun-drenched little Provençal town, entrenched in crumbling palatial mansions, were jealously guarding their time-honoured traditions against the onslaught of a new and ambitious trading class. Paul's father, Louis-Auguste Cézanne, was one such enterprising businessman: after arriving from Italy without a penny, he proved to have such financial flair that within ten years an established banker by the name of Cabassol took him into partnership.

By 1844, Louis-Auguste Cézanne's fortune was considerable enough for him to decide to marry one of his former employees, Anne-Elisabeth-Honorine Aubert, who had already borne him a son. He also stood as a candidate for the town council – unsuccessfully though, as the chauvinistic inhabitants of Aix mistrusted this tight-fisted and somewhat uncouth foreigner.

Paul Cézanne went to school at the Collège Bourbon (which has since become the Lycée Mignet), where the fathers gave him a heavy diet of classics and mathematics; he won several prizes, including on one occasion an honourable mention for drawing. During a school break in the courtyard of the Collège, Cézanne stopped the others bullying a new pupil who had a clipped Parisian accent: his name was Emile Zola. The two boys discovered a strong, deep-seated affinity, and soon became inseparable friends. Zola had lost his father, who was an engineer, at a very early age; his mother had to make terrible sacrifices in order to keep him at the Lycée. As for Cézanne, although he loved his mother, he was terrified of his highly critical, authoritarian father. They both loved to escape their family milieu and create a world of their own: their close relationship isolated them from the mediocre world around them – they were free to give full rein to their imagination. They read the Romantic poets and dreamt of a glorious future as they walked through the countryside round Aix. The town, which nestles in a hollow, is surrounded by a breathtakingly wild landscape: the barren slopes of the Montagne Sainte-Victoire overlook land that was once the scene of the Saxons' defeat at the hands of the Romans. As they tramped along paths that were fragrant with thyme and winter savory, Cézanne and Zola made grandiose plans: Paul decided he would become a poet, and Emile that he would be a novelist.

'Illusions are my wet-nurse', wrote Cézanne (BELOW), at the age of about twenty, to his friend Emile Zola (OPPOSITE), a great defender of realism in painting and standard-bearer for the Naturalist writers.

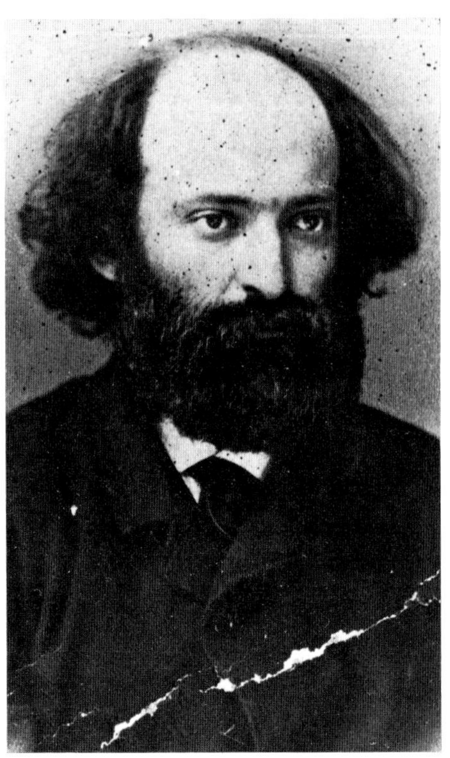

Cézanne felt completely at a loss when Zola left Aix for Paris in 1858. After half-heartedly completing his studies and taking his baccalauréat, he could not decide what to take up as a career. Aix was a town where the magistracy was powerful; Cézanne's father, whose philosophy was that 'with money you can eat; with genius, you die', insisted that his son read law. Paul got bored at the Law Faculty, and to cheer himself up took art lessons at the Académie of Aix. He dreamt vaguely of becoming a painter: 'I just thought to myself, we'd go to Paris, and I'd become an artist,' he wrote to Zola. 'I have been dreaming of pictures, a studio on the fourth floor, you and me, then we really would have had some fun.' Zola encouraged him to join him in the capital. But Cézanne was apathetic, anxious, shy and indecisive; and at home, he made life for his family quite unbearable by continually sulking.

The Cézannes were now living just outside Aix in the comfort of an old Provençal manor, the Jas de Bouffan, which was surrounded by extensive grounds and some magnificent plane trees. There, Paul installed a studio in the attic, but at the end of April 1861 his father finally gave in and accompanied him to Paris, where Paul promised to prepare for the entrance examination for the Ecole des Beaux-Arts.

From six in the morning until nine in the evening, Paul Cézanne drew and painted in the dusty Académie de Charles Suisse (where Pissarro and Monet were already working). But he was terribly depressed, not only because he had failed to renew his friendship with Zola but because the 125 francs (note: for a modern-day equivalent multiply by five) his father gave him each month scarcely covered his barest living expenses, and because in any case life in the capital did not at all agree with him. To crown everything, the scale of his artistic undertaking discouraged him, and he was convinced he had no talent. In September, his disappointment and despair got the better of him: he resigned himself to a lifetime in banking, and fled back to Aix.

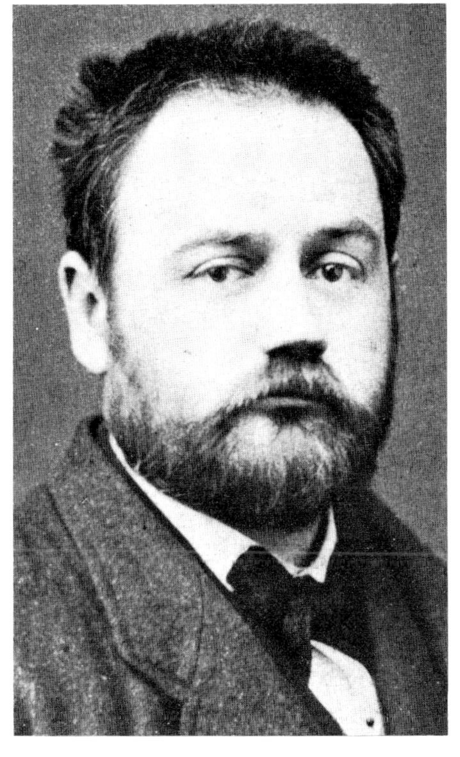

However, no sooner had he settled himself in his seat behind the counter of the Banque Cézanne & Cabassol than he began to dream of Paris and painting masterpieces. Nevertheless, his doubts vanished as the full horror of life in an office came home to him, and the future painter consigned his thoughts to his father's account books:

Cézanne le banquier ne voit pas sans frémir
Derrière son comptoir naître un peintre à venir.

(Cézanne the banker cannot behold without fright/Behind his counter a budding painter in sight.)

In the end Cézanne left his father's bank and took up painting again. One of his favourite spots was the delightful little village of Tholonet, a few kilometres from Aix, which he reached by foot along a rocky road at the foot of the Montagne Sainte-Victoire.

In November 1862, Cézanne returned to Paris, determined this time to stay there, enter the Beaux-Arts and become a painter. Even so, during the next thirty years he continued to travel back and forth between Paris and the South, submitting his paintings to the Salon every year.

Alfred Sisley, whose private life was the least eventful of all the Impressionists, was born in Paris on 30 October 1839. He was the second son of a well-to-do British family that had been living in France for many years. William Sisley, his father, owned a company which exported artificial flowers, chiefly to South America. His wife, Felicia Sell, was a cultured and very musical woman.

In 1857, when he was eighteen, Sisley was sent to England to become a businessman. But he spent more time in museums than in the office, where he admired Turner and Constable. Invoices, dockets and accounts, on the other hand, left him quite cold. Sisley returned to Paris in 1862. He managed to obtain permission to drop his business activities and try to become an artist. He enrolled right away at Charles Gleyre's studio to learn the basic skills.

Renoir and Sisley, who had met at Gleyre's studio, became inseparable friends. Sisley, a wealthy dilettante, often posed for his fellow painter. BELOW Photograph of Sisley. OPPOSITE Auguste Renoir: *Portrait of Claude Monet*, 1872 (Mr and Mrs Paul Mellon Collection, New York).

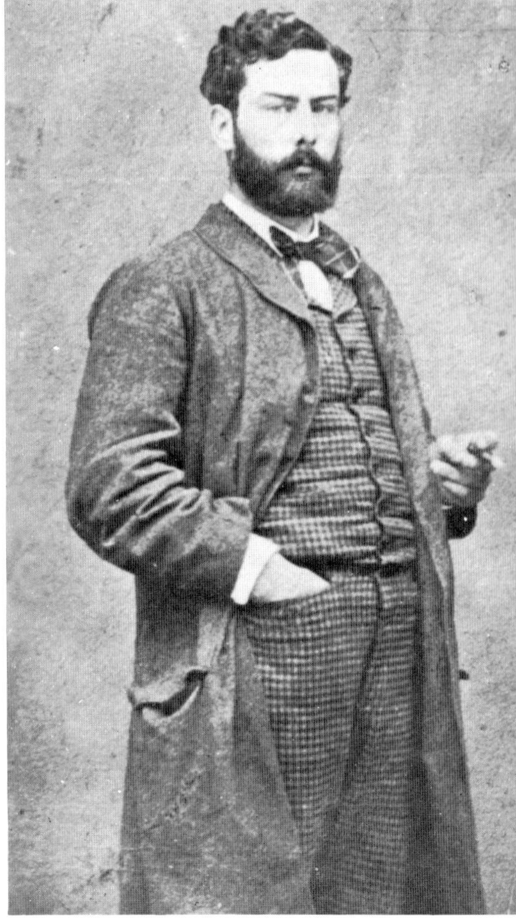

Enormously vigorous and self-confident, Claude Oscar Monet had none of Cézanne's nagging doubts. He was born on 14 November 1840, at 45 Rue Laffite, in Paris. His father, Adolphe Monet, who had been a sailor in his youth, was out of a job when Louise-Justine Aubrée bore him Claude, their second son. Four years later, Adolphe Monet moved with his family to Le Havre, where his half-sister, Marie-Jeanne Lecadre, asked him to manage her marine stores. The young Claude was fascinated by the spectacle of the harbour and its ships, and whenever he could he would slip out of school and stroll along the quayside or up the sidestreets, with their wealth of imported wares and other exotic treasures. He wandered through the surrounding countryside, or daydreamed on the beach. At school, he had no academic ambitions, and was liked by the other boys. But he did show a precocious talent for drawing – taught by François Orchard, a former pupil of David, who encouraged his pupil's natural abilities.

Claude's adolescence was a carefree time: often the house would be filled with the melodious sound of his mother singing – she possessed a quite exceptional voice. This happy period was brought to an abrupt end, however, when his mother died in 1857; Monet was then seventeen.

Unlike his brother Léon, Claude showed no aptitude for business. His school reports were disappointing, and his father thought him little better than a good-for-nothing. But Claude was fascinated by the art of caricature, and he spent hours poring over the page that every important newspaper would devote to the work of famous artists in that field (a considerable section of the public was illiterate and would buy the publication for its

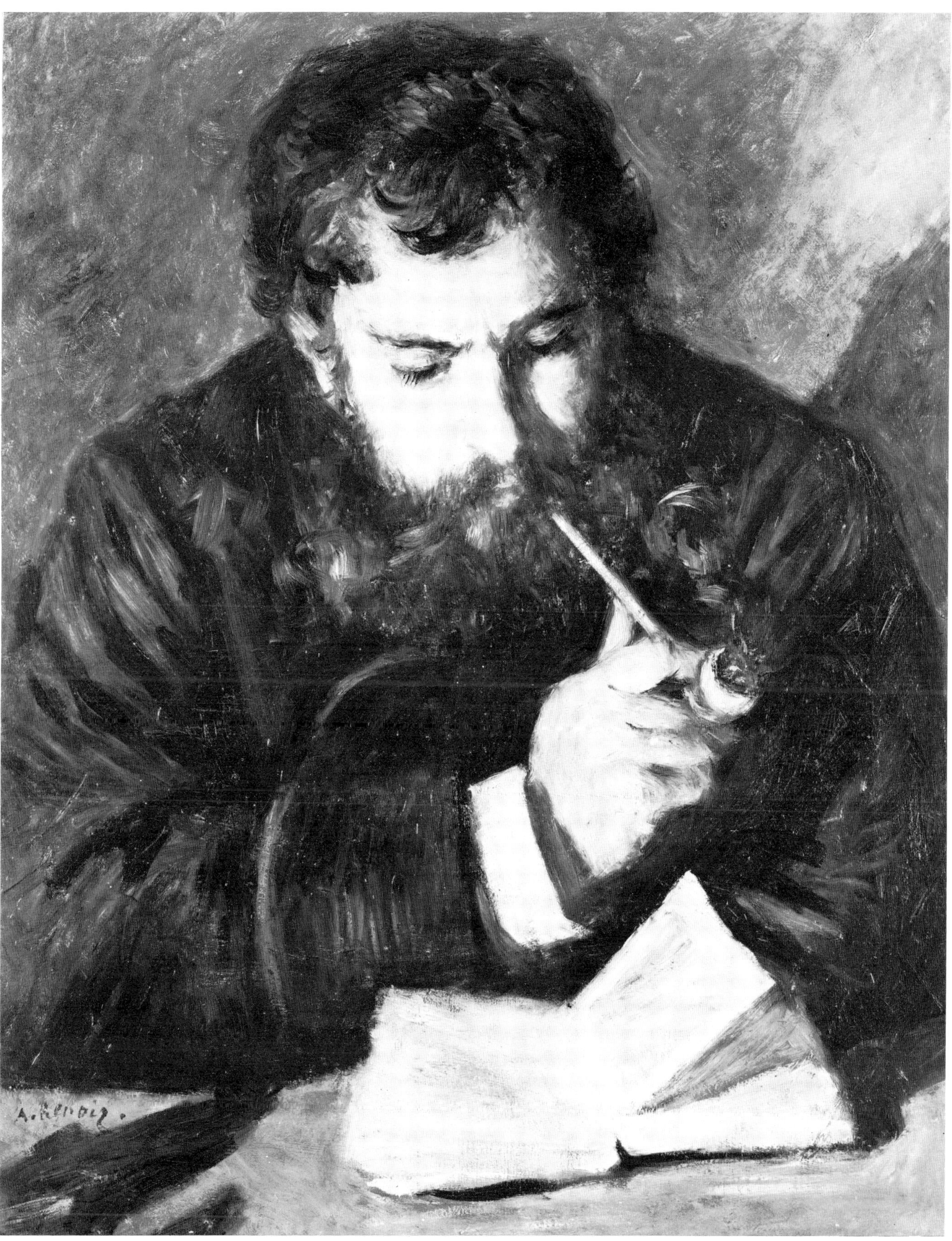

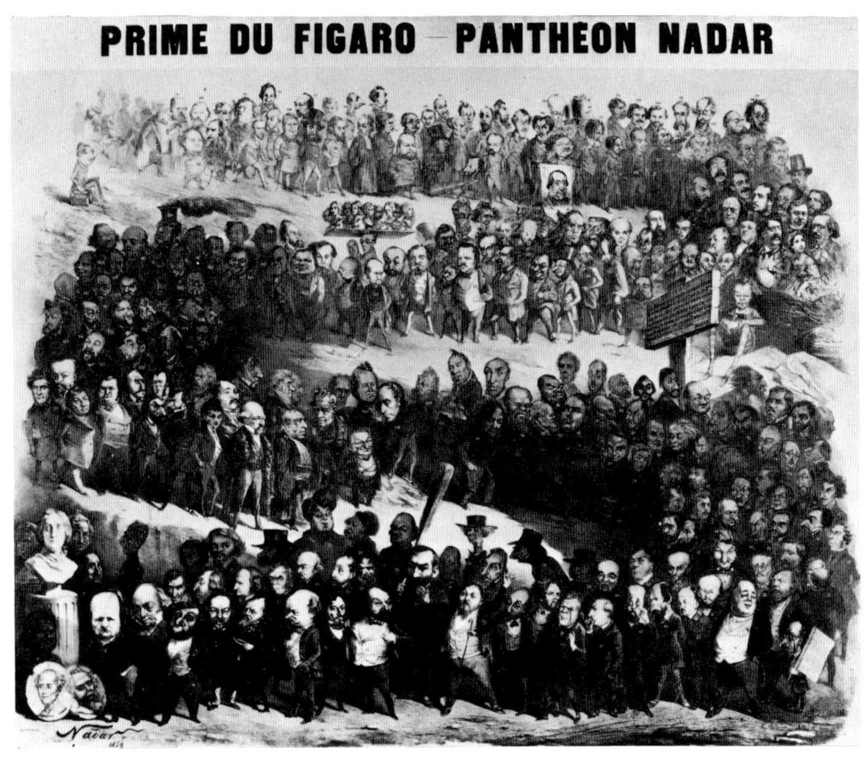

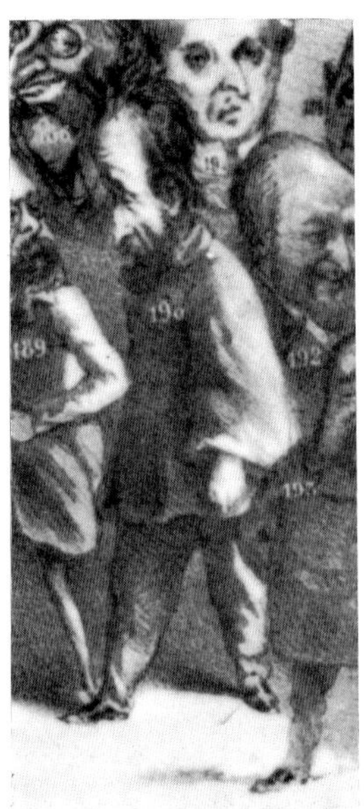

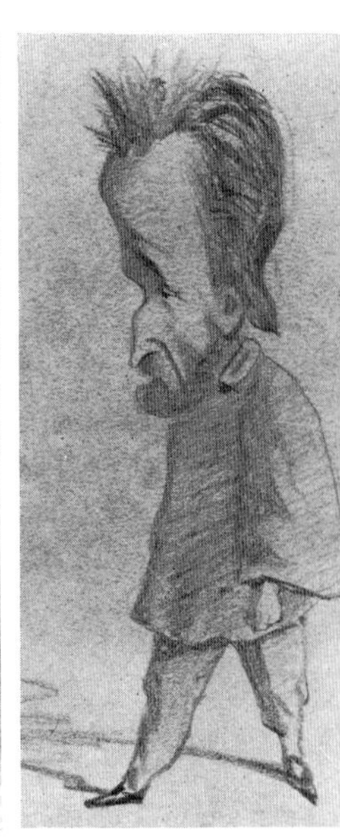

LEFT Nadar's caricature of famous Frenchmen. ABOVE Detail showing the journalist Théodore Pelloquet (LEFT), and the young Monet's copy of Nadar's caricature (RIGHT). BELOW Monet at the age of seventeen.

illustrations). Monet copied Nadar and others, and caught their style so accurately that his schoolfriends were soon clamouring for his caricatures. After school one day, he offered his drawings to the picture-framer in the Rue de Paris, who hung them in his window alongside some watercolours by a local painter, Eugène Boudin.

After working in Paris, Boudin had returned to Normandy to paint the landscapes he loved above all else. But this highly-gifted seascapist was not much appreciated by his fellow Normans. Even Claude Monet thought his pictures worthless daubs, and reacted rather snootily when Boudin complimented him on his own work. Nevertheless, it was Boudin who gave him the encouragement and advice he needed, and who urged him to go to Paris and learn drawing and painting there.

With the 2,000 francs he had got for his caricatures and a small allowance from his father, Claude Monet arrived in Paris in May 1859. His aunt, Madame Lecadre, had given him a letter of introduction to her friend the painter Amand Gautier, and Boudin recommended him to Troyon. In any case, Monet had certain immediate advantages: he was a good-looking young man of medium height, with a cheerful, resolute expression. He knew what he wanted and was bold enough to get it. It did not take him long to discover the Académie Charles Suisse, make several friends there, get down to work and familiarize himself with the major themes that were preoccupying artists at the time.

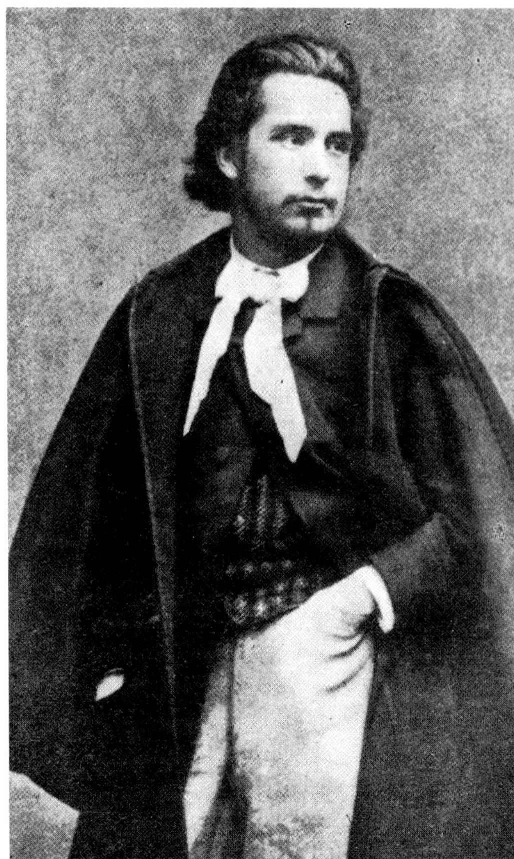

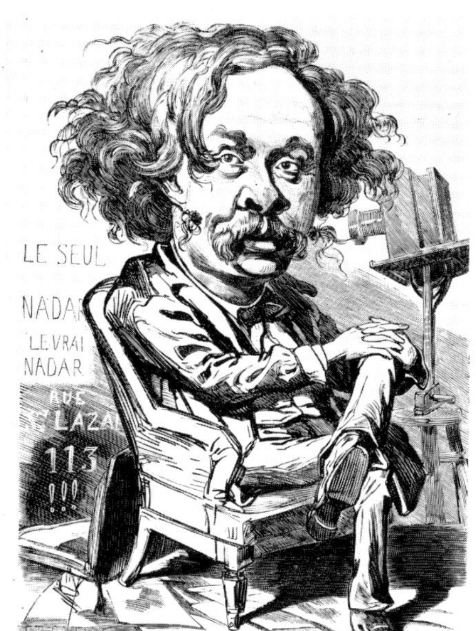

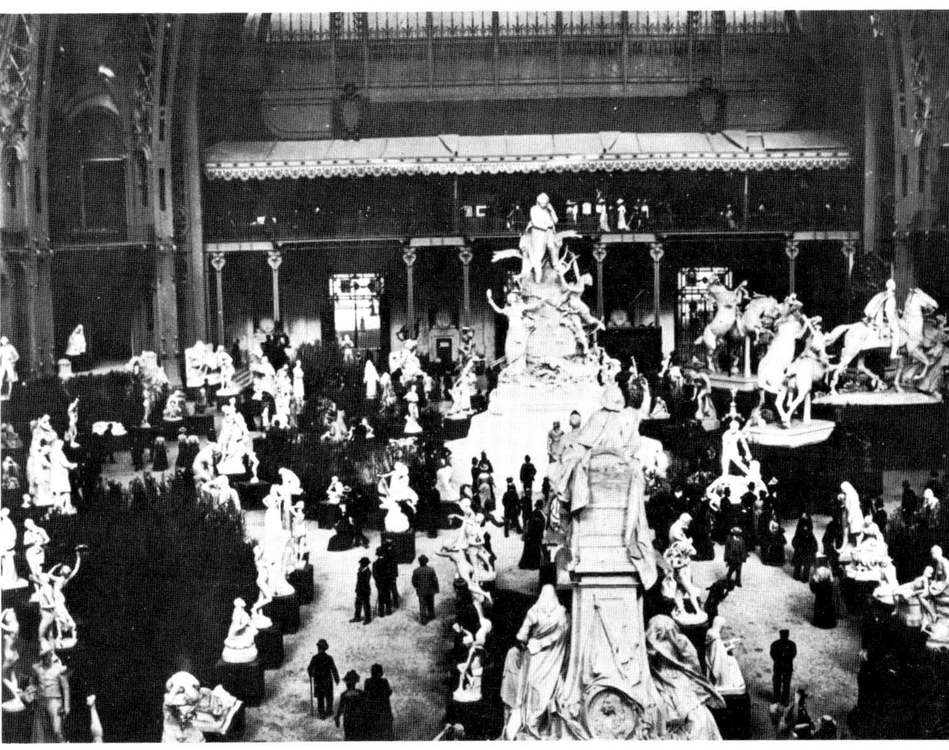

ABOVE Caricature of Nadar.
RIGHT Photograph by Emile Zola of the annual Salon de la Sculpture at the Palais de l'Industrie.

The big talking points among young painters were: the official Salon, where, because of the jury's bigoted traditionalism, it was so difficult to get shown, and where most of the painting was boring and conventional; photography, which had been exhibited for the first time as an art, like painting; and the realism of Courbet and Manet. Monet went to the Brasserie des Martyrs in Montmartre, where he could watch such already legendary figures as Courbet and Manet, accompanied by their friend Charles Baudelaire, dressed in black and made up with powder and red lipstick.

Monet's stay in Paris was also characterized by a problem that was to dog him throughout: he was a reckless spender and frequently got himself into debt. At the beginning of 1861, he suddenly had to leave Paris to do his military service. He had originally thought of getting his father to buy him out, but changed his mind as soon as he arrived in Le Havre: his father, who had been having an affair with a working-class girl of nineteen ever since he had been widowed, had just had a child by her. Probably prompted by jealousy, Claude decided it would be better for him to go away. He managed to get himself enrolled in the Chasseurs d'Afrique, a new corps that would enable him to visit the recent dominion of Algeria, a country that attracted many young people at the time.

Monet's spell in the army was brought to a premature end by a serious illness that required several months' convalescence, after which he was bought out by his aunt. As a result, in 1862, we again find the painter in front

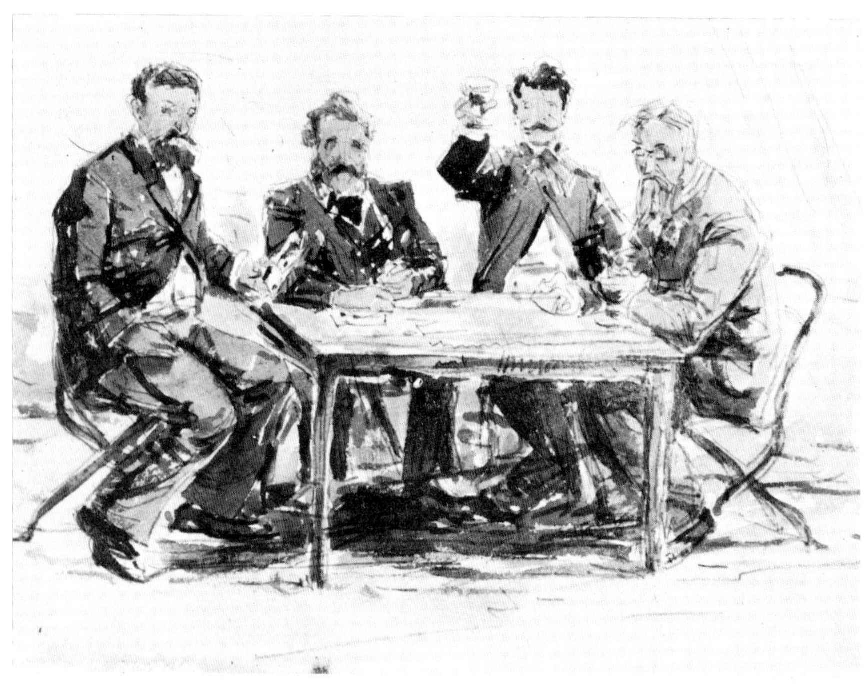

LEFT 'There are many of us at Honfleur at the moment . . . Boudin and Jongkind are here; we're getting on grandly', Monet wrote to Bazille, referring to their favourite retreat, the Saint-Siméon farm. Eugène Boudin: *At the Saint-Siméon Farm*, 1867 (Galerie Robert Schmit, Paris).
BELOW Berthe Morisot at the age of eighteen.
OPPOSITE Edouard Manet: *Portrait of Berthe Morisot*, 1872 (Rouart Collection, Paris). This is one of the last portraits Manet was to paint of the young woman who became his sister-in-law two years later.

of his easel in Normandy, working cheerfully throughout the summer with Boudin, or more often Jongkind, a talented landscape artist of Dutch origin, whose independent ideas suited Monet's temperament perfectly.

Early in 1863, Monet returned to Paris, this time convinced of his talent and determined, as he had promised his Aunt Lecadre and his father, to take lessons from one of the official teachers in the capital. Accordingly, he too enrolled at the studio of Charles Gleyre.

The only woman in the group, Berthe Morisot, not only held her own in a predominantly male world, but brought a distinct talent and a loyal temperament to it. She was born in Bourges, a prosperous town in the centre of France, on 14 January 1841. Her father, Tiburce Morisot, *préfet* of Bourges, had already passed his fortieth year when he seduced Marie-Cornélie Thomas, an exceptionally beautiful girl of sixteen. The couple, who adored each other, married and had two daughters, Yves and Edma, before Berthe.

Most of Berthe Morisot's childhood was spent in Limoges. She was aged fourteen when her father, out of loyalty to King Louis-Philippe, resigned from his post and settled in Paris. When he was appointed a Councillor of the Audit Office by the Emperor, Monsieur Morisot and his family took up residence on the Rue Franklin in the fashionable neighbourhood of Passy, in an attractive house surrounded by a large garden. The Morisot family was very well off, and the three girls were given an excellent education in a private school in Passy. Both Berthe and her sister Yves were fond of music,

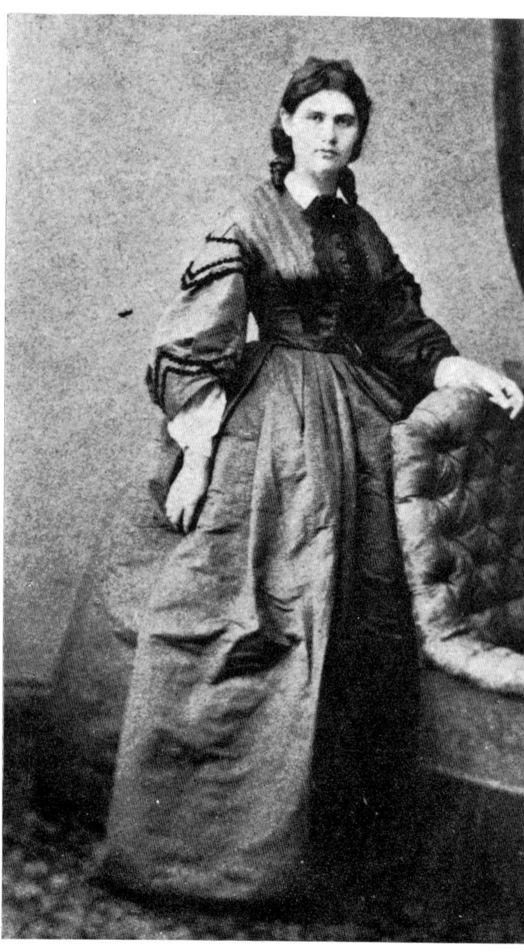

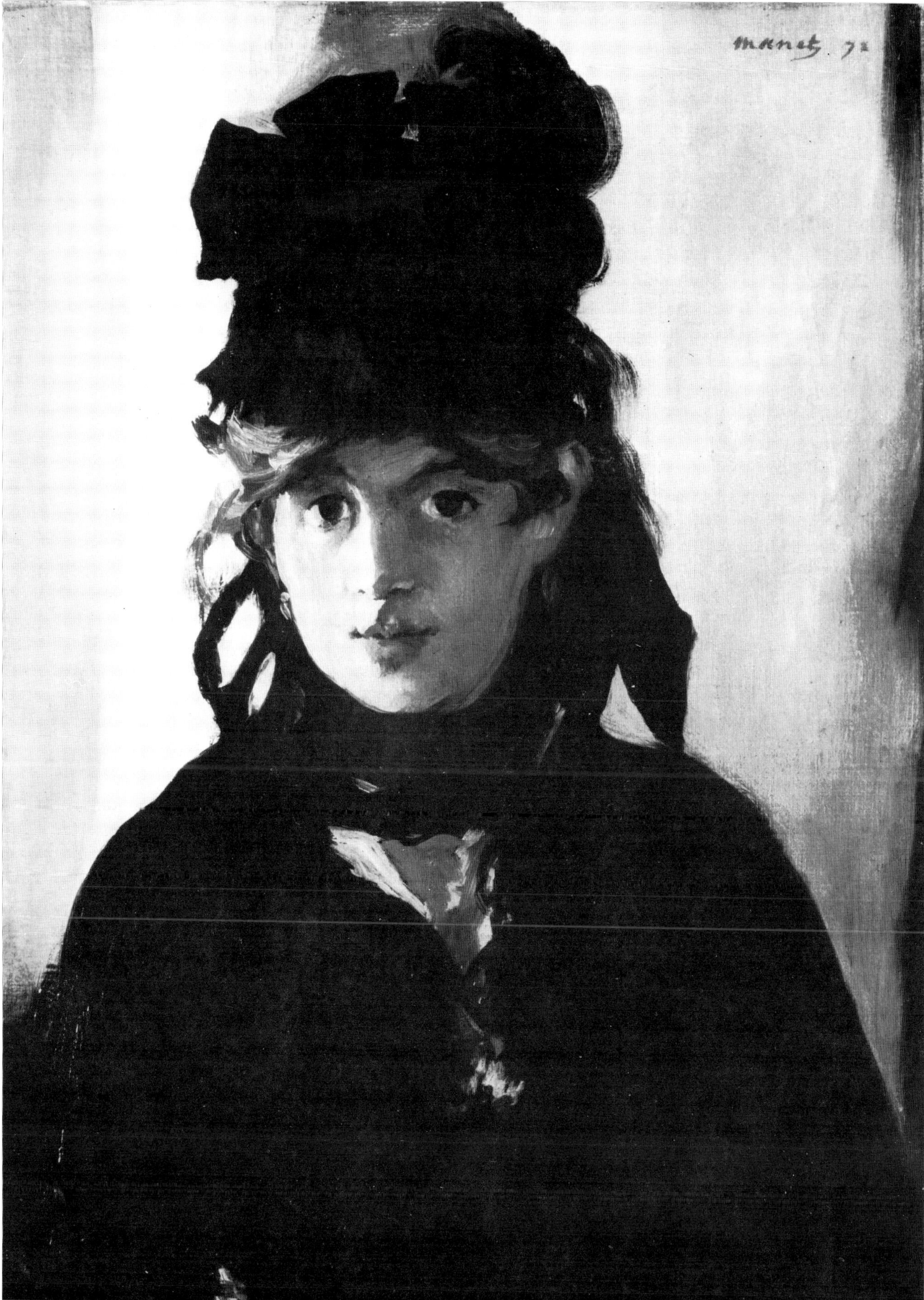
manet 72

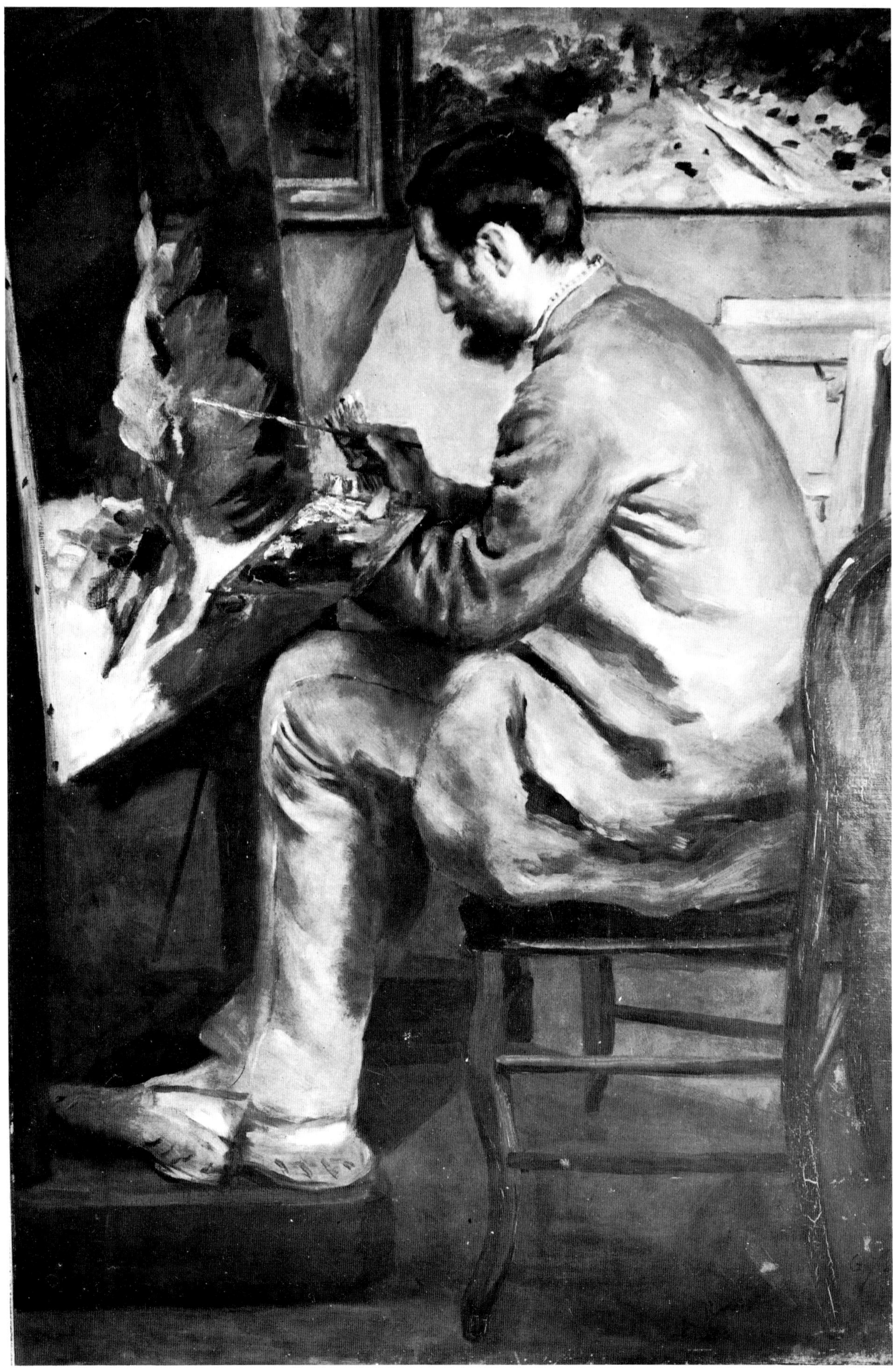

and took lessons with Stamaty, a well-known teacher (whose portrait Ingres had once painted). Then the three daughters were taken along to Chocarne's studio to learn drawing, for Madame Morisot had got it into her head that it would be a nice idea if her husband could be given, for his birthday, something *created* by his daughters.

After a few dreary sessions in Chocarne's dimly lit studio, where they had to make copies from plaster casts, Berthe and her sister insisted on changing teachers. Joseph Guichard, who was a poor painter but a good teacher, immediately spotted the unusual aptitude of his two pupils. He warned Madame Morisot, in an extremely roundabout way, that with the proper kind of lessons her daughters would become excellent artists – which could prove catastrophic for their prospects. Madame Morisot was an unbiased and intelligent person, and declared herself ready to cope with the situation. In fact, she felt herself bound to encourage her daughters' talents in every way. A roomy studio was built for them in their garden in the Rue Franklin; and soon they were introduced to several painters, among them Corot, Fantin-Latour, Stevens (a friend of Manet), and later on Puvis de Chavannes.

Every Tuesday evening, Camille Corot came for an informal meal at the Morisots'. Greatly impressed by the charms and talents of the two young ladies, he lent them some of his paintings for them to copy, gave them advice and generally guided their first efforts. Berthe Morisot, who was a keener and more audacious artist than her sister, worked away for hours on end in the main gallery of the Louvre, where, like Manet, Degas and countless other young painters, she copied the masters. She also sent her works to the Salon, where they were usually accepted.

LEFT Auguste Renoir: *Portrait of Bazille*, 1867 (Musée du Louvre, Paris).
BELOW The good-looking Bazille, intended by his father to pursue medicine as a career, had burning ambitions to become a painter. His early death in the Franco-Prussian War prevented him from establishing himself in either field.

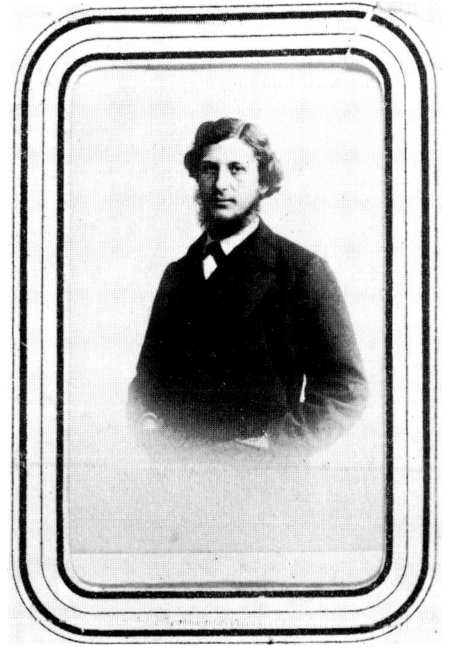

One of the most likeable and, in all senses, one of the best-endowed of the Impressionists was Frédéric Bazille. He was born on 5 December 1841, in Montpellier, where his family had been established for generations. His Protestant parents were rich, upright, and happily married. His mother liked the arts, music, and good company, while his father, although more austere, was not insensible to the pleasures of life.

Frédéric, like Marc, his younger brother by one year, spent a sheltered, pampered childhood in the family's fine old house on the Grand-Rue, in the heart of Montpellier. The former capital of Languedoc was a prosperous city, where ruins of a glorious medieval past were surrounded by broad avenues, promenades and superb gardens. The members of the bourgeoisie would go for a stroll around the Place du Peyrou in winter, but as soon as summer arrived they deserted Montpellier for their country houses amidst the fields or the vines.

Frédéric was sent to boarding school to receive a proper education, but he soon got bored there and became listless. His *joie de vivre* would return only during the summer holidays, which he used to spend nearby at Méric, on the estate belonging to his mother's family. There he found the warm atmosphere, the peace and the leisure he needed in order to blossom as a human being. He, his brother Marc, and their cousins would play games together, go for long walks across the arid heathland, or bathe in the River Lez.

Bazille passed his baccalauréat in 1859, and had to choose a career. His father wanted him to become a doctor, and had put him down for the illustrious and extremely ancient Faculty of Medicine in Montpellier. But Frédéric's interests lay elsewhere: he was mad about art, and spent all his spare time taking painting, drawing and modelling lessons.

From a very early age, Frédéric Bazille had known the famous Montpellier art collector Alfred Bruyas. Bruyas, a chronically ill bachelor, had devoted

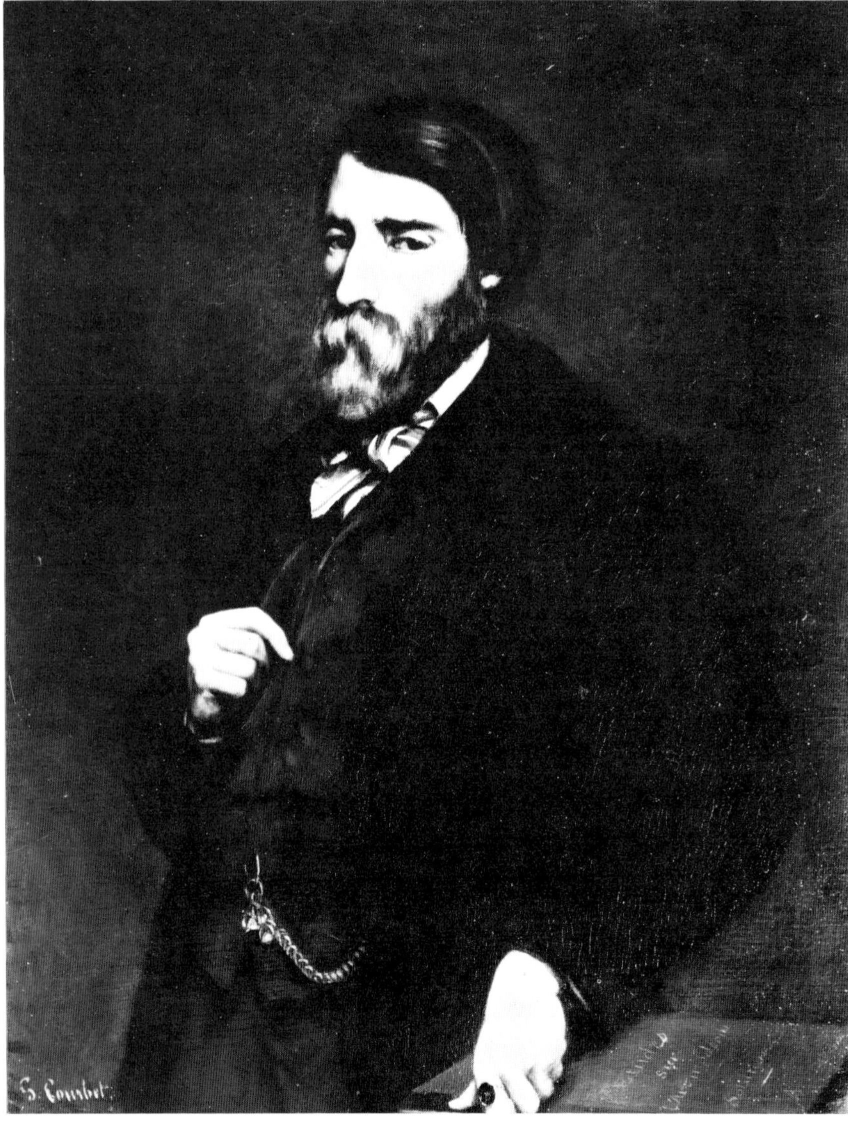

In spite of the general hostility shown towards the non-conformist, realist and Impressionist painters, they did find some defenders. LEFT Gustave Courbet: *Portrait of Alfred Bruyas*, 1853 (Musée de la Ville, Montpellier). Bruyas, a wealthy collector and patron of the arts, was a keen admirer of Courbet. OPPOSITE The dealer Paul Durand-Ruel (ABOVE), who became a supporter and friend of the Impressionists from 1871. Jules and Edmond de Goncourt (BELOW LEFT), aesthetes, critics and Naturalist novelists. Charles Baudelaire (BELOW RIGHT), who greatly admired Courbet, was quick to sense Manet's talent; he saw in him 'a marked predilection for modern truth . . . a very wide-ranging, sensitive and bold imagination'. This photograph was taken by Nadar.

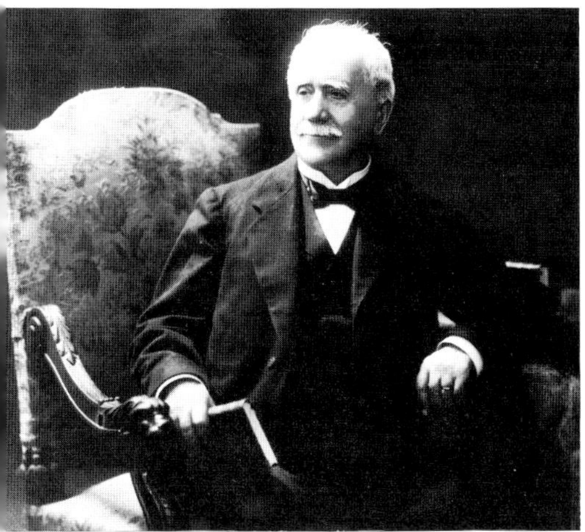

his whole life to art and artists. His house was a veritable treasure trove of rare furniture, old silver and paintings. He organized lively soirées to which art-lovers, artists, and the cream of Montpellier society were invited. Among the paintings that Frédéric Bazille admired at Bruyas' house were Delacroix' *Algerian Women* and *Daniel in the Lions' Den*, and Courbet's *The Meeting*, executed to commemorate the artist's stay with Bruyas.

In the autumn of 1862, Gaston Bazille authorized his son to go to Paris. On top of the art lessons he was taking in a studio, the young man would have to keep up his medical studies. Armed with letters of recommendation – for Courbet, among others – the tall, handsome Bazille left the family fold and set out to pursue his vocation, beginning by taking lessons at the studio of Charles Gleyre.

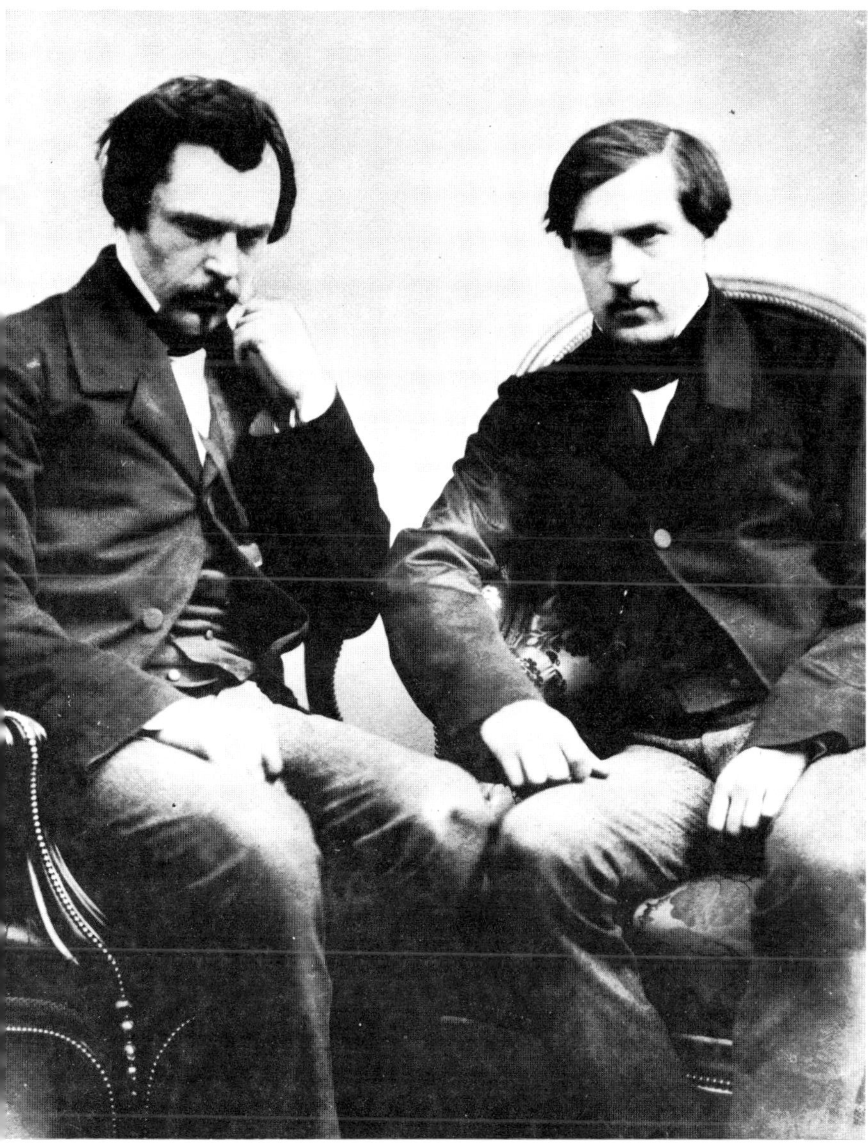

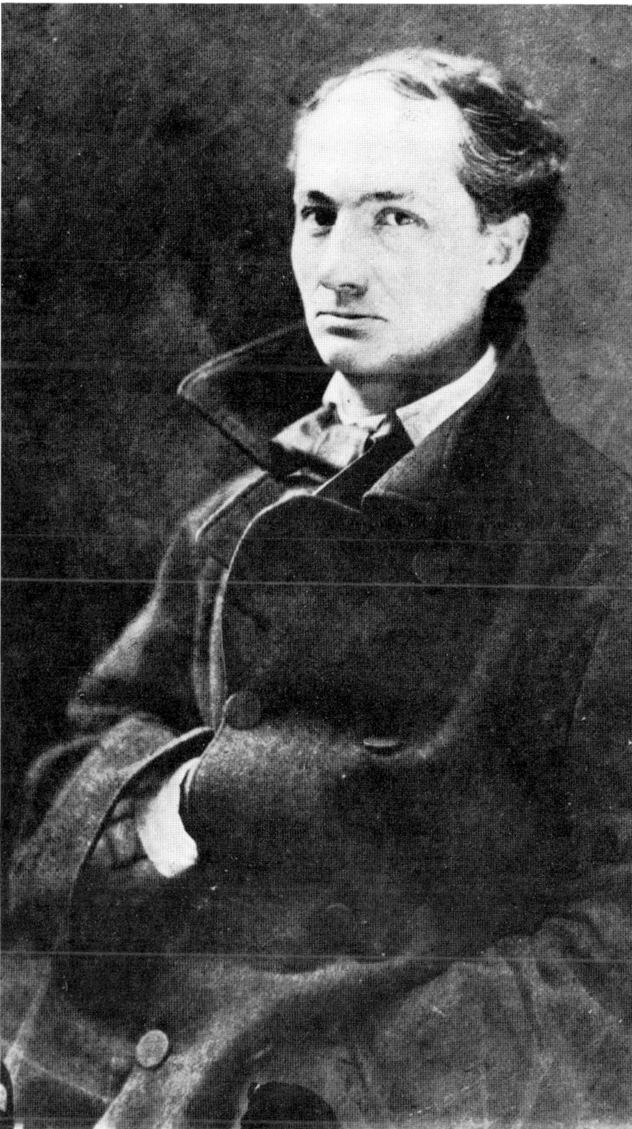

Pierre-Auguste Renoir, whose main concern in life was to be its simple joys and the best ways of recording them, was born on 25 February 1841, in Limoges, the capital of porcelain. His father, Léonard Renoir, was a tailor by trade, while his mother, Marguerite Merlet, who had been a dressmaker in her youth, now spent her time doing the housework and looking after their children. The last-born child was three when Léonard Renoir and his family moved to a quaint old building in the Tuileries area of Paris, almost opposite the palace of King Louis-Philippe and Queen Amélie. Pierre-Auguste was seven when the National Guard surrounded the palace, ejected the royal couple and France ceased for ever to be a monarchy. As he grew up, Pierre-Auguste heard his father complain how much he missed the good old days – his customers were deserting him and buying ready-to-wear clothes instead – and listened to his fearlessly militant sister Lisa and her friends as they talked of the class struggle.

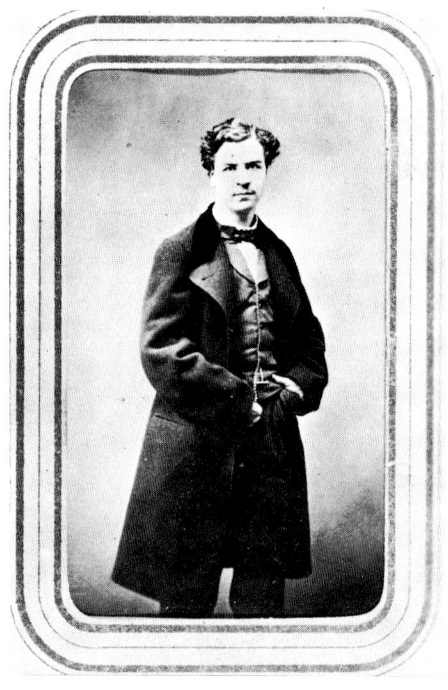

ABOVE Photograph of Renoir as a young man. OPPOSITE Frédéric Bazille: *Portrait of Renoir*, *c.* 1867 (Musée National des Beaux-Arts, Algiers).

The young Renoir was fun-loving, still carefree, and a bit of a daydreamer. He had a beautiful voice, and sang in the choir of Saint-Eustache Church, whose choirmaster was Charles Gounod. He did a few drawings with his father's coloured chalk, visited the Louvre with his mother, or simply wandered round the streets of Paris, which was being turned from an old into a modern city by Haussmann.

As soon as he was thirteen, Renoir had to leave school and don the long white smock of the apprentice painter. His father had managed to get him into a small factory where he was able to learn how to decorate porcelain. The young Pierre-Auguste's apprenticeship was soon completed, for he was attentive, hard-working and remarkably gifted. 'Monsieur Rubens', as he was nicknamed by his colleagues, liked his trade. He also adored art, and during his lunch hour he would nip into the Louvre for an all too short visit. Although he shared the life of his fellow workers all week, Renoir was beginning to harbour a greater ambition: to become an artist. He copied the old masters, and on Sundays in summer went to Fontainebleau to paint in the open air. But above all he saved up so he could one day afford to enter the Beaux-Arts.

Towards the end of the 1850s, mechanization forced the workshops dotted all over the Marais district to close down, and Renoir found himself out of a job. He desperately tried to get employment elsewhere – decorating cafés or painting shop blinds – and lived very frugally so as not to break into his savings. 'I used to walk on the earth in the middle of the street, to stop my soles from wearing out on the stone pavements,' he later recalled. At the same time, he prepared for the entrance examination to the Beaux-Arts. He was accepted. At the end of 1862, the young painter lived in a tiny room on the Rue Notre-Dame-des-Champs, just behind Montparnasse, and went down the street every day for lessons at Charles Gleyre's studio.

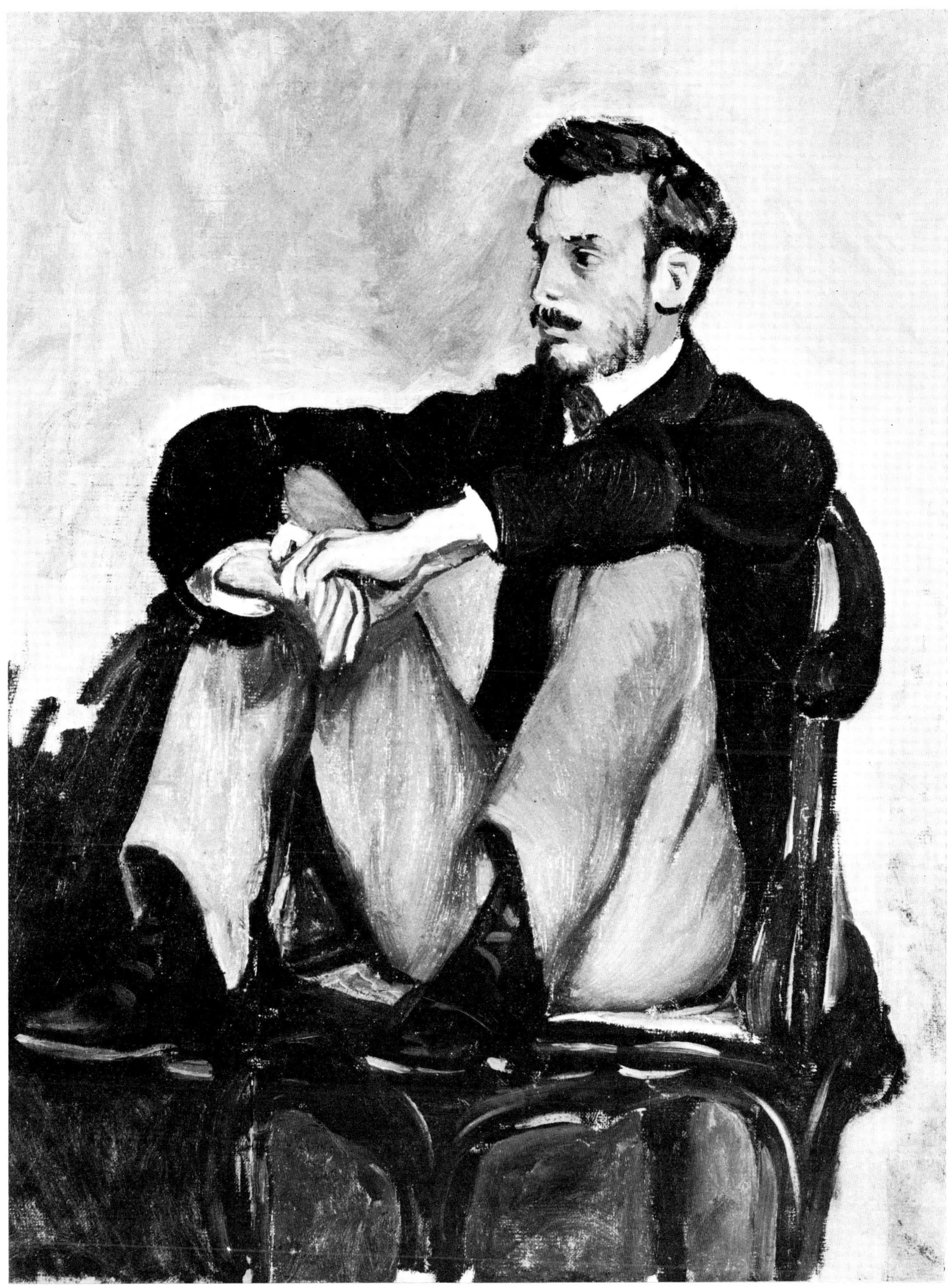

2 Fontainebleau

'To Hell with the Civilized World'

In the spring of 1863, Charles Gleyre closed his studio in the Rue Notre-Dame-des-Champs for a few weeks. Most of his pupils devoted their time to the Salon; but Renoir, Bazille, Monet and Sisley, who were only beginners and could not yet exhibit their work, left for the countryside. The spot they naturally chose for their first artistic attempts was the forest of Fontainebleau, 'the landscape painters' paradise' which for some thirty years had been used as a refuge by unorthodox painters.

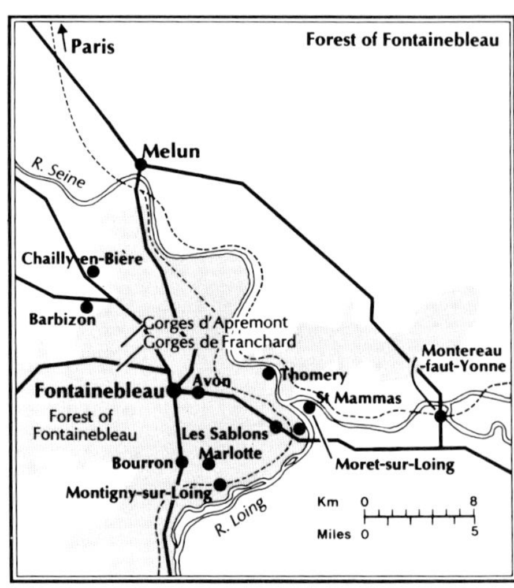

It had been out of a sense of silent protest that Diaz de la Peña, Daubigny, Rousseau, Millet and many others had moved at the beginning of the century from their Parisian studios to the country villages that bordered the forest. Although they had received a traditional artistic training, they felt unable to go along with the official line of the time, which held that only historical painting and classical subjects were of any value; they were tempted by neither the archaism nor the Romanticism of their predecessors. These artists chiefly wished to express their own feelings: they challenged the rules that had been handed down to them, and set off in search of a more truthful image of the world around them.

It was precisely at this period that the contrast between the new urban life forged by the recent industrial revolution and the artless rural world first began to be felt. Most painters were city-dwellers, and were therefore deeply struck by the direct beauty and authenticity of the countryside. Their instinct told them that they would have to escape city life, with its upheavals, political witch-hunts and epidemics, and opt for the freedom of nature if they were to express their emotions in a personal way. They adopted Rousseau's battle cry: 'To hell with the civilized world, long live nature and old poetry!'

The dense forest of Fontainebleau, which lies some forty miles south of the capital, forms a natural sanctuary. This massif consisting of 62,000 acres of crags and woods long remained a wild, mysterious place that according to ancient legends was inhabited by fantastic monsters. Travellers told of the dangers that lurked there, and artists on their way to or from Rome brought back descriptions of extraordinary scenery. According to one ancient account: 'In some places, awesome mountains can be seen which appear to be as high as the peak of Mount Olympus.' Such tales were reinforced by the huge rocks' grotesque shapes and by the risk run by any traveller who strayed there after dark of being attacked and robbed.

Daubigny, who was one of the first nineteenth-century painters to settle there, saw little else but stags, hinds, wildcats and foxes, which coexisted peacefully with the woodcutters, charcoal-burners and quarrymen who worked in the forest, often with only a ramshackle hut as protection at night. From time to time, the woods would be used as a hiding-place by a deserter until the police lost track of him, and probably more than one political refugee sought asylum there.

Claude Monet: *Le Déjeuner sur l'Herbe*, fragment, 1865–6 (Musée du Louvre, Paris). Fragment of the final version of the large composition which the artist never completed. In 1884 Monet recovered the canvas, which, along with several other paintings, had been seized by the landlord of his Argenteuil home, and after removing the right-hand part which had been spoilt by damp, hung it in his studio at Giverny.

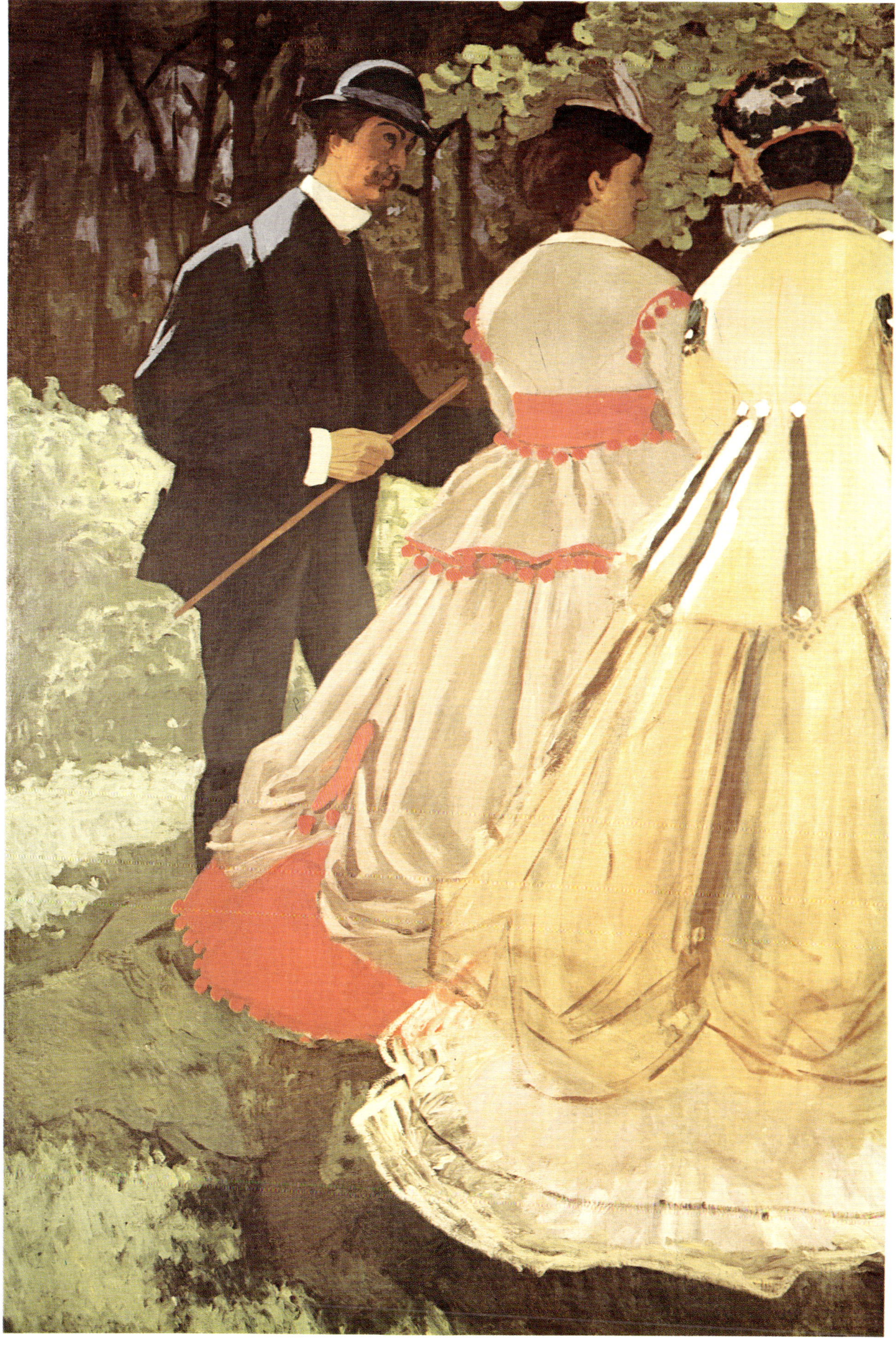

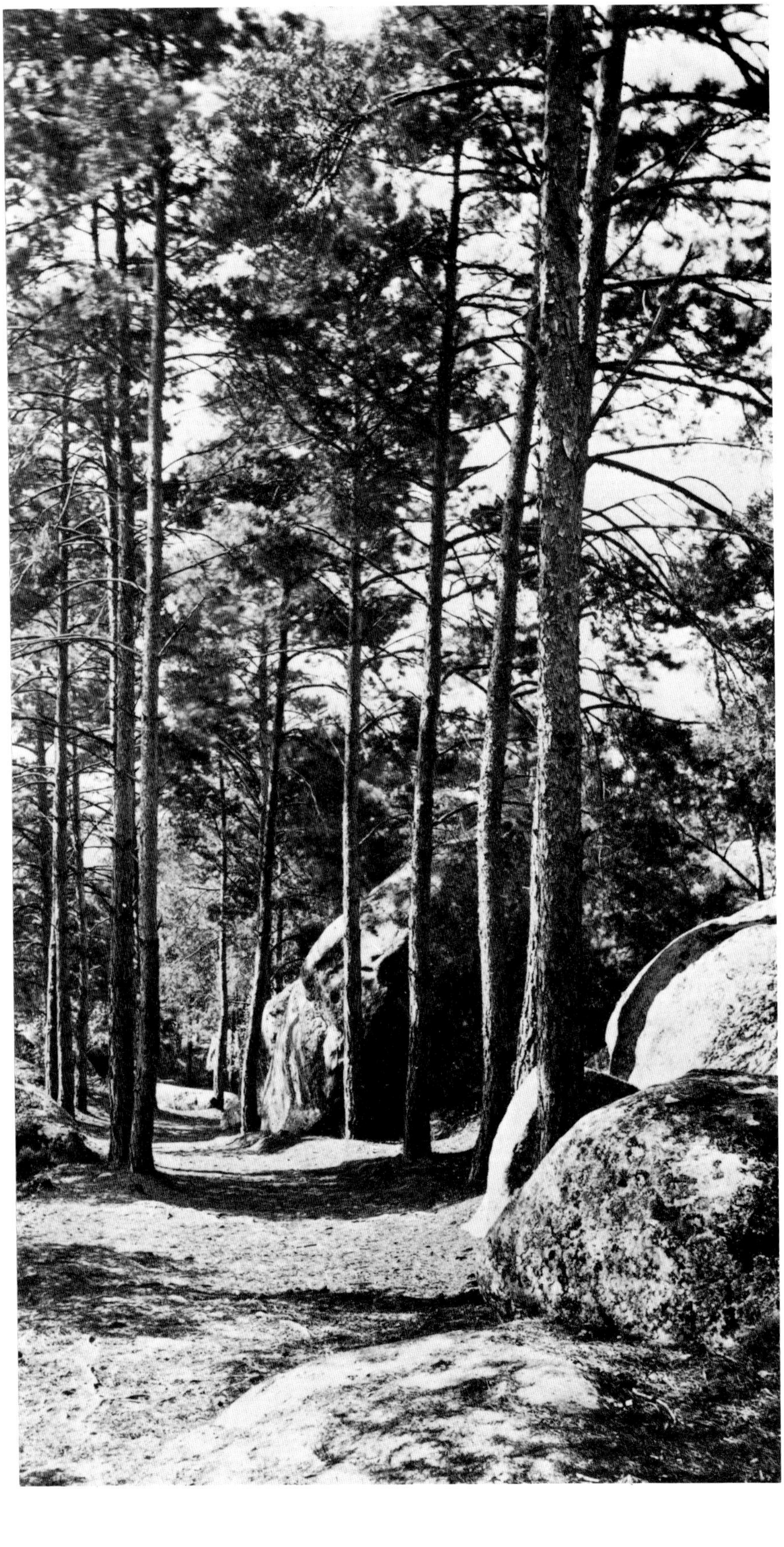

LEFT and BELOW The forest of Fontainebleau as the Impressionists knew it.

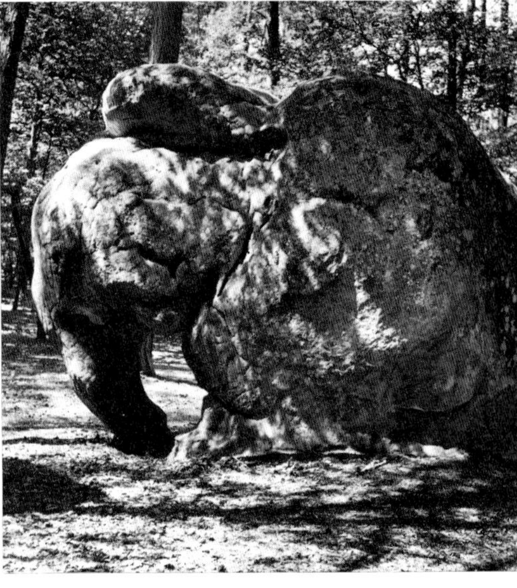

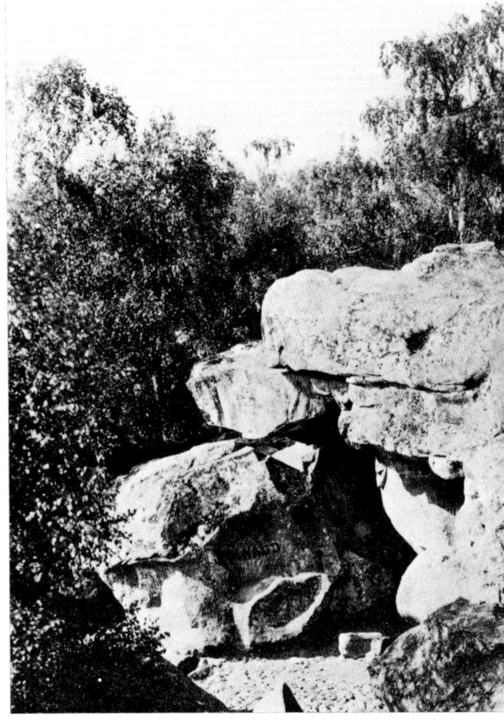

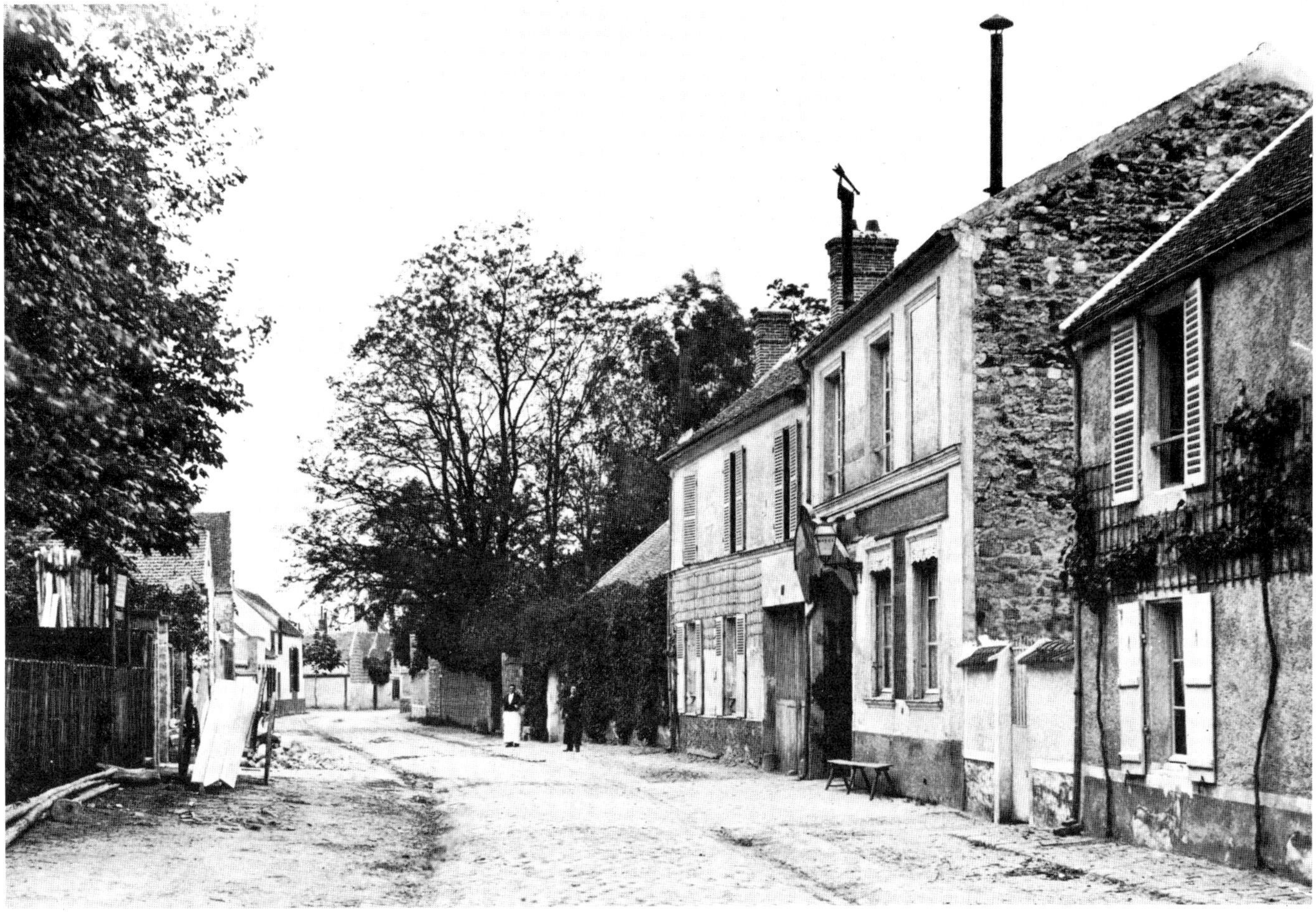

ABOVE The village of Barbizon, where artistic activity and rural life were closely interlinked. BELOW The rock formations were sometimes of forbidding aspect.

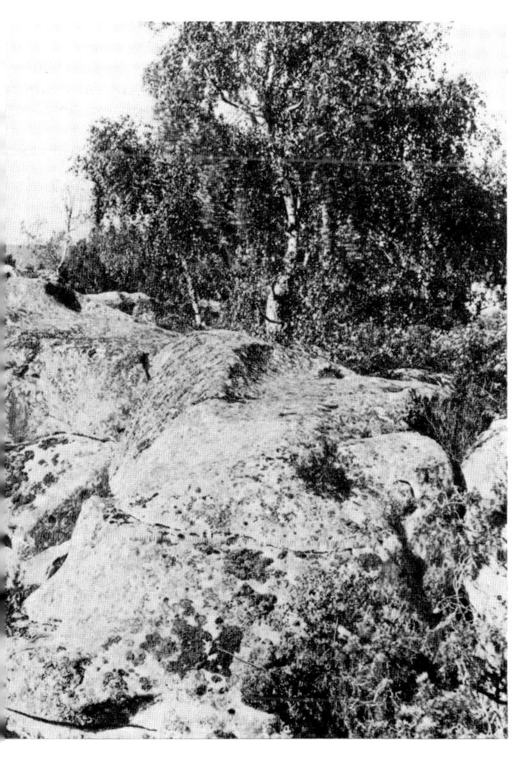

Renoir often went to paint there in the open air during his formative years as an artist. One day, to his alarm and surprise, he was suddenly confronted with a wild-eyed uncouth individual who was dying of exhaustion and begged him for a crust of bread. The painter took pity on him, rushed back to the village to get some bread, and then stayed to listen to the tale the man had to tell: he was a Republican journalist who, after escaping from the police of the Empire, had been wandering for several days completely lost in the forest. Renoir lent him a painter's smock, a wide-brimmed hat and a colour-box. Thus equipped, the fugitive was able to get back to Melun without awakening any suspicion.

A few small farmers had chosen to settle on the edge of the forest, just where the fertile plains of Brie begin. Their thatched cottages and sturdy farmsteads, clustered round the spire of a tiny church, formed hamlets that were to become the focus of an artistic counter-culture at the beginning of the nineteenth century. Legend has it that the first painter to appear at one such village, called Barbizon, was a colossus of a man wearing a three-cornered hat, an old grey overcoat and huge boots; he was accompanied on his visits by a diminutive manservant whom he got to pose nude in the woods and among the rocks.

The landscape painters who followed in the footsteps of this larger-than-life figure were of lesser stature. They lived in small cottages, rented rooms from the villagers or else boarded at an inn. They would rise at dawn, like the peasants, and disappear into the forest, their heavy kitbags bulging with an

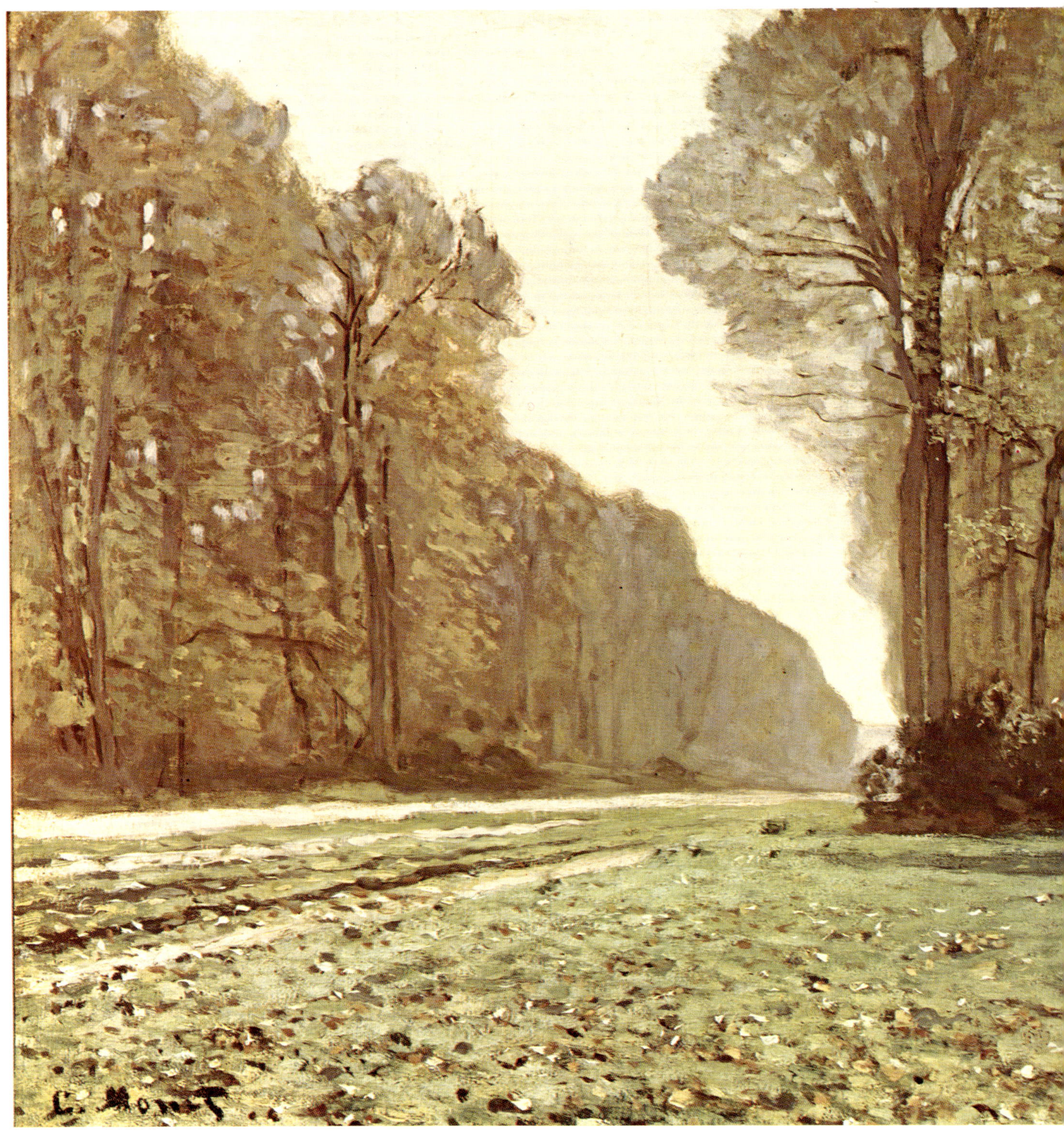

Claude Monet: *The Bas-Bréau Road*, 1865 (Musée du Louvre, Paris). The forest road from Chailly to Fontainebleau, lined with majestic beeches and centuries-old oaks, was one of the landscape painters' favourite subjects.

easel, canvases, brushes and colours slung over their shoulder, and a folding stool and a huge umbrella in their hands – for they scarcely had enough money for their own needs, let alone for a manservant. About 500 yards from Barbizon, in the clearing of Bas-Bréau, where hundred-year-old trees stood like monuments, in the dense woodland of Gros-Foutou, or in the gorges of Apremont near the Mare aux Fées, they would work until the light failed. Then in the evening they would get together round a huge bowl of steaming soup, and sit talking and singing to the light of candles. By nine o'clock, not

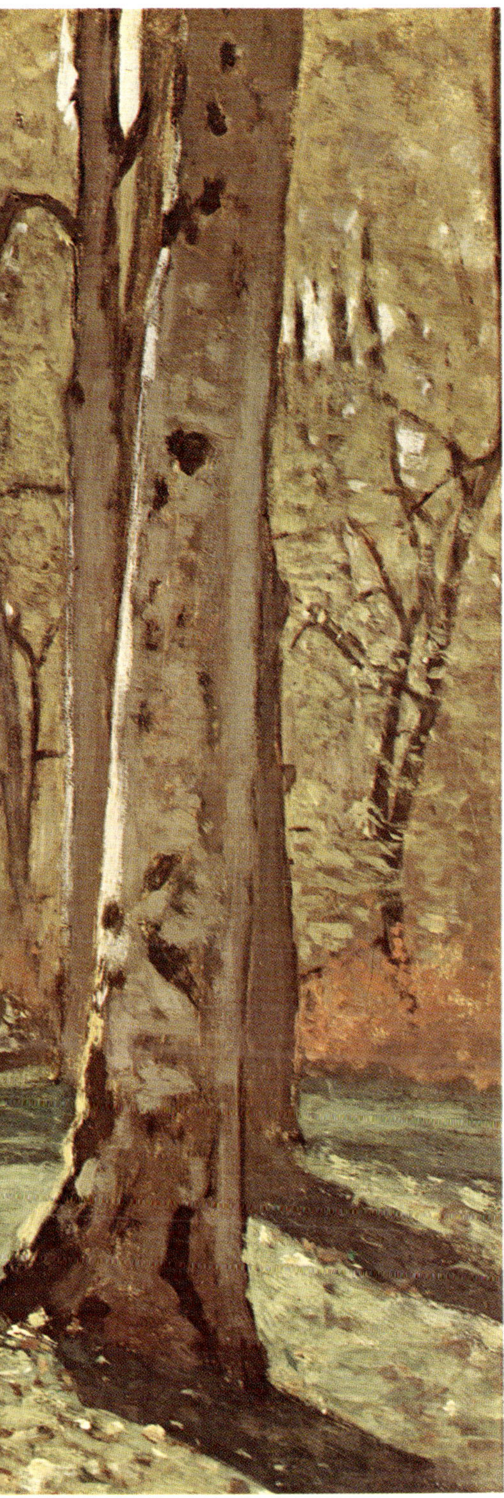

a soul was about in Barbizon, for everyone had to be up before six in the morning.

From August 1849 onwards, the forest of Fontainebleau lost its mystery. Whereas previously the coach journey had taken eight hours, the railway line that opened at that date enabled any Parisian to reach the woods in ninety minutes for the sum of 3 francs 65. Every Sunday, the haunt of the landscape painters was invaded by office workers, dressmakers' apprentices, drapers' assistants, as well as students and poets, who flocked from Melun station on foot in search of relaxation and fun. The Court, too, which spent every spring there, used to come by coach from the nearby Château of Fontainebleau to picnic in the woods. On his way through Barbizon, the Emperor Napoleon III once stopped in front of the village inn where the landscape paintings were on show and bought one (it was claimed) for the Empress Eugénie.

The landscape painters, whose numbers were swelling all the time, gradually began to impose 'nature' on the Salon. Official resistance

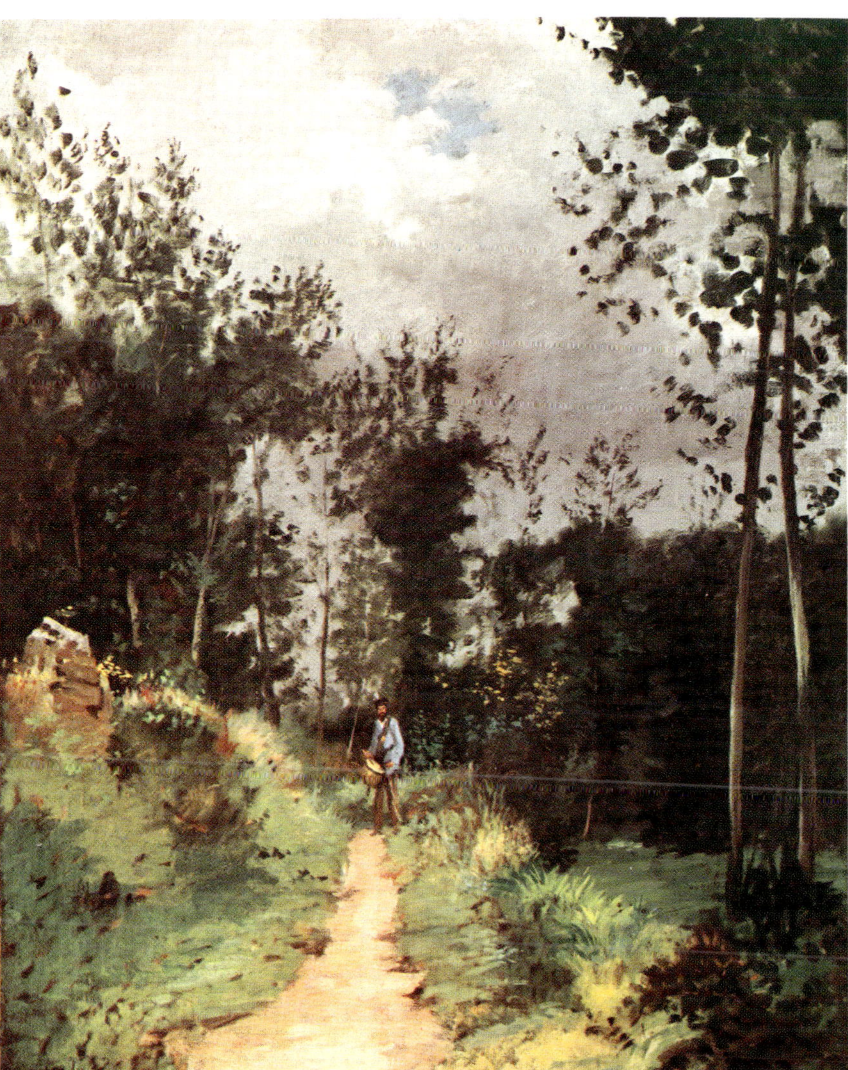

RIGHT Alfred Sisley: *Garde-Champêtre in the Forest of Fontainebleau*, 1870 (Private Collection, Switzerland). Sisley returned to Fontainebleau in search of subjects again and again throughout his life.

weakened, one or two landscapists like Charles Daubigny sat on the jury, and such influential critics as Baudelaire and Théophile Gautier praised the works of Théodore Rousseau, Troyon and Diaz. The only man to remain unyielding in his opposition was the powerful Intendant aux Beaux-Arts, the Comte de Nieuwerkerke, a man of unshakable political and moral prejudices, who repeatedly denigrated 'the painting of democrats, the painting of people who do not wash and see themselves as superior to gentlemen'.

The showing, amidst the Salon's usual plethora of gods and heroes, of two peasants painted by Jean-François Millet reciting the Angelus in the fields, triggered off a fierce controversy in 1859: the press, the whole of France, took sides for or against *The Angelus*. Executed between Chailly-en-Bière and Barbizon, it carried the fame of the two villages far beyond France's frontiers. American, German, English and Swiss painters visited Barbizon in order to imbue themselves with the new, direct method of interpreting nature. In June 1859, a Belgian artist wrote: 'From seven o'clock in the morning until the evening, I wander through the forest, it is magnificent and there I find all that I can wish for to make things easier to paint my picture. ... At present there are crowds of people gathered here, and everywhere exclamations of joy can be heard throughout the forest.'

Journalists, writers, and the simply curious converged in their turn on Barbizon, to watch the painters at work and describe their way of life and their setting for posterity. George Sand said she could hear 'the cry of the earth' there. Gustave Flaubert made Fontainebleau the setting of his first novel, *L'Education Sentimentale*. The very young Stéphane Mallarmé used to go on excursions there with the German girl who was later to become his wife. And the Goncourt brothers made Barbizon the home of the painter whose artistic development is charted in their realist novel *Manette Salomon*. In the interests of verisimilitude, Jules and Edmond de Goncourt felt it was essential they spend a whole month in a small house next to the old farmhouse that had been turned into an inn. They spent their time either savouring 'the immense delight of not being able to spend one's time or money', or else complaining about 'this mediocre inn, which reeks of the discomfort that is the lot of the painter's working-class nature, in bedrooms without fires, and at a dining table where Gruyère is devoured at the end of the meal and the boundless melancholy of dried fruit hangs over the gathering.'

For their first visit to the forest, Monet, Bazille and Sisley, probably on the advice of Renoir, who knew the area well, stayed in the village of Chailly-en-Bière, just over a mile from Barbizon. For 3 francs 75 they found board and lodging at the Hôtel du Cheval Blanc, a former coaching inn. Bazille found it 'excellent', and was enthusiastic about the scenery, so different from that of his native South of France. 'Some parts of the forest are truly admirable. We can't imagine oak-trees like that in Montpellier,' he wrote to his family immediately after his arrival.

The younger painters naturally kept to the same timetable as their elders. They would leave very early in the morning, so as to get the best light, and work on studies directly from nature. It was the first time that Frédéric Bazille had painted in the open air. Perhaps he felt the sense of exultation that apparently overtakes all beginners when they first come into contact with nature, but his letters to his father reveal nothing. He simply announces: 'I have worked a lot and will be able to show you my first paintings in August, six or seven of them.' No painting from this period in Bazille's life has survived. He had not yet received his parents' permission to give up his medical studies, and doubtless wished to impress on his father the importance of his stay in the forest.

Although Bazille did not produce any masterpiece during those few days, he did benefit from the advice of Claude Monet. Monet had forgotten nothing of the experience he had gained in Normandy with Boudin and Jongkind, and naturally passed on the gist of it to his fellow painter. He was clearly delighted to be able to counterbalance Bazille's social advantages – his wealth and his contacts with intellectuals and with high society – by drawing attention to his own skills and talents. During those few days, which marked the beginning of the two artists' friendly, though occasionally strained, relationship, Monet imposed himself unconsciously but decisively as the dominant force.

Each spring, Gleyre's young pupils would return to Fontainebleau. They got off the Paris train at Avon or at Melun, and walked to Chailly-en-Bière or Marlotte, avoiding the overcrowded Barbizon. Renoir and Sisley seemed to prefer Marlotte, and more particularly the Auberge de la Mère Anthony, where they were entranced by the beautiful eyes of the innkeeper's daughter, Nana. In Renoir's painting *At the Inn of Mother Anthony*, the dining-room of the inn at Marlotte seems tiny. It is virtually filled by a single table, at which all the painter's friends are grouped – Sisley wearing a huge straw hat, the painter Jules Le Coeur opposite him, Monet standing next to Nana and Toto, the lame dog. The plaster walls of the room are decorated with frescoes suggested to Renoir by *Les Scènes de la Vie de Bohème*, the autobiographical novel by Henri Murger describing the trials and tribulations of a young man who is driven from home by his concierge father when he says he wants to be a writer. Ever since its publication in 1848 the book had been enormously successful.

According to the description Renoir gave to his son, the film-maker Jean Renoir, Marlotte 'consisted of a few peasant houses scattered around the

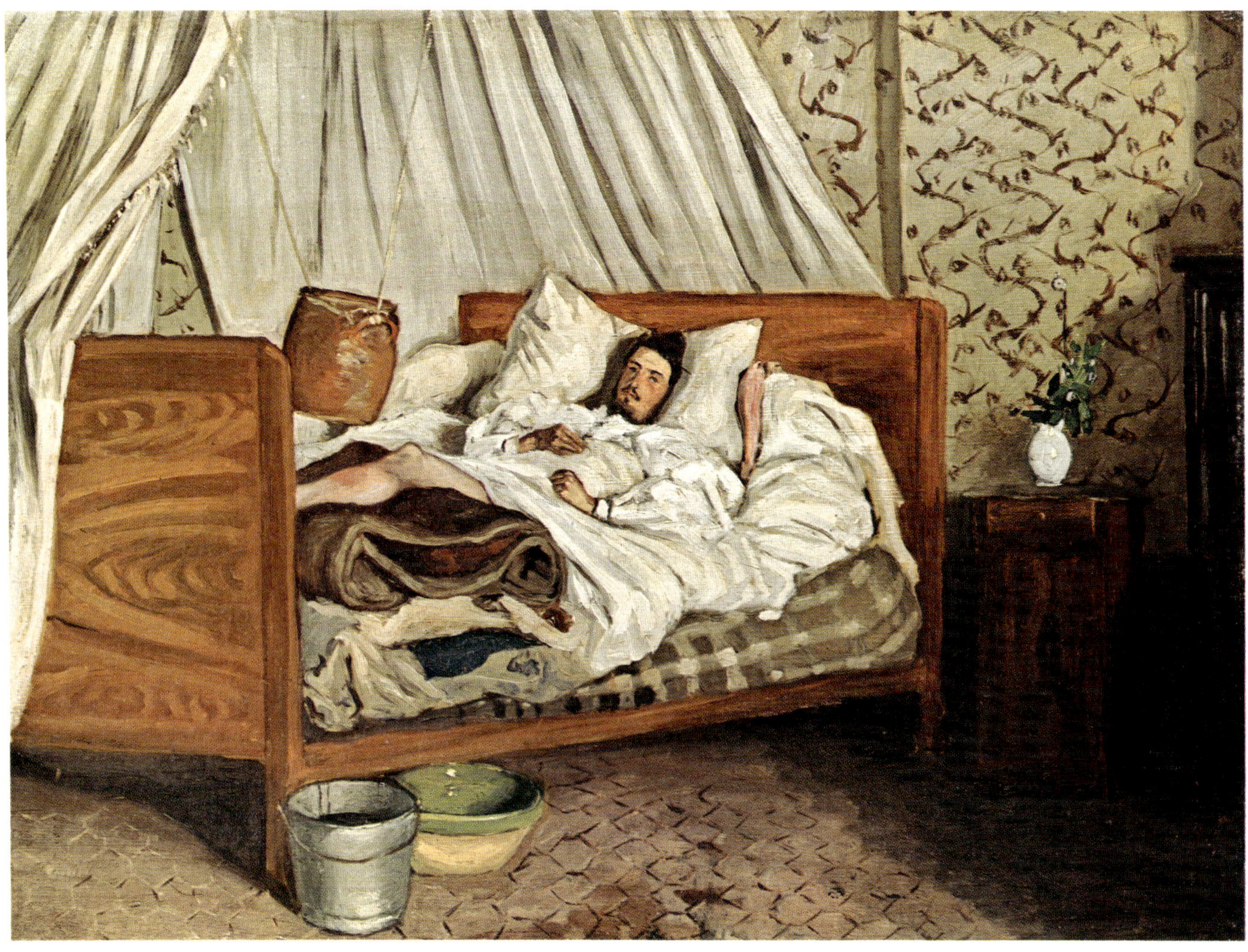

ABOVE Frédéric Bazille: *Monet after His Accident at the Inn in Chailly*, 1866 (Musée du Louvre, Paris). As soon as he arrived in Fontainebleau, Bazille, instead of posing for Monet, had to draw on his medical knowledge in order to treat his friend, who had injured his leg.

OPPOSITE Auguste Renoir: *At the Inn of Mother Anthony, Marlotte*, 1866 (Nationalmuseum, Stockholm). From left to right: Nana, the painter Jules Le Coeur, an unknown man, Mother Anthony, and Sisley. The caricatures on the wall behind were inspired by Murger's *Scènes de la Vie de Bohème*.

point where the roads from Fontainebleau and Montigny meet the road to Bourron. The woods ran up to the outlying houses, to the north. The houses on the south side overlooked the Loing valley.' The spot afforded artists not only a wide range of subjects, but a comparatively carefree existence. Nevertheless the necessities of day-to-day life were beginning to press upon Auguste Renoir. The young artist had completely used up the money that had enabled him to enter the Beaux-Arts, and was therefore forced, in order to survive in Paris, to work for a living. He turned out twopenny-halfpenny portraits, and painted the décor of a café in the Marais district of Paris, which scarcely provided him with enough to buy the canvases and paints he needed. He shared Bazille's or Sisley's studio, and his only food consisted of haricot beans that had cooked for hours on the stove which heated the room. So the forest was not only the biggest and best studio he could possibly have, but also a salutary place of escape, a refuge where, as it turned out, he was

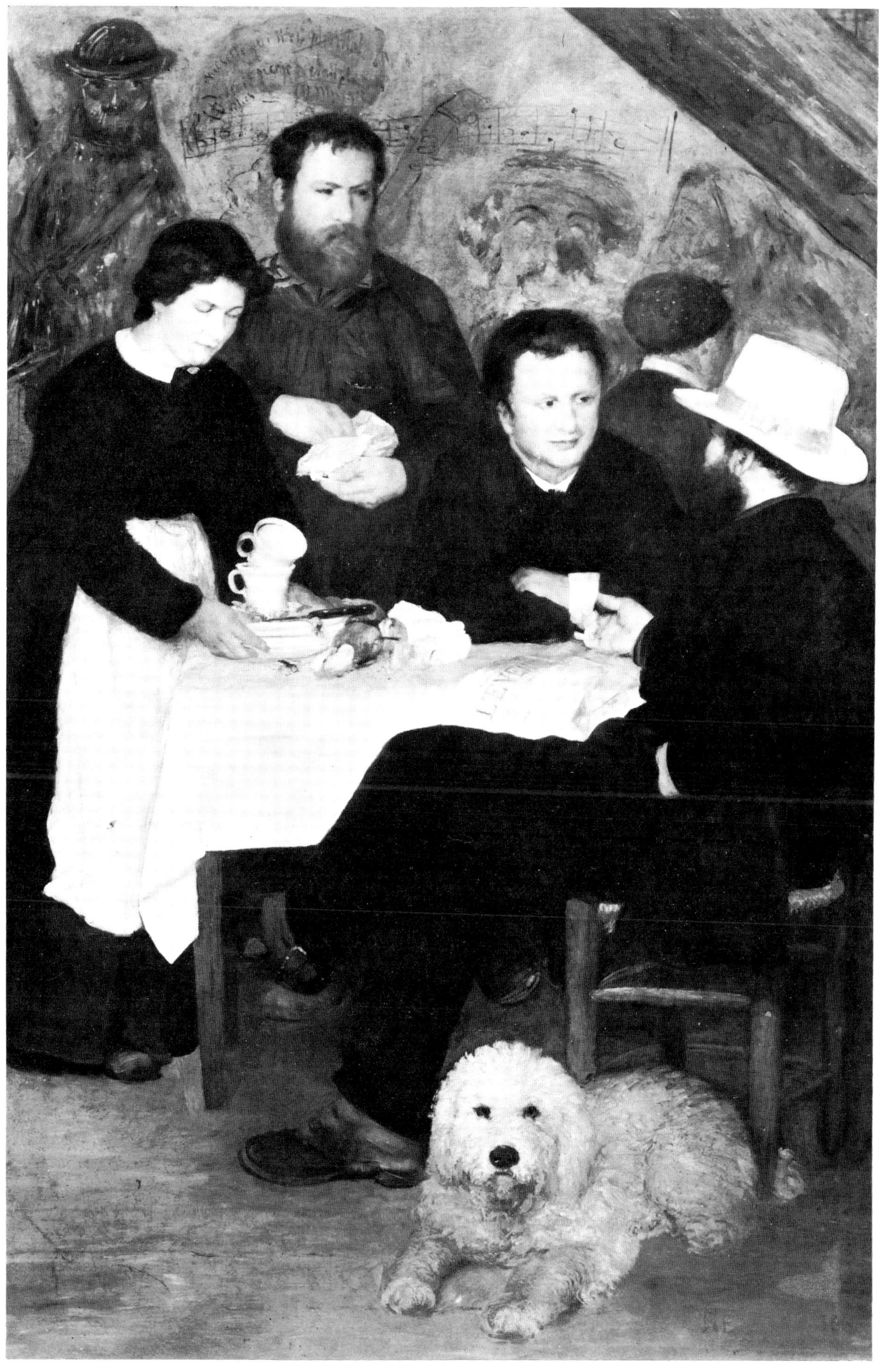

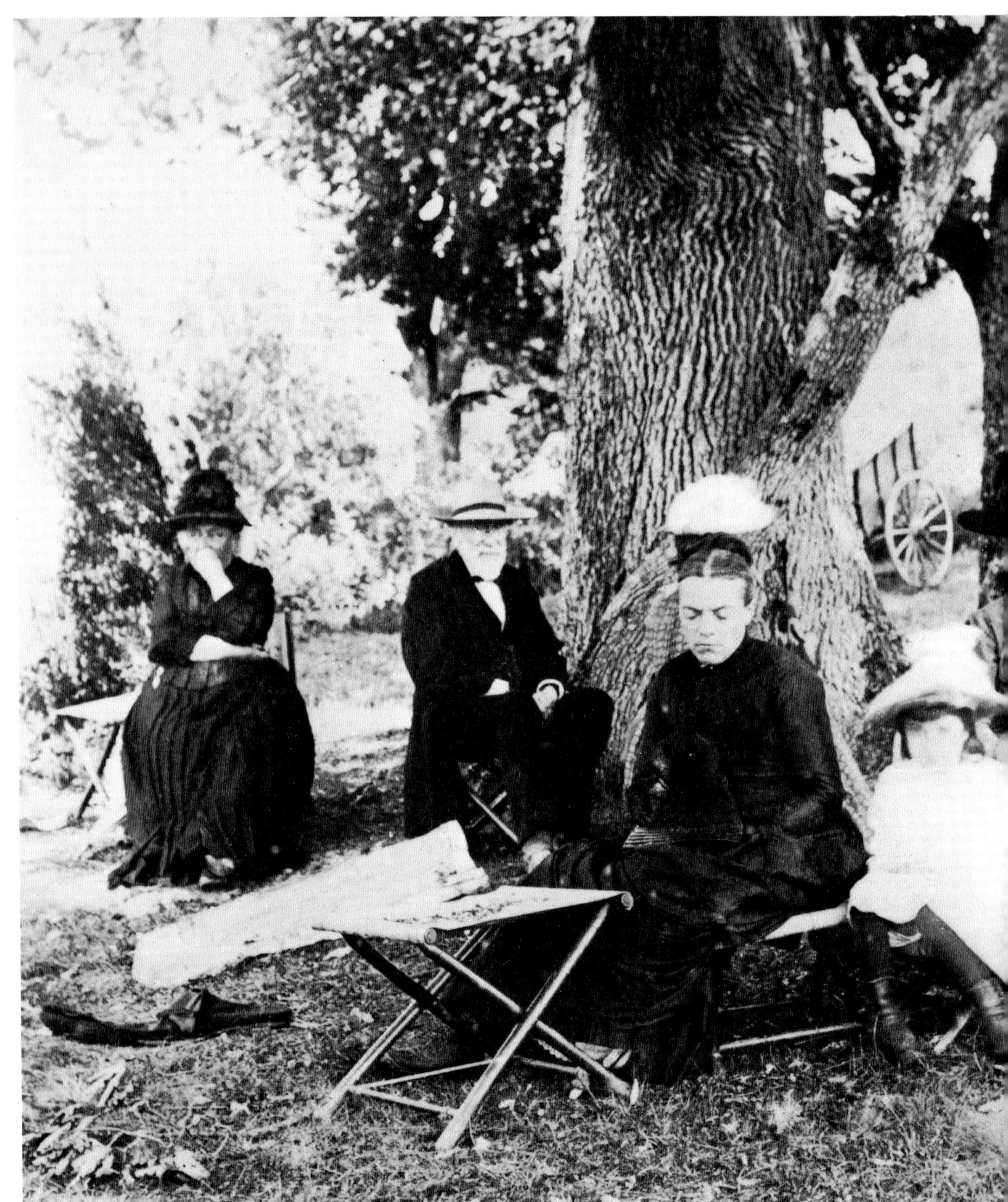

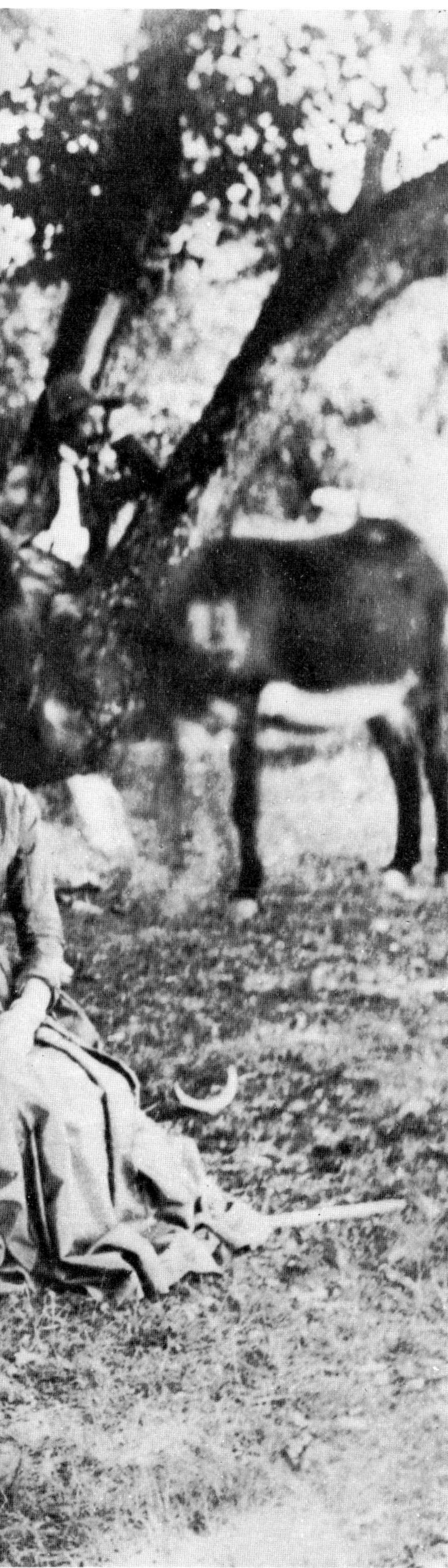

later blessed with some extremely fruitful encounters.

The most important of these was to help him in his development as a painter – indeed so important was it to him that shortly before his death he described it in detail to his son Jean: Renoir was painting alone in the forest, with a concentration that made him quite deaf and blind to everything that was going on around him, when a group of rowdy Parisians, obviously out to cause trouble, not only poked fun at the long white smock he was wearing but, creeping close, kicked his palette out of his hand. Renoir put up a good fight. It looked as though he was about to get the worse of it when a big old man came limping up to his assistance and routed the attackers with blows from his walking-stick and kicks with his wooden leg. Renoir's defender was none other than Narcisse Diaz de la Peña, one of the pioneers of landscape. He too had painted on china in his youth, and he was nostalgically touched by the smock Renoir was wearing. He decided to become his mentor and protector.

'You're gifted, very gifted,' said Diaz. 'By why do you paint so dark?' Renoir replied that many of the masters he admired painted dark. 'There's light even in the shade of foliage. . . . Bitumen is just a convention – it won't last,' retorted Diaz, who had already been singled out for praise by Baudelaire for the originality of his 'twinklings of busy light piercing vast patches of shade'. Diaz was not only an excellent artist, but a man of sunny disposition, optimistic and full of sympathy. He became interested in Renoir's talent and progress, and sensing his lack of means would unobtrusively leave behind half-used tubes of colour every time they met.

Renoir benefited from Diaz' advice, which happened to suit his temperament admirably and guided him in precisely the direction where his

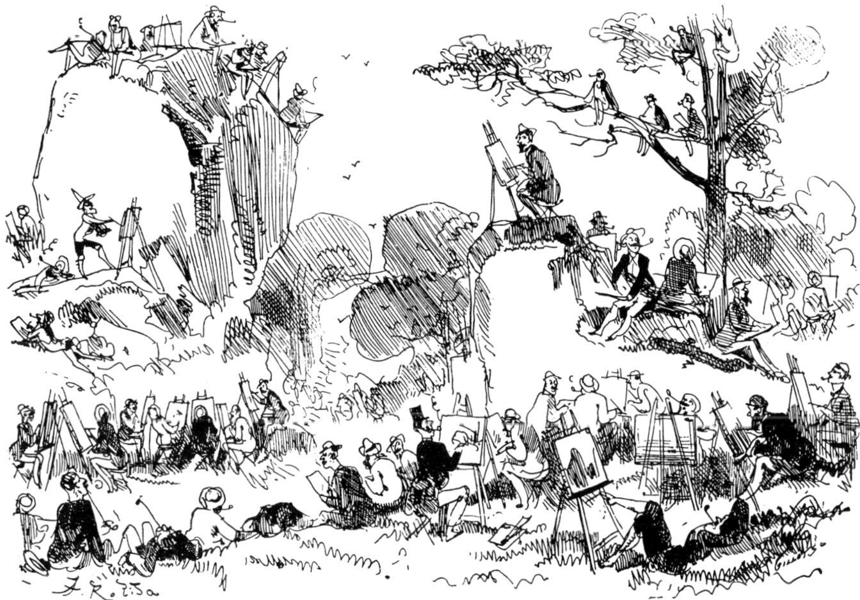

ABOVE Picnics like this were greatly enjoyed by Parisians in the mid-nineteenth century. RIGHT This cartoon appeared in the *Journal Amusant* of 4 September 1869. Art and artists were among the caricaturists' favourite targets.

genius was to come into full flower. Very quickly he disowned his earliest attempts; he destroyed *Diana the Huntress*, which he had painted in the dark tones that were fashionable in official circles and had been accepted for the Salon of 1864, as soon as it was returned from the exhibition. He made a renewed effort to observe directly from nature. Often he would curse the bad weather, wind and clouds that made the métier of landscapist so trying – patience was not one of his prime virtues – and he had not yet achieved the technical mastery that was to enable him to feel totally at ease with nature.

Renoir's development by no means followed a straight course. For a time he was influenced by Courbet, whom he must certainly have met at the same time as Claude Monet, and imitated his technique of applying thick colour with a palette knife. But much to Renoir's dissatisfaction this made retouching impossible, and he soon turned his hand to less heavily applied paintings of flowers and landscapes, using lighter combinations of colours more in the style of Fantin-Latour, whom he also admired.

Friendship, love and painting flourished together in that forest setting. The cheerful circle of artists attracted a bevy of young girls, who were either models or simply out of a job. The more solitary painters were often kept company by them, while the more audacious, older and wealthier had their own 'official' consorts. Of all the pretty girls who mixed with the small group of painters made up by Renoir, Lestringuez, Jules Le Coeur and Sisley, Lise Tréhot, whose sister was Jules Le Coeur's mistress Clémence, particularly caught Renoir's notice. She was barely sixteen, but her fully rounded figure, radiant complexion, and childish expression made her the model that tallied perfectly with Renoir's ideal.

He painted her sitting in the open air, chastely dressed and doing her needlework; he also painted her nude in his studio, as Diana, in a large composition he intended to enter for the Salon of 1867 (it was rejected). Renoir was still wavering between several influences, and was perfectly prepared, when he had the Salon in mind, to resort to archaic themes and a traditional style. But from 1867 on, he no longer made any compromises, and decided to work within a completely contemporary framework. He produced a portrait of *Alfred Sisley and His Wife* and a full-length portrait of *Lise* which he treated in a very personal manner. Lise, wearing a white organdie dress, with her face and neck screened from the light by a parasol, stands out against a background of verdure that casts a greenish tinge on her dress. 'The effect is so natural and so true that one might very well find it false,' remarked the critic Théo Bürger in his review of the Salon, 'because one is so accustomed to nature represented in conventional colours. . . . Does not colour depend upon the environment that surrounds it?' Renoir, Monet, Bazille and Sisley – those destined to become the Impressionists – soon drew revolutionary conclusions from that unsuspecting remark.

After 1868, Renoir no longer went regularly to Fontainebleau. He abandoned the depths of the forest, which filtered out the full strength of daylight, and joined his friends on the banks of the Seine.

While the forest served as a refuge for most of the painters, for Claude Monet it was the scene of his earliest ambitions, as well as the setting for his first professional setback, and his first successes in love.

In May 1865, after Gleyre had been forced by ophthalmia to close down his studio for good, Monet arrived at Chailly-en-Bière full of ambition. Ever since he had been confronted by Manet's *Le Déjeuner sur l'Herbe* at the Salon des Refusés, his keenest ambition had been to execute a work on the same scale, and of even greater realism, which would bring him to the attention of his contemporaries. The several months he had spent in Normandy painting with Jongkind, Boudin and Courbet had bolstered his self-confidence and consolidated his talent. He felt certain he could produce, in the open air, a very large composition which would feature half a dozen figures and one totally new ingredient: real, living light, just as it is found in woodland.

Obsessed by his grand design, Monet left very early in the morning in search of an ideal spot. As he strode along the forest paths and breathed in the sweet smells of the rustling trees, he again had the exhilarating feeling of freedom he so loved. Solitude and the rhythm of nature suited his temperament and stimulated his visual imagination and creative impulses: he observed, drew, and painted. When the light on which he relied for his work had faded, he was left with many hours of leisure which he spent with artists living at Chailly, Marlotte and Barbizon, and with the models and mistresses that supplied the indispensable feminine element. One of their favourite pastimes in Fontainebleau was to go from village to village at dusk calling on each other.

Then, in the words of the historian Hippolyte Taine:

> They would sit down on wooden benches and have supper on the bare table, to the light of four candles. . . . The light flickers on the ceiling's smoke-stained joists and covers the walls with grotesques. . . . Coffee is served and small glasses of rum are handed round. This is when literary discussions begin to get under way, and the philosophy of art is heatedly and noisily debated. When the contestants have no voice left, they go out and contemplate the moonlit woods. One will pick up his hunting horn, while another will imitate a troating stag. The air is thick with Rabelaisian anecdotes, while the listeners stretch on the sand and smoke their second pipes.

The day was over.

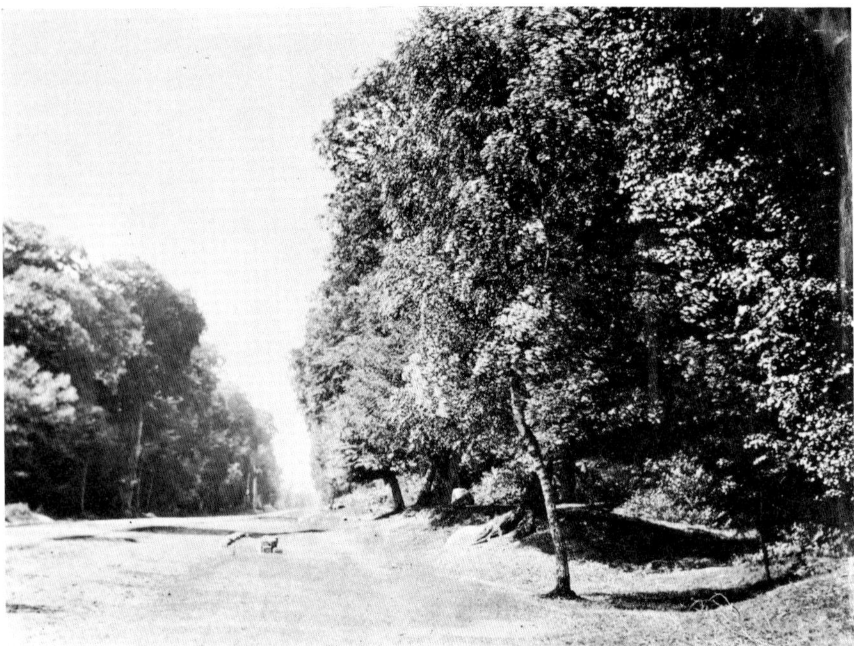

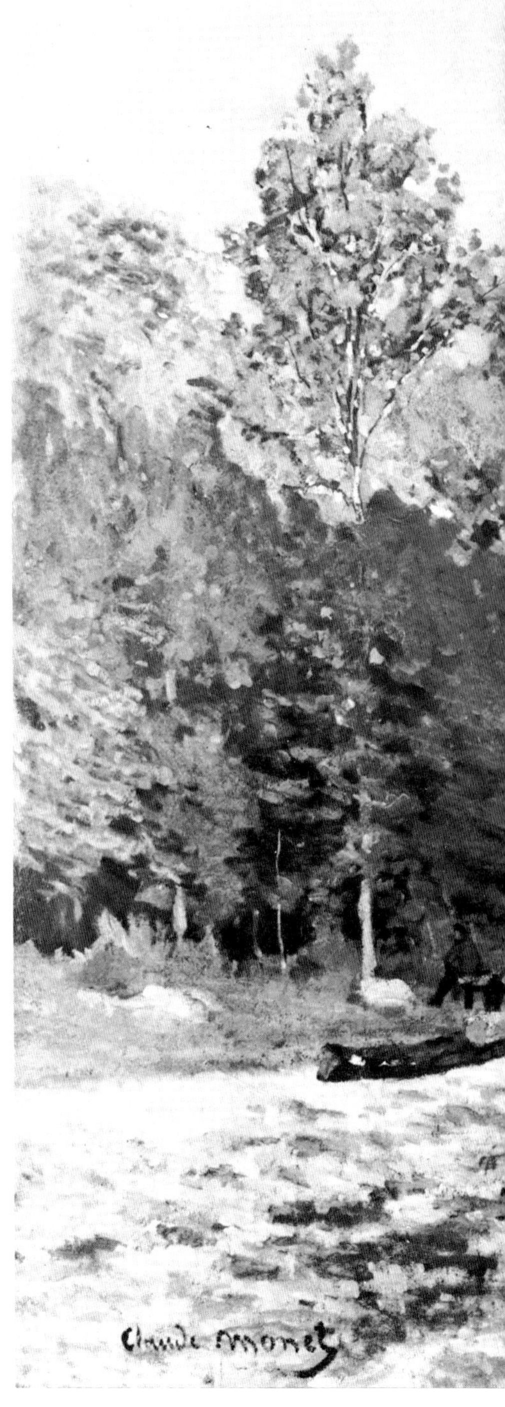

Gustave Le Gray, one of the pioneers of photography, often chose the same subjects as the painters. This photograph (ABOVE LEFT) was taken at the very same spot where Claude Monet was later to paint *The Road from Chailly to Fontainebleau* (ABOVE), *c.* 1865 (Private Collection).

To prepare his painting Monet needed not only Bazille, who had promised to pose for the male figures, but a female model. 'Little Eugénie', whom he had met at Chailly-en-Bière and mentioned twice in his letters to Bazille, would sit for him. But fortunately he also met the young Camille Doncieux at about that time: the distinction of her profile and the gracefulness of her tall, slender figure suited Monet admirably. She appears in all the drawings and numerous rough sketches he made in preparation for the great painting while waiting for Frédéric Bazille to arrive.

By the end of June, Monet was ready and dying to start on the picture. Only Bazille was lacking. He appealed to him in several short, impatient letters and tried to persuade him with every argument at his disposal. 'I want you to know that I am expecting you without fail for dinner with these gentlemen on Saturday. . . . The young Gabrielle will be arriving some time on Monday, it would be a pity if you were not here,' he wrote on 4 May. But Bazille, who was busy in Paris painting two decorative panels for his uncle's flat, kept on postponing his departure for Fontainebleau.

By the end of July, Bazille was getting desperate missives. 'All I can think of is my painting,' wrote Monet, 'and if I thought I was going to fail, I believe I would go mad.' Yet Bazille did not arrive until the middle of August, and even then stayed only a short time, for his family was clamouring for him to return to Montpellier. Then, as though to spite Monet, there occurred a series of mishaps. First, continuous rain made it impossible to work in the woods. Subsequently, when the painter was out walking, he was accidentally injured by a young English sportsman.

This incident, which laid Monet up in bed, has provided us with the only

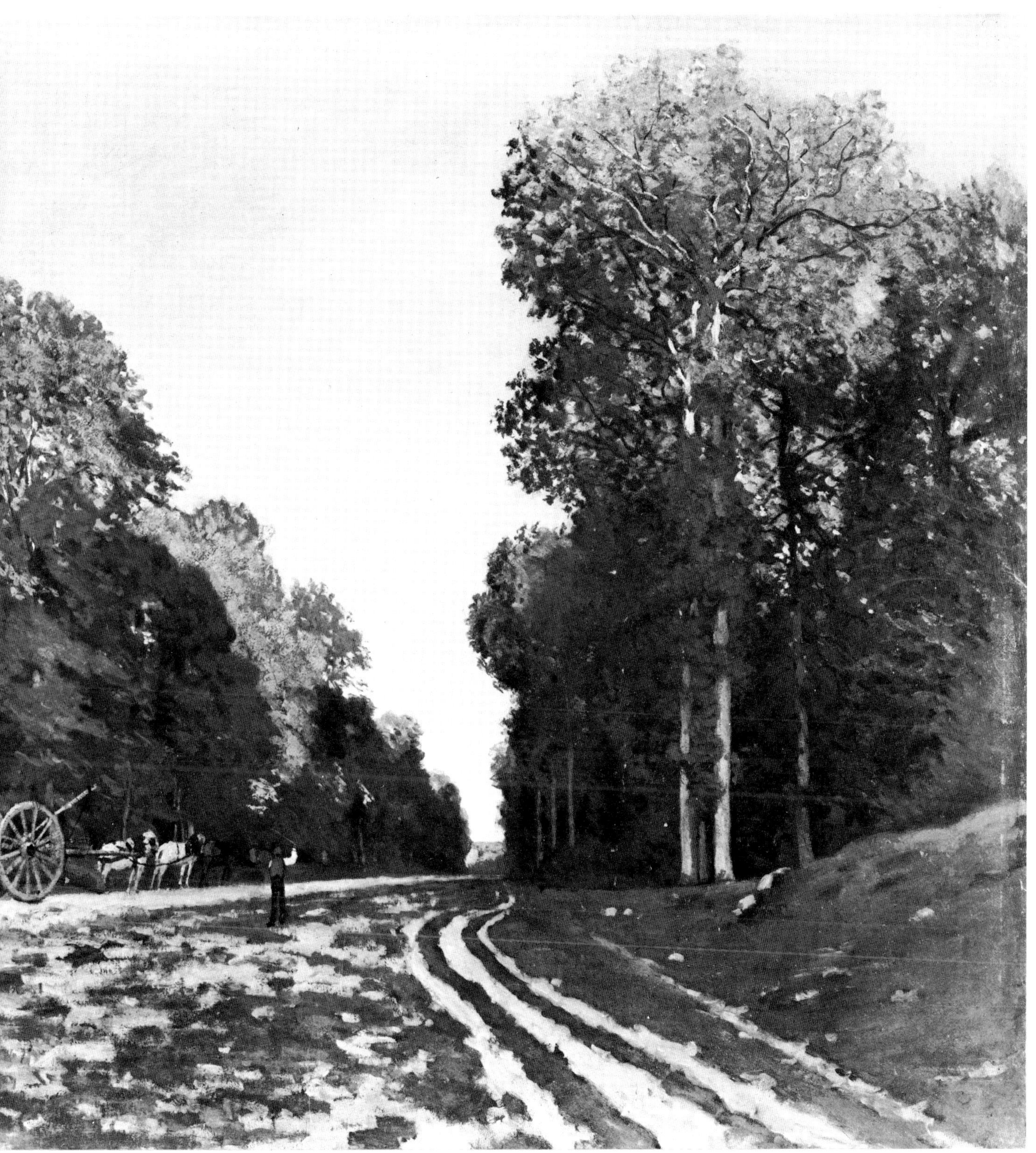

document that casts any light on the lodgings of artists at Chailly. Bazille, after doing what he could to make his friend comfortable, picked up paint-brushes and executed *Monet after His Accident at the Inn at Chailly*, which depicts Claude Monet lying on a large four-poster bed with his leg resting on a pile of blankets. The scene is portrayed with almost photographic realism: from the tiles on the floor to the wallpaper, every detail is depicted with a charming accuracy that perfectly reflects the intimate, impromptu quality of

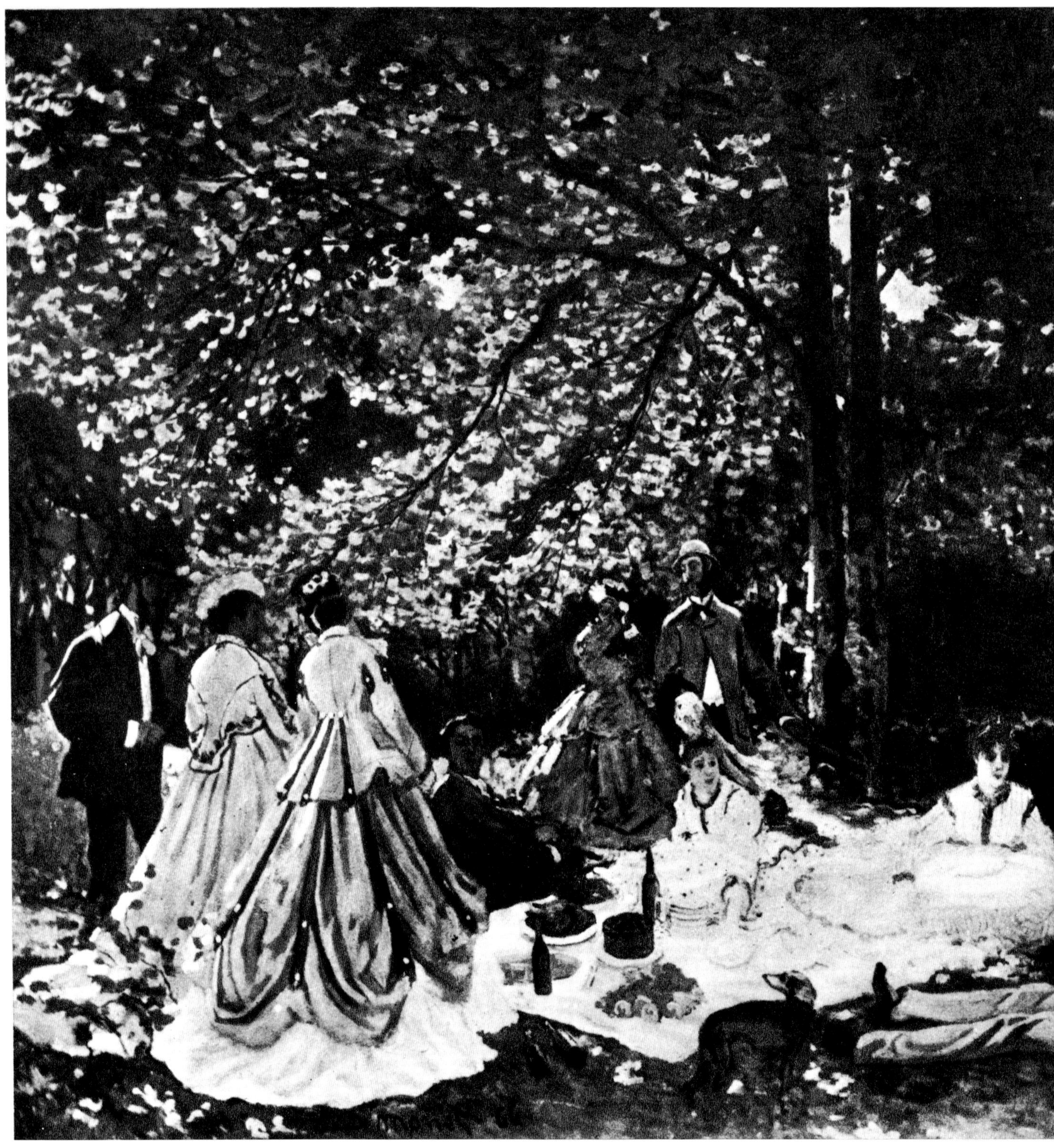

Claude Monet: Study for *Le Déjeuner sur l'Herbe*, 1866 (Pushkin Museum of Fine Arts, Moscow). This extensive study for the *Déjeuner*, begun in September 1865 in Monet's studio, was based on numerous sketches executed out-of-doors during the summer.

the scene. The rooms of the Hôtel du Lion d'Or seem far more comfortable in Bazille's painting than they do in the Goncourt brothers' description.

Once he had recovered, Monet led Bazille about half a mile from Chailly-en-Bière, on the Bas-Bréau road, to a spot where the beeches and oaks were less dense, forming a clearing that was ideal for one of those *parties de campagne* which were in such vogue at the time. Bazille posed patiently and lent his elegant figure to two (at least) of the men in *Le Déjeuner sur l'Herbe* – one of them standing by a sun-dappled tree-trunk, and the other, seen in

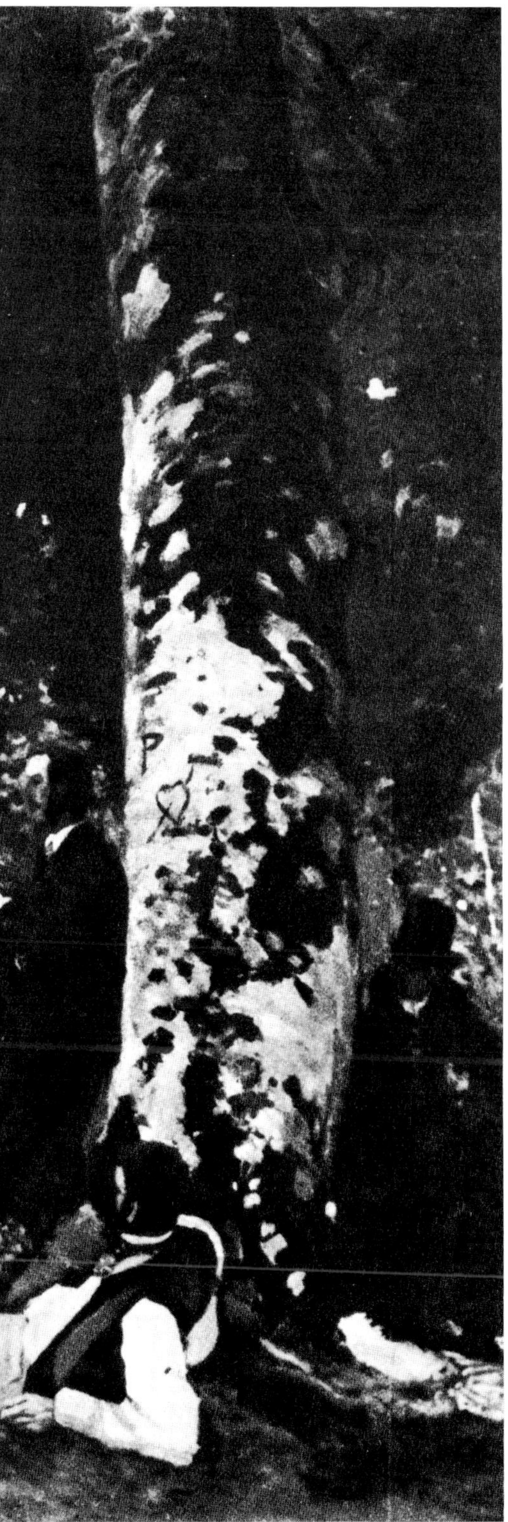

three-quarter face, on the far left between two women. The practical problems of painting the picture were made exceptionally complicated by the enormous dimensions that Monet planned for it. As it was impossible to carry such a vast canvas to the site, he decided to paint fragments of it each day from life, then copy them on to the final picture in his studio, without altering the light in any way. The only surviving fragment of the studies he carried out on the spot is *Les Promeneurs*, in which Bazille appears.

Claude Monet's unprecedented undertaking quickly drew the curiosity of the whole artistic colony of Fontainebleau. As soon as he got back from Le Havre, where he had been attending the regatta with Renoir, Sisley joined Monet and probably posed for the fourth male figure, seated on the left. Courbet, when visiting Fontainebleau to attend the races, showed interest in the project – he was of course fully aware of the problems it involved. Life at Chailly-en-Bière became increasingly hectic as friends and other people attracted by the news converged on the village. Bazille left at the end of August, and during September Monet worked indoors on a rough sketch of the complete painting, which is now in the Pushkin Museum in Moscow.

When the weather began to deteriorate, Monet wanted to return to Paris. But, as often happened, he was unable to pay his debts, and had to leave his personal belongings and a study for *Le Déjeuner* with the innkeeper. As soon as he got back to the capital, he installed himself in Bazille's spacious studio at 6 Place Furstemberg, a charming little square behind Saint-Germain-des-Prés, and began painting the final version of his composition on a canvas that measured 4.65 metres by 6 metres.

Monet certainly possessed the tremendous physical energy demanded by such a task, but once again he lacked the necessary money to buy colours and other materials. He begged from friends and acquaintances, but apparently without much success. Yet he fought tooth and nail to succeed in his venture, and numerous friends and older painters came to watch him in the throes of creating the painting. Some idea of the interest aroused by *Le Déjeuner* can be gained from a letter Bazille wrote to his parents in December 1865: '. . . First, I'm working well on my painting for the Salon, and have been complimented on it by Courbet, who dropped in on us to have a look at Monet's picture, which delighted him. Indeed, more than twenty painters have come to see it, and they all admire it greatly, even though it is not nearly completed. . . . The painting will be the talk of the exhibition.'

But all the difficulties Monet was encountering began to sap his self-confidence. Depressed by one or two critical remarks from Courbet he altered and retouched the work, and in so doing lost the spontaneity which, allied with inspiration, enables a creator to accept flaws in a work that otherwise possesses enormous qualities. After having had to move from Bazille's fine large studio to much smaller premises, and realizing about the middle of March that he would never be able to finish the painting for the Salon, Monet abandoned work on it so as to devote himself to the immediate and most important aim of all painters of the time, which was still to be exhibited on the walls of the Palais de l'Industrie.

Frédéric Bazille derived much benefit from Monet's example. He did not waste his time during the long sessions that he sat for his friend in that summer of 1865. Certain compositional details and the casual appearance of the figures in *Le Repos sur l'Herbe*, which he painted on the banks of the Loing during Sisley's stay there, were clearly inspired by Monet: the picture captures the memory of a moment of relaxation spent with friends on a fine summer day, and shows Monet in shirtsleeves leaning against the trunk of a chestnut tree next to his young mistress, Camille Doncieux, and Alfred Sisley stretched on the ground (like one of the figures in *Le Déjeuner*), reading his newspaper with his girlfriend beside him; but in the foreground Bazille pays homage to Courbet by including a still life made up of a bunch of flowers, a parasol, a hat and some clothes. Although Bazille returned to Fontainebleau, he never worked there again.

While his friends put their heart and soul into their work, Sisley painted lackadaisically, like the dilettante he then was. Art was just one of the countless pleasures that his parents' wealth had made accessible to him, and ambition was not something that concerned him overmuch. He did not attend Gleyre's studio very regularly, and although he spent long periods at Fontainebleau it was because work at the easel was made attractive by the concomitant pleasures of friendship, flirtation and the open air. As he was under no obligation to exhibit at the Salon, he followed the impulses of his sensitive and refined temperament, and was never tempted, like Renoir or Monet, to undertake large-scale compositions whose audacity and skill of execution would impress the members of the jury.

Sisley felt the beauties of nature very keenly; and in landscapes such as *Village Street at Marlotte* he renders harmonies of colours and shapes with great sureness of touch. The colours, however, remain sombre and lifeless, suggesting that he worked on the painting in a studio rather than in the open air. He was surprised when Renoir, on Diaz' advice, lightened his palette. But he rapidly followed suit.

Renoir was then Sisley's favourite companion. They went on long stays at Marlotte together and shared the same friends. Sisley very obligingly posed more than once for Renoir. In the large painting that Renoir executed for the Salon of 1868, *Portrait of Alfred Sisley and His Wife*, Sisley is seen offering his arm, with amorous attention, to his young wife. Both of them are dressed with the elegance that was *de rigueur* at the time: he is wearing light trousers

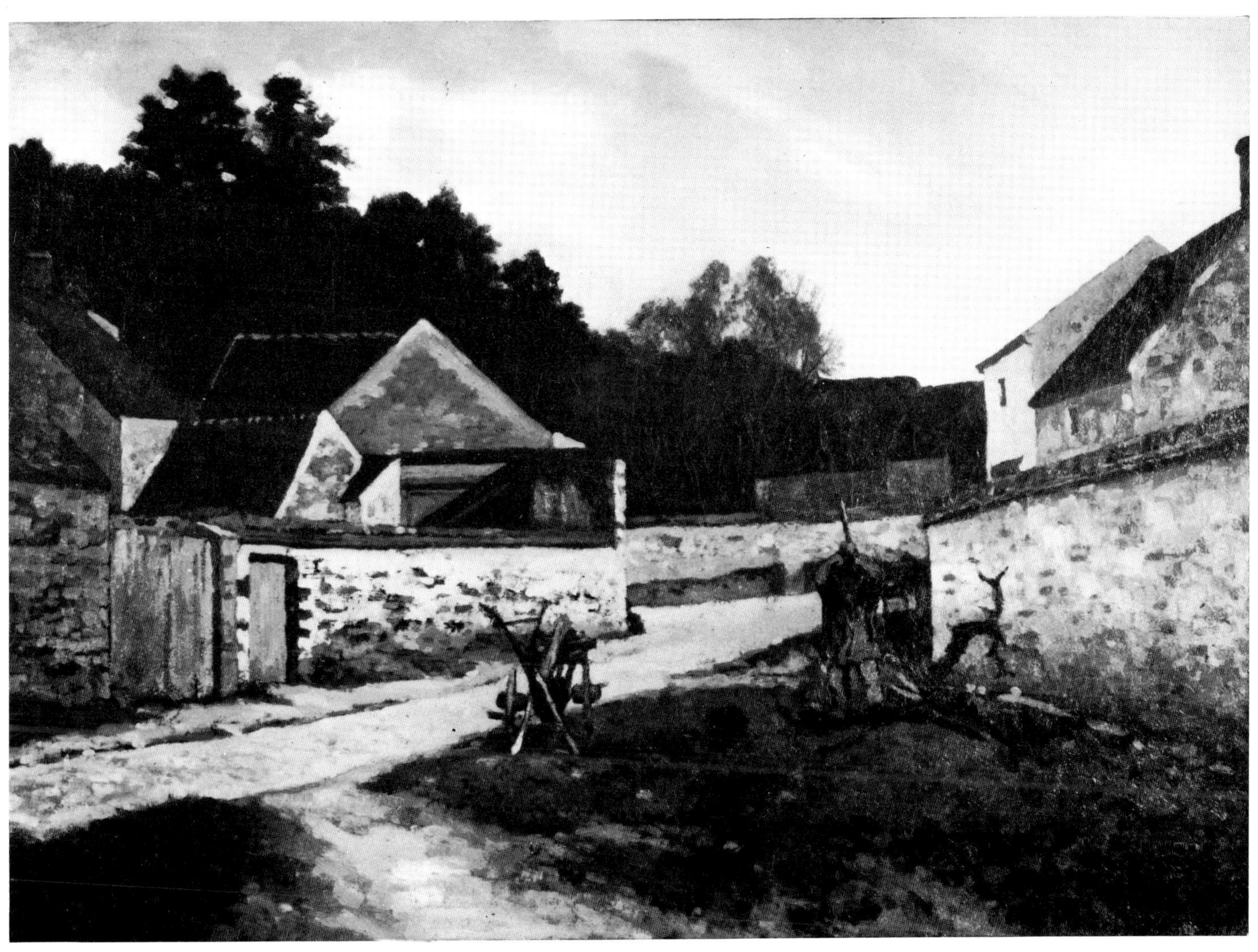

Alfred Sisley: *Village Street in Marlotte*, 1866 (Albright-Knox Art Gallery, Buffalo, New York). When Sisley and Renoir came to the forest they usually stayed at Marlotte, where Renoir's friend Jules Le Coeur had a house.

and a dark jacket, and holding in his hands the symbols of his class, a top-hat and gloves, while his wife's cumbersome crinoline is fully in accordance with the rules of contemporary fashion as laid down by the two women's magazines, *La Mode Illustrée* and *Le Magasin Pittoresque*. Nevertheless, the natural light that bathes the young couple quite outweighs such conventional details.

By the end of the 1860s Sisley was working mostly in Paris. It was about then that he went through a particularly harrowing period of his life: his father fell gravely ill and was no longer able to manage his export-import business, which as a result ran into serious difficulties. Sisley was left with no other income than what he could get from his painting. Then aged thirty, and already the father of two children, he was particularly ill equipped to cope with such a terrible change of fortune, coinciding as it did with the difficult times of the Franco-Prussian War and the Commune.

It was after an absence of more than fifteen years, in 1882, that Sisley came

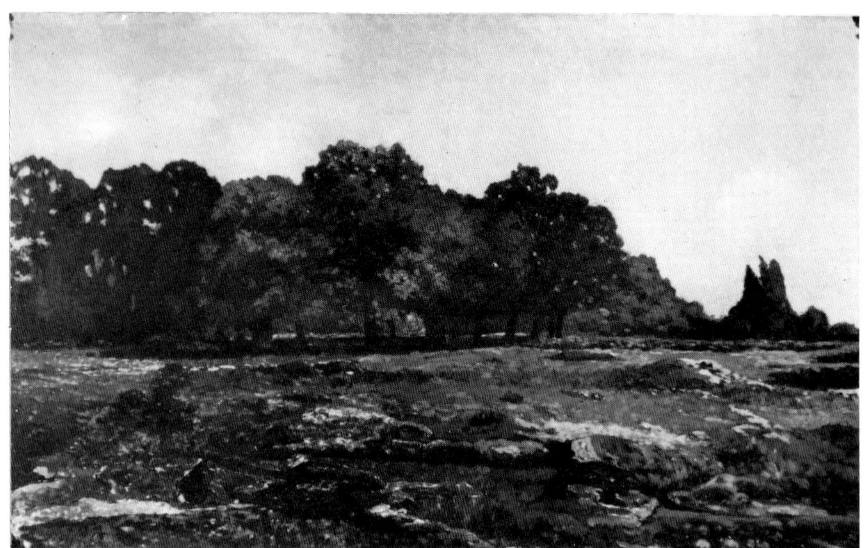

LEFT Alfred Sisley: *The Avenue of Chestnut Trees*, 1865 (Petit Palais, Paris). Sisley was later to lighten his palette like Monet and Renoir, but when he painted this landscape he was still conforming with the conventions of his time. OPPOSITE Auguste Renoir: *Portrait of Alfred Sisley and His Wife*, 1868 (Wallraf-Richartz Museum, Cologne). 'The man of antiquity created what he saw; create what you see!' was the advice of the critic Edmond Duranty to the young painters. Remembering his words, Renoir painted this thoroughly modern image of Sisley and his young wife.

back to the Fontainebleau area and settled in Moret-sur-Loing, to the south-east of the forest, on the opposite side to Barbizon. Traces of a certain nobility, such as the ancient Porte de Bourgogne and Francois I's house (which was later moved, stone by stone, to Cours-La-Reine in Paris), were reminders that the King of France had once appreciated the charms of that picturesque village. The beautiful river, spanned by an old bridge, and the fine trees that shaded its banks were just the sort of motifs that appealed to Sisley. And yet he did not feel at home there. Hardly had he arrived than he wrote to his dealer, Durand-Ruel: 'I've made up my mind to leave Moret as soon as possible, it doesn't agree with me. I won't go far, just to Les Sablons, a quarter of an hour from here, but I'll be more in my element.' So Sisley rented, on the outskirts of the village of Les Sablons, a small house surrounded by a garden in which he worked. He also often painted in Moret, or around the village and on the edge of the woods. Then, in 1889, he returned for good to Moret. The masterpieces he painted there were to immortalize for ever the little provincial streets, watermills, bridges, river banks and quaint church of that country town. Sisley's talent is to be found in his subtlety of nuance; his paintings, which are often dominated by infinite expanses of sky, reflect immense sensitivity and an atmosphere of delicate melancholy.

With the Fontainebleau experience, a basic pattern formed that was to characterize the lives of all the Impressionists except Manet and Degas. They oscillated continually between Paris and various parts of the French countryside. If Manet and Degas remained essentially painters of city life, the others were perpetually concerned with capturing nature in as direct and unidealized a fashion as possible. This preoccupation did not, of course, free them altogether from having to spend time in Paris. After all, it was only there that they could hope to make their name and fortune, quite apart from the other obvious attractions of the capital. But the taste for life in the country (where they could also exist for far less money) was to be with them throughout, as when it next took some of them to the fashionable coastal towns and soft green landscapes of Normandy.

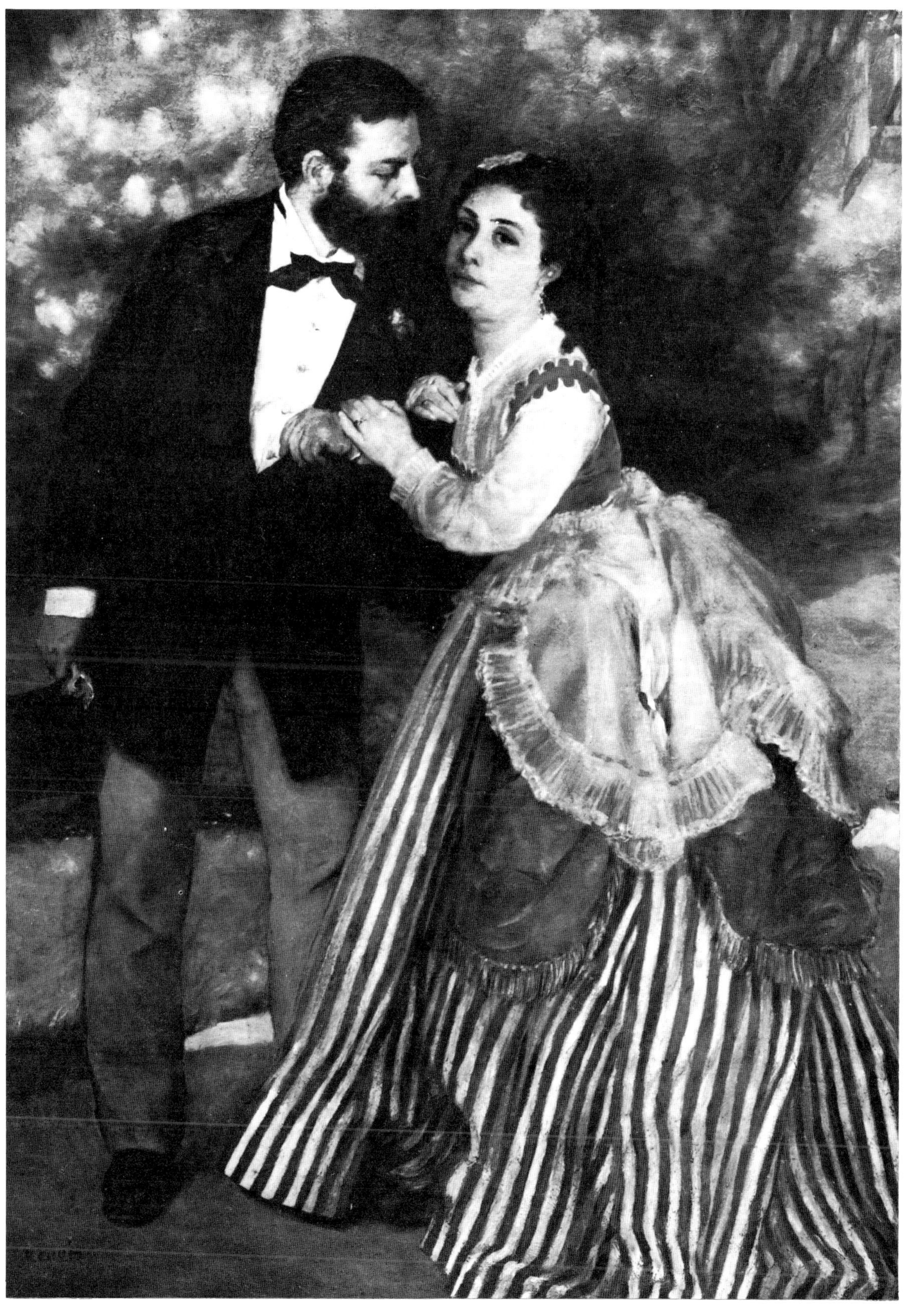

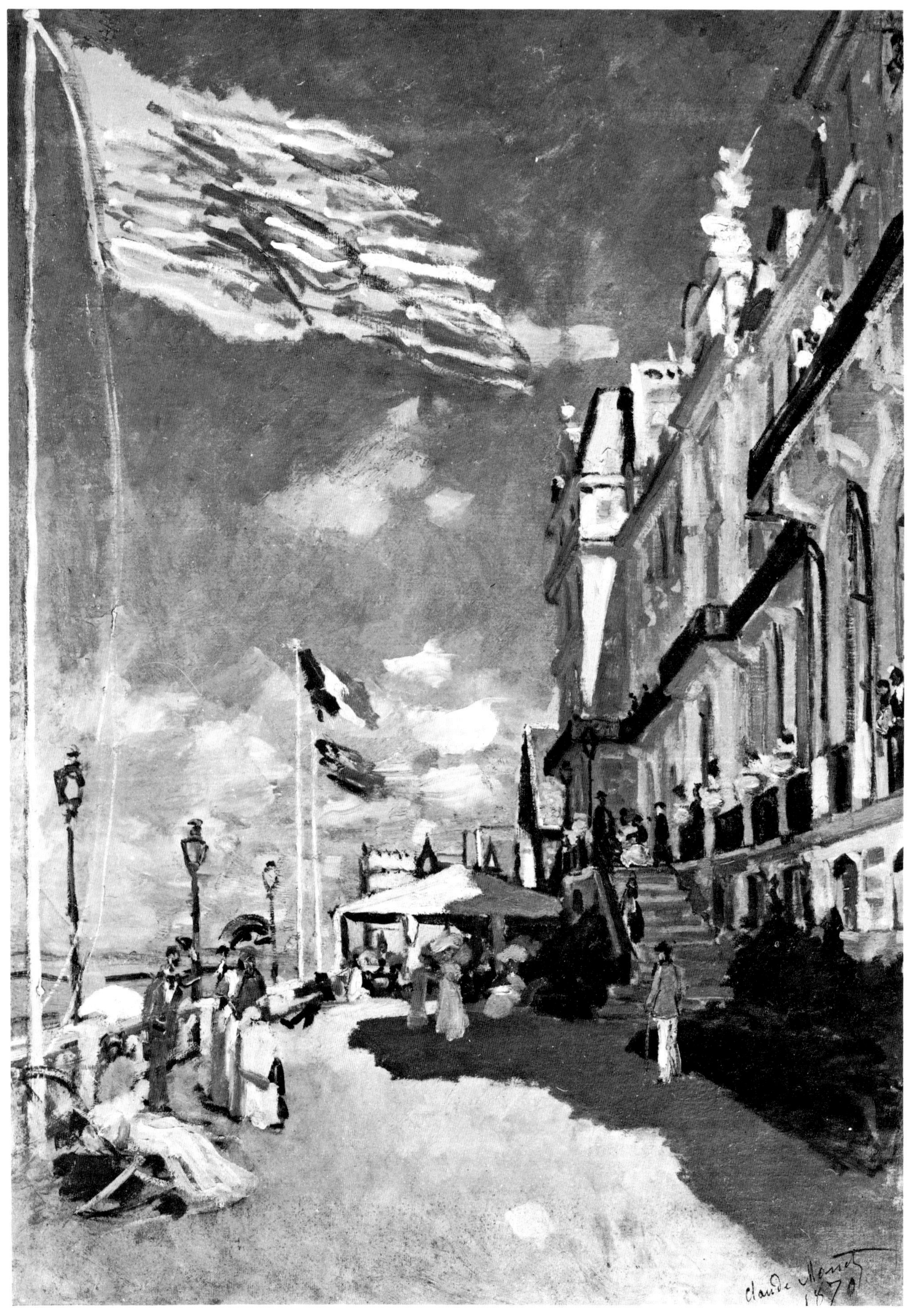
Claude Monet
1870

3 Normandy

Seascapes and Sophistication

There were several reasons why Normandy became a focal point for the Impressionists – none of them the visual reasons that one would tend to expect. The greatest champion of Normandy's spectacular coastline and damp lush countryside was, of course, Monet, for whom it was home. While studying at Gleyre's studio, he had lost no opportunity of singing its praises to his friends, all of whom went out there at one time or another.

The fact that the Normandy coast had become so fashionable also proved a strong pull. The new mania for sea bathing and fresh air had wafted across the Channel and become all the rage with the French. As a result, sophisticated seaside resorts blossomed all along the coast, luring the upper classes and the intelligentsia from Paris. Because of this, in addition to Monet, Bazille, Berthe Morisot, Renoir and Sisley, even the most Paris-bound of all painters, Degas, was tempted out there.

Monet himself made a habit of staying with his family in Normandy once or twice a year, right up until 1875. Having finished his spell out at Fontainebleau in the spring of 1863, he came back to Paris to visit the vast annual Salon and then began to prepare his summer trip. Although they were not on the best of terms, Claude's father was always willing to provide his son with bed and board – a fact of some importance to someone as impecunious as the young painter constantly was. The whole family used to spend the summer months on Madame Lecadre's estate at Sainte-Adresse, a seaside resort much frequented by holidaymakers from Le Havre. Madame Lecadre, Monet *père*'s half-sister, was interested in painting, and her daughters, who were of about the same age as Monet, had friends among the local intellectual bourgeoisie. All this made for a lively and enjoyable atmosphere.

In May 1864, Monet invited Frédéric Bazille to come with him to Normandy. They had always liked each other ever since they had worked together at Gleyre's studio, but had become firm friends during their visits to Chailly the previous year. Bazille admired Monet because he was a much more experienced and adventurous painter, while Claude appreciated the friendly disposition and generosity of his colleague.

Both men were in love with life and art. They adored boating, which was an enormously fashionable sport at the time, and decided therefore to turn their journey to Normandy into a pleasure cruise. A train would have enabled them to reach the coast in four hours; they chose instead to go by boat. The River Seine at that period was busier than a modern motorway, with steamers, three-masters, tugs and schooners plying their way to and fro between Paris and Le Havre.

Claude Monet: *L'Hôtel des Roches Noires, Trouville*, 1870 (Musée du Louvre, Paris). Monet uncharacteristically turns his back on the sea and produces a briskly executed, charming picture of Trouville, at that time a new and very chic seaside resort.

They stopped off at Rouen, Normandy's capital, which Emma Bovary, the heroine of Flaubert's novel, had found 'as still as a painting'. But for Monet and Bazille it was a bustling, modern city of quite spectacular aspect:

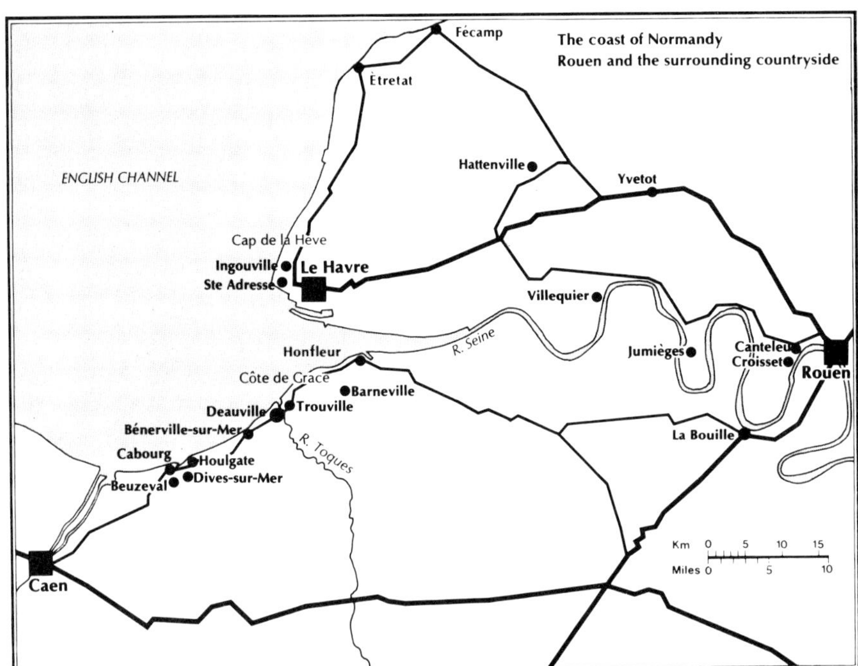

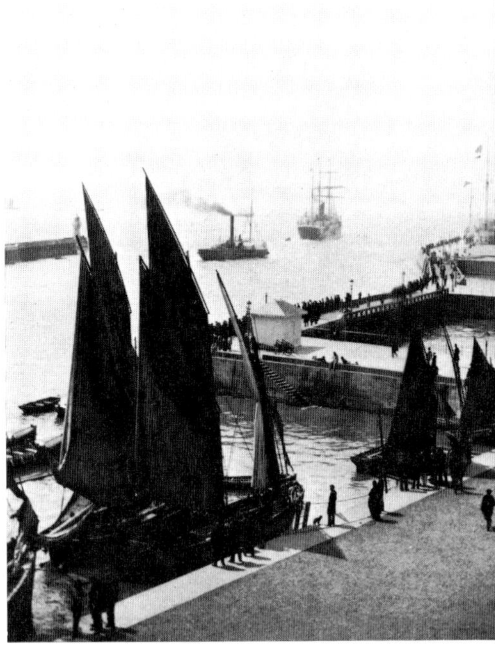

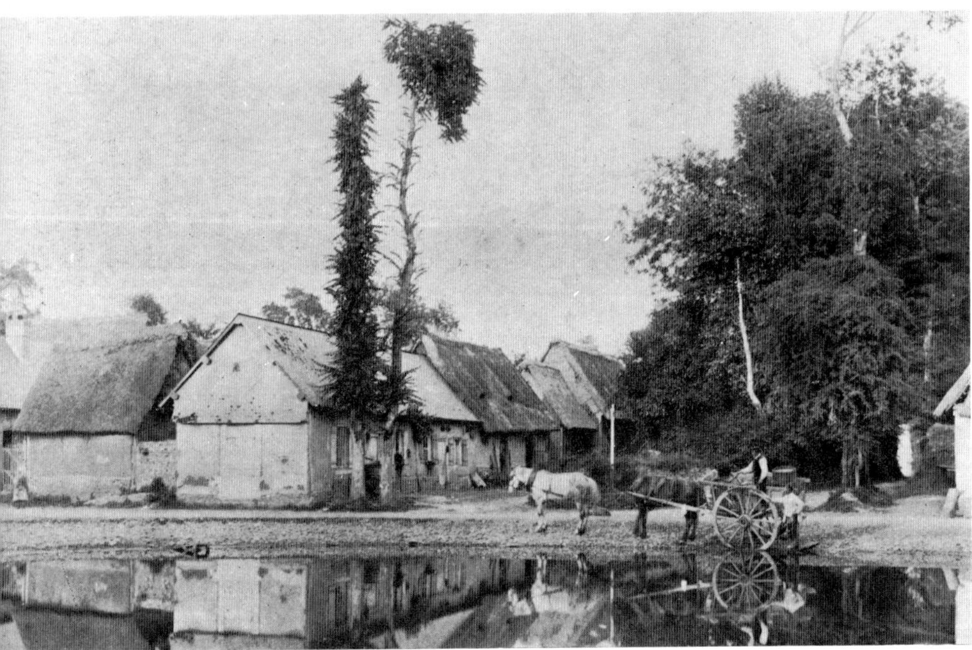

ABOVE The jetties of Le Havre, already a busy port, in the late nineteenth century.
BELOW LEFT Renoir loved the quiet little country village of Berneval near Wargemont. 'It is a real nest surrounded by trees and slopes, and with a pretty beach', said Pissarro, who much later went to work there too.
OPPOSITE Claude Monet: *Honfleur Ferry*, detail, 1864 (Professor Walter A. Johr Collection, Saint-Gall).

the finely sculpted Gothic steeples of the old quarter contrasted vividly with the countless smoke-belching chimneys of the new textile mills and chemical factories. The two artists visited Rouen's imposing cathedral, which after a fire in 1822 no longer had its celebrated steeple (it was rebuilt only in 1884); they looked at the beautiful Place du Vieux-Marché, where Joan of Arc was burnt at the stake; and in the Musée des Beaux-Arts they admired Delacroix' *The Justice of Trajan* and works by painters of Norman origin such as Poussin and Géricault.

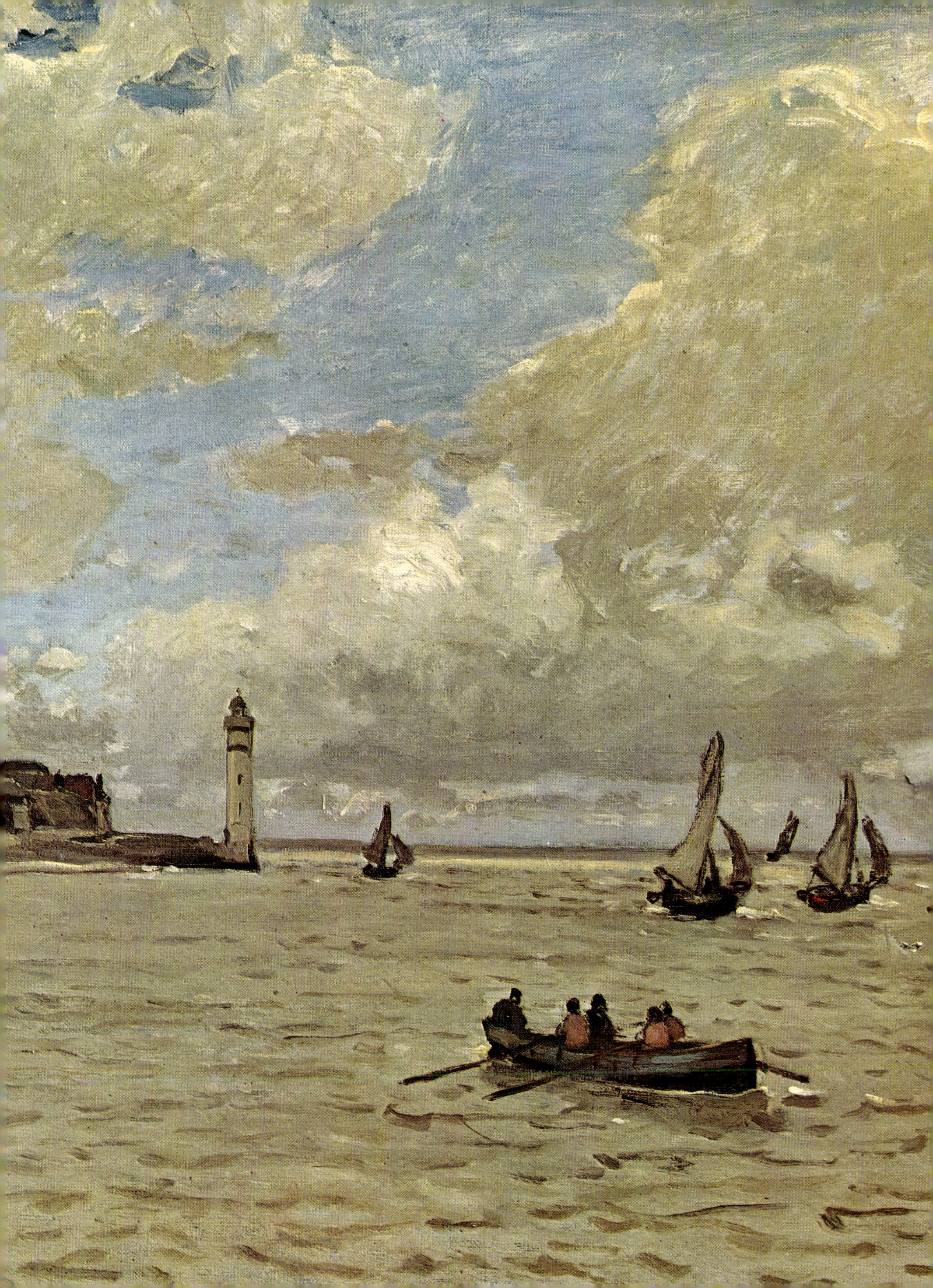

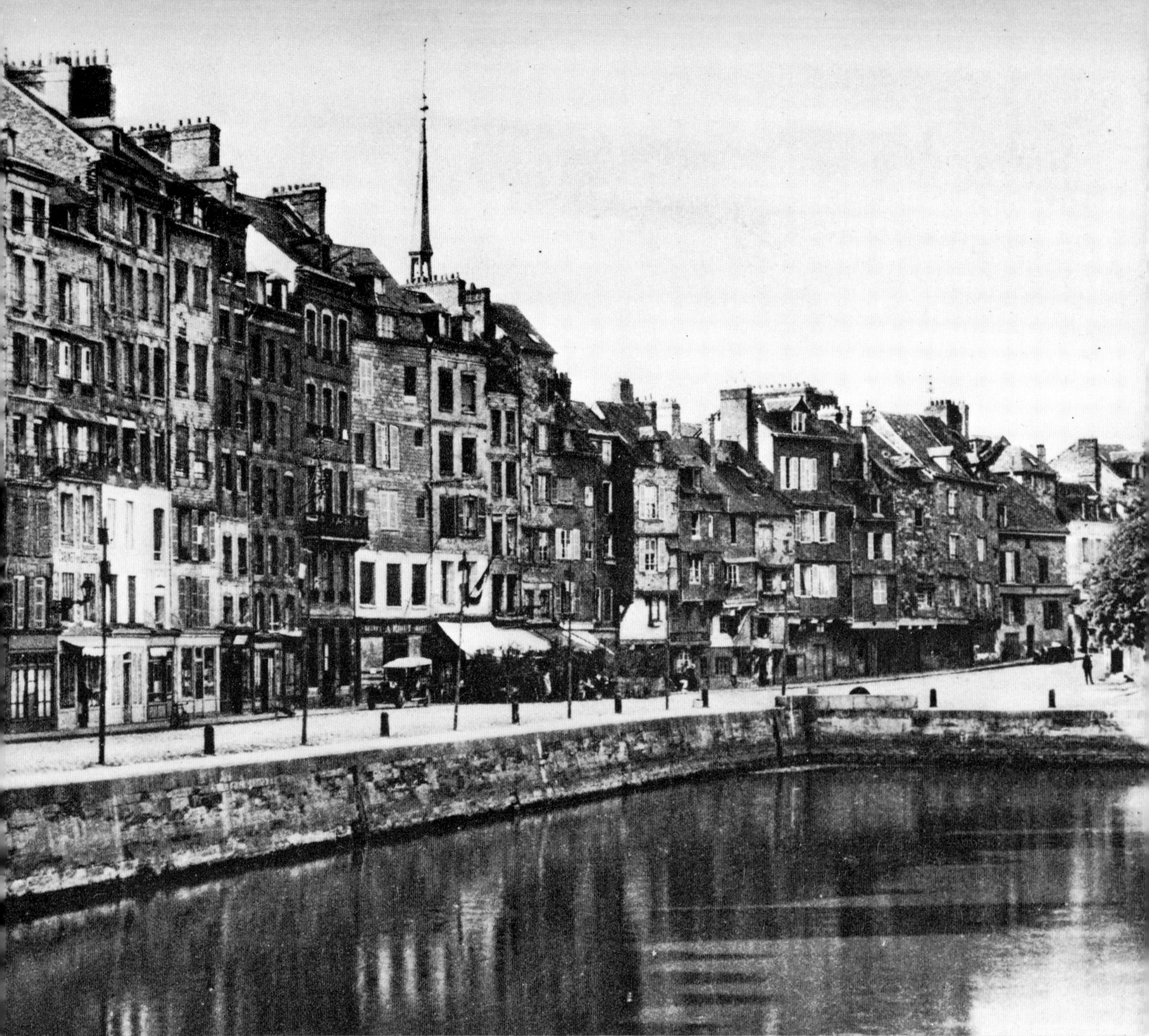

Every other day a regular steamboat service ran from Rouen to Le Havre in five to six hours with a shipment of locals and visitors (it cost five francs first class and four francs second class). Tourist guides, which were just beginning to appear at the time, warmly recommended the trip. Downstream from Rouen, the Seine twists and turns just as it does after passing through Paris, slicing its way through sheer cliffs topped sometimes with lush meadows, sometimes with thick woods. As the boat progressed, Monet and Bazille would have seen on the right bank the villages of Croisset, where Flaubert wrote *Madame Bovary*, and Villequier, which was well known for more tragic reasons: Victor Hugo had seen his daughter drown in the river there. Then they arrived at Honfleur, which is separated from Le Havre by the wide Seine estuary.

Monet could not have chosen a more attractive spot with which to introduce his guest to the Côte de Grâce, as this part of the Normandy coast

Honfleur, one of the most beautiful towns in Normandy, began to attract English and French landscape painters as early as the eighteenth century. ABOVE The basin of the Lieutenance, surrounded by old slate-fronted houses. OPPOSITE In the sixteenth century, the Lieutenance (ABOVE) was lived in by the governor of the port, which was then of considerable importance. Chapelle Notre-Dame-de-Grâce (RIGHT), a former place of pilgrimage, dominates the town.

OVERLEAF Edgar Degas: *At the Seaside*, *c.* 1876 (National Gallery, London). Degas was not interested in light, and he gave priority to unusual visual elements; the bathing costume sitting like a sloughed skin on the far right of the composition carries a very strong visual punch.

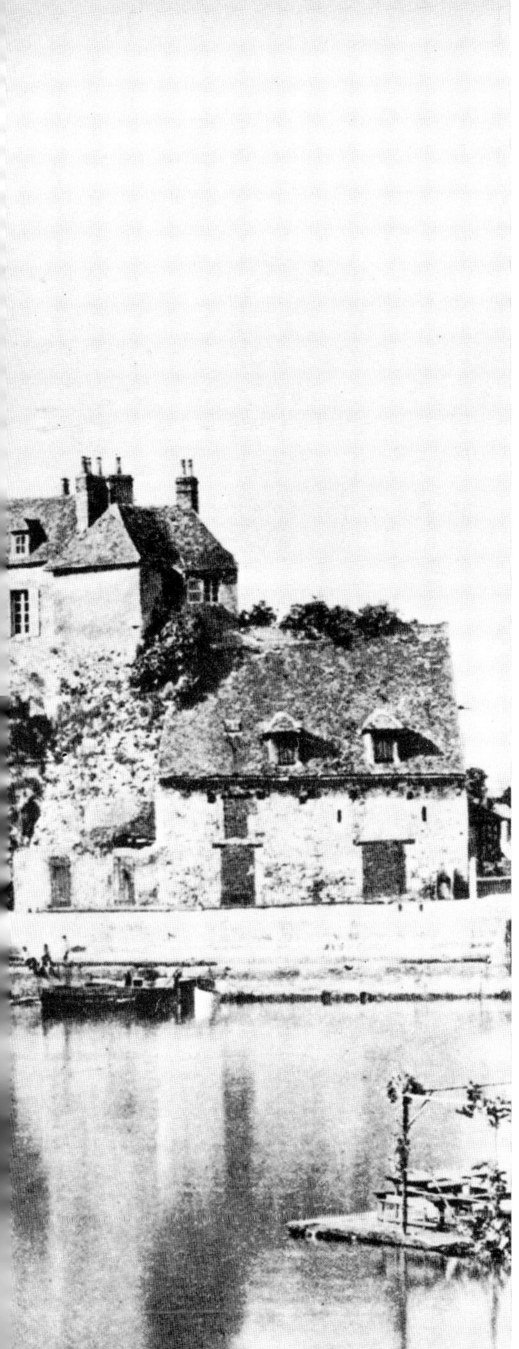

is called. Honfleur, little more than a village, had once been an important fortified harbour, as can be seen from its defence works and from La Lieutenance, the governor's residence, which dates from the sixteenth century.

The navy eventually moved elsewhere, but the town was taken up at the beginning of the nineteenth century by painters such as Isabey, Bonington, Corot and Courbet, who, with numerous other lesser-known figures, went there to paint seascapes. Boudin was a native of the place, while Jongkind never missed an opportunity to go and stay there. Even Baudelaire toyed with the idea of settling in Honfleur with his mother, who had been living there since the death of her second husband, General Aupick.

Bazille was much taken with the tall, narrow buildings that surrounded the harbour and the quaint church of Sainte-Catherine – built from old ships –

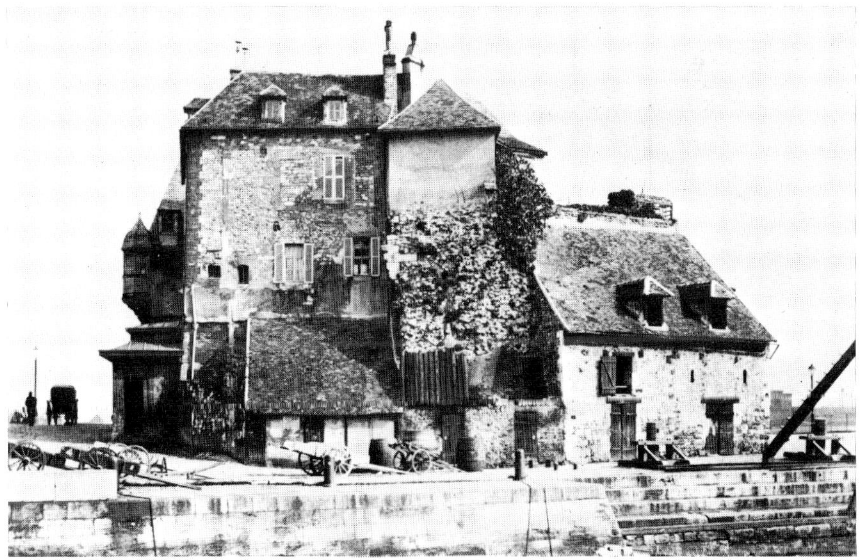

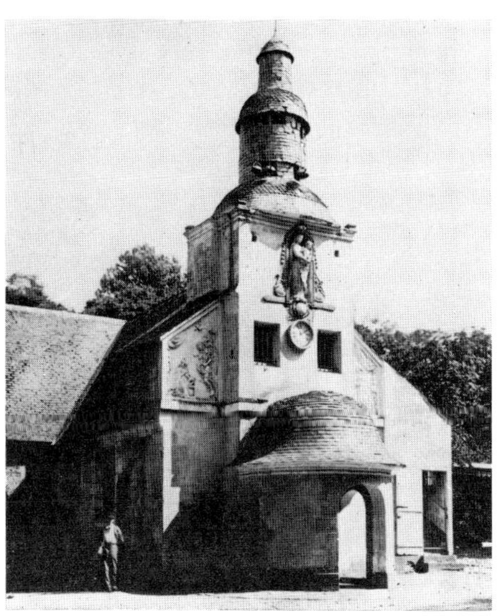

whose bell-tower stands opposite on the other side of the marketplace. To a man from the South of France such as he, everything seemed new – the moist light, the bracing air, the farmworkers' loose overalls and cotton caps, and the Norman women's attractive regional costumes and headdresses.

From the very start of their visit, the two painters rose early and left the little rooms they had rented from one of the village bakers to go and work in the open air. A steep road took them up to the Côte de Grâce, on which was perched the attractive Chapelle Notre-Dame-de-Grâce (which Monet was often to paint), with its sentinels of silent, towering trees. From there, they would tramp further up the winding, shaded track to the top of the hill where, set against a background of meadows, hedges and cows, stood La Ferme Saint-Siméon. In its courtyard, on tables laid out under the apple trees, old Mother Toutain the innkeeper would offer her wholesome local fare – cider, eggs, milk, and great bowls of fresh cream. Like Boudin,

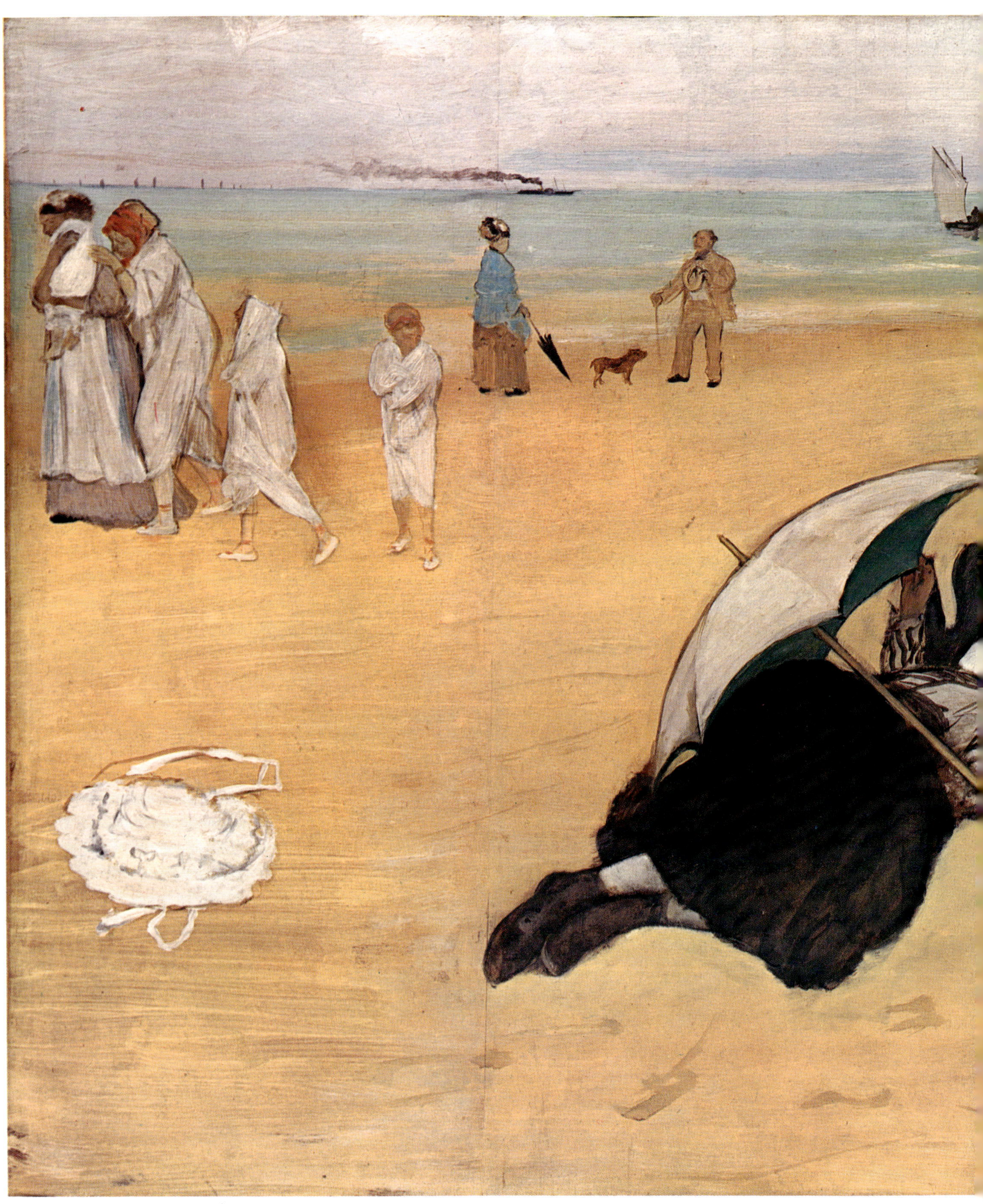

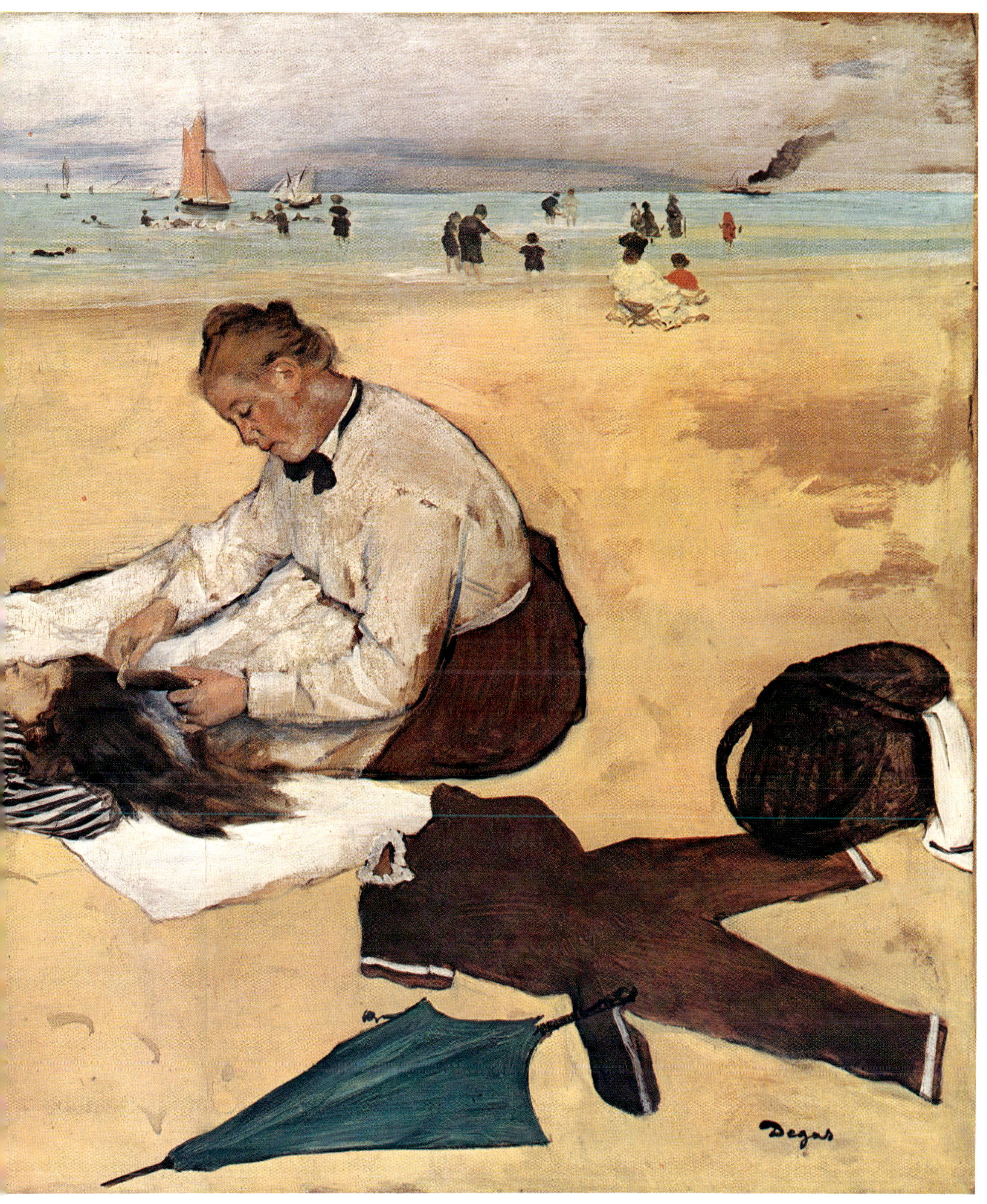
Degas

Courbet and Jongkind before them, Bazille and Monet often had lunch there, or waited to watch the sun set over the Seine estuary far below. Bazille set up his easel in the courtyard and painted *The Farmyard*, one of the few existing mementoes of their stay. It is an awkward, immature work. Monet himself painted *The Road by the Saint-Siméon Farm*, a well-composed canvas full of the self-confidence he had acquired at Chailly, but still rather sombre-toned.

A few days later, the two friends crossed the mouth of the Seine by boat to Le Havre, a trip which took them thirty-five minutes (by road the distance was fifty-seven kilometres). 'I lunched with the Monet family,' Bazille wrote to his parents. 'They are charming people, and have a charming estate at Sainte-Adresse, near Le Havre. I had to turn down their kind invitation to spend the month of August with them. I get up at 5 o'clock every morning, and paint throughout the day till 8 in the evening.' All that has remained of these long work sessions are versions by both artists of *The Seaside at Sainte-Adresse*.

Bazille was dissatisfied with his work. 'Don't expect me to come back with any good landscapes,' he told his parents. 'I'm making progress, and that's all.' This is hardly surprising: Bazille, who was still only a beginner, was probably put out of his stride by the sheer scale of the scenery and the unfamiliarity of the light. Green is always the dominant colour in Normandy, carpeting the ground, clothing the hedges and bordering the roads. And the delicate green of young leaves, the triumphant green of Normandy's open country, would have seemed a far cry from the deep green of Fontainebleau's sweeping avenues.

At the beginning of June Bazille left Normandy and returned to his family in Montpellier, leaving Monet in the grips of a feverish enthusiasm for work. The region was a kind of paradise for him, a source of power and inspiration. In the loneliness where land meets sea, in the fold of a gully leading down to the beach, or beneath a blue sky dotted with milk-white clouds, he rediscovered the vividness of his first sensations. A straightforward conviction that he was capable of putting his impressions on canvas filled him with sudden, heady energy. He wanted to paint everything within his field of vision, and if he was not satisfied he scraped off the paint and tried again. For he was convinced that 'one can express what one sees and what one understands.'

The landscapes produced by Monet at Honfleur, Sainte-Adresse and Cap de la Hève during the summers of 1864 and 1865 herald the startling blaze of colour to be found in two works he was to paint there in 1867, *Terrace at Sainte-Adresse* and *Regatta at Sainte-Adresse*.

That same summer of 1864, while Monet was working on the Côte de Grâce,

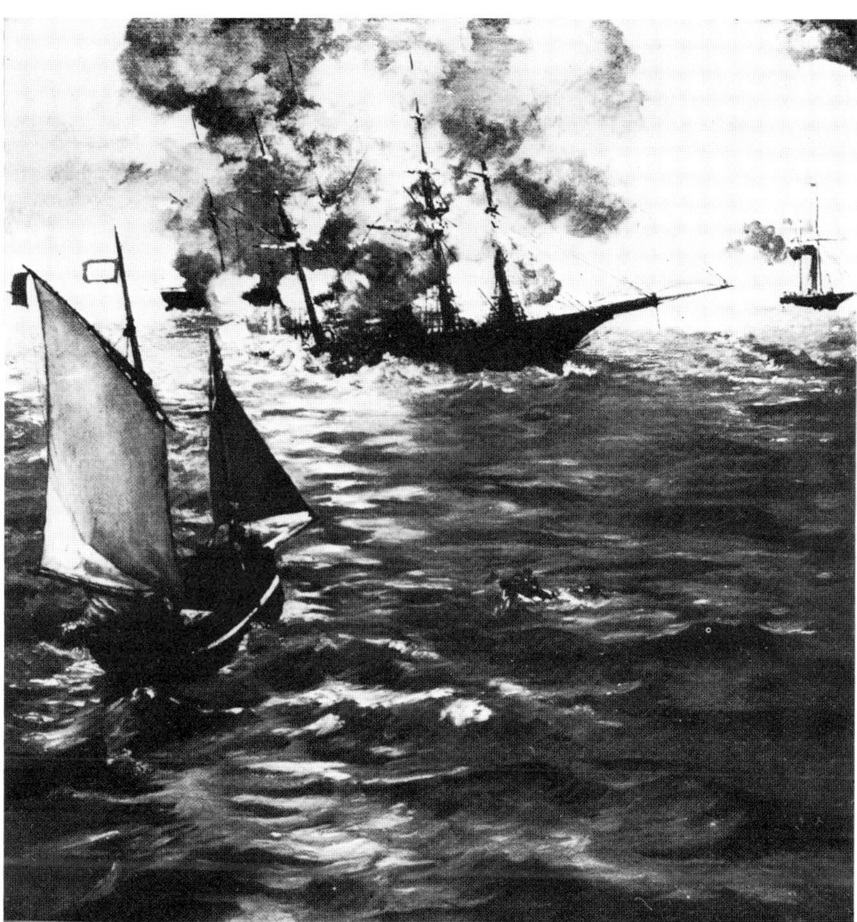

RIGHT Edouard Manet: *The Battle of the Kearsarge and the Alabama*, 1864 (Philadelphia Museum of Art, John G. Johnson Collection). Manet recorded one of the most talked about events of the year, the extraordinary battle between two American ships off the Normandy coast.
BELOW The captain of the *Kearsarge*, J. A. Winslow, and his crew aboard the ship on 18 June 1864, the day before the battle.

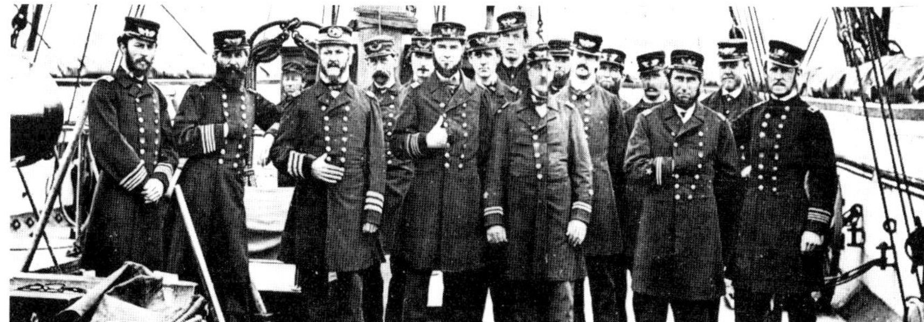

Edouard Manet travelled precipitately from Boulogne-sur-mer to Cherbourg, another Normandy port, to the northwest of Le Havre, in order to witness a preposterous episode in – of all things – the three-year-old American Civil War: a naval engagement between two American vessels.

From the beginning of June, the newspapers had been full of the affair: the *Kearsarge*, a Northern ship, had been giving chase to a Southern vessel, the *Alabama*, which had taken refuge in Cherbourg harbour. According to international conventions, it was impossible for the *Alabama* to stay there for very long. On 19 June, it would have to give battle to the Federal corvette off the French coast.

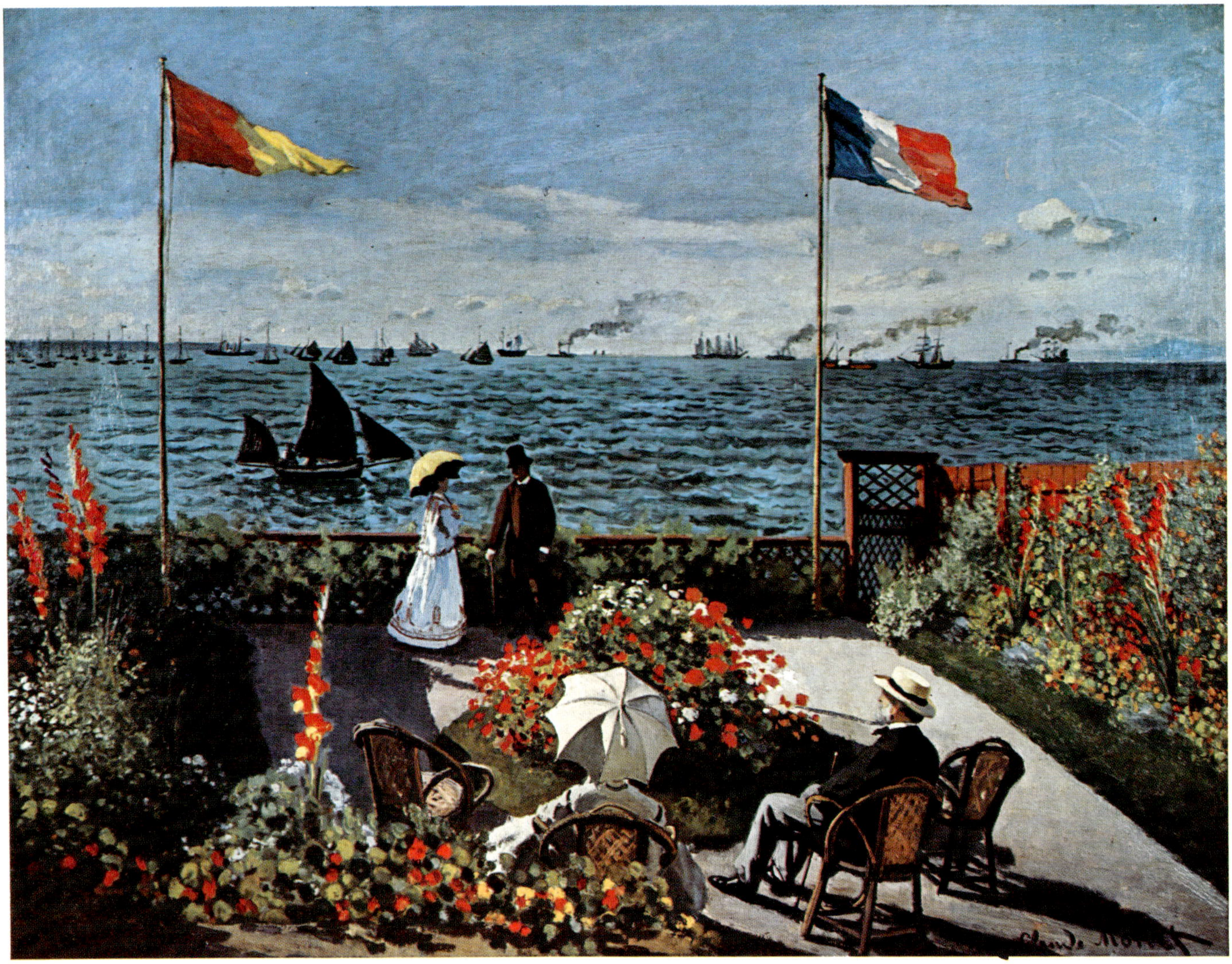

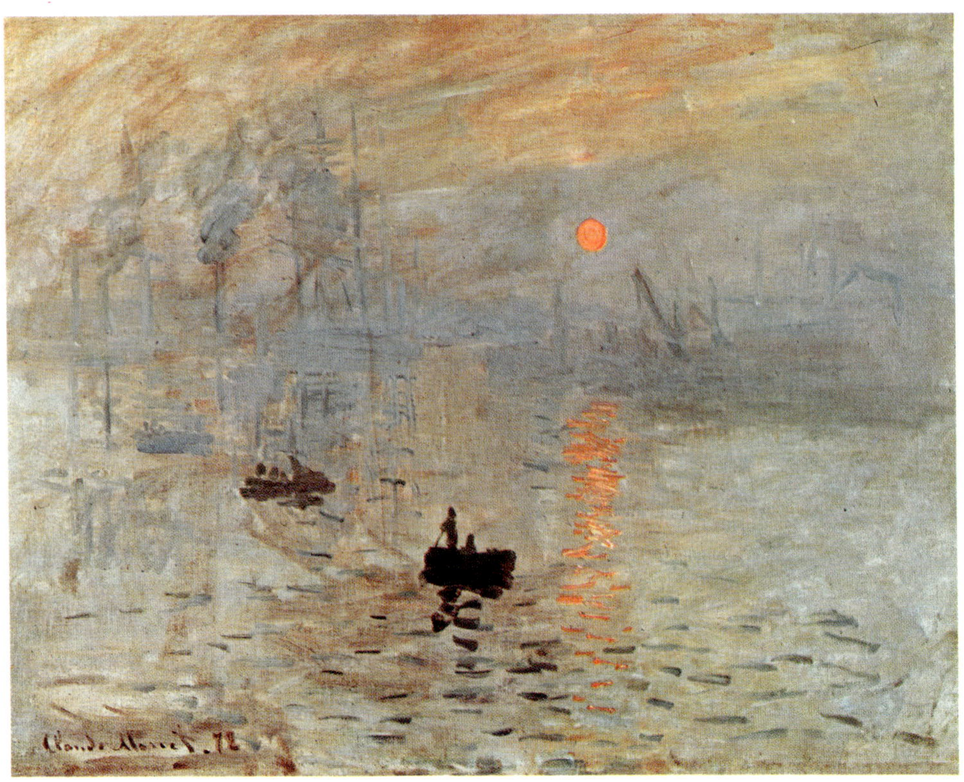

Crowds of interested onlookers gathered for what promised to be an extraordinary spectacle. Manet behaved as though he were covering the incident for a newspaper: from the bridge of a pilot-boat, he rapidly sketched the various stages of the battle (which proved disastrous for the *Alabama*). He then returned to Boulogne and polished off the painting in a few days. On 15 July, *The Battle of the Kearsarge and the Alabama* was put on display in Boulogne. Events were still fresh in people's minds when, in February 1865, the picture was exhibited at Martinet's gallery in Paris. Although far from flawless, the work was particularly successful because of its topicality.

That remained the only occasion on which Manet went to the coast in search of a subject. The influence of England was then at its peak, and had finally convinced the French of the benefits of fresh air and the virtues of sea bathing. It was, in fact, on doctor's orders that Manet spent the summer of 1865 in Boulogne. He returned there in 1869 with his family and was visited by Degas. Later, in 1873, it was in Berck that he chose to nurse his frayed nerves. Once there, of course, he yielded to the temptation of painting the subjects he came across, such as *Boulogne Harbour at Night*, *The Folkestone Boat* and *Déjeuner*.

Berthe Morisot was a frequent visitor to Normandy. As early as 1859, the year when on Corot's advice she began to paint from life, her stay near Dieppe is recorded in a landscape which features a Norman farmhouse.

Beuzeval, where the Morisot family spent the summer of 1864 in a former mill they had rented from the painter Léon Riesener (a cousin of Delacroix), is a hamlet separated from the seaside resort of Houlgate by the Drochon, a tiny but fast-flowing brook whose waters once drove the machinery of many watermills. It was a quiet place to stay, and ideally located as a point of departure for any number of excursions. A stroll along the embankment would bring one to Dives, a sleepy, picturesque old town that was an important port in the Middle Ages – it was from there that William the Conqueror and his men sailed for Hastings. The beautiful city of Caen and its monumental abbeys was only thirty kilometres away. The smart beaches of Cabourg were also within easy reach; it was there that the aristocracy of the Faubourg Saint-Germain, who didn't want to be seen at Dieppe, used to spend their summers in an atmosphere that Marcel Proust was to describe so brilliantly in *A l'Ombre des Jeunes Filles en Fleurs*.

Although Berthe Morisot did join in with the rest of the family's entertainment, we know from the recollections of her younger brother Tiburce (despite the fact that no painting has survived) that the startled villagers would be treated each morning to the incongruous sight of an elegant Parisian lady striding off – with a walking stick and a haversack full

OPPOSITE ABOVE Claude Monet: *The Terrace at Sainte-Adresse*, 1867 (Metropolitan Museum of Art, New York). 'I've spent the last fortnight with my family, and couldn't feel better or happier. They're all so nice to me: every brushstroke draws admiration', Monet wrote to his friend Bazille. He certainly succeeded in capturing the radiant, summery atmosphere of a Sunday with his family. The figures with their backs to the painter are probably Monet's father and Aunt Lecadre; his cousin, Jeanne-Marguerite Lecadre, is standing in front of the sea.
OPPOSITE BELOW Claude Monet: *Impression, Sunrise*, 1872 (Musée Marmottan, Paris). This painting, hastily given a title by Monet in time for the first exhibition of the group, was to give the Impressionist movement its name.

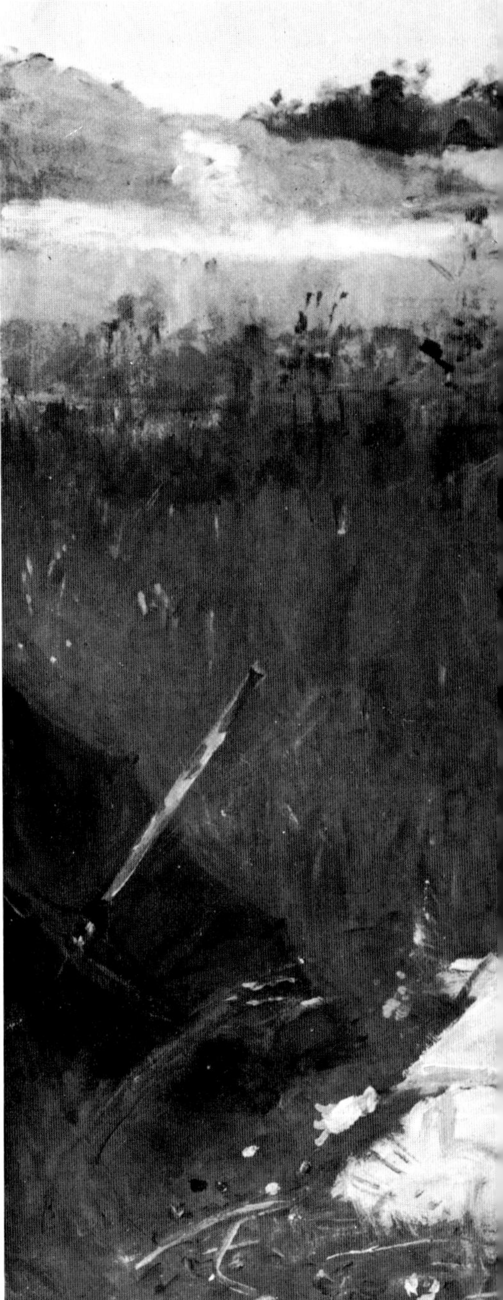

of the landscape painter's paraphernalia – to spend the day before her easel in the fields.

In her search for subjects, the young Berthe allowed neither the prejudices nor practices of her sex and class to stand in her way. According to Tiburce Morisot, one evening that summer his sister described how she had got into a fascinating conversation with a peasant because she found him brimming over with common sense. 'It's odd,' she said, 'how we underestimate people like that – they are not nearly as silly as a lot of people in society!' The presence of the same man next morning and for several days afterwards was just beginning to intrigue her when she found out that this so-called peasant was a former convict from Toulon prison. The news did not worry her unduly. She simply remarked: 'At last I understand why the same phrase kept on coming up in his conversation: "I don't like the South of France, I really don't".'

Three years later, at the little resort of Les Petites-Dalles, between Fécamp and Dieppe, Morisot painted her masterly *The Green Parasol*. It portrays her favourite sister Edma, sitting in a meadow and looking down at a book; the green parasol she has thrown down beside her makes a dark patch in the long grass. The light of a fine summer afternoon – Corot's influence can be felt here – envelops the scene with an impalpable, powdery texture of balmy tranquillity.

The elegant mottled organdie dress, the hat and the veil show the kind of attention that young women from the bourgeoisie of the Second Empire paid to their appearance. Even so, Les Petites-Dalles was little more than a family resort which could boast neither the diversions nor the smart society of the nearby beaches of Dieppe.

Empress Eugénie stayed at Dieppe twice, which sufficed to make it famous. Every Sunday, excursion trains (known as '*trains de plaisir*') arrived there with contingents of city-dwellers who could not wait to enjoy the delights of the first modern seaside resort. Visiting Parisian women set the fashion for bathing costumes which left the arms and calves bare, and had themselves carried into the water by strapping young sailors. (The job was nothing new, though perhaps more fun, for the sailors, who, in the previous century, used to have to immerse rabies victims in the sea three times a day.)

In between a visit to Lorient in Brittany and a trip to Spain, the much-travelled Berthe Morisot returned to Normandy several times, either to Les Petites-Dalles, to Fécamp, or to Cherbourg, where her sister Edma lived after marrying a naval officer friend of Manet's. Later, after her own marriage to Eugène Manet, the painter's brother, she spent a few days with her brother-in-law and his wife in Berck and in Boulogne. On each of these trips, she remained in front of her easel most of the time, and always returned to Paris with one or more completed canvases.

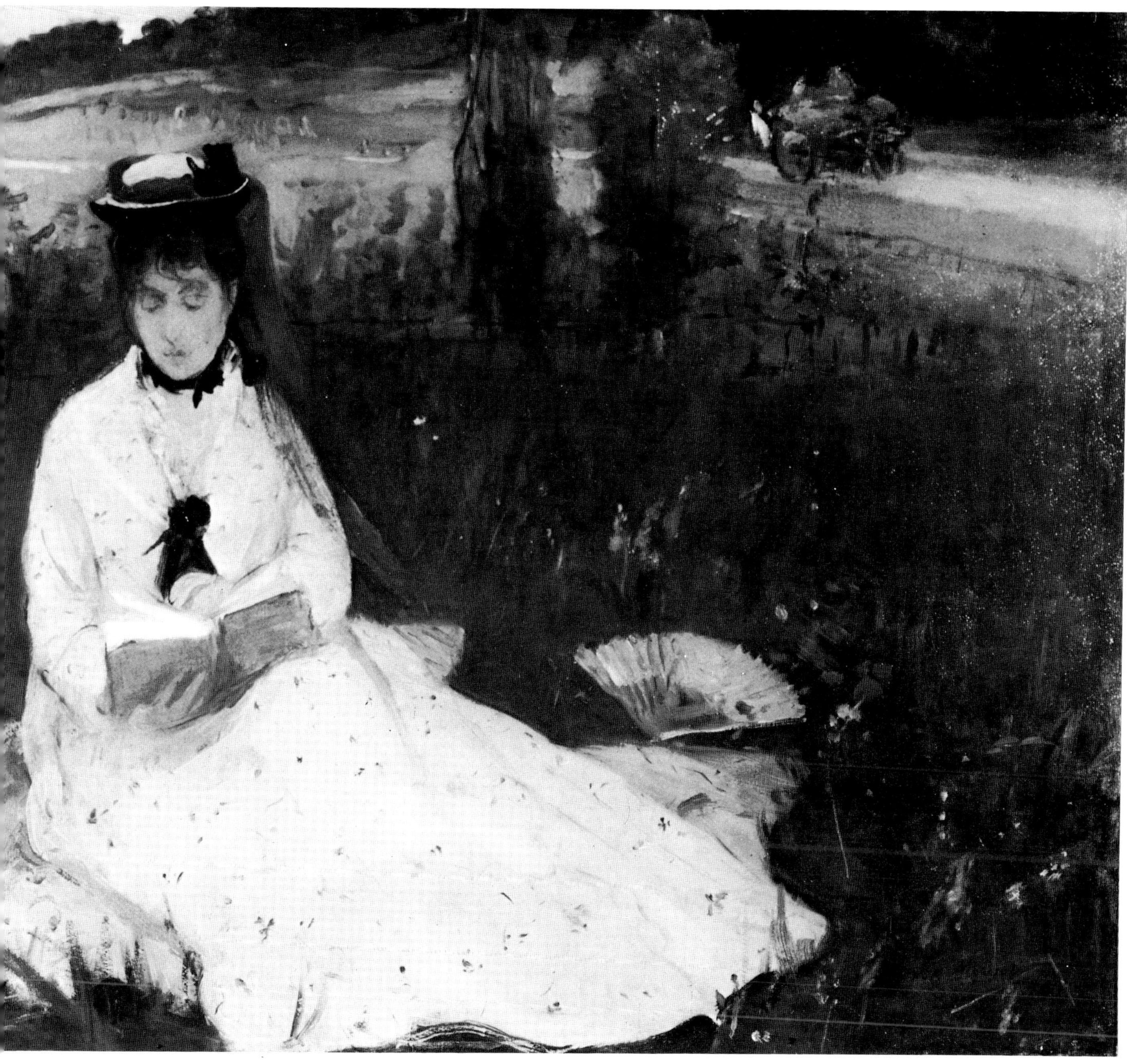

Berthe Morisot: *The Green Parasol*, 1873 (Cleveland Museum of Art). 'In the whole group there is only one impressionist, and that is Berthe Morisot. Her painting has all the freshness of improvization'—the critic Paul Mantz.

In 1865 Renoir and Sisley, like Bazille and Monet the previous year, left Paris by sailing boat for Le Havre in order to attend the regatta. This trip, which cost them no more than 50 francs apiece, was an extravagance for Renoir which he could not afford again: during most of his youth he was too poor to travel. But all of a sudden, in 1879, we find him in Wargemont, ten kilometres from Dieppe, as a guest at the château of the banker Paul Bérard.

Since 1876, the bohemian Renoir, whose friends up to then had come chiefly from the Parisian working class, had been frequenting the capital's smartest and most influential salon, that of Madame Charpentier, the wife of Emile Zola's publisher. In 1877 he painted a portrait of Madame Charpentier surrounded by her daughters, a large painting (1.54m. by 1.90 m.) which aroused the curiosity of Parisian society. Before it was shown at the Salon of 1879, Renoir sent a few privileged people who wanted to see it along to the

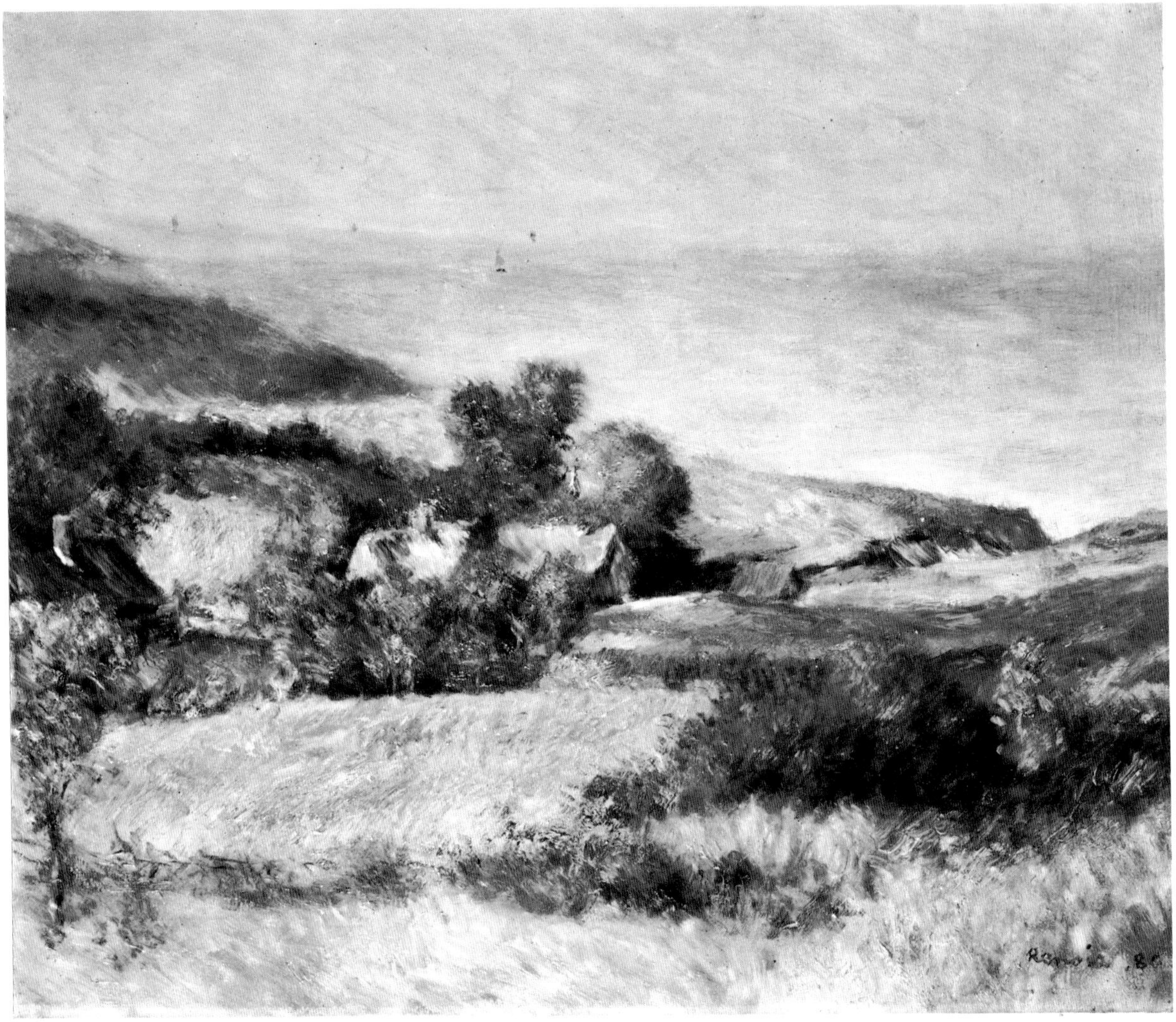

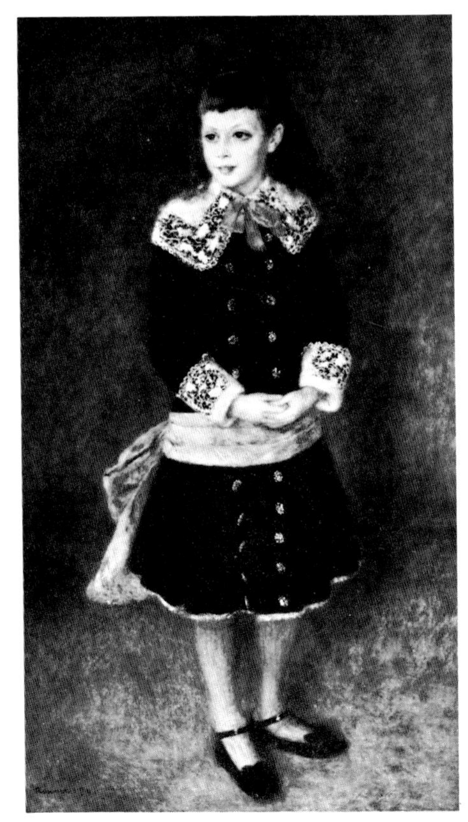

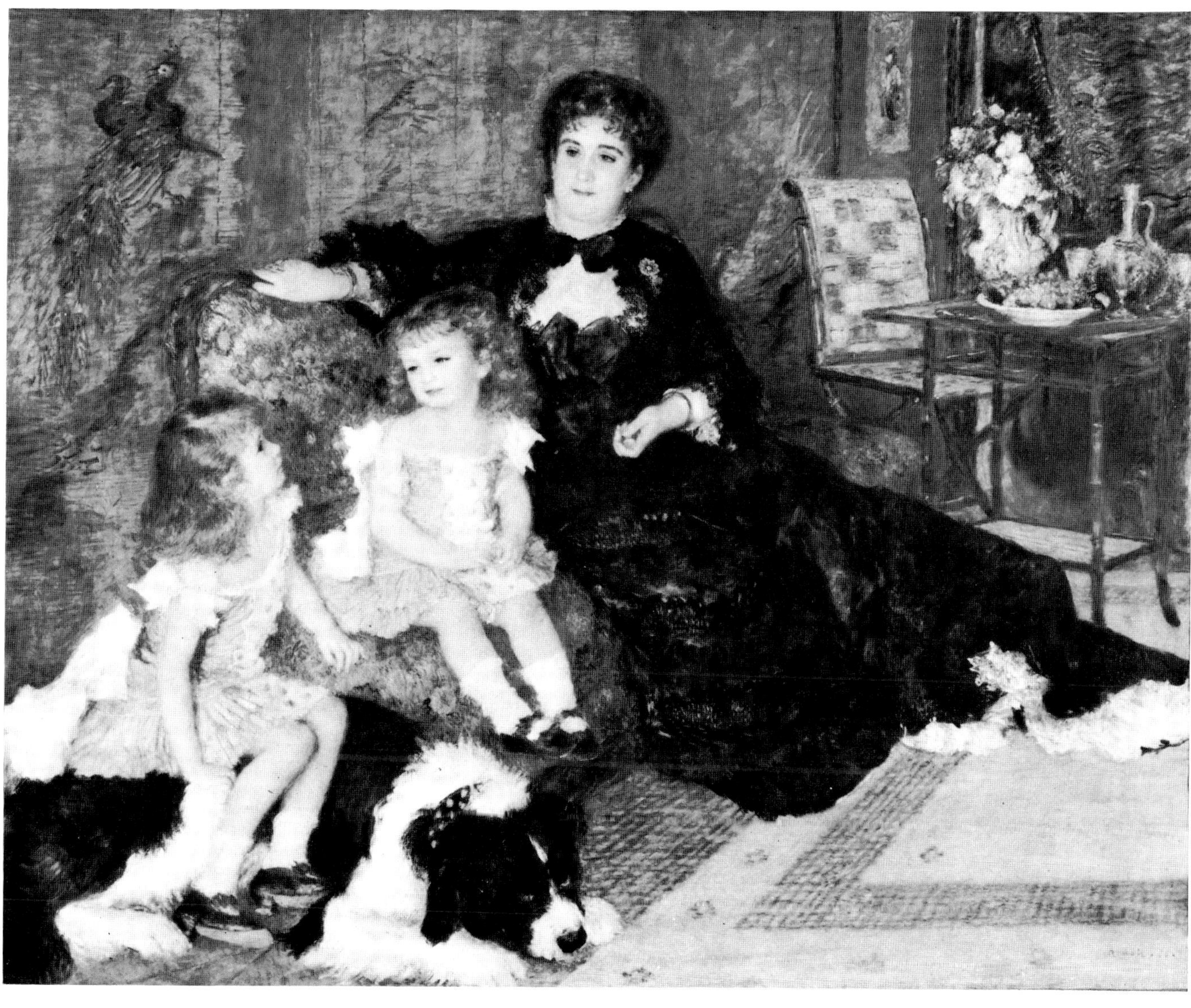

OPPOSITE Auguste Renoir: *View of the Seacoast near Wargemont*, 1880 (Metropolitan Museum of Art, New York, Bequest of Julia Emmons). While staying with the Bérards, Renoir painted in the gardens of the château and around the estate near the sea.
OPPOSITE BELOW Auguste Renoir: *Portrait of Marthe Bérard*, 1879 (Sao Paolo Museum). The Bérards were so delighted with this portrait that they asked Renoir to paint all the members of the family.
ABOVE *Madame Charpentier and Her Children*, 1878 (Metropolitan Museum of Art, New York, Wolfe Fund). Charpentier, Zola's publisher, commissioned this portrait of his wife and children, which was much admired by the Charpentiers' Parisian friends including the writer Marcel Proust.

Charpentiers' large town house on the Rue de Grenelle – Berthe Morisot, the influential banker Ephrussi, and Deudon, who collected Renoir paintings. Deudon described the work in glowing terms to Paul Bérard, and introduced Renoir to him.

The portrait Renoir painted of the Bérards' eldest daughter Marthe at the beginning of 1879 obviously sets out to please: it is pretty, soberly coloured, and classically executed. It satisfied her parents, who were completely won over by the good-natured, quick-witted and sociable Renoir, and remained firm friends with him for many years.

So at the age of thirty-eight Renoir was for the first time in his life able to enjoy the carefree, easy existence that suited his temperament so perfectly. The Bérards, like all rich bourgeois families of the period, had no qualms of conscience about the grand style of living that was the privilege of their class.

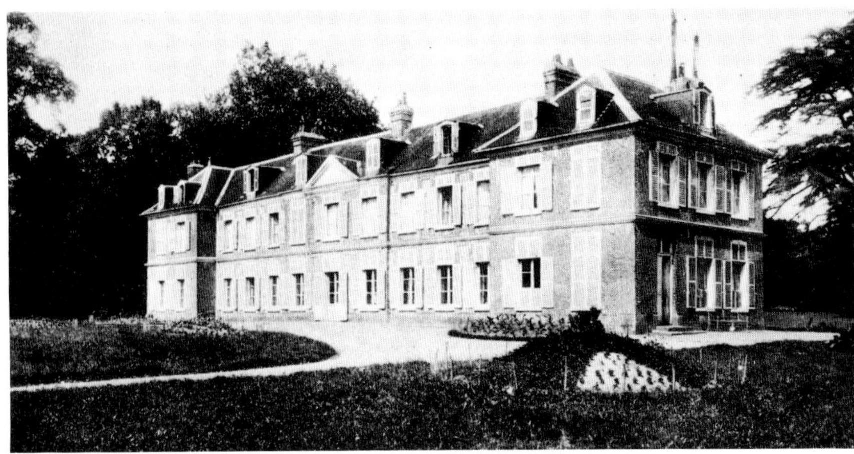

Paul Bérard devoted particular attention to the upkeep of the flowerbeds in the gardens surrounding the vast Norman manor where he and his family used to spend the summer.

The huge château that Paul Bérard had inherited from his family was surrounded by vast grounds that led right down to the sea. Everywhere there were lush lawns shaded by magnificent beeches. M. Bérard had a passion for flowers, and a wide variety of them grew in the borders along the paths, under the watchful eye of an army of gardeners. The Bérards were chiefly interested in getting the best out of life and its diversions; and their château was thronged with relations, friends and acquaintances who were on holiday in the area.

Renoir's stay there was one of unmitigated delight. He tossed off a series of charming decorative panels for his hosts, such as *Fête de Pan*, where, in the best eighteenth-century tradition combined with an Impressionist technique, graceful nymphs can be seen decking out the god's torso with garlands of flowers to celebrate the return of spring. In *The Rose Garden and the Château de Wargemont*, a few of the twenty-six doors and windows of the château's façade can be glimpsed behind a screen of roses and bright green vegetation.

Renoir was an easy-going, fun-loving man, and he used to join in the games of the three Bérard children and their friends, teasing them, making them laugh, and painting them. In *The Little Fisher Girl*, we see Marthe Bérard brandishing a shrimp-net and wearing the sort of beach clothes that were fashionable at the time – striped trousers, a long smock and a straw hat. Renoir's portrait so delighted the whole Bérard family that he had to make a copy of it secretly for the godmother of the child.

The artist's natural penchant for portraiture was stimulated by all the new faces he encountered there – the children, the parents, the trusty manservant. On the nearby Berneval beach he came across other models who enabled him to capture a completely different side of life by the sea. *The Mussel Gatherers* is a colourful painting which is given an almost disconcertingly aggressive tone by colours that are rarely used by Renoir. In *La Bohémienne*, the whole composition is dominated by the red hair of the little girl (also the model for

The Mussel Gatherers); the fiery background is treated in purely impressionistic fashion with a series of long, thin, flame-like strokes that look as though they are about to consume the strange little sorceress.

Renoir was invited to the Château de Wargemont every summer; he returned there in 1880, and again in 1885. His timetable was always more or less the same: during the week he would work in the open air, wearing canvas shoes and the broad-brimmed straw hat of the Argenteuil fishermen, and on Saturdays, with Léon, the Bérards' manservant, he would take an omnibus to Dieppe and go to market. He produced further portraits, including one of the Bérards' youngest daughter Lucie, in *Little Girl in a White Pinafore*, which is a little masterpiece. He also painted some still lifes, as well as a few landscapes around Berneval, which he found particularly picturesque. Another work from this period is *Children's Afternoon at Wargemont*: there is something static about this large composition, probably because Renoir was unhappy with impressionist techniques at the time, and had more or less abandoned intermingling optical effects and comma-shaped dashes in favour of a more precise and more traditional style. The light in which the scene is bathed is flat and uniform instead of shimmering.

During this stay, Renoir was again the life and soul of all amusements and outings. When he visited the famous mental doctor, Dr Blanche, at Le Bas-Fort-Blanc in Dieppe, he painted some lively designs on his drawing-room walls as a memento. He recommended his favourite walks to friends in the neighbourhood, as can be judged from this note he sent Madame Charpentier:

> A charming walk to go on: take the Dieppe road at Neufchâtel and go as far as Aucourt via Martin-Eglise. You must stop a moment at Aucourt Mill which is an adorable spot and not too far. If you have time come back via Sauchet-le-Haut, where there is the drive of a superb château, and you'll come back to Dieppe by the Auvernon-Dieppe road. You can do it all in two hours.

And he adds: 'I'm going on a two-day walk next Friday and Saturday to Saint-Saens.'

In 1893, Renoir again stayed briefly in Normandy, this time at Berneville near Deauville, where his friends the Gallimards, the family which was later to give France one of its most famous publishing houses, had a small château. He wrote to Berthe Morisot: 'I stayed only a very short time at the Manoir. No mistake about it, that part of Normandy doesn't appeal to me much, even though it's quite beautiful. So I have left the grand life and am exploring a corner of Normandy we don't know . . .'

By that time, all along the Côte Fleurie, which runs from Honfleur to Cabourg, the little fishing villages tucked away in the river estuaries had already been turned into seaside resorts. On the right bank of the Touques, Trouville (which Alexandre Dumas had discovered in 1821 – at that time so deserted he had been able to run naked from his house to the sea for his daily bathe), was launched in truly modern fashion by an English doctor in conjunction with the Duc de Morny. So successful was their venture that these imaginative developers decided to move to the other side of the river and build the Deauville racecourse that was to become the favourite meeting place of the international rich for the rest of the nineteenth and the beginning of the twentieth century.

While most of the publicity centred on Deauville and Trouville, the spectacularly situated town of Etretat to the north of Le Havre also had its

BELOW Les Quais de la Touques, Trouville. Only a few minutes away from the smart Hôtel des Roches Noires, Trouville still looked like a small fishing village.
OPPOSITE Claude Monet: *Beached Boats*, 1881 (Private Collection). Attracted by the sea and its wealth of subjects, Monet returned again and again throughout his life to work on the beaches of Normandy.

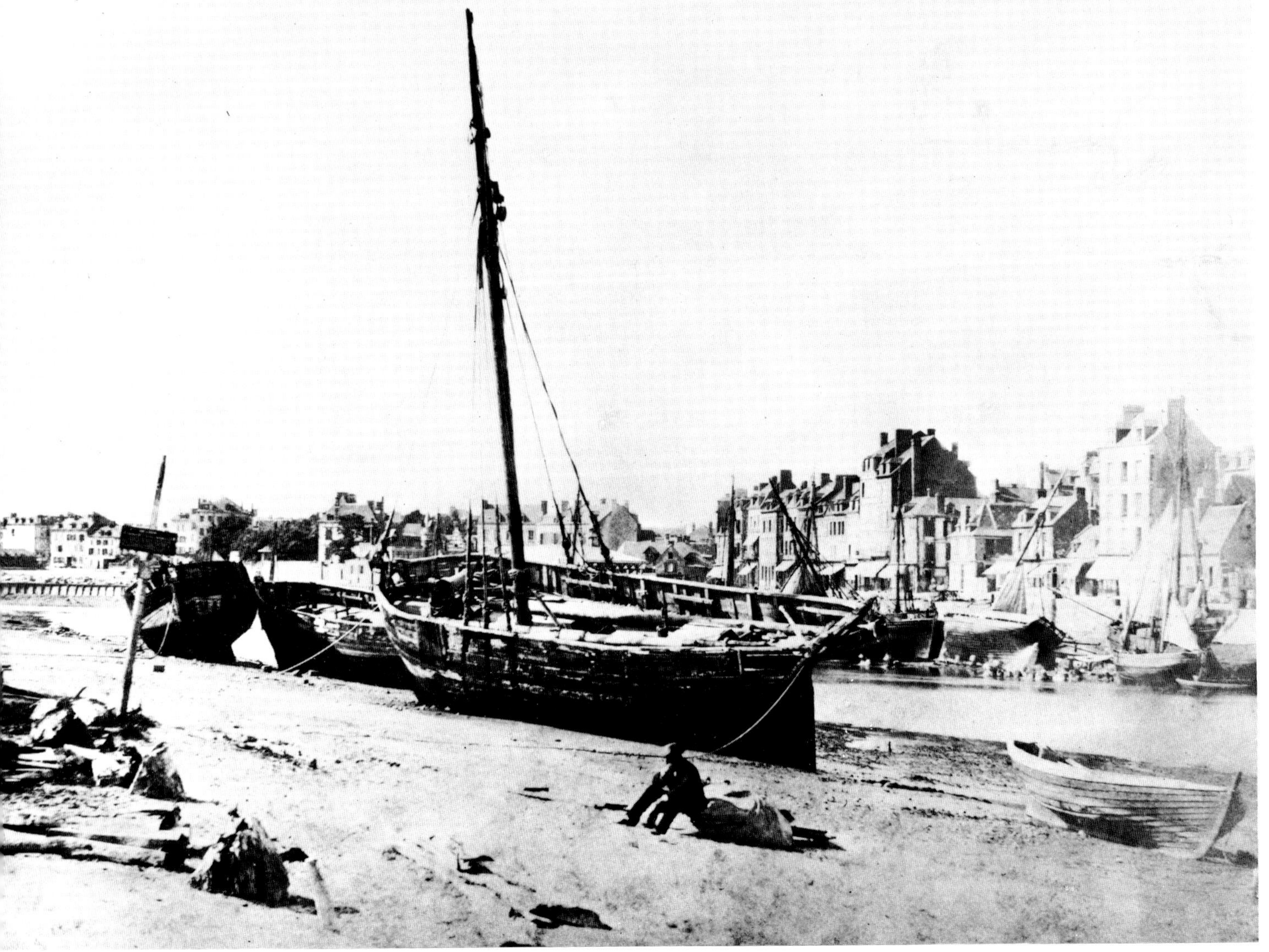

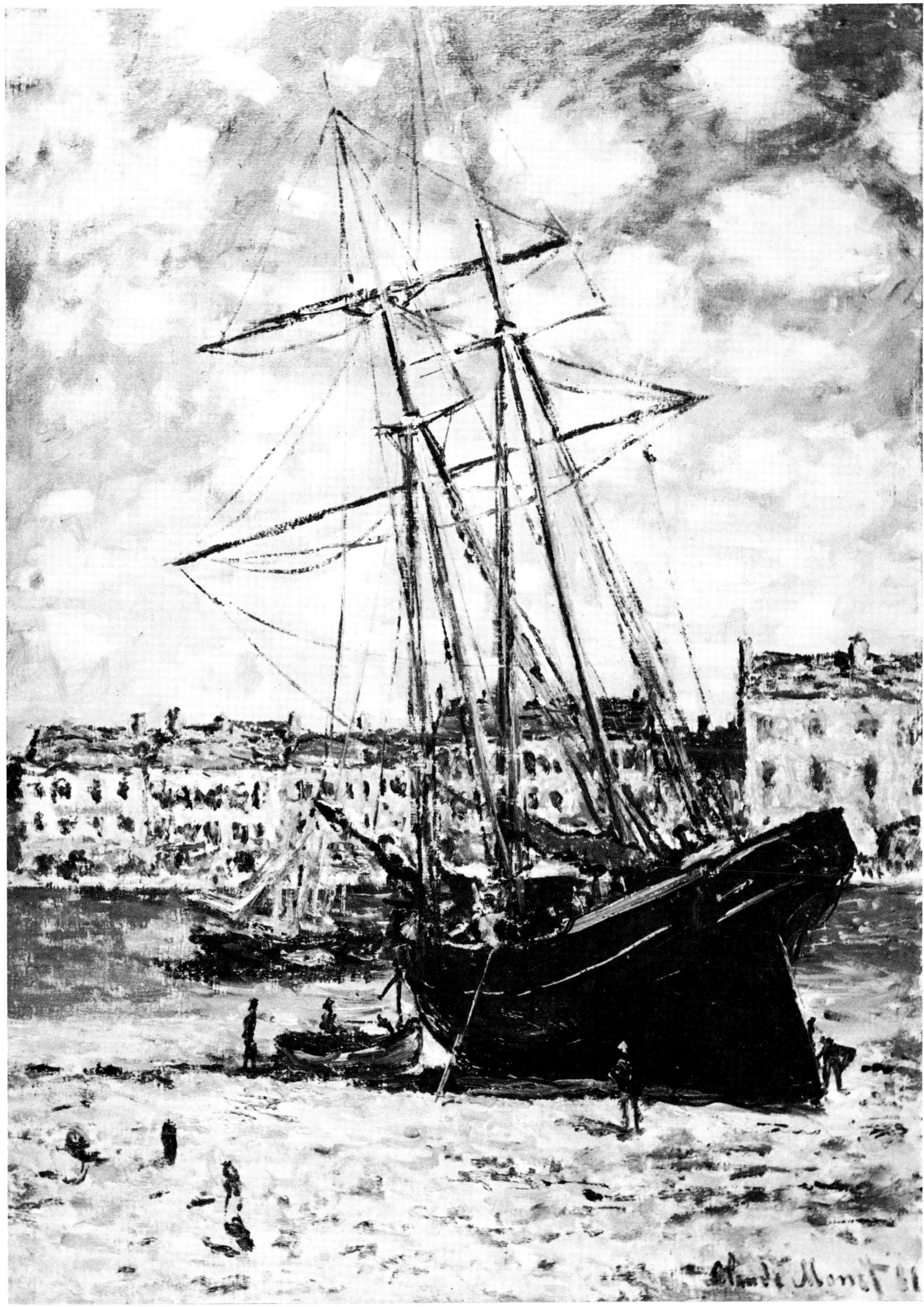

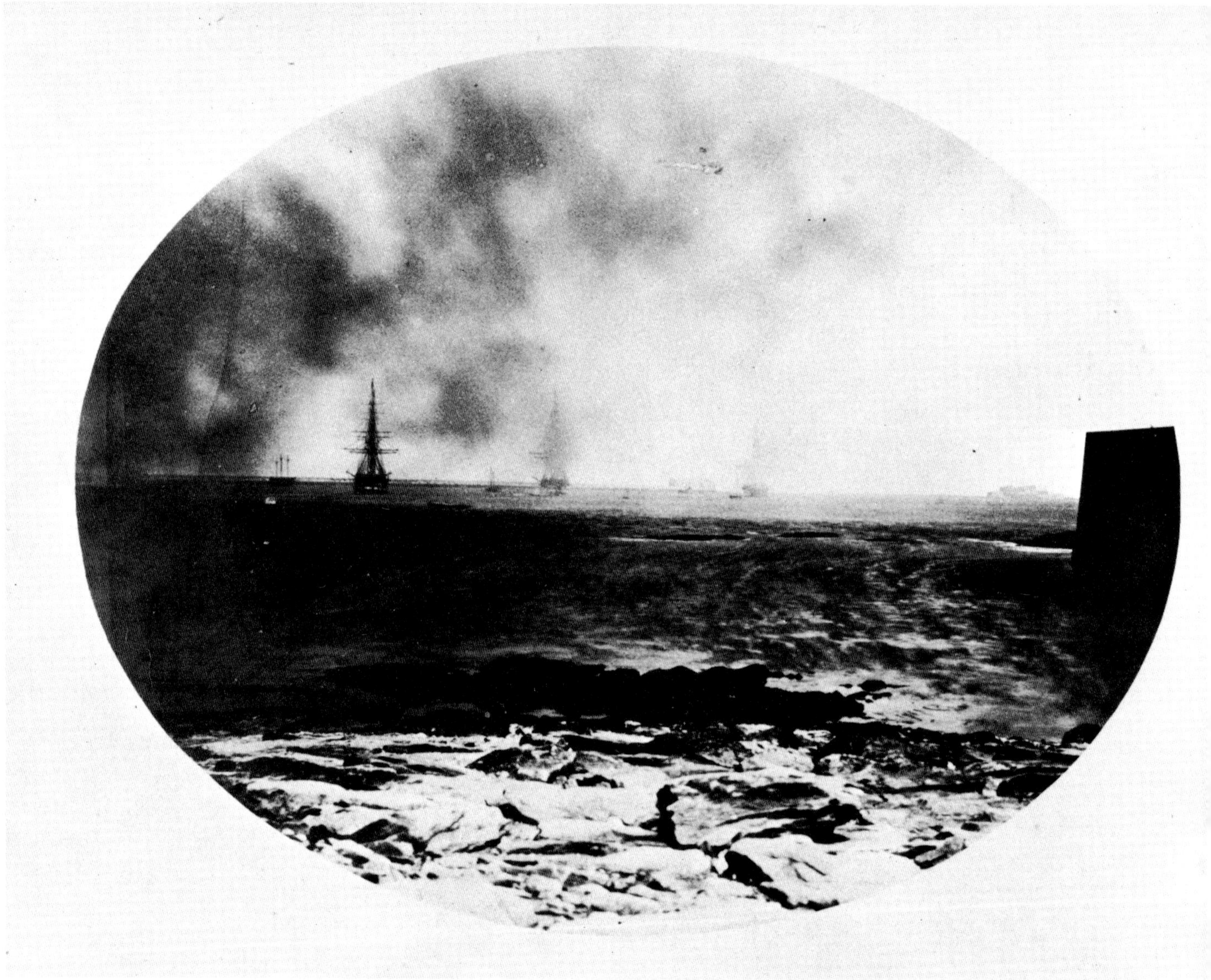

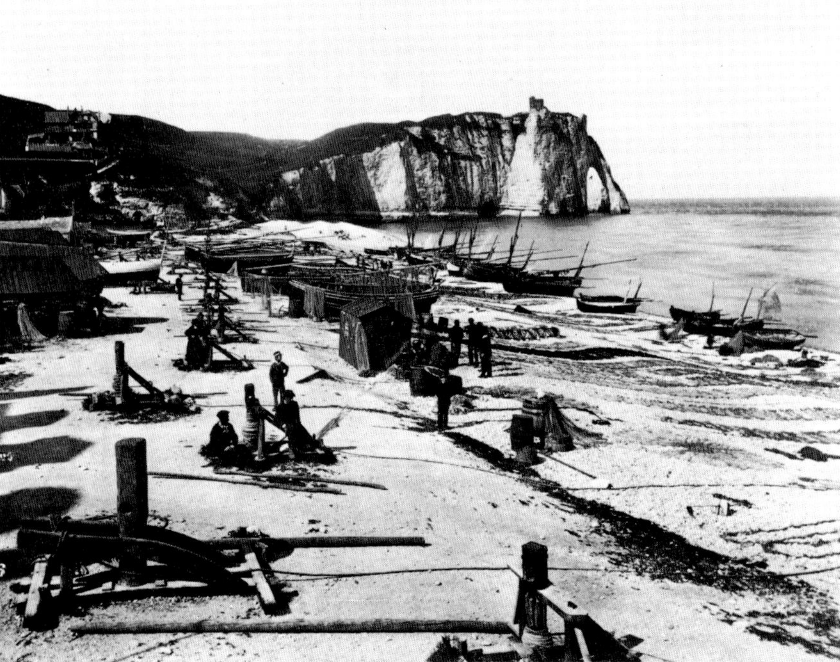

ABOVE Combination printing by Gustave Le Gray. 'This is the event of the year; in London these pictures are creating a sensation' – *La Lumière*, 1865.
LEFT At the end of the summer, when the members of high society had packed their bags and left, the fishermen again took over the beaches of Etretat.

devotees, most of whom were writers, musicians and theatrical people. The poet Alphonse Karr, who had been partly responsible for Etretat's new vogue, exclaimed with more than a touch of exaggeration: 'I talked so much about Etretat that I made it fashionable, and now it is just as accessible as the suburb of Asnières.' It is true that by then people used to come from all over the world to watch the sun set from the top of the astonishing 300-foot cliffs that overlook Etretat beach, or to stare at the comings and goings of the latest celebrities on the walkways across the shingle.

Surrounded by an atmosphere of scandal, the English poet Swinburne also lived there, with two companions – a man and a monkey. When Swinburne went swimming one day in a state of total drunkenness, he was saved from drowning by the very young Guy de Maupassant, who, as a token of gratitude, was invited to share a meal with the eccentric English trio. Alexandre Dumas, the trend-setter of the century, was also a frequent visitor, as was the darling of Paris, Offenbach, the celebrated composer of *The Tales of Hoffmann*. Famous actresses such as Mademoiselle Doche, the original *Dame aux Camélias*, would parade in crinolines beneath which one could just glimpse a pair of well-shod, high-heeled feet.

During the summer of 1868, Monet, who was still taking advantage of his Aunt Lecadre's hospitality at Sainte-Adresse, installed his mistress and their son (whom his family refused to meet) in a small flat on the Rue du Havre in Etretat, where he often came to visit them. Much later, after Camille's death in 1885, Monet returned to Etretat when he was invited there by the singer

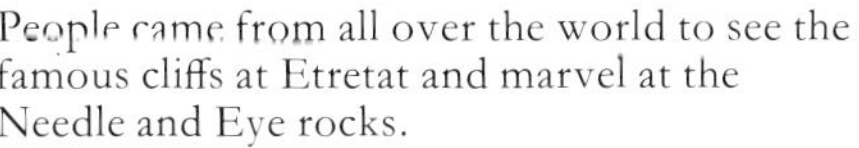

People came from all over the world to see the famous cliffs at Etretat and marvel at the Needle and Eye rocks.

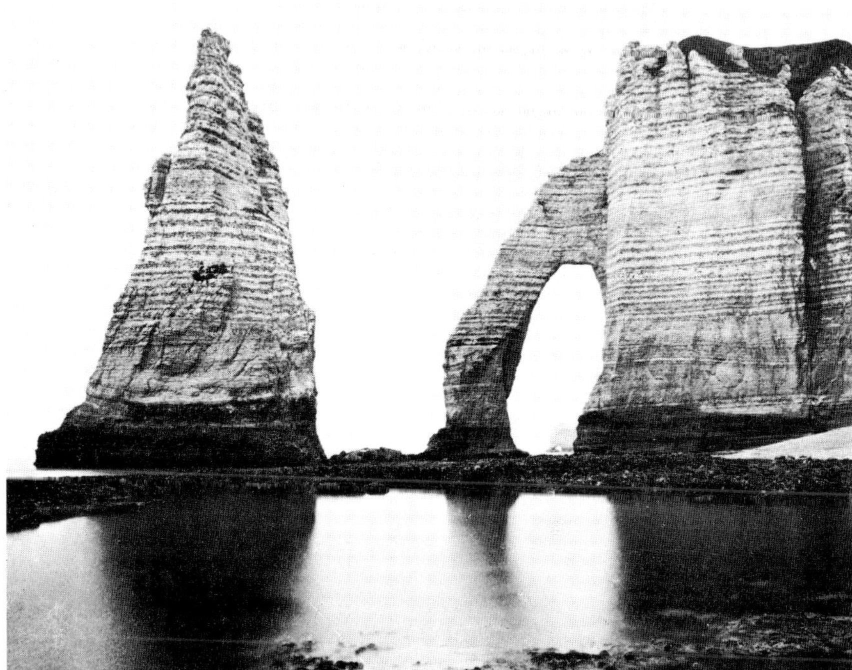

Jean-Baptiste Faure, who had long been collecting his paintings.

In an article which appeared in *Gil Blas* the following year, Guy de Maupassant described the artist at work, perhaps with more concern for poetic effect than for accuracy:

> I saw him seize a glittering streak of light on the white cliff face and capture it in a flow of yellow hues that rendered particularly well the startling, fleeting impression left by that almost imperceptible, yet blinding, dazzlement. On another occasion, he plunged his hands into a rainstorm that had swept down on to the sea and flung it against his canvas. And it was indeed rain that he painted in this way, rain and nothing but rain, obscuring the waves, the rocks and the sun so that they were barely discernible in the deluge.

Monet did in fact paint *Effect of Rain* that summer in Etretat.

Courbet, too, worked there at about the same time. Here is Maupassant's description:

> In a large, empty room a greasy, dirty, fat man was using a kitchen knife to stick layers of white paint on a large, empty canvas. From time to time he thrust his head against the window pane and watched the storm. The sea came so close that it seemed to be pounding the house, enveloping it with its roaring spray. The salt water lashed the window like hail and streamed down the walls. On the mantelpiece there was a bottle of cider and a half-empty glass. From time to time, Courbet walked over and took a few gulps, then returned to his canvas. Well, his canvas became *The Wave*, and caused quite a stir in society.

Shortly after the declaration of war in September 1870, the newly-wed Monets and their son Jean spent a few weeks at Trouville. The painter immediately knuckled down to work, probably to take his mind off the worrying situation in France. What chiefly interested him was the chic side of that little seaside resort. He turned out some brightly coloured canvases in which he used the same rapid brush-strokes he had recently exploited to such effect in his landscapes by the Seine. He painted the front of the luxury hotel Les Roches Noires, the avenues near the sea, and a few charming quick studies of Camille, wearing the graceful clothes that were fashionable at the time, while keeping an eye on Jean as he played on the beach.

After his self-imposed exile in England, then in Holland, Monet returned to Le Havre when the war no longer gave any cause for anxiety. His father had died while he was away, in January 1871, but his aunt Madame Lecadre was still living there. It was in Le Havre in 1873 that Monet painted a sunrise over the sea that proved to be a milestone in the history of art. When he sent the painting, along with four others and seven pastels, to the famous group exhibition in Nadar's studio in 1874, he hastily entitled it *Impression, Sunrise*. It was precisely the word 'impression' which was seized upon by those critics who sought to ridicule the new style of painting. But the painters who were dubbed the 'Impressionists' proudly adopted that ironical term as a true token of their identity.

Impression, Sunrise, in which the outlines of boats in Le Havre harbour can only just be glimpsed through the fog, was bound to infuriate a public that loved meticulously illustrated subjects. And yet the painting, which was a perfect example of what the new school was trying to do, did have a precedent: in 1829, some ten years before Monet was born, William Turner had painted a *Sunset* at Rouen with similar freedom of treatment, which Monet and Pissarro had much admired when they discovered the museums of London.

Even Edgar Degas, man of the world and painter of cities *par excellence*, stayed in Etretat several times. He was drawn there by his friend Ludovic Halévy, playwright and librettist for operettas, who could offer the sort of company that was to Degas' taste – a galaxy of actors, actresses, musicians and men of letters. It was impossible for anyone, even Maupassant, to catch Degas unawares while he was at work. His weak eyesight made it almost impossible for him to work in the open air, and in any case his ideas about art would hardly have encouraged him to do so even if he had been able to. To his mind a picture was the result of imagination, observation and thought, and could only be composed in a studio. 'Do you know what I think of painters who work in country lanes?' he used to volunteer. 'If I were the government I would have a special police squad to keep an eye on people who do landscapes from life.'

And yet he would occasionally note down in the sketchbook that he took almost everywhere the curve of a hill or the angle of a clump of trees bent by the wind; later, they would find their way into one of the canvases he painted in his studio. It is therefore impossible to pin down Degas' not very descriptive landscapes to this or that Normandy village where he paid frequent visits to his friends. From 1860 on, he often stayed in a rich, lush area of Normandy away from the sea, known as Suisse-Normande, where his childhood friends, the art-loving Valpinçons, had a château at Ménil-Hubert. In 1866 Degas painted *Children and Ponies in a Park* in the vast grounds of their estate, and produced countless landscape sketches.

One wonders whether he was thinking of the beach at Etretat or at Dieppe (where he once more joined the Halévys) when he painted *At the Seaside* – a work where the exquisite nuances of sun, sea and sand provide a background for the strongly contrasting colours of the bathing costume, the basket, and the dark skirts of the little girl and her nanny in the foreground. Degas was not particularly interested in light (which is here completely uniform); but he did, on the other hand, attach great importance to unusual visual elements. The body of the girl who lies as though crucified at the feet of her nanny while her long hair is combed, and the bathing costume sitting like a sloughed skin on the far right of the composition, carry a very strong visual punch. It was no mere chance, either, that the effect was very modern for the period. In a notebook of 1859, Degas saw as his appointed task: 'To treat every kind of ordinary object in such a way that it is as alive as a man or a woman, corsets which have just been taken off, for instance, and which still keep the shape of the body. . . .'

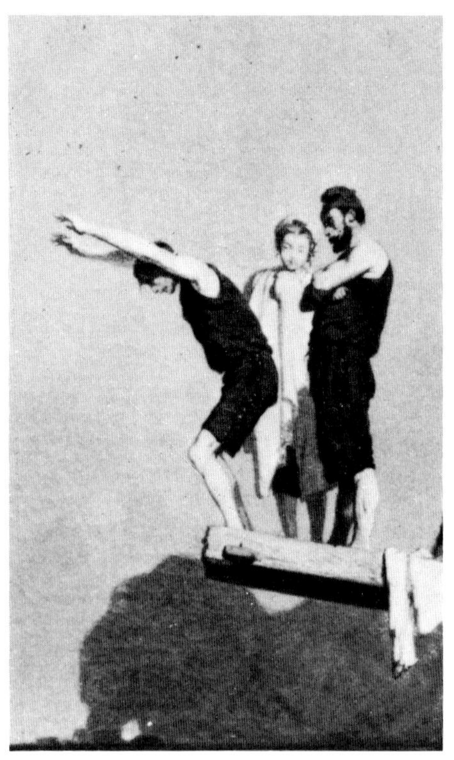

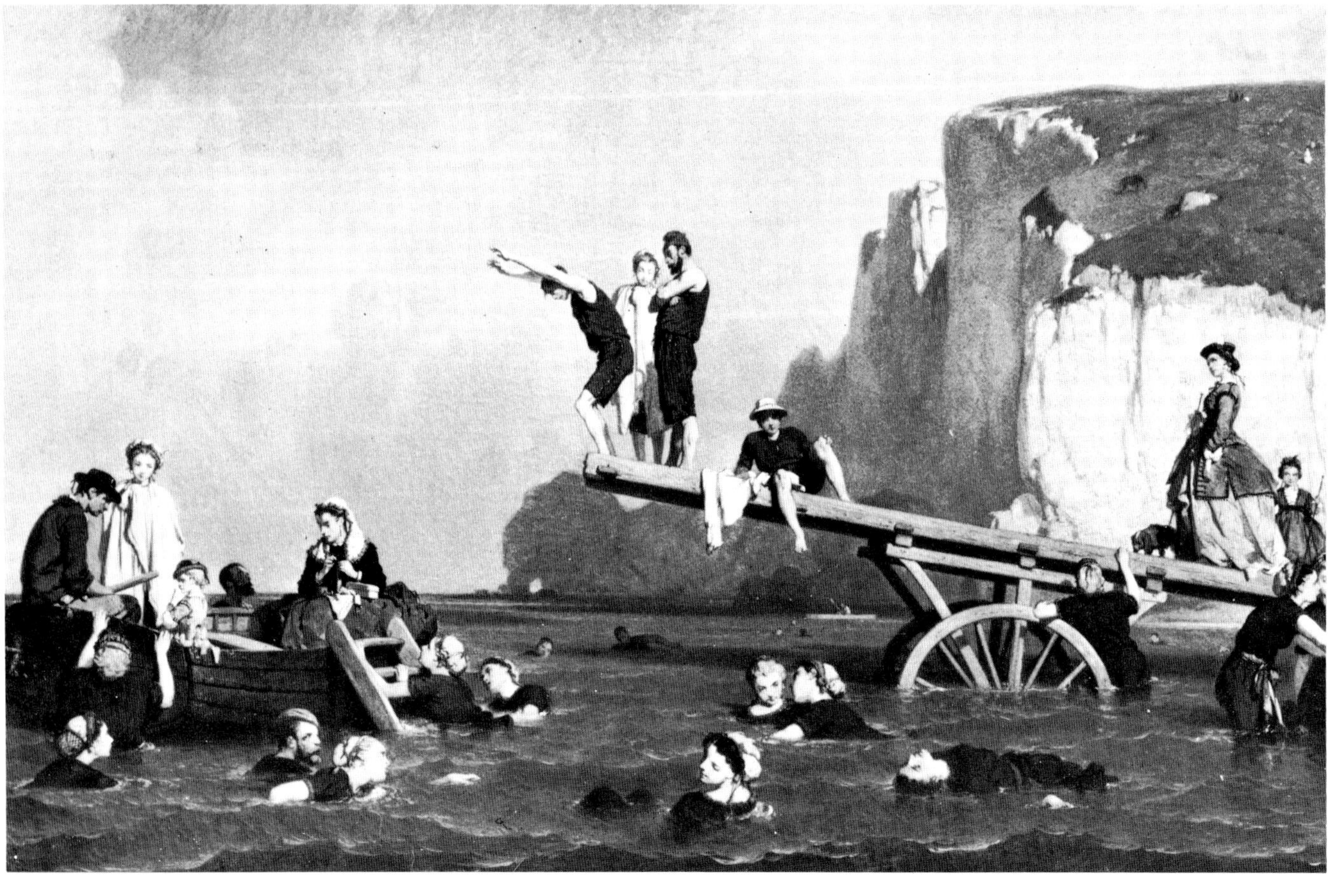

At the Seaside has as little to do with the experiments of the Impressionists as it has with the work of conventional painters of the time, such as Eugène Le Poitevin, for example, who hailed from the area and whose *Bathing at Etretat*, chosen for the Salon of 1865, is an excellent example of contemporary public taste. 'A very pretty painting,' the critic Gustave Privat wrote, 'in spite of its airlessness and lowering sky. There are elegant dresses to be seen, as well as the usual visitors to pleasure resorts.' Indeed one can even recognize the young Guy de Maupassant, about to dive into the water, and a little further away the famous actress, Mademoiselle Doche, looking on in full regalia.

Degas felt that a painting should never ape reality in such a literal way. 'It is a good thing to copy what one sees,' he said, 'but it is even better to draw what one can only remember. . . . In that way, your memories and your imagination are freed from the tyranny of nature.' Thus, various disparate elements of landscape he brought back from Normandy in his sketchbook were to serve as a framework for the studies of horses he painted so frequently later on. Memories of his trips to Saint-Valéry-en-Caux, Trouville and Boulogne, where he stayed with the Manets in 1869, turned into delicate pastel drawings where, in an almost abstract harmony of colour, only a few figures just discernible on the shore (in *Beach at Low Tide*) mark the dividing line between sand and sea, while on the horizon the sea fuses with the sky. In this series of studies of beaches and skies, Degas uses pastels with an extraordinary lightness of touch, and occasionally even allows the colour of the cardboard on which he is drawing to show through.

OPPOSITE BELOW Eugène Le Poitevin: *Bathing at Etretat*, 1865 (Musée de Troyes). Contemporaries of the Impressionists were also attracted by the beaches of Normandy, but they lent greater importance to anecdote and detail. Here, the young Guy de Maupassant is about to dive into the water, watched, from the right, by Mademoiselle Doche, famous for her title role in *La Dame aux Camélias*.
OPPOSITE ABOVE Detail of *Bathing at Etretat*, showing Maupassant about to dive.
BELOW Edouard Manet: *The Croquet Party*, 1871 (Private Collection).

Towards the end of the nineteenth century, Dieppe, ideally situated as it was halfway between London and Paris, became the favourite haunt of English

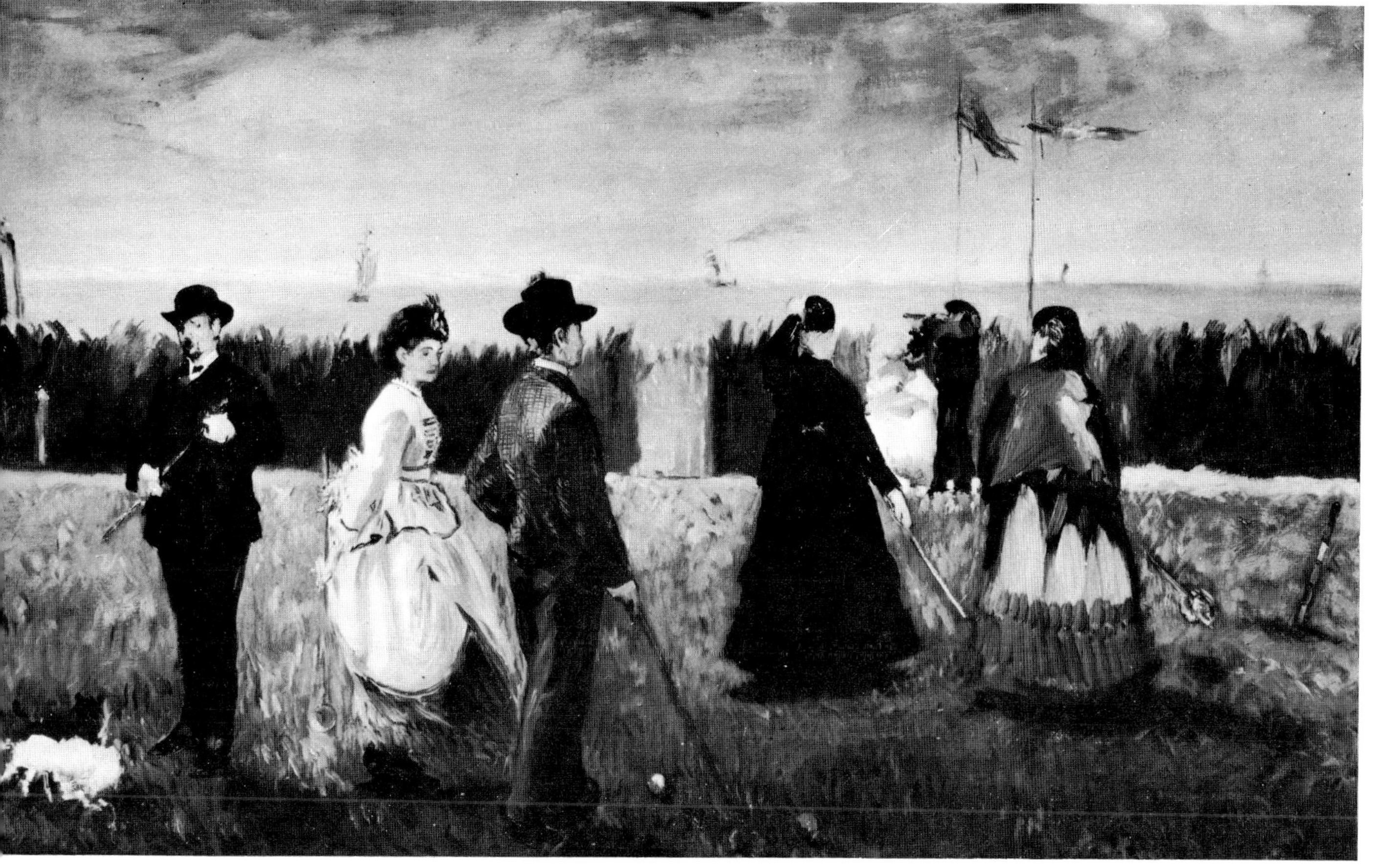

and American artists. Degas met and mingled with the members of that cosmopolitan colony when he went to visit Halévy there. French and foreign painters and writers were particularly fond of gathering at Le Bas-Fort-Blanc, the home of the celebrated mental specialist Dr Blanche. The Irish writer George Moore, the handsome young English painter and engraver Walter Sickert, 'Poor Barnes' – an English photographer who was put to work by Degas, then a budding photography enthusiast, the newspaper editor John Lemoisne and his daughters, Proust, and Madame Straus (Ludovic Halévy's cousin, who was one of the models for the character of the Duchesse de Guermantes) were all frequently to be seen in the studio of Jacques Blanche, the son of Dr Blanche, who was studying painting.

Neither the beaches of Dieppe and Etretat, with their elegance and gaiety, nor the sea and the balmy Normandy climate proved so attractive to the misanthropic Paul Cézanne, however, who remained very much a man of the South. Yet in the early autumn of 1882 he was to be found visiting the remote little village of Hattenville, in the depths of the countryside a few kilometres from Yvetot. Just as Renoir used to be the guest of the Bérards, and Monet of the baritone Faure, the unsociable lonely Cézanne was invited by a friend, Victor Chocquet.

Chocquet's hospitality was nowhere near as lavish as that of the Bérards. His salary as a civil servant with the Customs was scarcely able to satisfy his daily needs, let alone his collector's appetite, and he was consequently in no position to play the role of a patron of the arts. Yet Chocquet invited Cézanne to be his guest because he admired him intensely and was in some need of human and intellectual contact after several months of isolation in the heart of the country.

Victor Chocquet was a figure whose real originality emerged only long after his death. A very reserved, even secretive man, he would certainly be forgotten today had not Renoir and Cézanne painted his portrait many times. Chocquet already owned a large collection of works by Courbet, Daumier, and Corot, as well as a superb group of thirty-five watercolours and twenty-four drawings by Delacroix, by the time the Impressionists organized the first auction of their work in 1875. The idea for the sale had come from Renoir, who convinced his friends that it was the only way they could get any money from collectors, who had been completely nonplussed by their exhibition at Nadar's the previous year.

That afternoon of 24 March 1875, Victor Chocquet was among the crowd in the salerooms of the Hôtel Drouot. Although some members of the noisy throng were friends of the Impressionists, most of them made no bones about their hostility. Indeed, passions ran so high that the auctioneer had to call in the police to discourage brawling. The bidding was sluggish. Renoir's

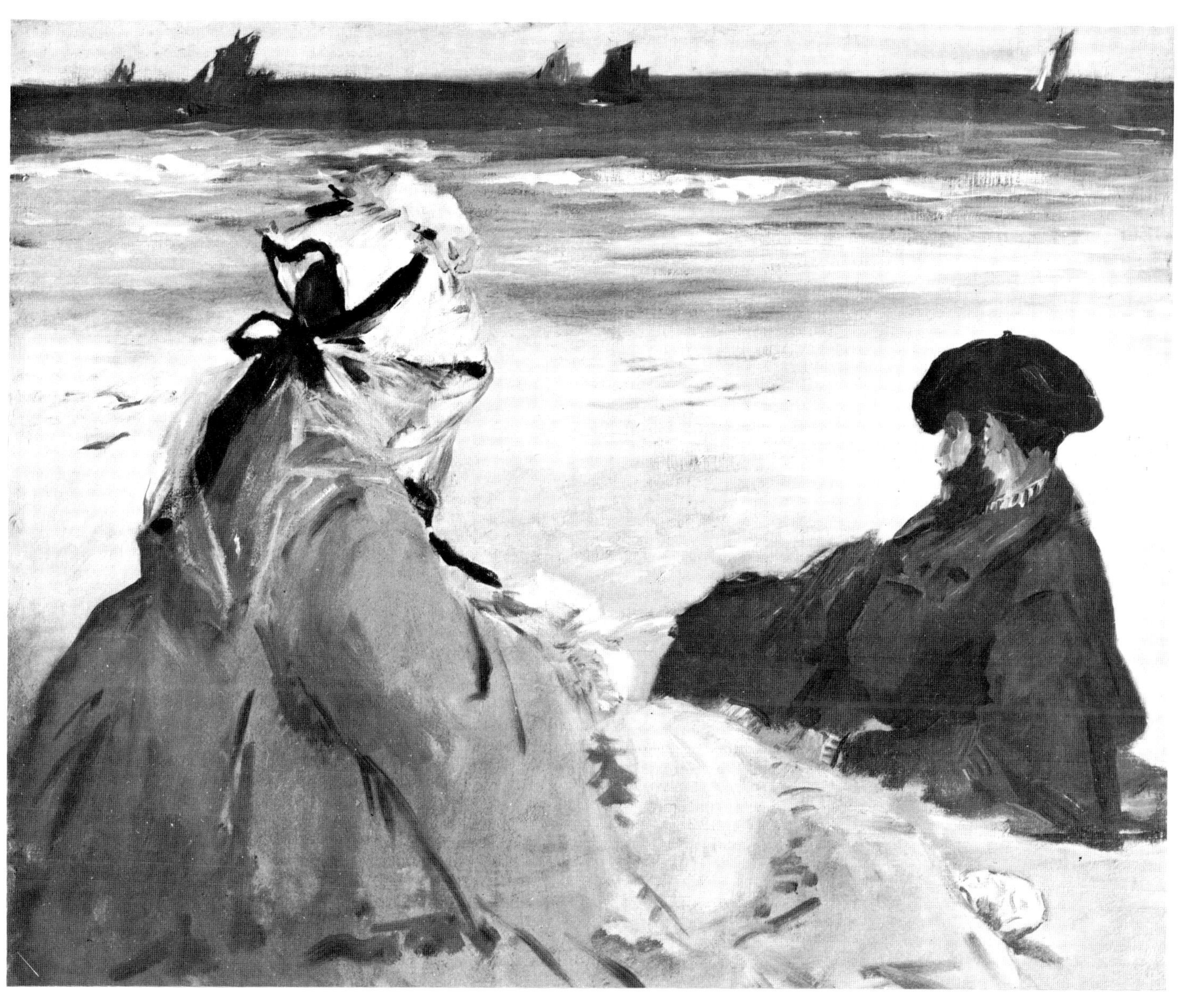

works had the doubtful distinction of being sold for the lowest price, while Berthe Morisot commanded the highest bids. It was in that electric atmosphere that Chocquet suddenly became enthusiastic about the Impressionists, and that he bought his first painting by one of them, Monet's *Argenteuil.*

Next day, Renoir was sent a note by the collector asking him whether he would agree to paint a portrait of his wife. While working on the painting in the couple's flat at 198 Rue de Rivoli, in front of an open window overlooking the Tuileries Gardens, Renoir discovered how exceptional a man Victor Chocquet in fact was. Unlike most of his contemporaries, he collected neither because it was fashionable nor because it was a speculative form of investment, but entirely out of a love of painting that was based on a

Edouard Manet: *On the Beach*, 1873 (Musée du Louvre, Paris). Suzanne and Eugène Manet, the artist's wife and brother, served as models for this painting which, with its solid colours and strong contrasts, is suggestive of the Japanese prints that Manet so admired.

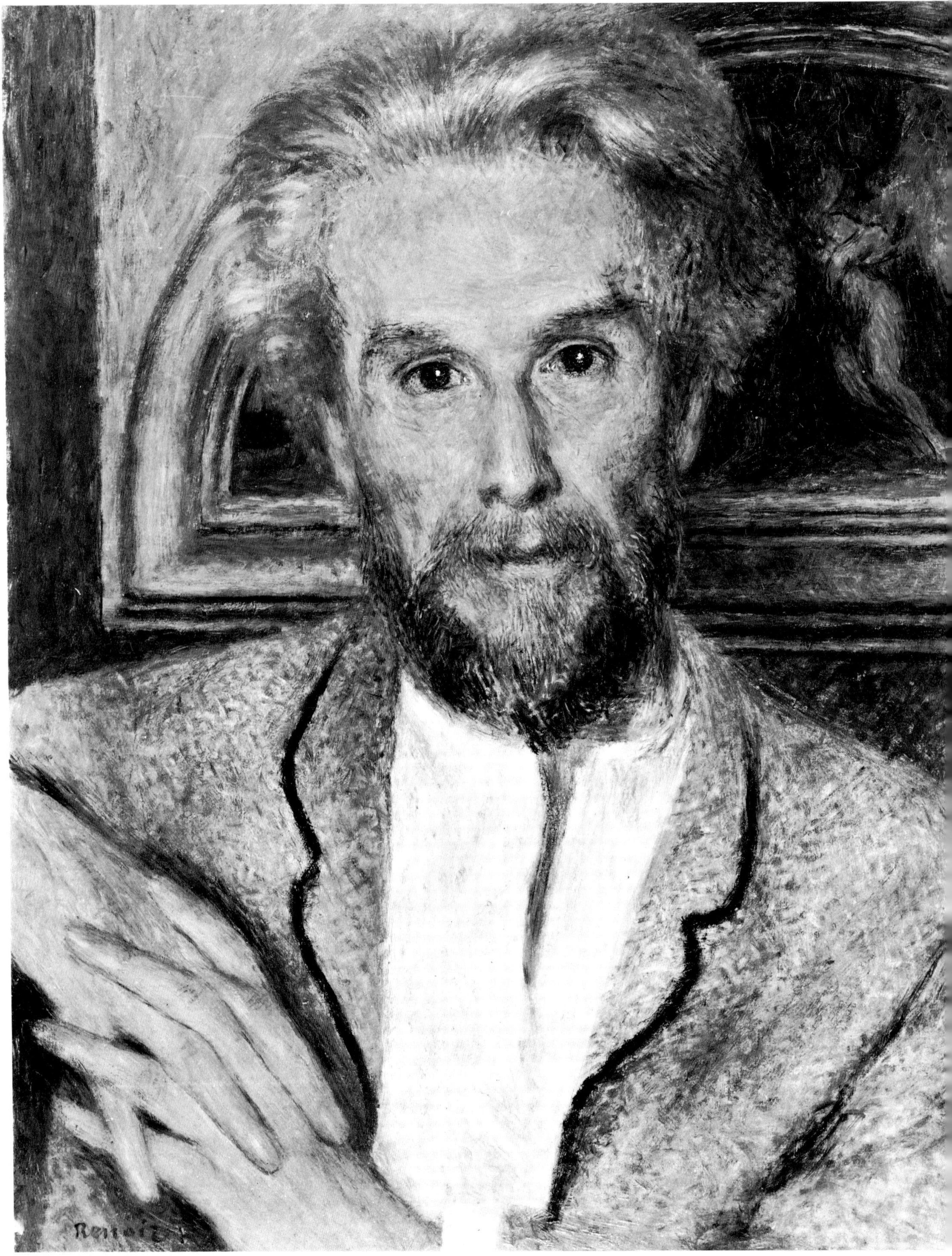
Renoir

OPPOSITE Auguste Renoir: *Victor Chocquet*, *c.* 1875 (Fogg Art Museum, Cambridge, Mass.). Chocquet was a connoisseur of unfailing taste and of striking appearance. Both Renoir and Cézanne, whom he admired, painted his portrait several times.

true understanding of art. Chocquet was a connoisseur of unfailing taste, whose passion for collecting extended to every kind of *objet d'art*, including furniture, porcelain and silver. According to Renoir, he was a modest, quiet man who was 'the purest expression of what an intelligent and determined collector should be'.

When the artists encountered a new collector like Chocquet in times as difficult as those, they felt like explorers who had just discovered a new continent. Renoir lost no time in passing on the good tidings to his friends: he introduced Chocquet to Monet, and took him along to see Cézanne's paintings in Père Tanguy's little shop in the Rue Clauzel. 'How good that will look between a Delacroix and a Courbet,' exclaimed Chocquet on seeing Cézanne's *Bathers*, which he bought on the spot. A deep affinity drew Victor Chocquet and Paul Cézanne together. Between 1876 and 1877 the artist produced three superb portraits of the collector – which was surprising on Cézanne's part, as he was usually thrown off balance by the presence of a stranger and for that reason tended to use members of his family as models. But Chocquet was also of striking appearance. His emaciated face, which looked even more elongated framed as it was by a fine head of hair, was remarkable for the burning intensity of his eyes. His long, thin limbs, which he seemed to move wearily, lent him a great distinction that emerges clearly from Cézanne's portraits.

It was only to be expected that during their sessions sitter and painter should discover a strong rapport, for they shared the same enthusiasms. They were both unqualified admirers of Delacroix, whose works Cézanne studied carefully every time he visited Chocquet's flat. Georges Rivière, the writer who defended the Impressionists and was Renoir's and Cézanne's close friend, described how he once went to see Chocquet with Cézanne, and witnessed 'those two hypersensitive people, on their knees, poring over faded sheets of paper, which for them were like holy relics, and weeping.'

At the age of fifty-three, Camille Pissarro felt a sudden and urgent need for new subjects, and it was in the hope of finding these that he decided to go to Normandy. Although the village of Osny (near Pontoise), where he lived, was a mere 130 kilometres from Rouen, it was not always easy for him to make the trip, for his movements were hampered by chronic poverty and a family of six, including himself and his wife. So until 1883 he had to content himself with the landscapes near where he lived. His eye adapted itself so wonderfully to this constraint that he was able to say, at the end of his life: 'I've found nothing to surpass what I have here – I mean, between Pontoise and Rouen.'

It was after his exhibition in May of that year at Durand-Ruel's that Pissarro felt dissatisfied with his work. His paintings struck him as dull and uninspired, and he felt the need for a change from his familiar green landscapes. Pissarro lived in the country throughout the year, so unlike his town-dwelling friends he chose as centre of operations for his holiday the beautiful city of Rouen.

This quiet family man had no contacts with any rich patron of the arts who might have asked him to be his guest. But his stay was facilitated by his friend, the eccentric Eugène Murer, who had previously run a restaurant in Paris. The painter Armand Guillaumin had taken his Impressionist friends along to Murer's Paris restaurant at 95 Boulevard Voltaire to taste his celebrated vol-au-vent. They often ate there, appreciating the warm welcome; in cases of extreme necessity they would sell off their paintings for a song to Murer, an anarchist-cum-Scrooge, who loved both art and literature. Murer had left Paris and retired to Auvers-sur-Oise, where he kept in touch with Pissarro and his friends through Dr Gachet. He subsequently bought the Hôtel du Dauphin et d'Espagne in Rouen, advertising the hotel as boasting 'a superb collection of Impressionists, on view every day from 10 a.m. to 6 p.m. Admission free.'

Pissarro occupied a 'superb' room overlooking the street in that 'top-class' hotel, which was located on the ultra-modern Place de la République, and gratefully took advantage of the comfort available there. 'The Murers have been very kind to me. They . . . have let me have full bed and board for 150 francs,' he wrote to his son Lucien shortly after his arrival.

Rapid industrial progress had turned the old Norman city into a bustling modern metropolis in no time. During the Second Empire, stations and bridges were built, and the harbour enlarged. The city had spread by then beyond the hollow in which it had originally nestled, and had swallowed up many of the surrounding villages. On the left bank of the Seine, a new housing area for workers had been created. Now factory chimneys were adding brown plumes of foul smoke to the fog. Like Monet in 1872, Pissarro was particularly attracted by the lively areas near the river: steamboats and barges were moored on its dark, oily waters, and the influence of the tides could be felt where muddy stretches of bank were bared – a favourite haunt of seagulls. 'I've begun a subject on the bank, on the way to Saint-Paul's Church,' the painter wrote to Lucien. 'As one looks towards Rouen, one can see the stone bridge in the distance, the island with its houses, factories, boats and launches on the left, and on the right a jumble of huge barges of every colour.'

Lucien Pissarro, who wanted to become a painter too and had just left home to go and live in London, was a perfect correspondent: every day his father would let him have his thoughts, his observations, the little incidents of his everyday life, and, certain of being understood, the details of his work. Camille Pissarro's letters, written in a slender, neat hand, suggest better than

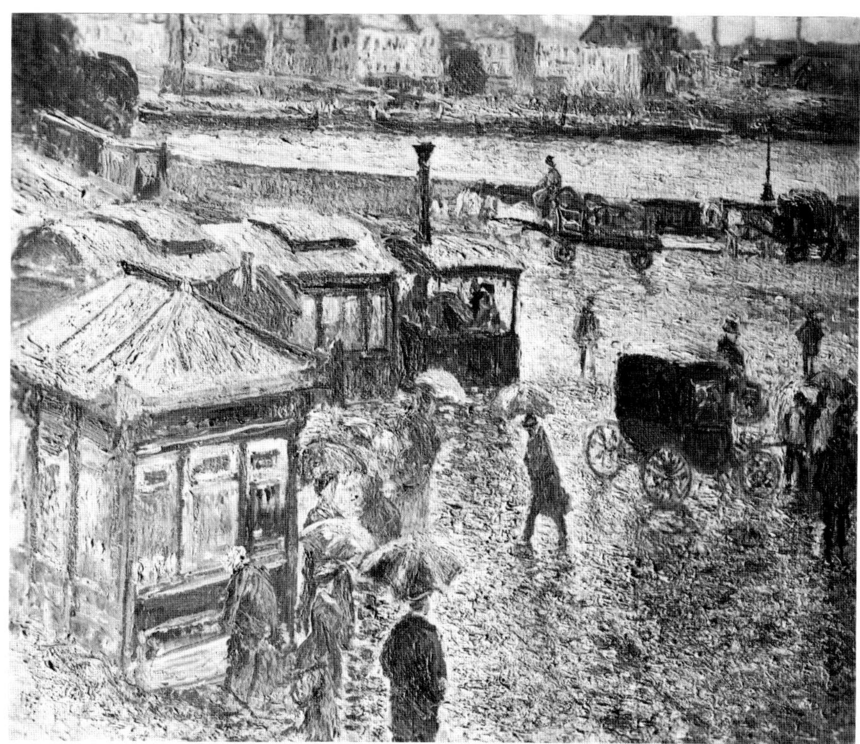

Camille Pissarro: *Place de la République, Rouen*, 1883 (Private Collection). Rouen's extremely variable weather made open-air work very difficult. Pissarro succeeded in rendering rain and fog effects in masterly fashion.

any diary the easygoing and natural rhythm of the man's life and thoughts, and show him to possess a quick inquisitive mind that contemplated the world without either bitterness or naivety.

In Rouen as elsewhere, painting was Pissarro's main occupation. Despite his experience and reputation, he still worked with the enthusiasm and self-doubt of a beginner. As he was more scrupulously faithful than ever in his observation of light, Pissarro was at the mercy of the weather, which can, of course, either create or screen a subject. In order to take advantage of every single moment of his stay, he used all the tricks of the experienced landscapist's trade to thwart the changeability of the skies. He would, for instance, start several paintings at once: 'I'm working on nine paintings now, at various stages of completion,' he wrote to Lucien at the beginning of his stay. 'I started one picture this afternoon on the Cours-la-Reine, in bright sunshine. But I'll need one more session on it in fine weather, to make it a little more convincing. Up to now I haven't quite found the effect I'm after.'

Pissarro tried whenever possible to complete his pictures in one sitting, for fear that his subject might disappear. Although the speed of application made possible by the Impressionist technique was particularly well suited to the demands of *plein-air* work, Pissarro often had to abandon a painting halfway through. But as he had noticed certain constant features of the weather, he sometimes decided to do several pictures of the same subject: thus, he depicted Rouen's nerve centre, the Place de la République, with 'a fog effect, for there's plenty every morning till about 11 or 12 o'clock,' and then painted the same subject in the sun, as soon as the fog had lifted.

When he was prevented by rain or lack of light from painting at all, Pissarro, a keen draughtsman, combed the narrow streets of old Rouen – which had already been visited by so many artists he admired – in search of the interesting visual motifs that were to be found there in profusion. 'I've drawn a few little carved wood motifs, pure gothic with little decorations – wonderful!' he told Lucien. Turner and Bonington, whose works Pissarro knew well, had worked in Rouen; and after drawing the arch of the Gros-Horloge, by the Place du Vieux-Marché, Pissarro was delighted to discover a lithograph of the same scene executed by Bonington in 1829 or 1830.

On 21 October, Claude Monet, his son and the dealer Durand-Ruel managed to tear Pissarro away from his easel. They all spent Sunday together at the house of Léon Monet, the painter's brother, a prosperous businessman who had moved into the beautiful countryside round Rouen. 'We had one day of superb weather at Canteleu, a village high on a hill, near Deville,' Pissarro wrote. 'We saw the most wonderful landscapes that a painter could possibly dream of: a view of Rouen in the distance, with a section of the Seine, as smooth as a mirror, sun-dappled slopes, and splendid foreground motifs. It was quite magical.' That rightly famous view was the one which Gustave Flaubert discovered on his way back and forth to his estate in Croisset, and which he described in such masterly fashion in *Madame Bovary*. It also drew the admiration of Corot, who painted it slightly shrouded in mist.

After that enjoyable interruption, Pissarro went off along the coast. In one of the frequent rainstorms that deluge the area, he painted two large studies of cliffs at Les Petites-Dalles. Not bothered at all by bad weather, he realized, with his experienced painter's eye, how wonderfully the grey light brought out the green of the meadows. 'It's a superb part of the country, with enough landscapes, farms, cliffs and woods to give one work day in and day out,' he wrote to Lucien.

Pissarro's enthusiasm was quite unquenchable. At the age of fifty-three, the beauty of a site still filled him with a strong fresh emotion that he was always ready to share with someone else. His communicative nature attracted beginners, those who were shy or who needed help. Reassured by his unruffled expression and patriarchal beard, perfect strangers would approach him. 'Yesterday, all the time I was working,' he wrote to his son, 'a little man kept on pestering me. The poor fellow told me about a youngster, aged nineteen, from Rouen, whom he would like to help. The young man is apparently full of enthusiasm and has unshakable faith in himself. The man asked me to go and have a look at what he has painted at his house – a portrait.'

Camille Pissarro: *The Roofs of Old Rouen (the Cathedral)*, 1896 (Toledo Museum of Art, Ohio).

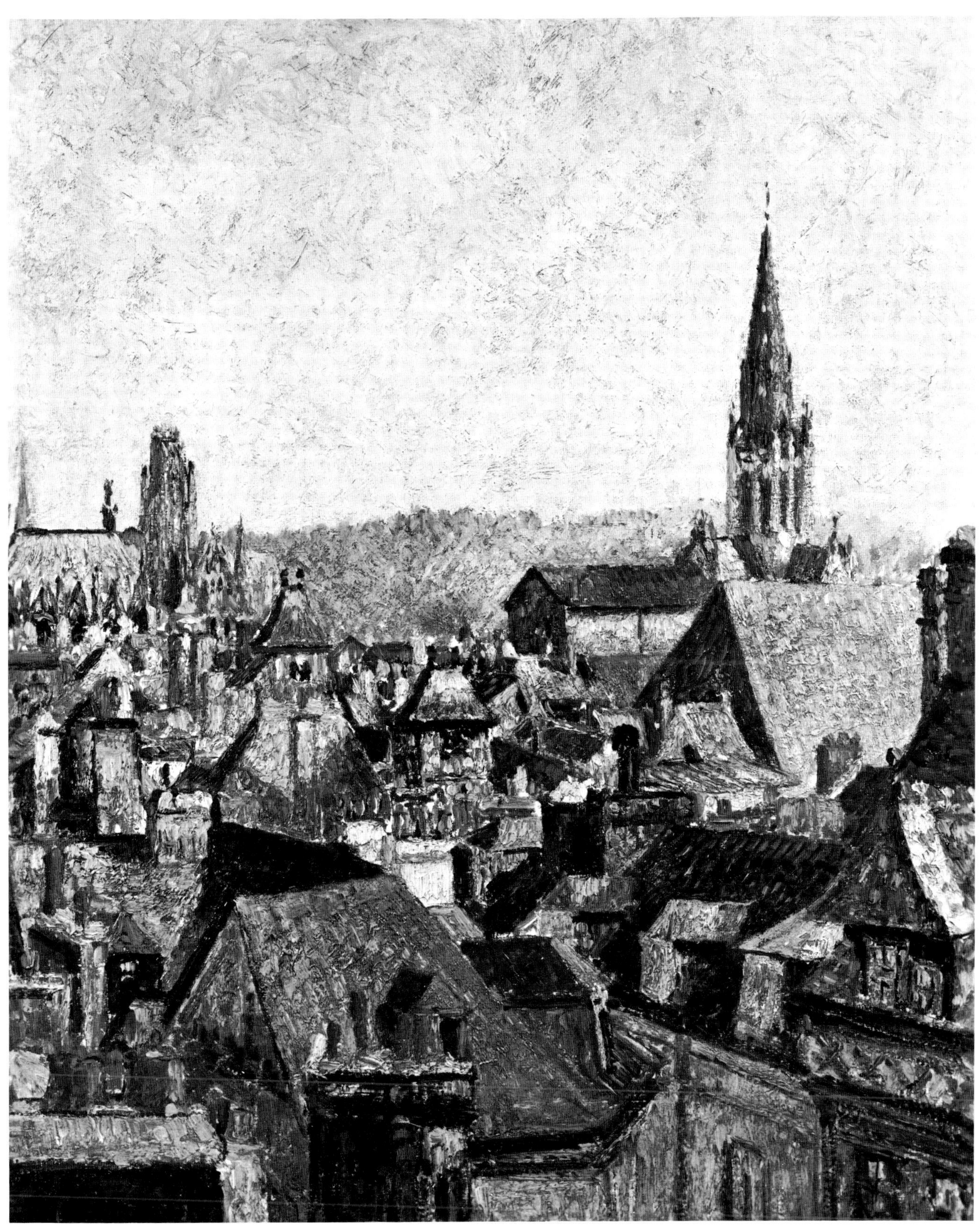

Pissarro agreed to go on that occasion because he was always touched by a sense of vocation in a young painter, just as he had been in the past by the ambitions of Paul Gauguin. In 1877, when Gauguin met Pissarro in Paris at the home of his godfather, the South American art collector Achille Arosa, he was still a prosperous stockbroker who on Sundays would turn out a few awkward pictures. In time, his passion for painting became more and more exclusive. He would often ask Pissarro's advice and spent several summer holidays working with him at Osny. The economic crisis had decided Gauguin to give up the world of stocks and shares: he was about to join his mentor in Normandy, 'to study the place from a practical and artistic point of view', as he told Pissarro, adding naively enough that, since the people of Rouen were rich, it might be easy to get them to buy at some point.

Pissarro's view, based on experience, was less optimistic than Gauguin's, as can be judged from a letter he wrote to Murer, who was thinking of organizing an exhibition of his works in the Hôtel du Dauphin et d'Espagne:

> I don't believe that paintings will sell in Rouen. You can rest assured, my dear friend, that when the collectors see some of my more recent studies, they will pelt me with baked apples. Remember that even in Paris we're considered to be black sheep, beggars. . . . No! No art which disturbs so many deep-rooted convictions could possibly gain general approval, and even less so in Rouen, where they don't dare admit Flaubert as one of their own. . . .

Gauguin spent several months in Rouen with his wife and children. His stay soon scotched his optimism and wiped out his savings. He left the city in December 1884, and never set foot there again. Pissarro, on the other hand, often went back. In 1896 and 1898 he produced some of his most famous paintings there. From his room in the Hôtel d'Angleterre he painted, one day when the sky was overcast, 'the whole of old Rouen seen from above the houses, with the Cathedral, the Eglise Saint-Ouen and some really extraordinary decorated roofs and turrets,' as he told his son.

The Roofs of Old Rouen, behind which the Cathedral can be seen looming, is an admirable work which Degas, who was so difficult to please, described as 'capital'. Pissarro would turn from such static subjects to bridges jammed with traffic, the quayside, or the little shopping streets in the centre of the town. In *La Rue de l'Epicerie*, he conjures up a delightful vision of the street, in which the vivid colours of tiles and slates, the pearly white and pale pink walls, dotted with posters, the dark shops and the passers-by form a harmonious and marvellously balanced whole.

The scientific discoveries which had been revolutionizing human activity ever since the beginning of the century began to influence art and artists in the 1890s. Young painters eager to go one better than the Impressionists paid increasing attention to the physical and chemical laws that govern light and colour. Even Monet, who lived instinctively at the tempo of the age, said in 1891 that he was no longer satisfied 'with facile things which come in a flash'. His insatiable need to create made him take his researches further and further. He naturally turned towards the quasi-scientific observation of light changing on a given subject. The haystacks near Giverny and the poplars lining the road gave him a fine opportunity to do this before he went on to tackle light's effects on stone.

In the following year, 1892, Monet began one of the most ambitious projects of his career: the great Cathedral of Rouen, seen under various conditions at different times of the day. From the room he had rented on the second floor at 81 Rue du Grand-Port, the painter was able to observe its astonishing Gothic façade closely. Changing canvases as often as the metamorphosis of his subject required, he produced a series of eighteen paintings which transformed the monolithic edifice into a succession of brilliant patterns of colour so skilfully assembled that the underlying structure always manages to emerge. Monet's friend and champion, the statesman Georges Clémenceau, went into raptures over his *tour de force*, and turning himself into an art critic wrote a laudatory article ringingly entitled 'The Revolution of Cathedrals'.

Sisley's next trip to Honfleur after his enjoyable cruise downstream with Renoir on their way to the regatta was a very short one in the summer of 1867 with his young wife and their new-born son Pierre. After that, more than twenty years were to elapse before he returned to work in Normandy.

In 1894, he also stayed at the Hôtel du Dauphin et d'Espagne, where he was welcomed by Murer, whom he had known for many years. He travelled from Moret to Rouen at the invitation of one of the very few champions of his work, François Depeaux, an important shipowner and friend of Léon Monet. Free for once from financial worry for a few days, Alfred Sisley was able to enjoy the admirable view from Canteleu and the other superb landscapes that abounded in the Rouen area. Like Monet and Pissarro, he painted the Seine, the hills of La Bouille, some still very rural scenery and one of the cottages that smallholders were beginning to desert for the towns.

In all these various ways, Normandy was bound up with the whole history of the Impressionist movement from Monet's youth to Pissarro's old age. For a shorter time, but with a considerably more specific effect, another area of France – a handful of villages on the banks of the Seine – was to dominate their lives. It was here that they were first to succeed in capturing that most elusive and essential aspect of their art: the changing effects of light.

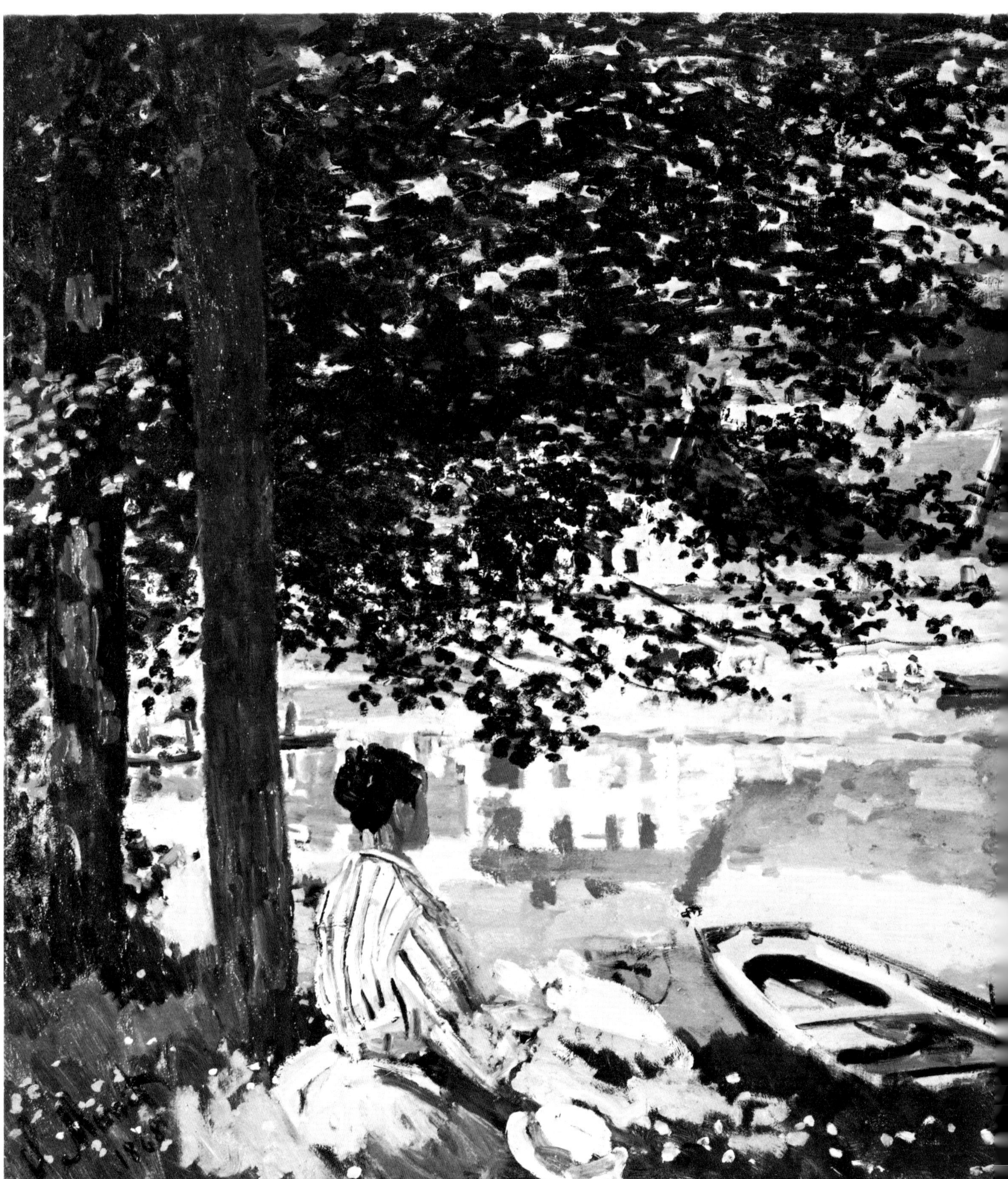

4 The Seine

A Cradle of Moving Light

Ideally situated beside the noble River Seine and conveniently near to Paris, villages such as Bennecourt, Bougival and Argenteuil were to occupy a very special place in the lives of the Impressionists. The period was above all a happy and artistically exciting one, even though it often lacked, for Monet, Renoir and Pissarro, the barest material necessities.

In its slow, winding course to the sea, the Seine was inexhaustibly fascinating to these young devotees of light and movement. It not only mirrored the changing scenery, but lent itself to a whole range of amusements, from boating to dancing in one of the popular café-restaurants along its banks.

The first time the Seine is given pride of place by a member of the group is in *The River*, a masterly landscape painted by Monet in the spring of 1868. Its light colours, and gentle, tender harmonies, make it an admirably well-balanced picture: in the foreground we see Camille, with her back to the artist, sitting on a patch of flowered grass; nearby there is the rowing-boat that brought Monet and his mistress across the arm of the river separating them from the hamlet of Le Gloton where they were living. Patches of sky and foliage, as well as the houses on the opposite bank, can be seen reflected in the smooth water of the river.

In March of that year Claude Monet, just back from one of his frequent trips to Normandy, was preparing his entry for the forthcoming Salon. Among the friends and colleagues he met as a matter of course at the Café Guerbois was Emile Zola, who announced his intention of writing an article about the painter. During his meetings with the writer, Monet doubtless mentioned how difficult it was for him to make ends meet: he had no studio, no home for his family, and now no income, since his aunt had decided – because of her nephew's 'irregular' situation with Camille – to cut off the small monthly allowance she had been sending him ever since he started out as an artist. Zola at once recommended the pretty village of Bennecourt and the adjoining hamlet of Le Gloton, with all the enthusiasm of his own happy memories of the place.

Two years before, Zola and his army of friends used to turn up every Sunday at that almost inaccessible spot on the Seine to visit their friend Cézanne, who, on the advice of Daubigny, had taken refuge there for a few months in the hope of finding new subjects, low prices and a little solitude. That pastoral setting, different though it was from the countryside in the South of France, offered a wealth of interesting subjects. Yet somehow Cézanne, the southerner, failed to work up any enthusiasm for the meadows, the golden cornfields, or the Seine with its shimmer of reflected light. At that time he was under the spell of Courbet, and could only dream of ambitious realist paintings such as the one he describes at length in a letter to Zola – for

Claude Monet: *The River*, 1868 (courtesy of the Art Institute of Chicago, Mrs Potter Palmer Collection).

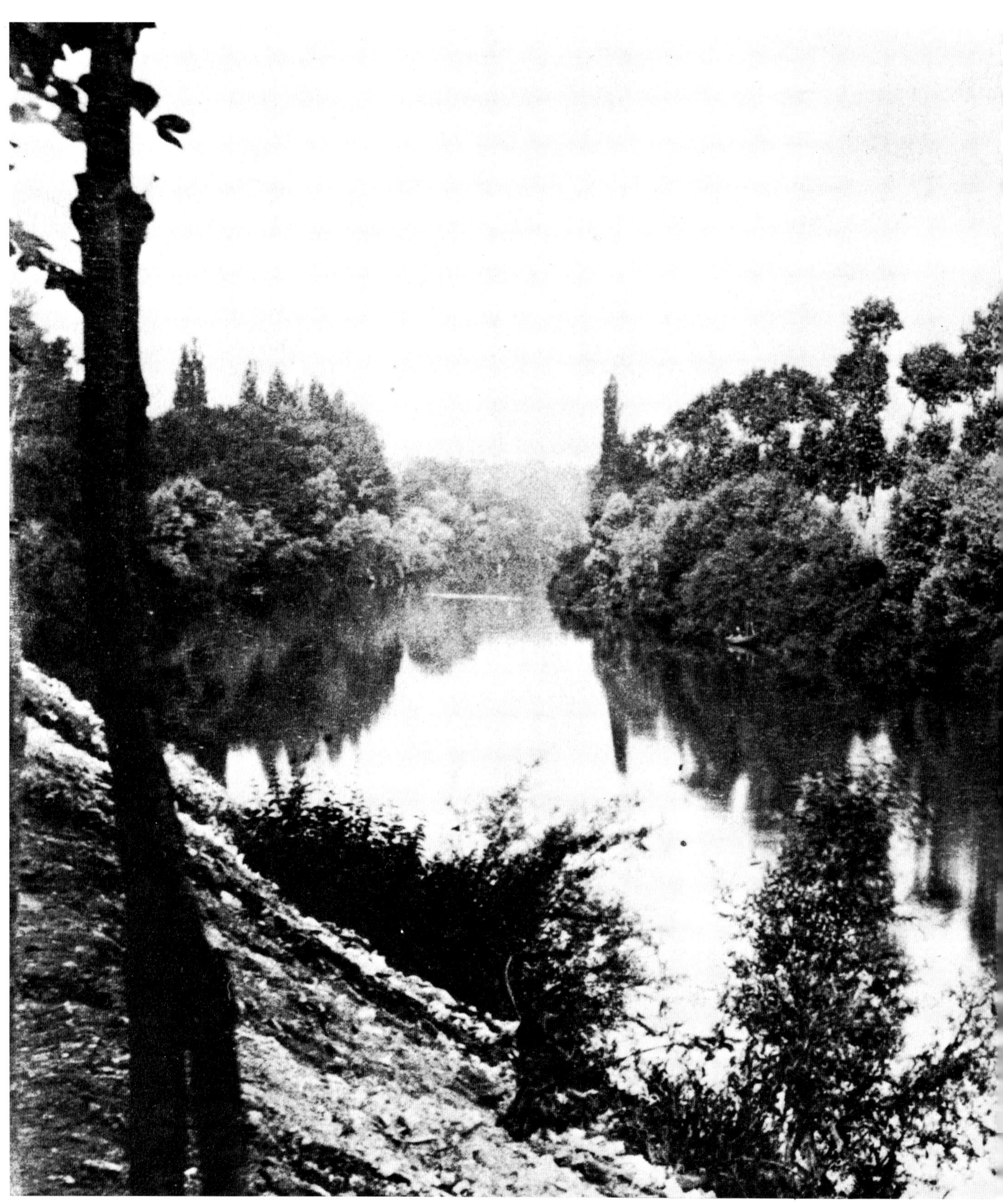

The Seine at Poissy, near Médan, where Zola lived. 'I believe I loved it as much as I did because somehow it gave me the meaning of life' – Guy de Maupassant.

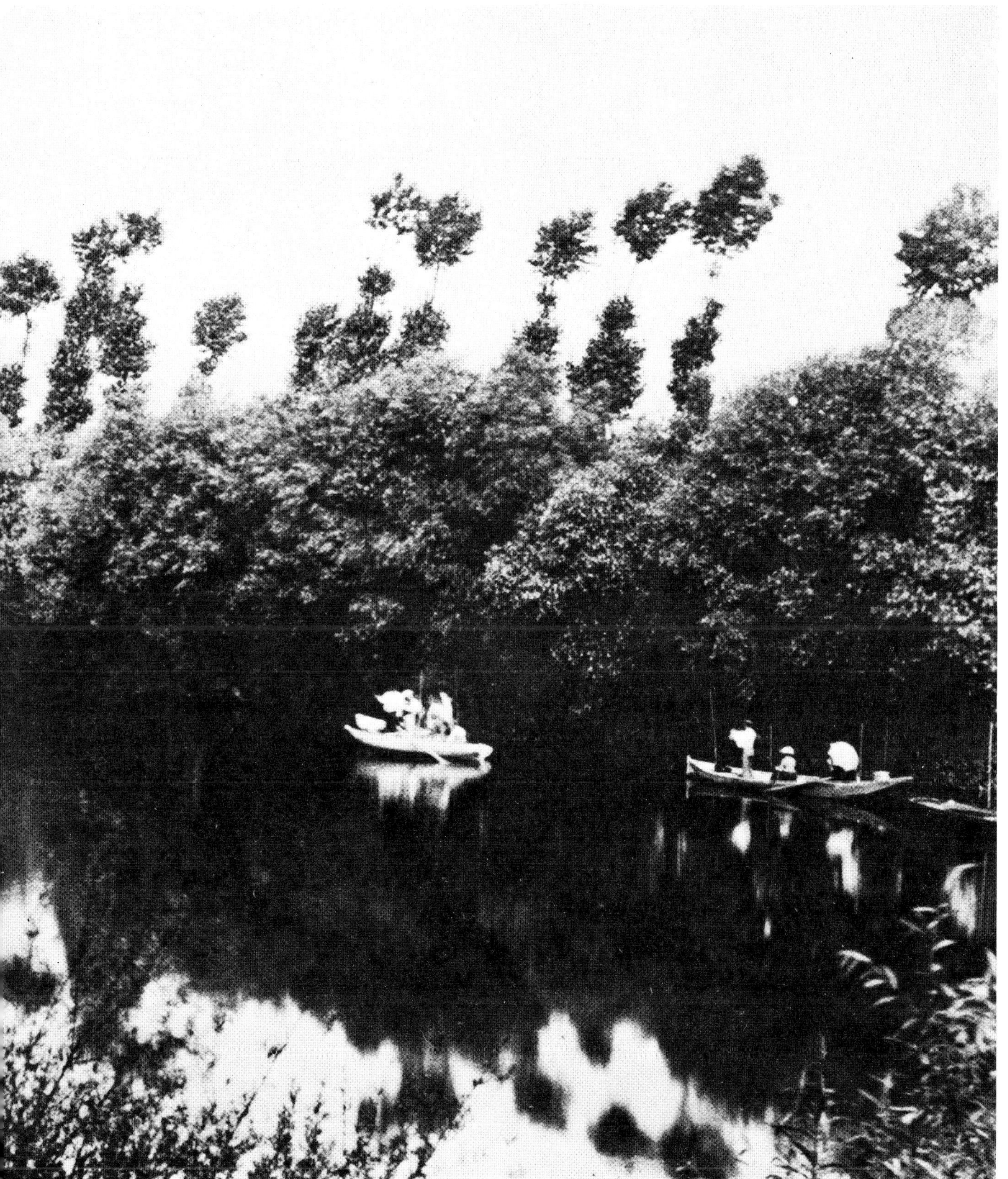

which he got his neighbours (the farrier Calvaire Levasseur and his two sons) to pose in their smithy. But Cézanne, who was as highly-strung as a racehorse, was ill equipped for the venture; the slightest problem would throw him off balance and prevent him from working. The scene was one that required rapid execution, but he was a slow painter. 'If I could work on it longer, it would get finished quite quickly,' he complained in a letter to Zola. 'Decidedly, it looks as though those people (the models) will have to come and sit for me in the studio.' That was a tacit admission that he had by no means mastered all the problems of painting outdoors.

Cézanne's worries were soon forgotten when, at weekends, Zola, his girlfriend the beautiful Gabrielle Melay, the sculptor Philippe Solari, the poet Antonin Valabrègue, the publicist Marius Roux and the budding novelist Paul Alexis invaded the hamlet and made its sleepy little streets resound with their exotic southern accents. 'They arrive wearing overcoats, but by evening their hats are crumpled, their smocks streaked with paint, and their trousers stained green by the grass,' Zola was to write later. The group went on endless walks across the countryside, outings as far as La Roche-Guyon and Jeufosse, and boating expeditions that were the occasion for a lot of horseplay and practical jokes. Then, after dinner, 'those young people . . . surrounded by the stillness of the night, conquered the world.'

Nothing has survived of Cézanne's stay at Le Gloton except a *Head of an Old Man*, the portrait of Père Roussel, the father of Madame Dumont the innkeeper. Zola, on the other hand, often evoked the village, the surrounding countryside and the memory of the exhilarating time he had had there with his friends in such novels as *La Rivière*, *L'Oeuvre* and *Une Farce*.

Few details are known of Monet's stay of a few months with the Dumonts, 'in that country inn,' as Zola described it, 'with its little grocery, large main room that smelt of washing, and huge courtyard full of ducks waddling around in the manure.' He was in the back of beyond: the trip to Paris was a veritable expedition that had to be undertaken in three stages. First, he had to go down to the foot of the steep embankment that protects Bennecourt, where Père Hayet ferried him across to the Grande Ile, an island in the middle of the Seine. Within a few minutes, he crossed the island to the far bank, where another ferryboat took him to Bonnières-sur-Seine. Then a two-hour rail journey would bring him to the Gare Saint-Lazare in Paris.

Monet felt as though he had been exiled – no visitor came to comfort him during his stay there – and on 29 June, in a letter to Bazille, he suddenly announced the end of that painful interlude in somewhat melodramatic terms:

> Dear Bazille, I am writing you a few lines in haste to ask for your speedy help. I was certainly born under an unlucky star. I have just been thrown

> out of the inn, and stark naked at that. I have found a roof for Camille and my poor little Jean for a few days in the country. This evening I am leaving for Le Havre to see about trying something with my collector (Gaudibert). My family have no intention of doing anything more for me. I don't even know where I'll have a place to sleep tomorrow. Your very harassed friend. Claude Monet.
>
> P.S. I was so upset yesterday that I was silly enough to throw myself into the river. Fortunately, no harm came of it.

This kind of abrupt and distressing dénouement seemed, with certain variations, to be the outcome of all Monet's stays, wherever he went. He was an unrepentant sybarite, and his pride refused to allow him to give up the advantages of bourgeois living even though he was poor. When he no longer had a penny, he would run up debts, convincing himself each time that somehow he would get out of his predicament. His family, his acquaintances, and his friend Bazille all had the money he so desperately needed; and he persistently begged for their help. When he failed to obtain it, he went through periods of terrible poverty which he bore bravely. And in the end, his lust for life and for art always managed to emerge unscathed.

In 1869, torn as usual between his yearning to get away from the bustle of the capital he hated and his concern to stay close enough to be able to look after his affairs there, Monet rented a cottage to the west of Paris, just off the main road that ran from the capital to Rouen via Saint-Germain-en-Laye. The village of Saint-Michel, where the painter and his family were to live for two years, was admirably located on the wooded hill that rose from Bougival on the banks of the Seine and went up as far as Louveciennes on the edge of

The Château de Monte Cristo at Port-Marly.

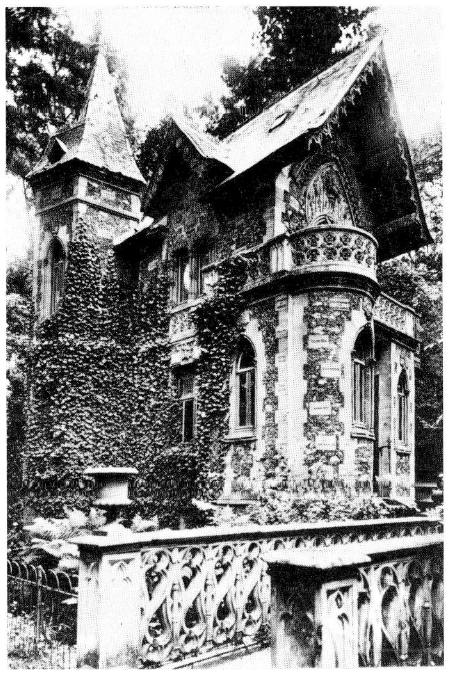

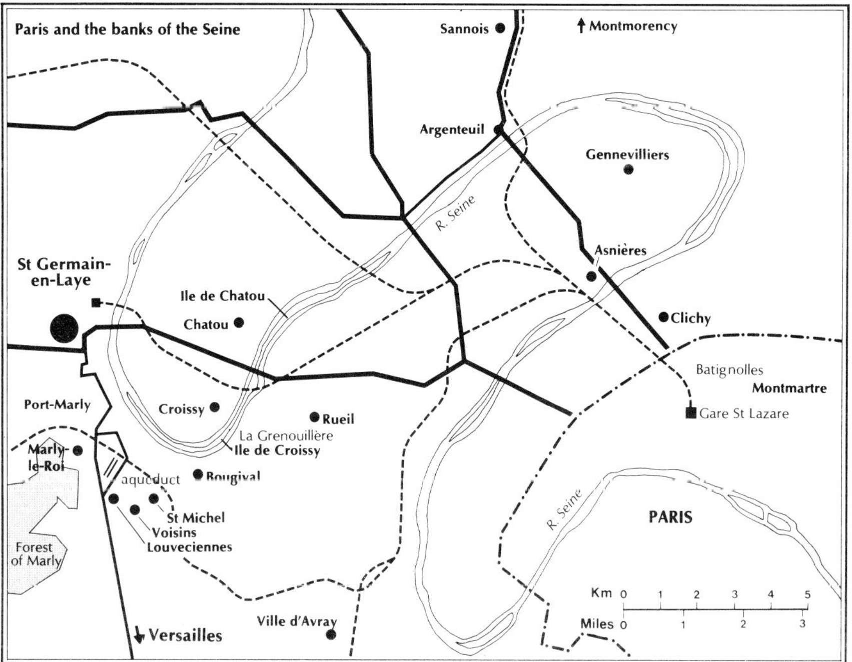

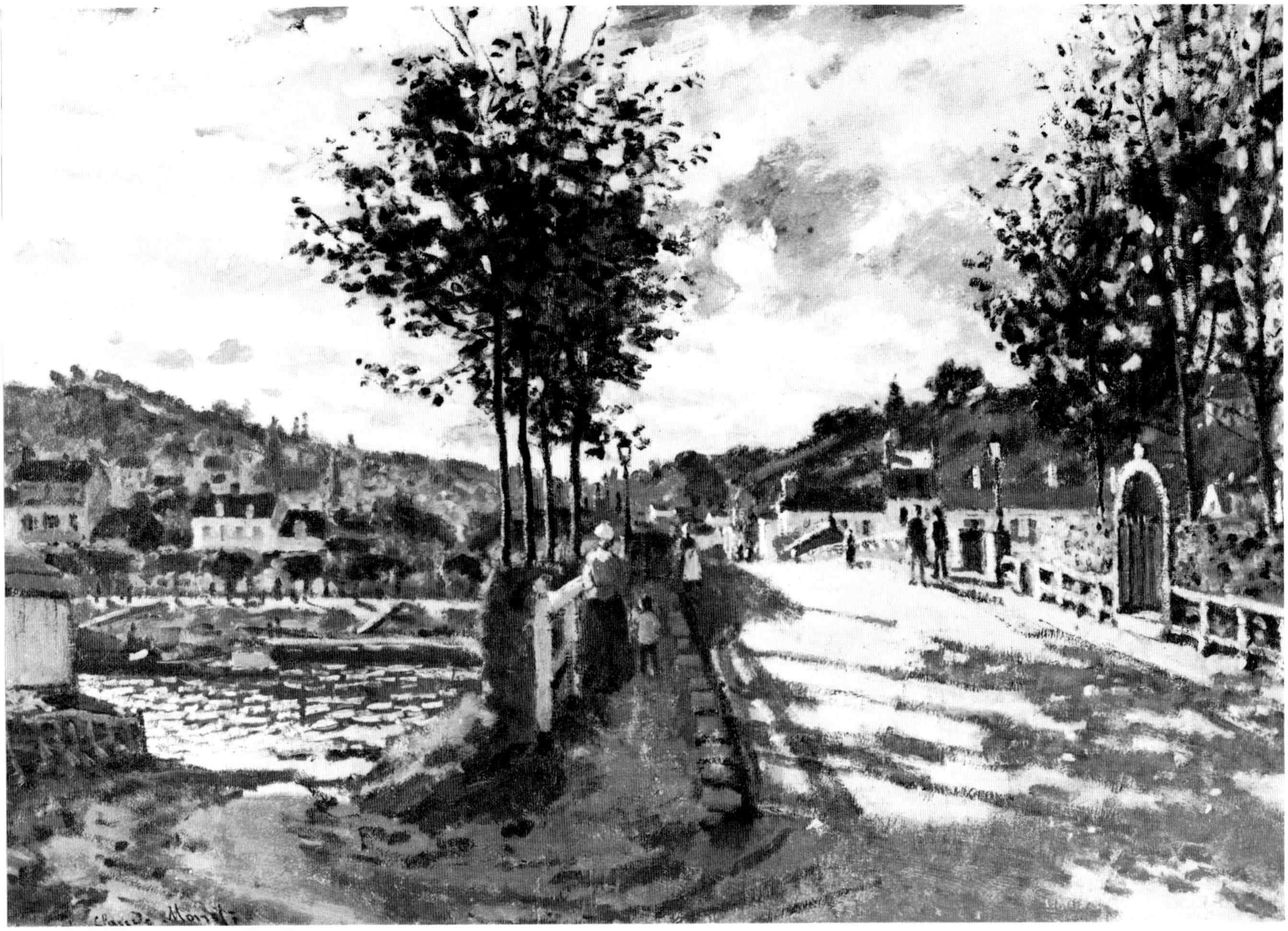

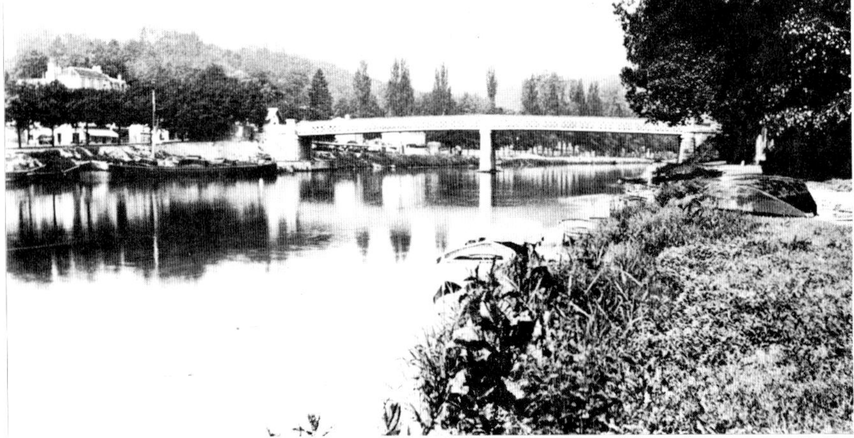

ABOVE Claude Monet: *The Bridge at Bougival*, 1870 (Currier Gallery of Art, Manchester, New Hampshire). 'This moment of life caught unawares will keep its charm, these immobilized gestures will testify to the grace of vanished figures amidst the masterpieces of art' – Gustave Geffroy.
LEFT Bougival – the river and the village.
OPPOSITE Berthe Morisot: *Quay at Bougival*, 1883 (National Gallery, Oslo). 'She is a sensitive colourist who brings everything into a general harmony of whites not easily attuned without lapsing into affectedness', said the critic Philippe Burty of Morisot.

the forest. From the beginning of the nineteenth century, artists, writers and musicians had sought to escape the harassments of city life by settling among the vineyards and smallholdings of that still countrified area. After his spell as director of the theatre at Saint-Germain-en-Laye, Alexandre Dumas went into hiding nearby in order to write his celebrated adventure story *The*

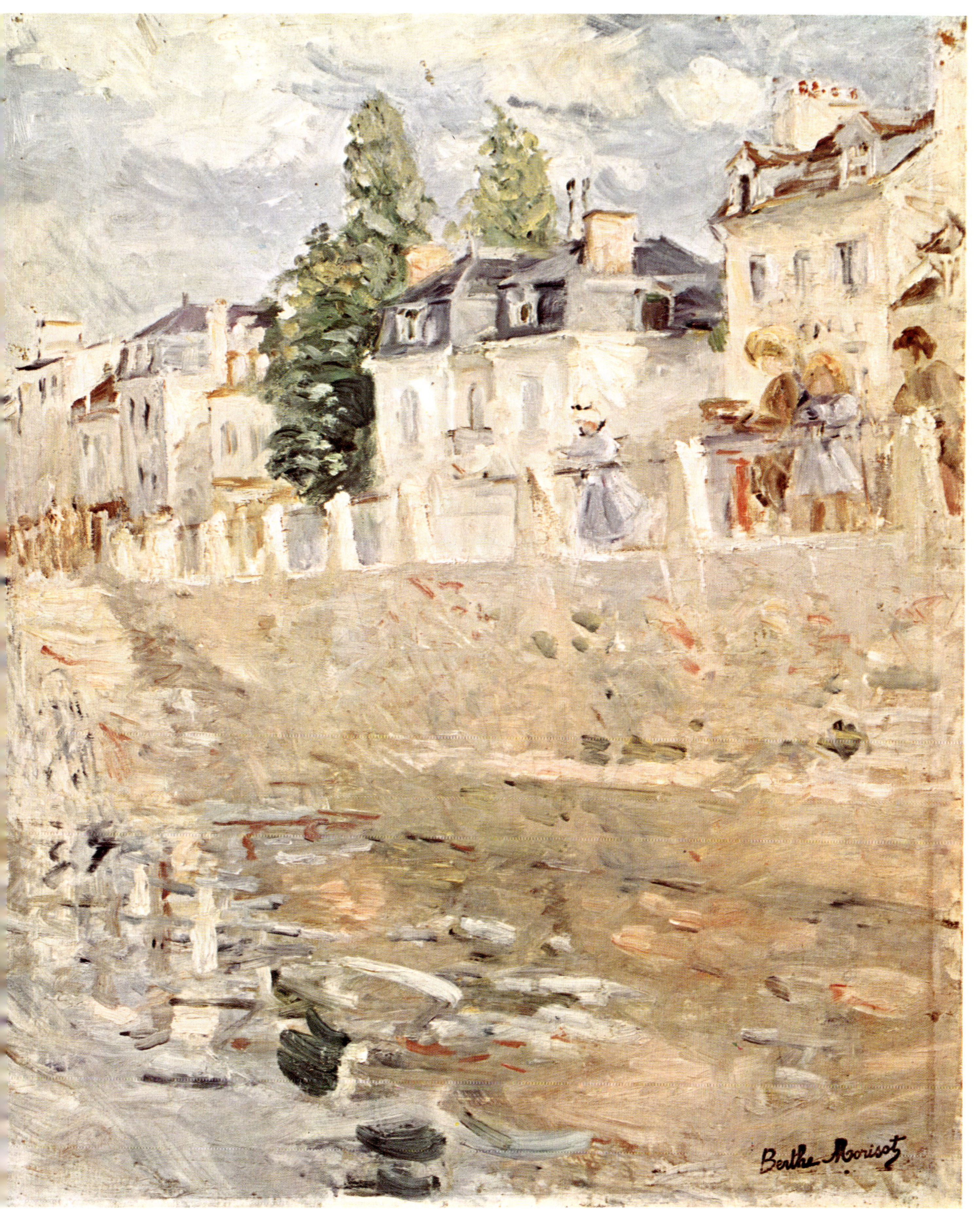
Berthe Morisot

Count of Monte Cristo. He subsequently built himself an extravagant, palatial home, the Château de Monte Cristo, where he quickly ruined himself by giving wild parties for the cream of Parisian society. The Russian novelist Turgenev stayed all year long with the singer Pauline Viardot at Bougival, as did Georges Bizet and his wife, Ludovic Halévy's cousin. Camille Saint-Saëns, who would spend day after day composing, cloistered in his house at Voisins, was thought mad by the villagers. It was in Voisins, too, that Renoir's parents had settled after their retirement.

Weekdays in that pastoral setting were quiet and undisturbed. But as soon as springtime arrived, hordes of Sunday trippers would flood out of Paris by train and road, and noisily enjoy their share of the pleasures that the river and the fields afforded them. Bougival, Chatou and the various islands that form a string down the Seine at that point became one vast amusement park for those who liked to go boating or have fun in the open air.

Like all young men of the period, Monet knew the spot well. In midwinter of 1867, he had painted *Ice on the Seine* and *Snow on the Seine*; and his decision to live there was certainly motivated by the variety of subjects offered by the neighbourhood. Thanks to the generosity of Gaudibert, his collector from Le Havre, Monet was in a position to set up house under less precarious circumstances than usual. Indeed, he would not have had a problem in the world if Bazille had kept his promise to send him 50 francs regularly each month in payment for *Women in the Garden*, which he had bought the previous year – or at least that is what Monet imagined. More than once he sent his friend a sharp reminder of his debt. But the habitually generous Frédéric Bazille, then staying with his family at Méric near Montpellier, was getting impatient with Monet's constant pathetic appeals, and did not answer.

A number of circumstances, on the other hand, drew Monet closer to Renoir, who had temporarily taken refuge with his parents at Louveciennes: a lack of money, a love of life and of painting, and an unquenchable thirst for recognition were things they both shared. What chiefly attracted Renoir to the Monets was Camille's charm and gaiety, the presence of their child, and the intimate family atmosphere – something that he himself was far too poor to afford. Renoir would often walk down through the woods from Voisins to Saint-Michel, his pockets bulging with bread pinched from his mother, and participate in his friends' frugal life, appreciating their good spirits and sharing their worries.

The two painters used to go together to Bougival where, just as at Bonnières, there was a string of islands in the middle of the Seine. The islands of La Loge, or of Croissy, between Bougival and Croissy, and, opposite Rueil, the island of Chatou, with the shade of its fine tall trees, were the most popular. The *guinguettes*, the cafés, the bathing establishments and the

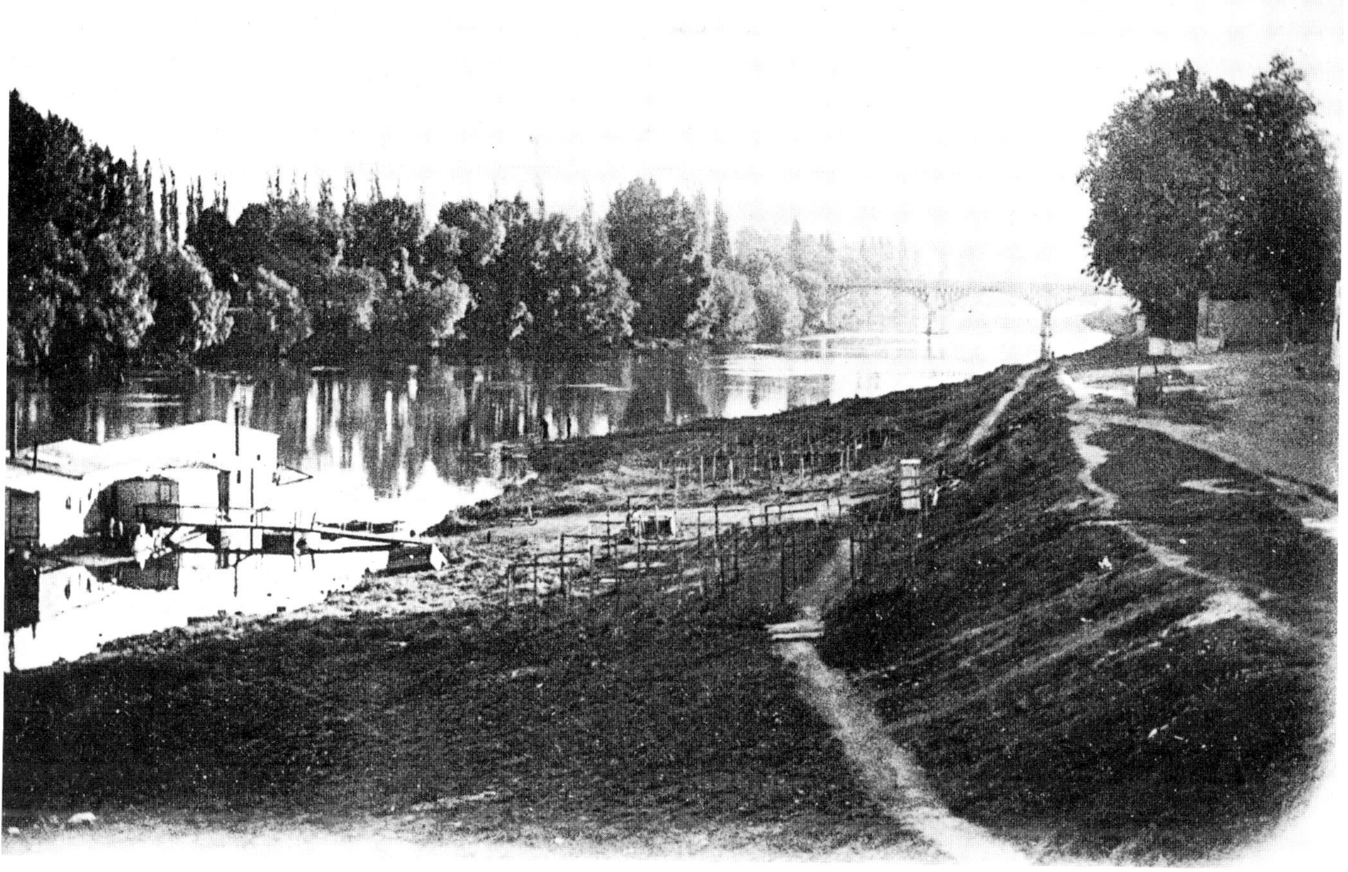

The Seine at Chatou.

pleasure-boat companies vied for the custom of a motley crowd of dandies, fast women (known as *grenouilles*), journalists, gentlemen and cocottes, flung into contact with each other either by chance or out of natural affinity.

Boatmen and their girlfriends, painters, poets and lovers would wait for the ferry to take them across to the island of La Loge. Guy de Maupassant, who loved to go boating and knew the place well, has left us a description of their favourite haunt, La Grenouillère, that displays the visual accuracy he considered a prime literary virtue: a 'huge raft, covered with a tarred roof which is supported by wooden posts, is joined to the charming island of Croissy by two gangways, one of which leads into the middle of that aquatic establishment, while the other runs from one end of it to a tiny island with just one tree, nicknamed the "flower-pot", and then on to the river bank by the bathing establishment's office.'

It was at that very spot, towards the end of the summer of 1869, that Renoir and Monet set up their easels side by side and tried to capture the spectacle of ephemeral enjoyment that lay before them. They worked very quickly. Just as someone taking notes allows his pen to dash across the page, caring little about the correct form of the letters, so Renoir and Monet gave their paintbrushes free rein in order to capture the ever-changing light and

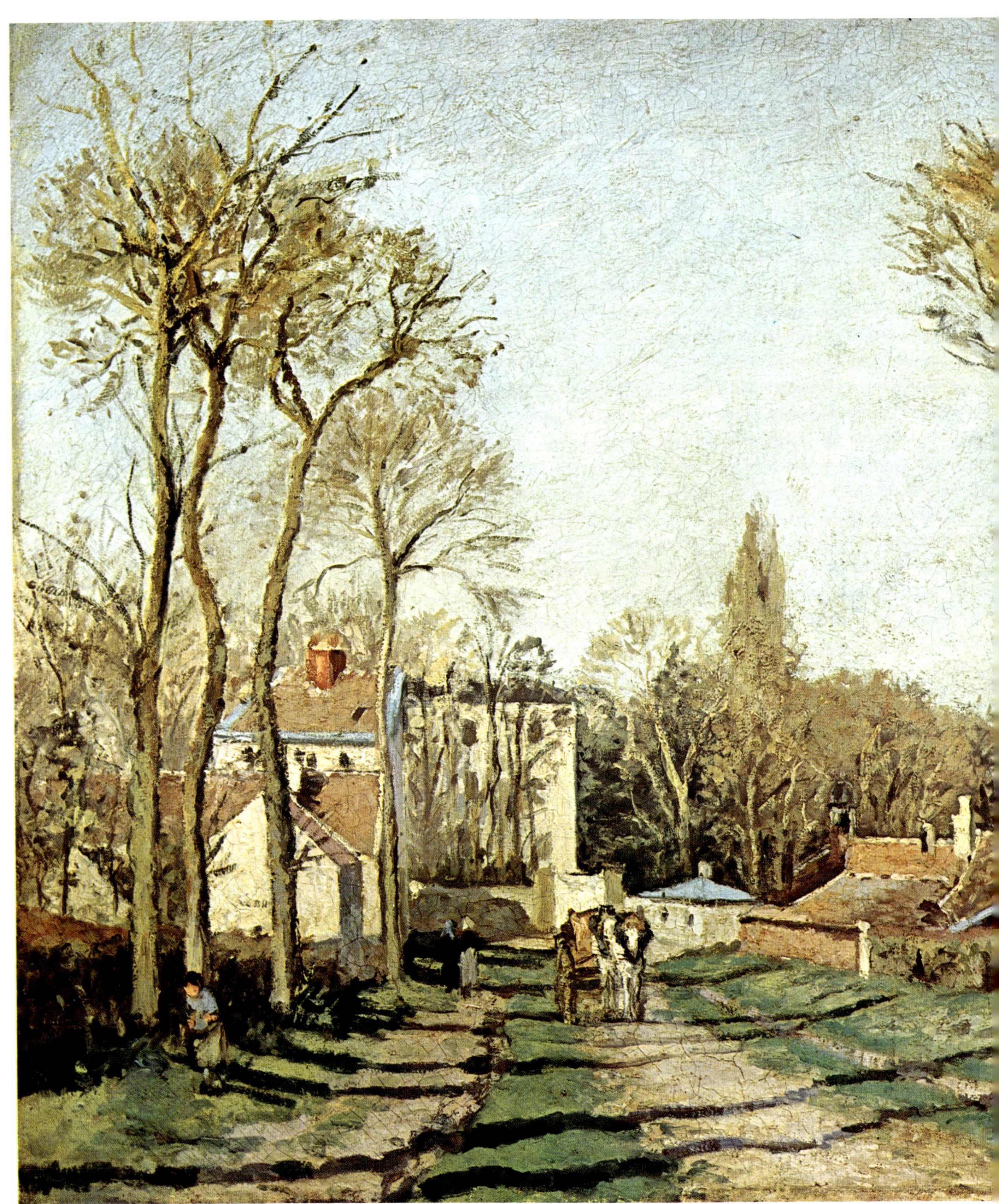

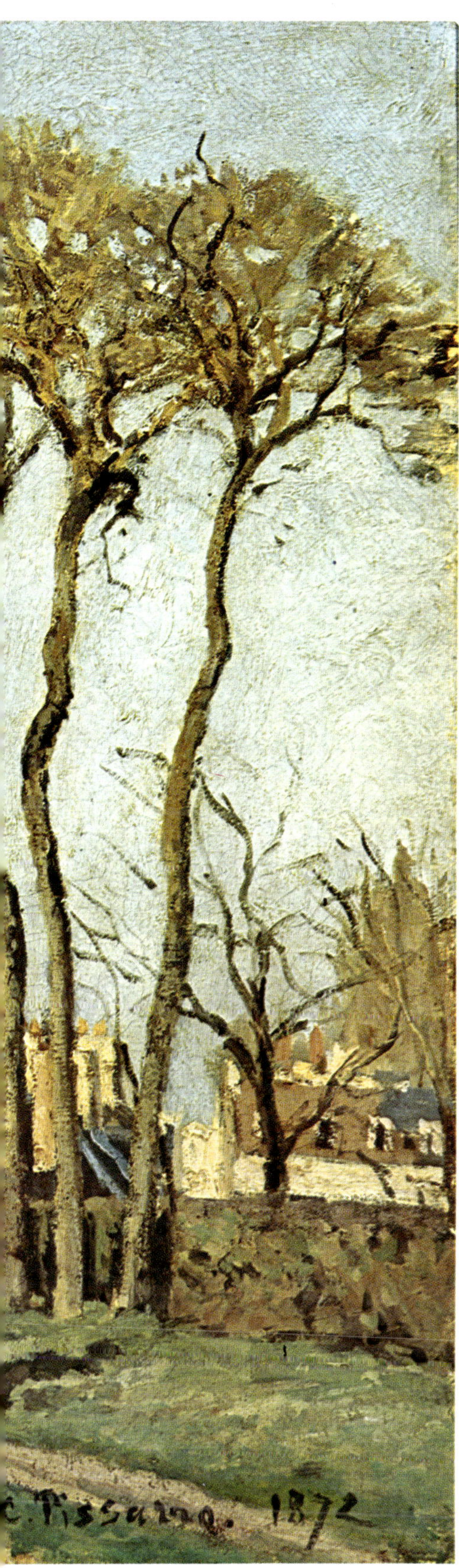

OPPOSITE Camille Pissarro: *Outskirts of a Village*, 1872 (Musée du Louvre, Paris – Jeu de Paume). With an exquisite subtlety and lightness of touch, Pissarro captures the light of a late autumn afternoon in the Ile de France.
BELOW Camille Pissarro: *The Seine at Marly*, 1871 (Private Collection).

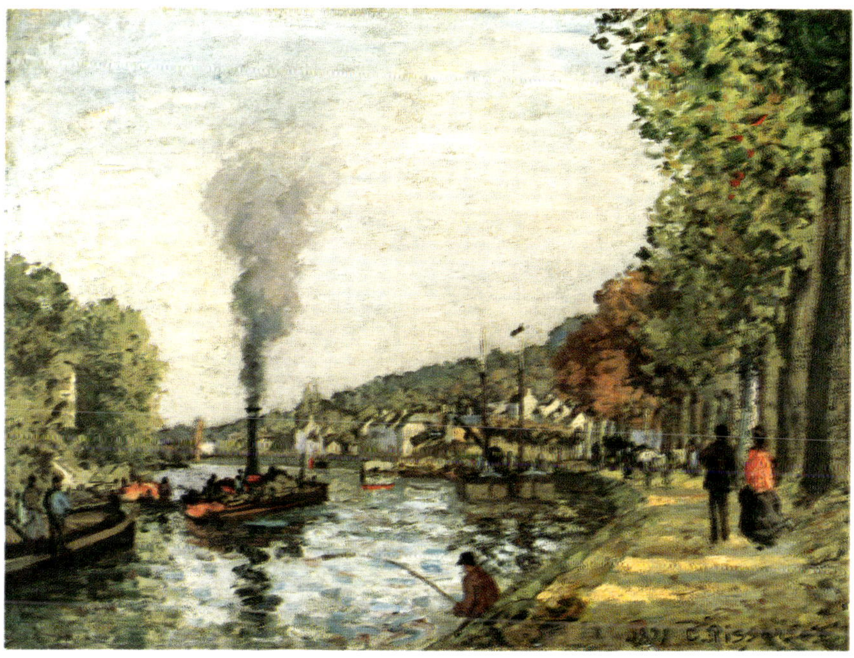

the moving human figures. The interplay of sun and shade on the river is rendered by long, thin strokes of colour, well separated from each other; little coloured dashes suggest the foliage, while the bathers are mere specks of black and white. The two painters literally invented a new way of painting in which form was sacrificed to light.

Renoir, who was always drawn towards people, treats his version of *La Grenouillère* as a setting for human figures: he lingers more than Monet on details of clothing, makes the girls' skirts billow, and adds a flounce or a hat here and there. His colours are brighter than those chosen by Monet, who evinces greater concern for the overall composition of the subject. They both made several studies of La Grenouillère and its surroundings, which were the first truly Impressionist paintings, and among the finest ever produced. Yet the two young painters had other, more immediate goals in mind, and felt unhappy that they had been unable, through lack of money, to buy the colours and canvases that might have allowed each of them to produce a possible entry for the Salon. In a letter to Bazille, Monet refers to 'one or two worthless rough sketches', while Renoir became so depressed that he began to talk of giving up painting altogether and finding a less frivolous occupation that would enable him to earn a decent living.

The fact was that once the summer came to an end Renoir and Monet were forced to move indoors to work, where they were soon overcome again by listlessness and worry. They set to work on still lifes and portraits, but their exhilaration had ebbed. Renoir, who had always felt the cold, soon retreated to Paris, but Claude Monet, whose extremely robust health enabled him to work under almost any conditions, trekked alone up the road leading to the forest of Marly in search of new natural subjects. With *Wooded Road, Effect of Snow*, he began a series of studies in which he observed the changes of light that occur in a snow-covered landscape. Occasionally, he went up as far as Louveciennes, where Pissarro lived.

At the end of 1869 Pissarro left Pontoise and moved to Louveciennes, to the house situated at Number 22 on the Route de Versailles that was to feature in so many masterpieces by him and his colleagues. The house, alongside the broad tree-lined avenue still used by the stagecoach service that connected up the local villages, had a tiny front garden which can be seen in *The Road from Versailles to Louveciennes*. This painting is composed in a fairly traditional manner, and is chiefly interesting for the way in which Pissarro uses colour. The work is divided diagonally in two, with lighter, airier tones to the right, while the left is filled with darker colours heightened, here and there, by clusters of red flowers. The stiffness of the figures shows how great a gulf still separated Pissarro from Monet in their respective developments.

Camille Pissarro: *The Road from Versailles to Louveciennes*, 1870 (Bührle Collection, Zurich). Madame Pissarro and her daughter Jeanne-Rachelle in front of their house.

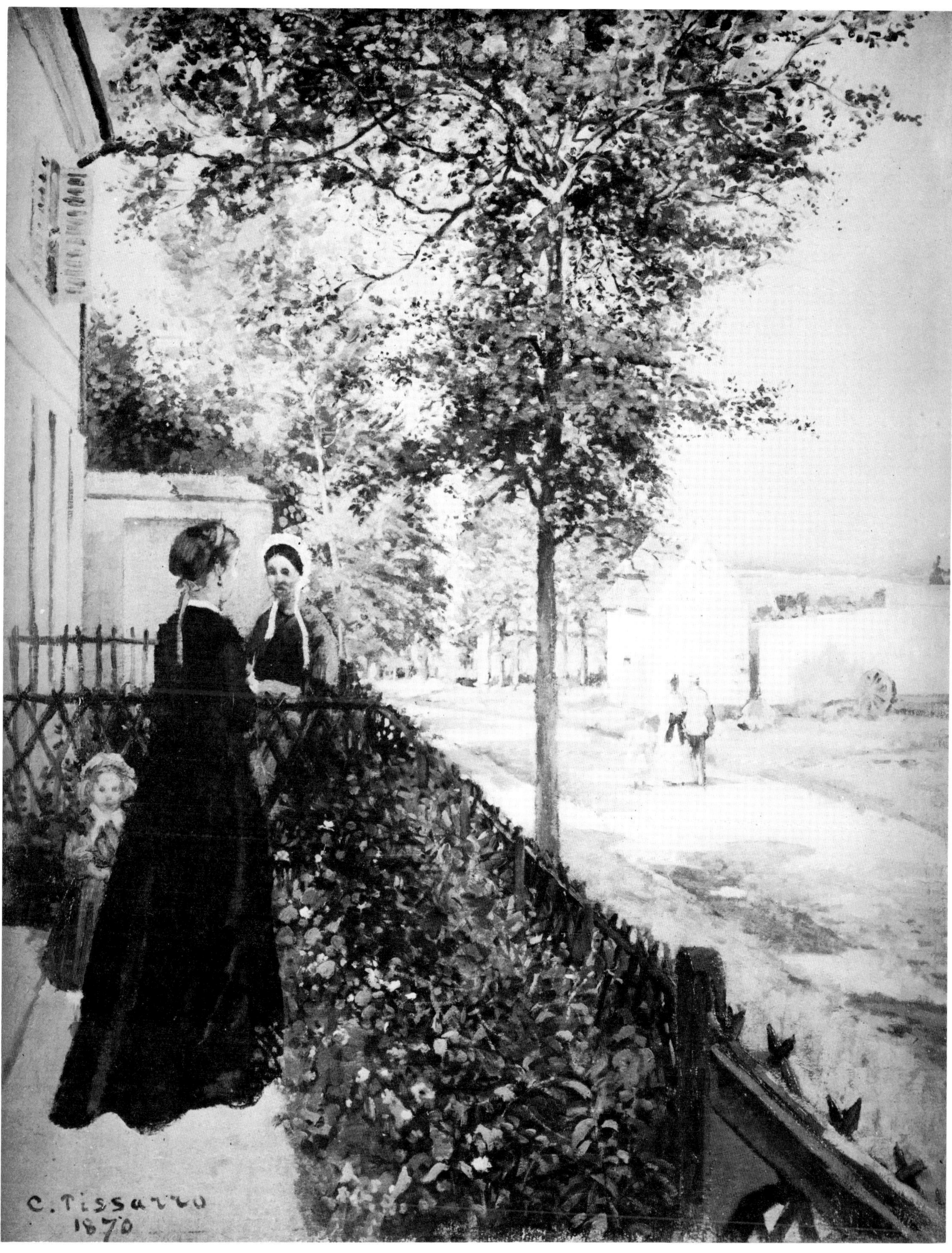
C. Pissarro
1870

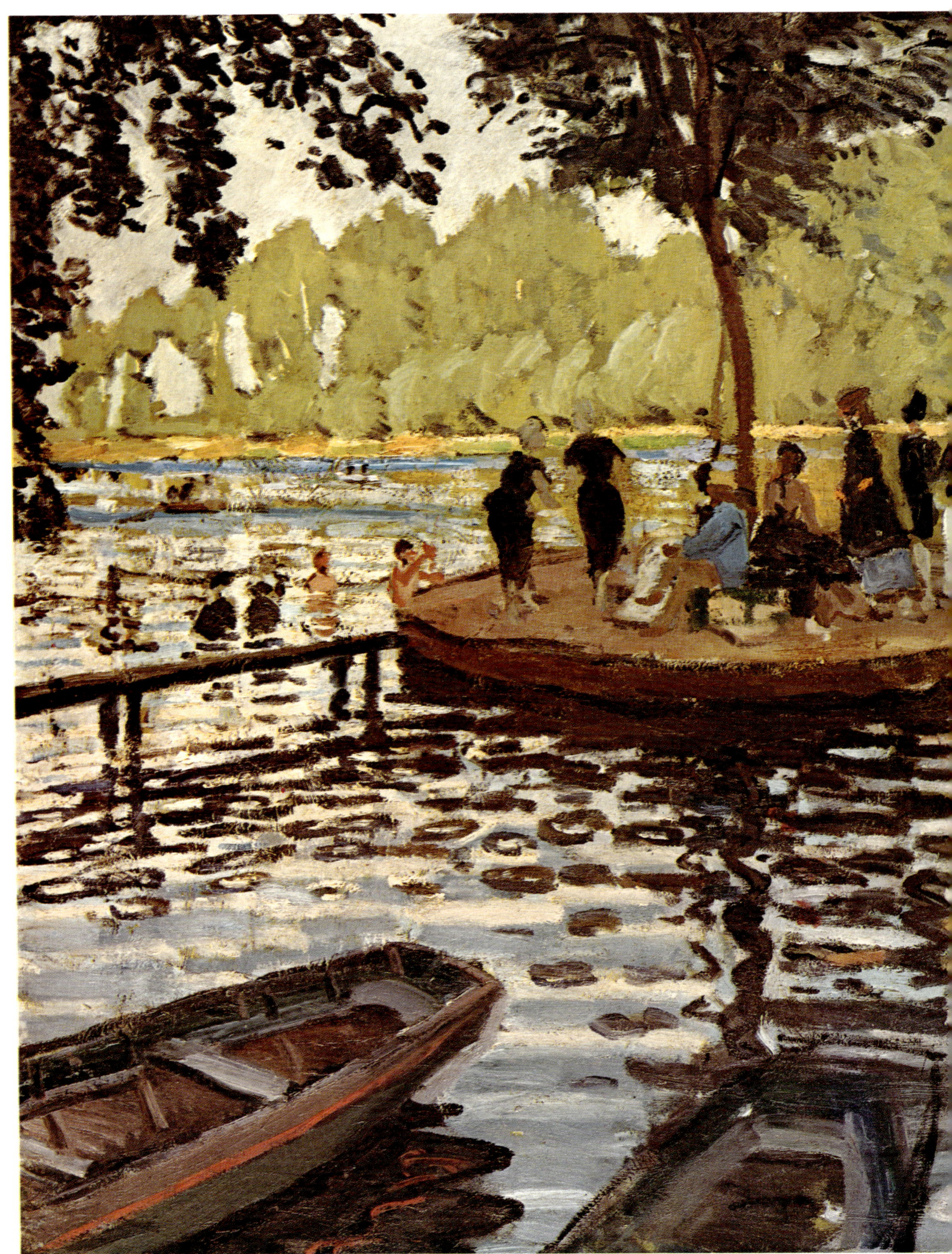

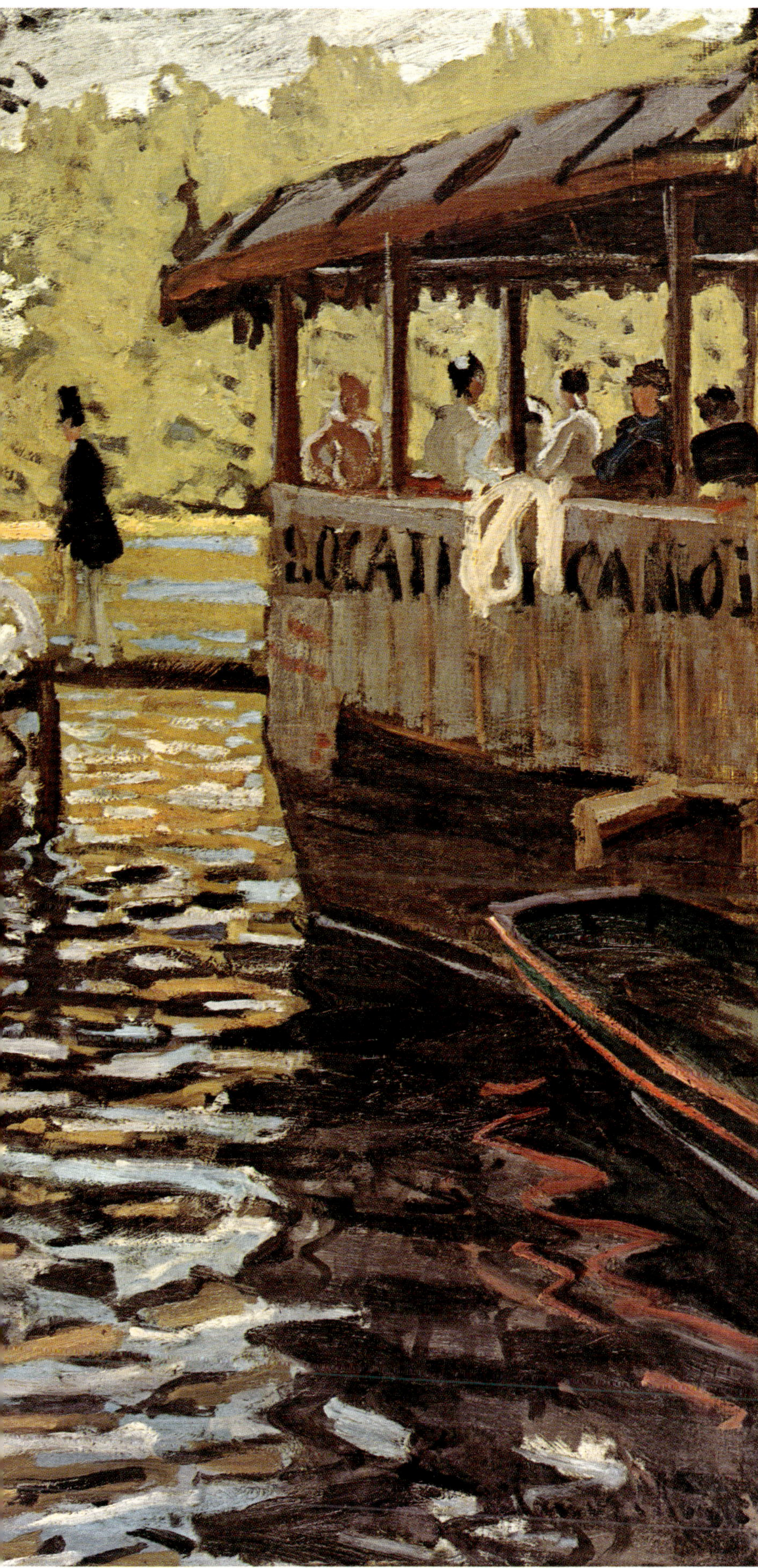

Claude Monet: *La Grenouillère*, *c.* 1869 (Metropolitan Museum of Art, New York, H. O. Havemeyer Collection). Just as someone taking notes allows his pen to dash across the page, caring little about the form of the letters, so Renoir and Monet gave their paintbrushes free rein in order to capture the ever-changing light and moving human figures.

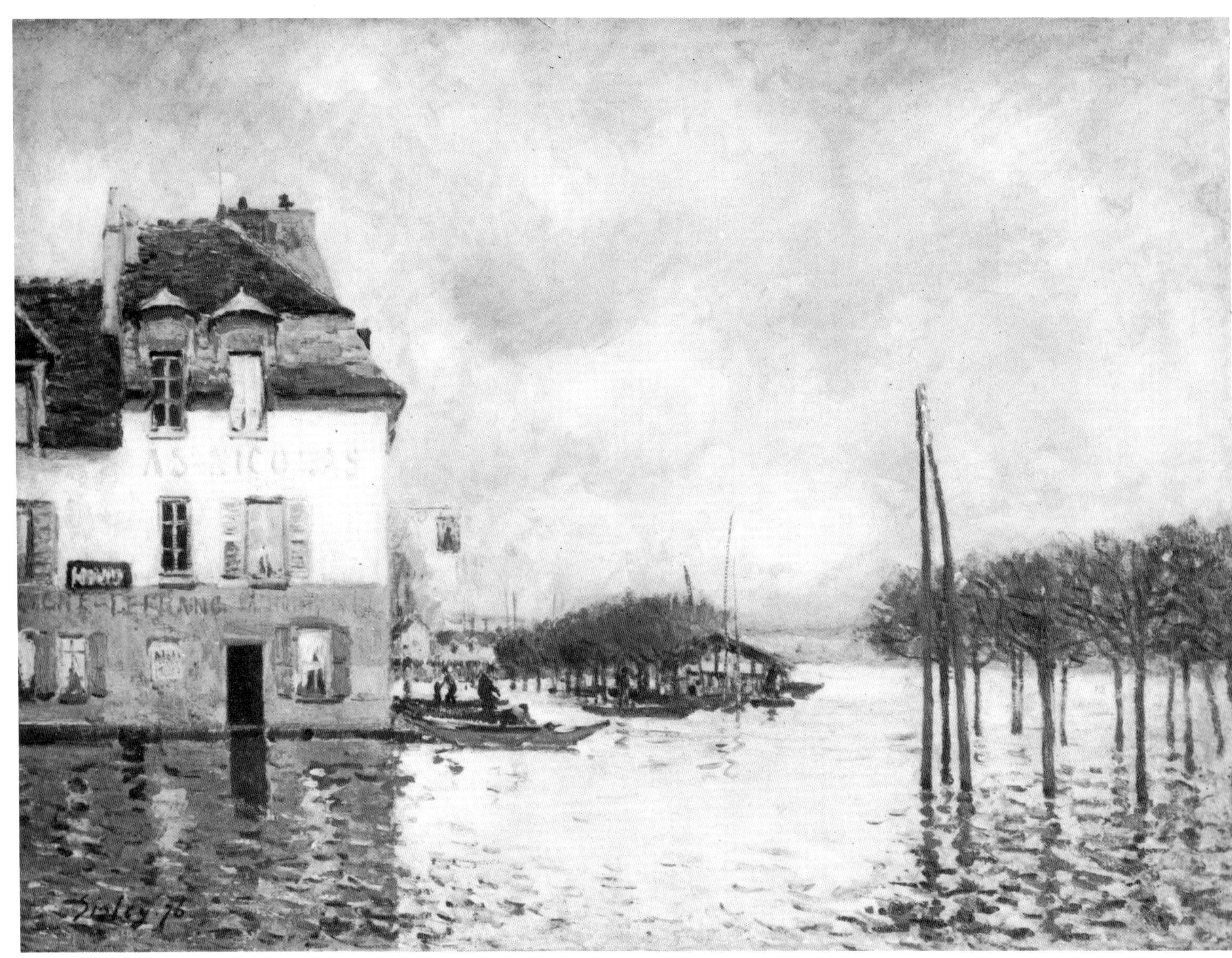

Pissarro was not nearly such a free or audacious man, in either his private life or his work, as Monet, who was ten years his junior. He lived a more restricted life, hardly travelling beyond the immediate environs of Paris and choosing his subjects in country villages where his wife could pick up some money from working on farms while he was painting. Pissarro was poor, like Renoir and Monet, but showed greater forbearance and stoicism about his situation. At that time, for instance, he used to make frequent trips to Paris, where he earned a living simply painting shop blinds.

Pissarro had met Monet at the Académie Charles Suisse, and subsequently saw him often at the Café Guerbois. Like all the painters who frequented the Batignolles area, he had admired Monet's study for *The Terrace at Sainte-Adresse* which was exhibited for a time in the front window of Latouche's

OPPOSITE Alfred Sisley: *Flood at Port-Marly*, 1876 (Musée du Louvre, Paris). Sisley is a great and beautiful artist, in my opinion he is a master equal to the greatest. I have seen works of his of rare amplitude and beauty, among others a *Flood* which is a masterpiece' – Camille Pissarro.
BELOW The long low building in the distance housed a hydraulic machine constructed on the order of Louis XIV to pump water into the fountains and ornamental lakes of Versailles and Marly.

gallery on the corner of the Rue Laffite and the Rue Lafayette. Pissarro, who had come in for criticism for tending to use dark tones and dull colours in his own paintings, had been particularly taken with the novelty of Monet's radiant colours. The even more luminous recent works of his younger colleague won him over completely to the cause of 'light' painting.

During the winter of 1870, Monet worked mainly in and around the woods of Marly and Louveciennes, and would often drop in on his older companion to warm his hands, numbed by long working stints in the cold and damp. Pissarro, who regularly attended meetings at the Café Guerbois,

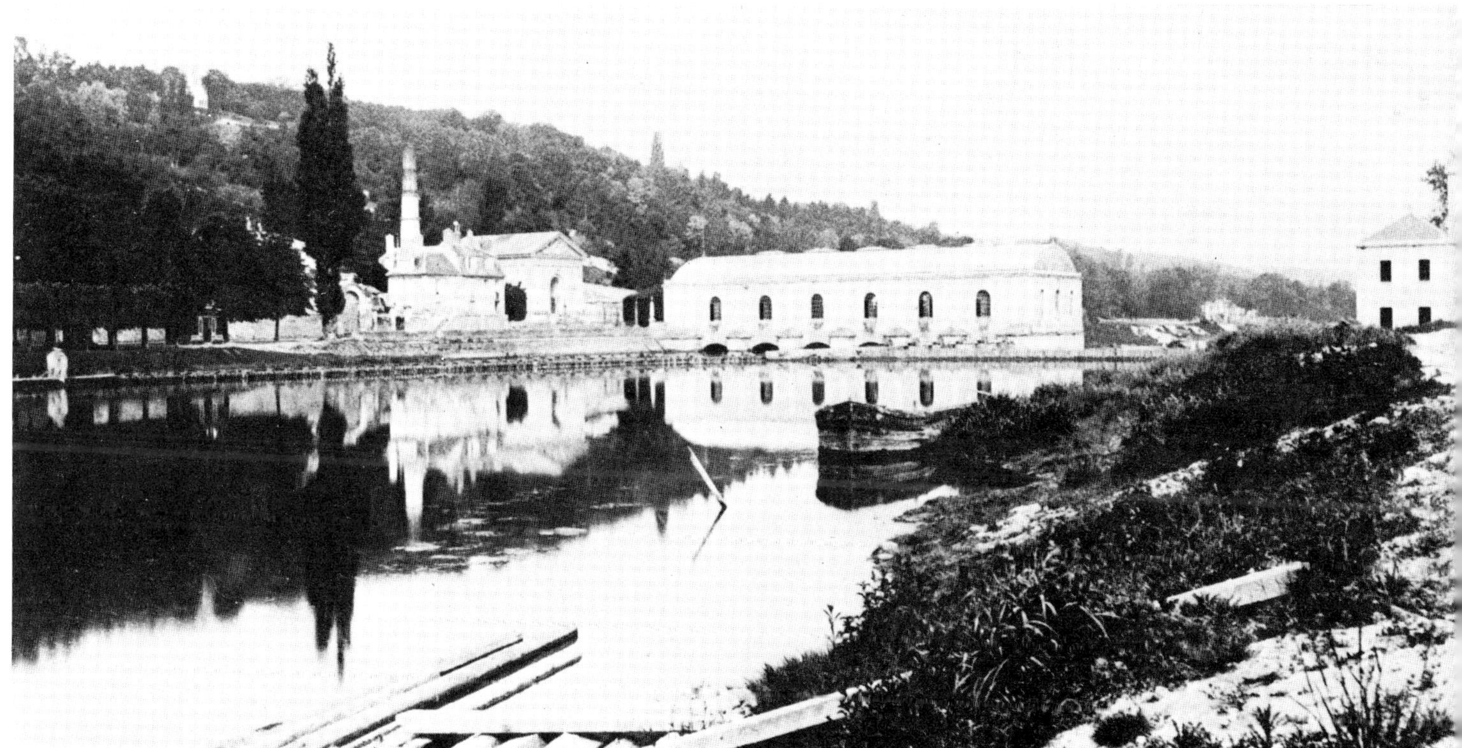

probably gave him the latest news about the various members of the group, and they would discuss their own difficulties and discoveries. On one essential point at least, Monet and Pissarro were in agreement: the only way to compose a landscape with every nuance of light was to paint in the open air. Well wrapped up in an overcoat (sometimes two overcoats), with heavy scarves wound round their necks, the two painters would study the way in which light could vary in rain or in snow, at dawn or at sunset. To paint *The Seine at Bougival*, Camille Pissarro installed himself opposite the island of Croissy, a little downstream from Bougival, at the precise spot where Monet was later to execute his own painting of the same title.

The whole area provided a wealth of subjects for Renoir, Pissarro and Sisley, who, attracted by Monet's dazzling discoveries, in turn produced

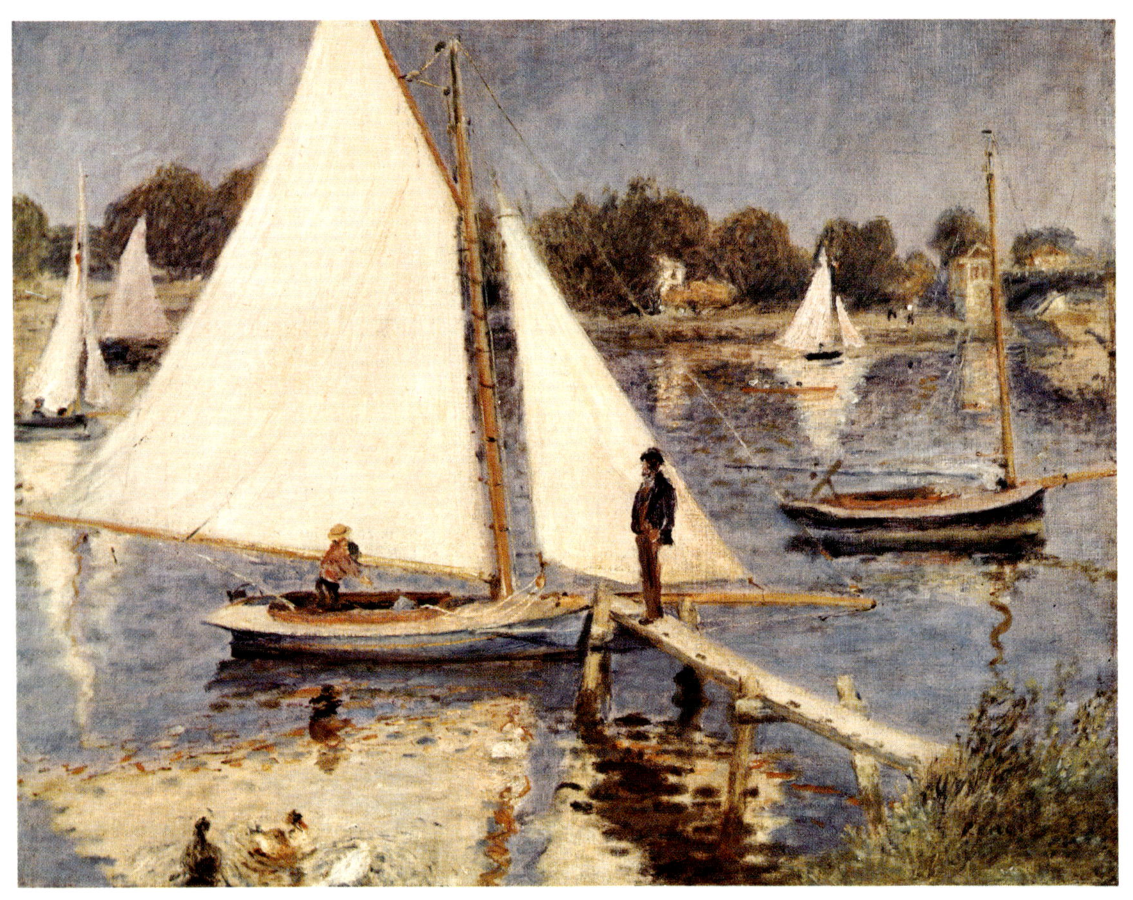

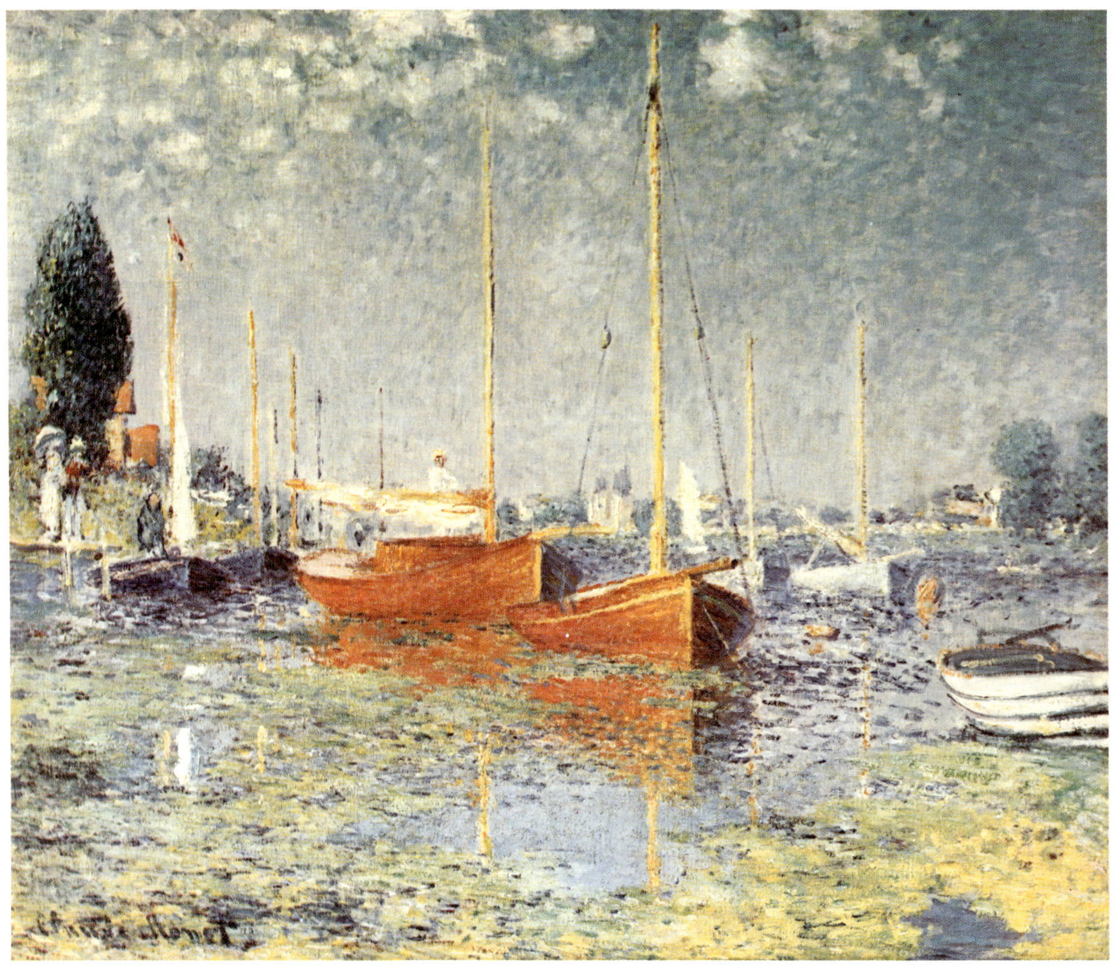

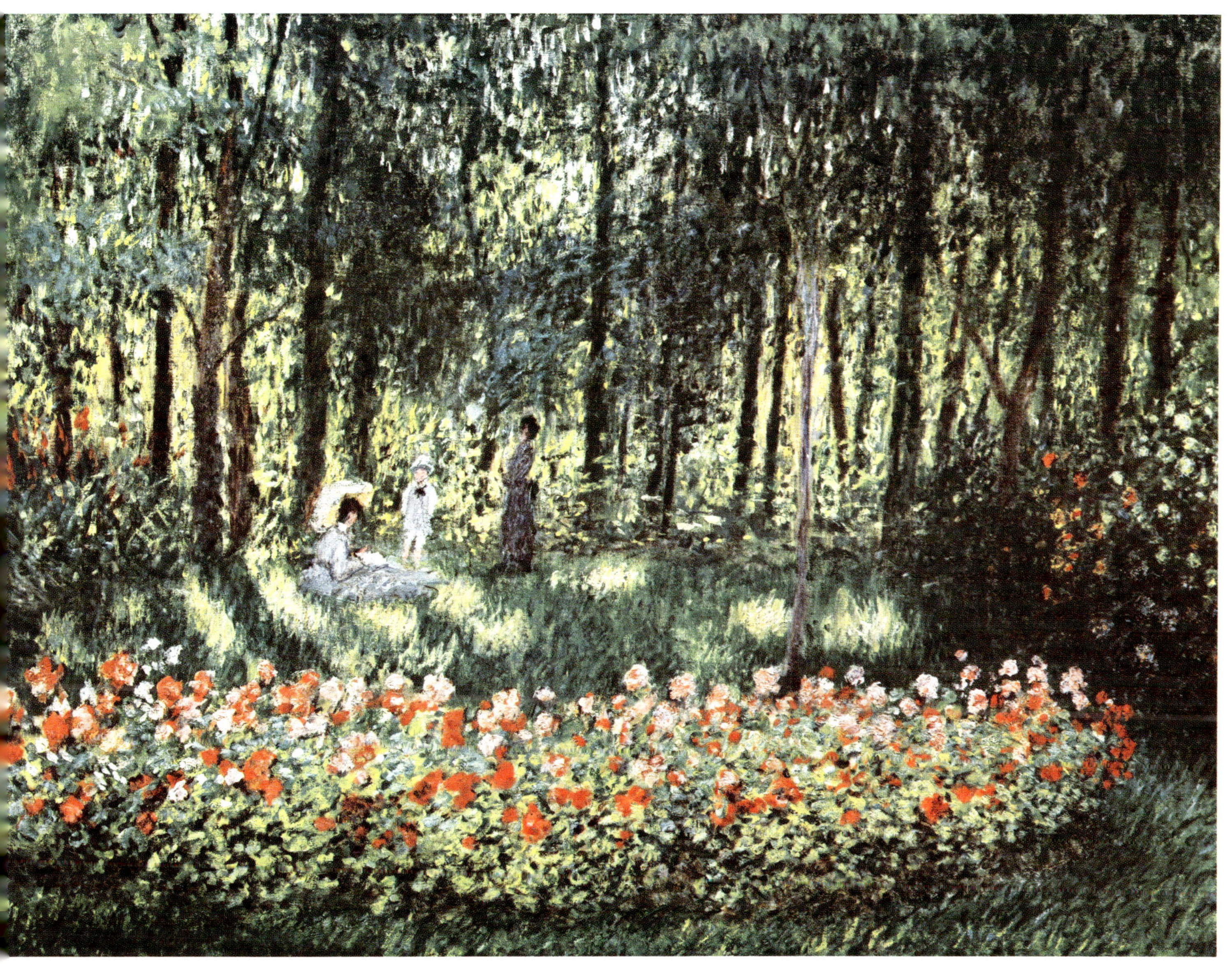

OPPOSITE ABOVE Auguste Renoir: *The Seine at Argenteuil*, 1873 (Portland Art Museum, Oregon). At Argenteuil, a meeting-place for boating enthusiasts, the Impressionists met Gustave Caillebotte, who loved both sailing and boating, and was to become an avid collector of their work.
OPPOSITE BELOW Claude Monet: *Argenteuil*, 1872–5 (Musée de l'Orangerie, Paris).

ABOVE Claude Monet: *The Artist's Garden at Argenteuil*, 1872 (Wildenstein Collection, Paris). Dazzling colours and a cascade of light transform the garden of Monet's house at Argenteuil, where he loved to paint his wife and son, into a paradise.

some of their best work there. All these artists, united in their common pursuit of self-expression, discovered almost ingenuously, during their heady yet difficult times there, a fresh way of looking at nature and the image of a new world vibrant with their own enthusiasm.

Monet and Pissarro had left France in 1870 in order not to have to fight in the Franco-Prussian War. Sisley, who, being English, had not been called up, came to look for lodgings near the banks of the Seine. His financially secure existence having been brought to an abrupt end by his father's illness, Sisley wanted to avail himself of the cheap cost of living and the numerous subjects the area offered. Towards the end of 1870, he rented a small house in Voisins, near Louveciennes, in the same street as the Renoirs. Accompanied by Auguste Renoir and his younger brother Edmond, Sisley began to work on a more regular basis than he had ever done before. Although less prolific than his friends, he possessed exceptional gifts which expressed themselves chiefly in the perfect balance of his compositions and in the very gentle harmonies of his palette.

Le Canal Saint-Martin, which he exhibited at the Salon in the spring of 1870, showed that he too had studied the way light was reflected by water. Although his technique was not yet as vigorous or as markedly original as that of Monet or Renoir, Sisley did however succeed in injecting genuine life into the various elements of his landscape. His colours were lighter and more subtly nuanced than those he had used at Fontainebleau. As he explored the area of Marly, with its vestiges of royal pomp, the Aqueduct and the Machine, as well as Chatou, Louveciennes and Bougival (all places his friends had already painted), Sisley discovered vast expanses of sky, delicate greens, dull browns and a kind of moist light that particularly appealed to his refined sensibility. During the considerable period he stayed there, although constantly hounded by a chronic lack of money, his talent well and truly blossomed.

It was not until 1880 that Berthe Morisot, who was by then Madame Eugène Manet and the painter's sister-in-law, also spent several summers in Bougival so that her husband would find it easier to visit his brother, who was receiving hydrotherapeutic treatment in a hospital at Bellevue.

Although by then newly built villas were beginning to encroach upon the woods, the area had not yet completely lost its rural character. And on Sundays, ever-increasing numbers of daytrippers would come to dance and drink at the *guinguettes* that lined the river banks. The Seine was still thronged with people in boats, and La Grenouillère was as popular as ever.

Berthe Morisot rented a house at 4 Rue de la Princesse, surrounded by a large and luxuriant garden where her daughter Julie could play and she

BELOW Eugène Manet, his wife Berthe Morisot and their daughter Julie in the garden of their villa at Bougival.
OPPOSITE Berthe Morisot: *Eugène Manet and His Daughter at Bougival*, 1883 (Private Collection). Morisot transforms the little impressionist dashes into long sweeps of colour that eliminate detail and reflect the intensity of her passionate nature.

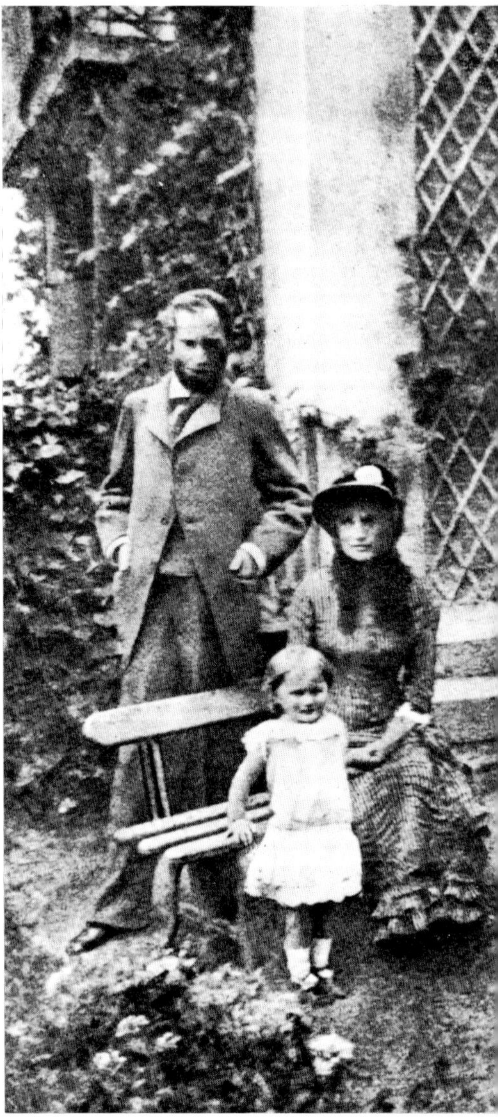

herself paint far from the madding crowd. Although her favourite models at that time were her daughter and her husband, Berthe Morisot found the banks of the Seine attractive enough to warrant *The Banks of the Seine at Bougival*. Julie Manet was aged five when her mother painted *Eugène Manet and His Daughter at Bougival* in their garden: the child, who is wearing a hat held in place by a broad ribbon tied under her chin, is playing on her father's knees. The picture is painted very freely with long sweeps of colour that eliminate detail, suggest a riot of greenery and reflect the artist's own feelings. The Impressionist technique was no longer an innovation by that time, and each member of the group used it in the way that best served the requirements of his or her personal vision. Quick little strokes and dashes of the brush are here forged by Berthe Morisot into a generous, calligraphic whole that reflects her unusual, impassioned temperament.

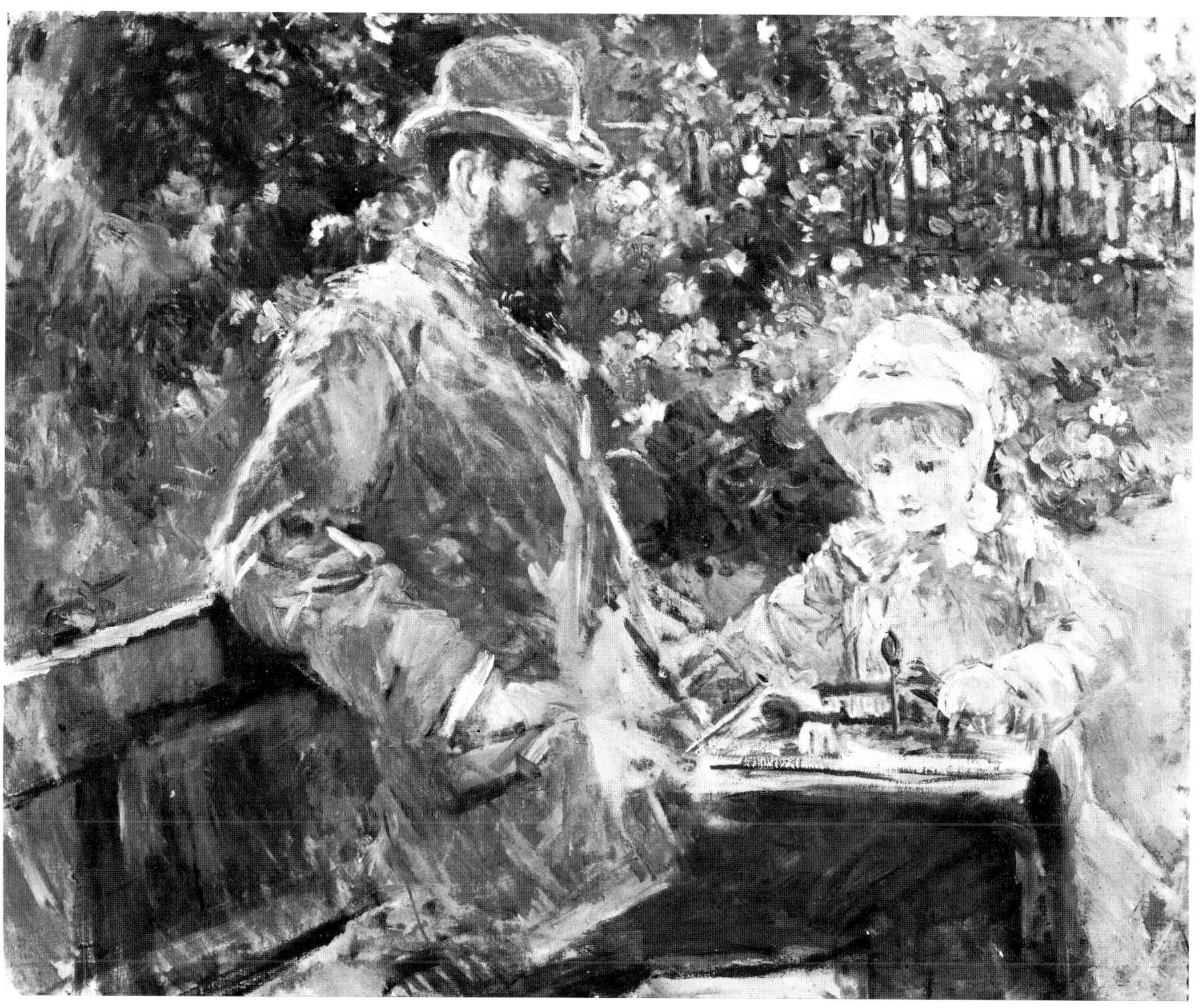

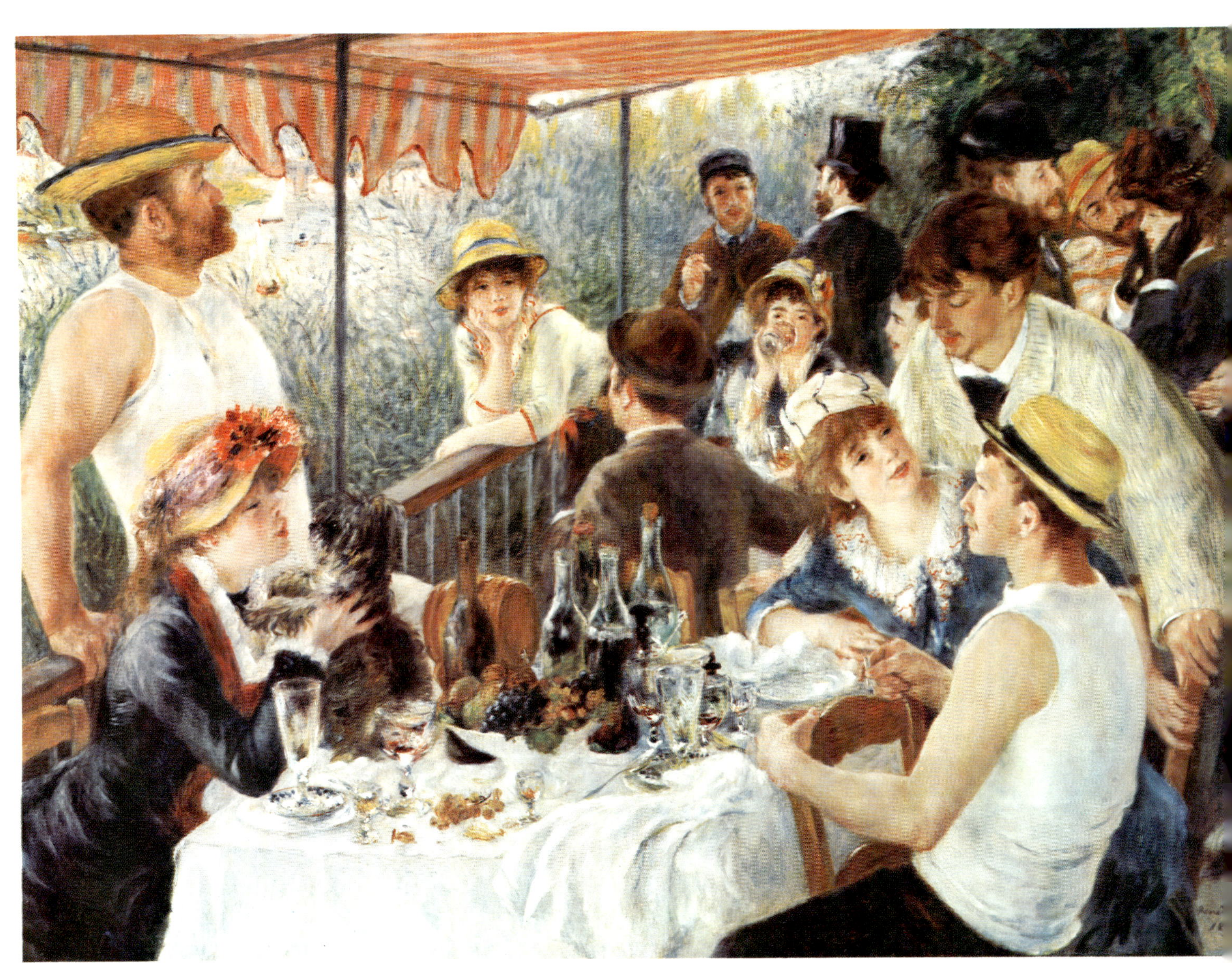

In this, as in most of her pictures, Berthe Morisot exploits a wide range of brush-strokes: small, light dots to make flowers stand out from banks of greenery, long hatching for the human figures and the left-hand part of the composition, and smooth surfaces for the faces. It is this variety of execution that lends such an admirable sense of animation to an otherwise static vision of a bourgeois garden – totally sheltered, it seems, from the hubbub of the world outside. Yet marriage and motherhood had not made Morisot any less enterprising than before: she still scoured the woods and fields for the landscape or light that would let her express her innermost feelings.

'I think Renoir has made it. Good for him!' exclaimed Pissarro in a letter to the critic Théodore Duret following the success obtained by his friend at the Salon of 1879 with his *Portrait of Madame Charpentier* (her husband published Zola, Flaubert and Maupassant). Although it was a fact that from then on his financial situation improved markedly, Renoir was still a long way from achieving glory and fortune. But he had succeeded in breaking down the wall of indifference that stood between the young painters and wealthy members of the public. Several well-paid commissions, which resulted from his friendship with the Charpentiers, enabled Renoir at last to tackle ambitious works such as *The Swing* and *Le Moulin de la Galette*, where all that counted for him was the pleasure of the act of painting. These two large canvases immortalize the amusements of the Parisian working class that he and a small group of friends themselves enjoyed. In the spring and during the fine summer weather, Renoir returned to Bougival and Chatou. The favourite rendezvous of boatmen, poets and intellectuals was at that time the Restaurant Fournaise, a fairly modest establishment where it was possible to lunch in the open air on the first-floor terrace overlooking the Seine.

OPPOSITE Auguste Renoir: *Le Déjeuner des Canotiers*, 1881 (Phillips Collection, Washington). 'The impressionists show their particular talent and attain the summit of their art when they paint our French Sundays . . . kisses in the sun, picnics, complete rest, not a thought about work, unashamed relaxation' – René Gimpel.
BELOW The Restaurant Fournaise on the island of Chatou, where Renoir painted *Le Déjeuner des Canotiers*, with (RIGHT) a view of the restaurant from the road.

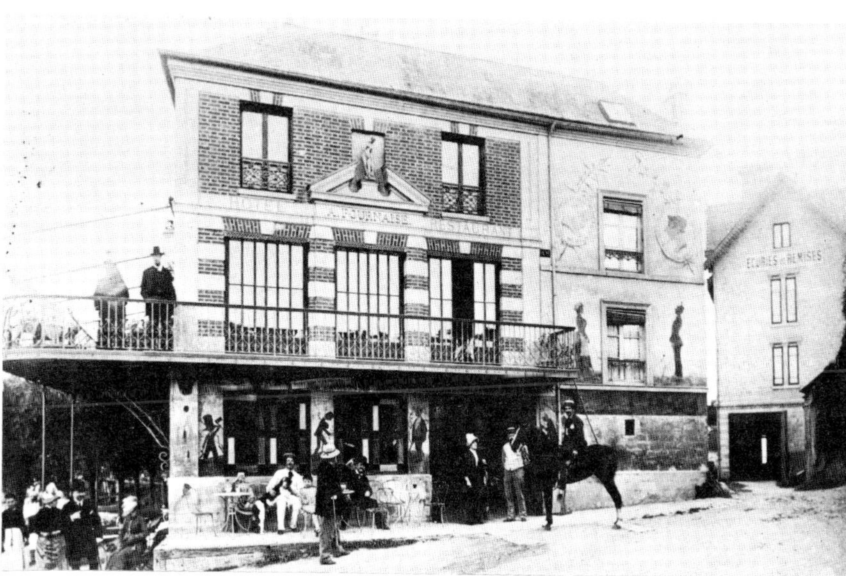

The place had the irresistible appeal of a family business. Père Fournaise, the man with a moustache and a florid complexion depicted in Renoir's *Man with a Pipe*, looked after his wine-cellar with loving care, and would gruffly retort to any question with a single, unvarying quip: 'It's up to the ladies!' Renoir, who was treated as a friend of the family, was asked to paint his portrait, for which he received 200 francs. Madame Fournaise was a well-organized woman who presided over the cooking and the accounts, and displayed equal proficiency in both departments. Their son, 'a big lad with a red beard, famed for his strength', deftly performed his duties, which consisted of giving his arm to pretty female customers while he held their bobbing boats steady. The daughter of the house was the ravishing Alphonsine, who had a host of admirers. Renoir painted three portraits of her which, according to a critic of the period, were 'vibrantly reminiscent of Watteau'. Degas too, while lunching with the beautiful Geneviève Halévy, Bizet's young widow, tossed off a pencil portrait of the girl's decidedly pleasing features. Alphonsine's grace and distinction, combined with the excellence of her mother's crayfish, attracted to Chatou a galaxy of bons vivants, ladies' men and fun-seekers such as Maupassant, his publisher Charpentier, Flaubert, the poet François Coppée, the spry retired cavalry officer Baron Barbier, bankers such as Baron Rothschild and people from high society or the theatre who kept the company of Geneviève Halévy.

Renoir's *Déjeuner des Canotiers* – a hymn to friendship, an encomium of happiness – shows his merry group of friends seated round a table laden with food (which incidentally forms a fine still life). In the foreground, Aline Charigot's pretty face can be seen for the first time in the painter's work. Renoir had met the girl shortly before in Montmartre: strongly attracted by her perfect complexion and refreshing naturalness, he had managed to get her to pose for him once or twice (their subsequent love affair led to marriage). A little further back Alphonsine Fournaise, with her elbows on a balcony, dreamily observes the assembled company, while in the background of the painting Baron Barbier, seen from behind and wearing a top hat, seems to be saying something to the Fournaises' son. On the right of the table, which divides the picture in two, a very relaxed-looking Gustave Caillebotte is sitting astride a chair in his vest. This young man, who was a keen boatman, met Renoir and Monet in 1874 in Argenteuil, and became their close friend as well as a collector of their works. Next to him can be seen Angèle, a pert and naive professional model who often sat for Renoir, amusing him with her mastery of slang and her whiplash repartee. A young journalist who occasionally joined the group completes the foreground of the painting. The background is made up of several figures whom it is difficult to identify. In this picture, painted from life, Renoir uses a purely Impressionist technique only for the foliage and the background; the faces

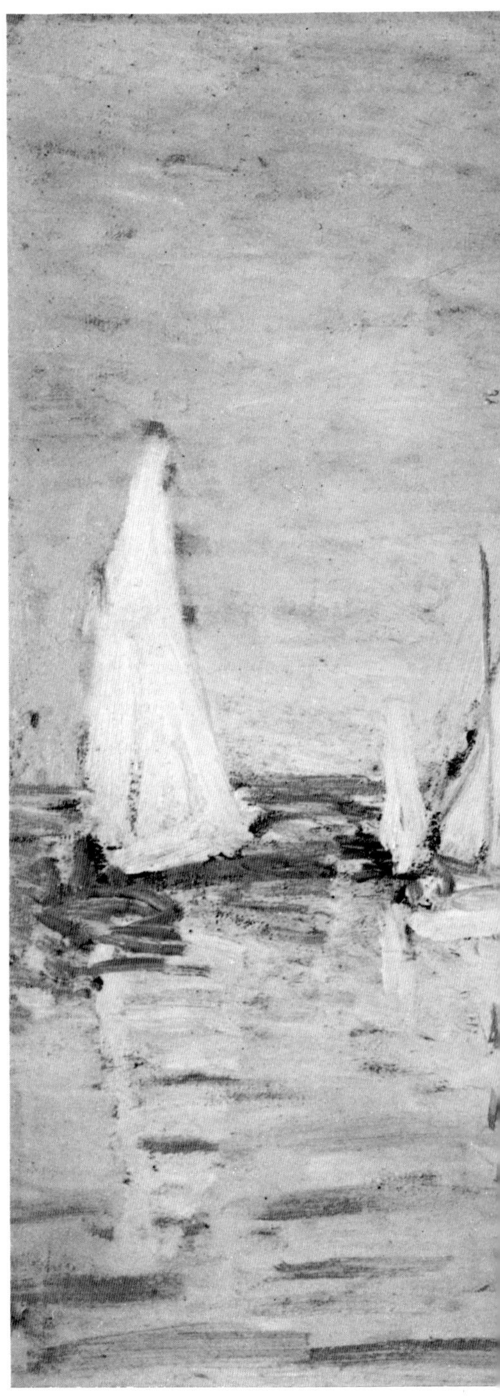

Claude Monet: *Regatta at Argenteuil*, 1874 (Musée du Louvre, Paris – Jeu de Paume).

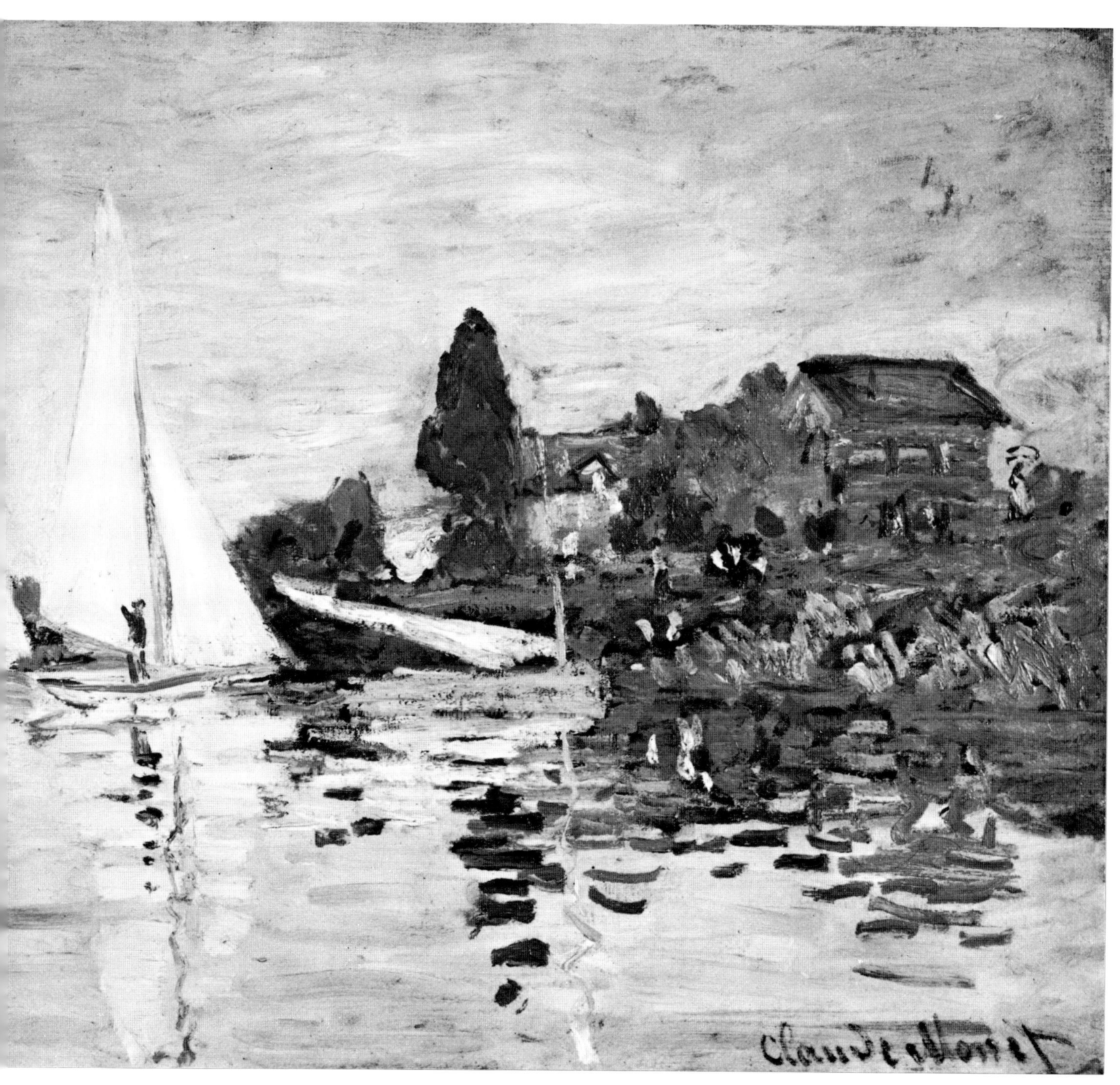
Claude Monet

are treated in conventional fashion, with smooth layers of colour contained by well-defined outlines.

Renoir retained a lifelong affection for the banks of the Seine, La Grenouillère and the Restaurant Fournaise, where masterpieces flowed so effortlessly from his brush. And he often returned there when visiting his mother, who lived in Louveciennes until November 1896.

One notable absentee from the banks of the Seine was Bazille, who had been working on *Young Man with a Fishing Rod* at the family's estate near Montpellier. When the Franco-Prussian war broke out, Bazille volunteered – even though his father had arranged things so that he would stay out. After a spell of active service he was killed on 28 November 1870.

At the end of 1871, Monet, who like most of his friends was back in France, began looking for a house not too far from Paris. In the meantime he stayed at a hotel, and then rented a studio on the Rue d'Isly, by the Gare Saint-Lazare. He had remained in correspondence with Pissarro, who had returned to Pontoise, and with Edouard Manet, whose studio was quite close. Life began to get under way again in the little villages around the capital, but only slowly, as they had been partly destroyed during the Commune. It was still difficult to find accommodation. Manet, who had many contacts in the Gennevilliers area, where his grandfather owned a considerable amount of land, recommended Claude Monet to the widow of a former mayor of Argenteuil, who let a house to him for 1,000 francs a year.

On 2 January 1872, Boudin was invited to a housewarming by his former pupil, whom he found comfortably lodged with his wife and son opposite the old alms-houses by the station. Monet used a lean-to by the side of the house as a studio, and to make things even better there was also a beautiful garden, where he painted his little boy playing with a hoop.

At that time, Argenteuil was a rather dull, well-to-do little town. The old convents which had made it prosperous had been demolished, and in their place there were broad avenues with rows of nondescript bourgeois residences. But the train service to Paris was excellent, with a departure every hour: this was a boon to Monet, who could reach the studio he still rented near the Gare Saint-Lazare within twenty-five minutes.

The painter was then having to spend a lot of time in Paris, showing his pictures around and trying to sell them: he and his wife had no other source of income. Fortunately the time seemed right: France was going through a period of prosperity just after the war, and some new as well as long-standing collectors were making the rounds of galleries and studios. There had been an optimistic atmosphere in Les Batignolles ever since the dealer Paul Durand-Ruel had begun to show interest in the artists of the new

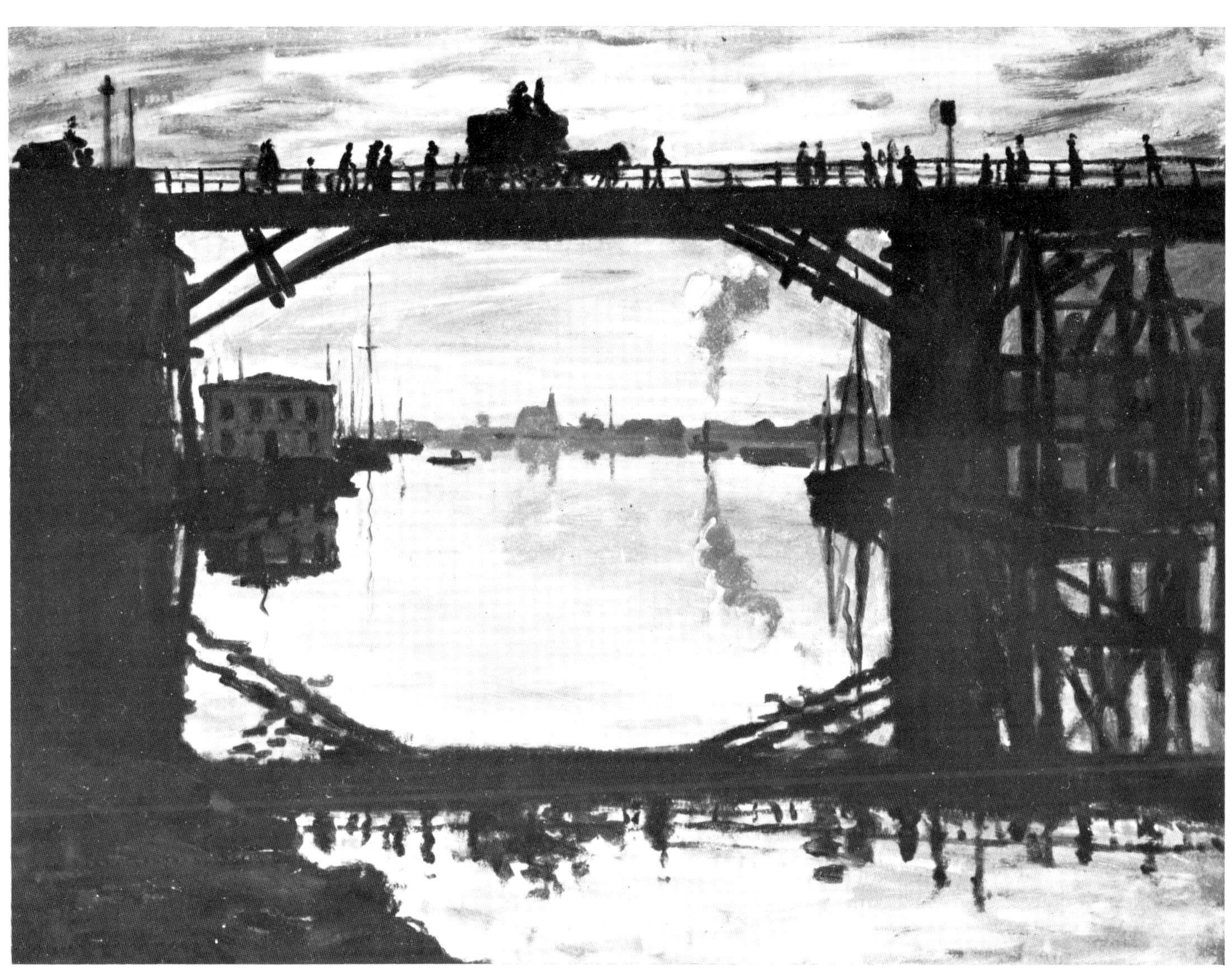

Claude Monet: *The Wooden Bridge at Argenteuil*, 1872 (Private Collection). Monet makes remarkable use of the wooden bridge, then in the process of being built, to frame the landmarks of the Argenteuil landscape.

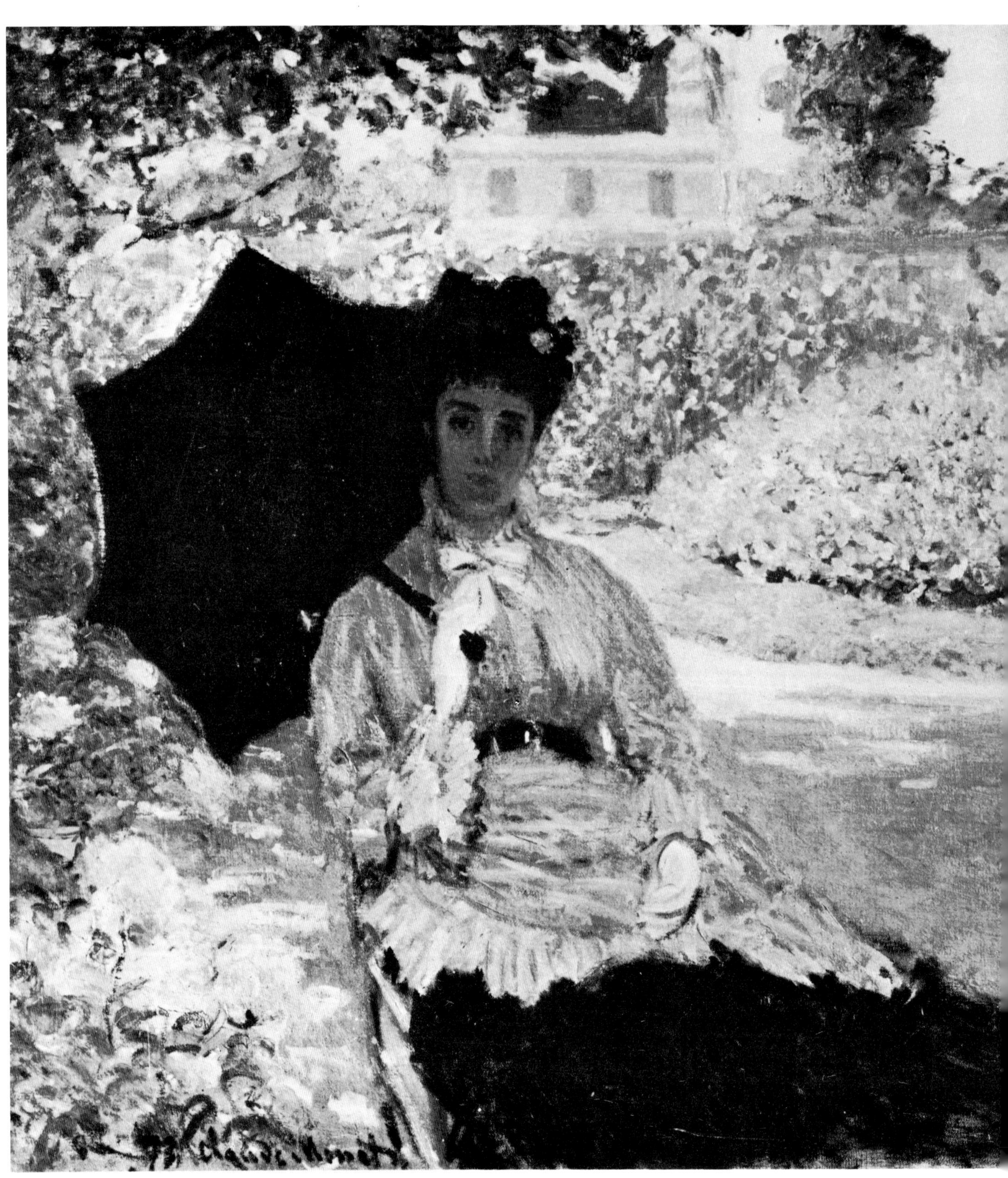

Claude Monet: *Camille in the Garden with Jean and Her Maid*, 1873 (Bührle Collection, Zurich).

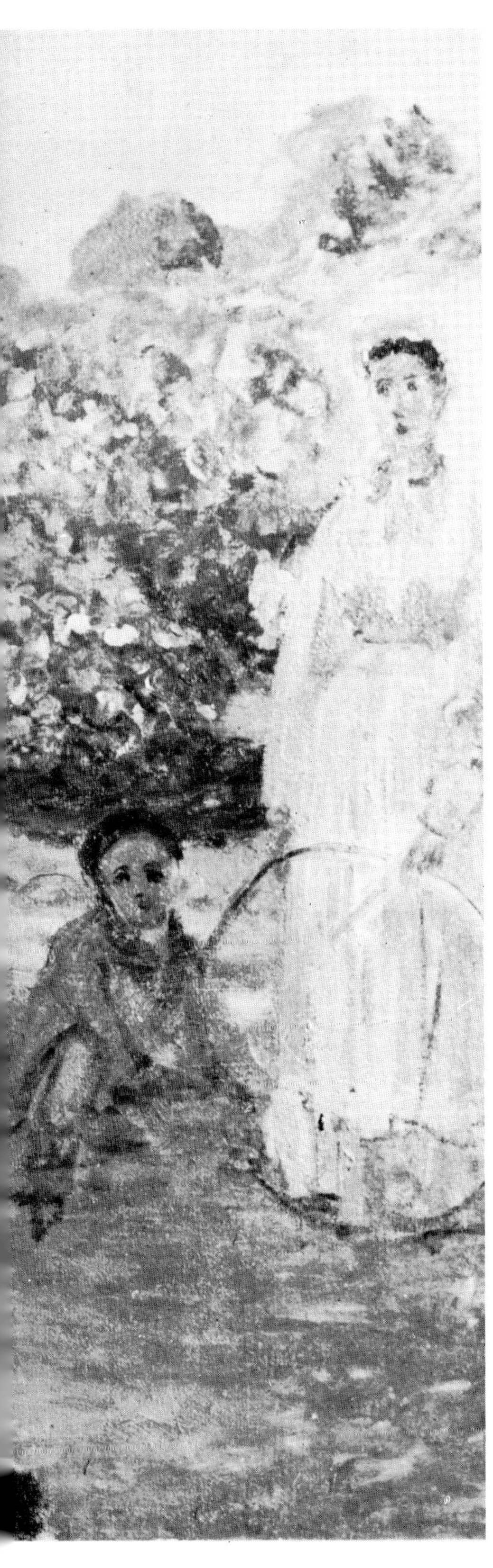

generation – he had paid Manet 1,600 francs, for instance, for several of his earlier paintings. The artists were hoping that lesser dealers such as Latouche, Père Martin and Portier would be bound to raise their prices.

At all events, 1872 was a very profitable year for Monet: Durand-Ruel purchased at least twenty-nine pictures from him, which brought in 9,800 francs. Latouche, the dealer on the Rue Lafayette, continued to buy his works, as did his brother Léon (who had become a successful businessman) and one or two other collectors. Monet's overall income (according to his notebooks) rose to the considerable sum of 12,100 francs. Although he was not yet really famous, he could pride himself on the fact that by the age of thirty-two, thanks to his talent and to his excellent business sense, he had carved out quite an enviable niche for himself. His wife was helped by two maids, one of whom probably looked after their son Jean; and a gardener tended the superb flowerbeds that were so important to him. The cuisine served at the Monets' table was of a high standard, and far from disgraced by the fine wines ordered direct from Bordeaux and Montpellier.

Monet also enjoyed great prestige in the eyes of his colleagues. 'Monet's talent is to my mind a very serious and a very pure one,' Pissarro wrote to the critic Théodore Duret. 'His art is based on observation, and is utterly original in feeling – poetry produced by the harmony of true colours.' And Manet, whose fame Monet had once envied, now admired his talents so much that he bought one of the first works he produced at Argenteuil, *The Wooden Bridge*. It is hardly surprising that this striking picture, with its powerfully contrasted touches and daring simplifications reminiscent of Japanese prints, should have appealed to Manet. In it, the Argenteuil landscape (which Monet was to paint again and again – factory chimneys, a public bathing establishment, and a boat or two) is framed to the right and left by scaffolding which is supporting a road bridge under repair, while the bridge itself, the traffic crossing it, and its reflection in the water complete the framing along the top and bottom edges of the composition.

Monet's peace of mind was no doubt helped by his happy domestic life. The couple's prosperity increased when Camille was left 6,000 francs by her father. During the spring of 1872, she was her young husband's favourite model: in orchards not far from the town or simply in their garden, Monet painted several pictures of his wife. Attracted once more by the theme of the woman in the garden, he painted her and a friend (or possibly their maid) sitting beneath a pink and white cascade of lilac flowers: the very dense trees form an area of shade behind the figures, who are tinged with the violet pink of the flowers, while in the foreground some immaculate linen reflects the intensity of the surrounding colours. It is a luminous, airy, transparent work that magically metamorphoses a small suburban garden into a corner of paradise.

The Old Embankment at Argenteuil, The Hospice, Sloping Street, and *The Gare St-Lazare* show that no subject was too commonplace for Monet. The technique is not always as unfettered as in *Festival at Argenteuil*, where he almost exclusively uses purely Impressionist dabs of colour, but everything he painted there is light and vivacious, and only rarely shows a smooth surface. In summer, the silver-green Seine, sluggishly gliding its way past Argenteuil, again became a major attraction for Monet. He would go a little downstream from the village so as to be able to include the little island of Marante, which can be seen in the background on the left, as well as two factory chimneys – the first industrial blots on the landscape. On another occasion, he set out from Argenteuil towards Bezons and painted *Basin at Argenteuil*, in which a row of old plane trees lends immense depth to the composition and casts a dark, melancholy shadow along the length of the embankment.

BELOW Claude Monet: *Basin at Argenteuil*, 1872 (Musée du Louvre, Paris). Monet's eye took in the whole panoramic view, various elements of which were often depicted separately by Manet, Sisley and Renoir. The artist, here in top form, lends the sky, earth and water an intensely transient quality that creates an overall impression of the ineluctable passage of time.
OPPOSITE ABOVE View of the road-bridge at Argenteuil.
OPPOSITE BELOW Claude Monet: *The Bridge at Argenteuil* 1874 (Musée du Louvre, Paris – Jeu de Paume). 'It was Argenteuil that was to sharpen Monet's perceptions and to provide the point of departure for the most decisive evolution of his art' – Arsène Alexandre.

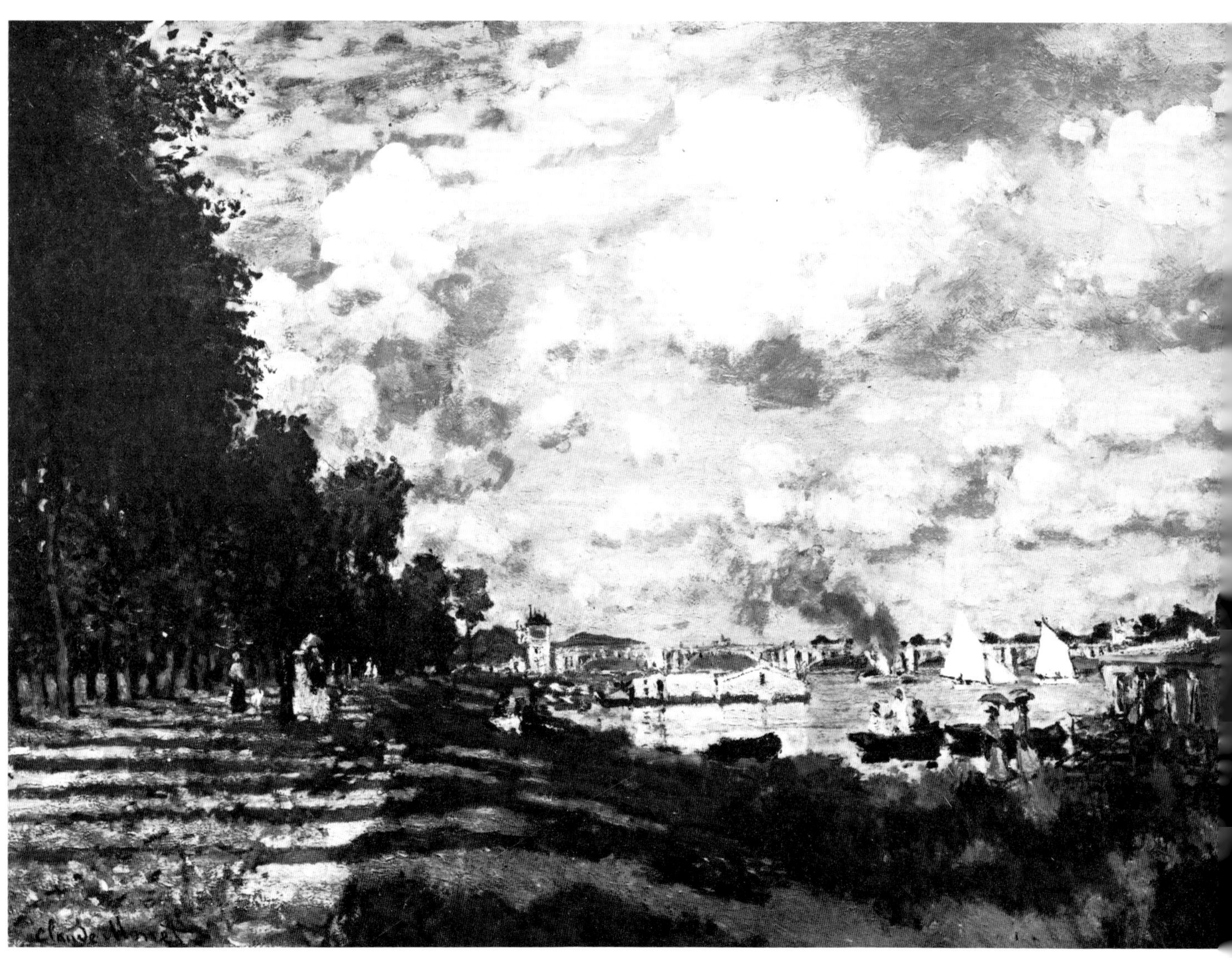

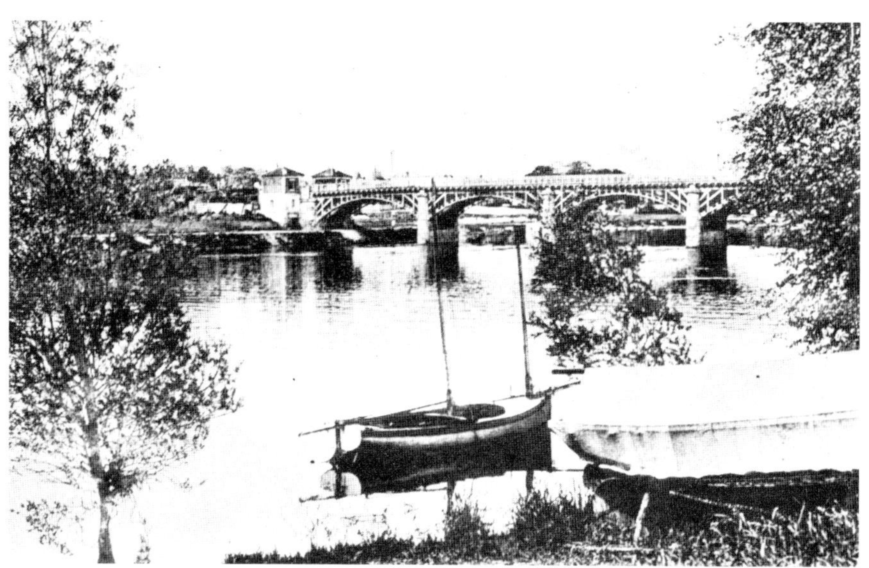

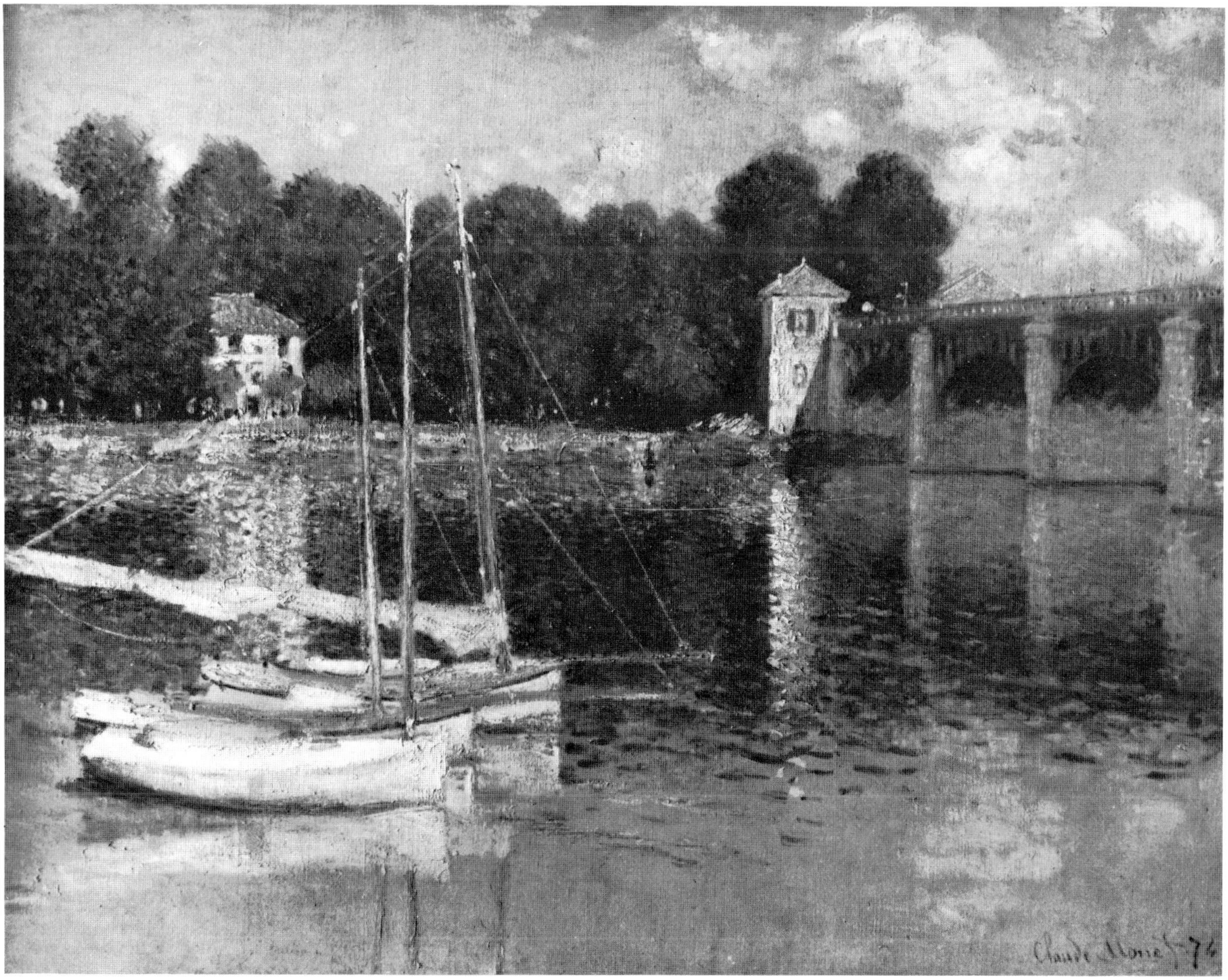

The frenzied brush-strokes that injected such life into Monet's vision of La Grenouillère here give way to a more controlled manner: the Argenteuil paintings, which radiate calm and light, are among the finest examples of the Impressionist technique. Argenteuil was just as lively as Bougival: boatmen and their lady companions would have boisterous get-togethers over a bottle or two of the famous white wine from the area, while the *guinguettes* blared out quadrilles and mazurkas. But Monet, now a contented husband and father, and never much tempted by such popular entertainment, had given himself up totally to artistic creation.

In order to vary the angle from which he approached his subjects, Monet bought a boat and had it fitted out with a cabin large enough to accommodate his easel, as Daubigny had once done. In that way, he could satisfy his appetite for new subjects; thus he was able, for instance, to concentrate on the river and the embankment on the Argenteuil side, or else direct his attention towards the wilder banks of Petit-Gennevilliers.

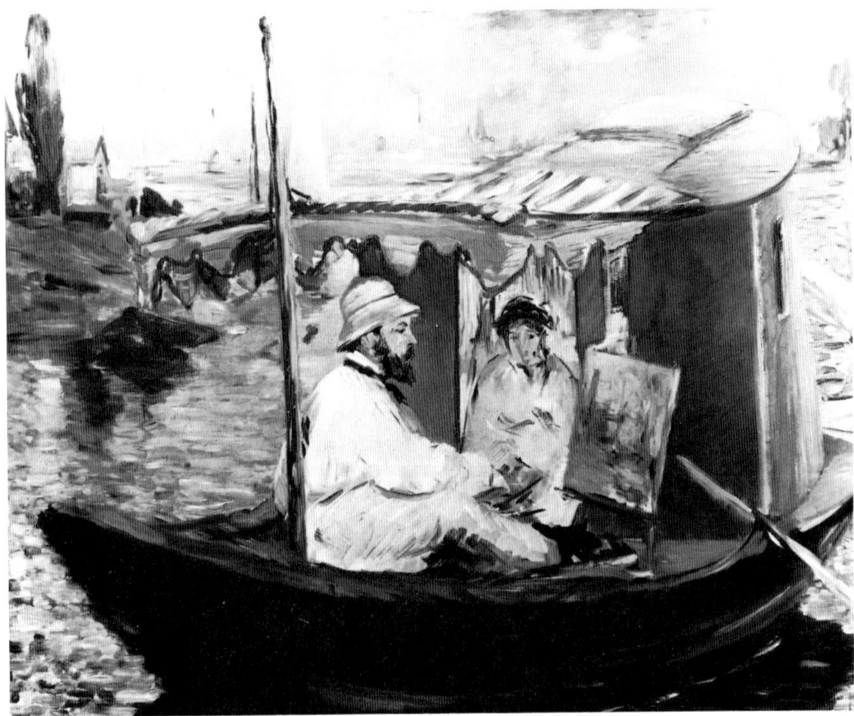

LEFT Edouard Manet: *Monet Working on His Boat in Argenteuil*, 1874 (Neue Pinakothek, Munich). 'A successful sale suddenly brought in enough money to enable me to buy a boat and build a wooden cabin on it that was just big enough for me to set up my easel', Monet later explained to Thiebault-Sisson.
OPPOSITE Edouard Manet: *Argenteuil*, 1874 (Musée des Beaux-Arts, Tournai). 'Behind the figures, a river of indigo, as solid as an ingot and as straight as a wall.' This painting, which allowed a chink of Impressionist light to penetrate the Salon of 1875, met with a very unfavourable reception.

Manet was staying there with one of his cousins in the summer of 1874. After achieving a notable success at the previous Salon with his very conventional *Bon Bock*, he felt he could now try his hand at *plein-air* painting without any risk of damaging his reputation with the public of the Salon. He had worked outdoors on the beach at Berck during the few weeks' rest he had just spent there.

His *Argenteuil* shows a young couple in a boat outlined against the waters of the river, with the famous scenery of Argenteuil in the far distance. The

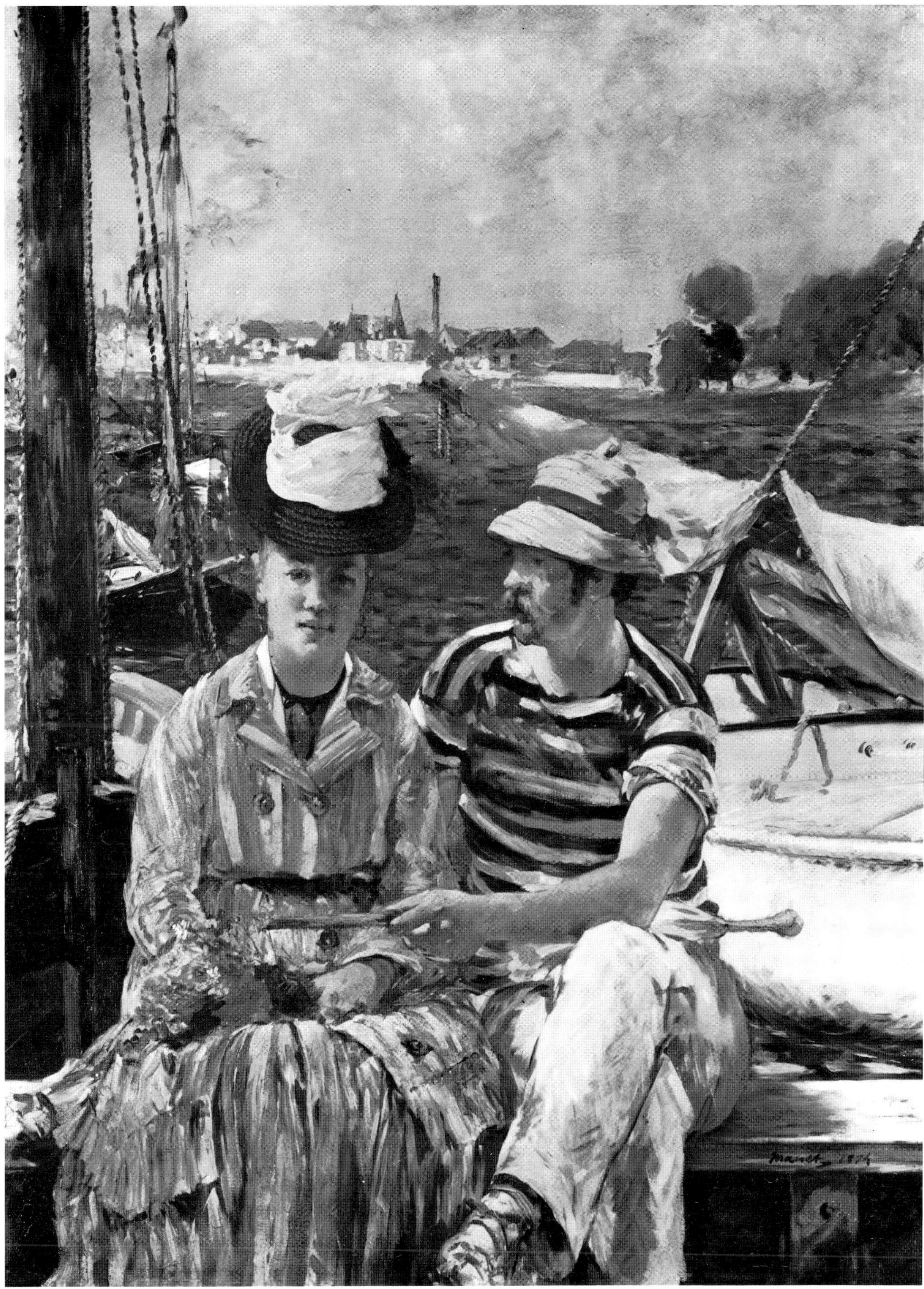
Manet 1874

critics were scandalized by the painting's brilliant colours when they saw it at the Salon of 1875, and immediately lumped Manet together with the Impressionists, even though his precise technique and sharply defined contours remained quite classical. But the appearance among the Salon's usual mythological subjects of this burly boatman (the model was the painter's brother-in-law, Rudolph Leenhoff) in a short-sleeved striped vest, clasping a buxom young lady with his bare arms, was like a shaft of light from the Impressionist world.

Manet found Monet's floating studio rather quaint, and immortalized it in *Monet Working on His Boat at Argenteuil*. The picture shows the painter at work with his wife, while in the background a few sailing boats, the familiar

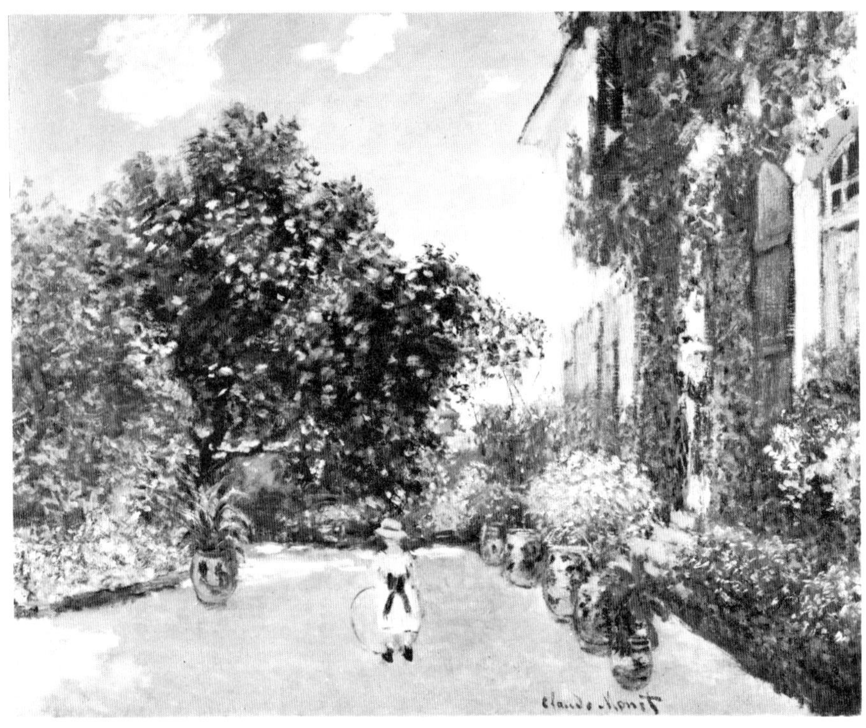

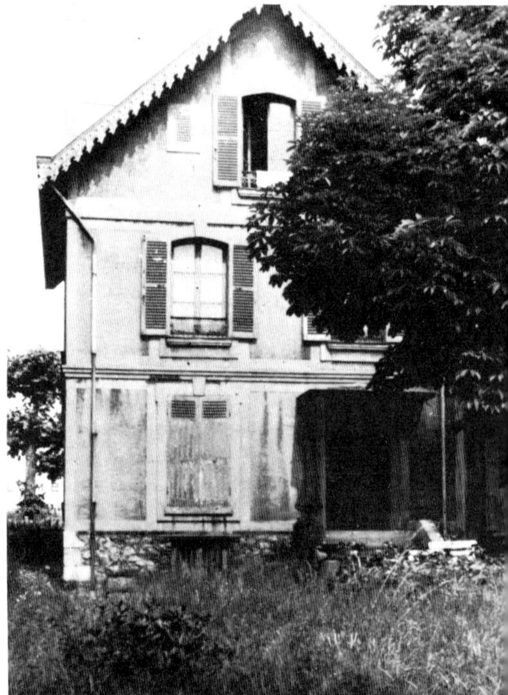

factory chimneys and a section of bank can be seen. It is a colourful, charming and spontaneous work that records the friendship of those two very strong and very different personalities.

Although the close ties that existed between Monet and Renoir at Bougival were not as close as they had been (for the latter was often kept in Paris by his work), from 1873 on, and during the summer of 1874, Renoir joined his friend quite often. Sometimes they worked again side by side, and their treatment was so similar it is difficult to tell them apart.

In Renoir's *Monet Painting in His Garden*, Monet's second home in Argenteuil can be seen, 'a pink house with green shutters, 2 Boulevard Saint-Denis, opposite the station', as its tenant described it when sending an invitation to the collector Victor Chocquet in 1876. It was a new building

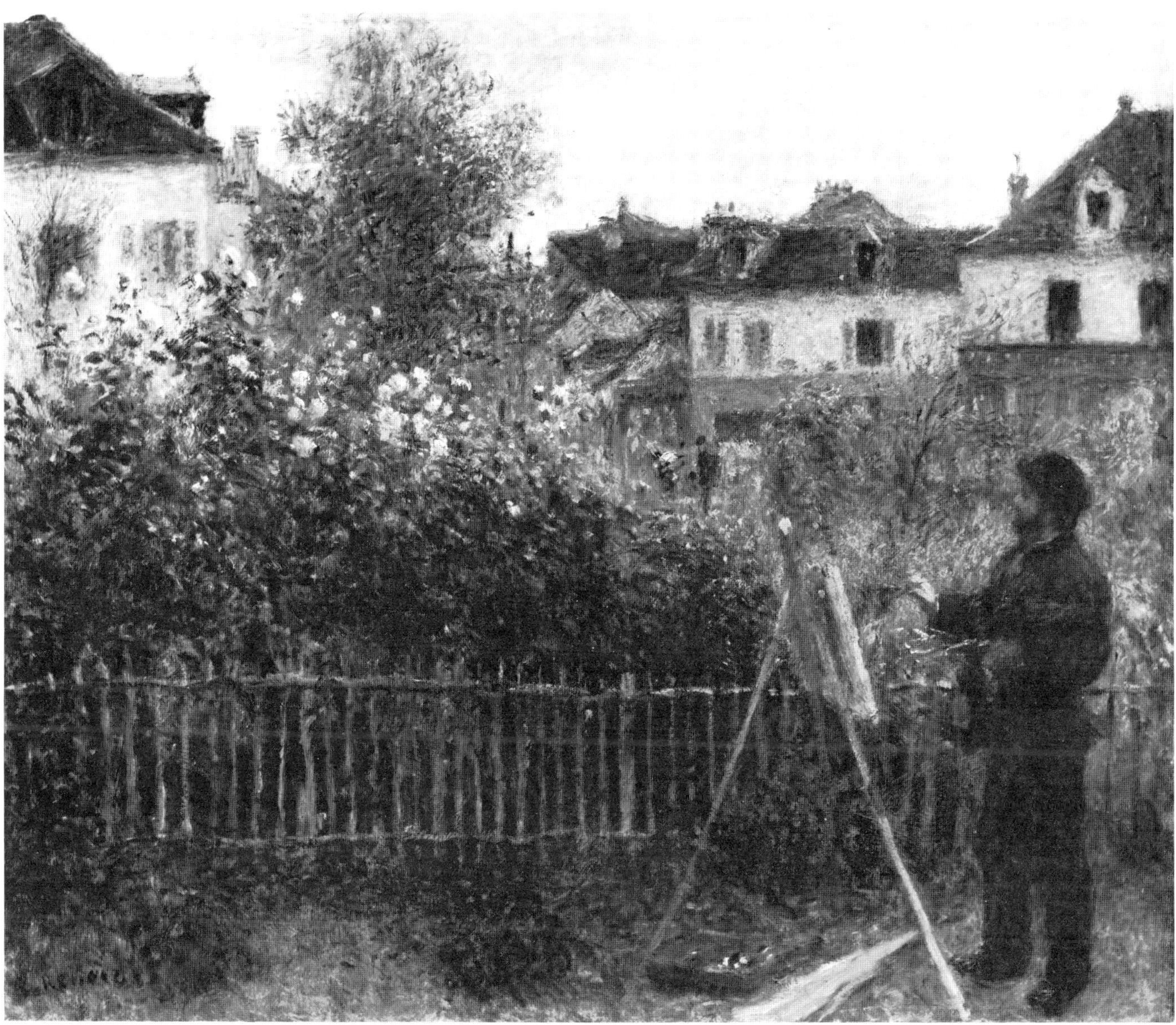

OPPOSITE LEFT Claude Monet: *The Artist's House at Argenteuil*, 1873 (courtesy of the Art Institute of Chicago, Mr and Mrs Martin A. Ryerson Collection). In 1872–4, Monet experienced a period of unusual stability and financial prosperity. Camille and his son Jean, whom he often painted in his flower-filled garden at Argenteuil, were living proof of his happy and well-balanced existence.
OPPOSITE RIGHT Photograph of Monet's second house at Argenteuil, 'a pink house with green shutters, 2 Boulevard Saint-Denis'.
ABOVE Auguste Renoir: *Monet Painting in His Garden*, 1873 (courtesy of the Wadsworth Atheneum, Hartford, Conn.). Monet and Renoir often worked side by side at Argenteuil; Renoir, who preferred painting human figures, sometimes took his friend as a model.

that looked like a two-storied chalet, and like his previous house was surrounded by a garden where on Sundays the painter entertained his friends. It was there that Manet painted *The Monet Family in the Garden*, while a few yards away Renoir worked on a *Portrait of Madame Monet and Her Son*. From time to time, Manet would glance at what Renoir was doing, then whisper to his host: 'The fellow doesn't have much talent. You're his friend, why don't you tell him to give up painting?' Manet, who had a natural admiration for classical painting, was ill equipped to understand Renoir's spontaneous, sensuous and capricious art.

Sisley, who was still living at Port-Marly, near Bougival, or in the neighbourhood, also came to visit Monet. He produced a fine series of landscapes around the docks of Argenteuil, often choosing the same angle as

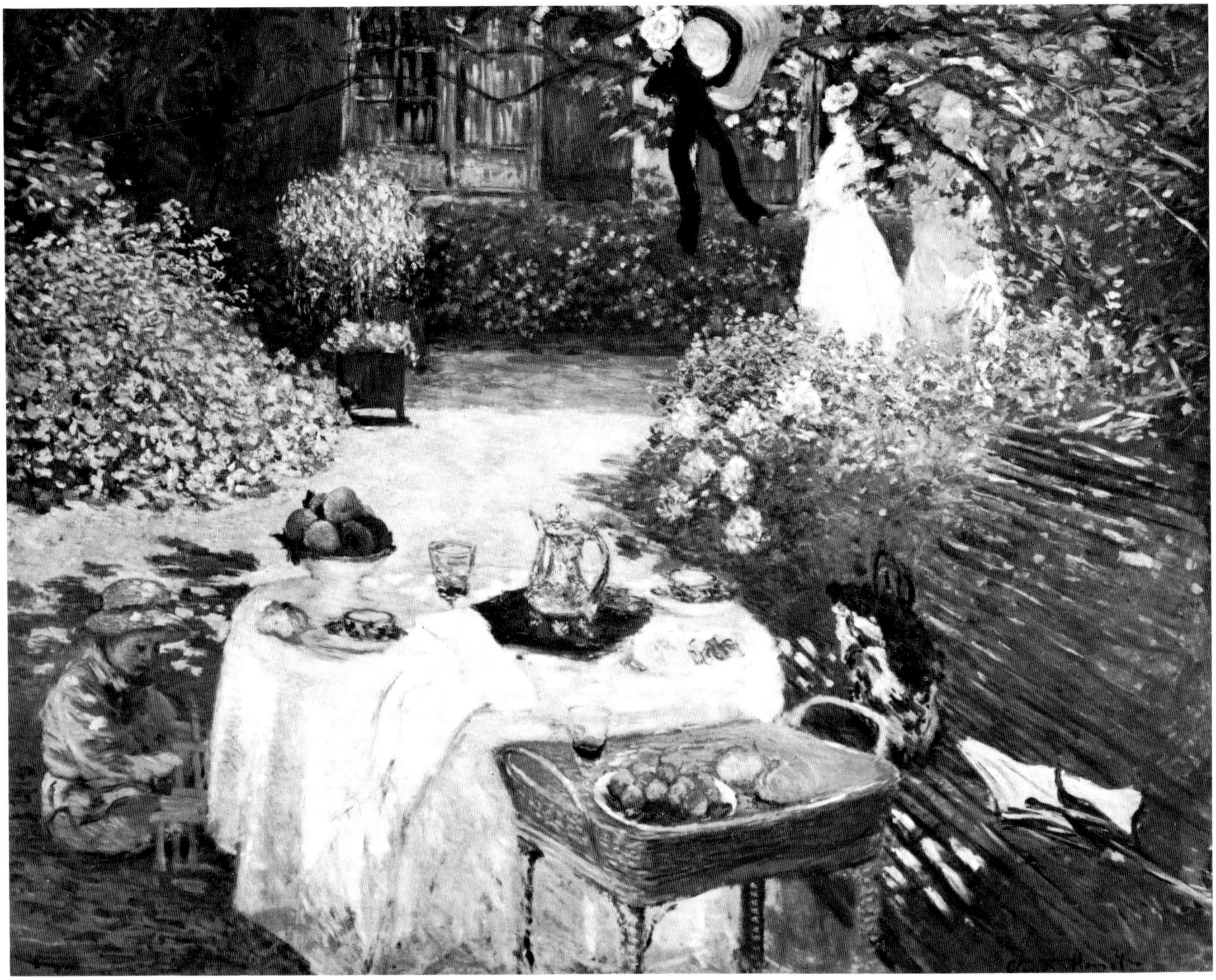

Monet. Although his colours were very light and clear, his paintings were less radiant than Monet's: they were bathed in a kind of opaline light of ineffable charm and just a hint of melancholy. The reserved, shy Sisley was going through a period of poverty made all the more unbearable by his wife's delicate health. But despite his worries, his talents flourished and he turned out some of his best work at Argenteuil.

The particularly productive Argenteuil period was further enriched, as we have seen, when Renoir and Monet had the good fortune to meet a young man of leisure, artistic tastes and considerable means, Gustave Caillebotte, who was ten years their junior, and whose wealth enabled him to collect the works of his new-found friends. Out of generosity, he would select precisely those paintings that had little chance otherwise of finding a buyer, thus providing invaluable help at the time of their direst need. On his death in 1893, Caillebotte left his collection of masterpieces to the state, ensuring in

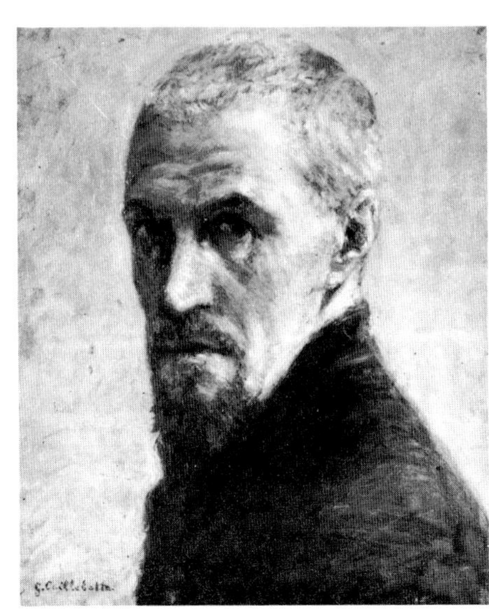

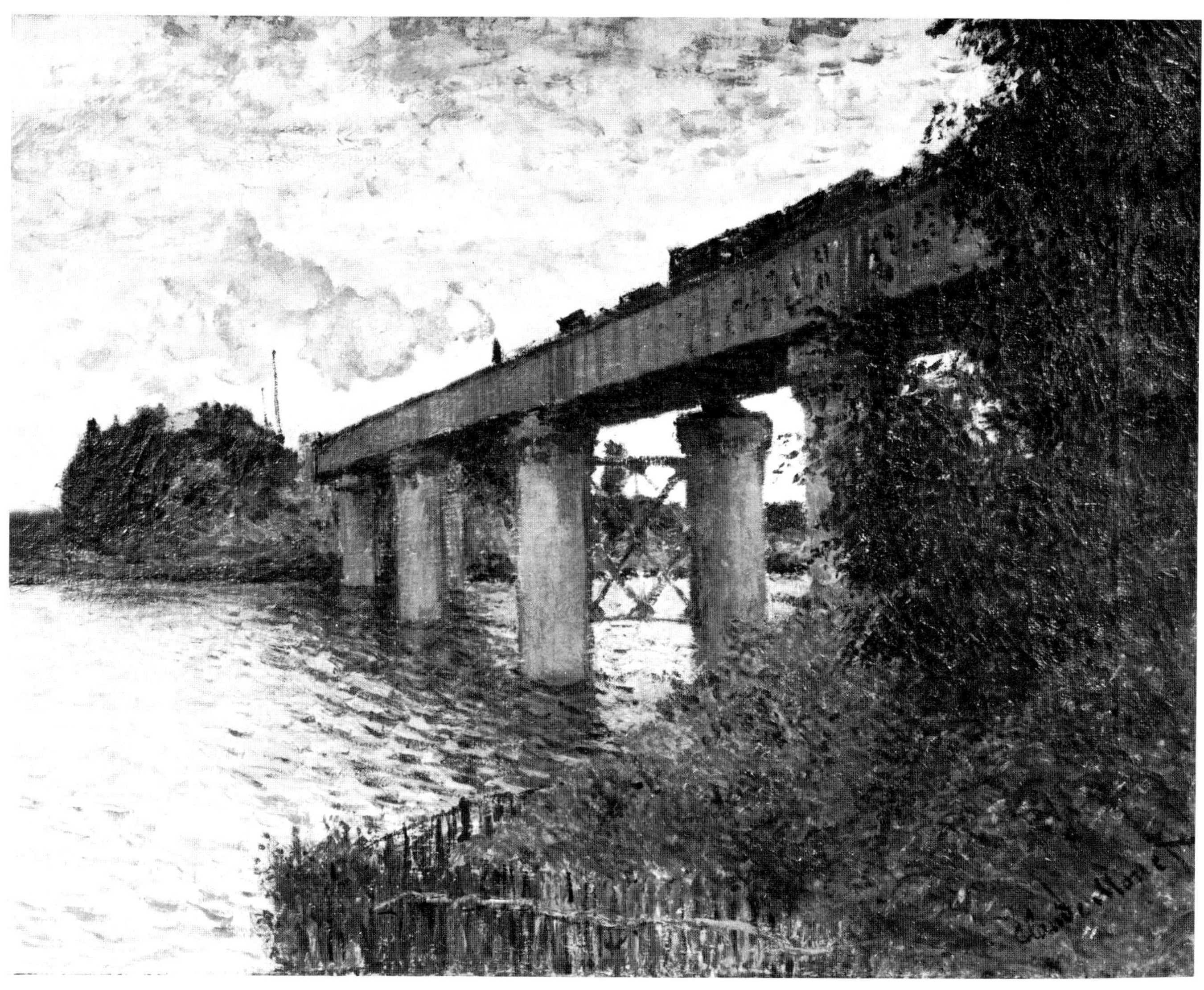

OPPOSITE ABOVE Claude Monet: *Breakfast*, 1872–3 (Musée du Louvre, Paris – Jeu de Paume). This work, which was shown as a decorative panel at the Impressionist group's second exhibition, was bought by Caillebotte in 1878 when Monet was in particularly severe financial difficulties.

OPPOSITE BELOW Gustave Caillebotte: *Self-Portrait*, c. 1889 (Musée du Louvre, Paris – Jeu de Paume). On his death in 1894, Caillebotte bequeathed his collection to the State. This set of some sixty Impressionist works ran into such hostility in official circles that it was only accepted several years later.

ABOVE Claude Monet: *The Railway Bridge at Argenteuil*, c. 1873 (Musée du Louvre, Paris). This bridge was a familiar landmark which appears in numerous paintings by Renoir, Monet and Sisley.

this way that the works of the Impressionists would find their way into French museums. (Despite considerable opposition, they were eventually accepted by the Musée du Luxembourg, and later by the Louvre.)

Monet's stay in Argenteuil ended under a cloud. In 1877, Camille's pregnancy was complicated by illness. On top of that, the Monets, who had changed nothing in their life-style since they had first experienced a period of relative wealth, were by then deeply in debt. Monet appealed more than once to Manet's generosity, and sold paintings to Murer and the collector Ernest Hoschedc, without being able to satisfy his numerous creditors. The artist also still owed a tidy sum to his picture-framer, a certain Monsieur Braque (great-uncle of Georges Braque). Monet left the pink house for good without paying a number of debts. His laundress pursued him for the rest of her life in an attempt to secure the 1,200 francs he owed her. But Monet never paid up, even when his means would have easily allowed him to!

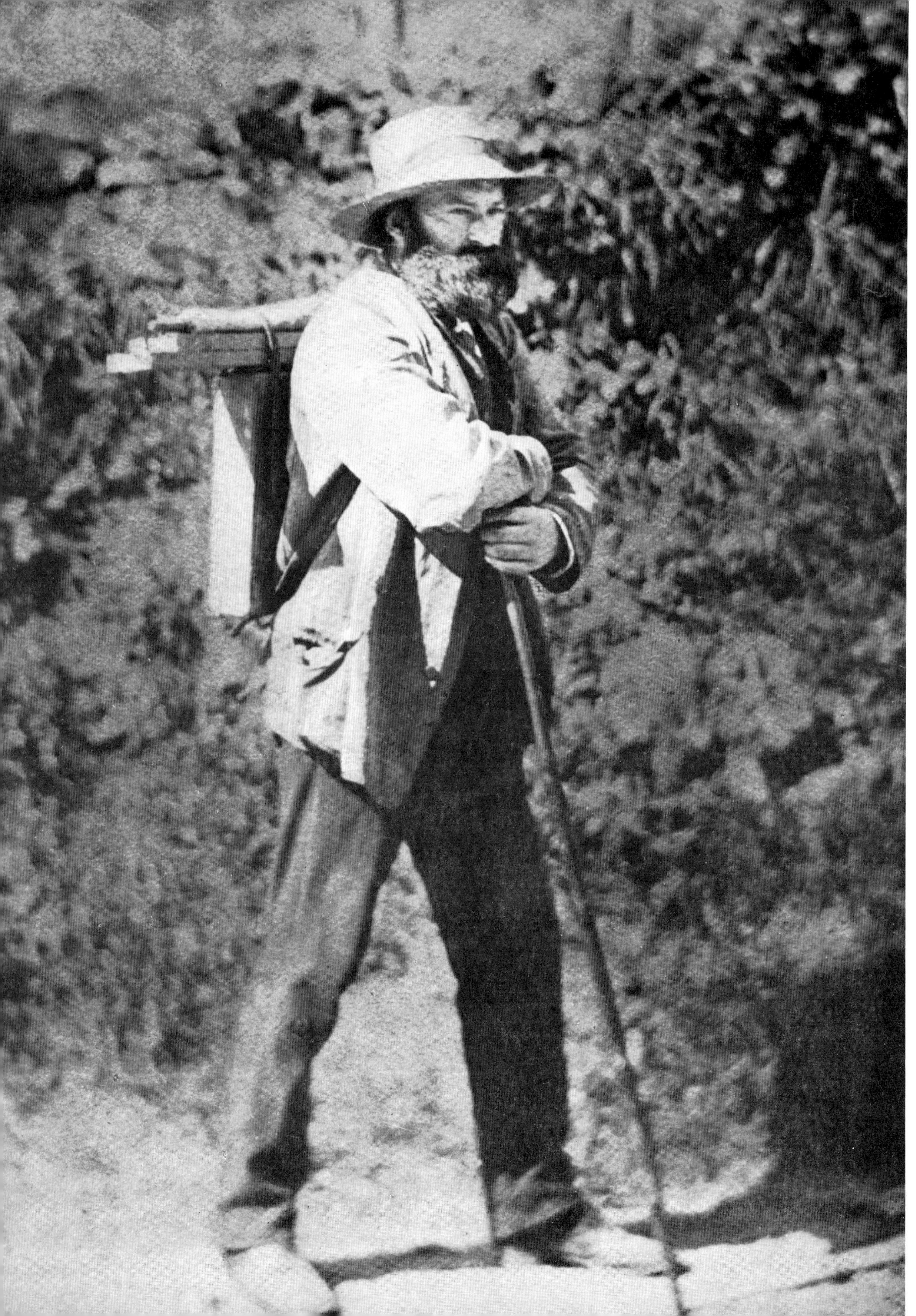

5 The Vexin

Rich Pastures for the Restless

Situated between Normandy and the banks of the Seine, the rich fertile region of the Vexin shares with them the privilege of having been one of the four main areas of the French countryside (with Fontainebleau) to have been lived in and recorded by the Impressionists.

Like Normandy, it is bound up with the lives of the painters over a long period, if often sporadically. It was from here, as we shall see, that Pissarro began to organize the decisive 1784 group exhibition; here, too, that Cézanne painted his first truly Impressionist work. With the Vexin, we begin to see fully how unsettled and restless the Impressionists were, constantly on the move from lodging to lodging in search of reasonable conditions of life and work.

From the early nineteenth century a number of landscape painters had been attracted by the calm of the Vexin's pretty villages. Daubigny chose it as a place to spend his retirement after years of wanderlust, and both Corot and his pupils worked there. During the second half of the century, Camille Pissarro settled there, drawing in his wake two painters who were later to become famous, Paul Cézanne and Paul Gauguin.

In 1863 Corot had urged his young pupils Berthe and Edma Morisot to paint outdoors. As he was too busy to supervise their studies himself, he entrusted them to his disciple, the painter Achille Oudinot, who at that time was working on the banks of the River Oise. Madame Morisot rented a country house for the summer at Le Chou, a village some fifty kilometres from Paris, close to the former capital of the Vexin, the little town of Pontoise. Sometimes alone, and sometimes chaperoned by their mother, the

OPPOSITE Cézanne in landscape painter's outfit at the age of thirty-four. He had come to the Vexin to work in the open air at Pissarro's suggestion.

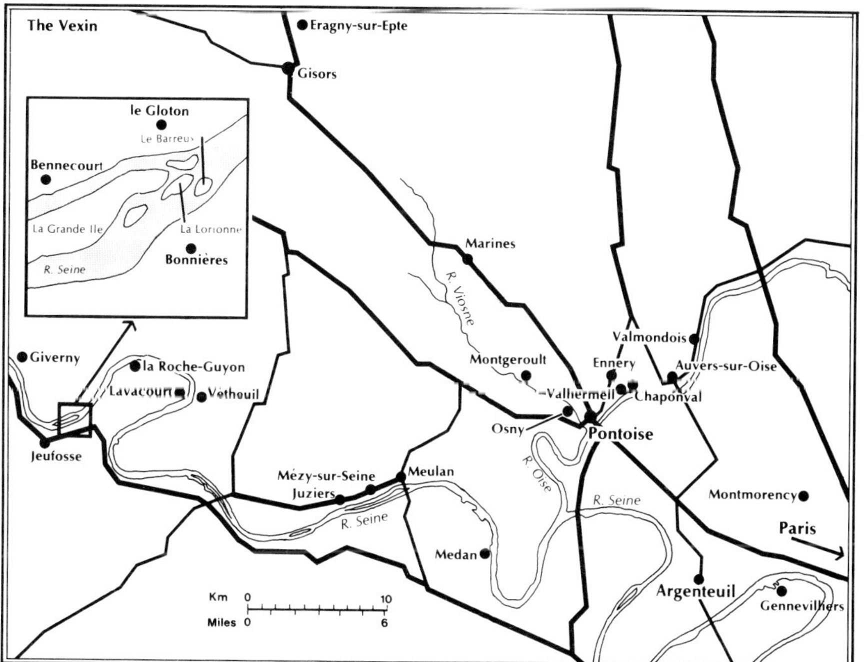

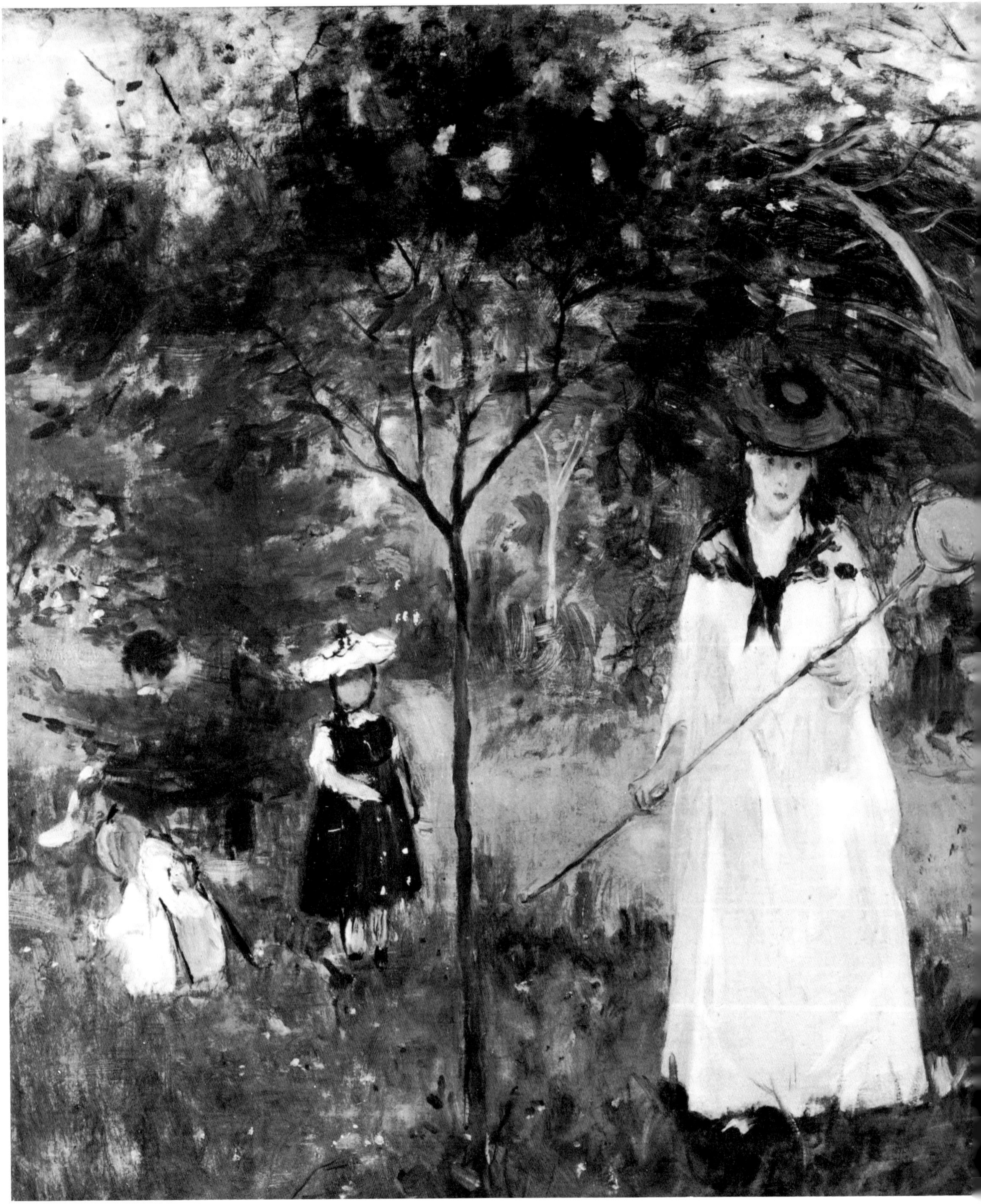

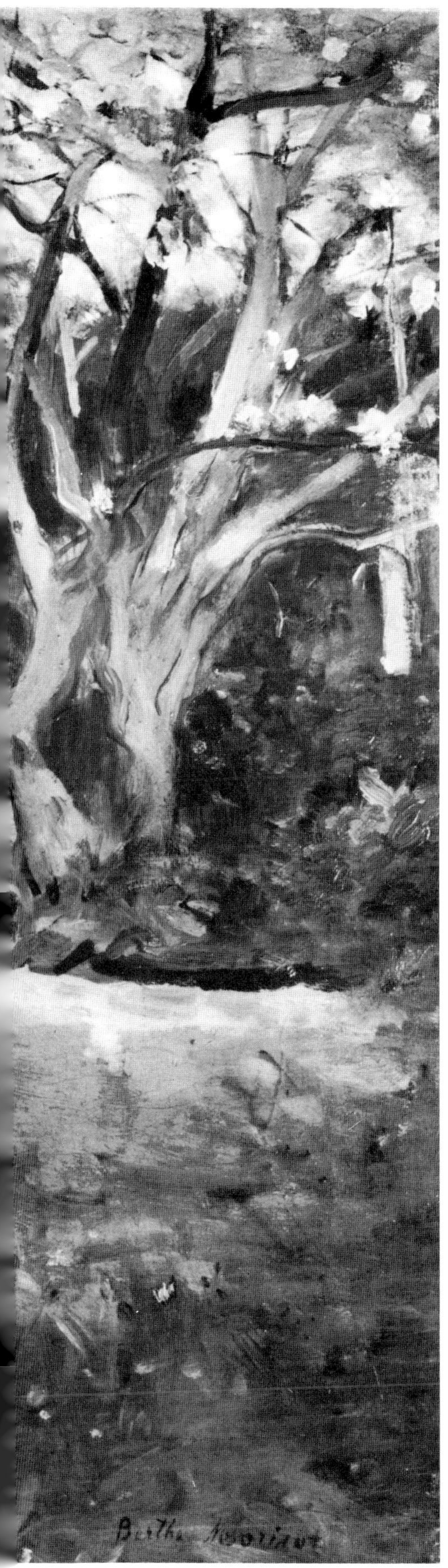
Berthe Morisot: *The Butterfly Hunt*, 1874 (Musée du Louvre, Paris). Morisot's congenial universe was inhabited by her sister, Edma Pointillon, and her daughters Jeanne and Blanche.

two young girls would leave early in the morning to work from nature. They did not have to go far: beyond the farmyards and kitchen gardens of the village, fields and woods stretched as far as the eye could see. Such work sessions, which lasted until lunchtime, were a pleasure, not a chore: the two pretty young pupils were twenty years old and extremely gifted, while their teacher, a perfect man of the world, was only ten years their senior. There very soon sprang up an atmosphere of friendly camaraderie between the three of them, and this was encouraged by Madame Morisot, a woman of the world with a taste for light-heartedness. Berthe Morisot nevertheless worked diligently, and completed two small canvases, including *The Old Road at Auvers*, a delightful landscape heavily influenced by Corot, which was accepted for the Salon the following year.

The most memorable event of their working holiday was an invitation to lunch at the Daubignys'. His son Charles and several young painters were present, but the guest of honour was Honoré Daumier. The famous caricaturist had unceasingly attacked the previous regime, which had retaliated by fining him and sending him to prison more than once; now, greatly aged, he was spending his last years at Valmondois in a little house given to him by the very successful painter, Meissonier. After lunch, everyone admired the frescoes with which Daumier had decorated the Daubignys' old cottage.

Much later, in 1890 and 1891, Berthe Morisot, who was worried about her husband's health, returned to the Val d'Oise: she rented for six months a large, comfortable mansion called La Blottière in the pretty village of Mézy, overlooking the Seine valley. There was a superb view from the loft of the house, which provided her with a marvellous studio. Moreover, the orchard was not only a perfect place for her daughter to play, but a haven of peace and quiet for the convalescing Eugène Manet. Family life did not prevent Berthe Morisot from painting – far from it, the grace and spontaneity of her daughter Julie, as well as her cousins and the girls from the village with whom she played, inspired paintings where the verve of the artist's talent is heightened by the charm of the models. *The Cherry Tree*, which portrays Julie Manet and one of her friends, is perhaps the finest example of the work of an accomplished artist and happy mother.

Berthe Morisot's artist friends (most of them her comrades in arms, the Impressionists), as well as several writers, were frequent guests both in the country and at her town house in the Rue Villejust. Since 1874, she had taken part in all the exhibitions of the group and kept on particularly friendly terms with Monet, Degas and Renoir. From 1886 on, Renoir made a point of never missing a single one of the celebrated Thursday dinners at the Manets' in Paris. He was also, of course, invited to Mézy, where in 1890 he spent three

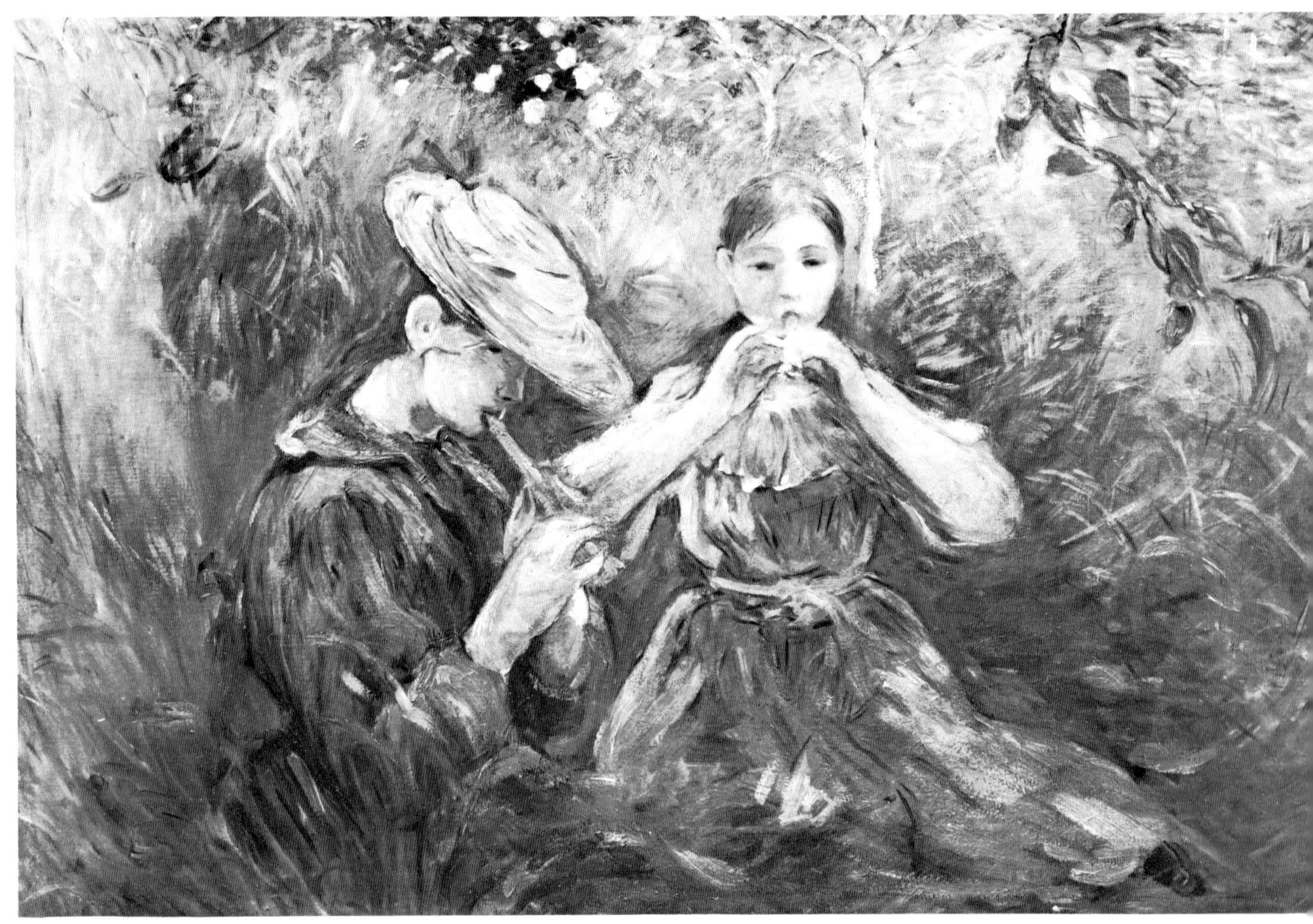

weeks painting with Berthe Morisot, just as he had done in the past with Monet beside the Seine. The following summer Renoir paid his friends another visit, accompanied this time by his wife and his son Jean – which was the most natural thing in the world, except that with typical vagueness Renoir had failed to tell his hostess about his long liaison with Aline Charigot (which had just been officialized by marriage), and in all the excitement of meeting Berthe again he had forgotten to make the necessary introductions. Berthe Morisot was embarrassed by the inexplicable presence of a strange woman, whom she judged to be neither a 'lady' nor a model. 'I cannot tell you how taken aback I was by so ungainly a person – somehow I had imagined her to be just like her husband's painting,' Berthe Morisot wrote shortly afterwards to Stéphane Mallarmé.

Mallarmé, who had been Edouard Manet's great friend and on close terms with the painter's brother and sister-in-law ever since Edouard's death, was also a guest at Mézy. He once announced he was coming to La Blottière in a whimsical note that must have alarmed the postman but delighted his friends:

In 1890 and 1891 Berthe Morisot rented La Blottière in the pretty village of Mézy.
ABOVE Berthe Morisot: *The Recorder Players*, 1890 (Private Collection). Julie Manet (facing the artist) and her cousin in the garden of La Blottière.
OPPOSITE Berthe Morisot: *View from La Blottière, Mézy*, 1890 (Private Collection). The view from Morisot's studio over the plateau of Le Gibet, from which the banks of the Seine could be seen.

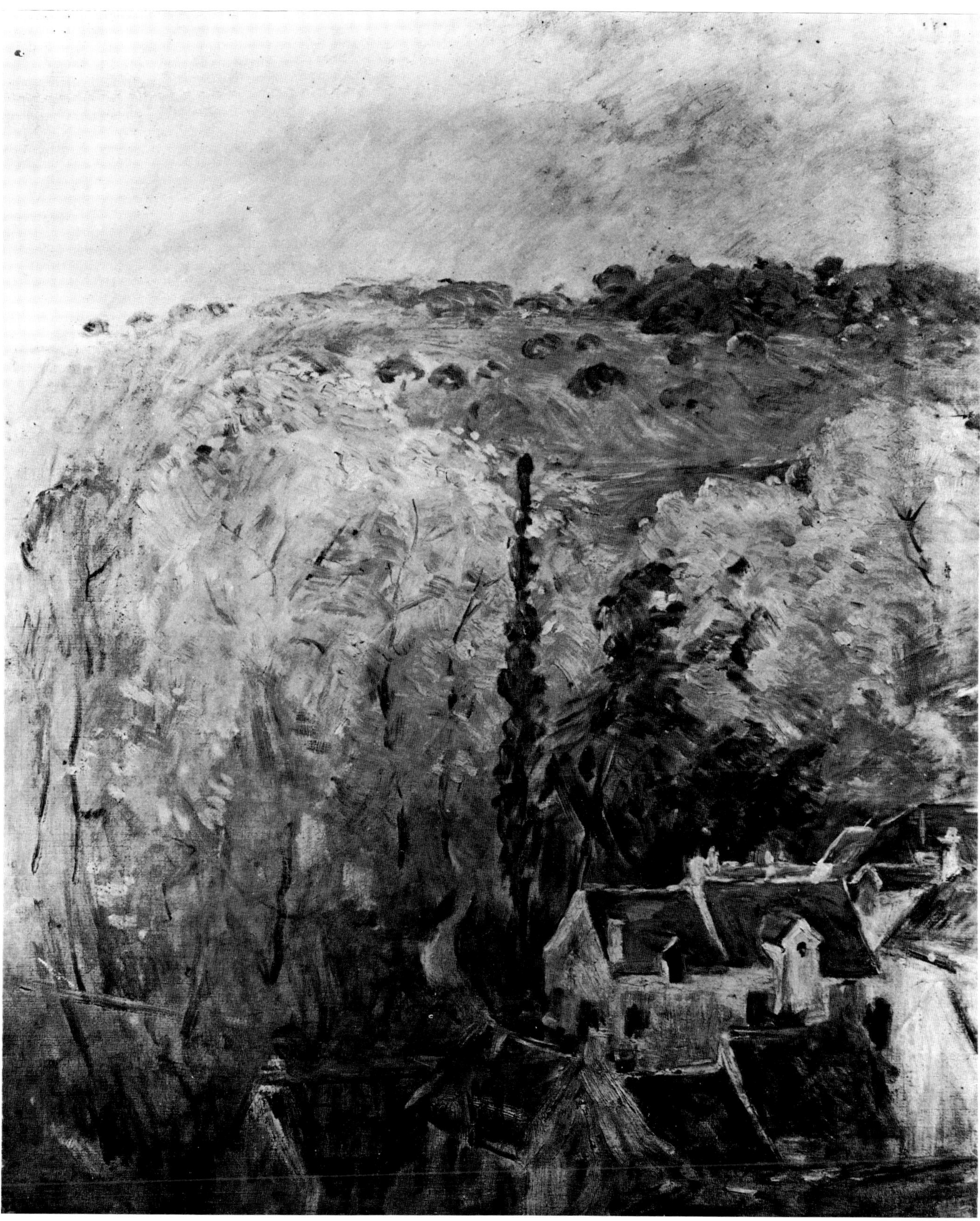

Sans t'endormir, dans l'herbe verte
Naïf distributeur, mets-y
Du tien: cours chez Madame Berthe
Manet, par Melan, à Mézy.

(In the green grass don't doze away/Simple postman: run along/Quickly to Madame Berthe Manet/At Mézy, close by Melan.)

During his stay there, the Manets and their famous guest all piled into a horsedrawn carriage and drove a few kilometres to Giverny, where Monet had been living for the last seven years.

In the course of their outings around Mézy, the Manets discovered a delightfully proportioned little eighteenth-century manor, Le Mesnil, near the village of Juziers. They succeeded in contacting the owners, and ended up by buying it in the winter of 1892. Unfortunately Eugène Manet died in Paris the following April without having been able to enjoy his new home. His death was a cruel blow to Berthe Morisot. Shortly before, she had committed her anxiety to her diary. 'I must plunge as deep as I can into unhappiness,' she wrote, 'because it seems to me that one can only rise out of

BELOW General view of Pontoise, dominated by the twelfth-century church of St-Maclou. OPPOSITE Camille Pissarro: *View of Pontoise, Quai du Pothuis*, 1868 (Kunsthalle, Mannheim). Pissarro set up his easel on the corner of the Boulevard des Fossés and the Route de Dieppe in order to produce this realist view of the town in which he had just settled.

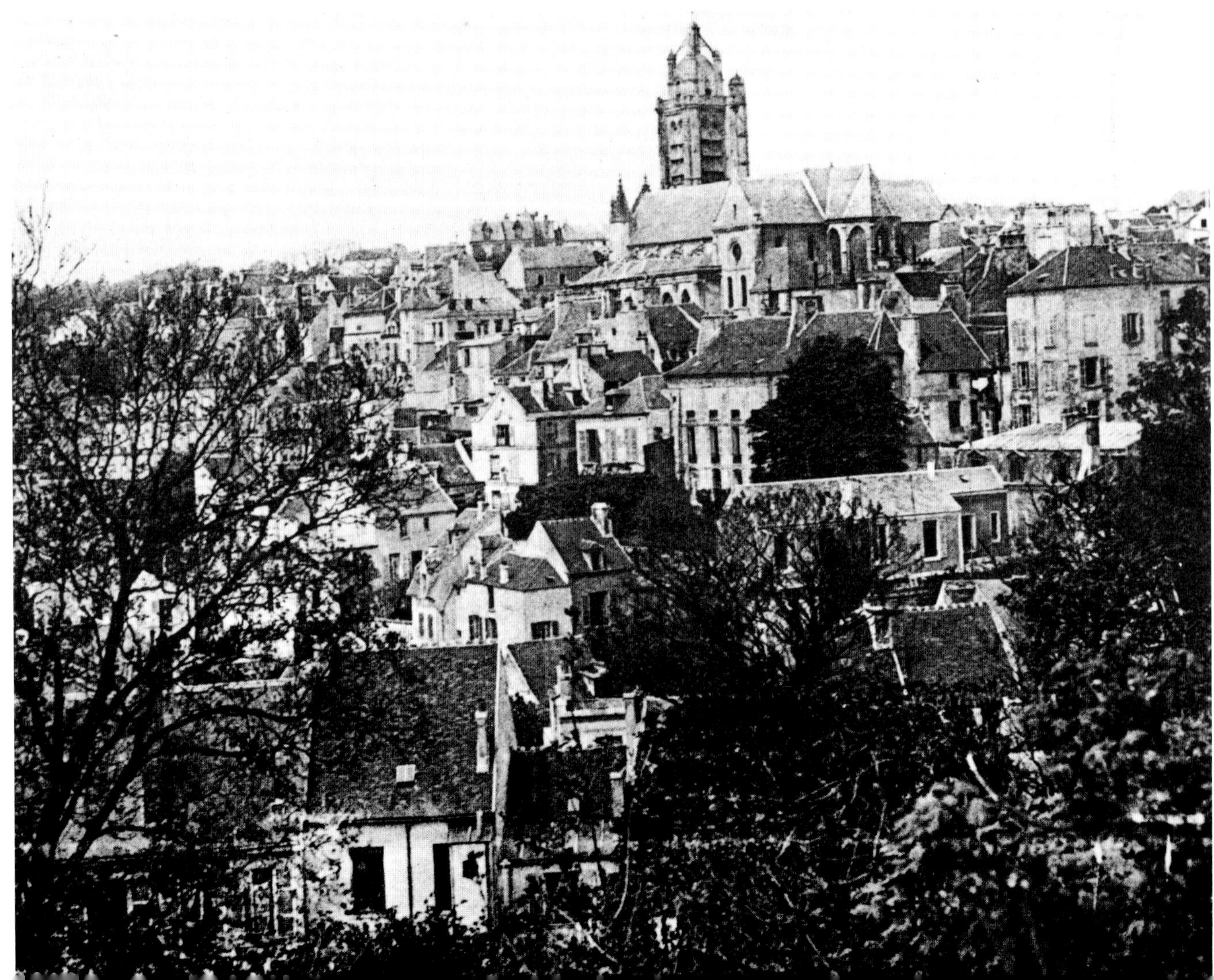

it afterwards. But I have spent the last three nights crying: "Please God!"' She took refuge at the new house during the months following her loss. *The Dovecote at Le Mesnil, Alley at Le Mesnil* and the fine portrait of *Julie Dreaming* show that she was still working as before, if only to forget her grief.

But the principal figure in this haven of peace was Pissarro, who lived and worked in the Vexin for over three decades. As early as 1867, he settled in Pontoise, a small town thirty-two kilometres from the capital, which clings to the side of a hill and is overlooked by a ruined castle where kings of France once stayed. For almost twenty years afterwards, he was a familiar figure in its narrow winding streets. Six kilometres away, at Auvers-sur-Oise, lived Daubigny, who was now a member of the jury of the Salon; he was favourably disposed towards Pissarro and one or two other young artists such as Guillemet and Cézanne.

As soon as he arrived at his new home, Pissarro set up his easel on the embankment alongside the Oise and painted *The Quay and Bridge at Pontoise*, a picture in which the colours – reds, greens and browns – are deadened by a lowering sky. The thickly applied paint, the stiff human figures, and the

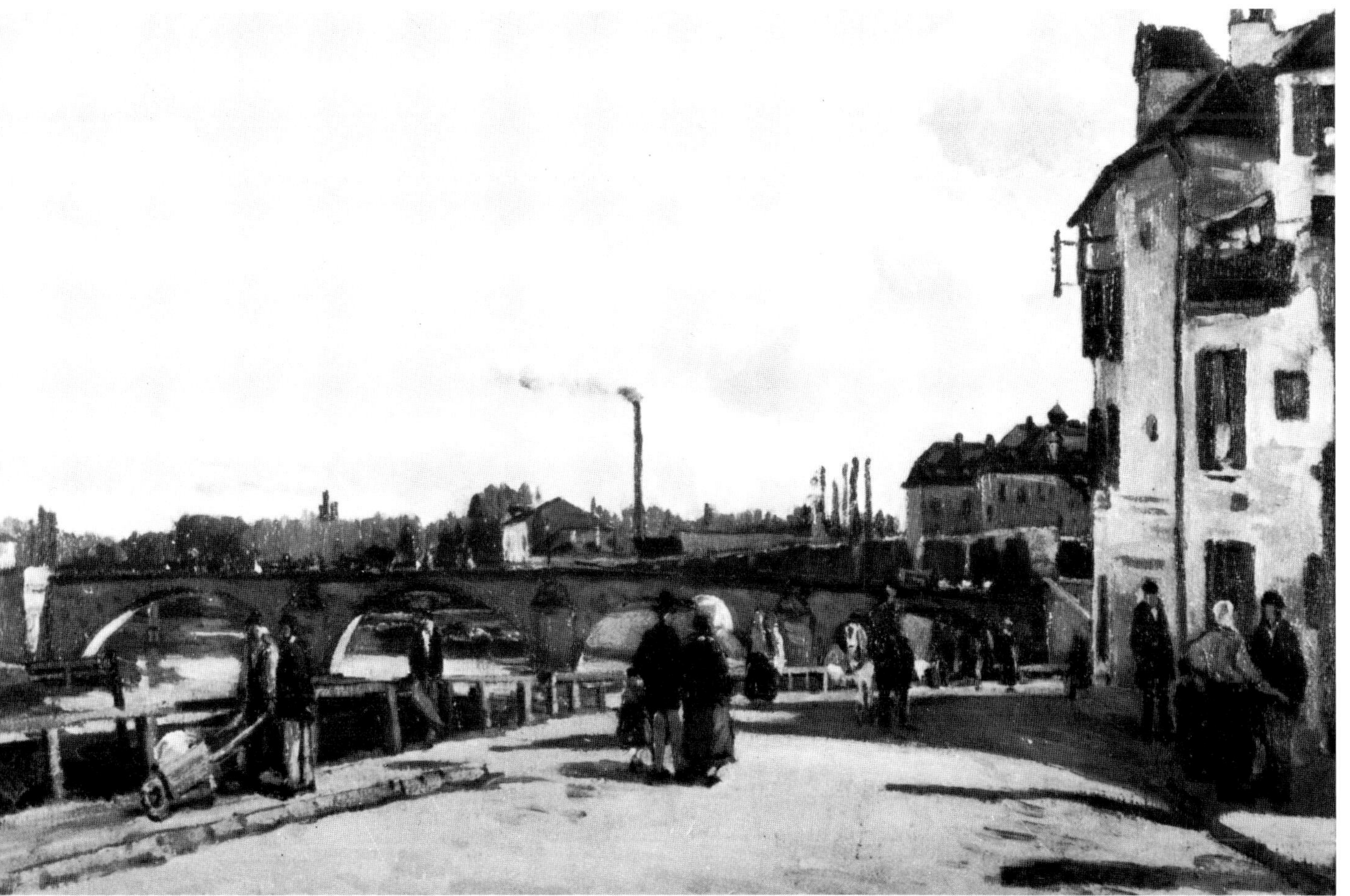

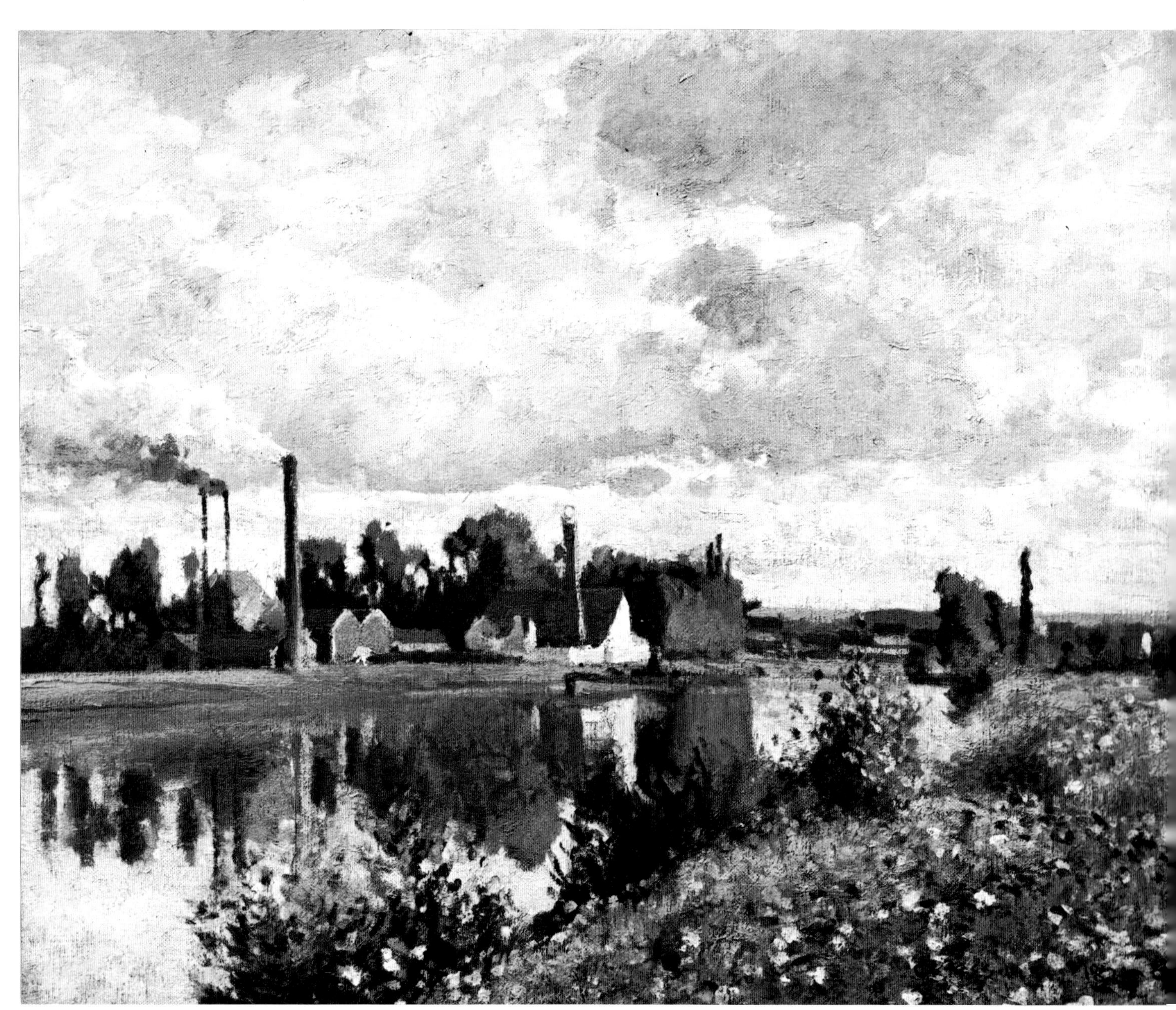

rather over-rigid composition lend the work an air of provincial melancholy. Pissarro, who had been working alone for several years, still displayed a certain awkwardness. But his aim was always to express his own sensations as faithfully as possible. At this point in his development, however, he was not yet ready to start inventing, and had to rely on the language of his predecessors in order to render what he felt. Even so, he already possessed striking personal qualities. 'One of the three or four painters of our time. He has solidity and broadness of execution, he paints generously, following the traditions, like the masters. A beautiful picture by this artist is the act of an

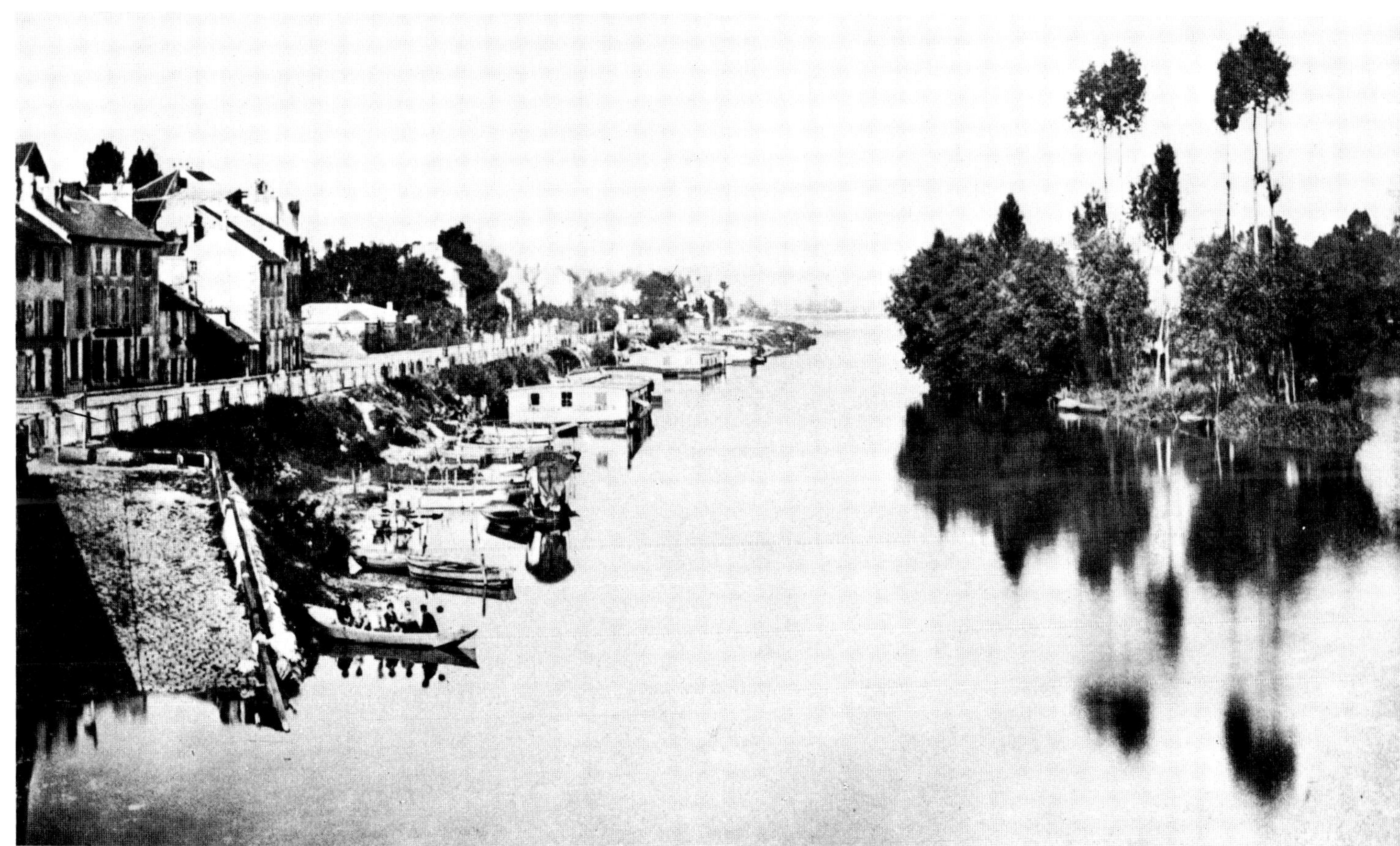

OPPOSITE Camille Pissarro: *The River Oise near Pontoise*, 1873 (Sterling and Francine Clark Art Institute, Williamstown, Mass.). Pissarro saw no reason not to include, in this bucolic landscape, the chimneys and graceless building of the distilleries and flour mills that had been built at the end of the eighteenth century at Saint-Ouen-l'Aumône, a village near Pontoise, on the left bank of the river. ABOVE View of the island of Pothuis. As on the banks of the Seine, a restaurant hidden away among the island's tall trees was a favourite rendezvous for boating enthusiasts.

honest man. I could not define his talent better than that,' remarked Zola in front of *La Côte du Jullais*, which thanks to Daubigny's support had been put on show at the Salon that year. The hill in question, which runs along the horizon of a landscape distinguished by its gently rounded contours and perfectly arranged planes, is just one of the countless subjects to be found all around Pontoise.

Pissarro lodged in the Rue du Fond de l'Hermitage with his mistress Julie Vellay and his two young children. From there he had only to walk a few steps to reach the orchards, fields and sunken ways lined with walnut and chestnut trees that surrounded the town. Pissarro's whole life revolved around painting; he left home at six in the morning, and while the farmers would reassuringly go about their usual jobs he used to come to grips with nature – alone, and totally engrossed in the terrifying task he had set himself: to reveal the beauty of the world around him with a few colours and

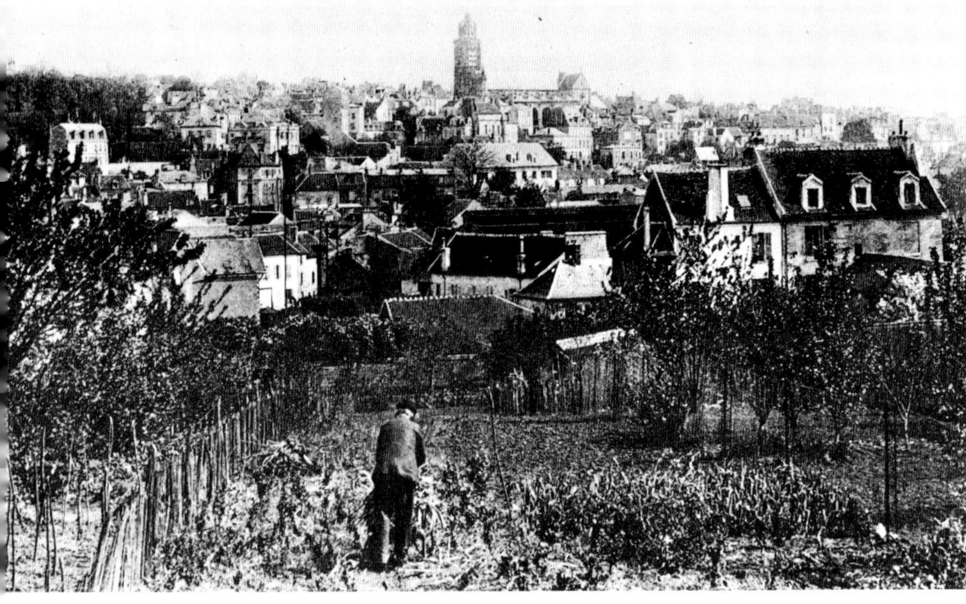

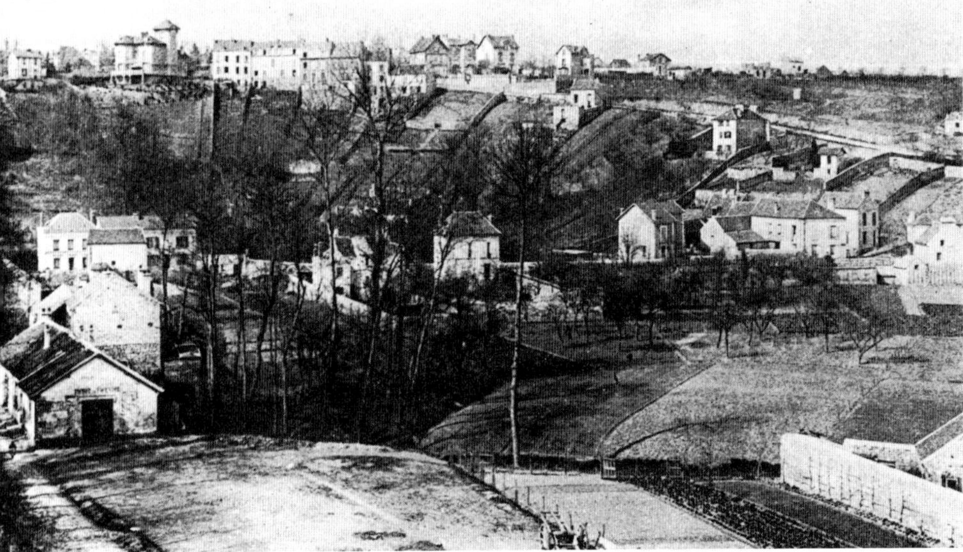

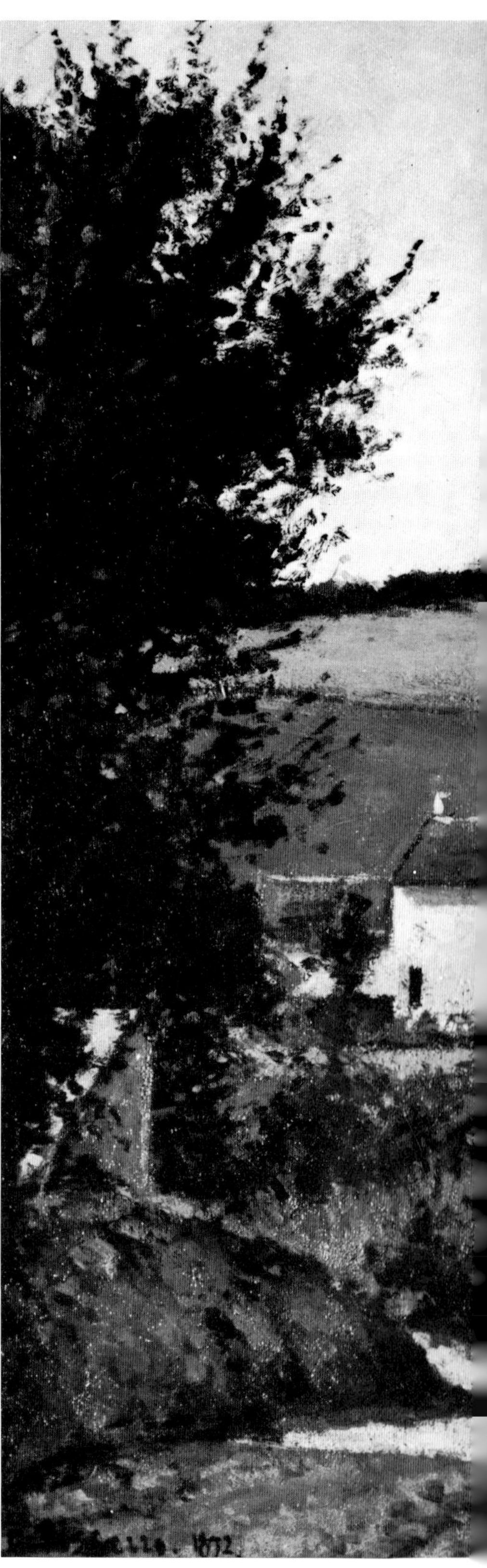

paintbrushes. He worked for as long as he could at a time, and, whenever possible, would try to capture the essence of his picture in one sitting. But he often had to wrench himself away from his easel, clean his brushes and jump on the Paris train earlier than he would have wished. For it was in Paris that he tried to show his work, arouse some interest, or, when it became necessary, borrow money in order to keep his family alive.

LEFT Two views of Pontoise, from the Haut St-Martin (ABOVE) and from the Hermitage quarter (BELOW). The town was surrounded by a profusion of orchards and market gardens.

ABOVE Camille Pissarro: *Le Chemin de l'Hermitage*, 1872 (Wildenstein Collection, New York).

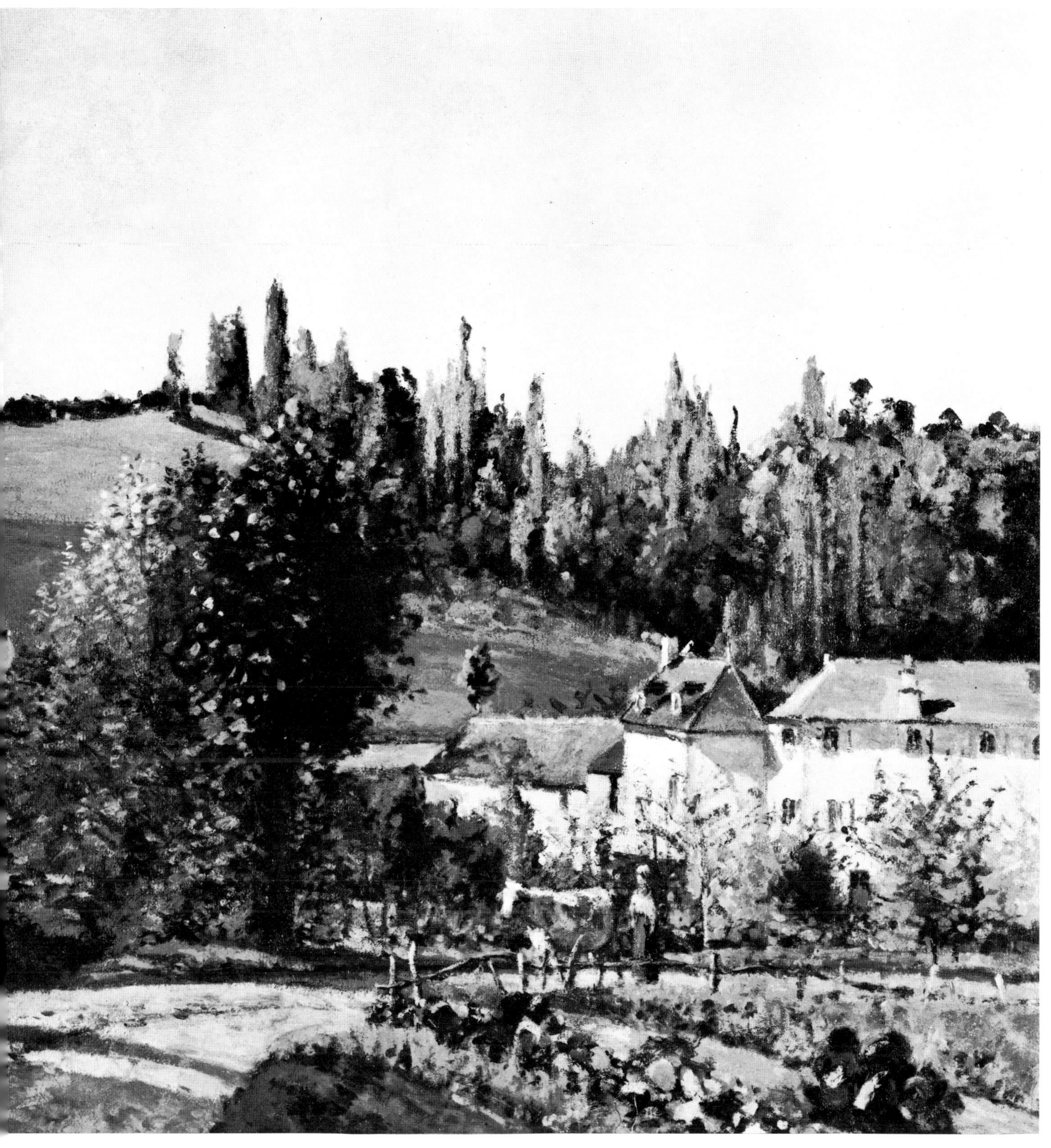

Sometimes Pissarro visited his wealthy bourgeois mother, who had been widowed since 1865 and still entertained the sort of guests who might, he hoped, throw up a collector or two. He did the rounds of the dealers who sometimes bought from the young painters: the former painter Latouche, on the corner of the Rue Laffite and the Rue Lafayette, Portier, who occupied an entresol on the Rue Lepic, or Père Martin, on the Rue des Martyrs. His intensively rural landscapes, they said, did not have much appeal; and he was rarely able to get more than 20 to 40 francs.

After walking all over Montmartre, Pissarro would drop into the Café Guerbois, near the Place Clichy, where he knew he would find friends with whom he could talk about the things that really mattered to him. The company of painters, and the discussions that used to set the champions of different aesthetic schools at loggerheads, delighted Pissarro: as well as being naturally curious, he was a good listener and must certainly have learnt as much in the course of such evenings as he could have done in any studio.

But the long and expensive journey from Pontoise to Paris prevented him from attending the meetings as regularly as Manet or Degas, for instance, whose studios were round the corner in Les Batignolles. During the summer, Pissarro scarcely came to Paris at all, but devoted all his time to landscape painting.

After an absence of three years, which he spent – as we have seen – at Louveciennes, then in London, Pissarro settled again in Pointoise in 1872, this time at 16 Rue Malebranche. He had by then married Julie Vellay, who had given him a third child. He was also now a painter in full possession of his artistic abilities, and looked at the unchanged countryside of the Val d'Oise through new spectacles, for while away he had learnt to see 'light'. This change in him had started at Louveciennes with Monet and continued in London when Pissarro discovered Turner's astonishing watercolours, in which colour explodes like a firework display and destroys all form. The dark brown earth of the Val d'Oise looked lighter to him, the wheat fairer and more radiant with light. In and around the village, he picked the same subjects as before – vegetable patches, alleys, hillocks dotted with a few houses surrounded by trees – but now he treated them with a range of colours from which his usual sienna and dark green were conspicuously absent.

The paintings of Pissarro brought back from London caused a sensation in Paris. 'I've been along the Rue Laffite and looked in on all the dealers, including Durand-Ruel,' his friend Antoine Guillemet wrote to him exultantly, 'and what I must tell you is that everywhere I saw your charming things – in other words, light, varied, lively paintings that gave me the

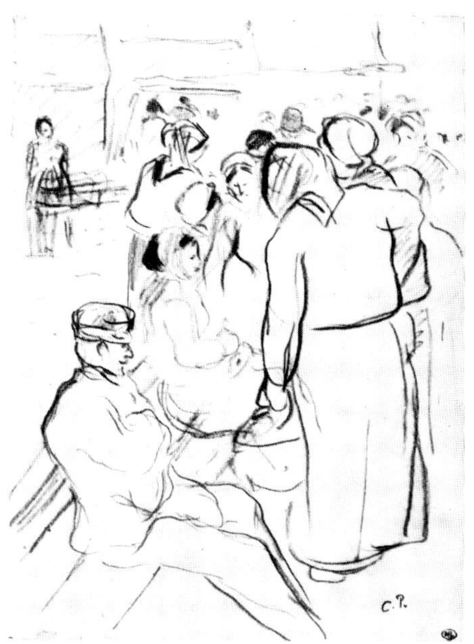

Camille Pissarro: *Market Shoppers in Pontoise*, drawing, 1880 (Musée du Louvre, Paris).

greatest of pleasure'. For a time, Pissarro was indeed in favour with the dealer Durand-Ruel (who had met him in London and recognized his talents) and with a fair number of collectors. His pictures fetched up to 950 francs in 1873, and his financial situation, which until then had been very shaky, improved a little. 'Reactions to the sale at the Drouot salerooms can be felt as far away as Pontoise,' Pissarro wrote to his friend the critic Théodore Duret. And yet he did not change anything in his habits or way of life: at dawn he would be out and about in the fields, dressed like a hunter with high boots protecting his trousers from the dew, a wide-brimmed felt hat, a haversack, an easel over his shoulder, and a walking-stick in his hand. Pissarro was indeed a tireless walker. Often he would trek east along winding paths until he reached little villages on the Oise such as Le Chou and Auvers, where there were still a few old cottages with thatched roofs. To the north, he walked as far as Ennery, Montgeroult, Valhermeil and Chaponval. He would set up his easel on a towpath by a river, or in front of a very commonplace view whose subdued poetry only he could spot.

Pissarro still had to travel frantically to and fro between Pontoise and Paris, and was kept constantly on the hop by the forthcoming joint exhibition at Nadar's studio, due to open a fortnight before the Salon of 1874. 'Pissarro is delightfully enthusiastic and confident,' remarked Degas; as well he had to be if he were to convince the timorous, win over the lukewarm and change the opinions of those who were fiercely opposed to the undertaking if only because they believed the jury's word was God.

Pissarro's best friends urged him to act cautiously and advised him not to shock the public, whose favours he was only just beginning to enjoy. 'The reform you are trying to carry out is a useful one, but it is impracticable,' wrote his friend the painter Ludovic Piette. 'Artists have no spunk in them.' And the shrewd Théodore Duret, who had been following the fortunes of the Impressionists from the very beginning, added: 'You must go one step further forward and make a real name for yourselves. You'll never succeed in doing that by organizing private exhibitions.'

But nothing in fact could have persuaded Pissarro to abandon a venture which he sensed, intuitively, to be of enormous importance. He was, however, cruelly treated by destiny: in March, scarcely two months before the exhibition was due to open, his only daughter Jeanne-Rachelle died just before her ninth birthday. 'La petite Minette', as she had been nicknamed, inspired two very fine portraits (a genre otherwise rare in his *oeuvre*). In 1872, Pissarro painted the little girl in her blue school smock, with the gloomy expression of all children who are forced to pose, standing in a bare-walled room in front of a table, on which a tea-pot and a sugar-tin form a skimpy still life. The other portrait of her, in her best Sunday clothes, is a masterpiece of tender affection: she is seated holding a bunch of flowers which, like the rest of the painting, is treated in pastel pink and pale yellow hues, while her melancholy young face is shaded by a large romantic straw hat.

As the defeatist wiseacres had predicted, the exhibition of the Independents was a disaster for Pissarro. He naturally had to put up with his fair share of jeering insults, and his sales began to decline, for at precisely the same time Durand-Ruel and the select band of private collectors had been hit by the economic crisis and were no longer buying pictures. Money became scarcer and scarcer in the Pissarros' Pontoise home: Madame Pissarro, struggling with the problems of housework and the delicate health of her infant children, kept up a constant stream of complaints, while Camille continued to paint despite severe bouts of depression. He attempted to enliven his landscapes by placing human figures in them, but unfortunately for him they looked nothing like Monet's smart young ladies in crinolines sheltering from the sun in flower gardens, or the charming Parisiennes whose complexions Renoir so loved to heighten. All Pissarro could offer were peasant girls picking apples, pork butchers at their market stalls, a young maidservant or a lass with her flock of geese. However unfashionable it made him, the artist was determined to stand by his country-loving temperament and simple tastes. Although still living in straitened circumstances, he gave his wife two further children, Ludovic-Rudolphe in 1878 and Jeanne in 1881, both born in Pontoise.

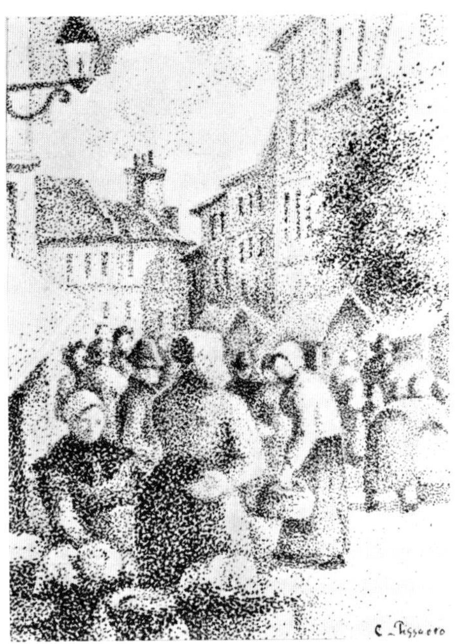

ABOVE Camille Pissarro: *Pontoise Market*, watercolour, *c.* 1886 (Private Collection).

BELOW Market day in Pontoise in the 1880s.

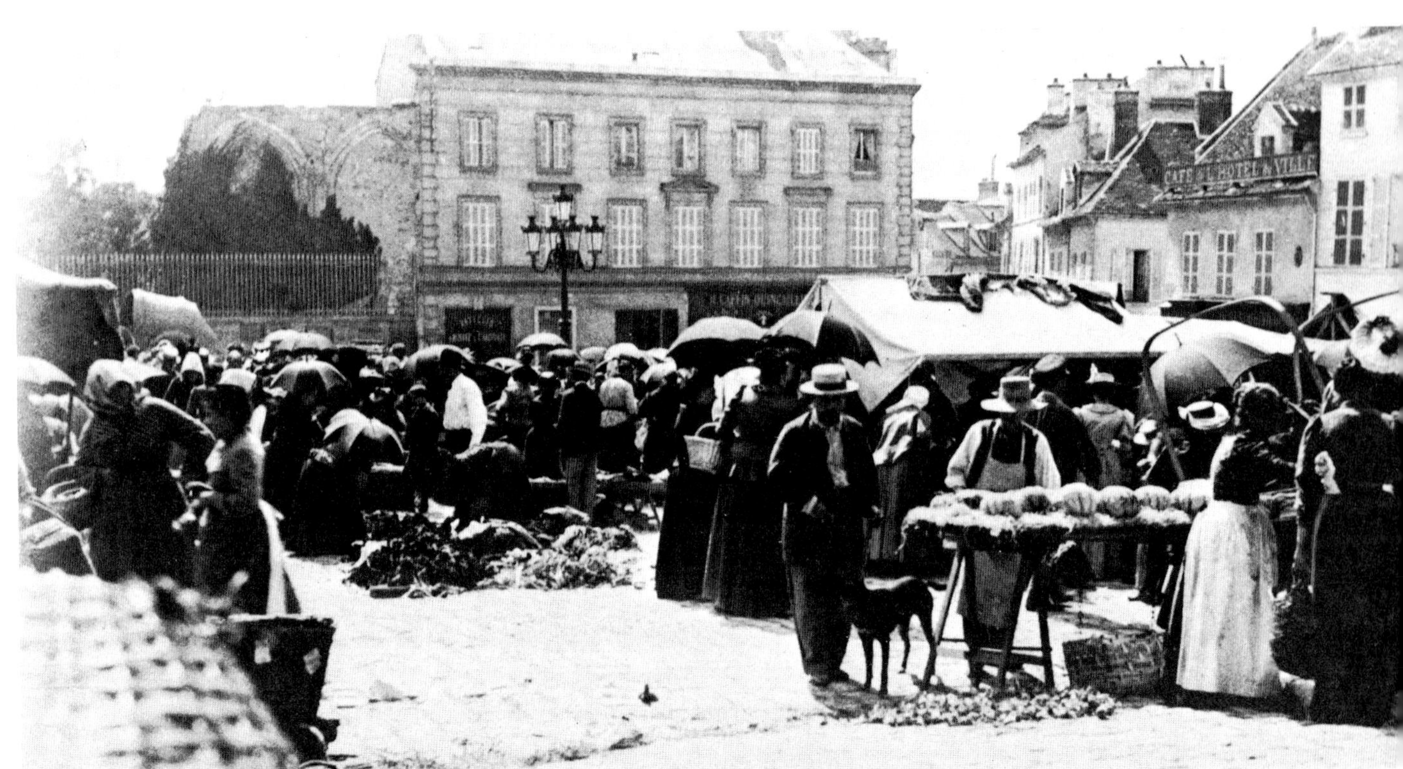

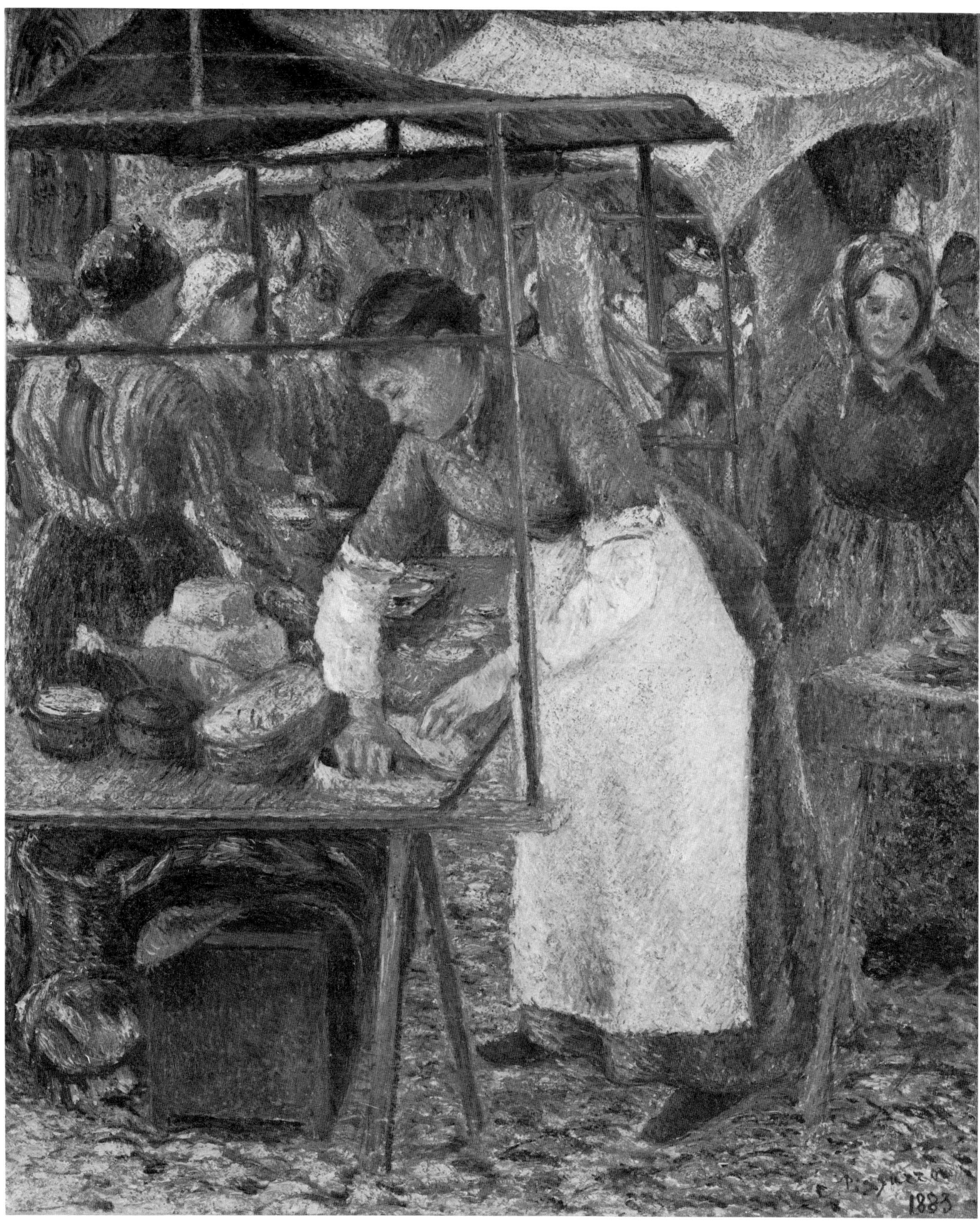

Camille Pissarro: *The Pork Butcher*, 1883 (Tate Gallery, London).

Pissarro's quiet confidence and warm, communicative nature drew a group of painter friends to Pontoise. Antoine Guillemet, whom he had met at the Académie Charles Suisse, Edouard Béliard, Armand Guillaumin, Paul Cézanne and Paul Gauguin all in turn became his friends or pupils.

Cézanne returned from the Midi at the end of 1871, after spending the period of the War and the Commune in hiding at L'Estaque with Hortense Fiquet, his model and mistress. They had a child in January 1872; but, as we have seen, Paul had not told his father, and so he still had to live on his bachelor's allowance.

In Paris, they could only afford a tiny flat. The baby's crying prevented Cézanne from either working or getting any sleep, and he became deeply depressed. Pissarro took sympathy on him and advised him to try the solution that had worked in his own case – live in the country, where rents were lower and where he would have plenty of space and above all the tremendous advantage of being able to work outdoors without the exasperating distractions of Paris streets.

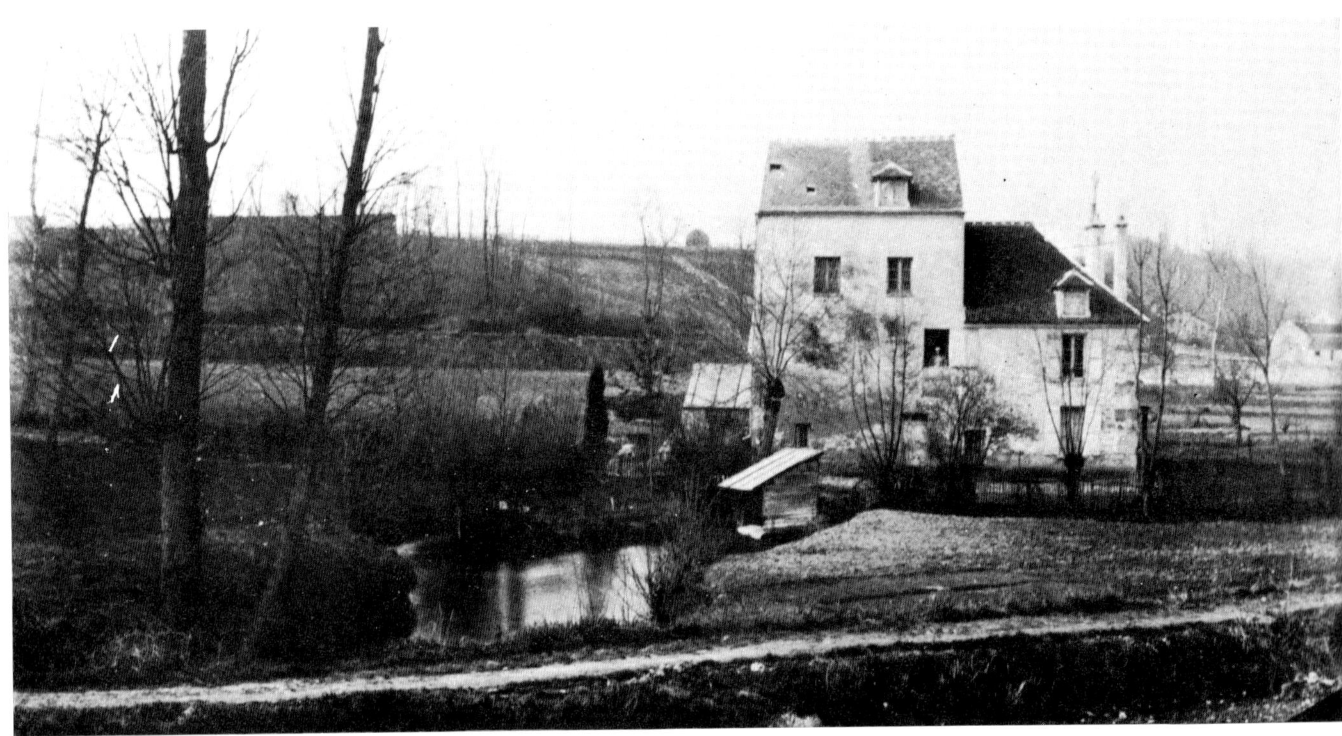

ABOVE Water-mill on the Couleuvre. The Oise and its tributaries supplied water for the numerous mills and tanneries in Pontoise and the surrounding area.
OPPOSITE Paul Cézanne: *The Mill on the Couleuvre at Pontoise*, c. 1879 (Staatliche Museen, East Berlin). The sturdy construction of this former mill had a rustic simplicity reminiscent of the Provençal farms that were familiar to Cézanne.

Pissarro ended up by convincing Cézanne; and he moved to Pontoise at the beginning of 1872, to 31 Quai du Pothuis, just down the road from the Pissarros. Cézanne was to spend some of the most important months of his whole career in that unassuming little town. As often as he could, he used to set out at dawn with Pissarro and plant his easel before the same subject as his elder. But whereas Pissarro was used to the specific problems of working in

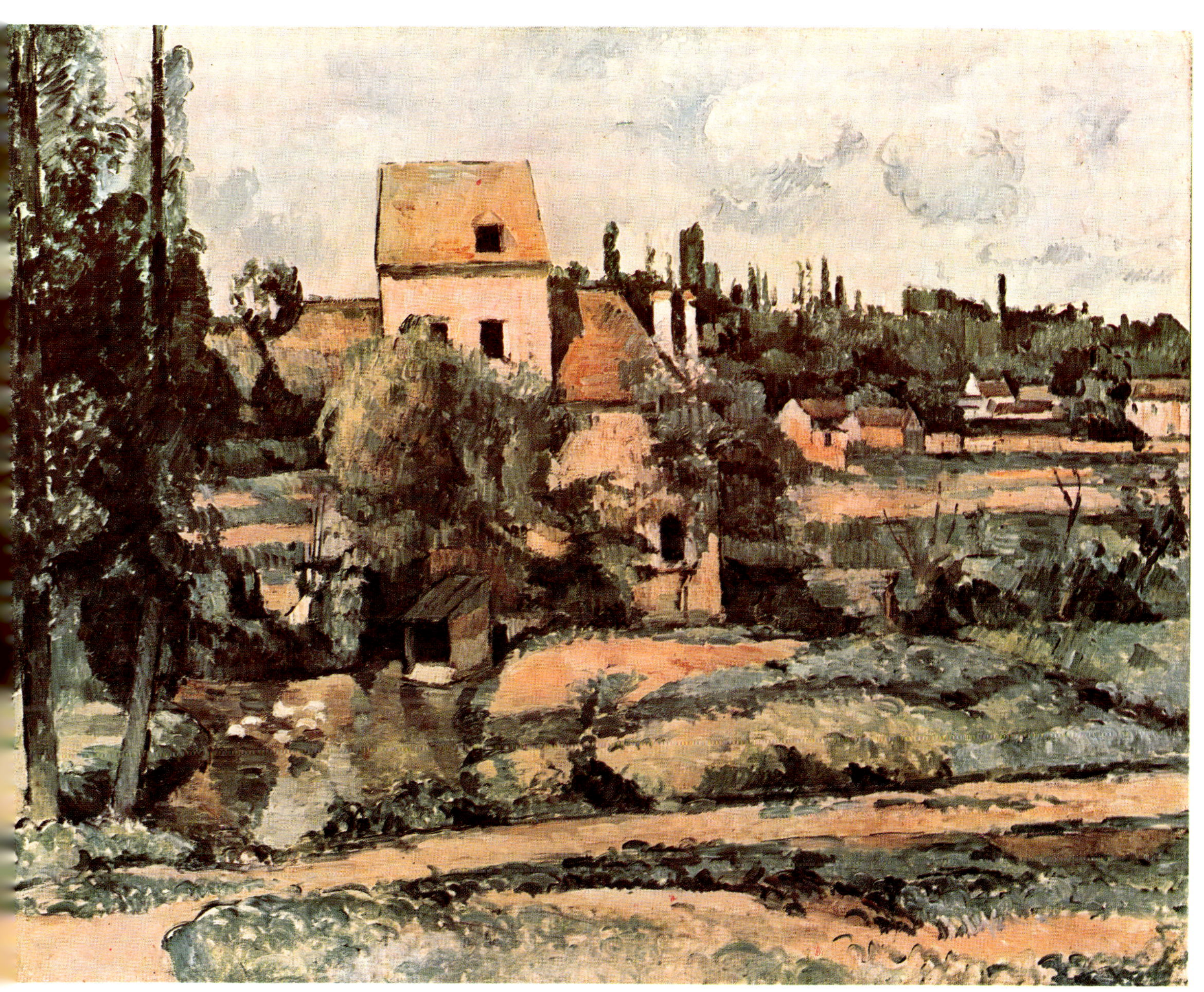

the open air, and would quickly organize his composition with a few light touches of colour, his friend still painted slowly, applying thick patches of paint that were slow to dry and difficult to alter – and Cézanne was constantly hesitating, rethinking, changing.

As well as being interested in changes of light, Cézanne also tried to express something that was quite his own: a sensation of the permanence of nature, and of the solidity of its masses. 'Nature is always the same, but nothing of it remains, nothing of what appears to us. Our art must register the quivering of its duration with the elements, and the appearances of all its changes,' he was to say much later. In an attempt to solve that paradox, Cézanne strove to master the Impressionist technique, whose advantages he implicitly recognized. With a modesty that may seem startling today, he copied one of the landscapes Pissarro had painted at Louveciennes several years before. Within a few months, thanks to the influence of the 'colossal' Pissarro (as he called him), Cézanne took something of the heaviness out of

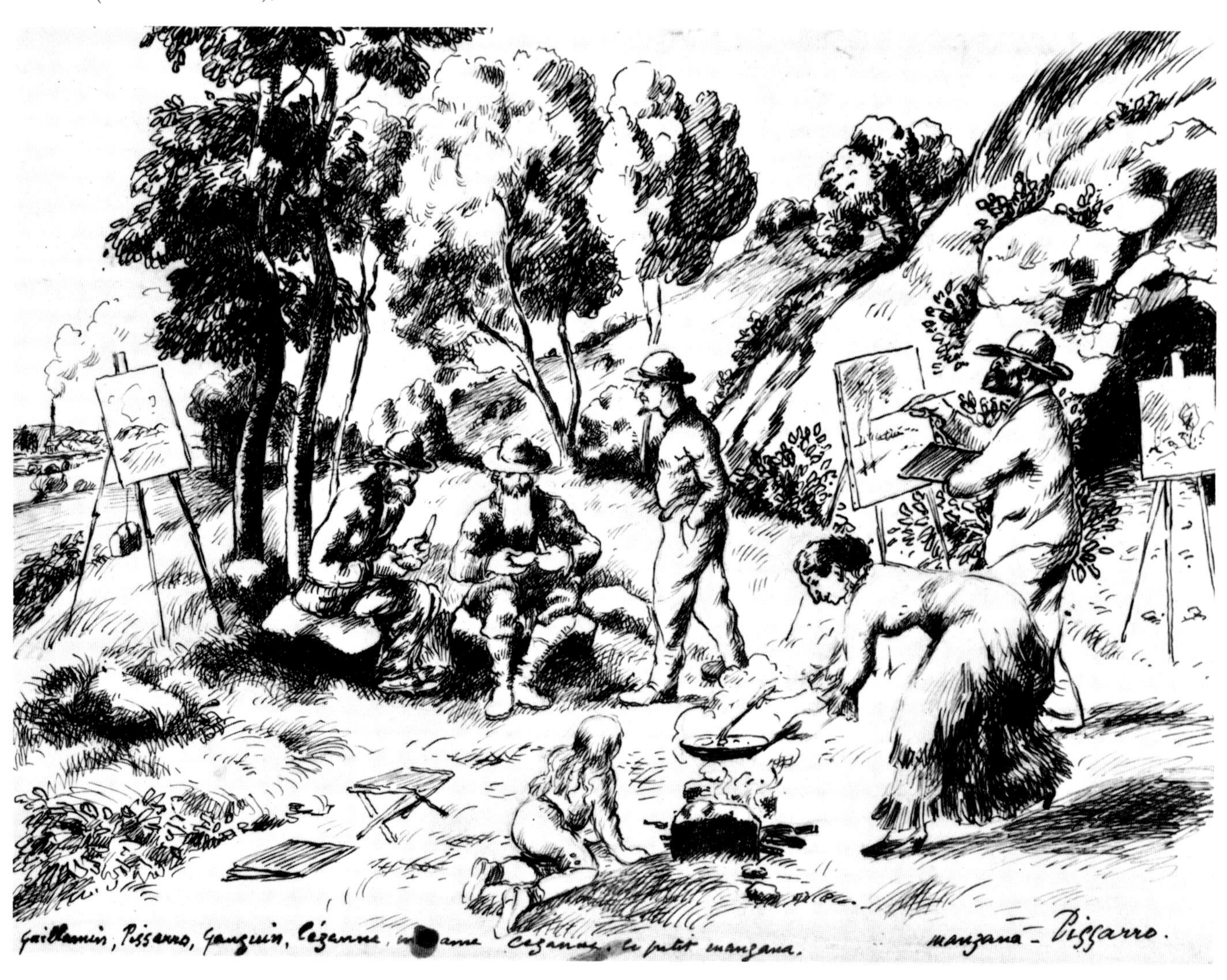

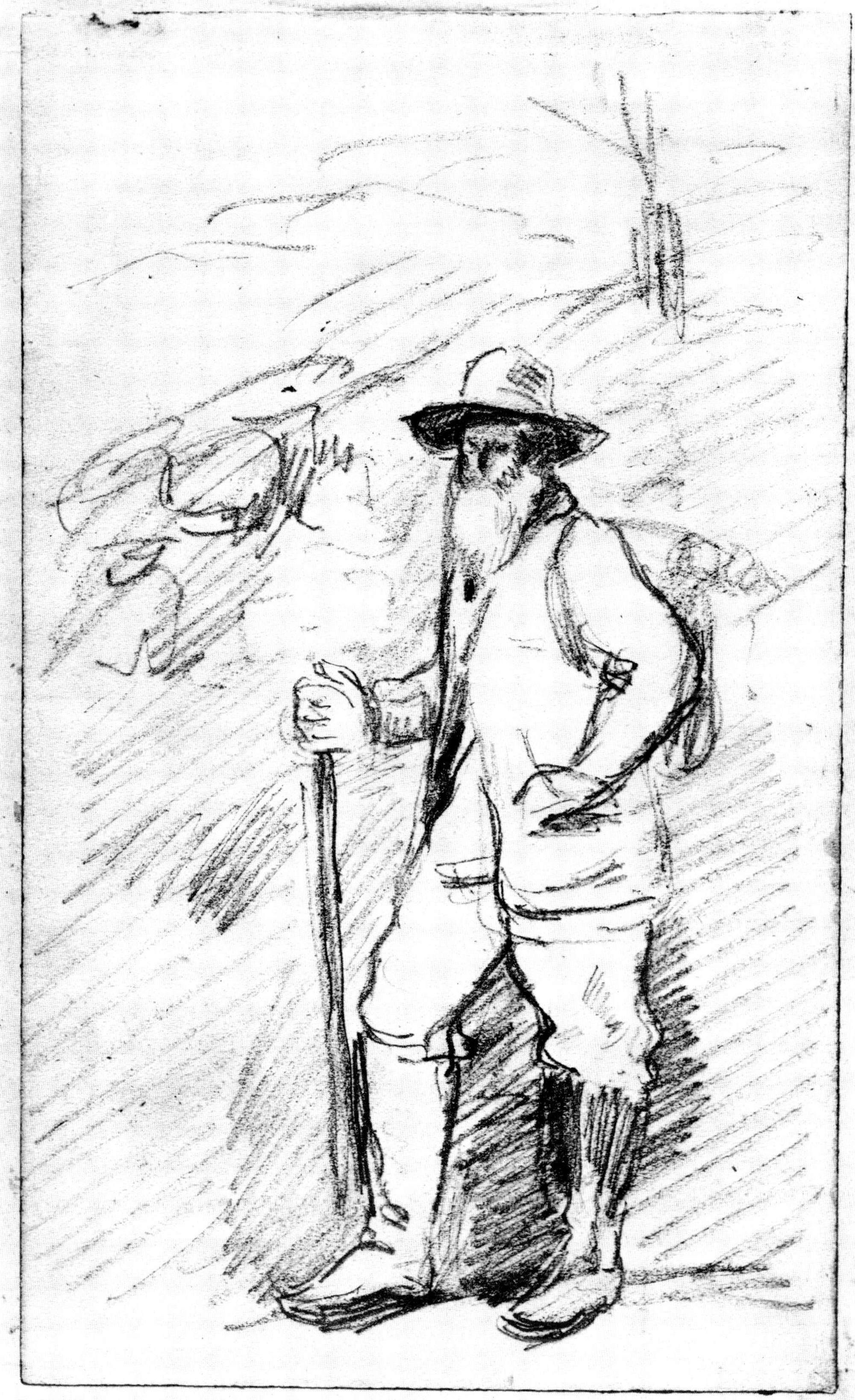

OPPOSITE *An Impressionist Picnic* in 1881, as seen by Manzana Pissarro, the child in the foreground. This remarkably accomplished drawing shows Guillaumin, Pissarro, Gauguin, Cézanne (painting) and Madame Cézanne in the countryside, with the gasworks chimney of Pontoise in the distance. (Courtesy André Watteau, Paris.)
RIGHT Paul Cézanne: *Pissarro on His Way to Work*, pencil drawing, *c.* 1874 (Musée du Louvre, Paris). Pissarro and Cézanne frequently worked in the countryside near Pontoise, often painting the same subject.

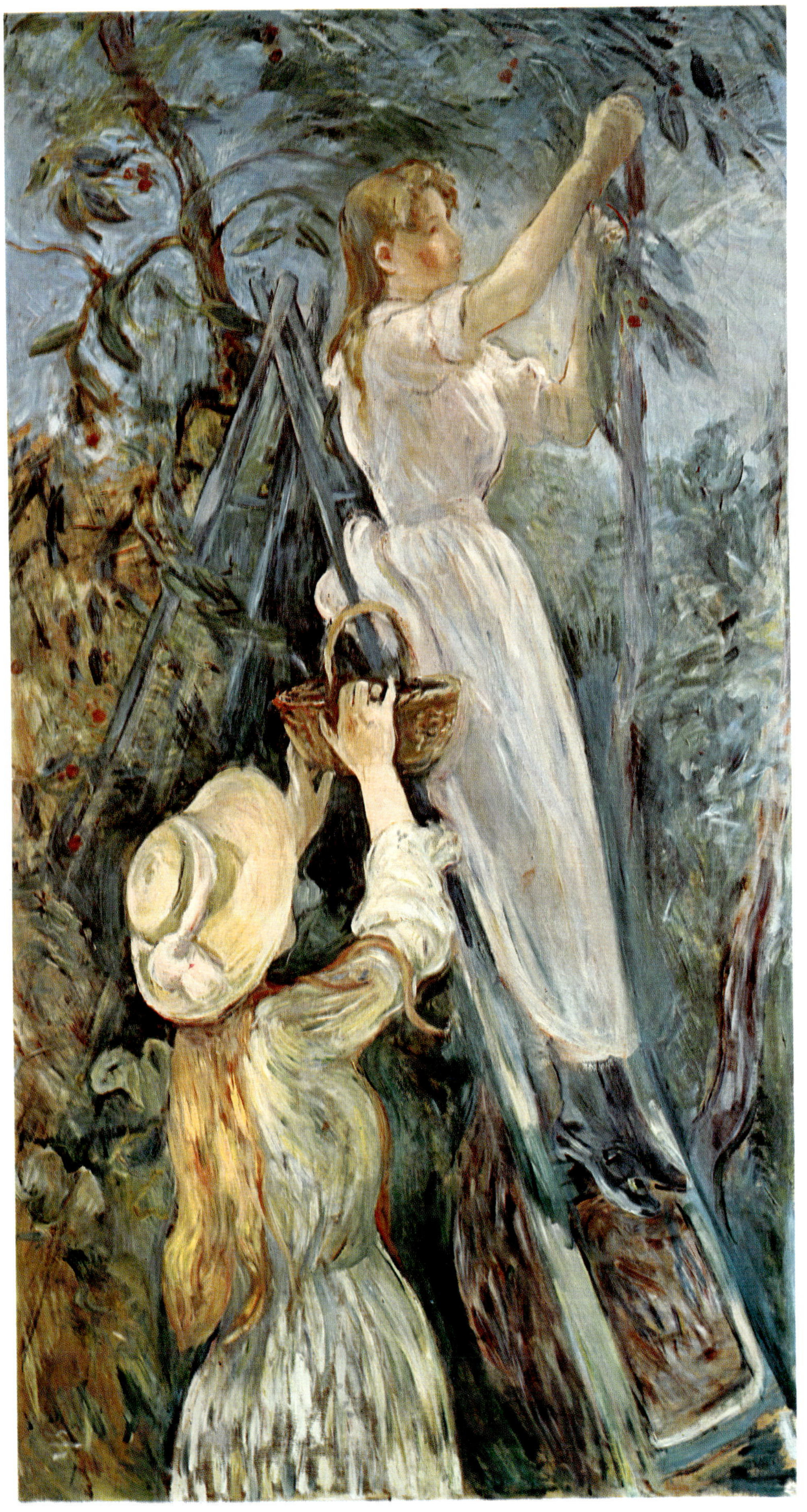

LEFT Berthe Morisot: *The Cherry Tree*, 1890 (Rouart Collection). The games and pastimes of her daughter Julie provided Morisot with inspiration for most of the paintings she executed at Mézy during the summers of 1890 and 1891.
OPPOSITE Camille Pissarro: *The Road to Rouen, Pontoise*, 1872 (Private Collection). One of the few examples where Pissarro forsakes his working peasant figures in favour of a better dressed mother and child going for a walk.

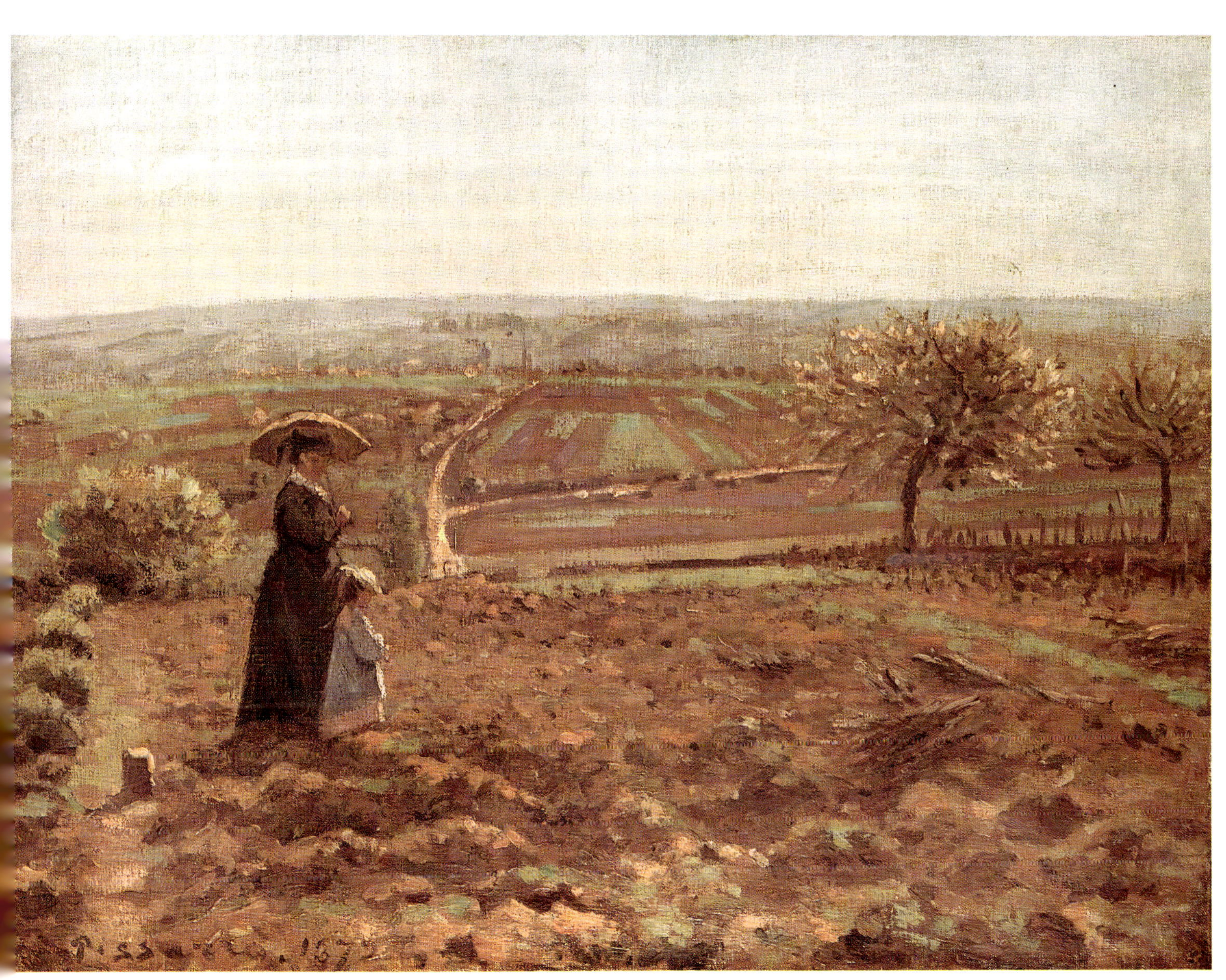

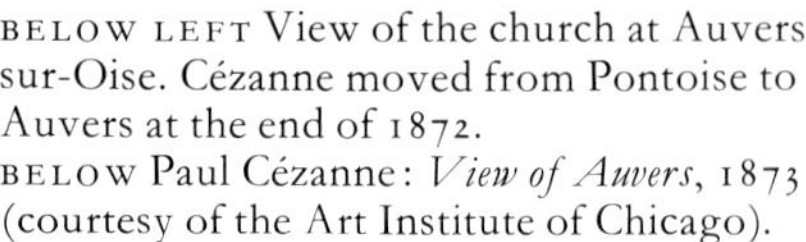

BELOW LEFT View of the church at Auvers-sur-Oise. Cézanne moved from Pontoise to Auvers at the end of 1872.
BELOW Paul Cézanne: *View of Auvers*, 1873 (courtesy of the Art Institute of Chicago).

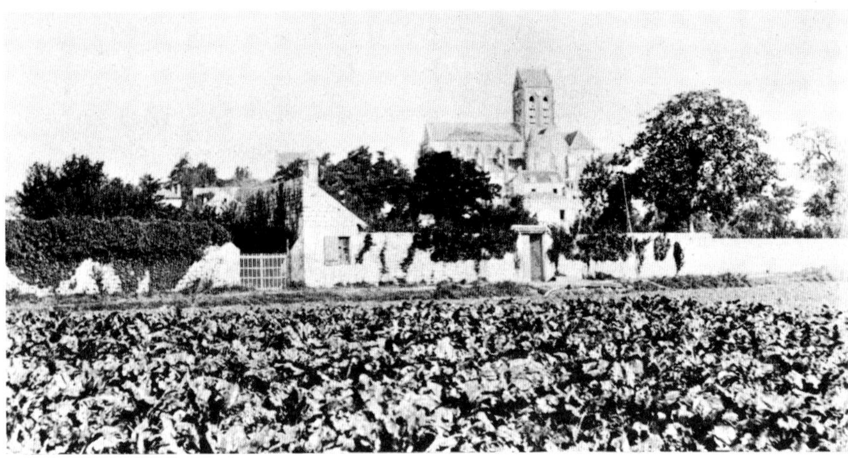

his compositions: the violent contrasts disappeared and his pigment became lighter, as though the inner confusion that had somehow prevented him from responding to light had begun gradually to dissipate in the open air.

At the end of the year, the restless Cézanne moved from Pontoise to the nearby village of Auvers-sur-Oise, drawn there perhaps by the eccentric Dr Gachet. The doctor had been an habitué of the cafés and brasseries frequented by the Impressionists ever since he had left Montpellier, at whose famous medical school he had qualified. He adored avant-garde art, and was himself an enthusiastic amateur engraver (he even installed his own press at home). Dr Gachet knew most of the Impressionists, bought their paintings, and on occasion gave them medical treatment. And his villa overlooking the valley of the Oise was always an open house to them.

Cézanne used his press to produce two engravings that are quite unique in his *oeuvre*: *Portrait of Guillaumin* and *Landscape on the Banks of the Oise*. He also painted *The House of Dr Gachet*, which shows the doctor's house at the top of a road that curves up a hill towards the horizon. A little farther along the same street, Cézanne depicted a small thatched house, *La Maison du Pendu*, a work of romantic inspiration and light colours, in which he used a genuinely Impressionist technique for the first time. *The House and the Tree*, *Village Street* and *The House of Père Lacroix at Auvers* are powerful, complex landscapes in which the painter attempts to strike a balance between his own emotions and a more objective vision of reality.

After an absence of several years, Cézanne joined Pissarro again at Pontoise in 1877, and produced *The Path at La Ravine*, *View from the Hermitage* and *La Côte des Boeufs*, which shows his considerable penchant for strongly visualized volumes. In 1881 he again spent the spring with Pissarro, this time also in the company of Paul Gauguin and his wife. As Hortense Fiquet had probably had to stay in Paris to look after their boy's schooling, Cézanne came alone. He was a difficult husband who seemed to dislike the constant presence of a woman. The bald, ill-kempt Cézanne looked much

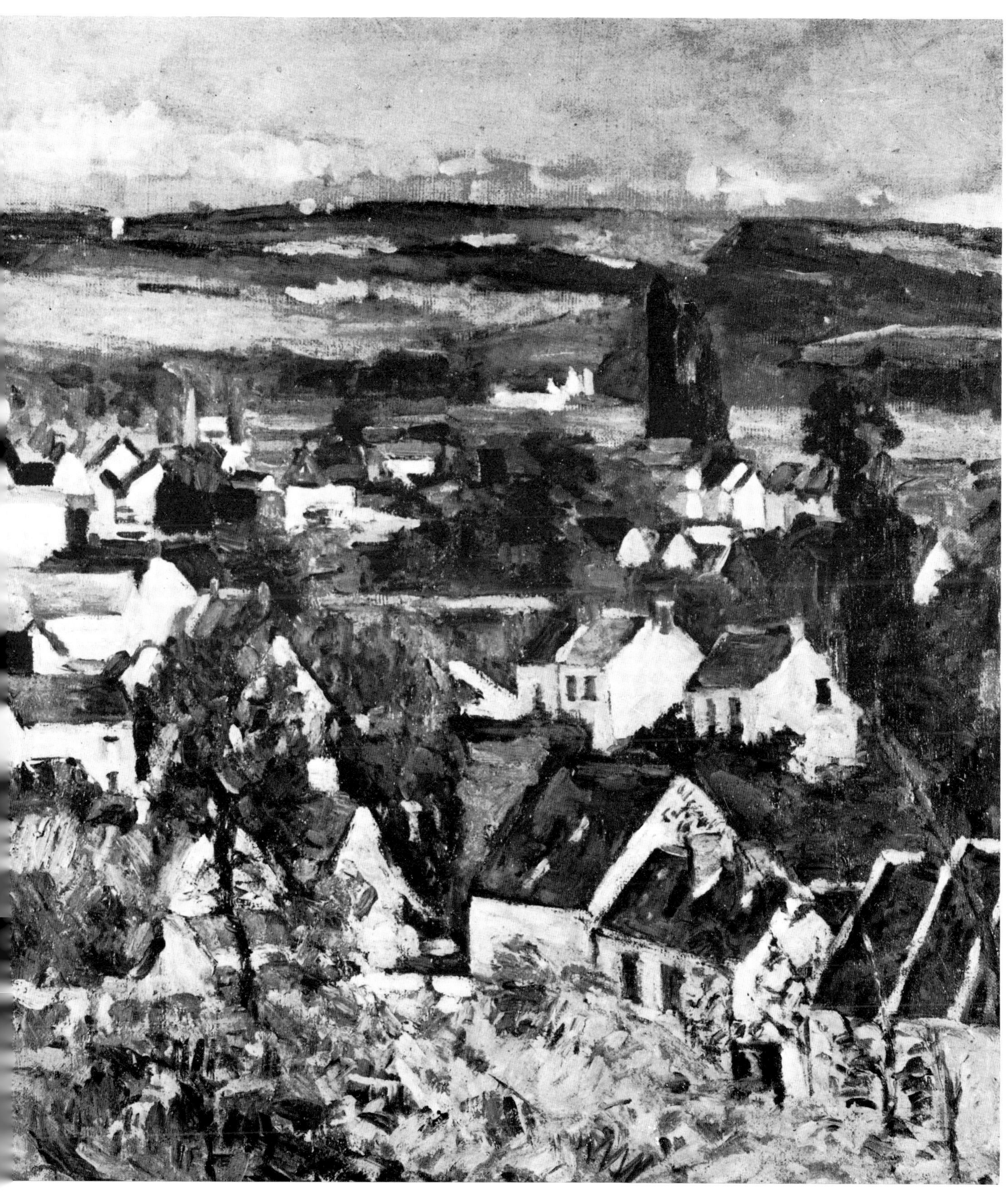

Paul Cézanne: *Le Château de Médan*, 1880 (Glasgow Art Gallery, Burrell Collection). Zola's house near the castle at Médan was at least fifteen kilometres from Pontoise, but this did not deter Cézanne from going on foot to visit his childhood friend.

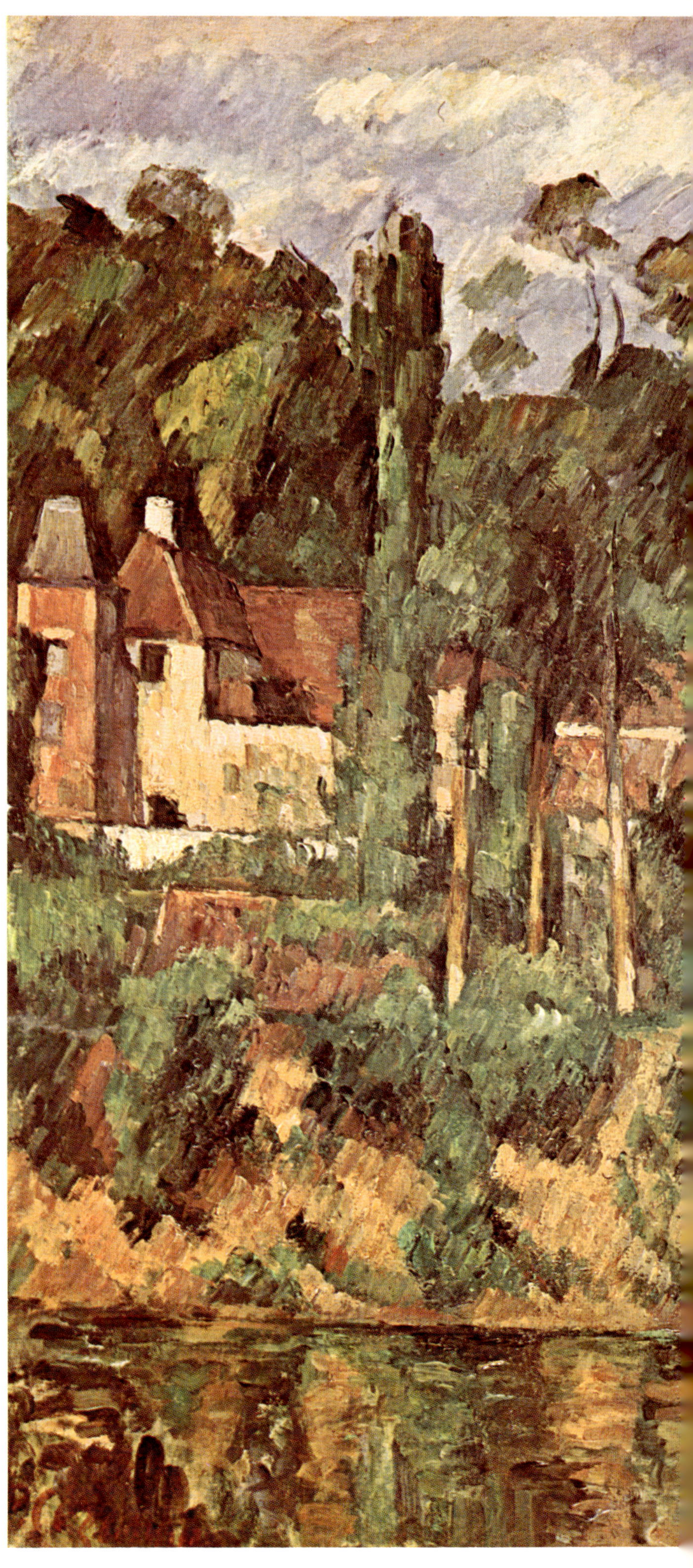

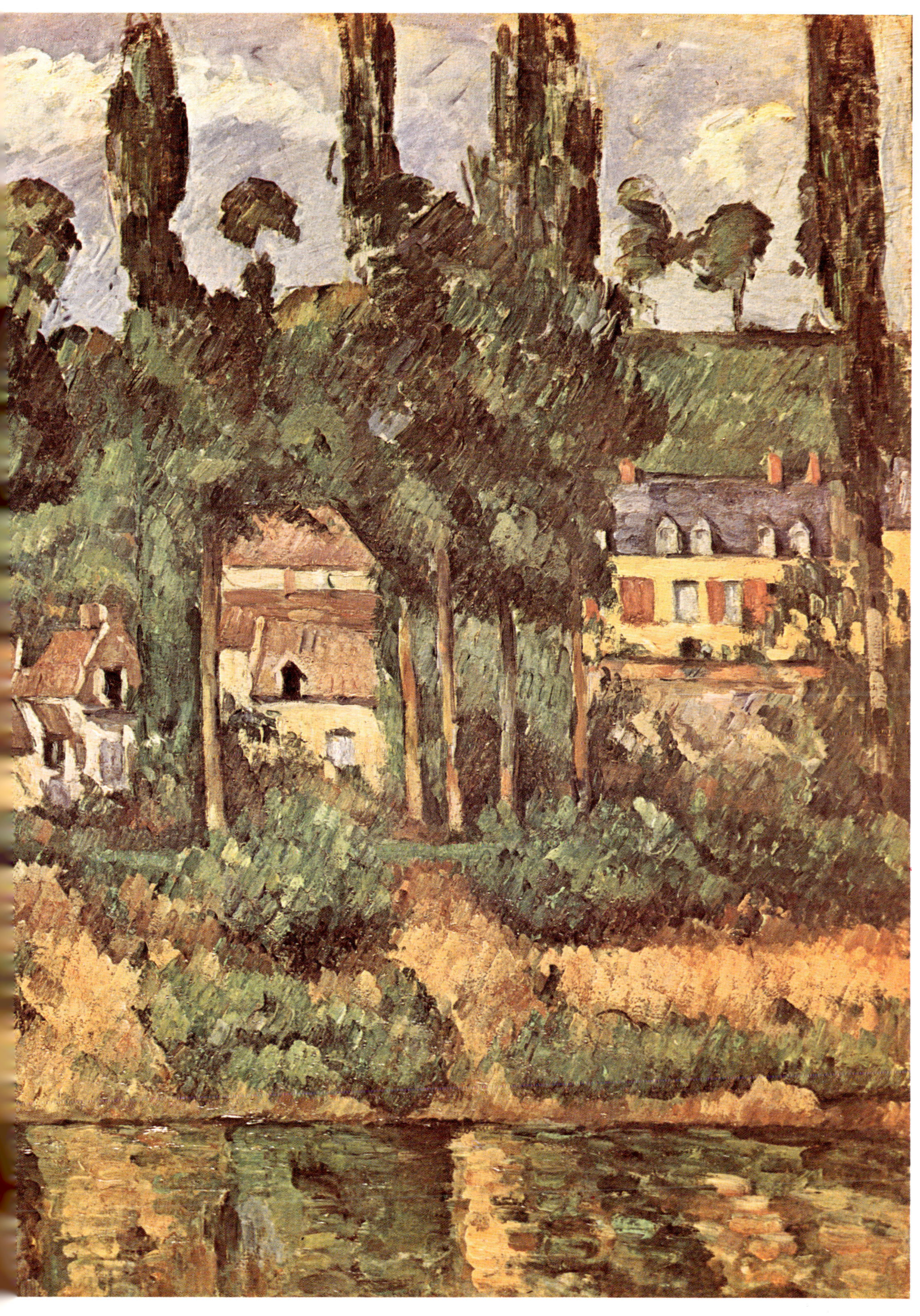

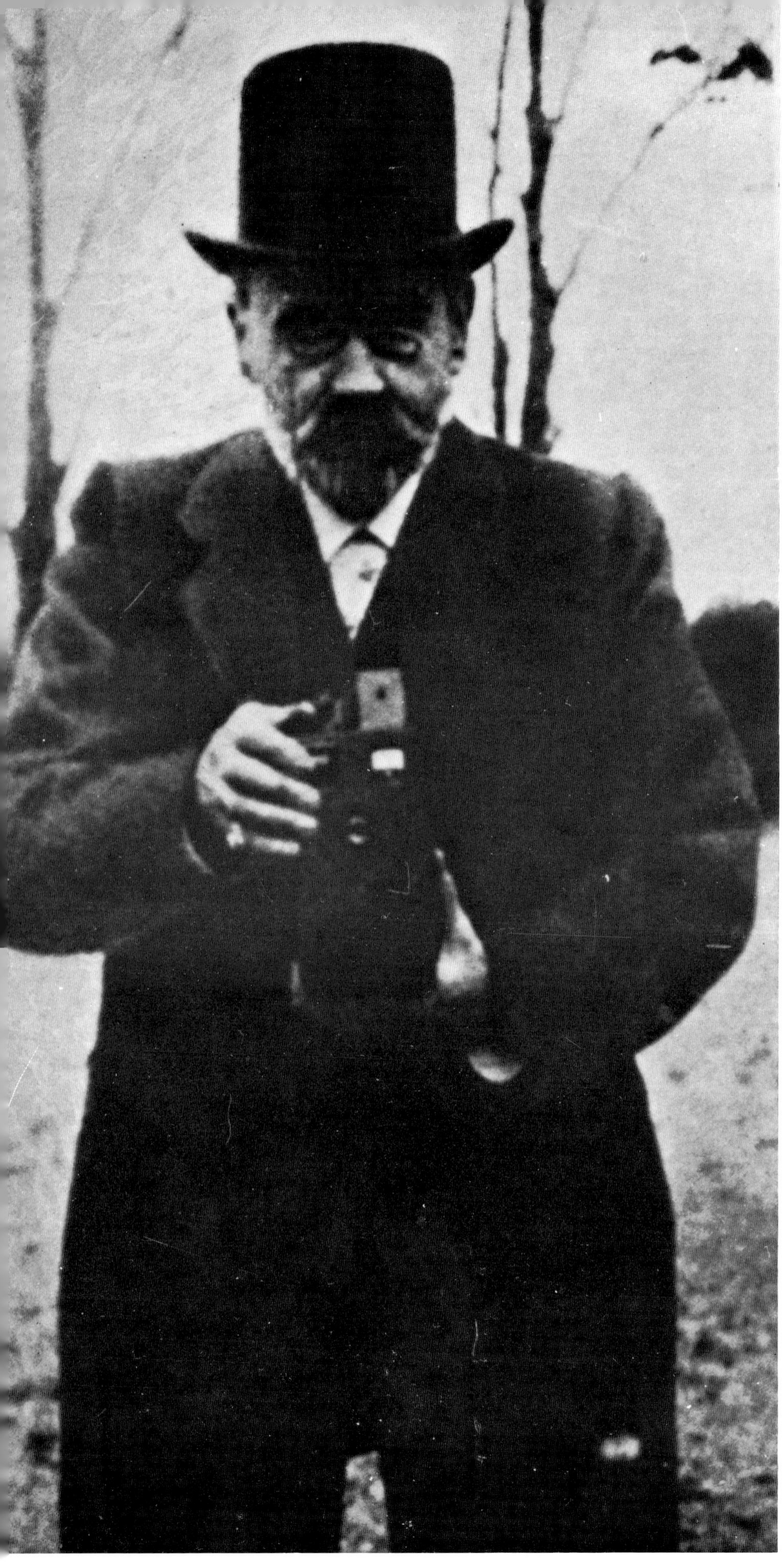

LEFT Zola, a keen photographer, behind the camera.
BELOW A wide-angle view of Médan taken by Zola.

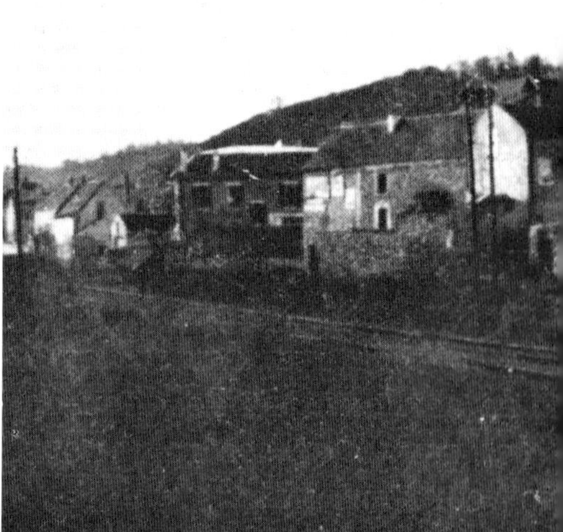

older than his age (fifty-one), but was energetic enough to get great pleasure out of walking fifteen kilometres to Médan to see his friend Zola.

The Vexin and its environs continued to attract Cézanne for many years to come. In 1885, he burst in on the Renoirs at La Roche-Guyon with an obsessive problem on his mind. Cézanne was at that time madly in love with a mysterious woman to whom he had written a passionate love letter on the back of a drawing – almost as though he wanted unconsciously to leave a trace of his passion. So desperate was he for a reply, which Zola was to

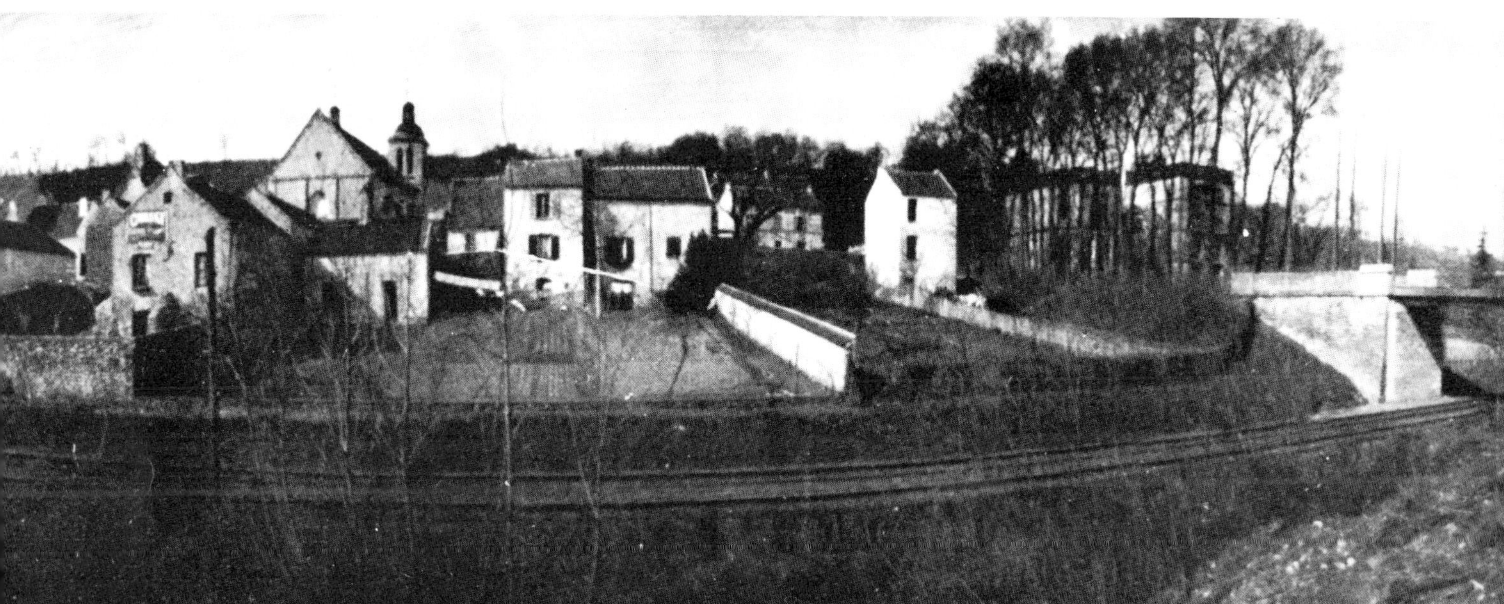

forward to him at the poste restante, that his nerves were completely in shreds. The intensity of his love was so overwhelming that he could no longer control himself. The panic-stricken Hortense Fiquet and her bewildered young son Paul sought solace from the Renoirs, who were helpless to do anything. This passion, which was unprecedented in Cézanne's life, gradually subsided as it emerged that there would never be any requital. And he returned to his first and only love: painting.

In 1899, at Montgeroult and Marines, Cézanne found that little had changed in that greenest of regions, which had provided him with such different subjects from his native Provence. But he had by then completely lost touch with Pissarro, whose style had, in his opinion, changed for the worse, and he did not go to visit him.

Cézanne and Pissarro were frequently joined in Pontoise by Armand Guillaumin, who had met them both at Suisse's studio in 1863, where he would come to draw whenever he had any spare time from his job as a civil

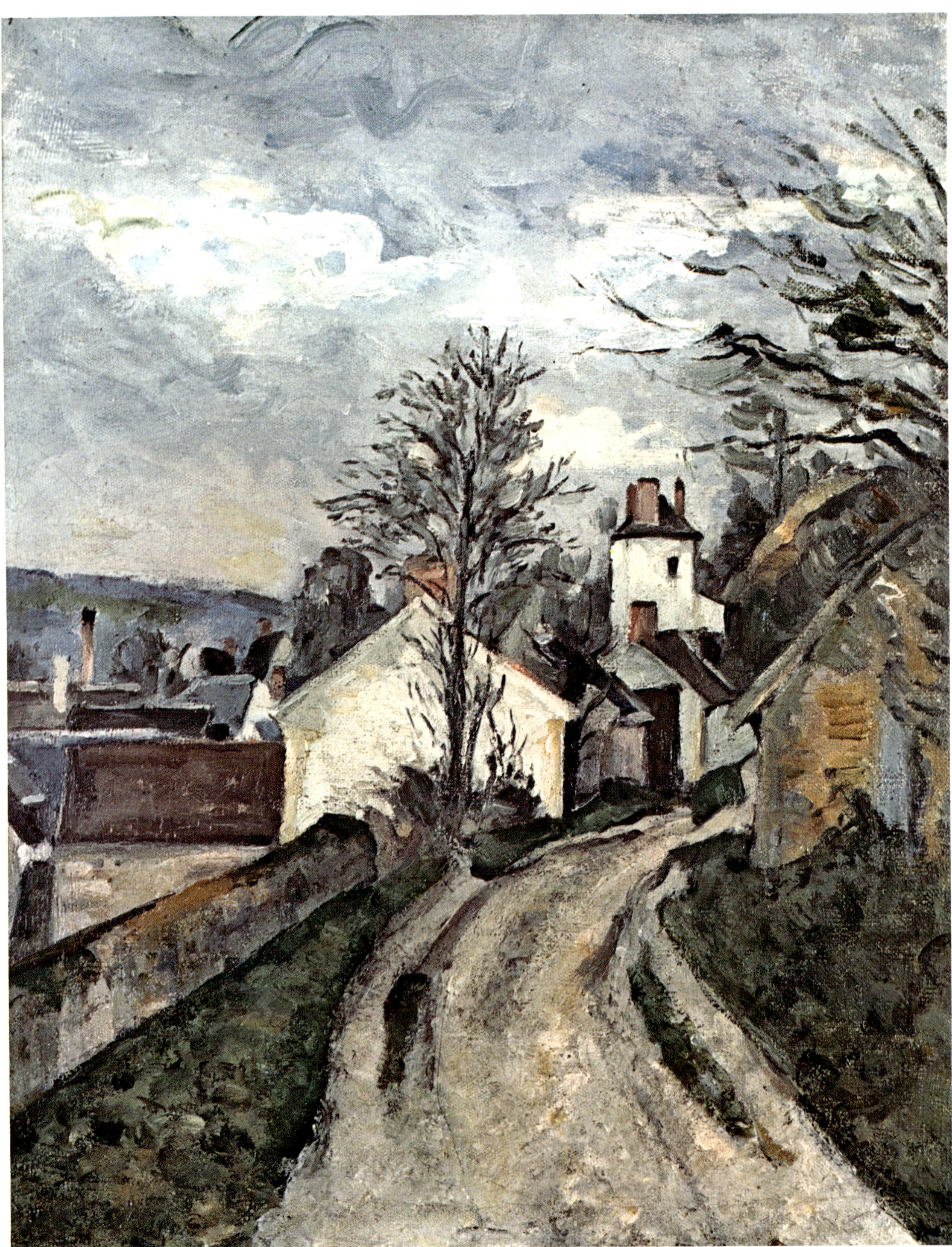

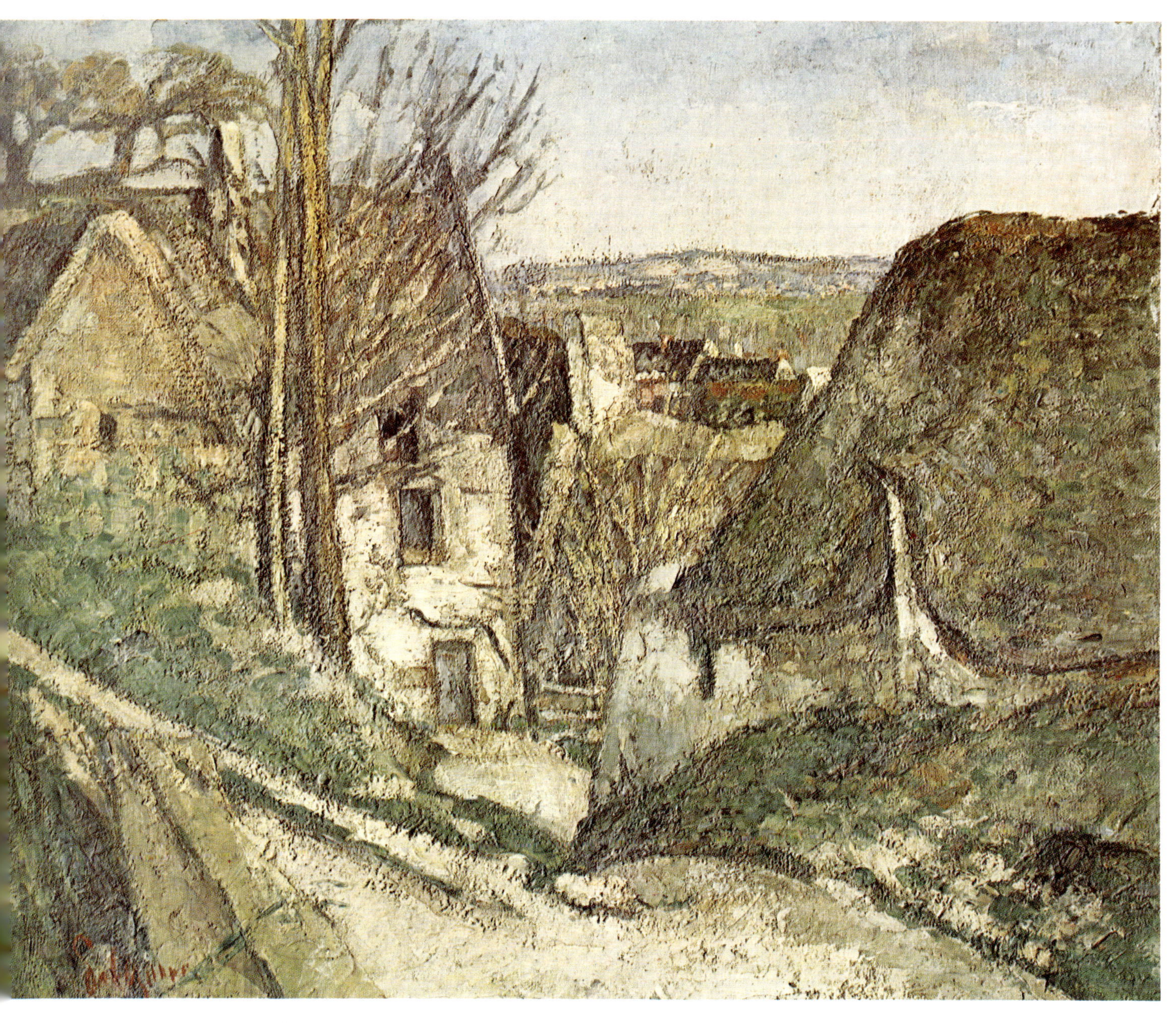

OPPOSITE Paul Cézanne: *The House of Dr Gachet*, 1873 (Musée du Louvre, Paris). Paul Gachet, nicknamed 'Dr Saffron' because of his dyed hair, was an enthusiastic admirer of the Impressionists. His house at Auvers was open to all artists, and Cézanne, Pissarro and Guillaumin went to work there.
ABOVE Paul Cézanne: *La Maison du Pendu*, 1873 (Musée du Louvre, Paris). It was at Auvers-sur-Oise, where a few old thatched cottages were still standing, that Cézanne painted his first truly Impressionist work. It infuriated the public when it was shown at the group's first exhibition in 1874.

servant in the Department of Civil Engineering. Guillaumin, who came from a poor family, had lost his parents very young, and had to support his grandparents. So he was unable to devote himself as completely as he would have liked to his painting. All his life he remained on very good terms with most of the Impressionists, but above all with Cézanne and Pissarro. When, in 1872, he was sent to the Vexin to supervise the sinking of public drains, he worked three nights a week and spent the rest of his time with a paintbrush in his hand. Cézanne, like Pissarro, admired Guillaumin and copied one of his Paris landscapes, *The Seine at Bercy*, for Guillaumin, although only marginally an Impressionist, expressed his own very personal vision of the world with undoubted talent.

In 1881, Paul Gauguin arrived at Pontoise with his young Danish wife, Mette. The couple had come to share Pissarro's frugal and simple life for a few days, although Gauguin could have afforded to go to an expensive

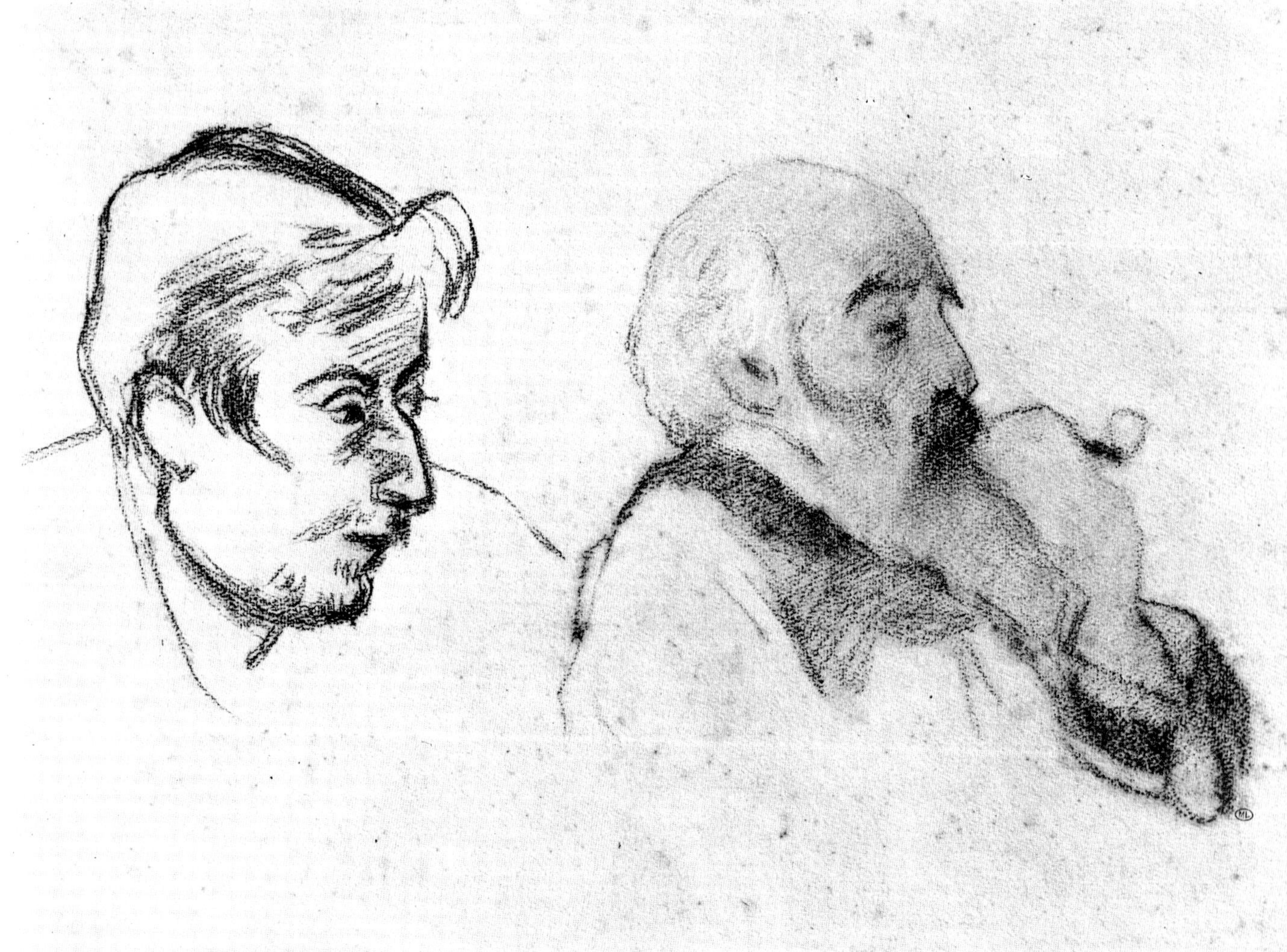

Camille Pissarro: *Portrait of Gauguin*; Paul Gauguin: *Portrait of Pissarro*, pencil, *c.* 1881 (Musée du Louvre, Paris). Gauguin stayed on several occasions with Pissarro, who gave him advice and encouragement.

resort. It was a great honour for the young man, as he himself fully realized, to work in the company of his elder.

Gauguin had met Pissarro several years before, as we have seen, at his godfather Achille Arosa's house, and he had felt immediately attracted by the older painter's upright and generous personality. Gauguin was a Sunday painter of some dexterity – one of his pictures had been accepted for the Salon of 1876 – but he was dissatisfied with himself, lacked self-confidence, and was eager to make progress.

Their working sessions in the open air, the long conversations in the course of which Pissarro would unstintingly pass on his experience and bestow advice, as well as the example of Cézanne, who was gradually managing to structure his compositions, taught Gauguin a great deal that he was never to forget. He direly needed someone to guide him at that point, and Pissarro was an ideal mentor. So in the spring of 1883, when his growing interest in painting looked very much as though it was going to swamp everything else, Gauguin went back to Pissarro for advice.

Yet although he addressed Pissarro as 'my dear master' in his correspondence, Gauguin was unable totally to repress his natural sense of irony, as can be judged from a letter which he sent Pissarro on his return to Paris in 1881, and which amused its recipient while alarming Cézanne. 'Has Monsieur Cézanne found the exact formula for a work that is accepted by all and sundry?' he wrote. 'If he has found the recipe for telescoping the exaggerated expression of all his sensations into a single device, then please try to get him to blurt it out in his sleep by giving him one of those mysterious homeopathic drugs, and come post-haste to Paris and tell us all about it.' This harmless joke about something that was no doubt constantly on Cézanne's lips resulted in making him extremely mistrustful of Gauguin: Cézanne suspected him of wishing to steal his 'little sensation', as he modestly described his prodigious originality.

At the end of 1882, Pissarro moved from the Oise valley to Osny, a little village on the River Viosne. Although the countryside was virtually the same as in Pontoise, his professional eye spotted some new subjects for masterpieces: *Bridge on the Viosne*, *The Little Bridge* and *La Rue de Pontoise*. He stayed there only about a year. After a visit to Rouen, Pissarro began to look for a new place to live. He found it difficult to make up his mind, and investigated every nook and cranny of the Val d'Oise. 'I went to L'Isle-Adam, to see the house with the large garden,' he wrote to his son Lucien, who was in London. 'I find the place horrible – long, long streets, dismal walls, silly bourgeois houses . . .' A few days later, he was eighty kilometres from Paris, in Compiègne, 'a boring, bourgeois, pompous place, a much duller, smaller version of Versailles'. We then find him to the north of

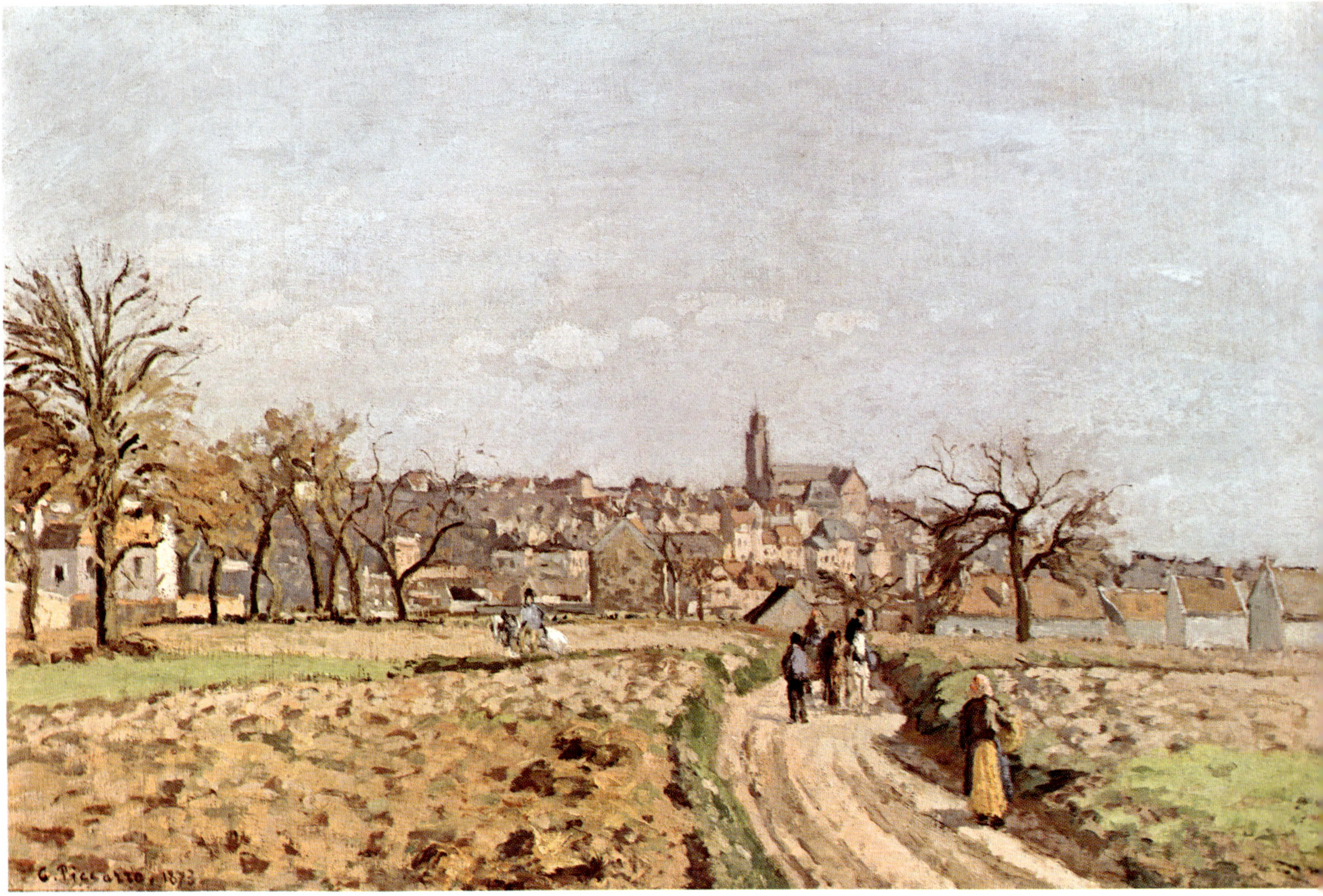

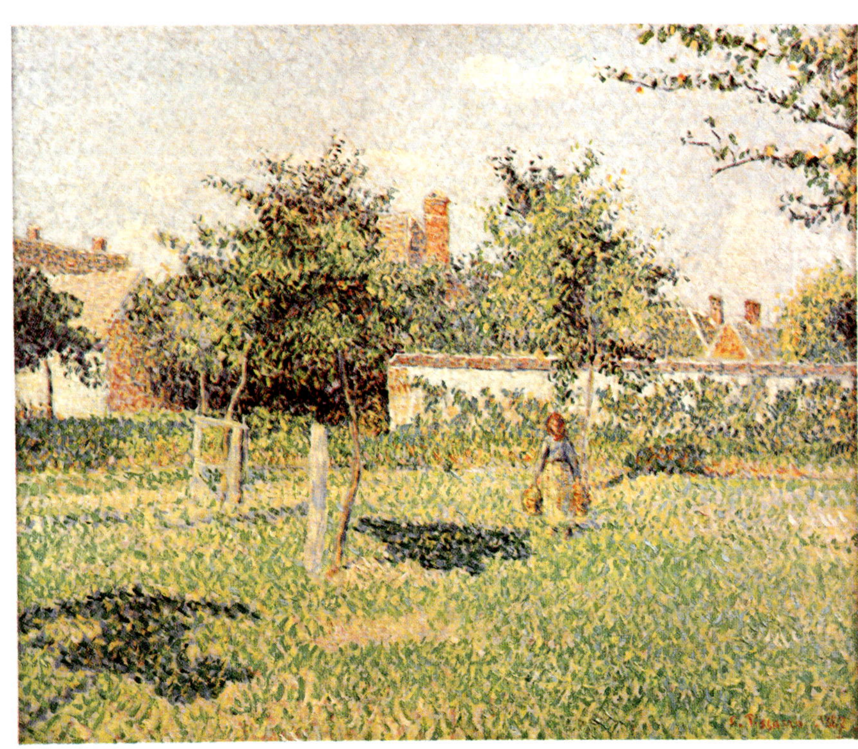

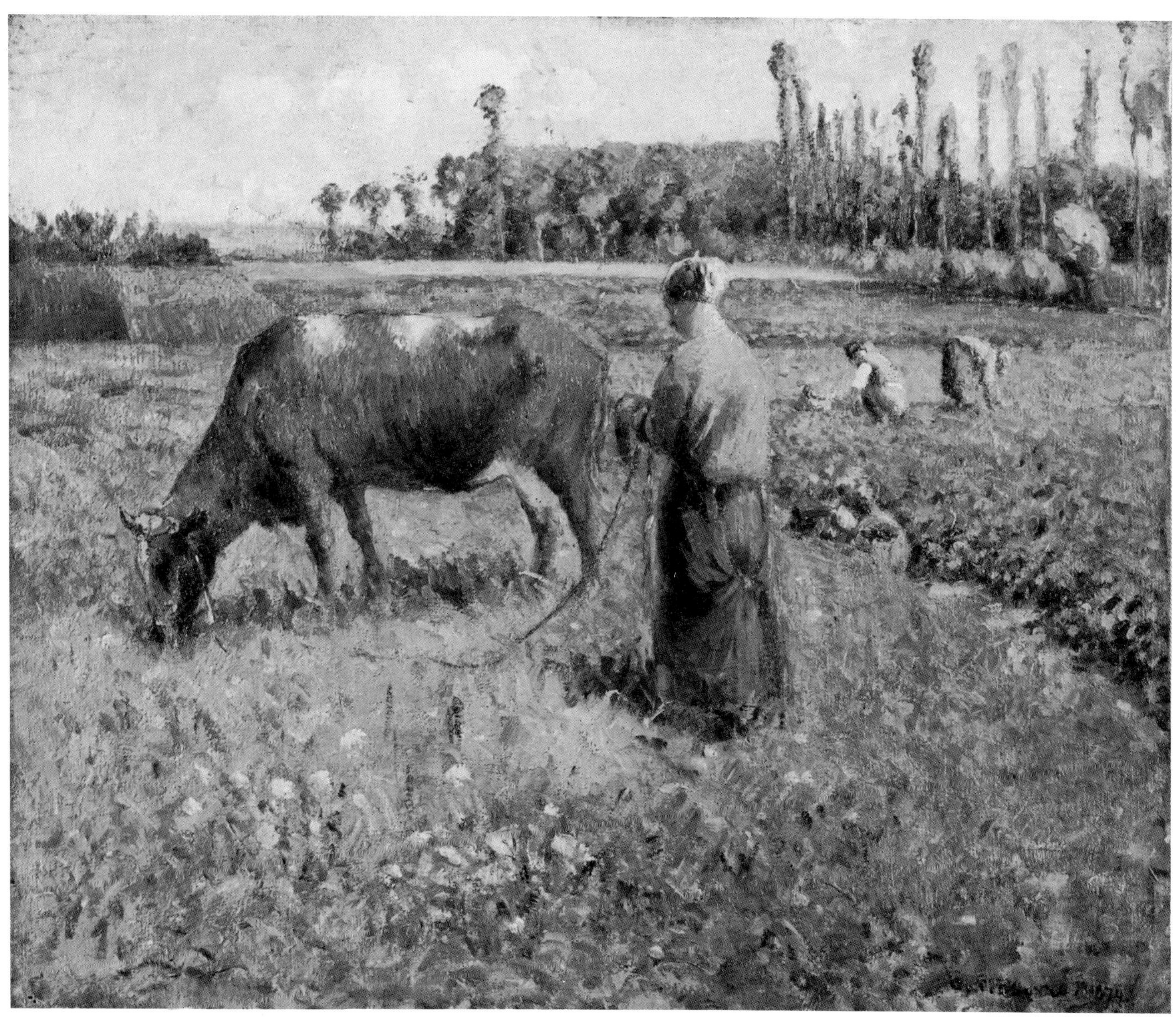

OPPOSITE ABOVE Camille Pissarro: *View of Pontoise*, 1873 (Private Collection).
OPPOSITE BELOW Camille Pissarro: *Woman in an Orchard*, 1887 (Musée du Louvre, Paris – Jeu de Paume.
ABOVE Camille Pissarro: *Woman Guarding a Grazing Cow*, 1874 (Private Collection). 'I have started to do figures and animals. I have several genre paintings, but I am venturing timidly into this field of art which has been distinguished by artists of the first order' – Pissarro to Duret.

Pontoise, in Gisors, a town he liked so much he stayed three days, 'wonderful differences of ground level, a few old streets and three little rivers full of interesting subjects'. But he could not find anything there that suited him, and in the end opted for Eragny-sur-Epte, just nearby, where he rented 'a superb house, and cheap at that: 1,000 francs with a garden and fields. It's two hours from Paris.' The artist, who later bought the house with money his wife borrowed from Monet, was to spend most of the last twenty years of his life there.

His seventh child, Paul-Emile, was born in that village at a time when Pissarro, then fifty-four years old, was entering one of the most tumultuous periods of his professional life. Dissatisfaction with Impressionism had plunged him into a long bout of depression. Once he had found a more

Camille Pissarro: *The Orchard*, 1879 (Musée du Louvre, Paris).

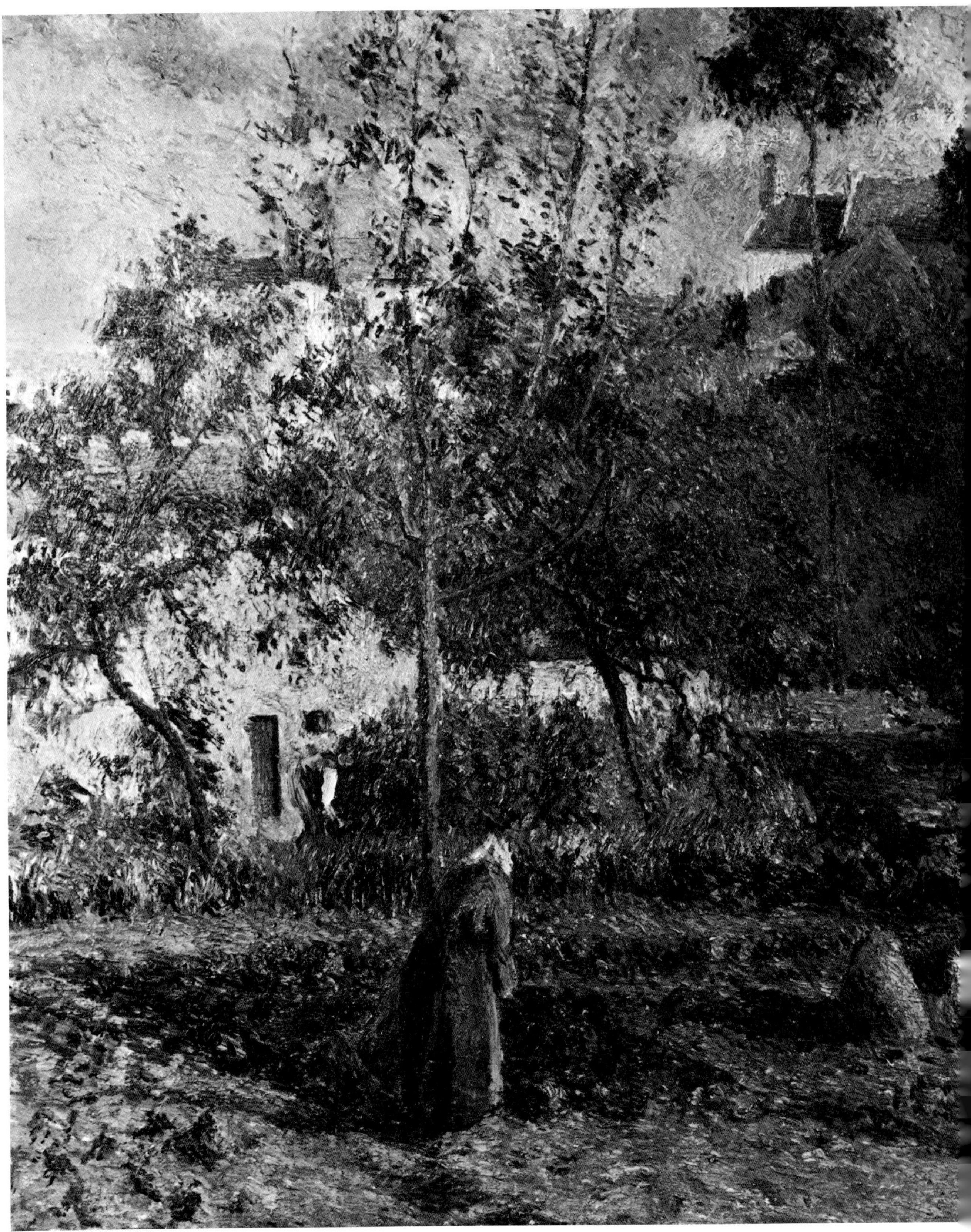

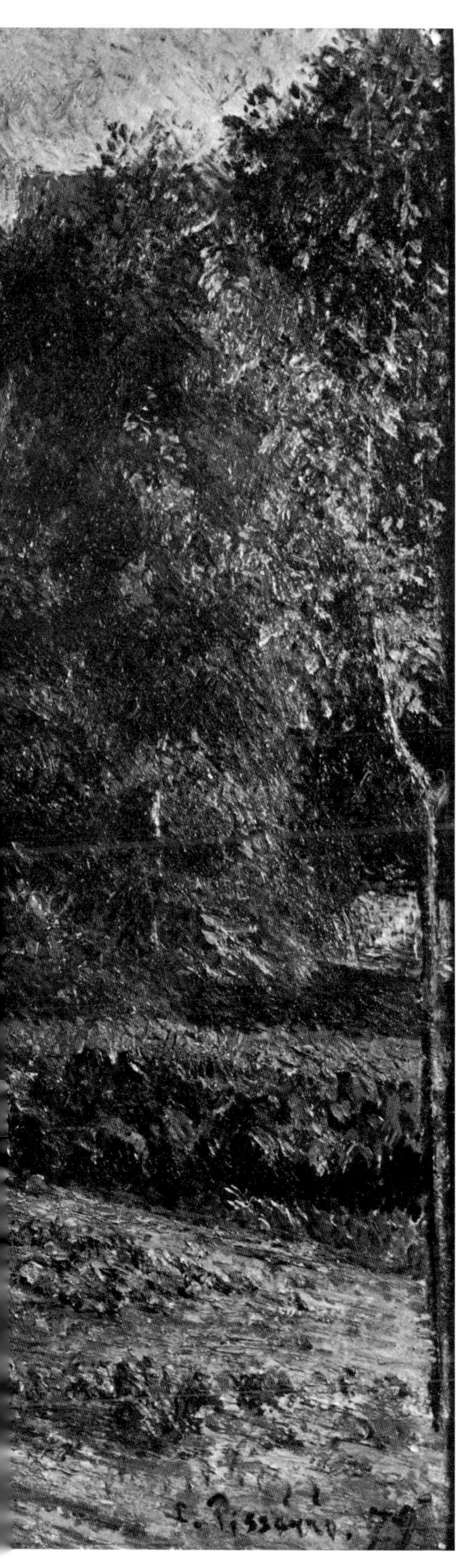

scientific basis for painting in the divisionist technique, however, his habitual enthusiasm came flooding back. He executed his first Pointillist pictures at Eragny, Gisors and the surrounding area. Although he was the eldest of the 'romantic Impressionists' – as he called his former colleagues – it was he who formed the link between the two generations. It was a difficult role: Pissarro again found himself going through a period of great financial need, as his new manner was not much appreciated. And his family life was not made much easier by the continuous complaining of his wife, who had to bear the daily brunt of their money problems. 'Your poor father is really an innocent. He doesn't understand the problems of life,' she wrote to her son Lucien. 'He knows I owe 3,000 francs, sends me 300, then tells me to wait. What can I do? There are eight of us to feed every day.' But Pissarro, driven on by his insatiable passion, continued to 'slog away furiously', as he put it. Even when he contracted an eye infection and was no longer able to paint outdoors, he sought out hotel and apartment rooms in Paris and Rouen from whose windows he could observe, well protected from the inclemency of the weather, 'nature's wonderful, fleeting effects'.

Vital as the Vexin, the banks of the Seine, Normandy and Fontainebleau were to the development of Impressionism, they were not, of course, exclusively so. Two of the greatest individual achievements were produced in quite other surroundings: in Cézanne's Provence and in the brilliant, vibrantly alive Paris captured, above all, by Degas.

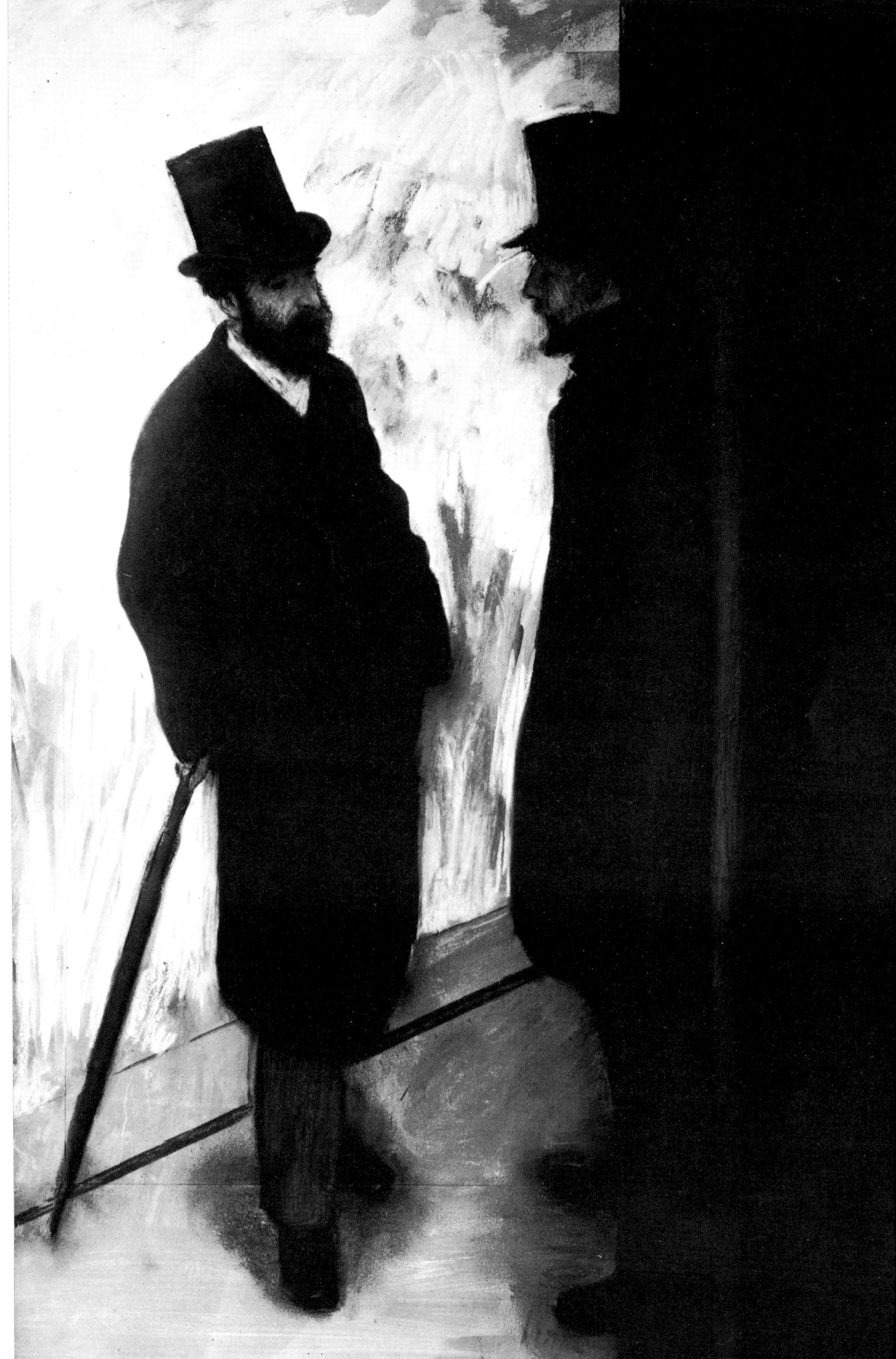

6 Paris

Capital of the Universe

Having provided a meeting-place, then a rallying-point, for the Impressionists, Paris continued to be vitally important in their lives and art. Clearly it was to Paris that they had to come for everything that would further their career. But the capital also had a place apart in their work. Berthe Morisot, Renoir, Pissarro and Monet have left memorable images of its charm and vitality behind. Even so, when one thinks of Paris of the time, it is Degas, the city's great visual poet, who comes first to mind.

Unlike most of his artist friends, Degas was fortunate enough to come from a wealthy family. As the son of a banker with an aristocratic pedigree, he moved in high society and in business circles. His father was more interested in music than in finance, and the young Edgar met many of the big names in the musical world. And no sooner had he made up his mind to become a painter than he was put in contact with all the most fashionable artists of the period. In his new enthusiasm, he seems to have been everywhere at once: in the Louvre, studying and copying the great masters; in the Luxembourg Museum, lost in admiration before paintings by Ingres; and at his friends', the Valpincons, who owned *La Grande Odalisque* (now in the Louvre).

Degas was also to be seen at the races at Longchamp, the finest, most modern racecourse in the world, haunt of the richest men and most illustrious beauties of the century. At Longchamp, he would continue work on drawings and sketches he had begun at the Valpinçons' stud at Le Ménil-Hubert, suggesting with just a few deft strokes of his pencil a volume, or the slender strength of a horse's articulation. He also worked in the studio of the sculptor Cuvelier, who specialized in equestrian portraits, so as to pick up the rudiments of an art that would enable him to model horses.

Towards noon – it was not done to be seen out and about before then on the fashionable *grands boulevards* – Degas would meet his smart friends and acquaintances at cafés such as Tortoni's, the Maison Dorée and the Café Anglais. In the evening, he would go up to Montmartre to the Brasserie des Martyrs or the Café Guerbois and listen to the enthusiastic discussions and theorizing of the rumbustious independent artists, who came from a social background completely different from his own. The heated arguments that set the champions of the various schools at each other's throats struck a chord in Degas' mind: his secret ambition, like theirs, was to depict the novelty of the contemporary world. The change had been particularly striking for Degas, who, having been brought up under the Restoration, was aged eighteen when, under Napoleon III, new notions of progress utterly changed the lives of the Parisians.

During the Second Empire, nobody could afford to miss one of those extravagant evenings in the sumptuously decorated restaurants of the Boulevards – neither the cocottes, who were always on the lookout for

Edgar Degas: *Ludovic Halévy at the Opera*, 1874 (D. Halévy Collection). The writer and librettist Halévy was Degas' lifelong friend.

potential protectors, nor the writers, journalists and artists who vied with each other in wit, inventiveness and sartorial elegance. Fashionable people went to concerts, to the Opera, to the theatre and to balls. The French of the period were gregarious, high-spirited and communicative, and their conversation sparkled with puns, jokes and witticisms. They were the envy of foreigners, the wealthier of whom came whenever they could to enjoy the imperial festivities in Paris, 'capital of the Universe'.

Degas, however, blamed himself for 'having the time neither to live nor to draw'. He was impatient to create: when his friend, the bassoonist Désiré Dihau, took him along to the Opera, Degas vowed that he would undertake a series of paintings 'on instruments and instrumentalists – their shape, the contortions of the violinist's hand, arm and neck, the cheeks of the bassoonists and oboists puffing and blowing. . . .' He succeeded brilliantly in putting across the originality of his vision in two remarkably powerful compositions. In *The Orchestra of the Opera*, the musicians' faces can be seen like pools of light shining forth from the orchestra pit, between their starched white shirts and the footlights, in a forest of bows pointing up towards the stage, which is alive with the ballet dancers' pink skirts and pale legs. In *Musicians of the Orchestra*, on the other hand, the contrast between the dark mass formed by the backs of the three musicians in the foreground and the dazzling pink light of the stage with its dancers is heightened by a variation of technique: the whole of the fully-lit area of the picture is painted very freely, whereas the darker parts are given a thicker, smoother application of colour.

The painter's attention was soon monopolized by the *corps de ballet* at the Opera: he was fascinated by the mysterious charm and graceful movements of the dancers. After a while the slim figure of Degas became a regular sight at rehearsals in the Rue Le Peletier, in the company of the portly bankers and rich tradesmen who flocked there to extend their protection to the dancing girls, who were usually working-class and had no security against the hazards of their profession. Degas, however, was more interested in discovering the secret of their arabesques, entrechats and other ballet positions. Ludovic Halévy, the painter's best friend, whom he had known since school, later wrote a novel, *La Famille Cardinale*, which described how the mother of one such ballet dancer, wishing to guarantee her daughter's fortune, sold her to a rich old man. When the book was republished in 1880 it was only natural that Degas should illustrate it with a magnificent series of monotypes.

As always when he approached a subject, Degas wanted to become familiar with every detail. He had to know everything about that 'dainty little collection of girls, with their *décolletés* and their silk and satin dresses', who spent the whole day leaping about in such a seemingly arcane way. He

OPPOSITE ABOVE Edgar Degas: *The Foyer de la Danse at the Rue Le Peletier Opera*, 1872 (Musée du Louvre, Paris). The composition of this painting, with its large area of empty floor and prominently placed chair, was strikingly original.

OPPOSITE BELOW Edgar Degas: *Rehearsal for a Ballet*, 1878–9 (Metropolitan Museum of Art, New York, H. O. Havemeyer Collection).

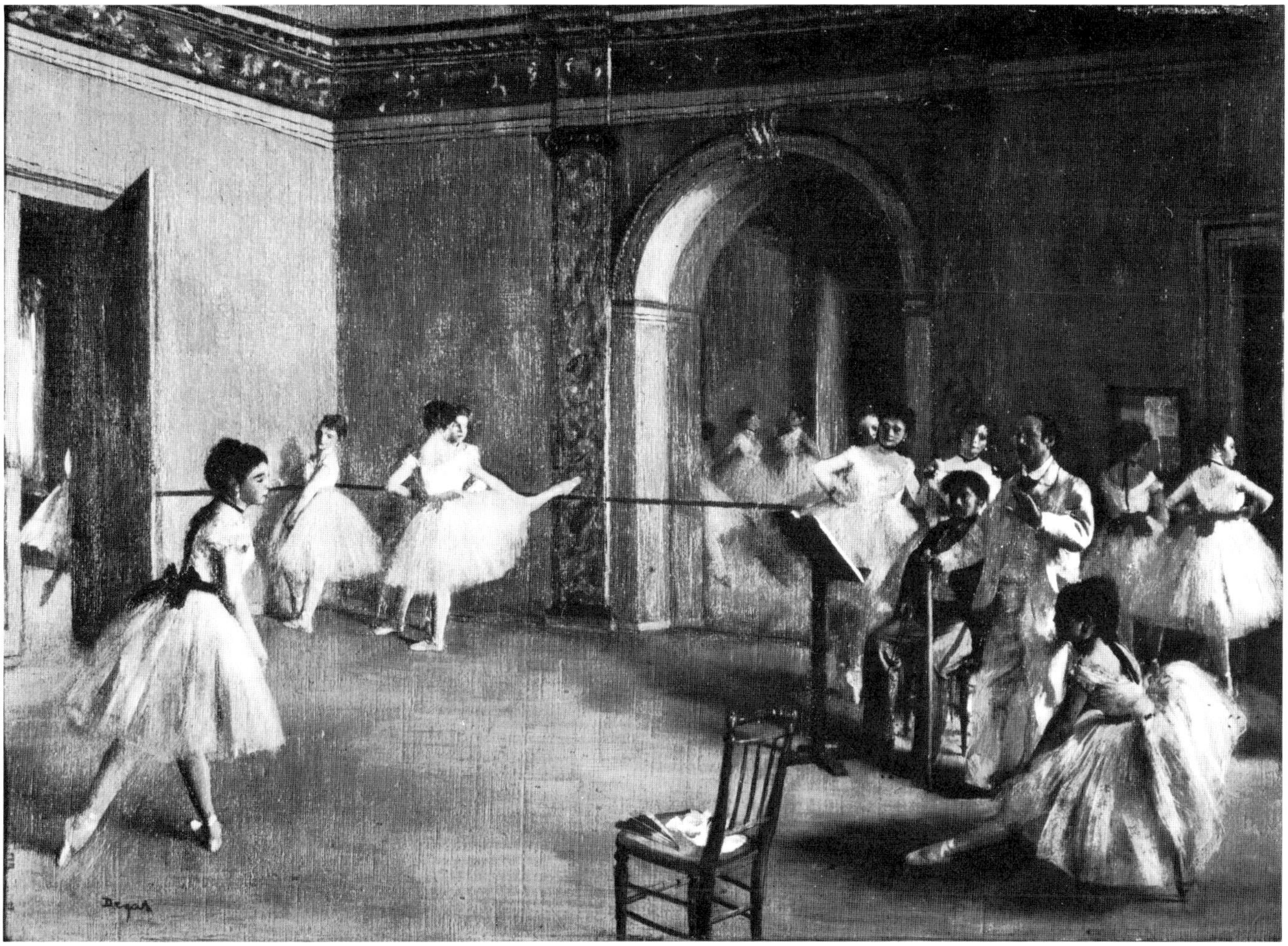

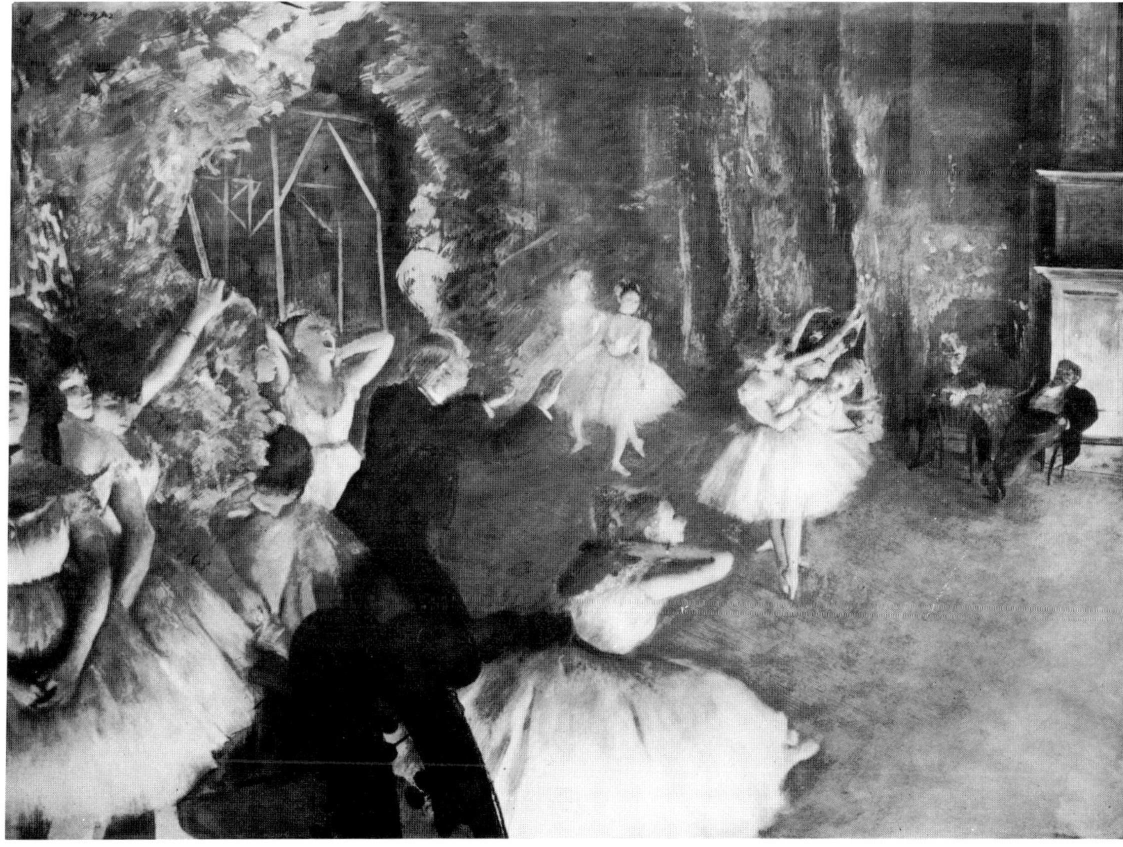

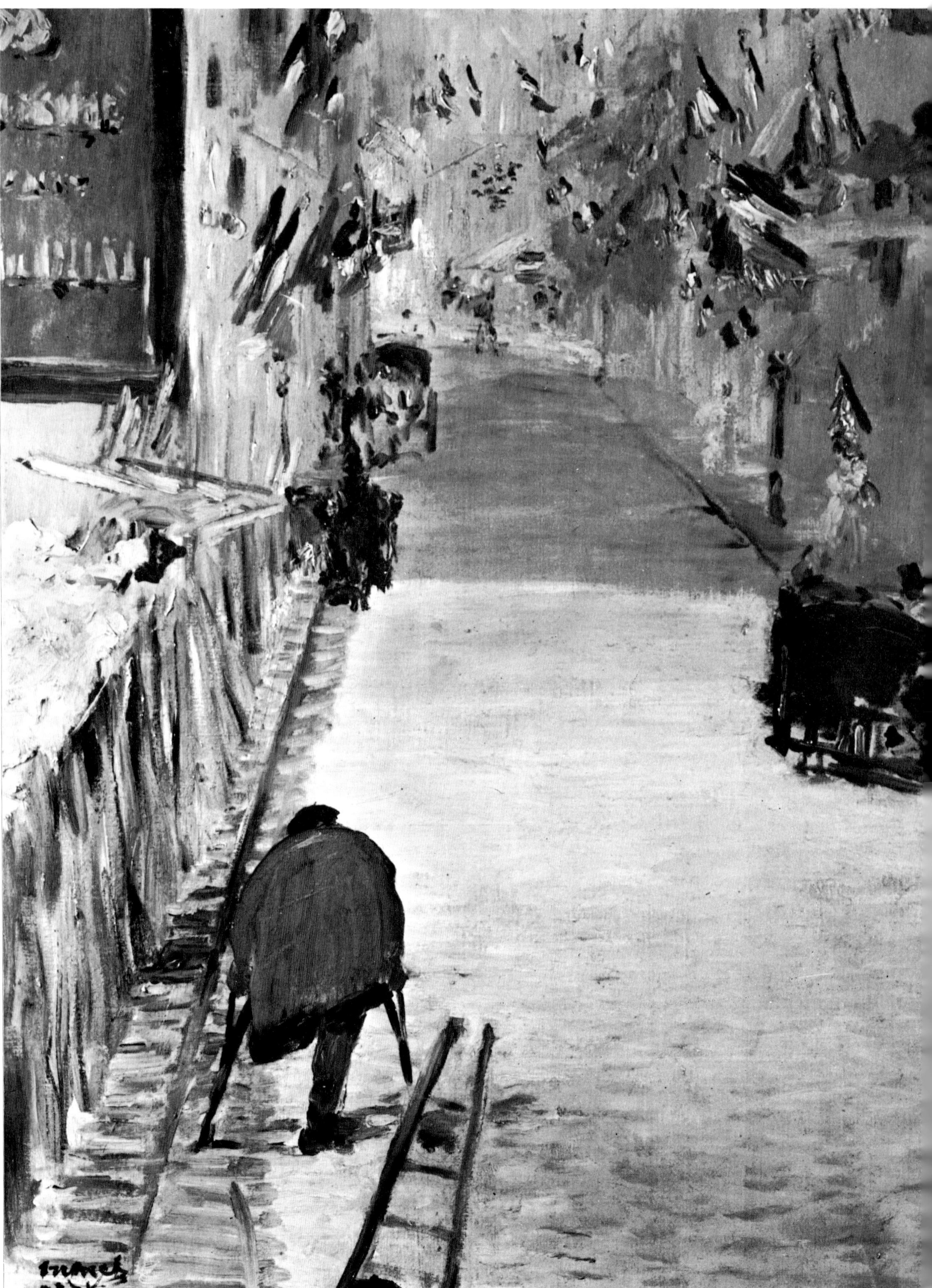

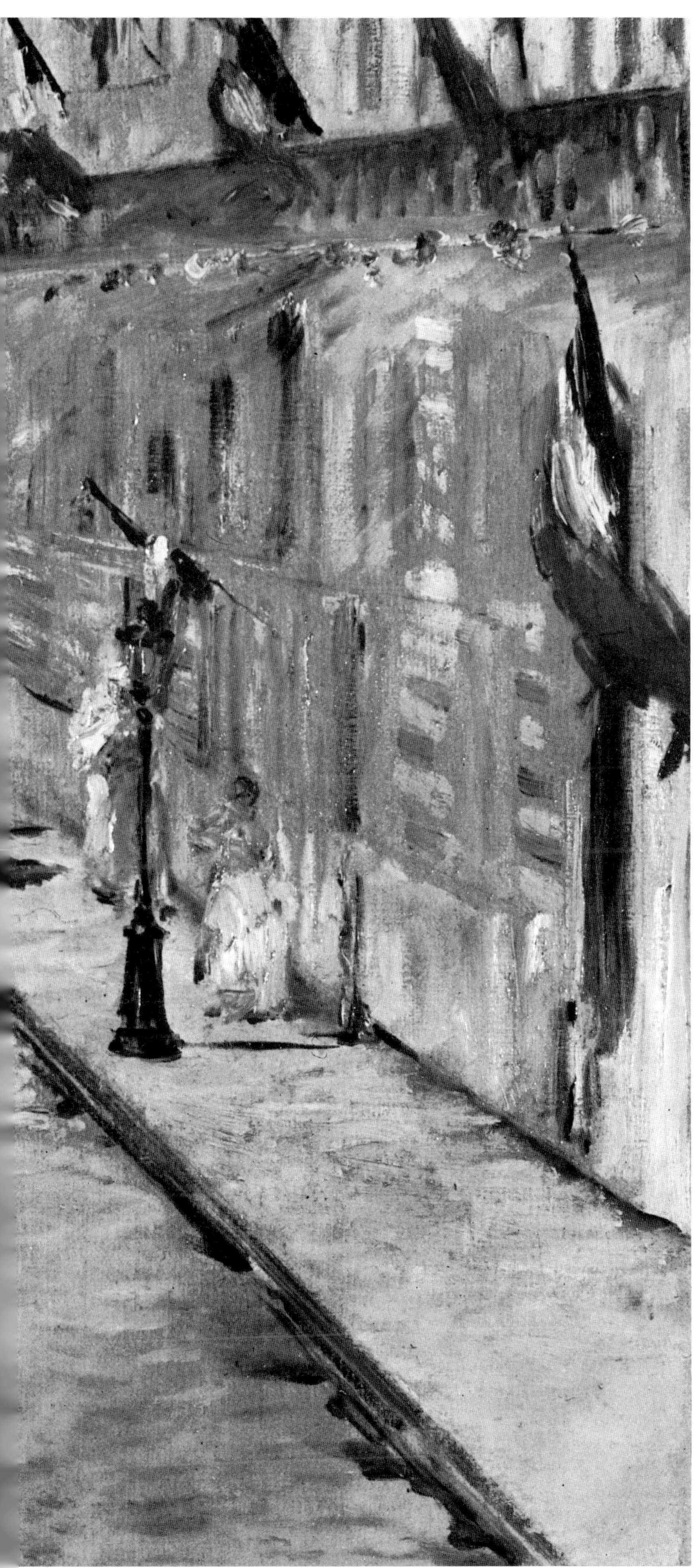

Edouard Manet: *Rue Mosnier with Flags*, 1878 (Goldschmidt Collection, Chicago). The view from Manet's studio of the Republic's first *Fête Nationale* since the Franco-Prussian War, on 30 June.

was everywhere – at rehearsals, at the Opera at performances, at exams. He even caught the dancers when they were resting in the greenroom. He dashed off hundreds of sketches on the spot, and filled notebook after notebook with accurate details of what he had observed:

> Whole theatre dark, with huge green and grey covers on the boxes and stalls. Six large reflectors in the entasis of the orchestra. They begin. The men in little black or blue jackets, short trousers, white stockings. Look like little boys. Monsieur Mérante stands playing the violin, extremely out of tune . . . It's an age when dancing is pretty, it's naive, primitive, compact . . .

Such highly detailed notes as these enabled Degas to recapture the singularity of the figures and the originality of the atmosphere when he was back working in his studio.

Unlike the young painters of Les Batignolles, Degas painted solely in his studio. His sight was too weak for him to stay for long in full daylight, but on top of that he was a man of traditional views who felt that painting was an art of observation and reflection. As an aid to his prodigious memory, he would get models to pose in his studio, or occasionally use one of his own sculptures, as he did, for instance, to represent Mademoiselle Fiocre's horse in his painting of the *Ballet 'La Source'* in 1866. Most of the time, décor played a minor role in his compositions, which were always very simple. Often, the parallel lines of the floor suffice to set off the audacious foreshortening of a ballet dancer's body seen from above; or, to take another example, the enormous corolla of a dancer's skirt as she bends down to fix her shoe is admirably heightened by the plain colour of an ordinary wall.

The war of 1870 deeply affected Degas, who volunteered as soon as hostilities broke out. Madame Morisot, whom he visited, told her daughter: 'Monsieur Degas has joined the artillery, and says he has not yet heard a gun being fired: it's a noise he wants to hear, for he would like to know whether he will be able to bear the sound of his own guns firing.' His eyes had already suffered cruelly from the cold when he had been on night duty as an infantryman. When she saw him again in July 1871, at the Manets', Madame Morisot could not help remarking, in a letter to Berthe: 'He seemed completely drowsy – your father looked younger than him.' Degas had been deeply shocked by the loss of several friends in battle, and revealed an extreme sensitivity to death, which he was to retain even when he was much older.

To take his mind off such unpleasant memories, Degas decided at the end of the year to accompany his brother René back to New Orleans, where their mother's family lived. During his stay, he produced no less than fifteen

Edgar Degas: *The Collector of Prints*, 1866. Metropolitan Museum of Art, New York, H. O. Havemeyer Collection). Degas' quick eye was fascinated by the many differing aspects of contemporary life.

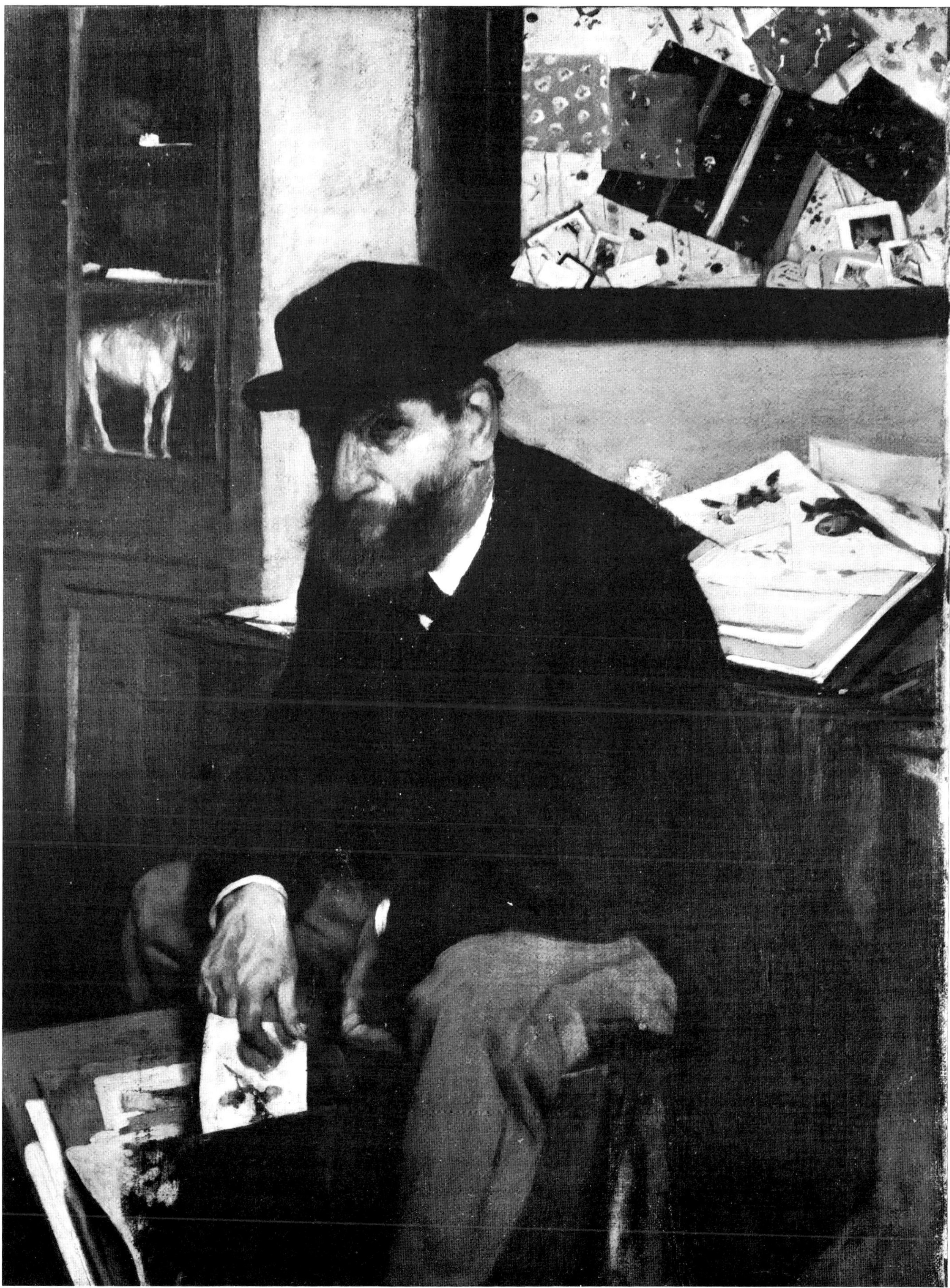

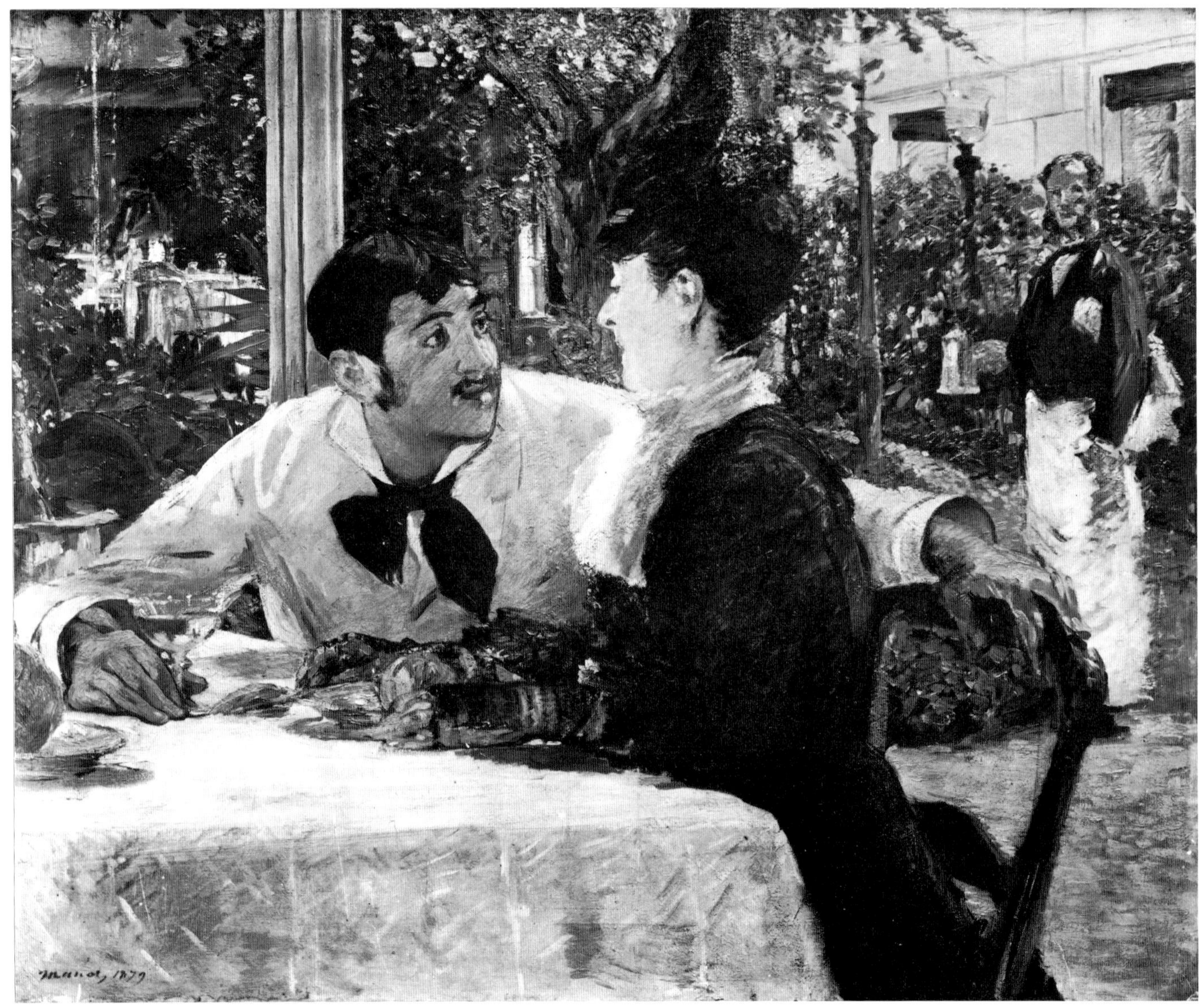

paintings, including several portraits of Estelle, his blind sister-in-law, of whom he was very fond. Mainly in the hope of attracting an English buyer, Degas used a startlingly realistic manner to render the interior of his brother's office. *The Cotton Office in New Orleans* shows his younger brother Achille leaning against a window, René reading a local newspaper, and his uncle Michel Musson examining a cotton sample. 'A fairly vigorous picture which is destined for Agnew (the London dealer) and which he should place in Manchester,' he wrote to his friend, the painter James Tissot. 'For if a spinner ever wished to find his painter, he really ought to hit on me!' This painting was the first work by Degas to find its way into a museum: thanks to the curator Paul Lafond, it was bought by the Pau Museum in 1878.

A year after Edgar's return to Europe, in February 1874, his father died in Naples, leaving his business affairs in an extremely parlous state. Later on,

ABOVE Edouard Manet: *Chez le Père Lathuille*, 1879 (Musée des Beaux-Arts, Tournai). 'Here it is, the modern style I have been talking about – life rendered just as it is, without emphasis', wrote the Symbolist novelist J. K. Huysmans. OPPOSITE Édouard Manet: *Café-Concert*, 1879 (Private Collection). The café-concert was a unique kind of popular entertainment that sprang up in Paris after 1870.

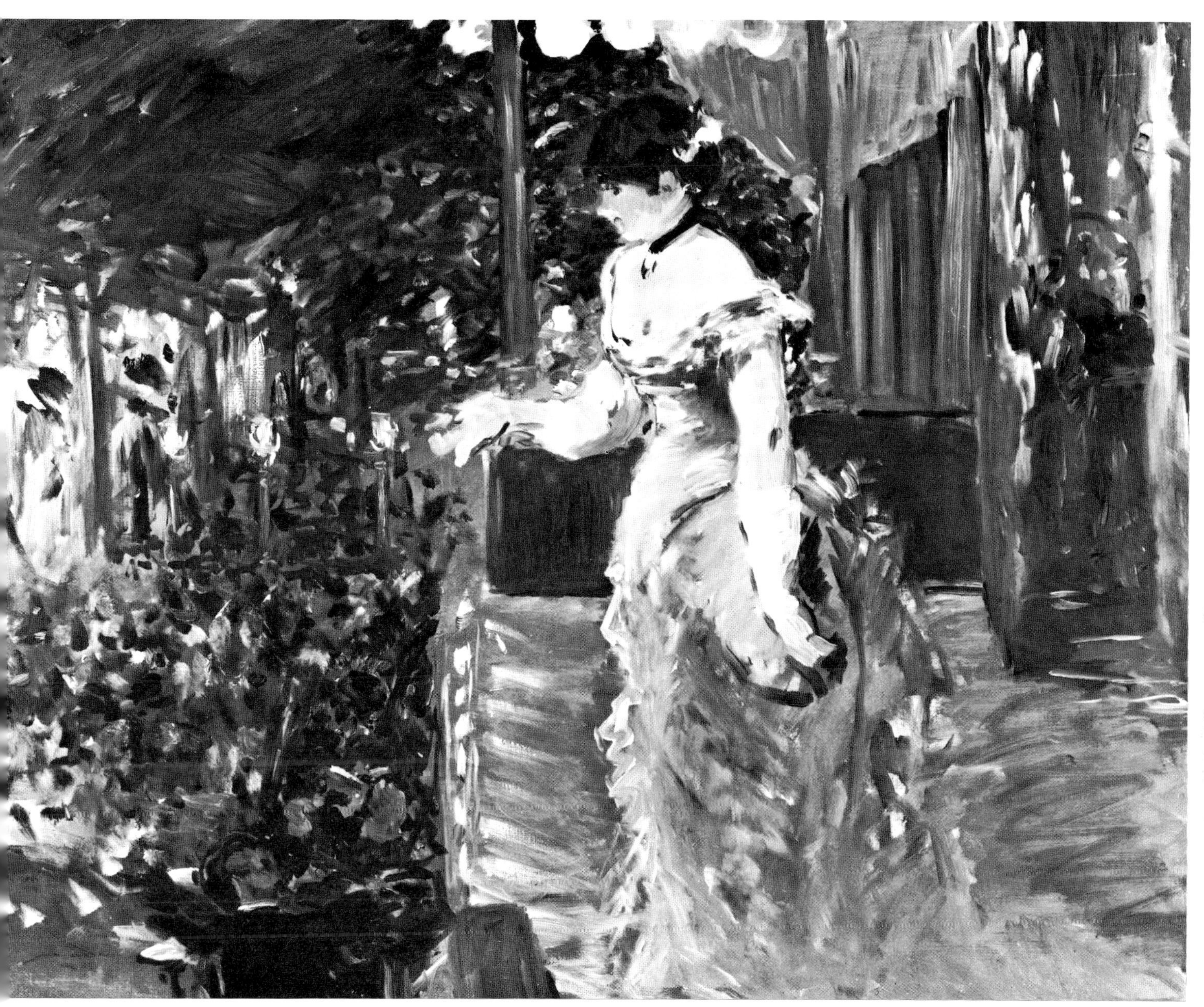

his brother Achille was ruined by the cotton crisis in the United States. Degas, a stickler for the honour of his family's name, behaved as any gentleman would have at the time and paid off all his brother's debts. This act of generosity changed his life completely. Whereas he had enjoyed the benefits and security of wealth ever since his birth, he was now forced to earn a living and help his brothers and their children.

This reverse of fortune affected Degas' self-respect. He became moody, was no longer to be seen in society salons, and shunned his former friends. But his change of circumstances brought him closer to Monet, Renoir and Pissarro. He enthusiastically agreed to exhibit in the 1874 group show, and urged his friends de Nittis, Rouart and Meyer to do the same. He himself put five paintings on show. In spite of their originality, they displayed certain features of classical technique which appealed to the critics. Not only was Degas less severely lambasted than his friends, but he was the only member of the group to effect a sale: the baritone Jean-Baptiste Faure bought a masterpiece, *The Dancing Examination*, for 5,000 francs.

To cut down on his expenses, Degas left his small private house on the Rue Blanche and went to ground in a studio hidden away in an alley off the Rue Pigalle. He sold the greater part of his remarkable collection of drawings and paintings, stripped his way of life of anything that did not directly benefit his art, and increasingly restricted his circle of friends to a few intimates. From a society gentleman, he had suddenly turned into a professional artist, who spent more and more of his time in his studio working with a feverish energy that was to abandon him only in the very last hours of his life.

Degas' concern was to capture Parisian men and women as they went about their daily life: laundresses, bent double with the weight of their washing, two or three businessmen discussing stock prices, a wide-mouthed singer bawling out the verse of some ballad, a billiard player, an art-lover, a woman at the milliner's or at the dressmaker's. The extraordinary richness of his visual genius enabled Degas to transform such commonplace scenes into superbly gripping paintings. They stood as the most eloquent proof of his consummate skill as a draughtsman, perfect grasp of colour, and innate mastery of pictorial technique.

None of the new visual experiences made available by the prosperity of the Empire – such as the oriental art that was now regularly imported – had escaped Degas' attention. He belonged to that very nineteenth-century breed, the aesthetes: men with refined, eclectic tastes, curious minds and a love of all that was exotic. Like the Goncourt brothers and the Comte de Montesquiou, whose extravagances and whims were a feature of the second half of the nineteenth century, Degas adored oriental art and was a frequent visitor to La Porte Chinoise, the shop in the Rue de Rivoli where Madame

BELOW Edgar Degas: *Absinthe*, 1876 (Musée du Louvre, Paris – Jeu de Paume). A friend of Degas', the engraver Marcellin Desboutin, and the actress Hélène André posed for this picture.
OPPOSITE The spacious and ornately decorated cafés where the French spent much of their time during the eighteenth and nineteenth centuries often caught the attention of Manet and Degas. ABOVE Edouard Manet: *A Café on the Place du Palais-Royal*, 1881 (City Art Gallery, Glasgow). BELOW Edouard Manet: *Bar at the Folies-Bergère*, 1881 (Courtauld Institute Galleries, London). This superb composition caused a sensation at the Salon of 1882.

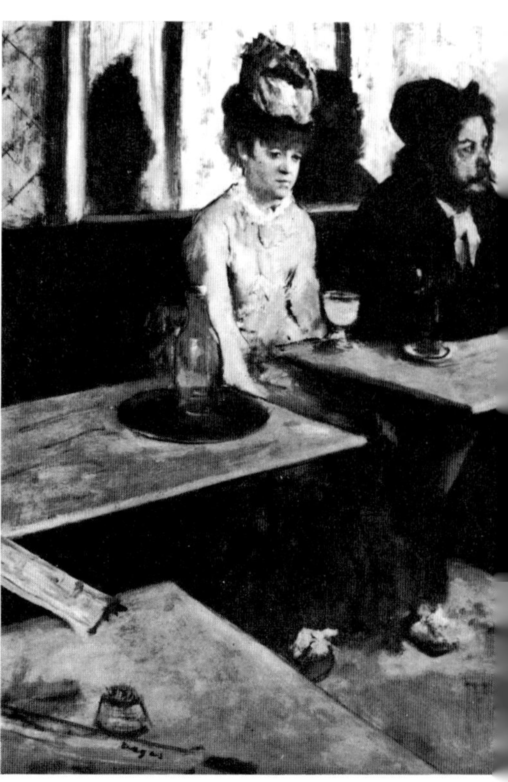

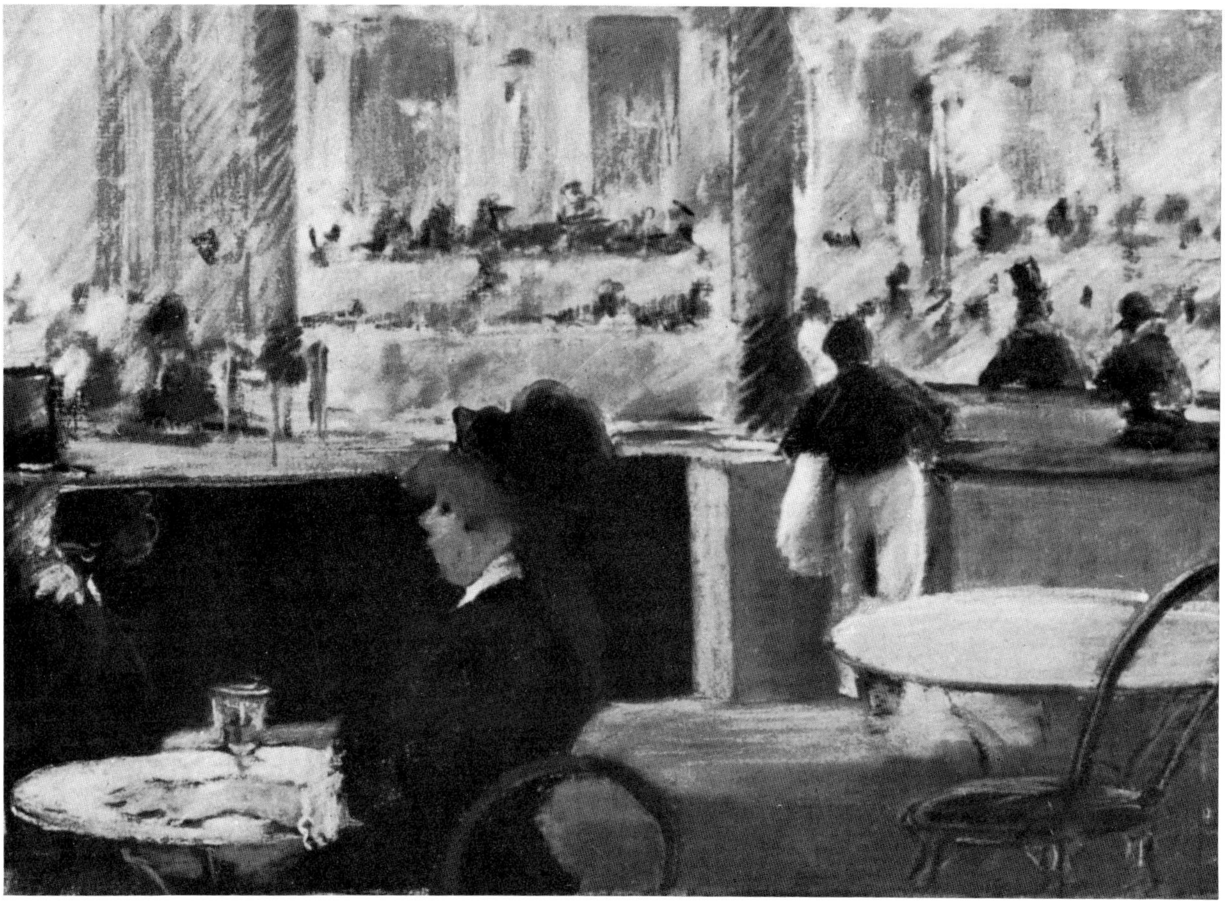

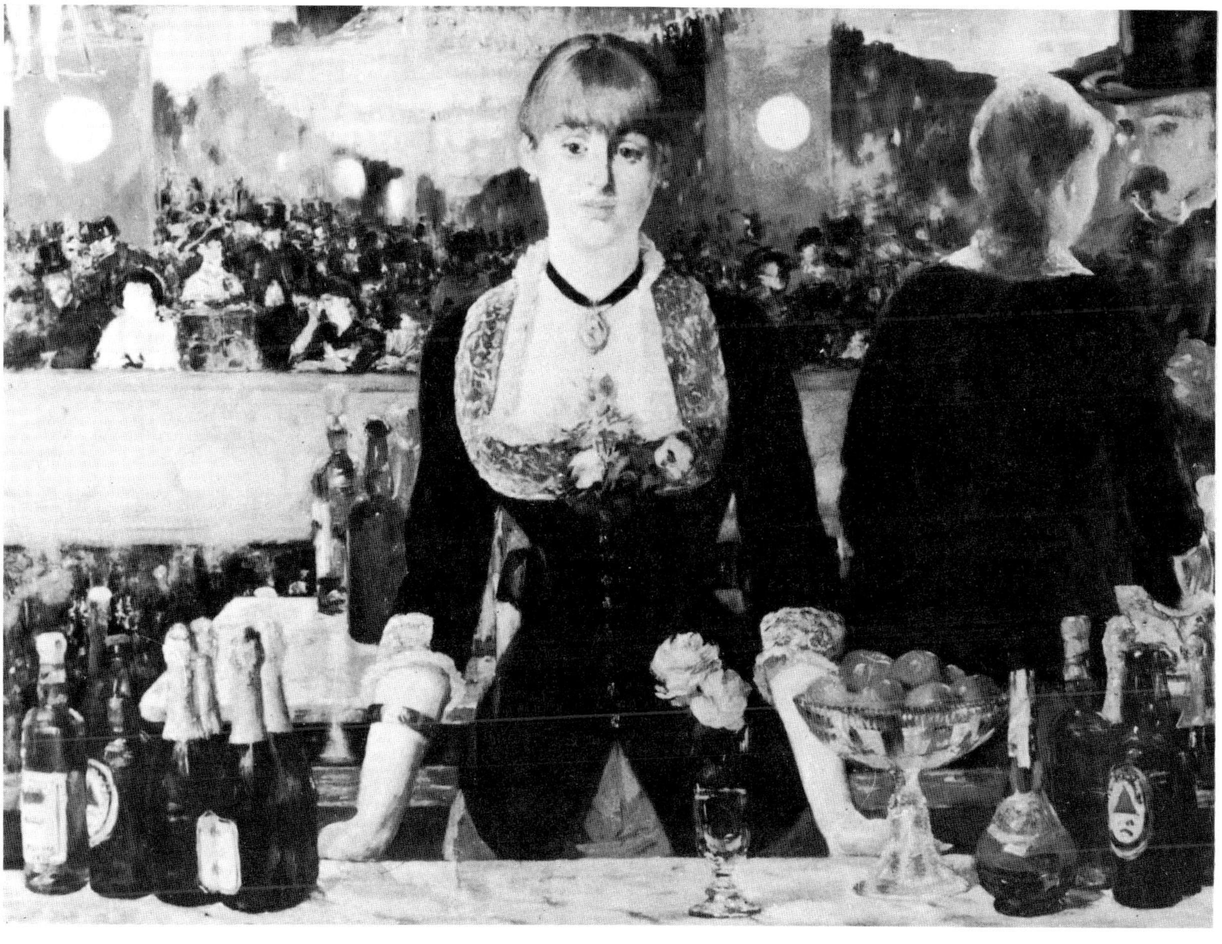

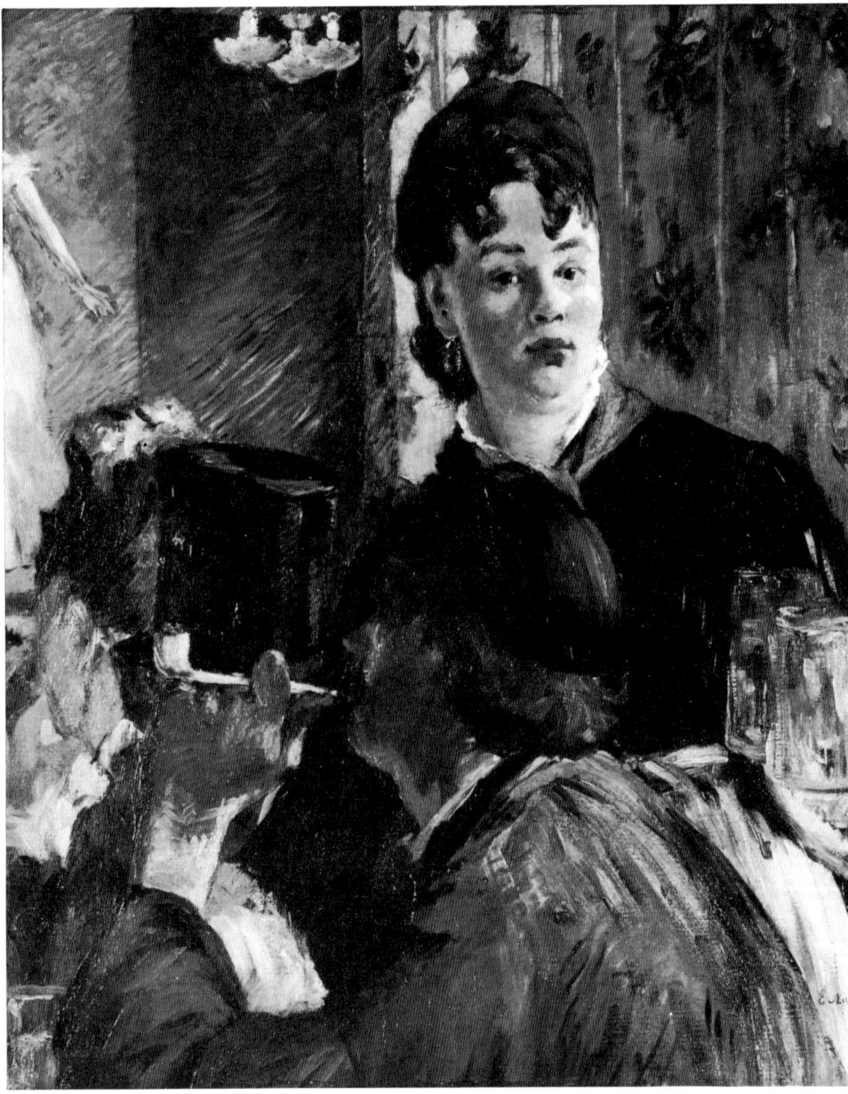

LEFT Edouard Manet: *La Servante de Bocks*, 1878–9 (Musée du Louvre, Paris).
OPPOSITE Edgar Degas: *Miss La La at the Cirque Fernando*, 1879 (National Gallery, London). Degas approached his subject from an unconventional angle for a painter at that time, but one which would later become a common technique in photography.

Desoye sold oriental *objets d'art* and Japanese prints. Whenever Le Bon Marché, the luxurious department store, received a shipment of Persian carpets, Degas was always among the throng of admirers. And although it was only in 1880, when the first Kodak cameras appeared, that Degas became an enthusiastic amateur photographer, he had always been fascinated by the medium from the beginning; after his death numerous photographs of landscapes that he had probably used as a basis for some of his pastels were found among his belongings.

However that may be, his strange painting entitled *At the Races* makes a pioneering use of the close-up, which was later so overworked by the cinema. Although more closely attached than the other Impressionists to the classical tradition and to an eighteenth-century conception of life, Degas was far more adventurous than any of them when it came to integrating the

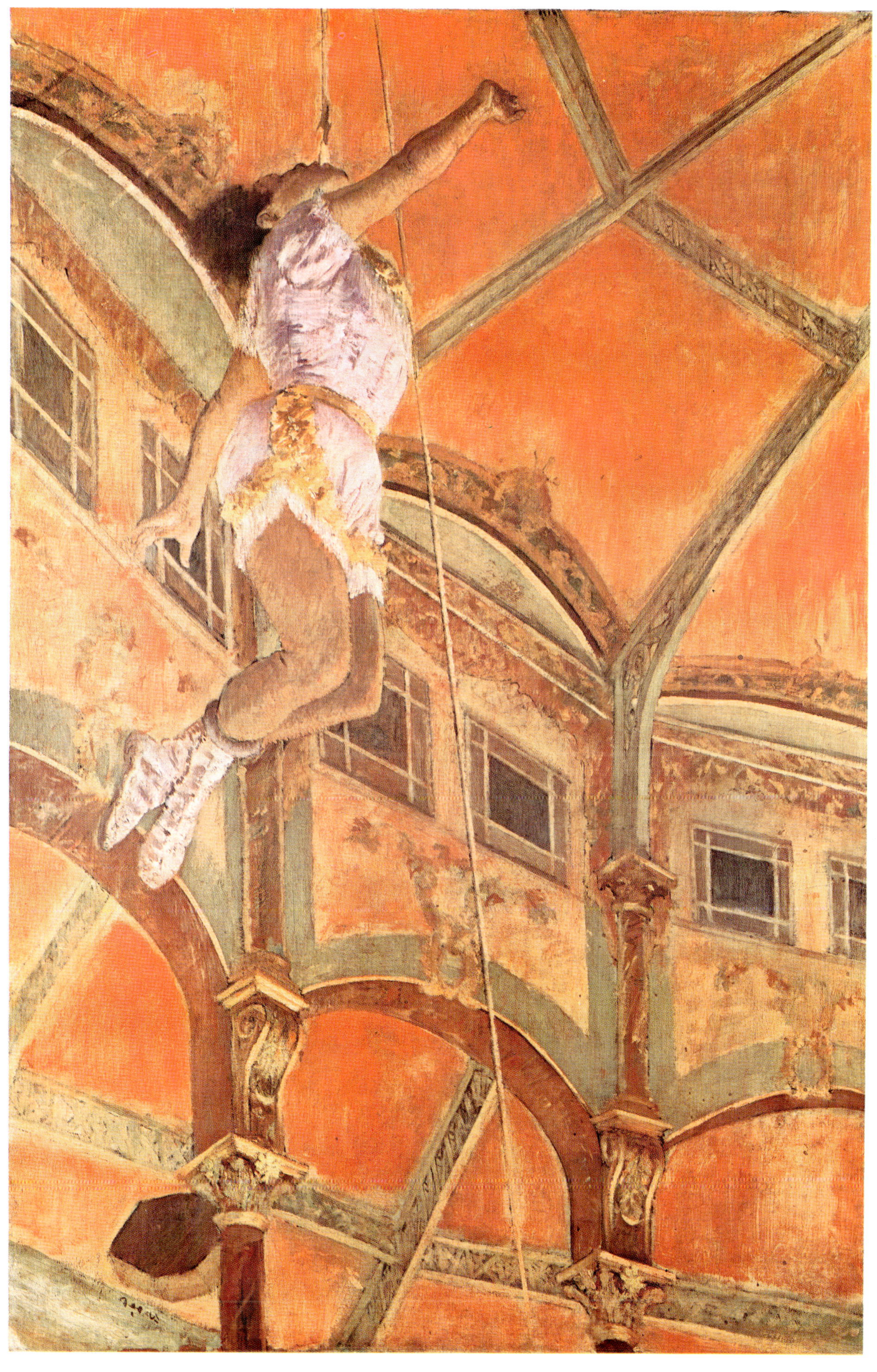

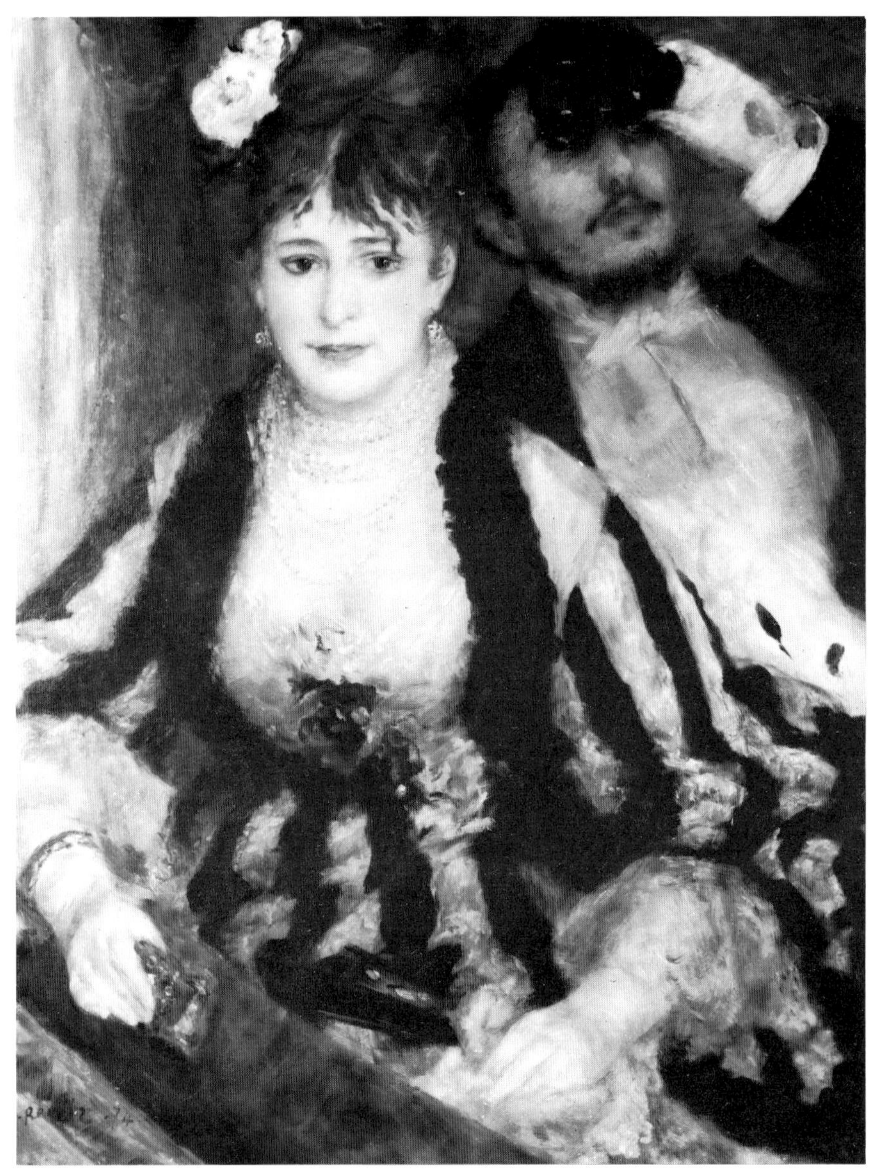

LEFT Auguste Renoir: *La Loge*, 1874 (Courtauld Institute Galleries, London). The models Renoir used for this passive-looking couple were his own brother Edmond and a girl called Nini.
OPPOSITE Edgar Degas: *Singer with a Glove*, pastel, 1878 (Fogg Art Museum, Cambridge, Mass.). What chiefly interested Degas here was the spectacular and dynamic attitude of a café-concert singer in action.

innovations of the century into his painting. From Japanese prints he derived simplification of composition, single-colour backgrounds and bright hues; and from photography a certain way of distorting his figures. At a time when the camera was still very unwieldy, Degas approached his subject from angles that later became the common currency of photographers. In *Miss La La at the Cirque Fernando*, for instance, he shows the acrobat from below, hanging from the ceiling like some monstrous insect, and framed by a network of curved lines that was very characteristic of *fin de Siècle* architecture. Degas was the only painter to use details in a way that not only emphasized the oddness of his angle of vision, but situated his subject in space and in time. Miss La La was a superb mulatto woman who performed amazing acrobatics hanging from her jaws. Her feats and a famous troupe of

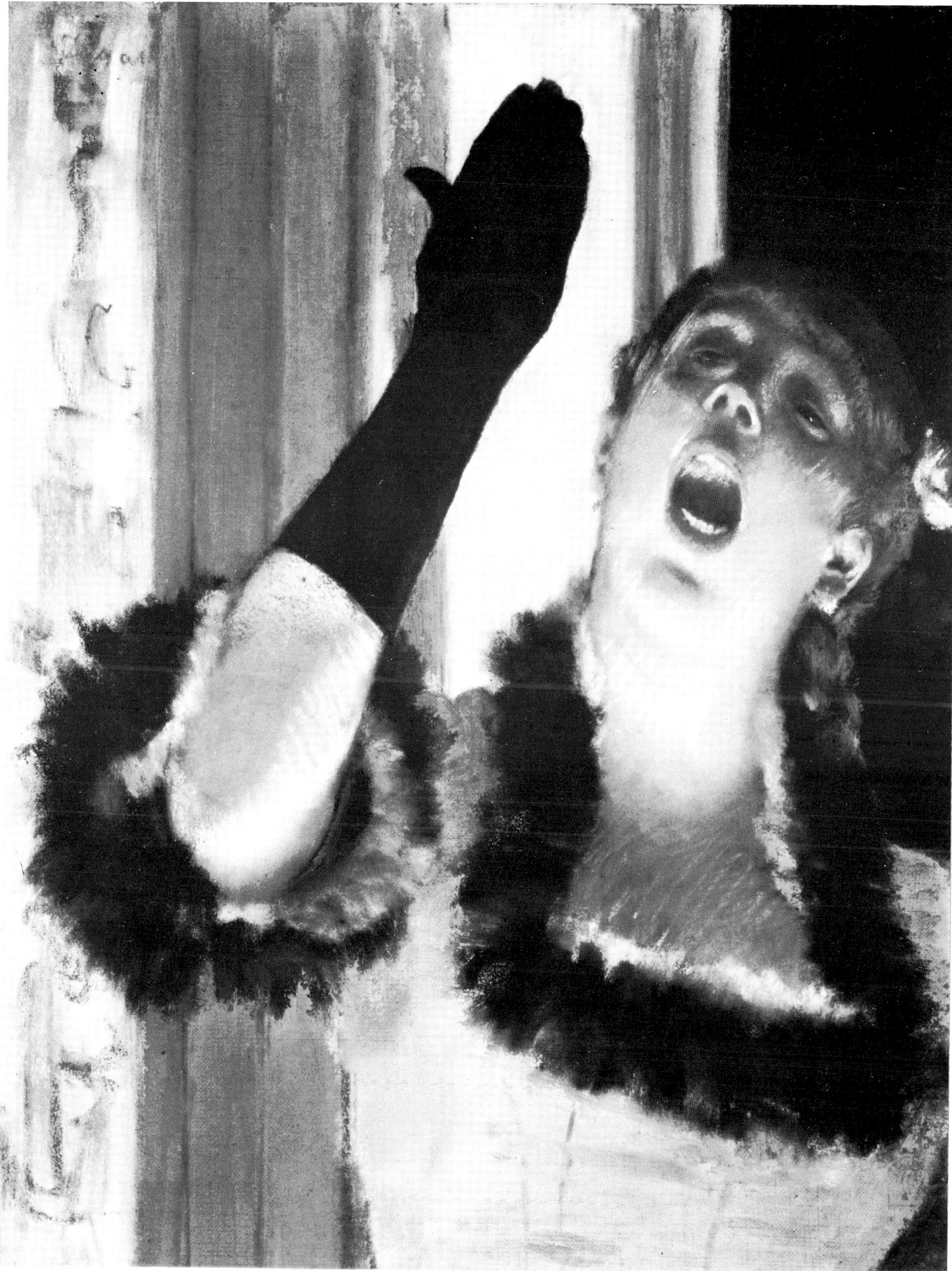

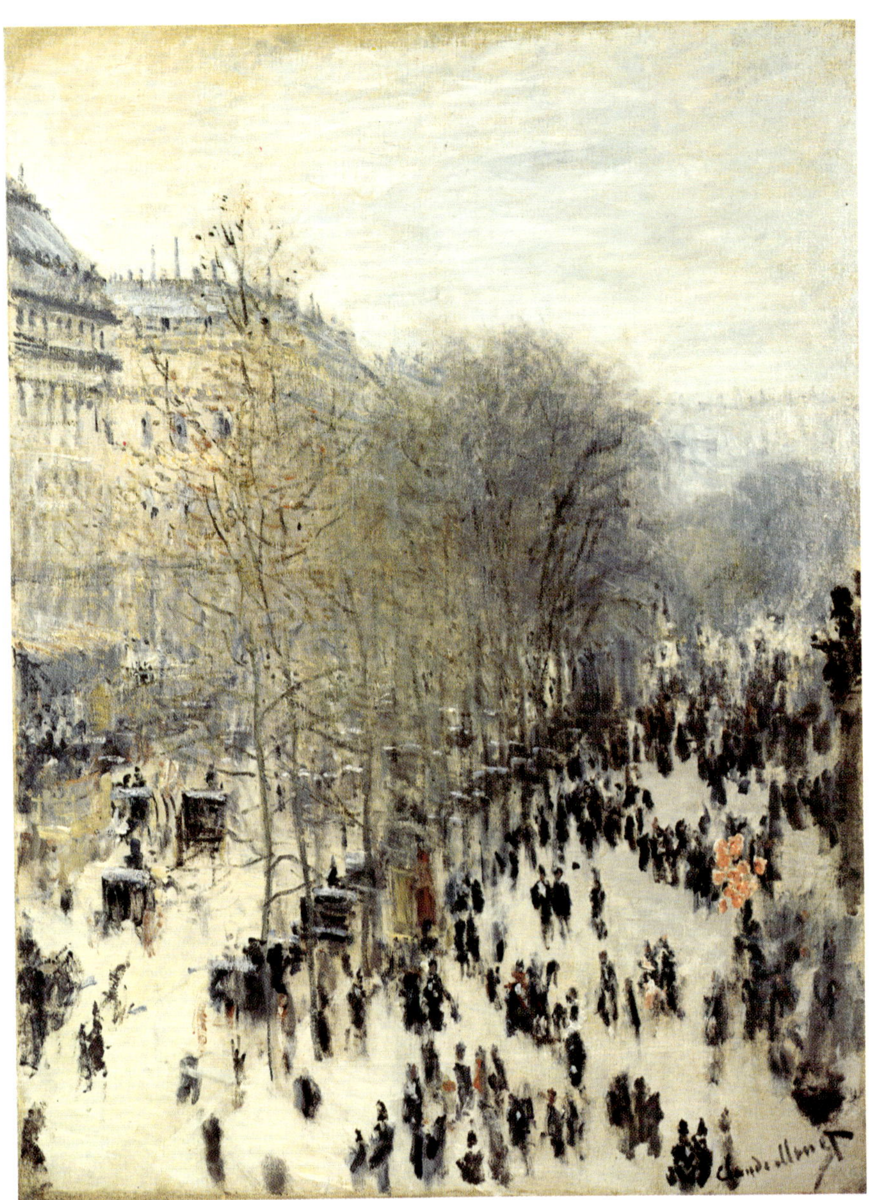

LEFT Claude Monet: *Boulevard des Capucines, Paris,* 1873 (Gallery of Art, Kansas City, Miss., William Rockhill Nelson Collection). 'Never has the elusive, the fleeting, the instantaneousness of movement been caught in its incredible flux, and fixed as it is' – Ernest Chesneau, a contemporary critic.

BELOW Photograph of the Pont des Arts by Adolphe Braun. Photography, which alarmed some painters towards the middle of the century, inspired others to strive after a more immediately gripping representation of movement in their paintings.

OPPOSITE Claude Monet: *Rue Montorgueil, Paris, 30 June 1878*, 1878 (Musée des Beaux-Arts, Rouen).

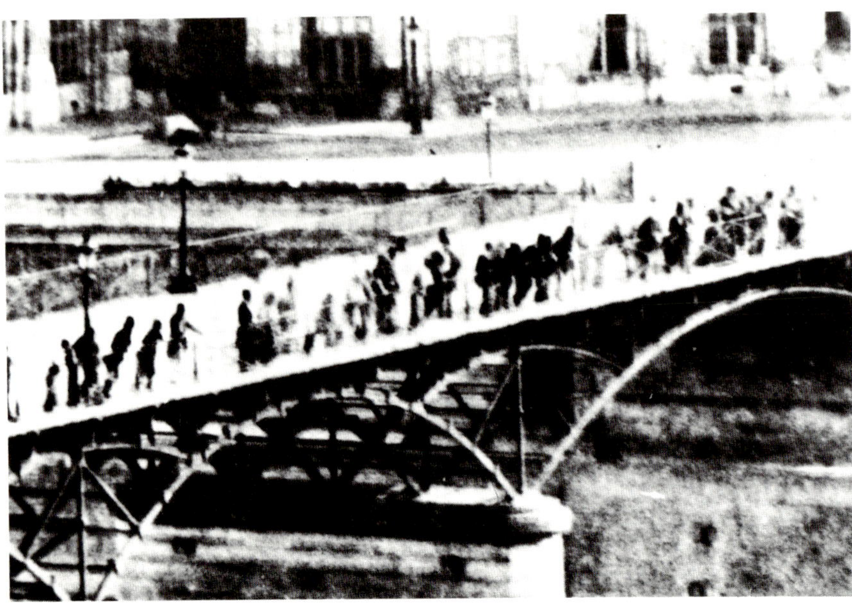

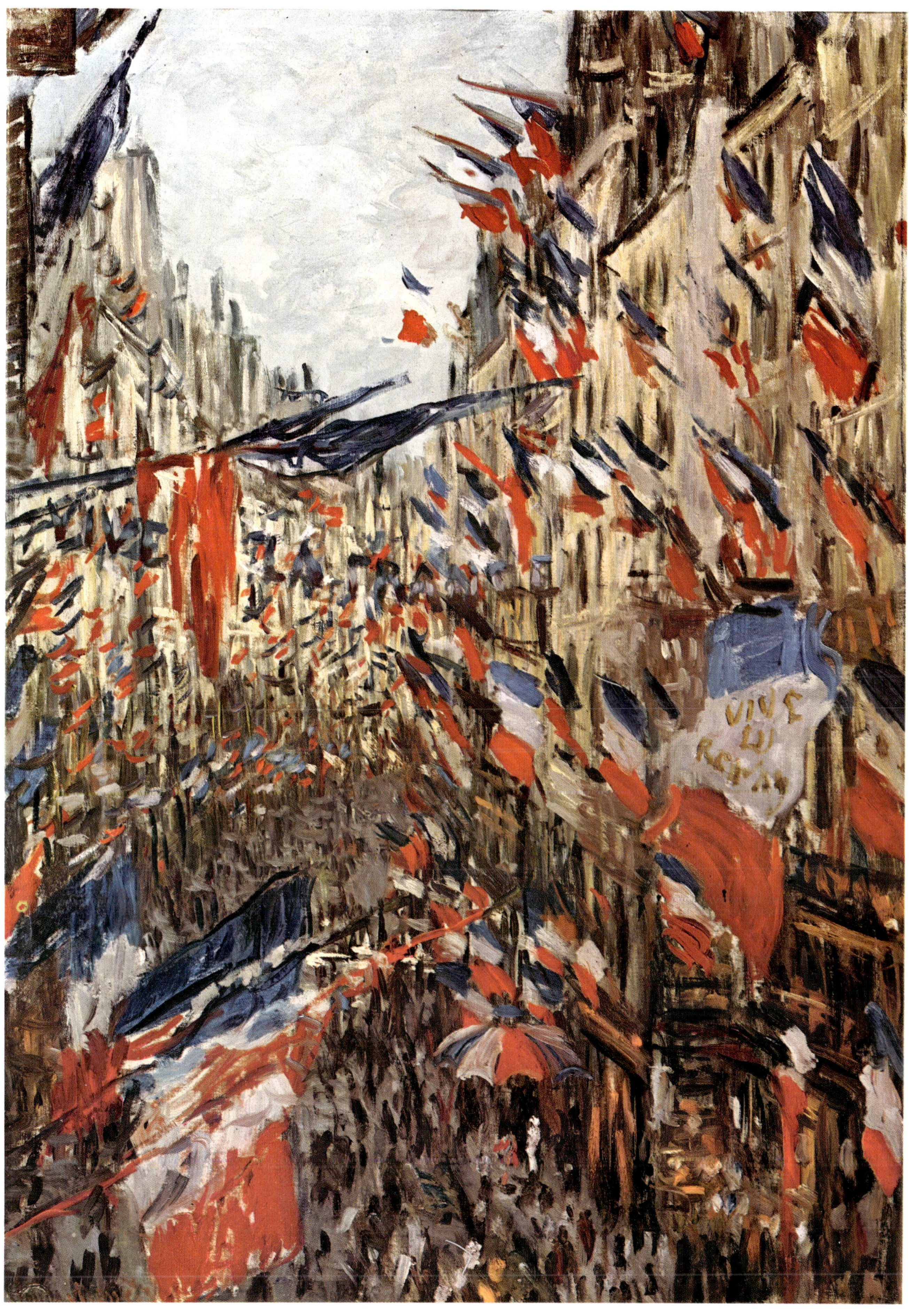

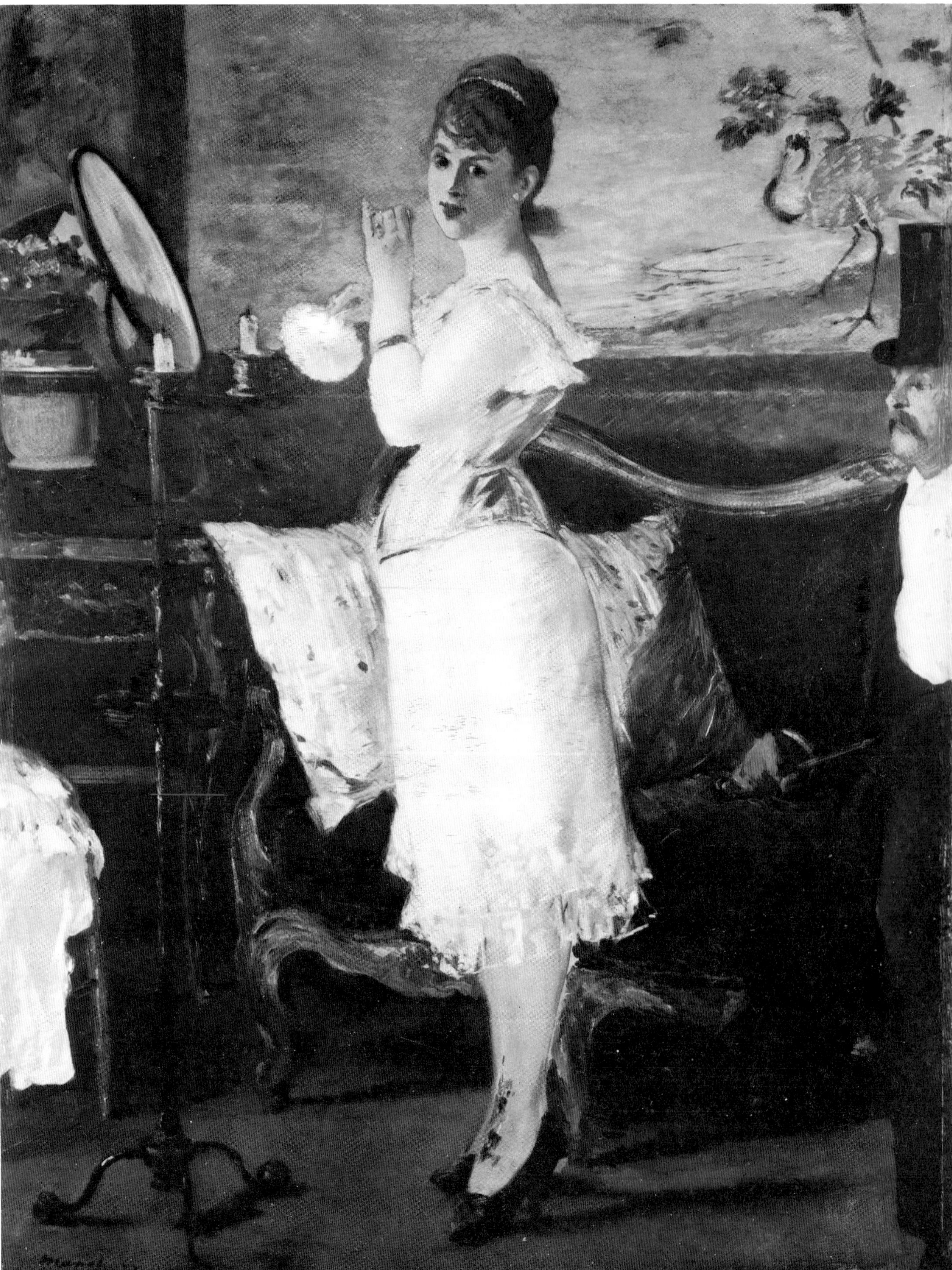

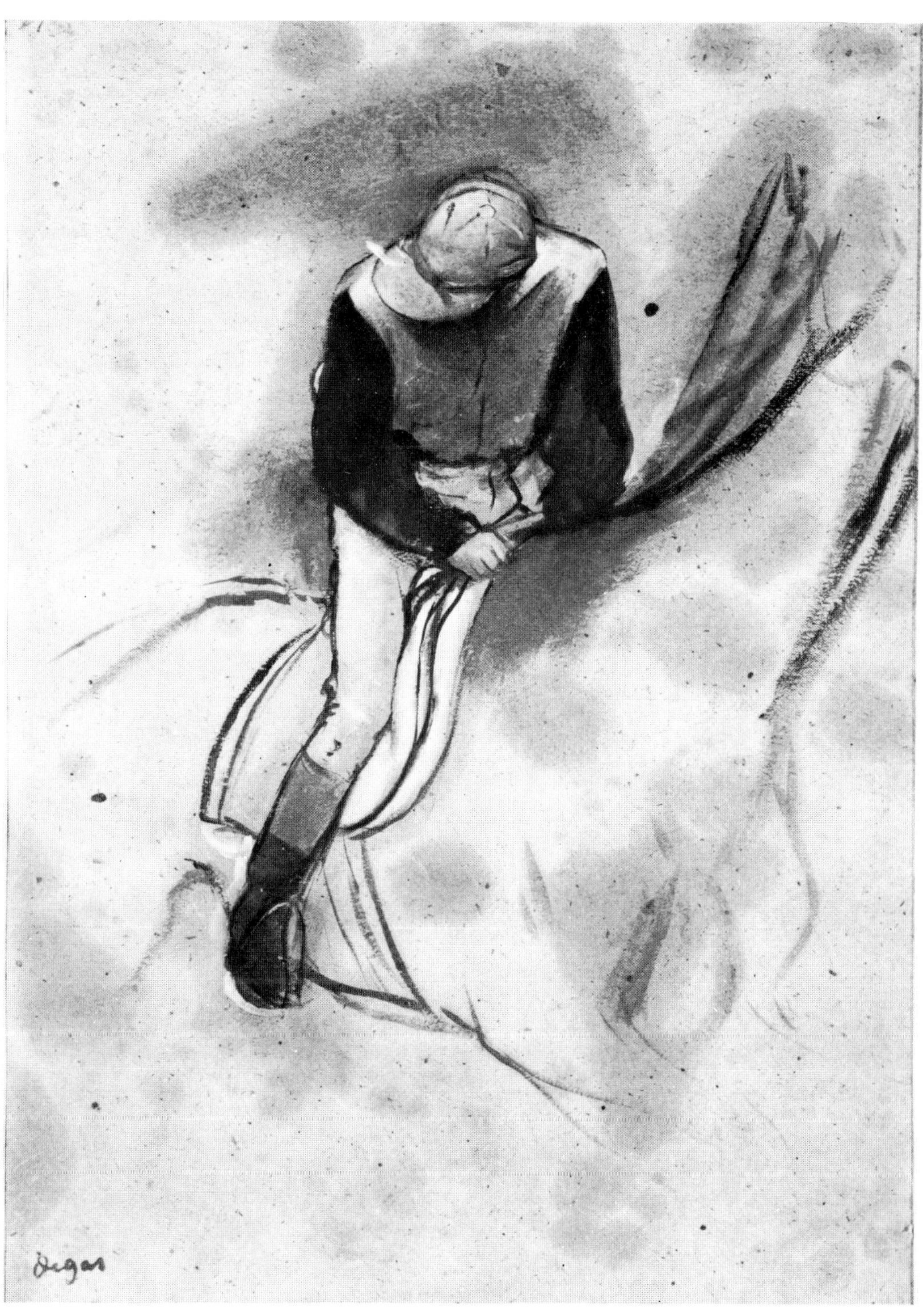

OPPOSITE Edouard Manet: *Nana*, 1877 (Kunsthalle, Hamburg). Cocottes played an important role in the social life of nineteenth-century France – Zola made one of them the heroine of a novel. Manet's wonderful painting caused extremely violent reactions when it was put on show in the Rue des Capucines.
ABOVE Edgar Degas: *Jockey*, 1868 (Private Collection, Zurich). Degas and Manet made numerous studies of the Longchamp races.

clowns made the Cirque Fernando a favourite with artists and general public alike right up until the turn of the century.

Between 1872 and 1882, Paris ceased to be the exclusive territory of Degas. Renoir, Berthe Morisot and Monet often came to work there. But as light was of prime importance for them, they painted Paris in a very different way from Degas. As a result of the widely differing temperaments of the artists belonging to the group, we have an image of the capital in all its diversity.

Renoir, for instance, painted his luminous, teeming view of *Le Pont Neuf* from the first floor of a café. Similarly, Monet produced his *Boulevard des*

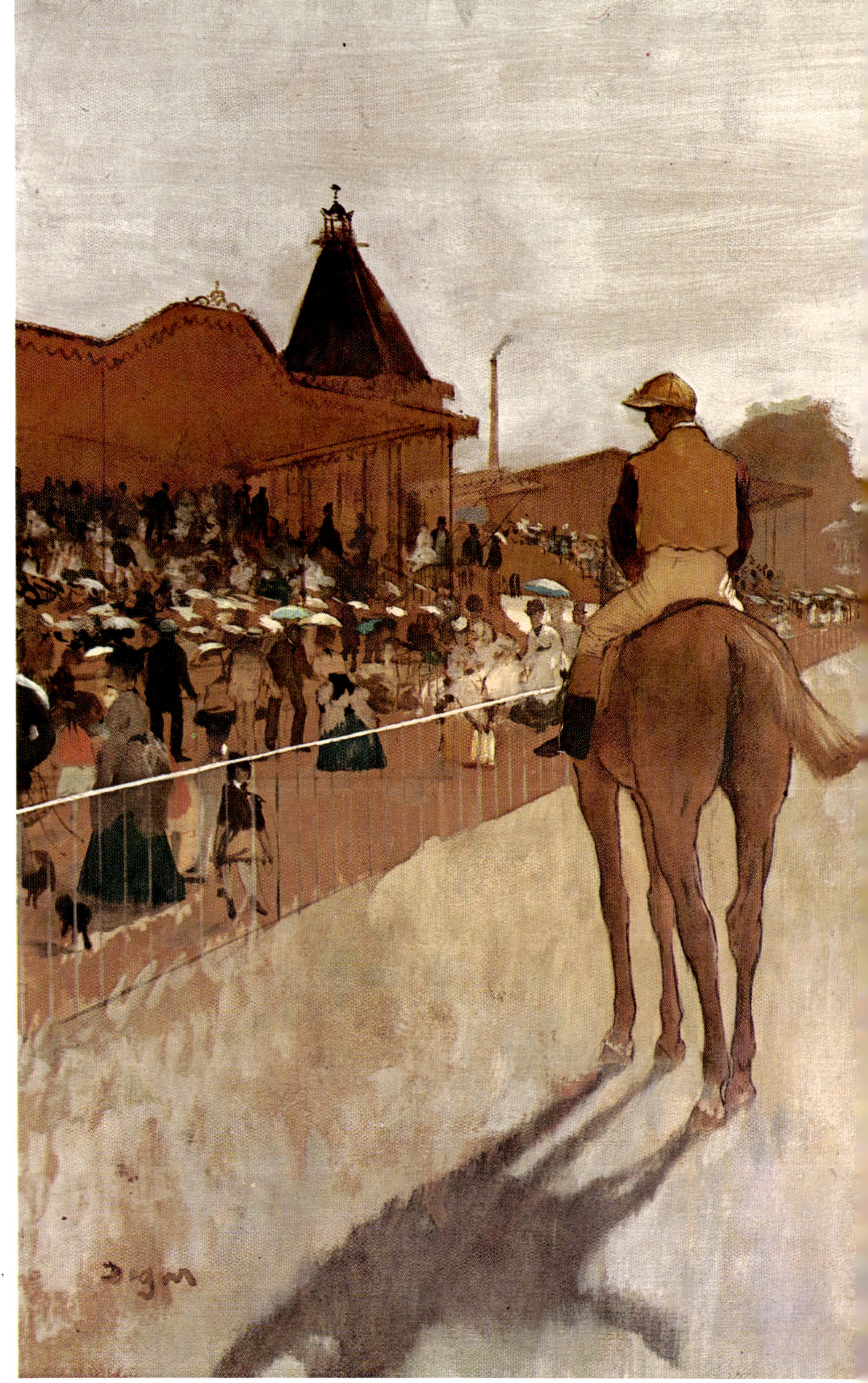

Edgar Degas: *At the Races, in Front of the Stands*, c.1869–72 (Musée du Louvre, Paris – Jeu de Paume).

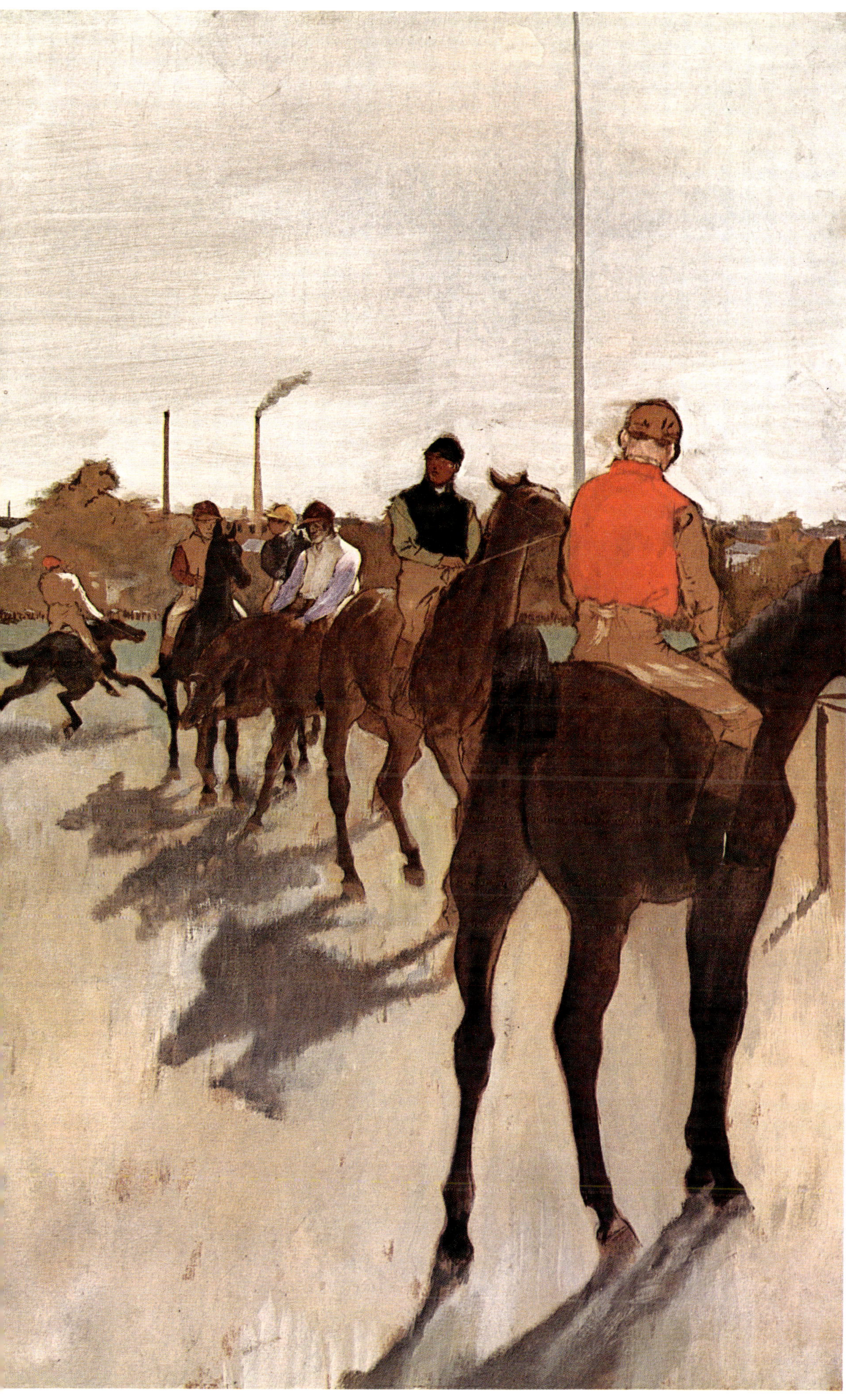

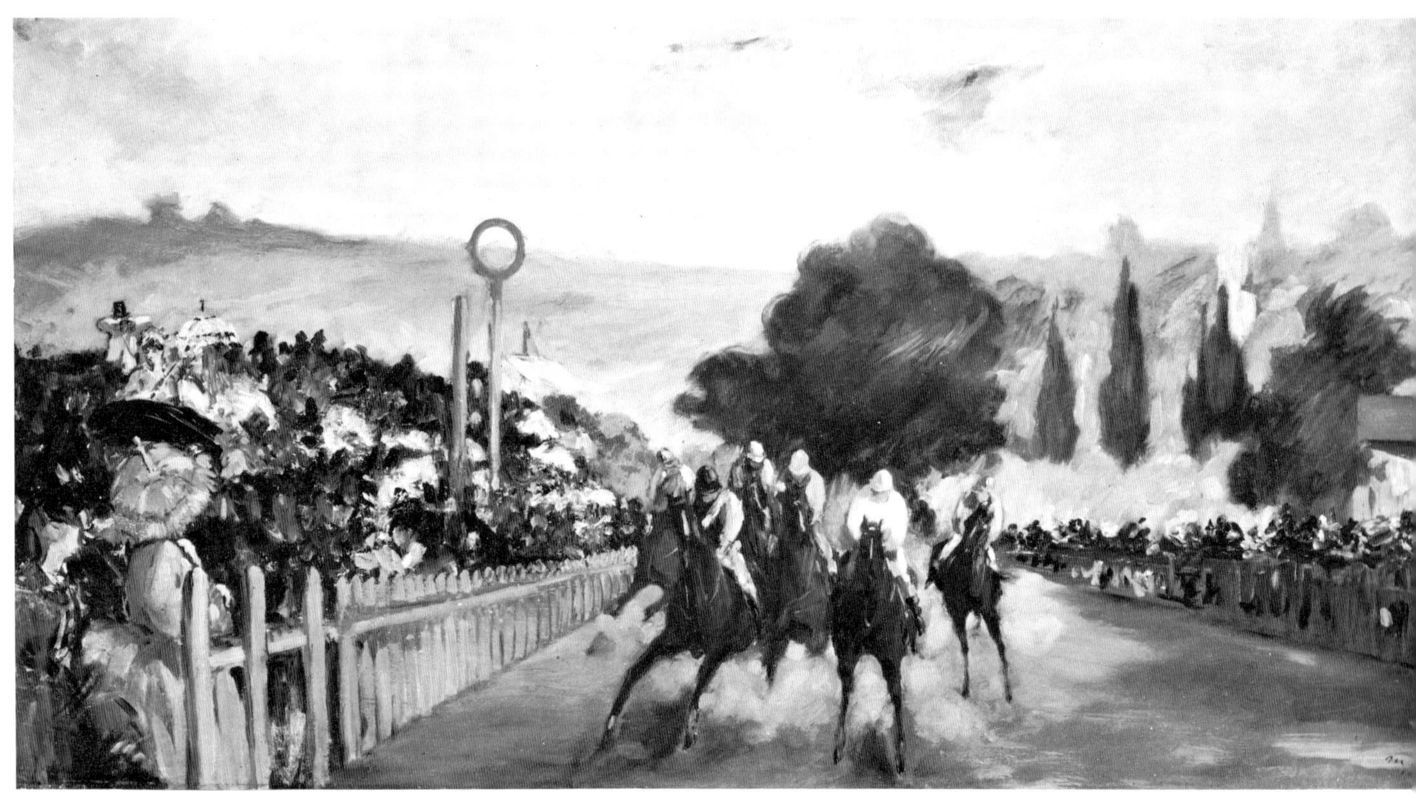

ABOVE Edouard Manet: *Racecourse near Paris*, 1864 (courtesy of the Art Institute of Chicago, Mrs. Potter Palmer Collection).
OPPOSITE ABOVE Edgar Degas: *Study of a Racehorse in Full Gallop*, *c.* 1889 (Galerie Robert Schmit, Paris).
OPPOSITE BELOW Edgar Degas: *Carriage at the Races*, 1870–2 (Museum of Fine Arts, Boston).

Capucines while preparing the famous 1874 group exhibition in Nadar's studio. Later, he carefully chose a balcony in the clothiers' quarter from which to paint his colourful *Rue Montorgueil with Flags*, on 30 June 1878, the day the new Republic had chosen to celebrate the national holiday. Manet, although by no means fascinated by outdoor scenes, recorded the view from the window of his studio in the Rue Saint-Pétersbourg, just before leaving it, in *Rue Mosnier with Flags*, a very lively rendering of an unusually attractive little street.

Berthe Morisot set up her easel not far from her parents' house to paint *Paris, Vue du Trocadéro*, a sweeping panorama over the city. Later, while her house in the Rue Villejust was being built in 1878, she took off to the Bois de Boulogne and executed a series of paintings around one of the lakes. Monet, meanwhile, in his *Le Parc Monceau*, depicted a group of nannies with white bonnets sitting in an avenue running through the gardens, which he enlivened with an interplay of light and shade. The numerous restaurants and cafés, which loomed large in the social life of the time, were a source of great attraction for Manet: in his *Chez le Père Lathuille*, he creates such a bright, lively and modern image of the restaurant in the Avenue de Clichy, not far from the Café Guerbois, that the young critic, and later famous novelist, J.K. Huysmans, was moved to write: 'The young man and the young woman are superb. This is a rendering of life as it really is, without

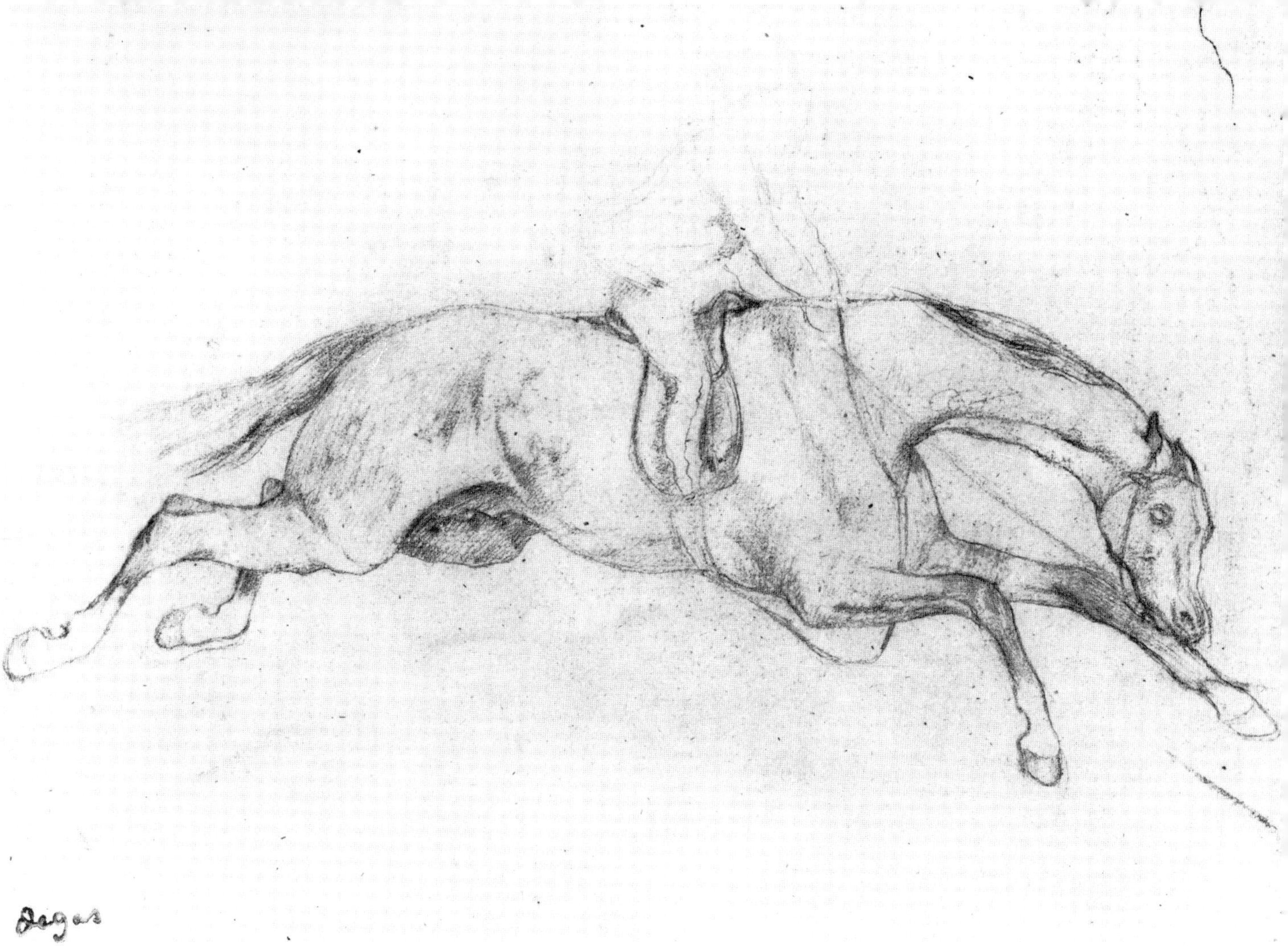

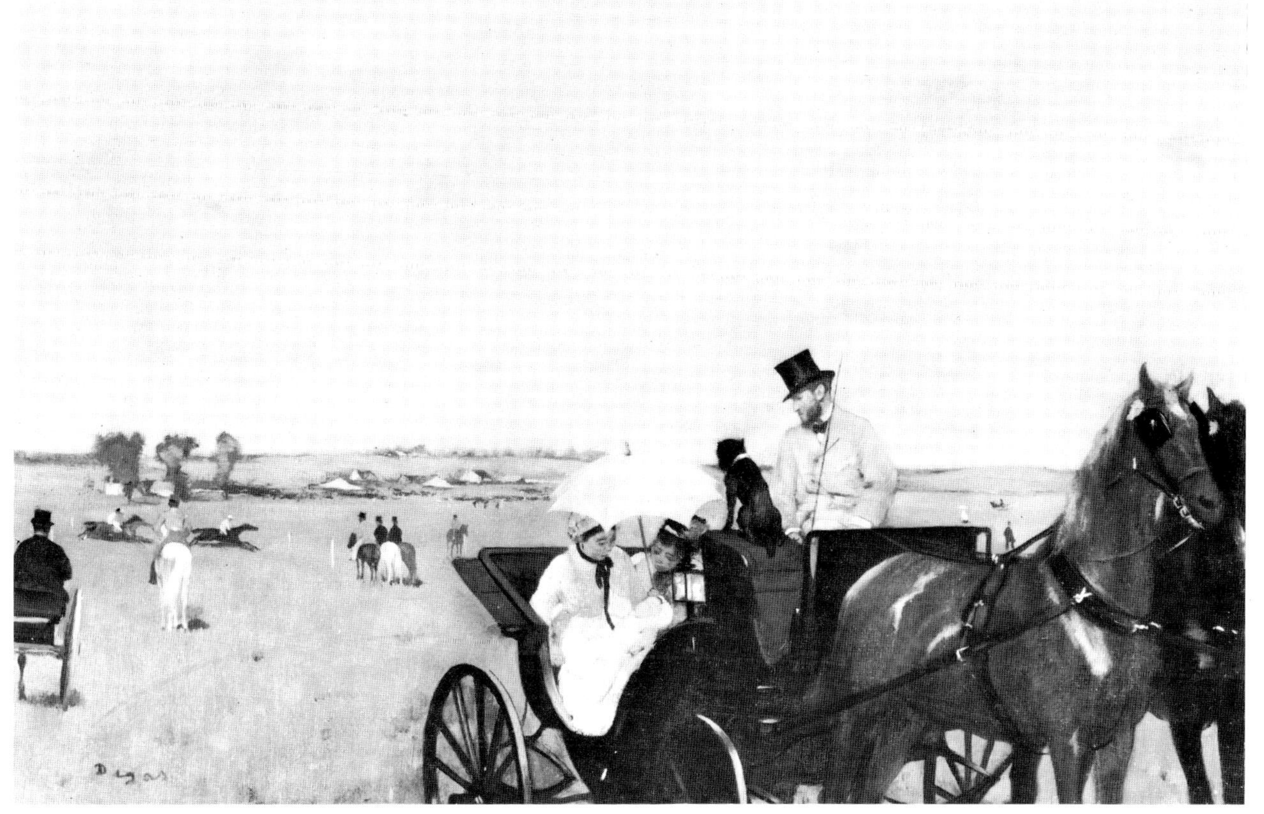

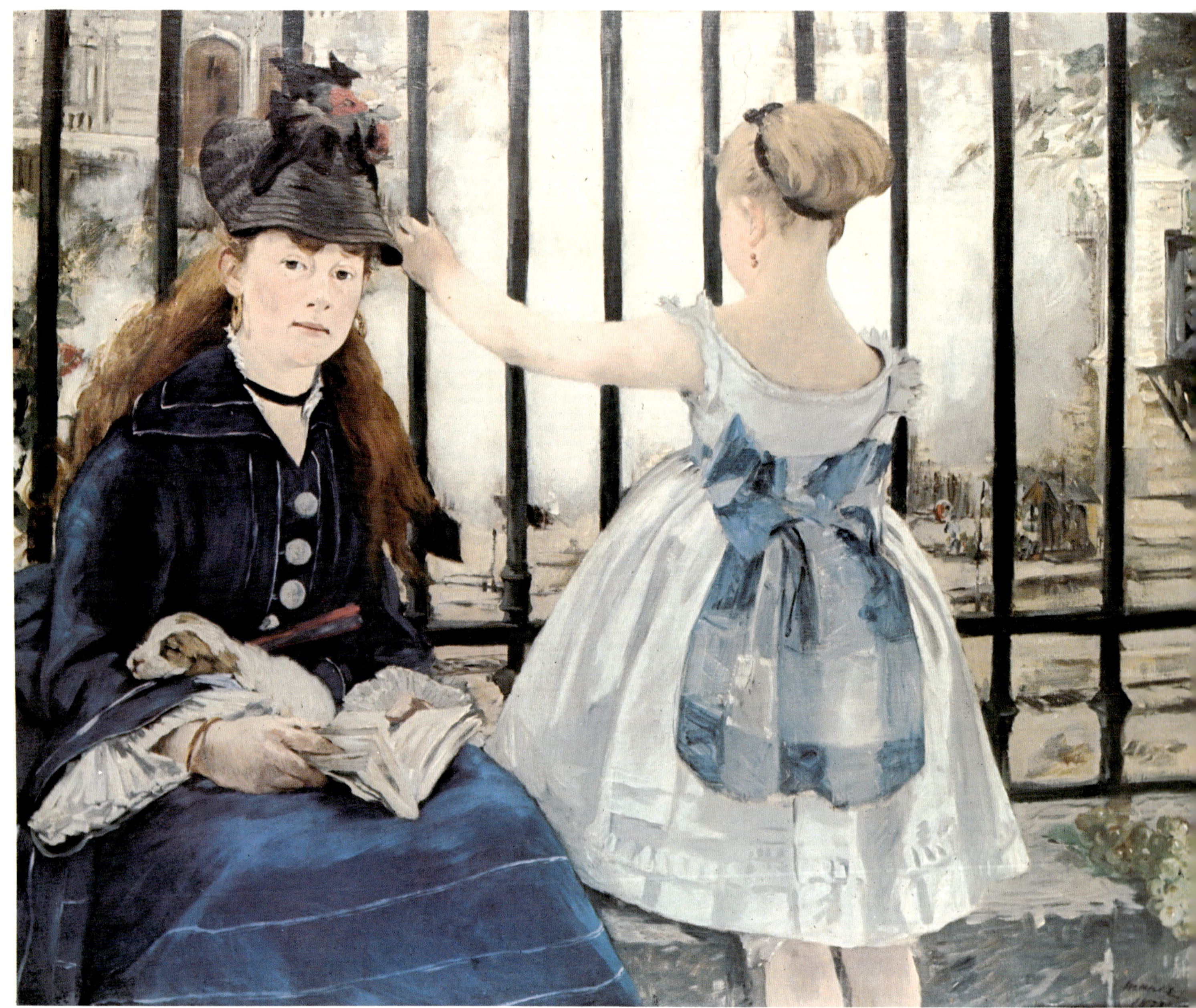

ABOVE Edouard Manet: *The Gare St-Lazare*, 1873 (National Gallery, Washington). Manet, who painted this picture from a private garden in the Rue de Rome, concealed the industrial aspect of the subject behind a thick cloud of smoke which suggests the passage of a train.
OPPOSITE Claude Monet: *The Gare St-Lazare*, 1877 (Musée du Louvre, Paris). With customary audacity, Monet aims to give a detailed portrayal of the 'new cathedrals of humanity'.

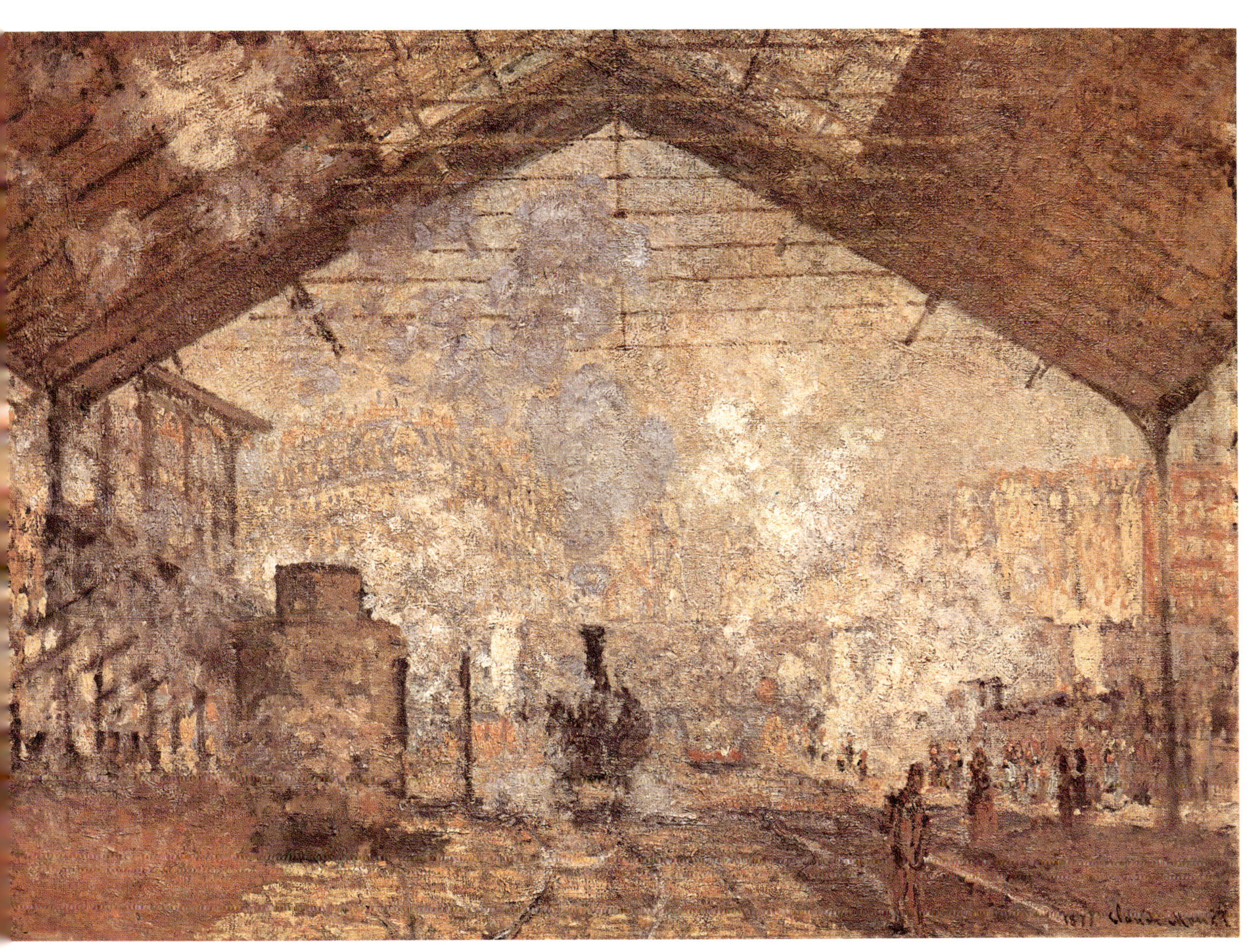

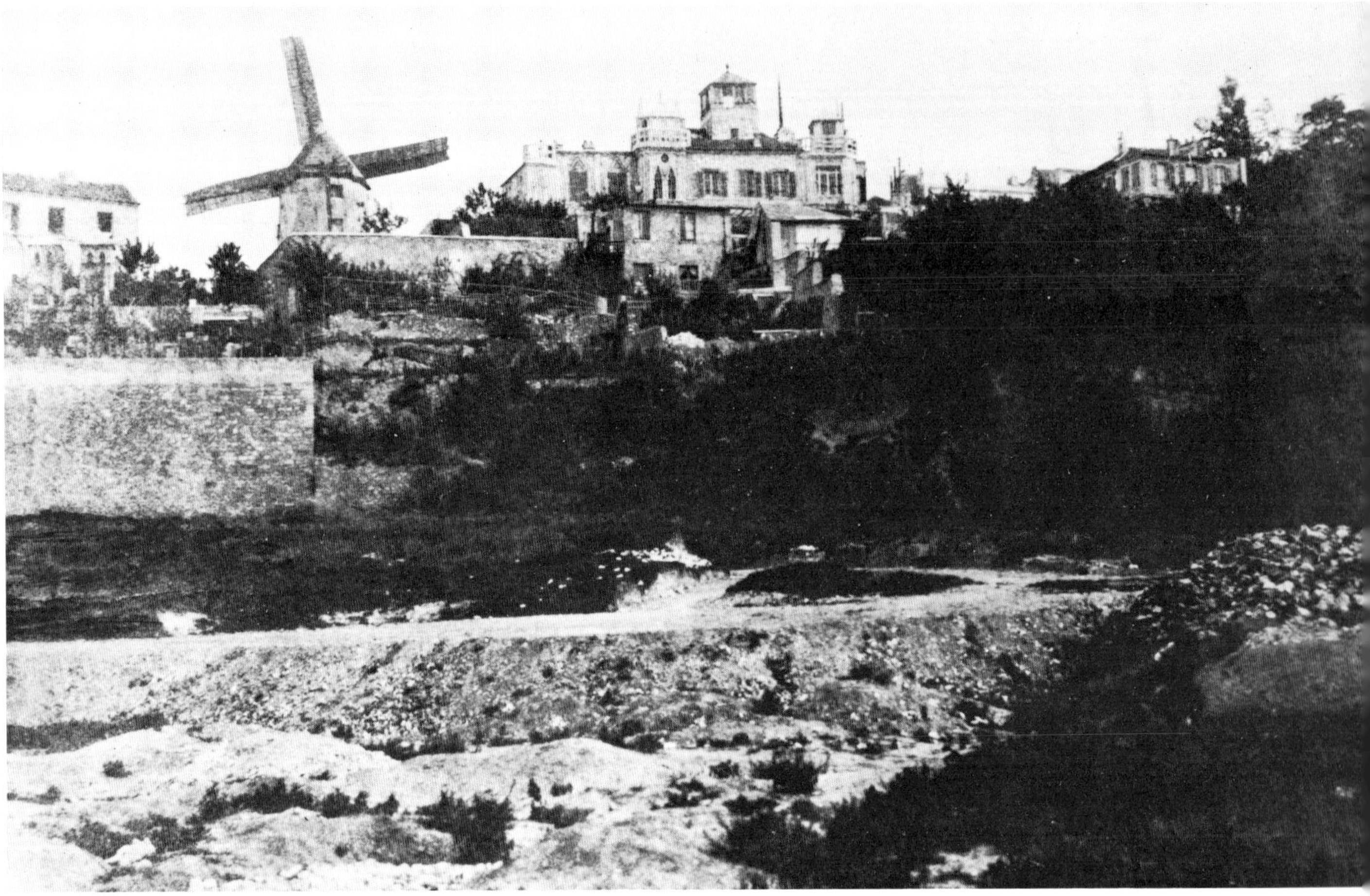

any over-emphasis.' The subject also attracted Degas, who produced numerous versions: in *Absinthe*, he depicts a besotted, desperate couple in a bare, angular setting, whereas the crowd surrounding his *Two Women on the Terrace of a Café* creates an utterly natural, relaxed and cheering atmosphere. He also made a charming pencil sketch of a corner of La Nouvelle-Athènes, the famous café where he often went to meet his Impressionist friends. Renoir frequented the gardens of the Moulin de la Galette, where he was fascinated by the way the sun caught the faces of his fellow Parisians, and painted such unforgettably moving works as *The Swing* and *The Dance of the Moulin de la Galette*.

Renoir, Monet and Degas also differed in their approach to the theatre. What interested Renoir, in *La Loge* for instance, was the elegance and attractiveness of the young couple and the sumptuousness of their setting. The more sophisticated Manet, drawing on all his prodigious skill, sought after subtle effects in *The Bar at the Folies-Bergère*. Degas, who adored the artificial light of the stage, produced countless variations on the theme, and recorded the quite unique atmosphere of the cafés-concerts, a new kind of entertainment that was all the rage after the war of 1870.

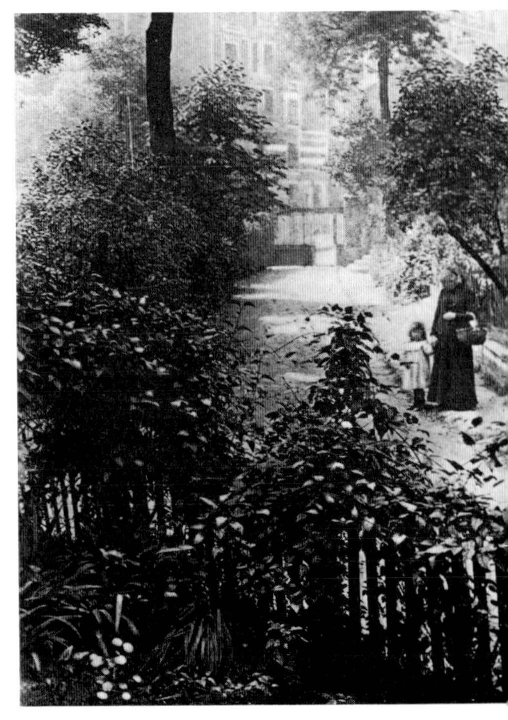

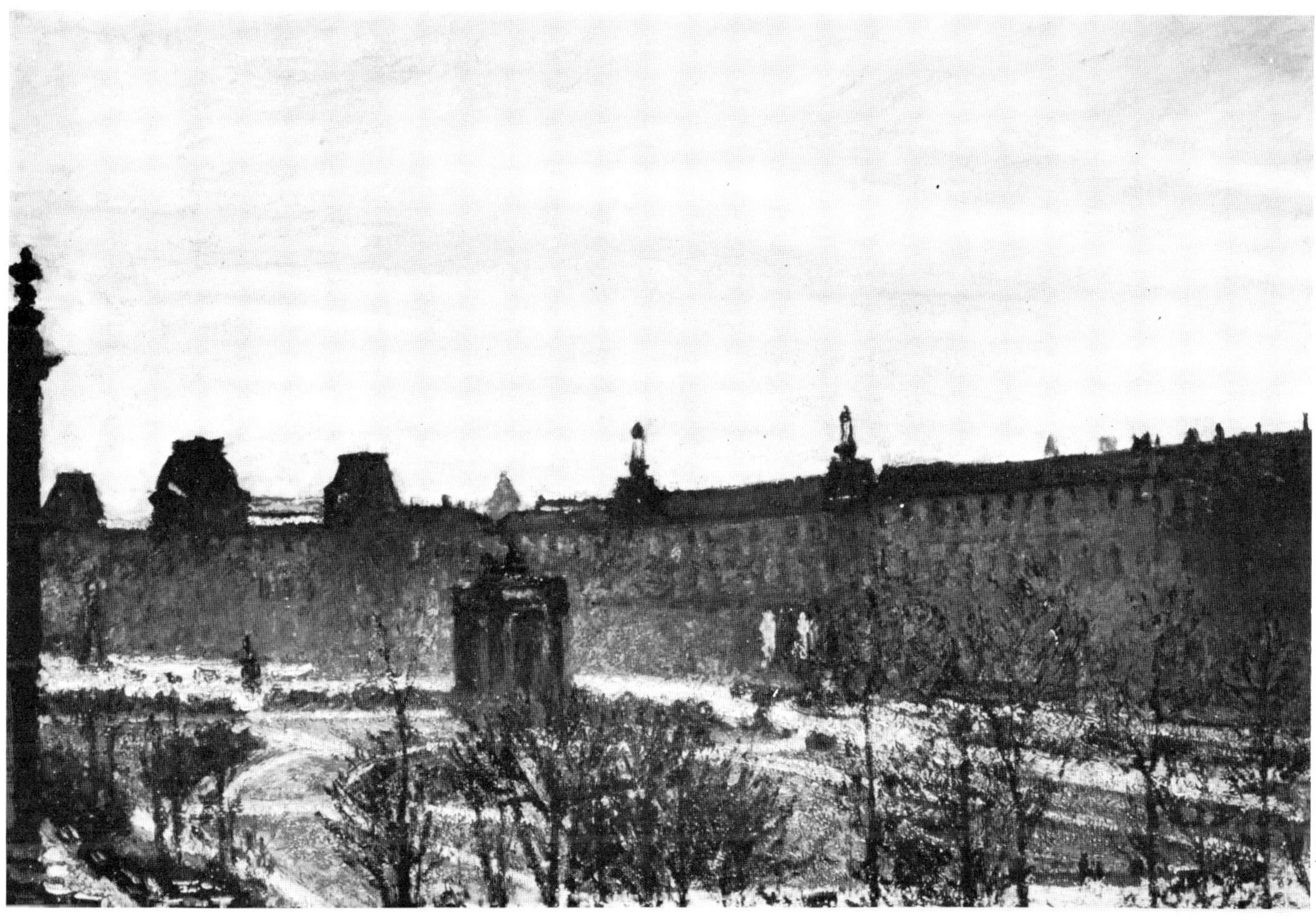

OPPOSITE ABOVE To the north of Paris the village of Montmartre, with its old windmills and leafy gardens, long retained its rural charm.
OPPOSITE BELOW The Allée du Château des Brouillards, where Renoir lived for a time.
ABOVE Camille Pissarro: *The Tuileries*, c. 1900 (Private Collection).

In 1877, Monet tackled an undoubtedly novel subject – an invention which had totally transformed people's lives at the beginning of the century: the train. He executed a series of superb paintings inside the Gare Saint-Lazare and in neighbouring streets. He had to go to considerable lengths before obtaining permission to plant his easel where he wanted, but Monet was not easily thwarted once he had got an idea into his head. He convinced the station master that he was a Salon celebrity, with the result, Renoir was to tell his son Jean, that 'the trains were halted; the platforms cleared; and the engines were crammed with coal so as to give all the smoke Monet desired.'

With the same scrupulous accuracy that he had applied to his observation of storms or of the Argenteuil landscape, Monet painted views of the main lines, suburban departures, and two locomotives chugging into the huge iron and glass shell amidst clouds of smoke. He also took up position outside the station, and produced *Exterior of the Station, Effect of Sun*, and *Le Pont de l'Europe*, in which, through a screen of smoke from two locomotives, the Rue de Rome and the track running past the Rue Legendre, near Les Batignolles, can just be glimpsed. Manet had chosen an utterly different appoach, five years earlier, when he had painted *The Gare St-Lazare*

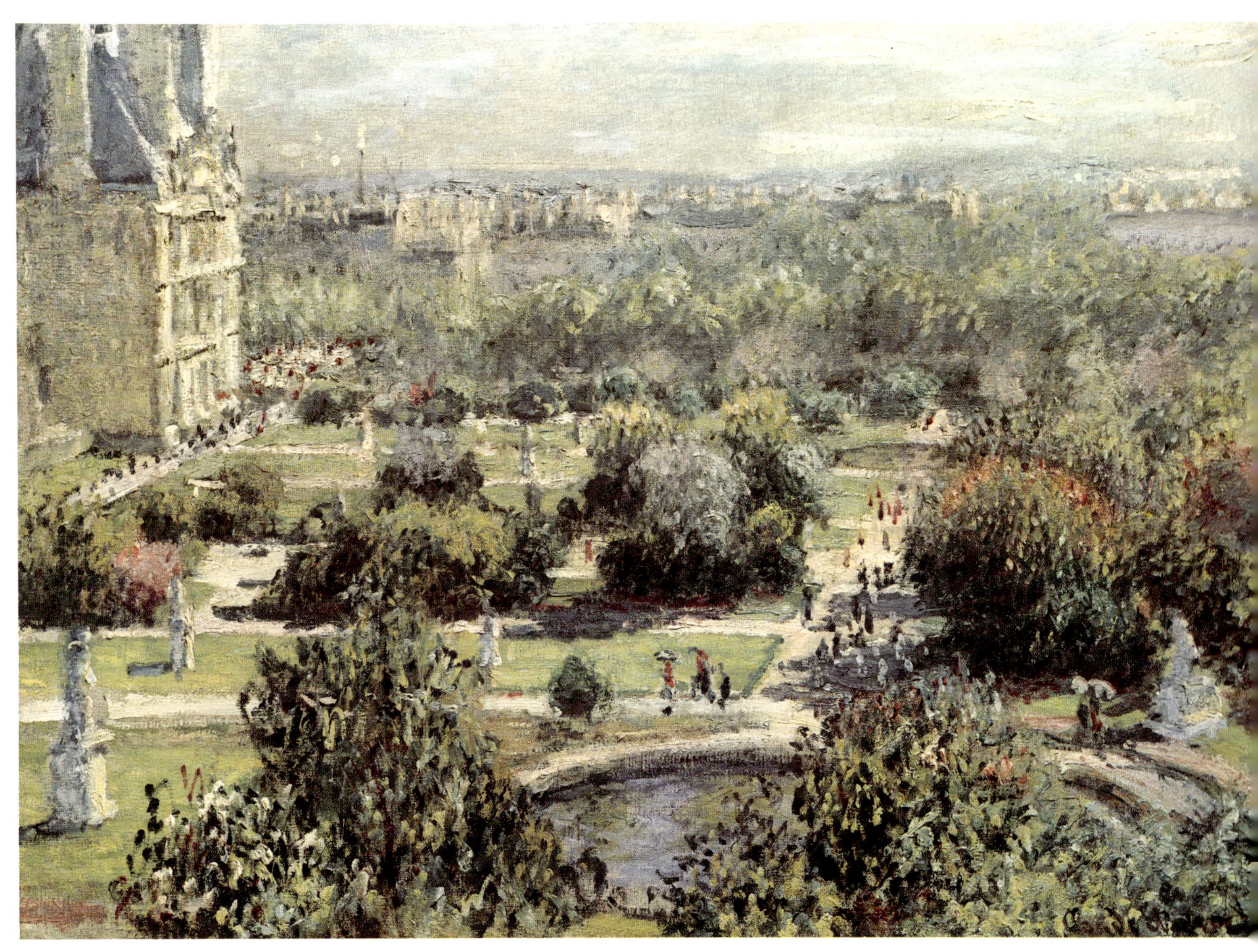

ABOVE Claude Monet: *View of the Tuileries*, 1876 (Musée Marmottan, Paris).
OPPOSITE Auguste Renoir: *Les Tuileries*, 1875 (Private Collection).

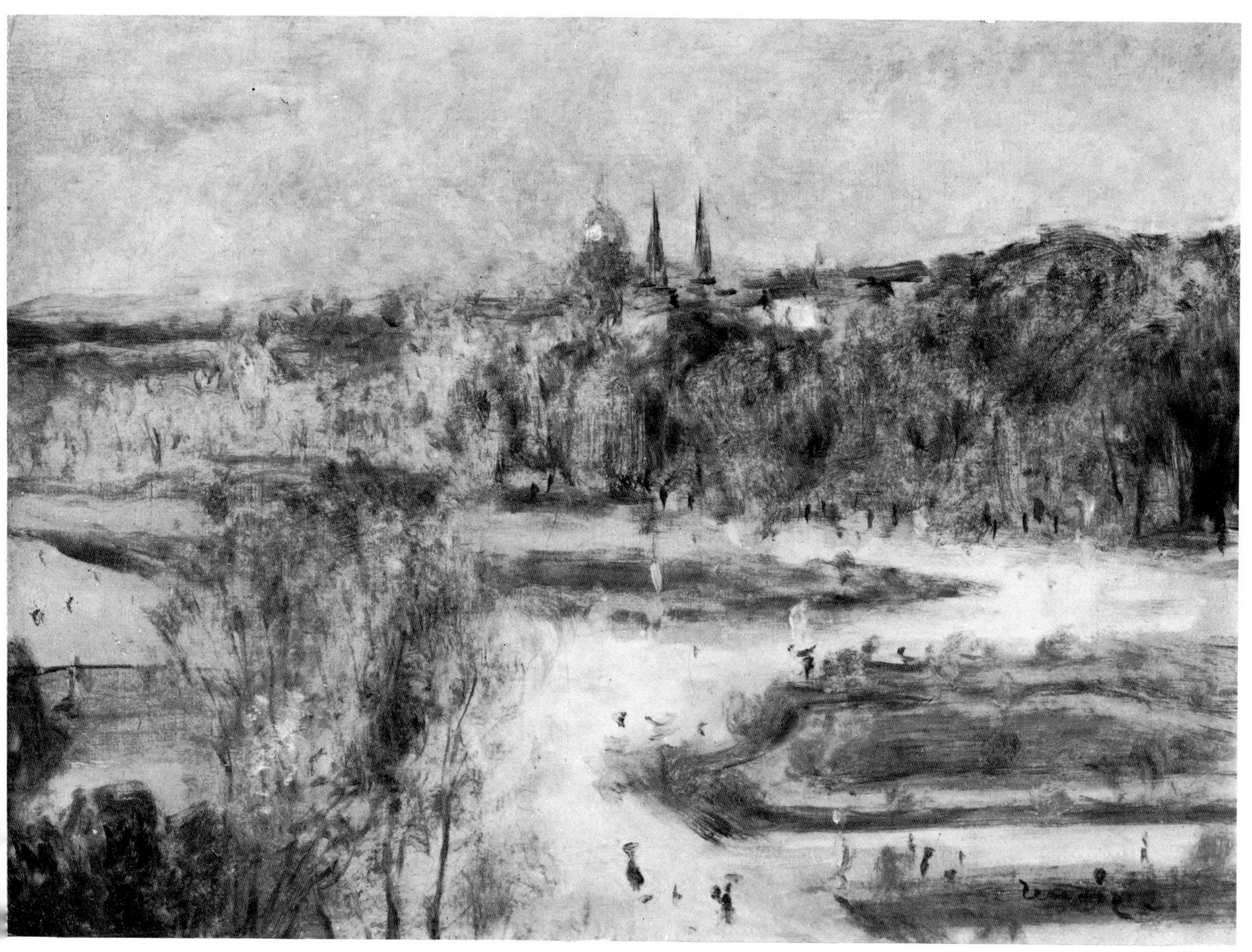

from a garden belonging to one of his painter friends on the corner of the Rue de Rome and the Rue de Constantinople. His composition was a very subtly suggestive one: he shrouded the realistic aspects of the subject in a thick cloud of smoke, justifying the picture's title solely via the little girl who, with her back to the artist, is staring – one imagines – at a railway train. The common denominator between these otherwise very different works was the subject, which for the first time was taken straight from contemporary life – and consistently rejected by the jury of the Salon.

Although Degas' painting did not attract much less criticism than the others', he had no difficulty in finding buyers and making a reasonable living. His problems lay elsewhere: he could not bring himself to part with his pictures, which often failed to satisfy him, and the whole idea of selling

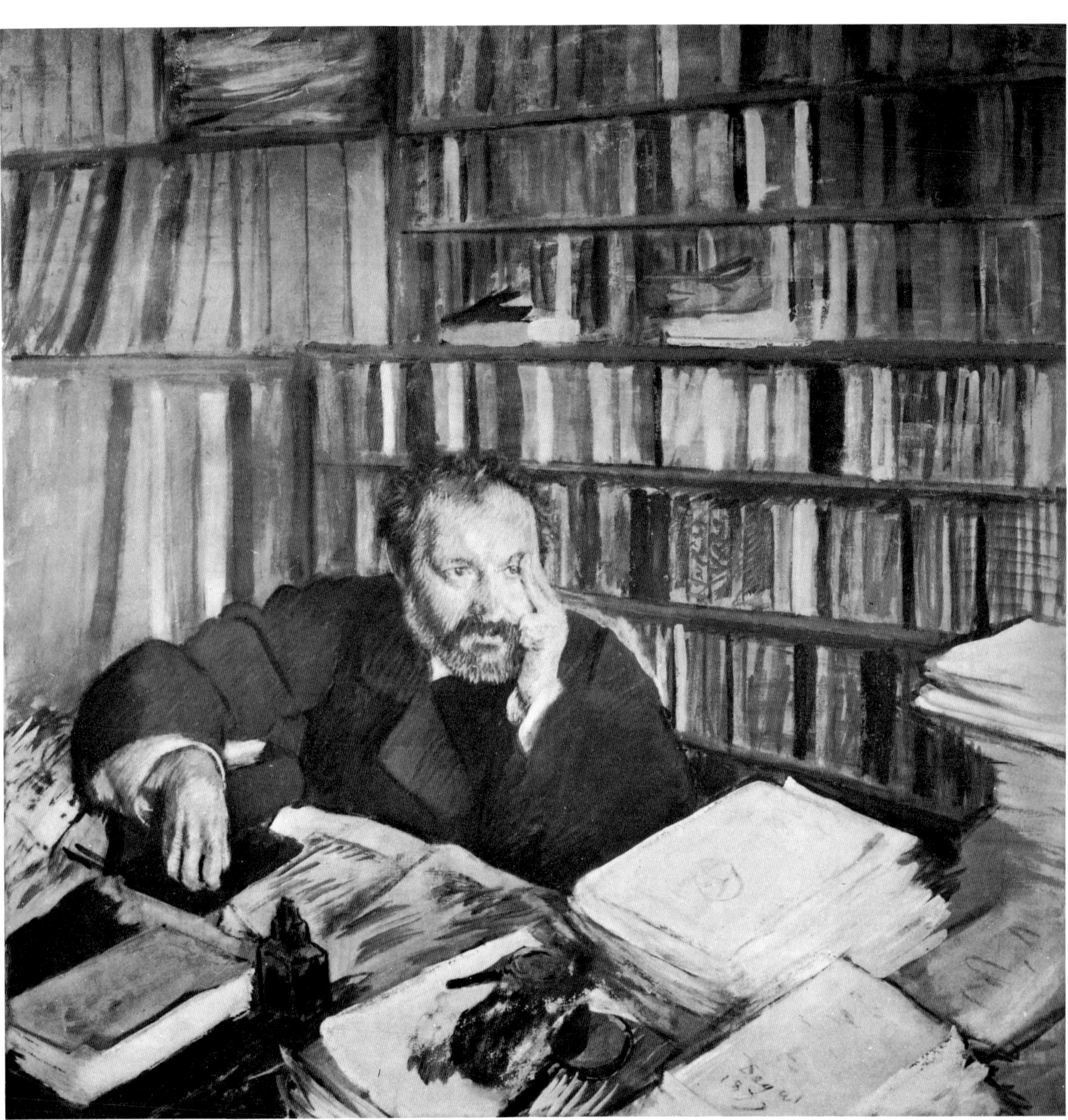

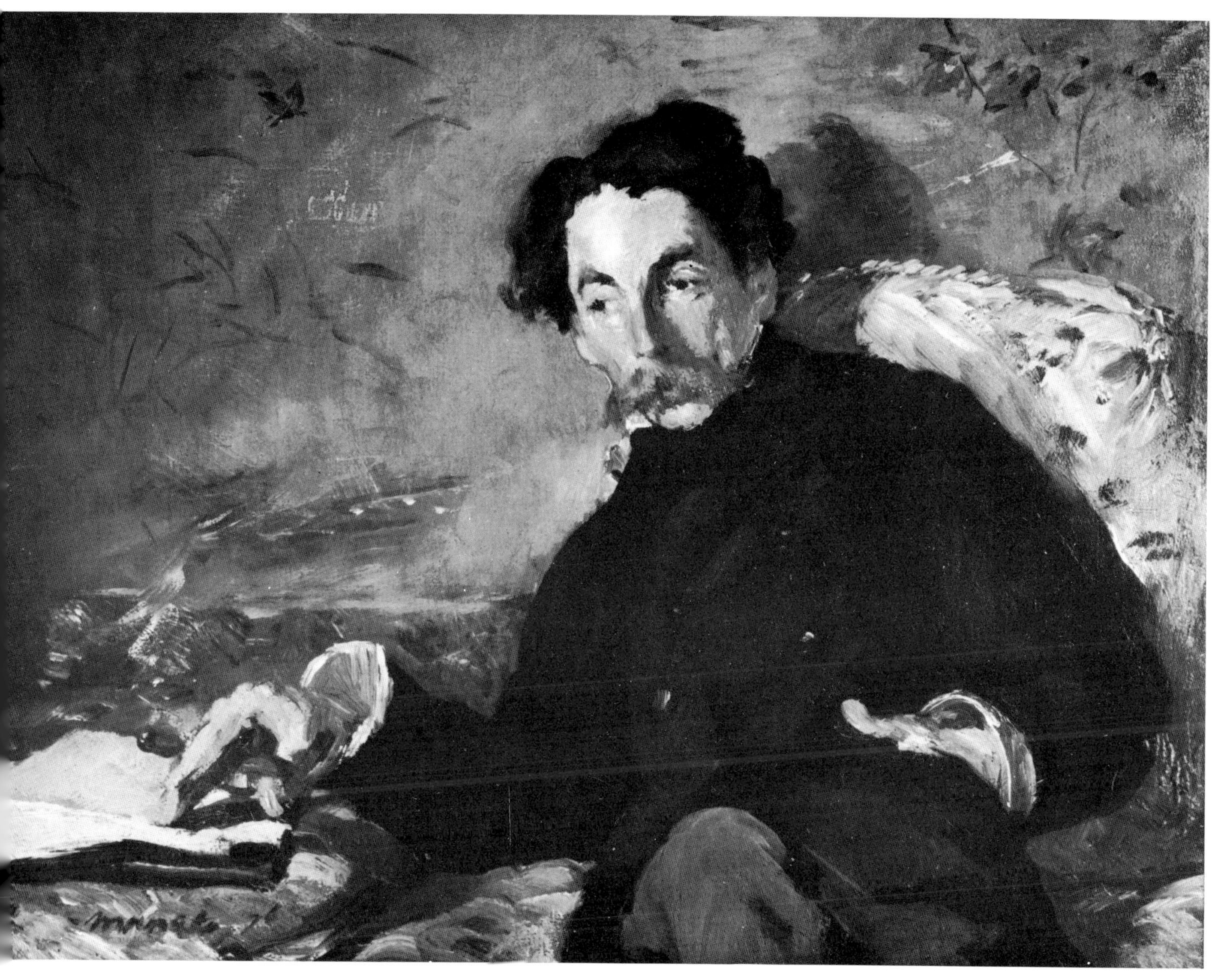

OPPOSITE Edgar Degas: *Portrait of Edmond Duranty*, 1870 (City Art Gallery, Glasgow, Burrell Collection). The novelst and critic Duranty was a champion of realism. An *habitué* of the Café Guerbois, and a close friend of Degas, he put forward the latter's views in an article which appeared in his own review, *La Nouvelle Peinture*, in 1876.
ABOVE Edouard Manet: *Portrait of Stéphane Mallarmé*, 1876 (Musée du Louvre, Paris – Jeu de Paume). Every day, on his way home from the Lycée Condorcet where he taught English, the poet would call on Manet, who during their conversations executed this marvellously spontaneous portrait.

his 'articles', as he called them, disgusted him. Whenever he had a chance, he would try to recover from their rightful owners paintings which he felt were not up to standard. For instance, he took back a pastel he had given his friends the Rouarts, with a view to improving it; but instead he destroyed it by working too much on it.

Durand-Ruel, Degas' dealer for many years, had enormous difficulty in wheedling pastels, paintings and drawings from the artist who, like the other Impressionists, had to make a living from his pictures. Yet Degas' needs were small: he was a bachelor, and had resigned himself to living on a modest scale. When Madame Halévy urged him to make a few improvements to his flat – such as taking the bathtub out of the bedroom – Degas refused. 'I am a well-off poor man,' he told her, to close the subject.

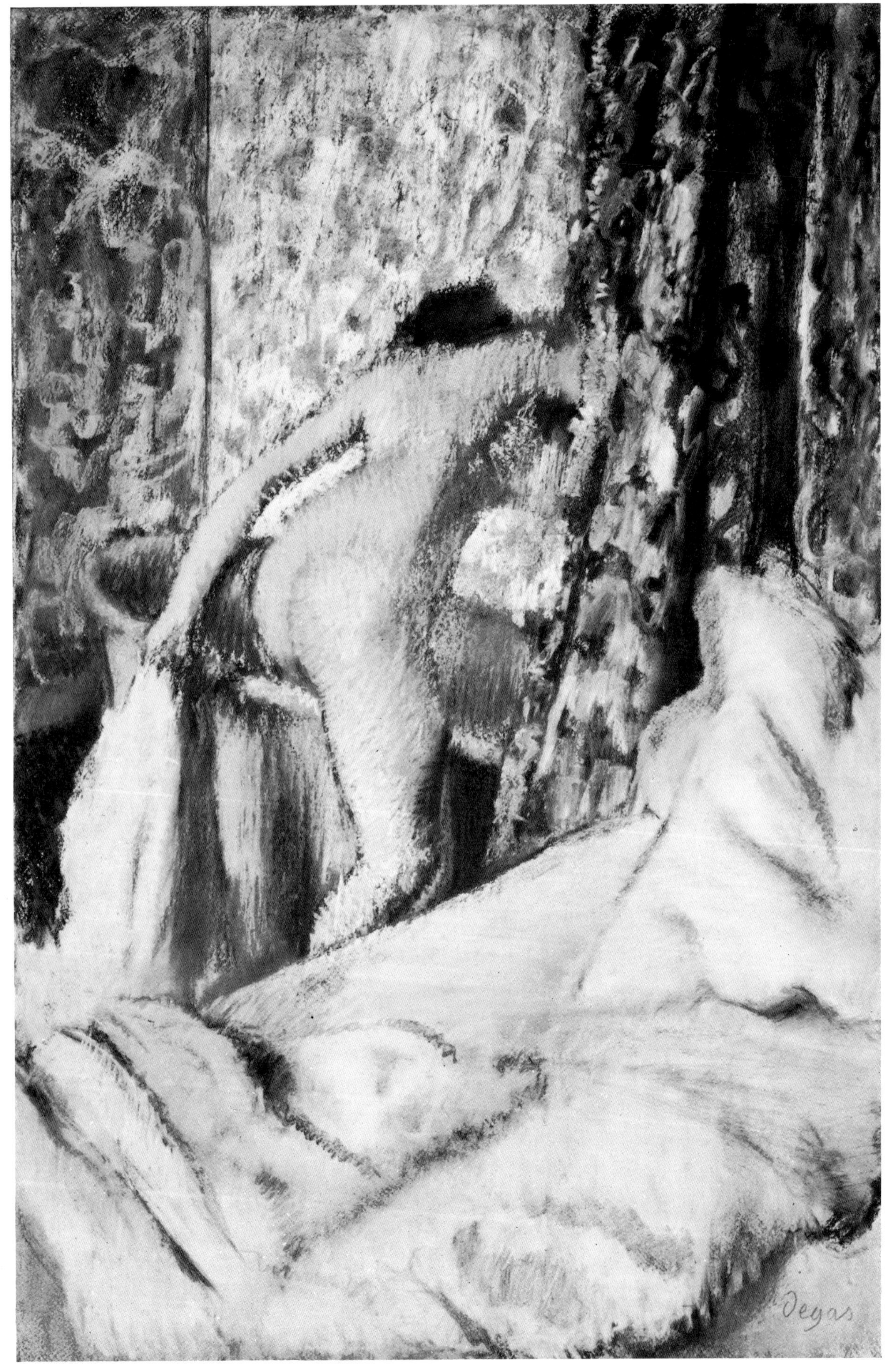
Degas

7 The Terrible Degas

OPPOSITE Edgar Degas: *The Morning Bath*, pastel, 1883 (courtesy of the Art Institute of Chicago). One of a series of striking studies of women washing and dressing.
BELOW Edgar Degas: *The Pedicure*, 1873 (Musée du Louvre, Paris – Jeu de Paume). The unusual subject of this picture emphasizes Degas' modernity.

Degas spent his whole working life at the foot of the hill of Montmartre. In 1889 he left the Rue Pigalle and moved not far away, to 37 Rue Victor-Massé, where he occupied all three floors of the building. At eight o'clock in the morning he would clamber up to his studio in the attic, where he was once again surrounded by the chaos of his beloved painting equipment and by the creations that were his, and his alone. A thick layer of dust on the panes of the bay window softened the light that filtered into the long room and alighted on the jumble of half-finished wax statuettes, bulging portfolios, and easels with a pastel, a charcoal sketch or an oil painting in position. In one corner, a bath, a zinc tub and a frayed bathrobe waited ready for the artist's model. On a narrow shelf that ran along the walls, there was a motley collection of boxes, bottles, pieces of chalk, etcher's needles and old copper plates, all ready for use as soon as the artist needed them.

Throughout the day Degas worked feverishly, surrounded by a muddle that was completely familiar to him, and repeating, without any trace of irony: 'I like tidiness.' One day, a scrap of paper fell from a packet that the

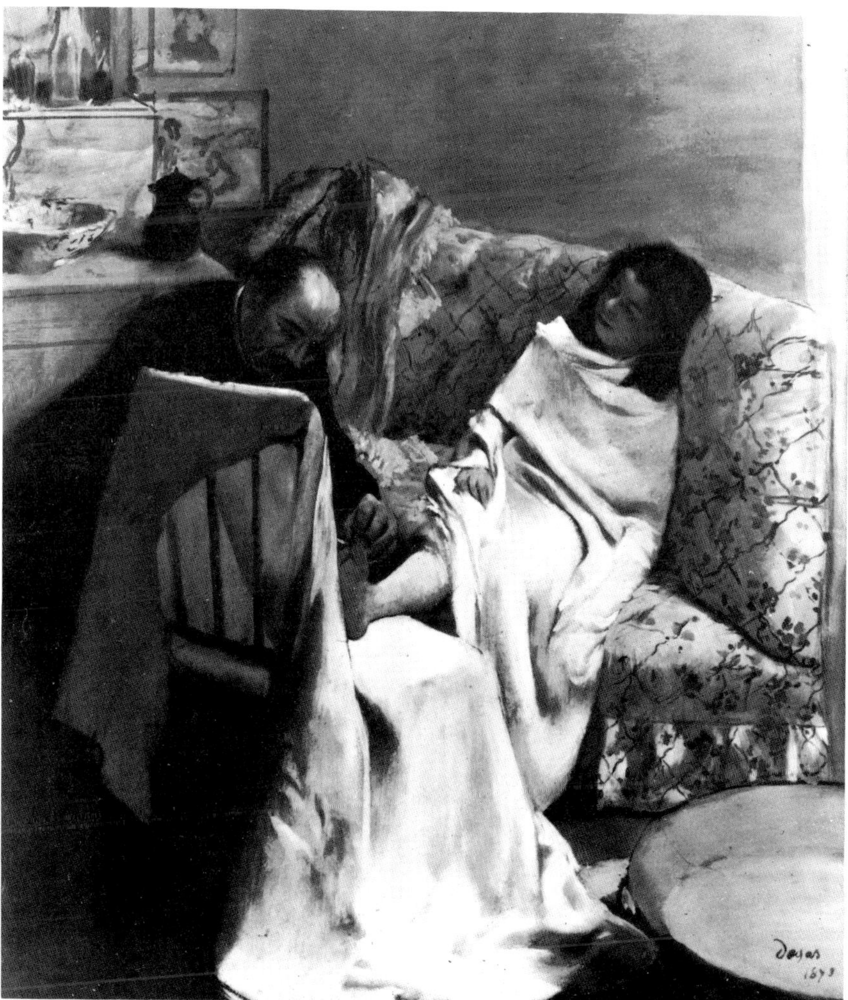

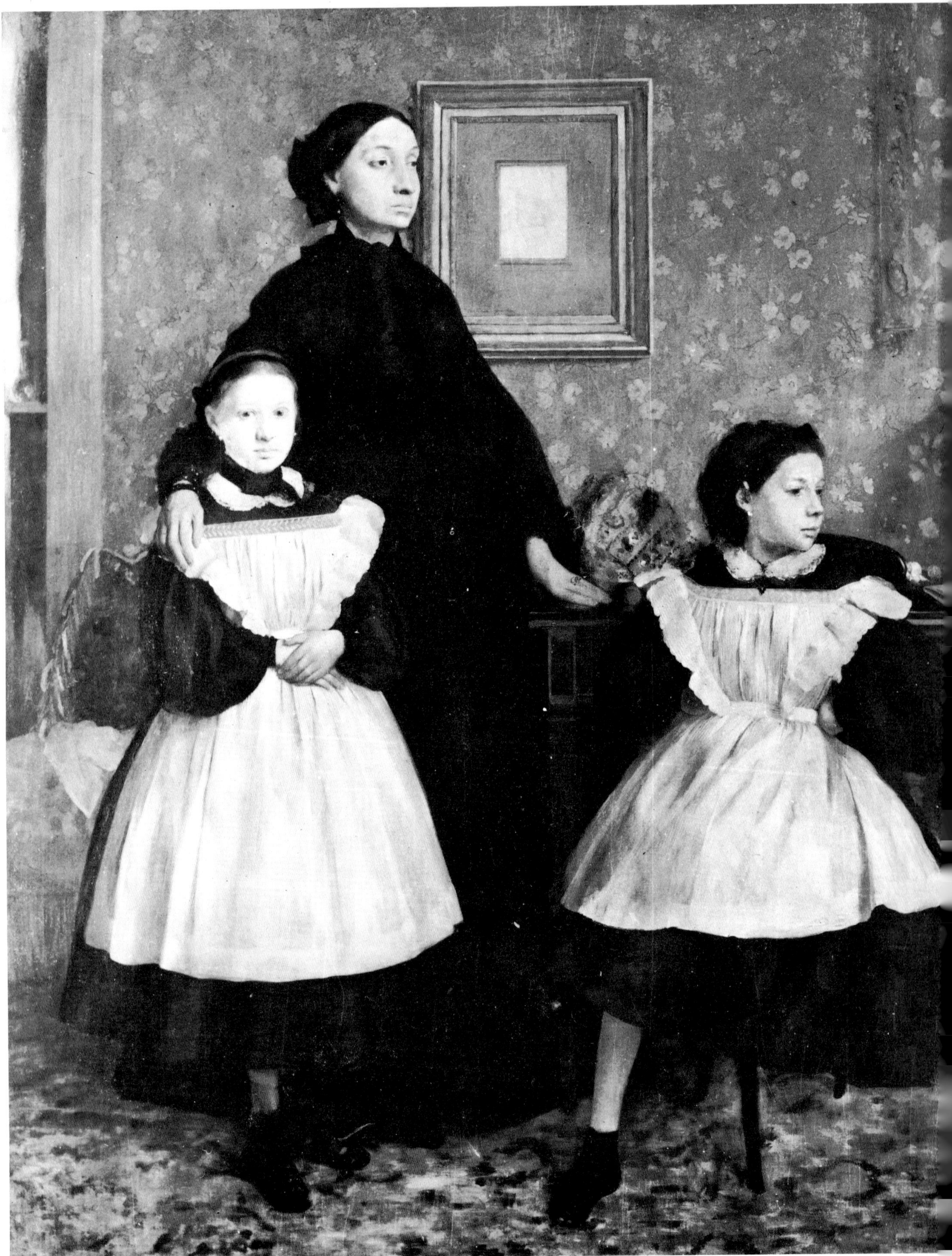

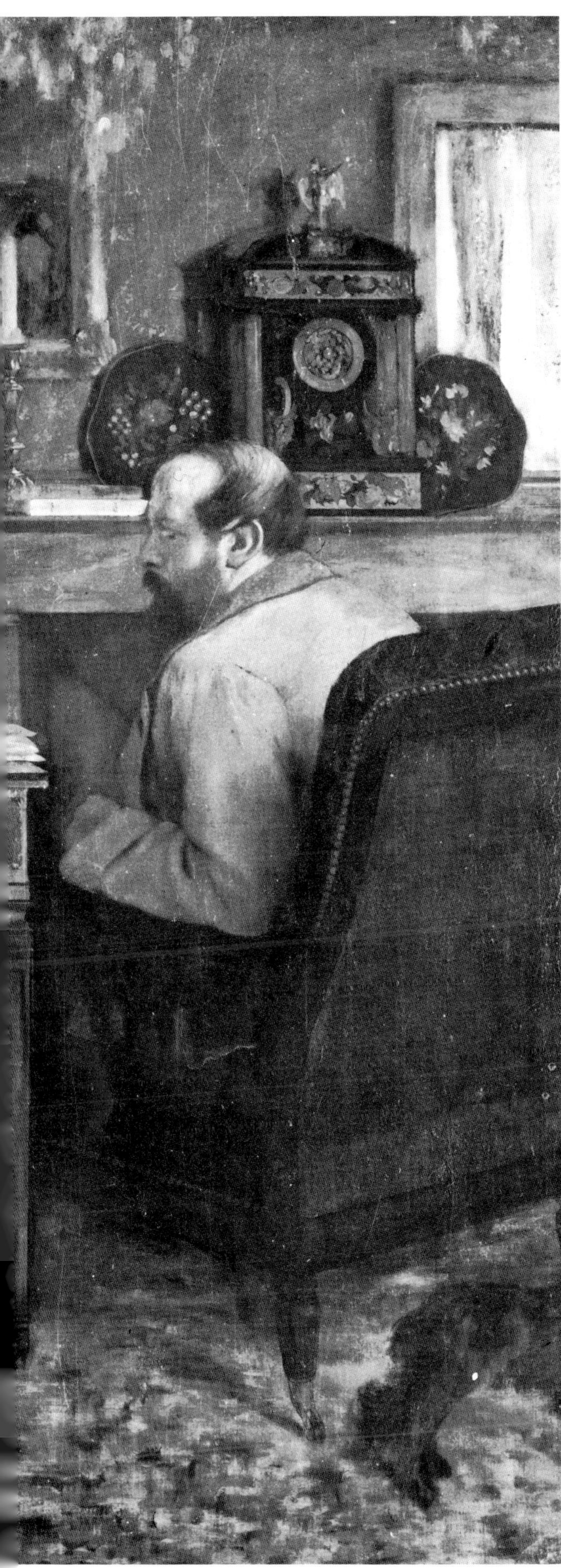

Edgar Degas: *The Bellelli Family*, *c.* 1858–9 (Musée du Louvre, Paris). Degas made many sketches for this portrait of his aunt, Laura Degas, and her family while staying with them in Florence.

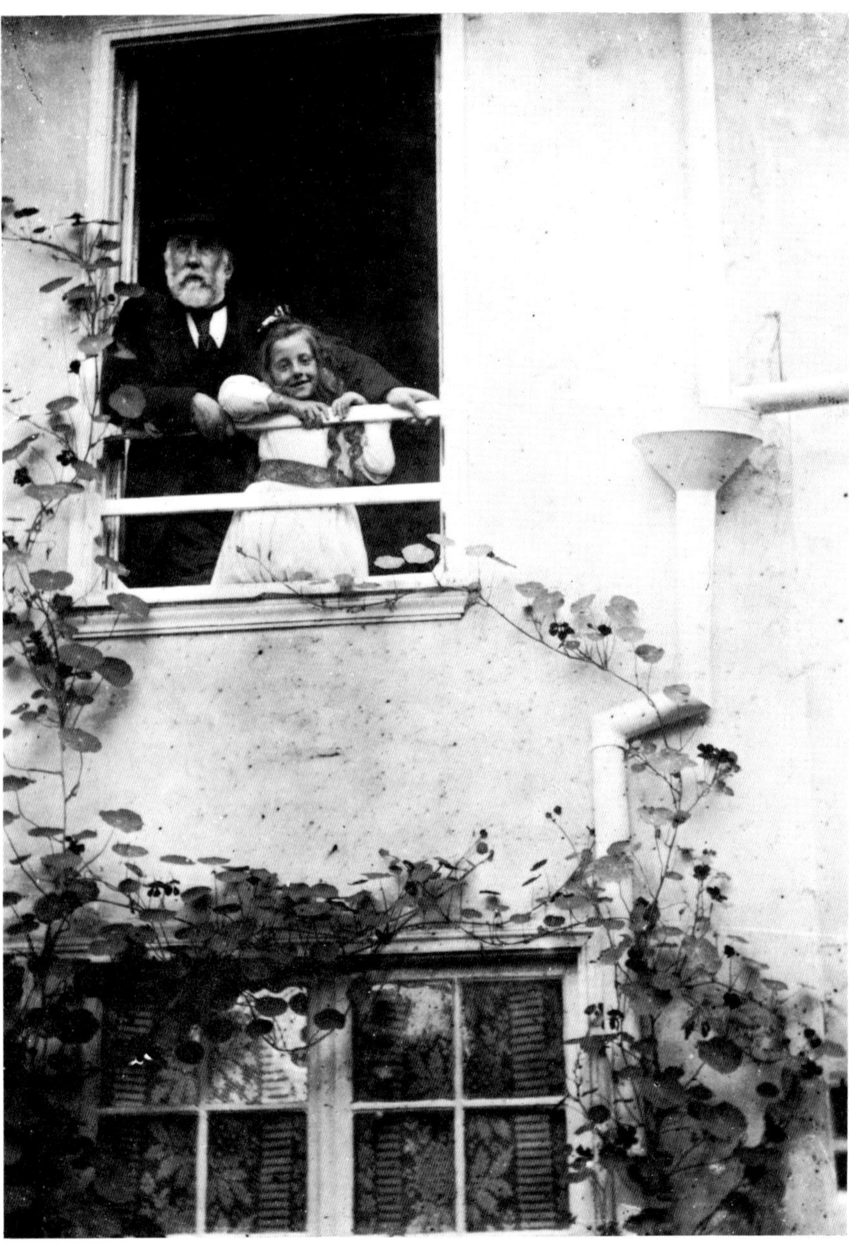

LEFT Degas at a window with a child.
BELOW Photograph of Degas, in visiting card format, by Barnes, an English photographer working in Dieppe.
BOTTOM Photograph taken in the painter's flat.
OPPOSITE LEFT Degas standing in front of the Château du Ménil-Hubert, which belonged to his friends the Valpinçons.
OPPOSITE RIGHT Self-portrait of Degas wearing his painter's smock.

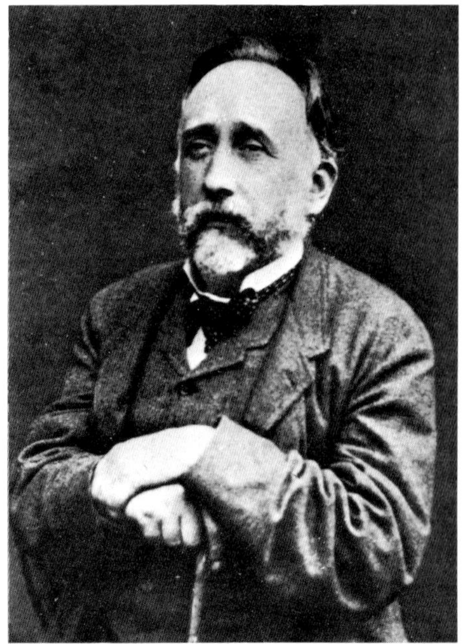

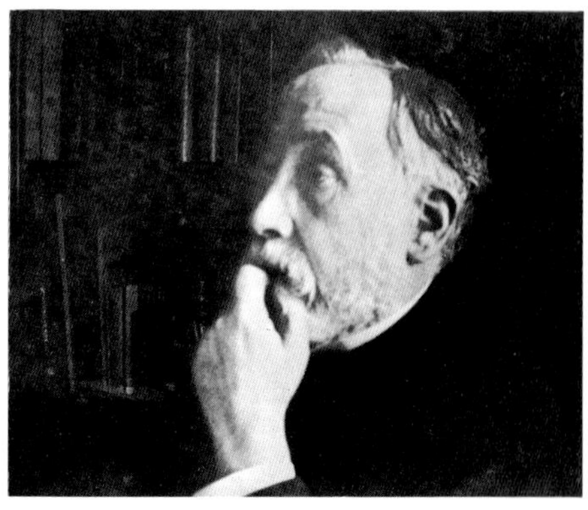

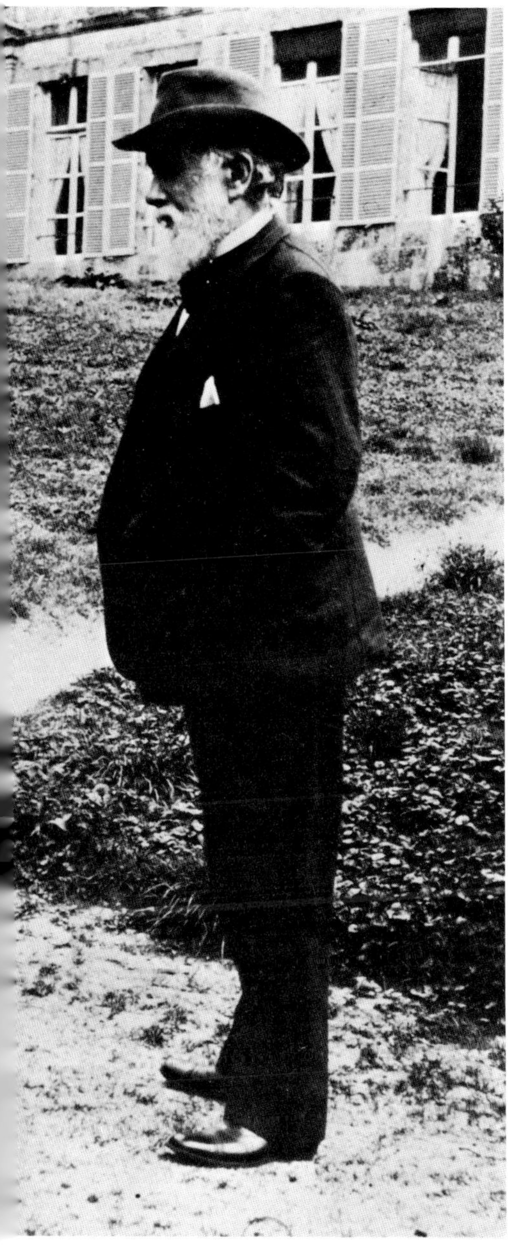

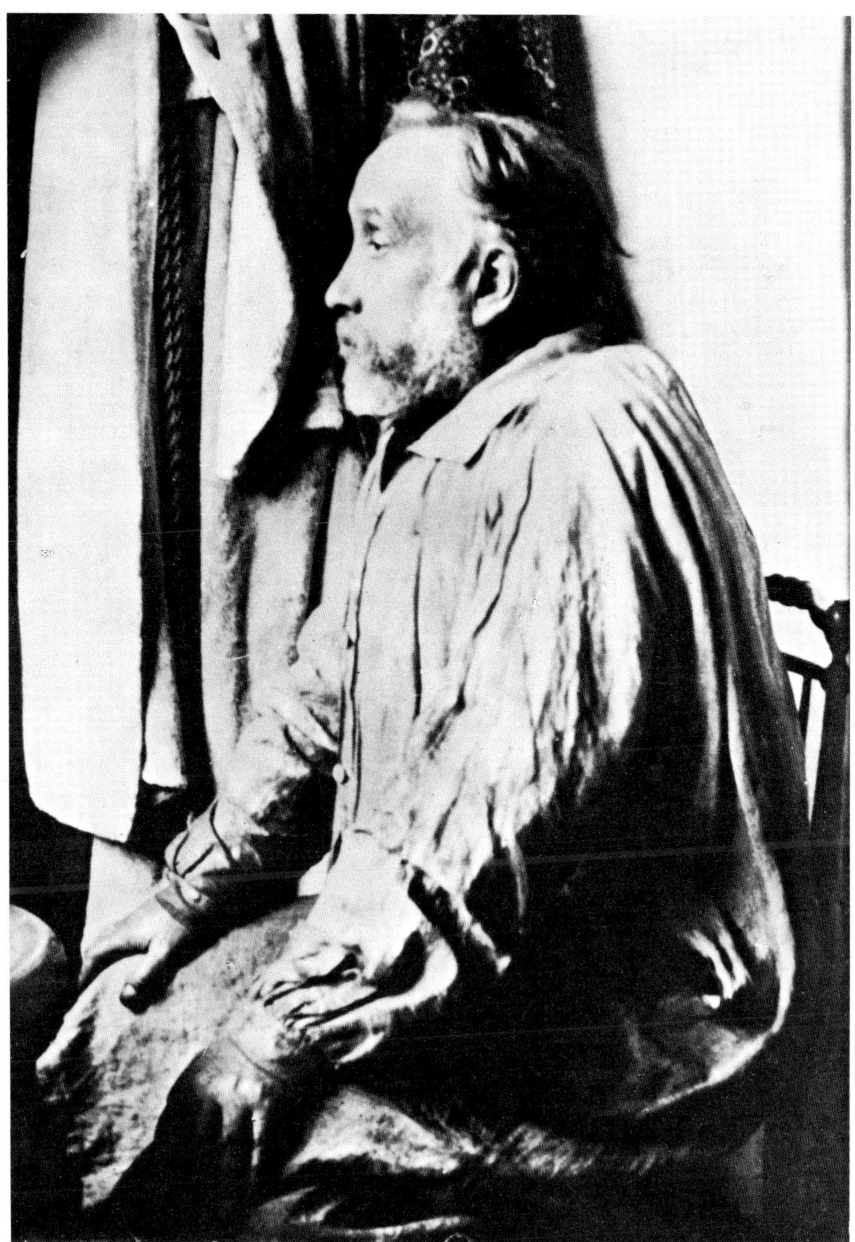

dealer Ambroise Vollard had brought him, and got stuck between two floorboards. According to Vollard, Degas went to the trouble of winkling it out and tossing it into the fire, probably because he could not bear the idea of the slightest intrusion from the outside world. Access to Degas' lair, which, it goes without saying, was never dusted or swept, was strictly forbidden to anyone except models and dealers.

Degas usually had lunch at a little restaurant in the Rue Notre-Dame-de-Lorette much frequented by artists. Renoir, who had a tiny studio in the nearby Rue Saint-Georges, used to go there with such friends as Marcellin Desboutin, the bohemian engraver, who served as a model for Degas'

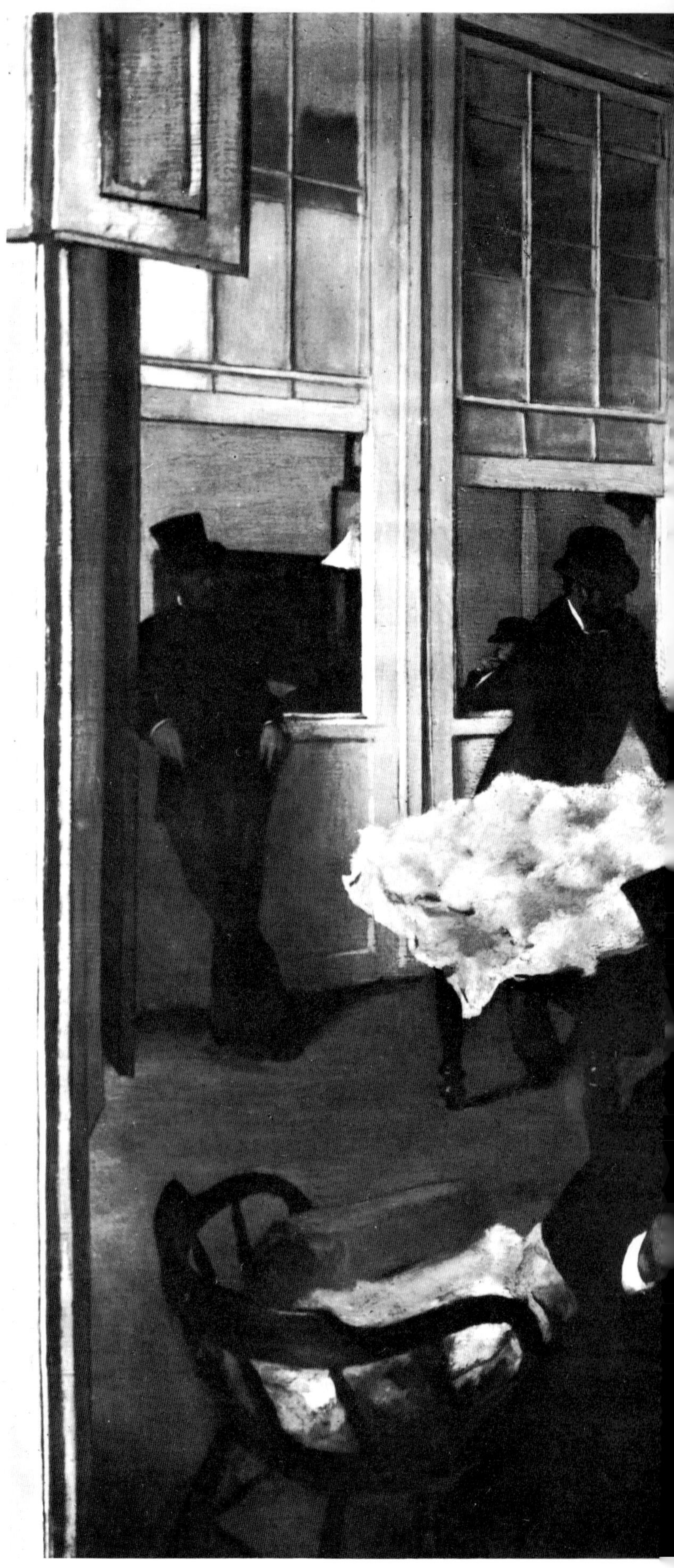

Edgar Degas: *The Cotton Office at New Orleans*, 1873 (Musée Municipal, Pau). Degas visited New Orleans, his mother's home town, in 1872. This painting of the family business shows Achille leaning against the window, their uncle, Michel Musson, in the centre foreground, and René reading a newspaper.

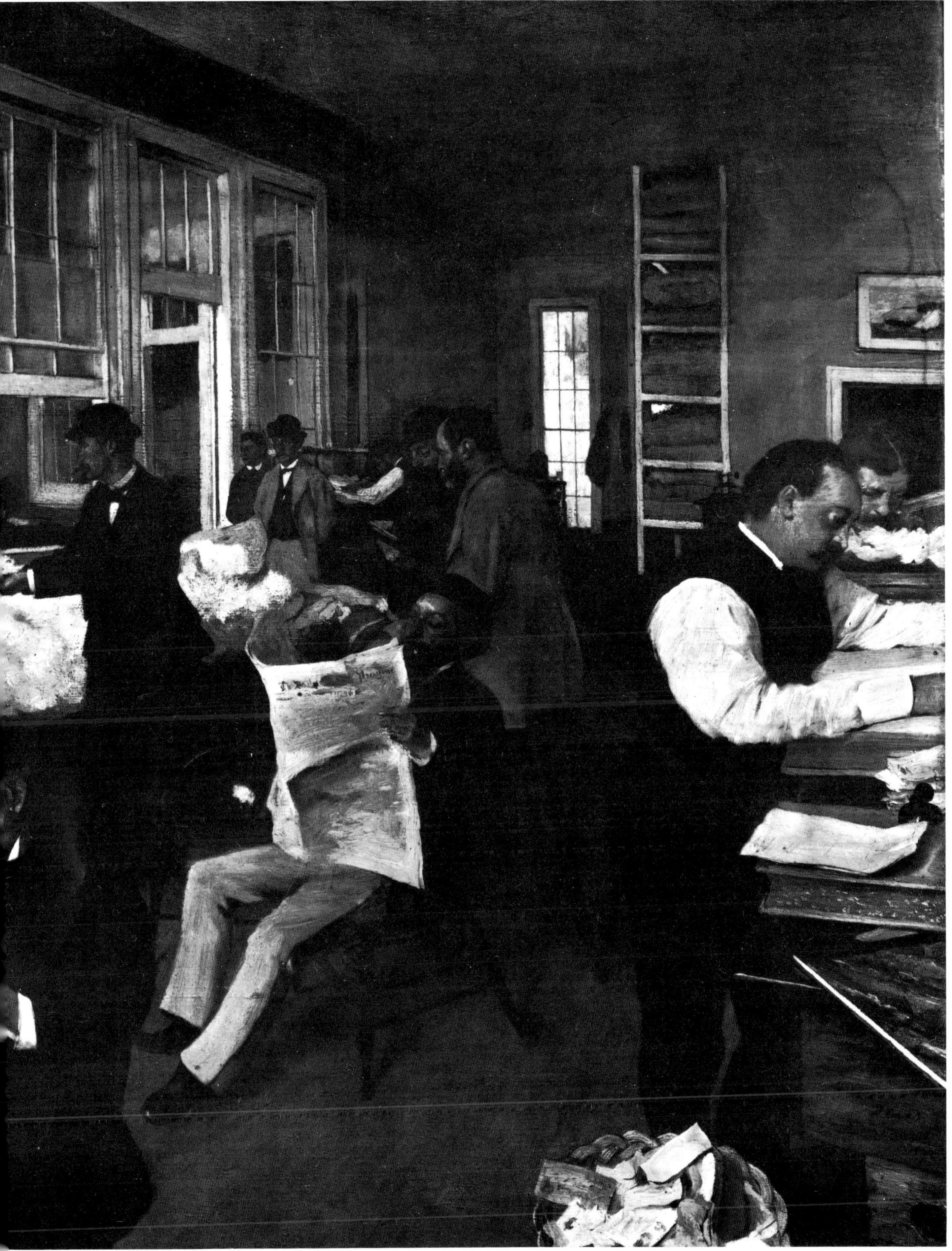

Absinthe, and sometimes the writer Georges Rivière or the composer Emmanuel Chabrier. If he was in a good mood, Degas took part in the conversation, contributing damning judgments and mordant witticisms that he would always follow up with a 'What d'you say, eh?' But his unpredictable temperament, which made him sometimes friendly but more usually grumpy, meant that on the whole people tended to have little time for him.

Degas spent almost all his time outside the studio with the handful of friends who remembered the days when he had been a charming young aristocrat. Every Thursday, with eager expectation, he walked to the Halévys', where he knew he would be listened to with respect and admiration by distinguished table companions he had known for years. The lady of the house, Louise Halévy, had been the best friend of his favourite sister Marguerite De Gas ever since childhood. Her youngest son Daniel was passionately interested in Degas, and later published reminiscences of their conversations.

LEFT Photograph of Ludovic and Louise Halévy taken by Degas in front of one of his paintings. The Halévys remained the painter's most loyal friends until the Dreyfus Affair in 1897.
BELOW Ludovic Halévy.
OPPOSITE Edgar Degas: *Degas and Valernes*, *c.* 1864 (Musée du Louvre, Paris). Throughout his life Degas remained a devoted friend of Evariste de Valernes, an older painter whom he had met at Louis Lamothe's studio.

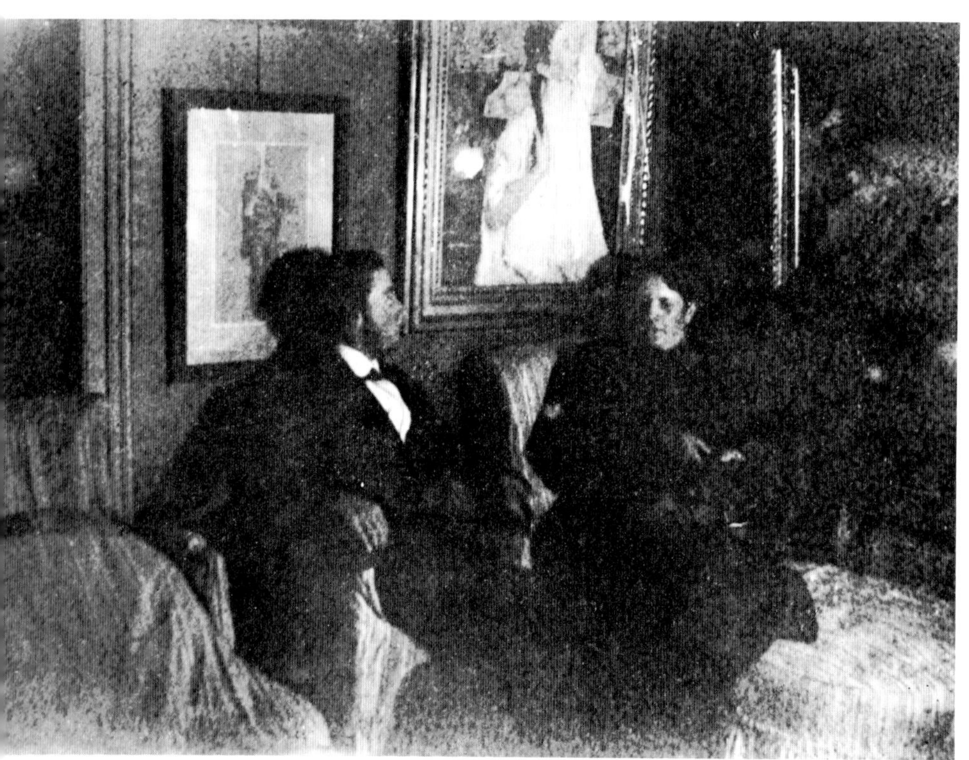

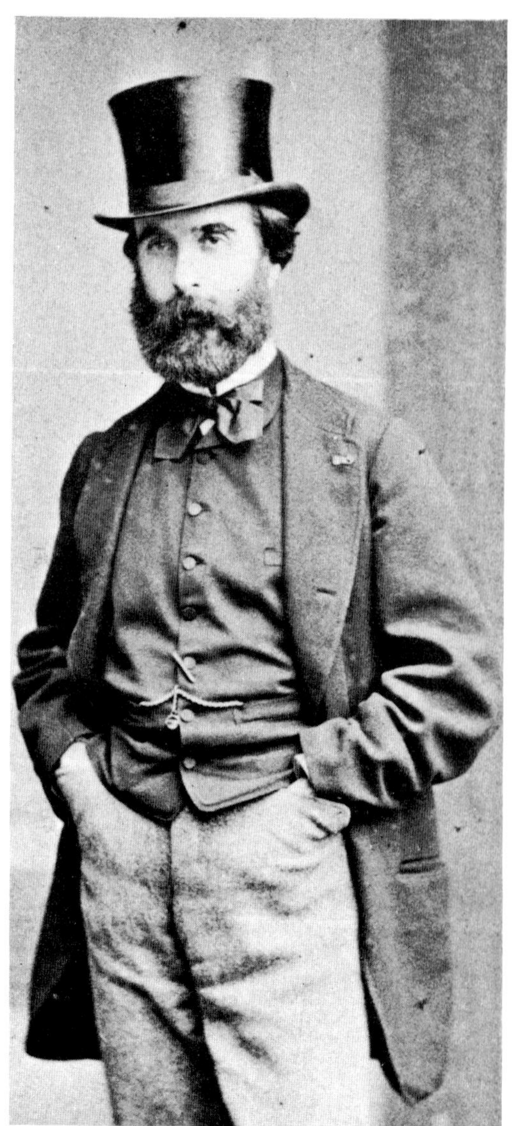

Among the other regular guests were Jacques Emile-Blanche, a friend of the young Marcel Proust (who studied to be a painter before becoming a brilliant chronicler of his times), Albert Cavé, a witty, unstable and whimsical dilettante, the Academician John Lemoisne, who edited the newspaper *Les Débats*, the American painter Whistler and the singer Rose Caron. Degas would refer lovingly to the eighteenth century, saying how

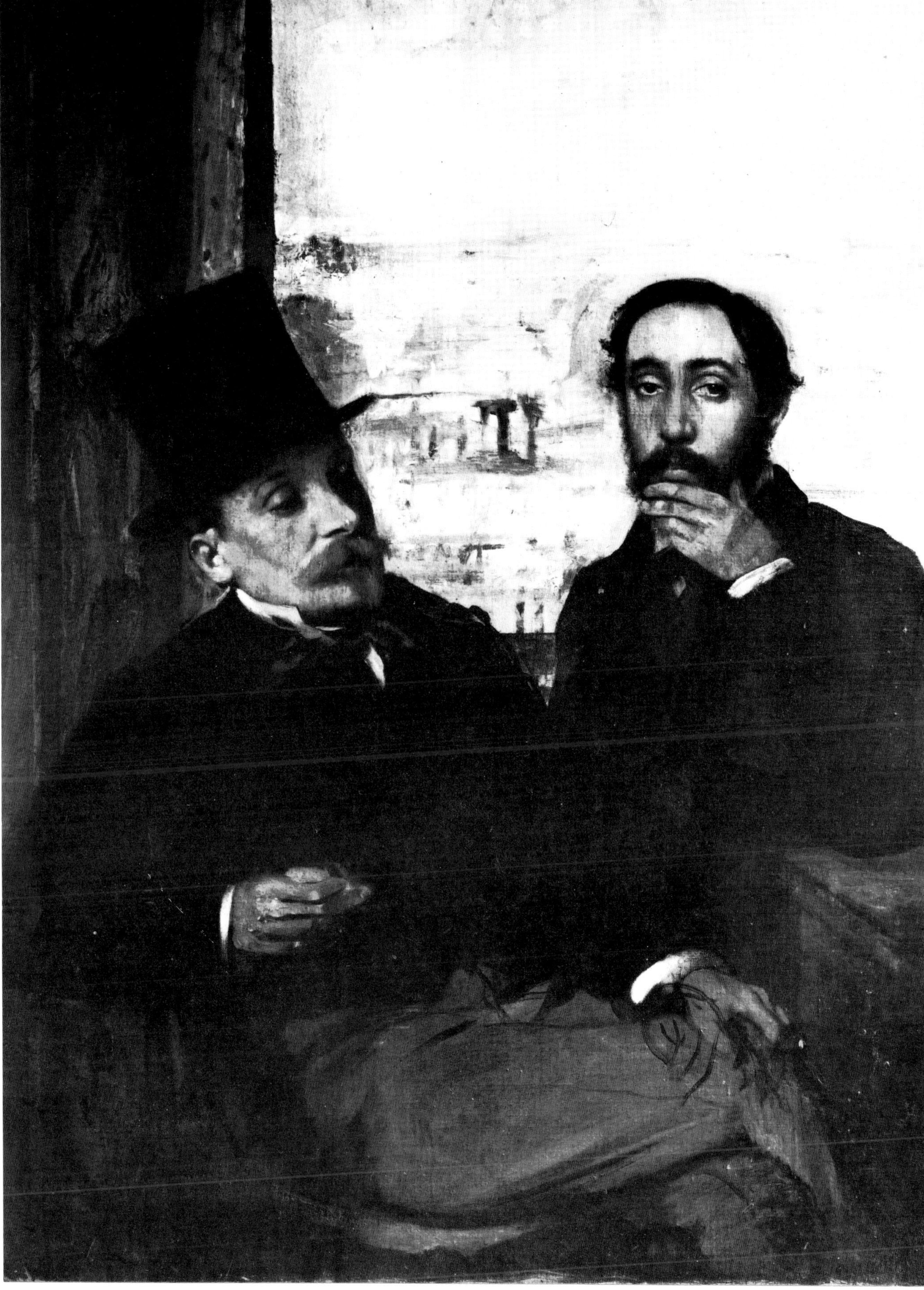

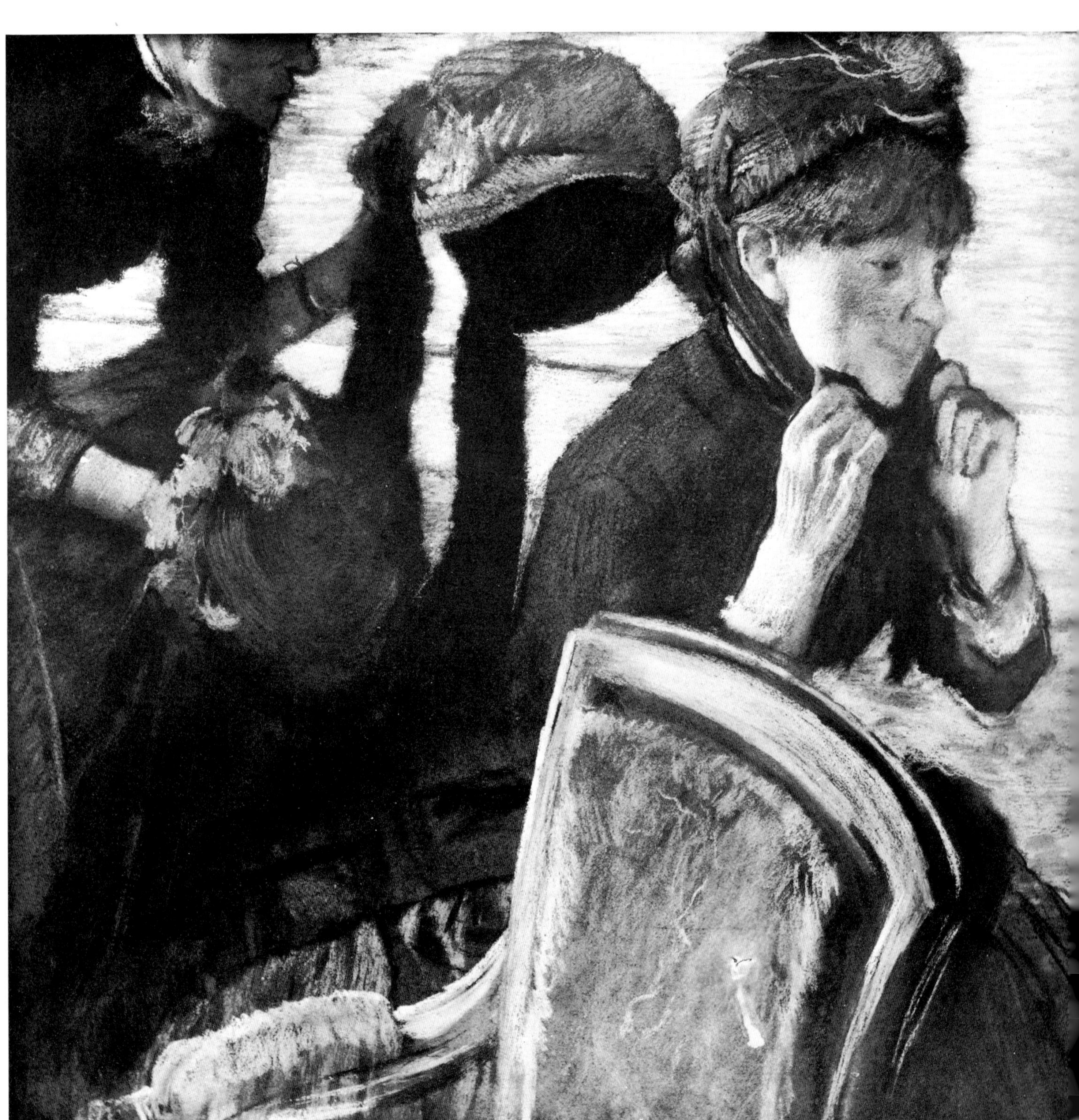

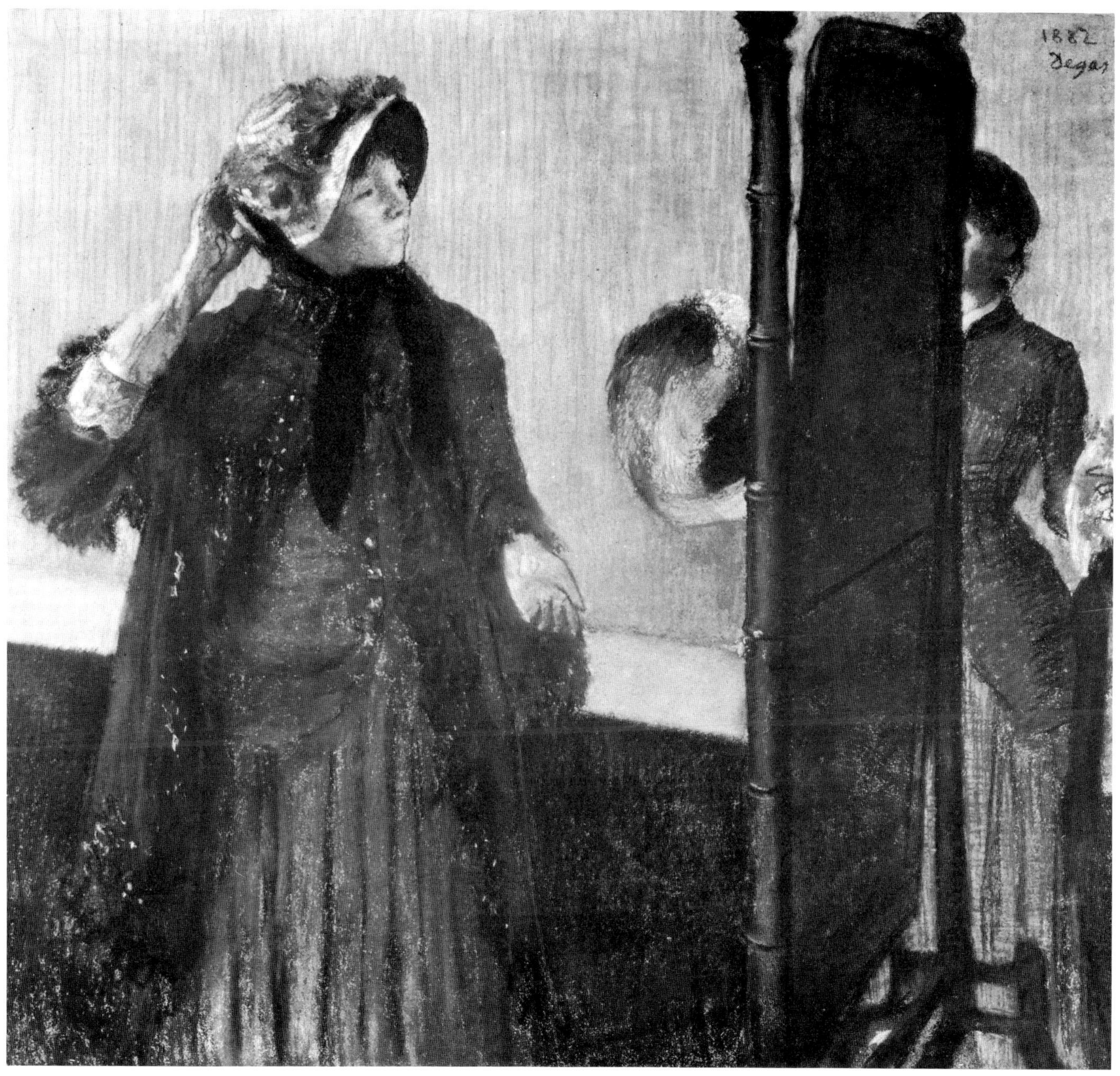

OPPOSITE Edgar Degas: *Trying Hats at the Milliner's*, pastel, *c.* 1882 (Gompel Collection). ABOVE Edgar Degas: *At the Milliner's*, pastel, 1882 (Metropolitan Museum of Art, New York, H. O. Havemeyer Collection). Mary Cassatt, the American painter who much admired Degas' work, posed for both these pictures.

much he missed the naturalness and simplicity of women who could make a faded dress look elegant. He talked about music, which had been one of the great joys of his childhood and adolescence, and discussed literature and philosophy. In order to give an anecdote a particular zest, Degas was quite prepared to make faces or play the fool. His judgments were passed with a bias that was appreciated because it was so uniquely his own.

On Fridays, Degas would join the company of scientists, well-read bourgeois and collectors for dinner with Henri Rouart, an engineer who had

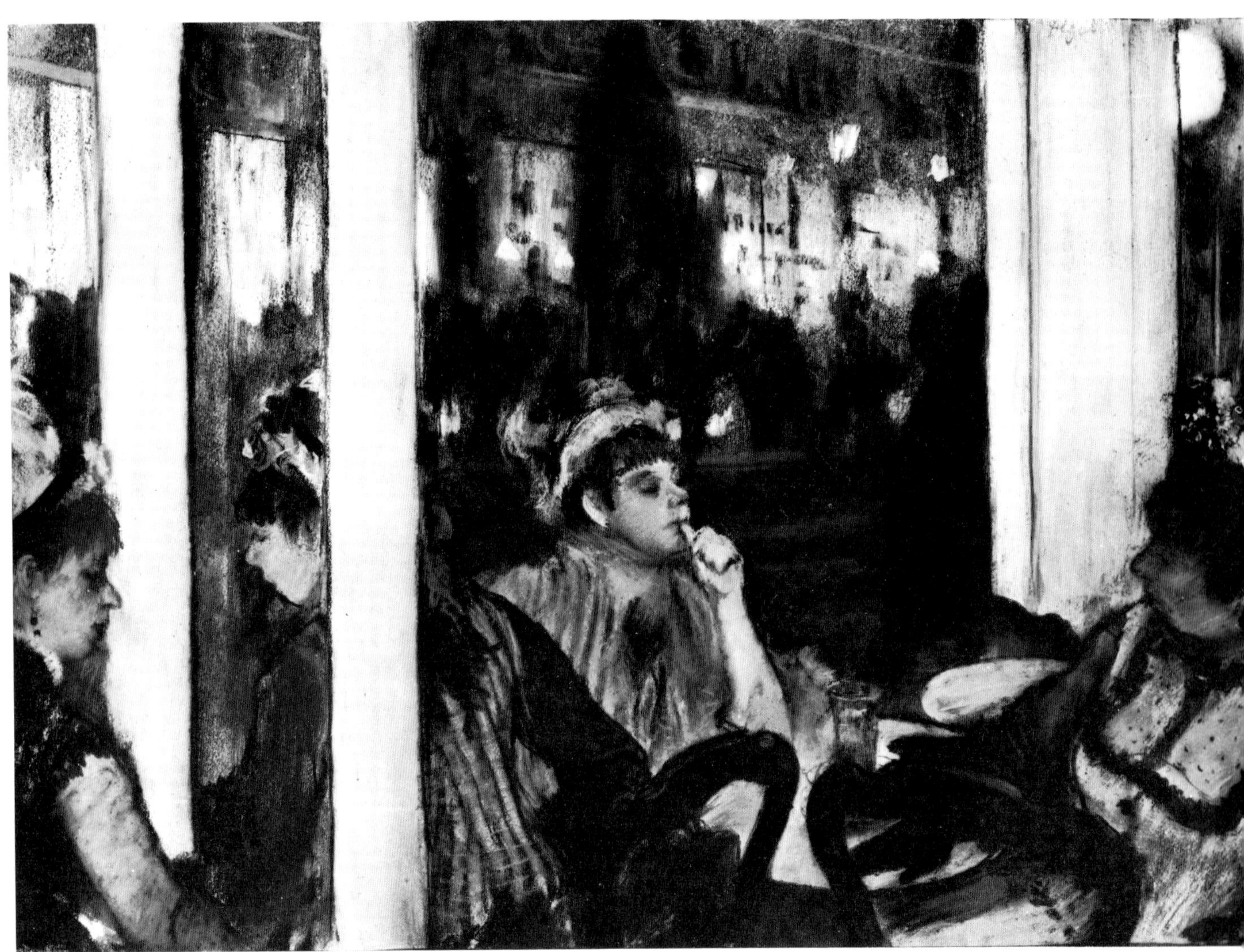

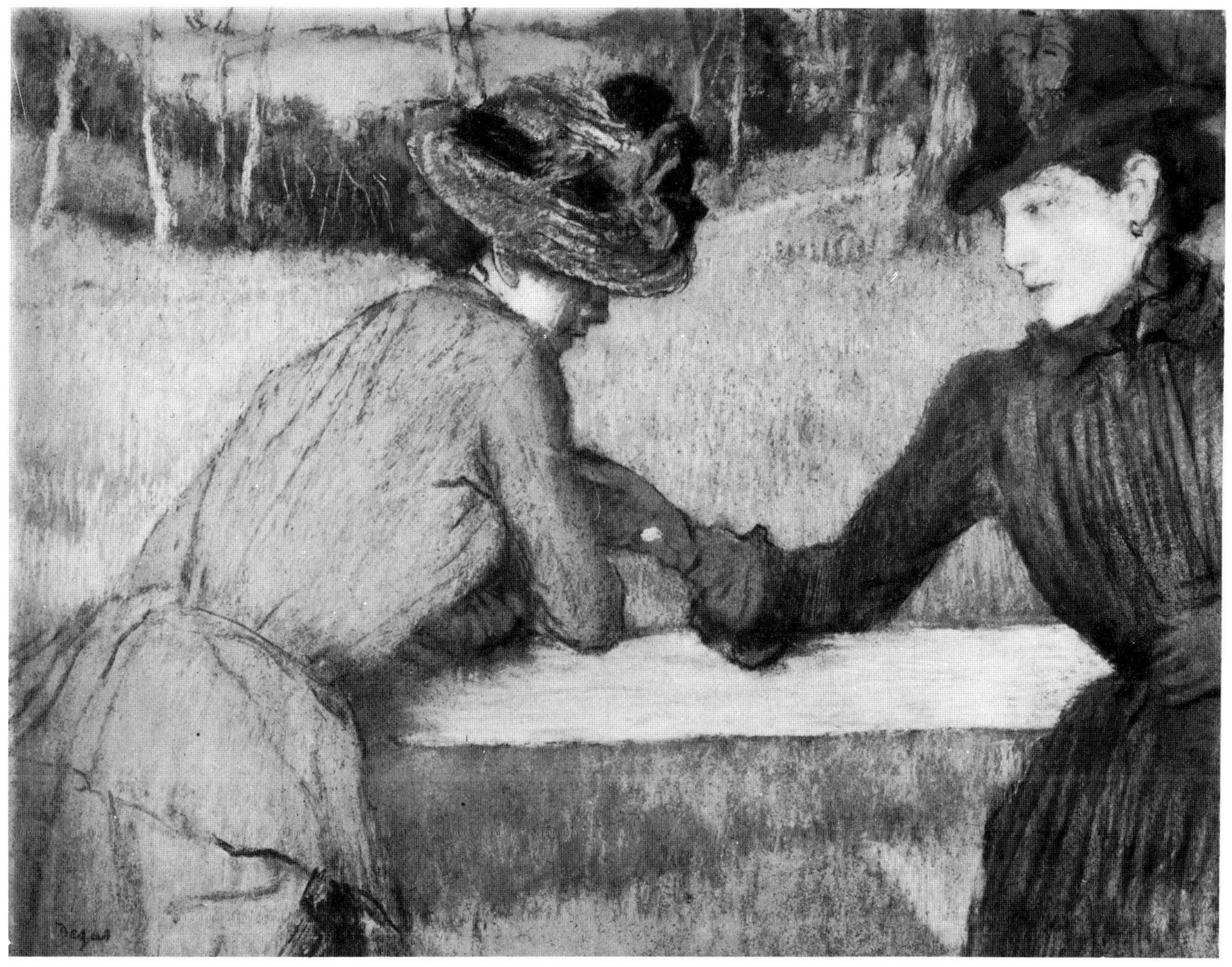

OPPOSITE Edgar Degas: *Café in the Boulevard Montmartre*, pastel, 1877 (Musée du Louvre, Paris). The boldness of the composition is reminiscent of Japanese prints, while the relaxed, casual attitude of the models suggests they have been caught by a camera.
ABOVE Edgar Degas: *The Conversation*, pastel, 1882–5 (Private Collection).

been to school with Degas at the Lycée Louis-le-Grand. He would have spent the previous evening at Alexis Rouart's – for every self-respecting host had 'his day'. This attractive custom, which made for very close relationships, was taken up by almost all the groups of intellectuals of the period.

To rest his weak eyesight and improve the sorry state of his lungs, Degas used to travel to all four corners of France. He would relax with the Halévys' brilliant galaxy of friends in Dieppe. At La Queue-en-Brie, a small studio in the house of his friends the Rouarts was always waiting for him, and he made frequent use of it; the dealer Ambroise Vollard, who once turned up there unannounced, found it difficult to believe that the old man wearing duck trousers, a straw hat and thick glasses whom he met there was in fact the 'terrible Degas'. From time to time, Degas would go into hiding with his friends the Braquavals at Abbeville, forcing their daughter Louise, who unlike Degas loved animals, to shut up all the dogs and cats before he arrived. And, as we have already seen, he also stayed frequently with the Valpinçons at Le Ménil-Hubert.

Several times Degas visited the obscure little village of Monieux, near Avignon in the Vaucluse, to see Evariste Valernes, a painter older than himself, with whom he had made friends while still a pupil at Louis Lamothe's studio. Degas had kept up a correspondence with him ever since he had gone back to his native village after losing his fortune. Degas did his best to give some discreet financial help to Valernes, whom he admired, and who scraped a meagre living as an art teacher. In a letter he wrote to him at the end of his life, Degas reveals a touching sincerity. He attempts to justify himself against the charge of harshness, and explains his behaviour as follows: 'I was, or I seemed, harsh on everyone, through a kind of training in incivility that arose from my own self-doubt and bad temper. I felt so – ill-formed, so ill-equipped, so spineless . . . I was sulky with everyone and with myself. I beg your forgiveness if ever, on the pretext of this damned art, I have wounded your most noble and intelligent mind, perhaps even your heart.'

As soon as cameras became less unwieldy, in about 1880, Degas took his own with him on all his travels and became a keen amateur photographer, displaying the same perfectionism in the pursuit of that technique as he applied to everything he did. When in Paris, he himself supervised the printing and enlarging of his negatives, and while he was travelling he

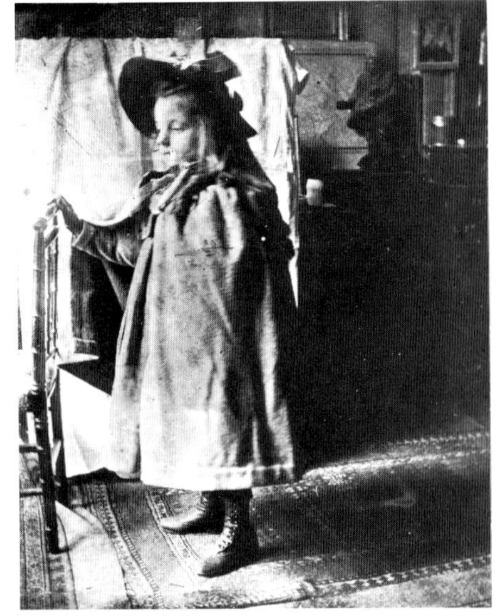

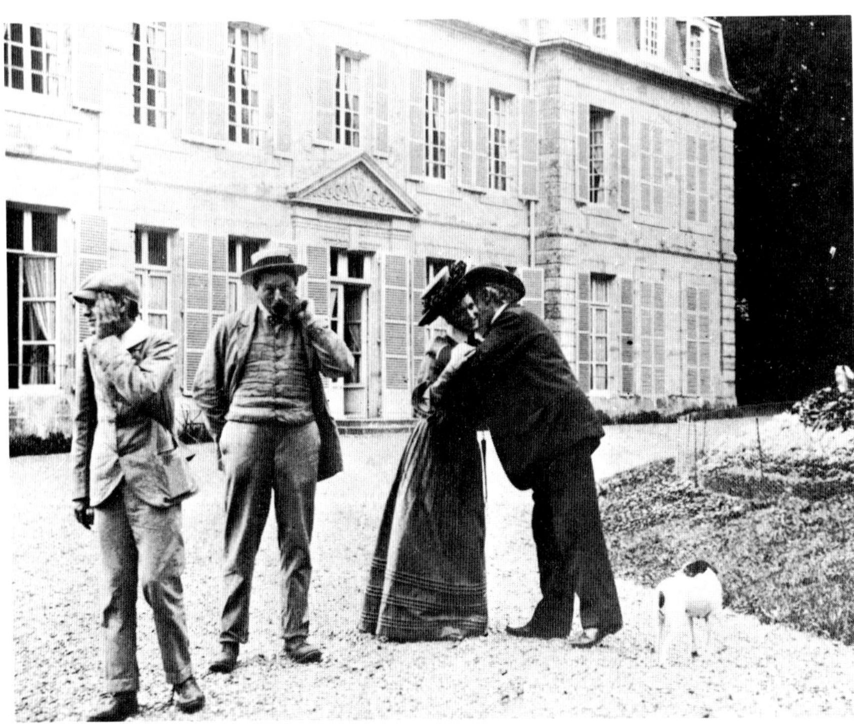

Degas loved to photograph his friends and relations, and forced them to endure lengthy sittings.
ABOVE and LEFT Two portraits of the painter's niece, Odette Fèvre-Degas. OPPOSITE ABOVE LEFT Madame Howland, a friend of Degas and the Halévys. ABOVE RIGHT A child in Degas' studio. BELOW LEFT Degas kissing Madame Valpinçon. BELOW RIGHT A posed parody of Ingres' *Apotheosis of Homer*, with Degas in the centre as Homer.

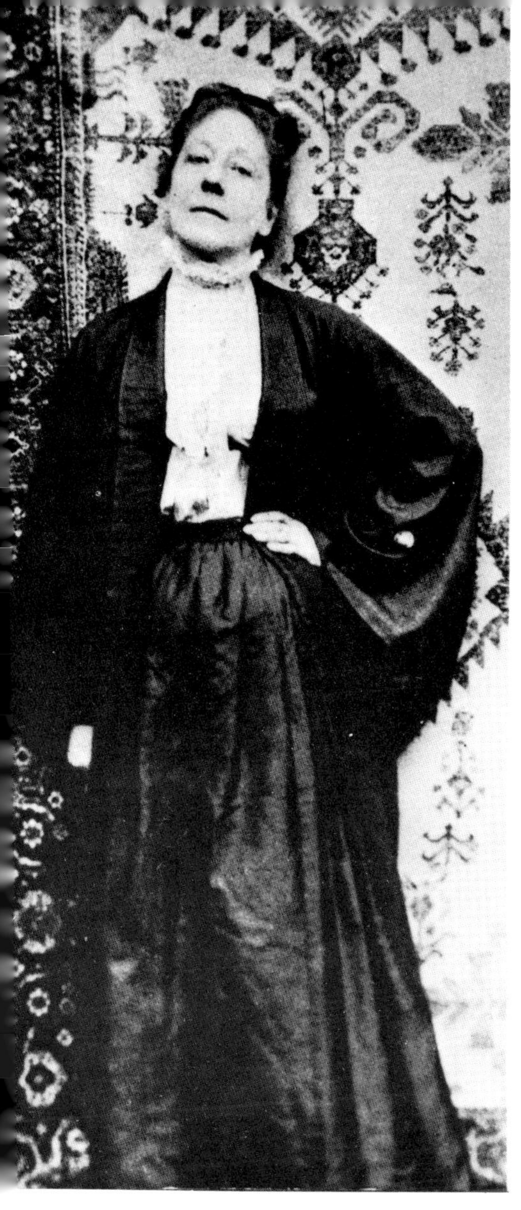

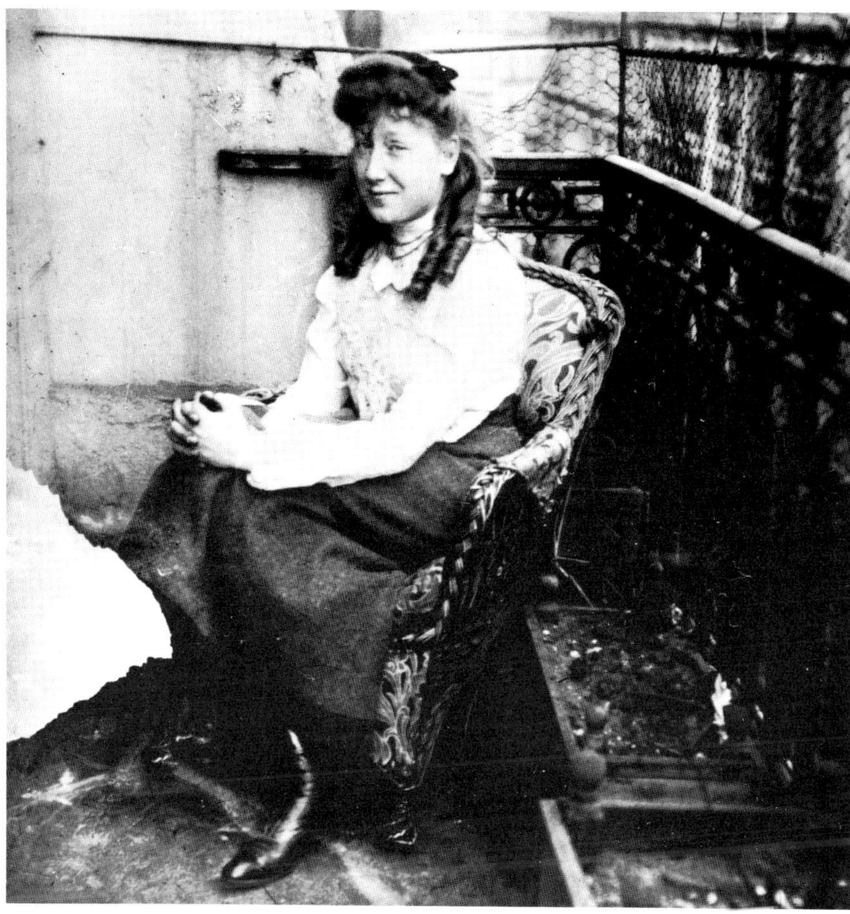

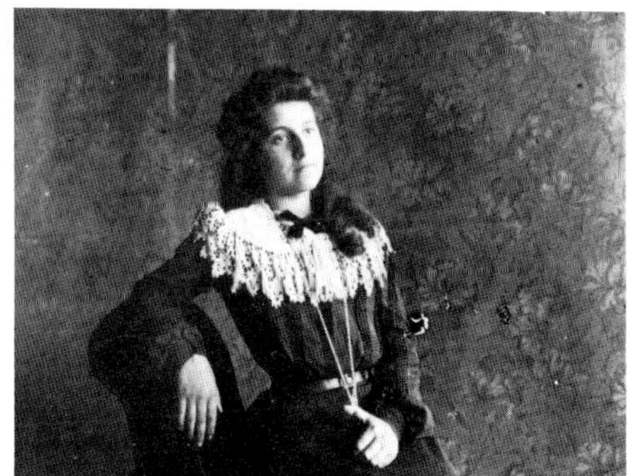

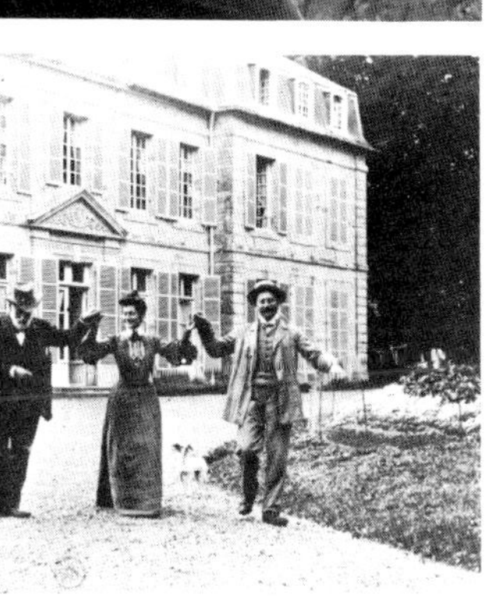

remained in constant touch with his suppliers, Tasset & Lhote, in the Rue Fontaine. The series of eight photographs he took in the Valpinçons' garden, to demonstrate a dance step to his friends, suggests that Degas would have made an excellent film director. His playfulness also inspired him to conceive an amusing *tableau vivant* – a parody of Ingres' *Apotheosis of Homer* – in which he appears wearing a laurel wreath and surrounded by

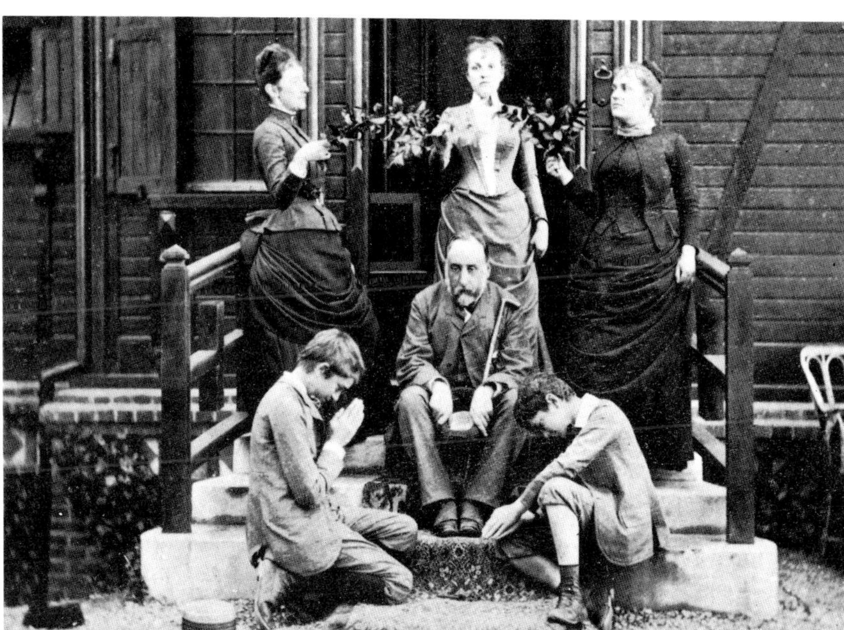

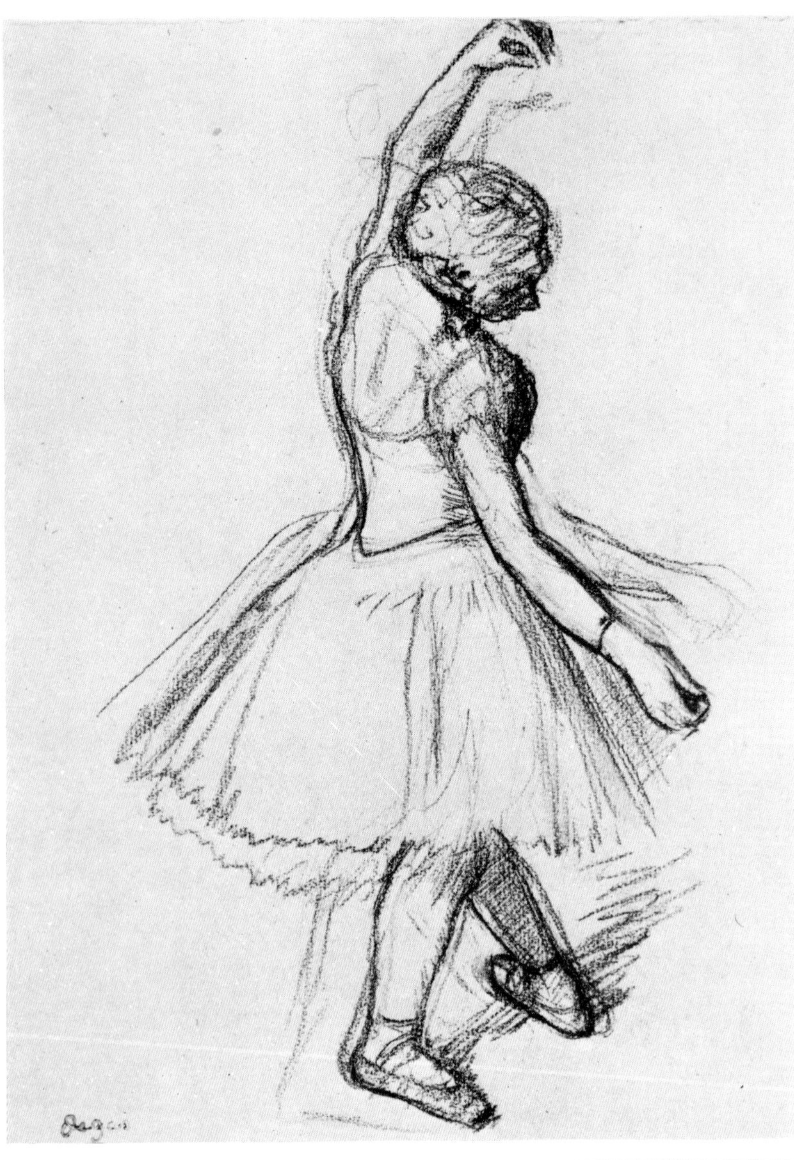

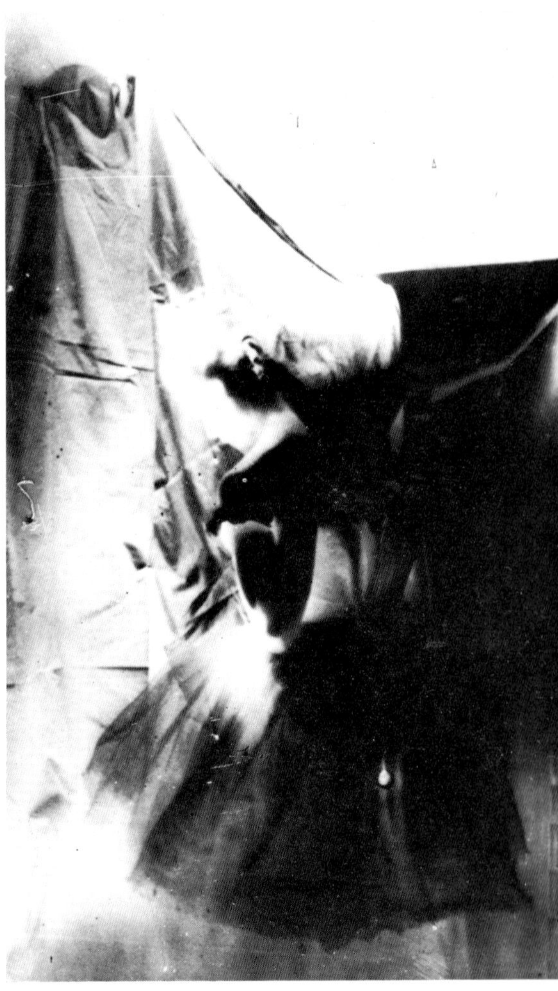

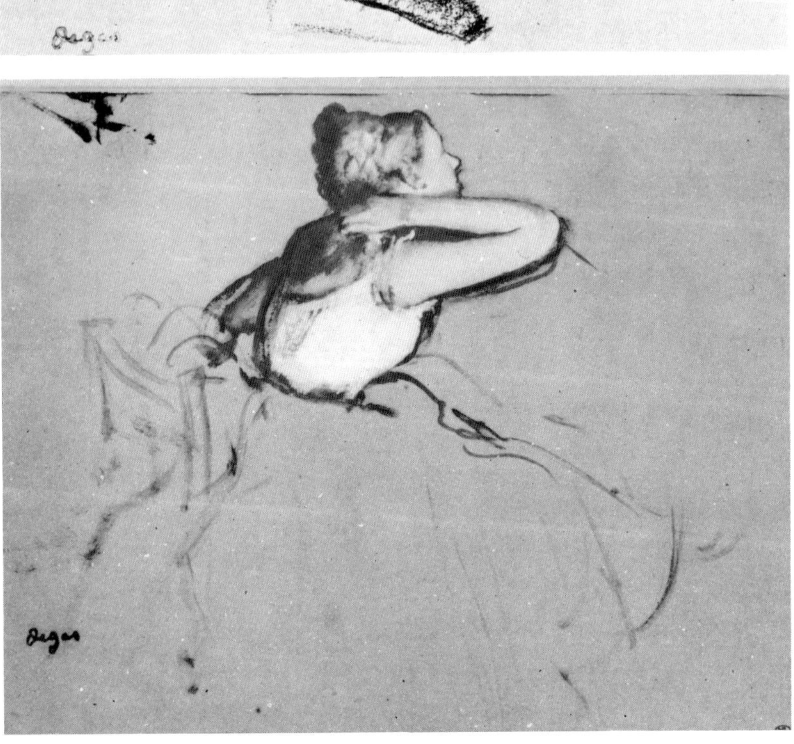

ABOVE LEFT Edgar Degas: *Dancer with a Raised Arm*, sanguine, *c.* 1879 (Private Collection). Degas made numerous sketches and paintings of dancers throughout his career, turning more and more to pastels as his eyesight began to fail him.
ABOVE Photograph by Degas of a ballet dancer posing in his studio.
LEFT Edgar Degas: *Seated Dancer*, sketch, *c.* 1878 (Musée du Louvre, Paris).
OPPOSITE Edgar Degas: *Dancers*, pastel and charcoal, 1895 (Private Collection).

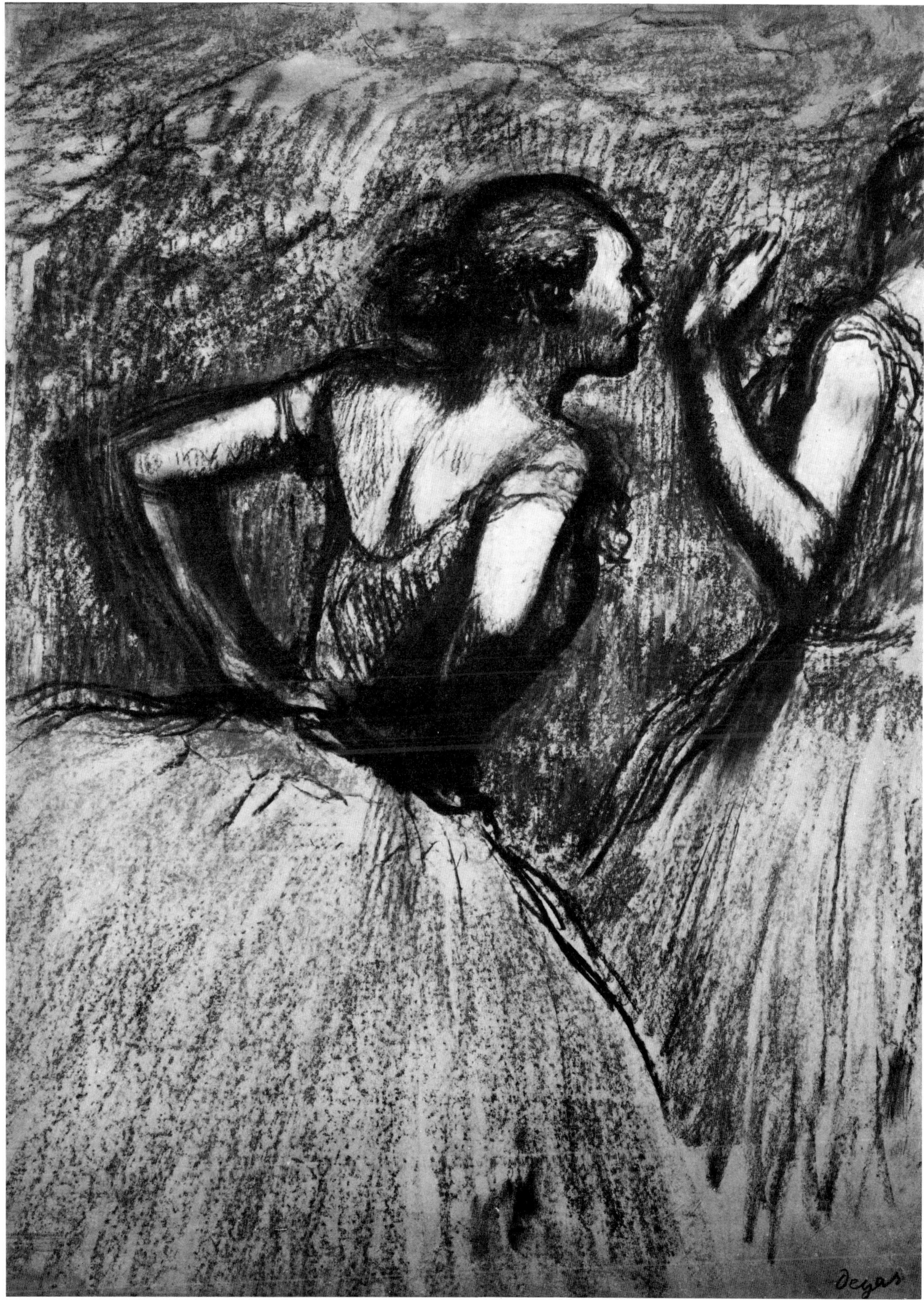
Degas

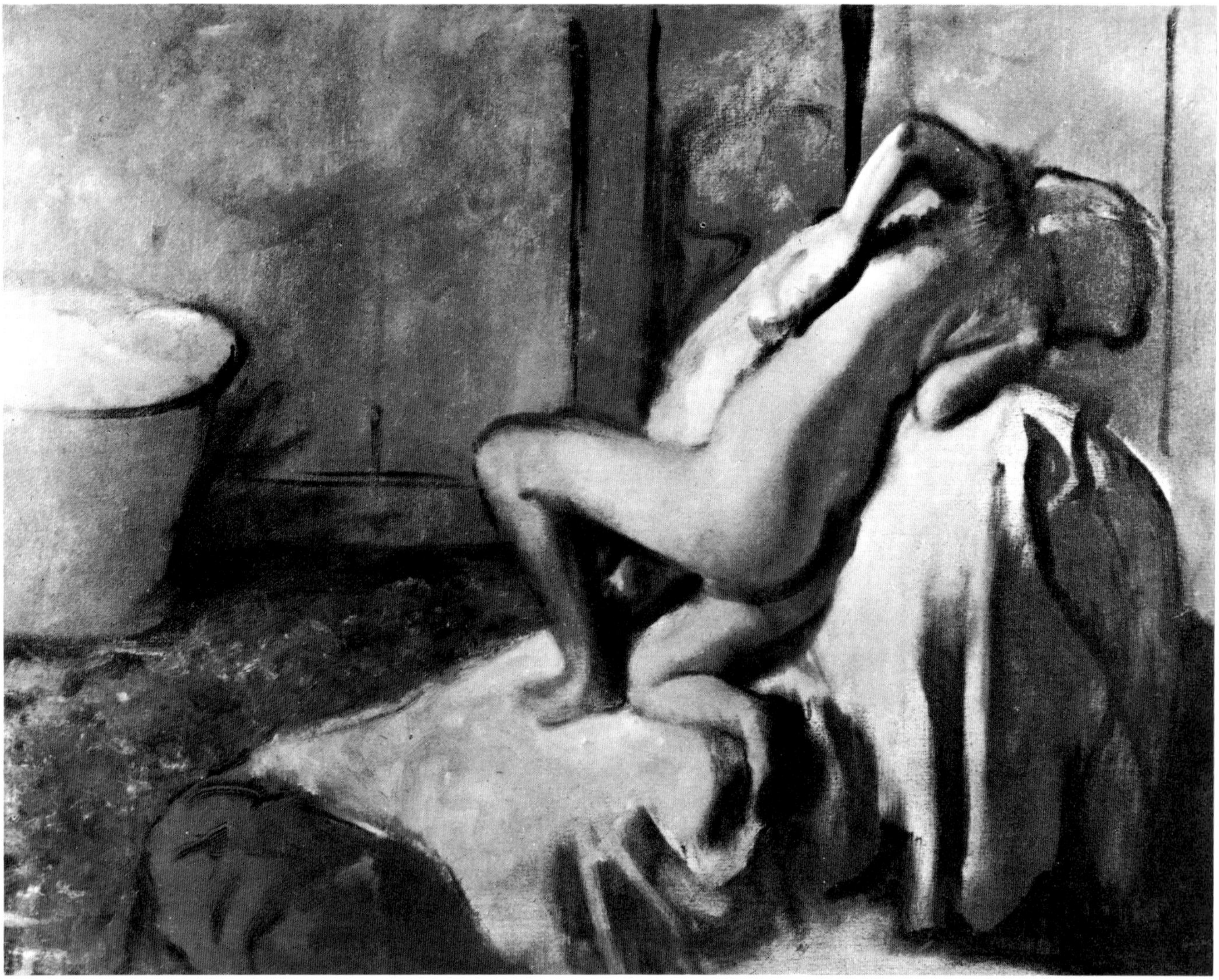

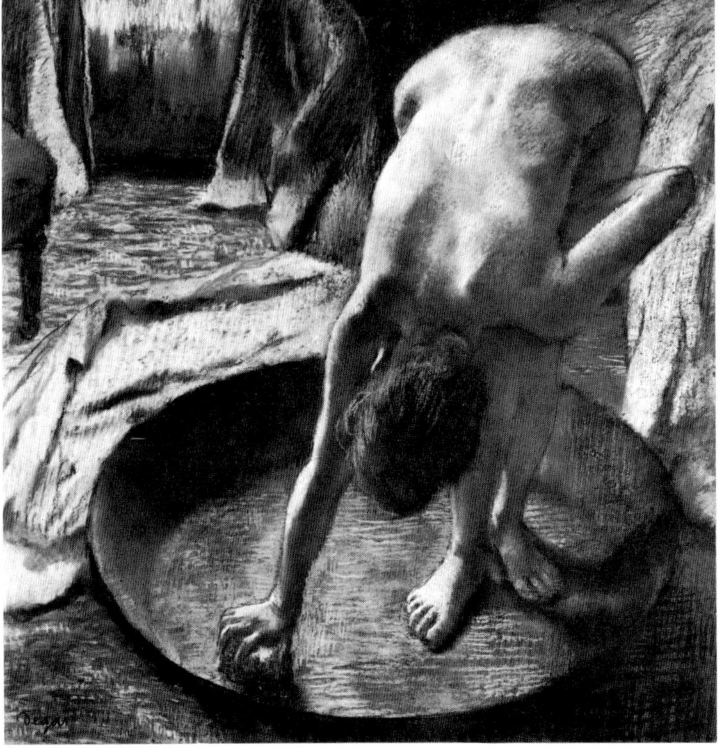

ABOVE Edgar Degas: *After the Bath – Woman Drying Herself*, oil sketch, *c.* 1883 (M. Lutjous Collection). Degas' nudes shocked the public. The Symbolist writer J. K. Huysmans sensed in Degas the desire 'to throw in the face of his century the most excessive outrage, the destruction of the invariably respected idol: woman'.

LEFT Edgar Degas: *The Tub*, pastel, 1886 (Hill-Stead Museum, Farmington, Conn.). Another example – and a very different one – of the many 'bath tub' pictures painted by Degas.

OPPOSITE Edgar Degas: *Woman Ironing*, *c.* 1885 (Private Collection).

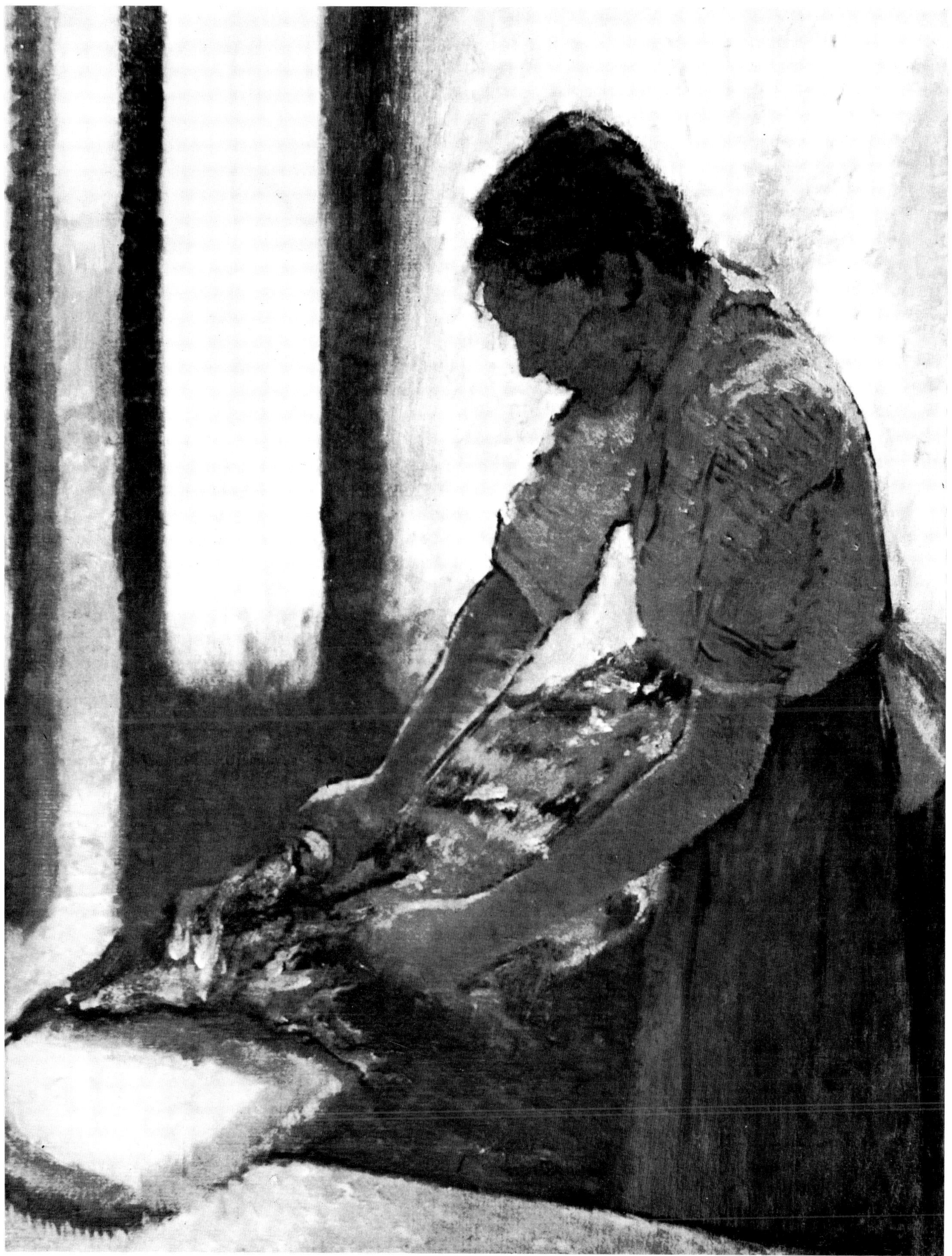

his young friends, John Lemoisne's daughters and the Halévy children. Once he got away from his studio and was able to forget the distressing deterioration of his eyesight, Degas could play and make believe like a child.

Giving in to one such childish whim, in 1890, Degas managed to persuade his friend Bartholomé to accompany him on a somewhat hare-brained adventure: a tour of Burgundy in a horsedrawn trap. As exuberant as two boys playing truant, the artists left Ivry, on the ouskirts of Paris, on 30 September, and drawn by a white horse at a trot that was 'gentler than a woman's gait' set out on their long journey to Dienay, a village where a painter friend, Jeanniot, was expecting them. Their first stop, after travelling through the autumnal woods of Fontainebleau, was at the Halévys', in Montgeron, where they had lunch. Then, after a leisurely trot of thirty-eight kilometres, they arrived at Melun, where they stayed the night at the Hôtel du Grand Monarque. Before retiring, they got through the following Gargantuan meal:

Sheep's trotters
Fried gudgeon
Sausage with mashed potatoes (admirable)
Beef steak with water-cress
Cheese, fruit, biscuits (admirable)

And they followed it up with an equally copious lunch next day.

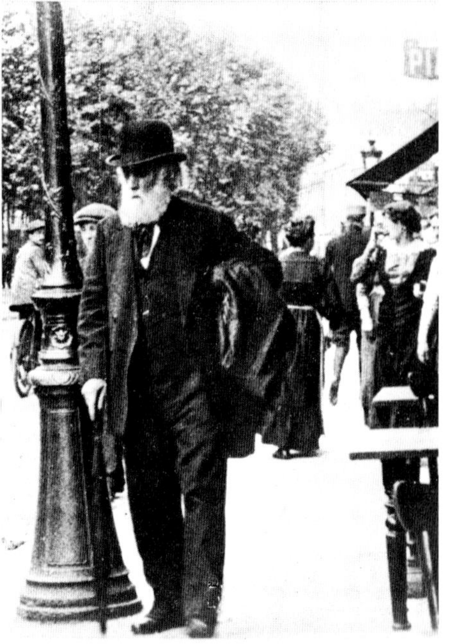

The short letters that Degas sent the Halévys every day of their trip reveal that behind the cranky, cantankerous townsman there lurked a cheerful gourmand and bon vivant who genuinely liked the countryside. 'There's only one country, Sir: ours!' exclaimed Degas in one of his letters, after tasting at Aignay-le-Duc 'some unbelievable gherkins – a garden in vinegar', the day before they were due to arrive at their destination. In the Yonne valley, lined by woods in the last phase of their autumnal splendour, Degas was only fifty kilometres or so from the village of Essoyes, where Renoir had just bought a small house.

On 7 October, at five o'clock in the afternoon, the travellers were welcomed with great pomp and circumstance in Dienay, where the *sous-préfet*, escorted by a gendarme on horseback (Jeanniot and a friend in disguise), presented them with the keys of the city, while young girls wreathed them with flowers. 'It's only when one has been sad and gloomy for a long time that one can enjoy oneself as much as this,' Degas remarked delightedly. In the loft that Jeanniot used as a studio, Degas immediately recorded his impressions of the journey in front of his friend, who later described the experience as follows:

> With his strong but beautifully shaped fingers, his hand seized the objects, the tools of his genius, and manipulated them with uncanny skill; and

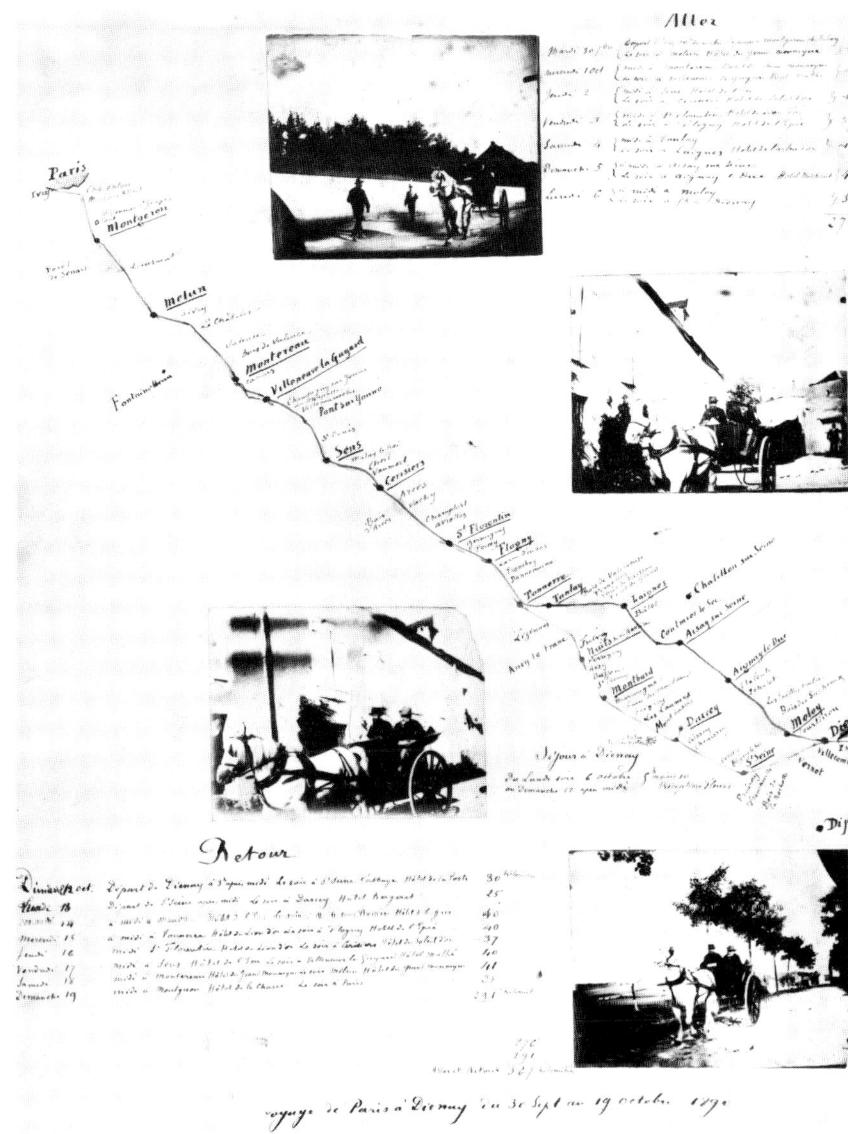

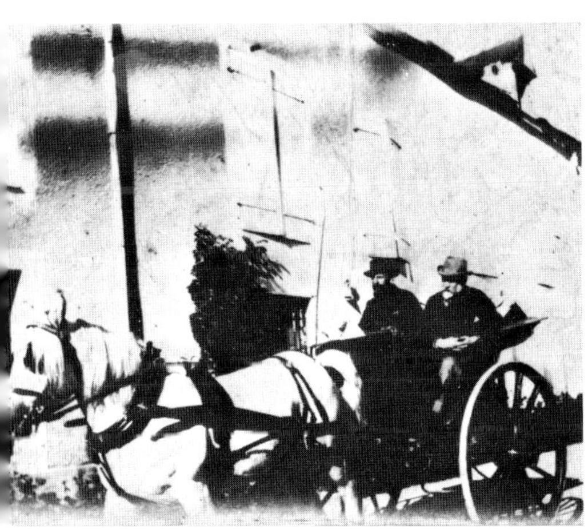

OPPOSITE Degas in old age – a lonely, irritable man with failing eyesight and an indestructible will to work.
ABOVE RIGHT Map of Degas' journey from Paris to Dienay from 30 September to 19 October 1890. Degas was accompanied by his friend Bartholomé.
ABOVE Degas and Bartholomé on their trip.

gradually one could see, emerging on the surface of the metal, a little valley, a sky, some white houses, some trees with dark branches, a few birches and oaks, ruts full of water from a recent shower, orange clouds scudding across a spectacular sky above the red and green earth . . . Such beauties sprang from his hand seemingly without effort, as though he had the model before his eyes.

Those landscapes – captured, reworked and transformed by Degas' inimitable genius – were to form the bulk of the only show he had at Durand-Ruel's gallery in 1892. 'It looks like colour printing, it's very strange . . . tremendously subtle tones,' Pissarro wrote in a letter to his son Lucien.

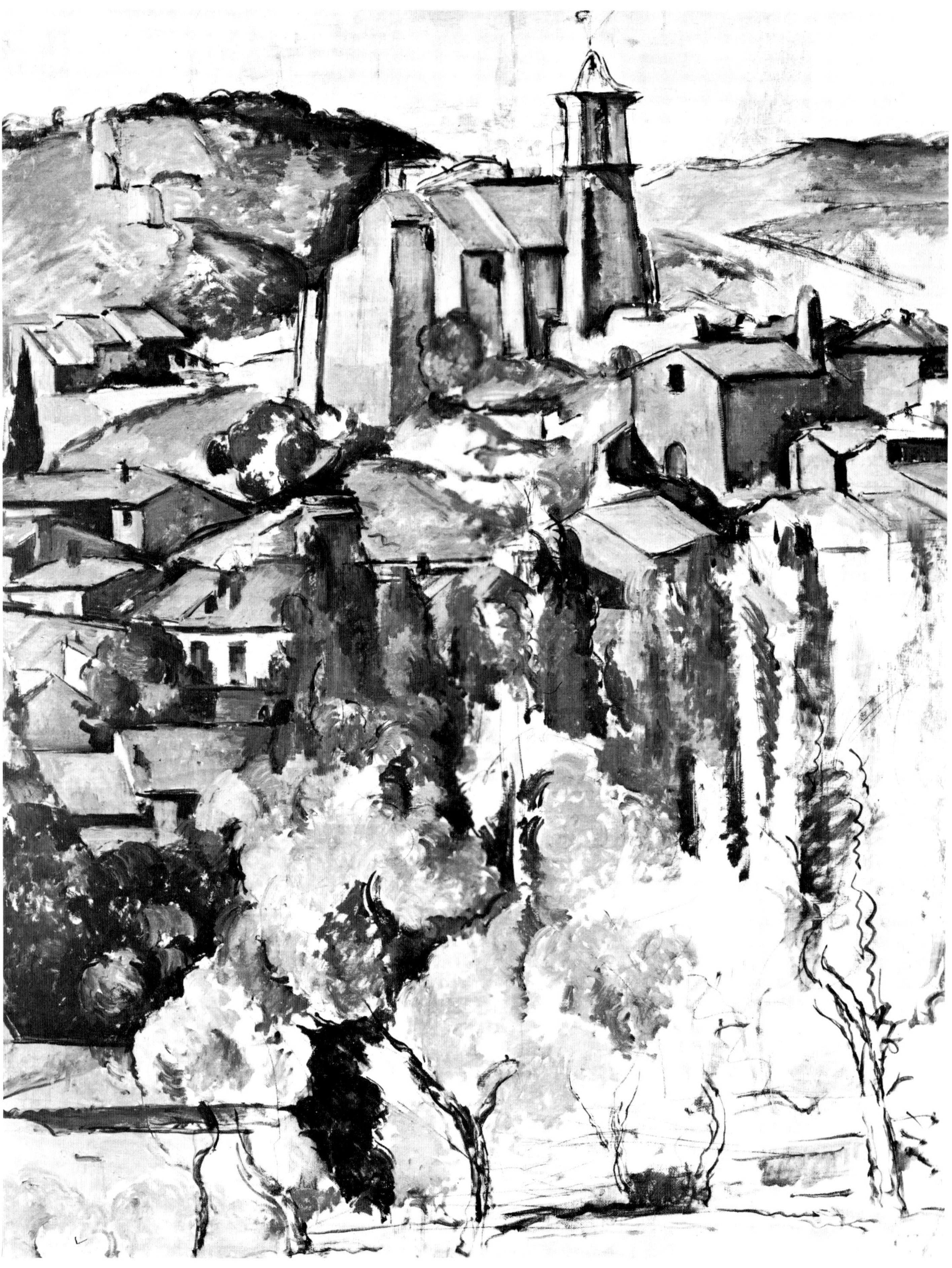

8 Cézanne in Provence

Between the Mistral and the Sun

Cézanne remained ferociously attached to Provence. 'When you were born there,' he once put it, 'nothing else has any meaning.' Having failed to find his artistic identity in Paris, Cézanne returned to his native Provence to become the great poet of southern light, red earth, tortured pine trees and the mysterious contours of the Montagne Sainte-Victoire. His achievement is all the more considerable when one thinks that, at the beginning of the century, his beloved region was associated mostly with baked earth and outbreaks of plague and cholera.

After trying in vain to make a name for himself at the Salon and enduring swingeing attacks from the critics in 1874 and 1877, when the group's first and third exhibitions were held, Cézanne actually despaired of ever being understood by the public and gradually spent more and more of his time in the South. The Jas de Bouffan, Cézanne *père*'s huge estate, was hidden away amidst vineyards and pinewoods some twenty minutes' walk from the babbling fountains and imposing mansions on the Cours Mirabeau in the centre of Aix-en-Provence. Cezanne found a wide variety of subjects there, both in the well-kept area around the house itself and in the sweet-scented wilderness of the rest of the estate.

The painter's artistic preoccupations at that time can be judged from the attention he pays to geometric lines in his treatment of *The Lake at the Jas de Bouffan*, an ornamental lake presided over by stone lions and dolphins. But occasionally he would paint quite different subjects, such as the magnificent chestnut trees of the *Avenue of Chestnuts*, or a few isolated clumps of trees on the edge of the estate. He also depicted, in predominantly ochre tones, the

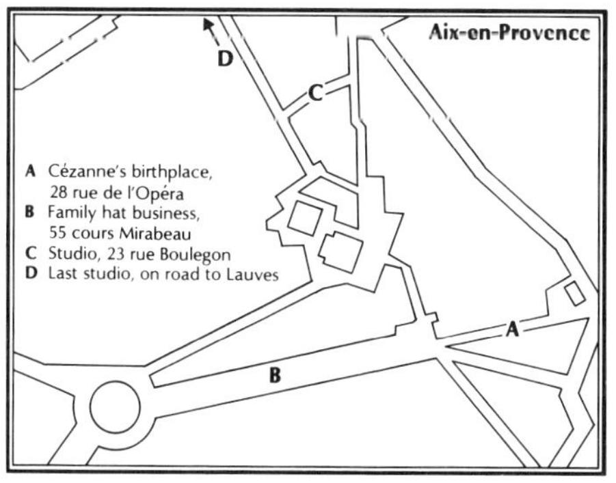

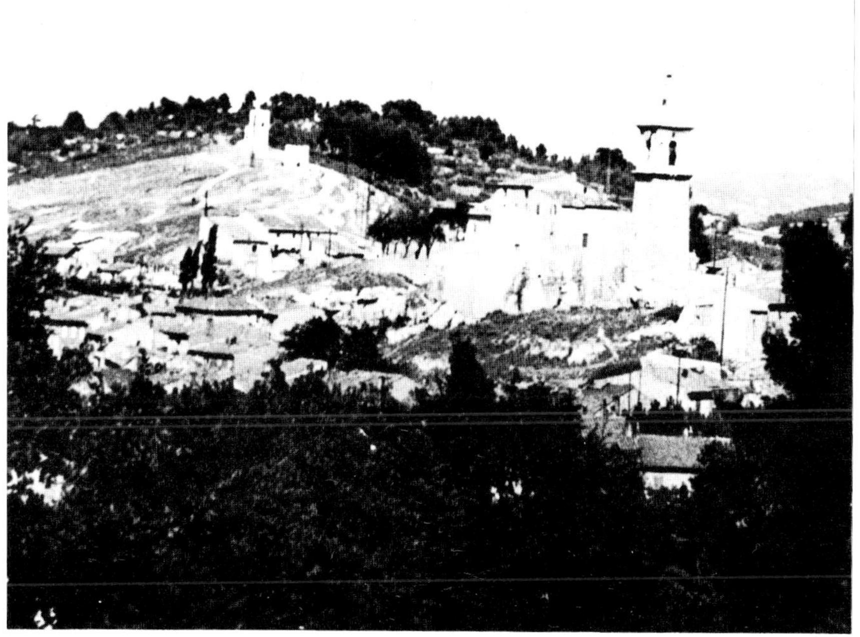

OPPOSITE Paul Cézanne: *The Village of Gardanne*, 1885–6 (Brooklyn Museum, New York, Ella C. Woodward and A. T. White Memorial Funds). Cézanne often went to Gardanne, and produced several paintings of the hill-top village.
RIGHT Photograph of the village of Gardanne.

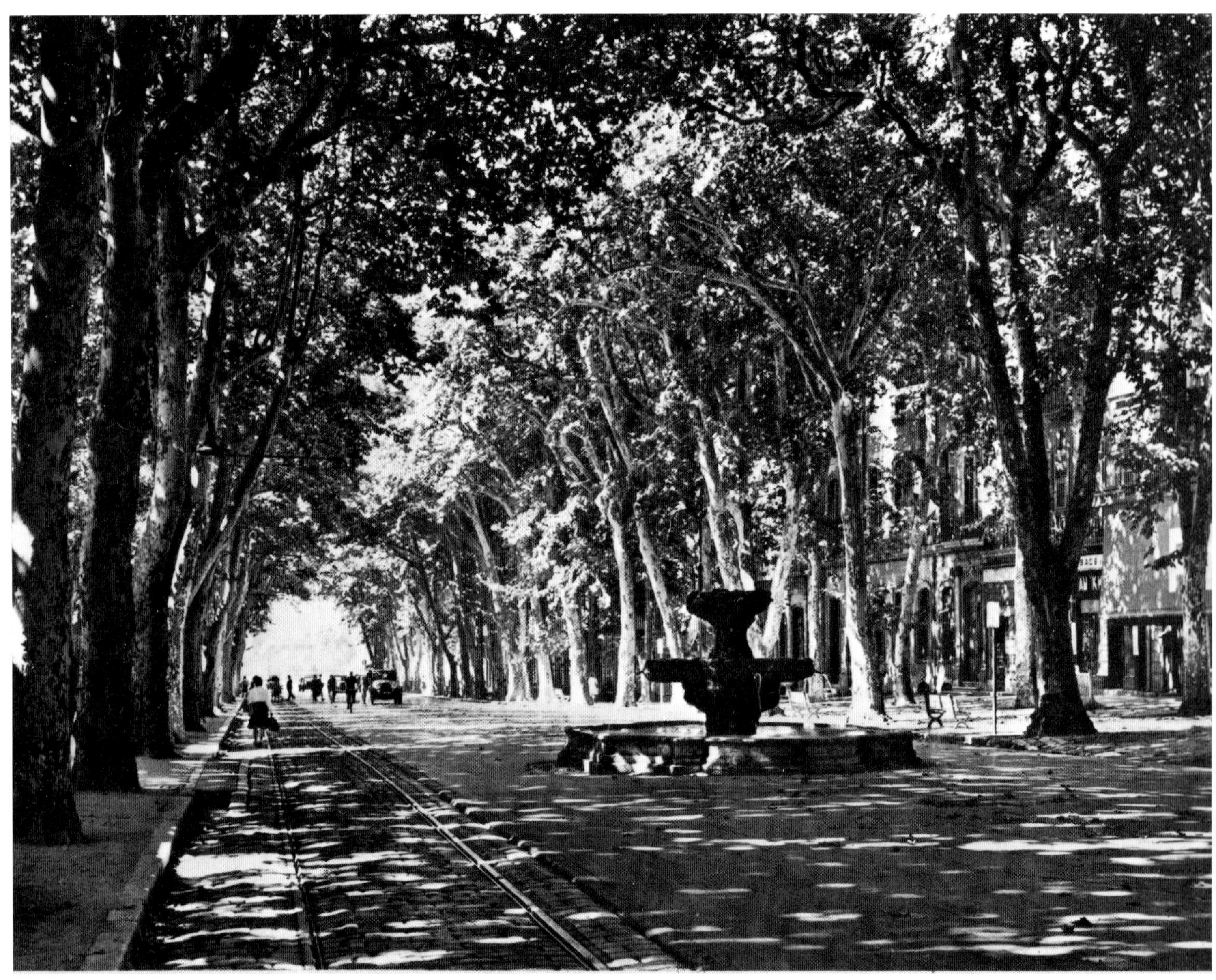

ABOVE Cours Mirabeau, the centre of Aix-en-Provence.

OPPOSITE Paul Cézanne: *The Jas de Bouffan*, 1875–6 (Private Collection). Cézanne *père*'s huge estate was hidden away among vineyards and pinewoods a few minutes' walk from the town.

noble façade of the *Jas de Bouffan* and of the *Farm at the Jas de Bouffan* and its outbuildings, scarcely visible behind a screen of mulberry trees.

The Jas de Bouffan would have been the ideal place for Cézanne to live and work, had it not been for the overbearing presence of his father, who kept a close control on his finances and his mail, and was always breathing down his neck or spying on him. He seemed to derive a bitter satisfaction from the submissiveness of his son, who was so unlike himself. Even though he was near forty, Cézanne had not dared to tell his father about his liaison with Hortense Fiquet and the existence of their son Paul. But he found solace and understanding with his mother, whom he adored; the family atmosphere,

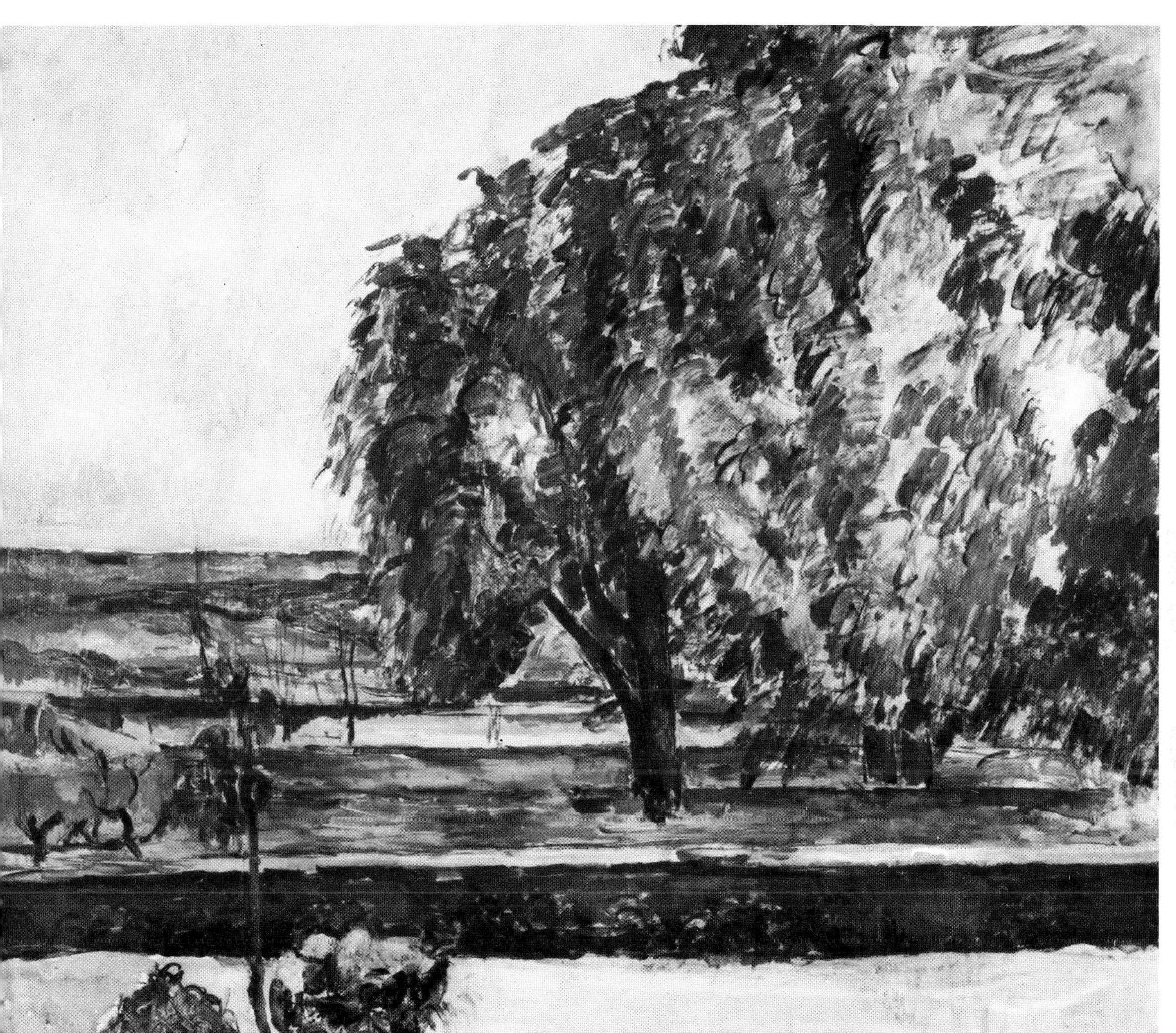

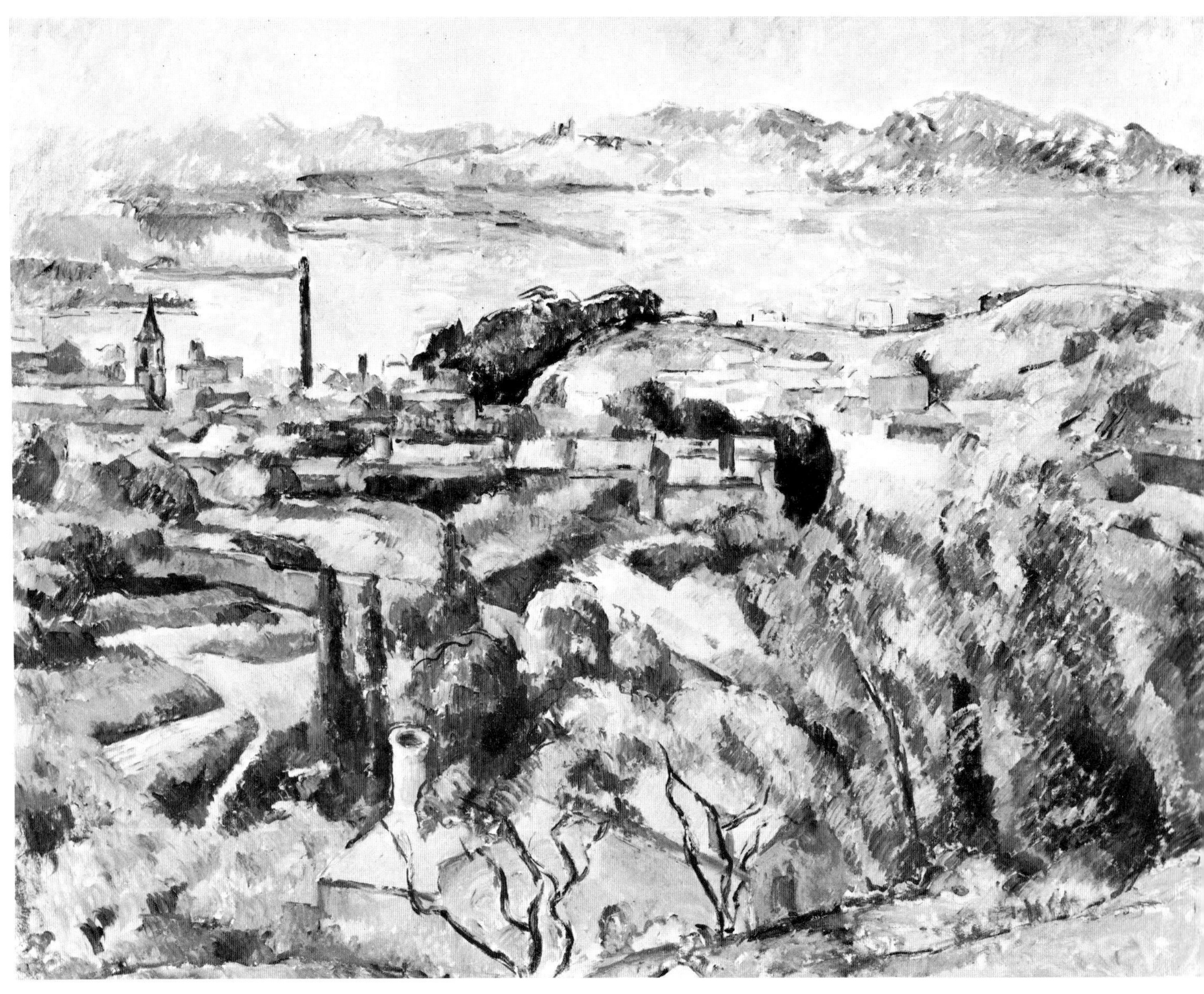

for all its bickering, was still preferable to the monotonous gloom of life in Paris.

In order not to be separated from his mistress and his son for too long, Cézanne found them lodgings in villages near Aix, such as L'Estaque or Gardanne, where, under the pretext of painting, he was often able to join them. In 1878 Cézanne left Hortense and his son hidden away in a flat on the Rue de Rome in Marseilles as a precautionary measure (his father's suspicions had been aroused by a letter to Paul from Chocquet), and made his way every morning to L'Estaque, about ten kilometres away. That extraordinary village, huddling between the sea and a vertiginous succession of rocks and ravines, provided a superb view. Cézanne wrote to Pissarro: 'I have found subjects there which would need three to four months' work,'

OPPOSITE Paul Cézanne: *L'Estaque and the Gulf of Marseilles*, 1882–5 (Philadelphia Museum of Art). In one of his short stories Zola described L'Estaque as 'a little town on the outskirts of Marseilles, at the end of the cul-de-sac of cliffs that bound the end of the gulf'.

ABOVE Paul Cézanne: *The House and Garden of the Jas de Bouffan*, 1885–7 (National Gallery, Prague). The Jas de Bouffan was a fine eighteenth-century building whose noble façade overlooked a large garden shaded by venerable trees.

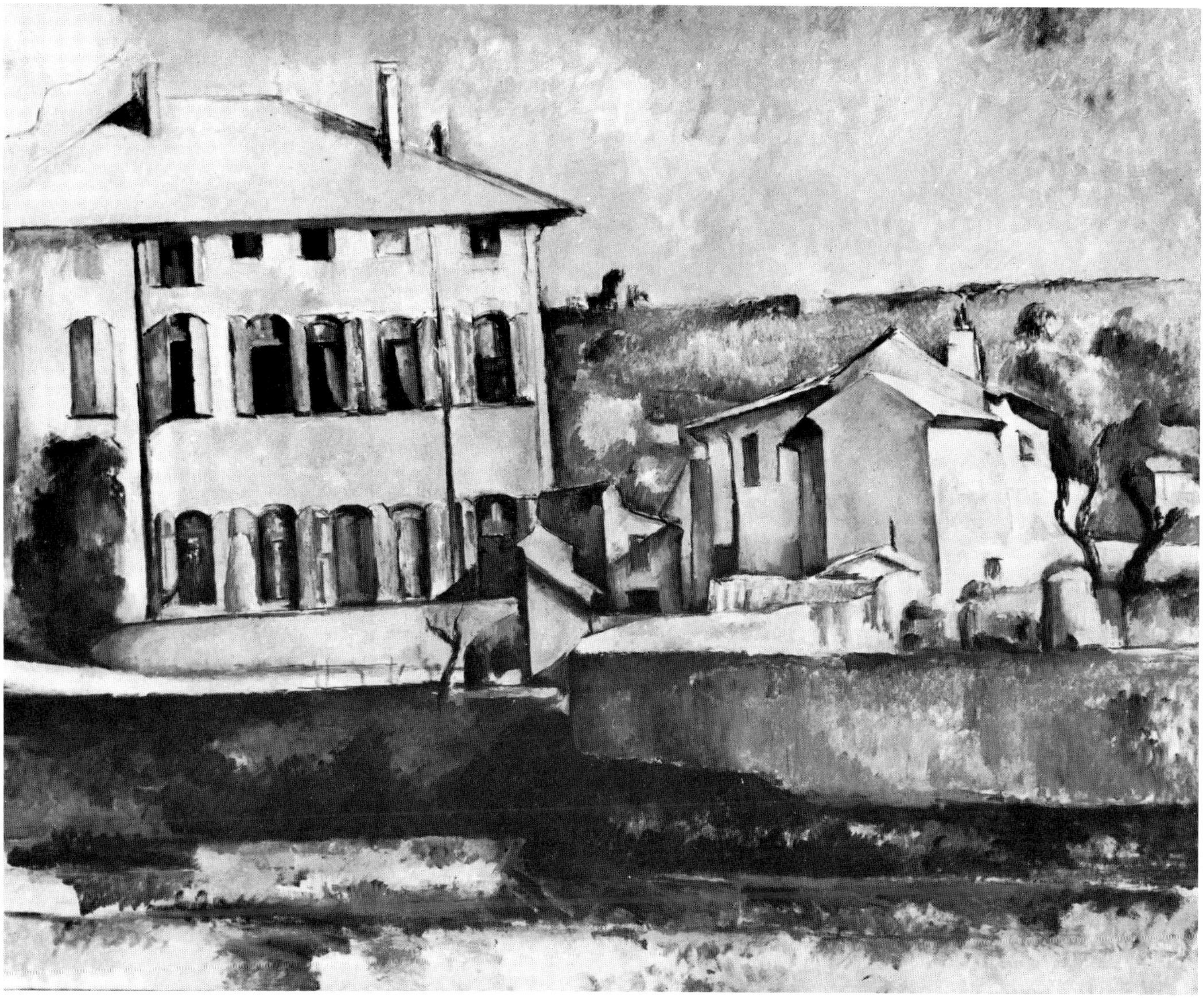

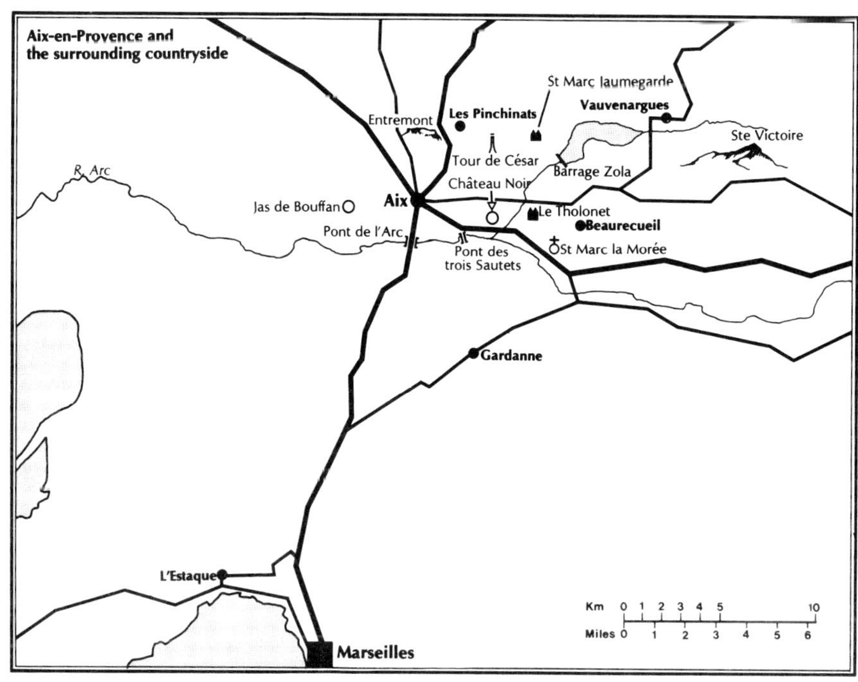
Aix-en-Provence and the surrounding countryside
St Marc Jaumegarde
Vauvenargues
Entremont
Les Pinchinats
Ste Victoire
Tour de César
Barrage Zola
R. Arc
Château Noir
Jas de Bouffan
Aix
Le Tholonet
Beaurecueil
Pont de l'Arc
St Marc la Morée
Pont des trois Sautets
Gardanne
L'Estaque
Marseilles
Km 0 1 2 3 4 5 10
Miles 0 1 2 3 4 5 6

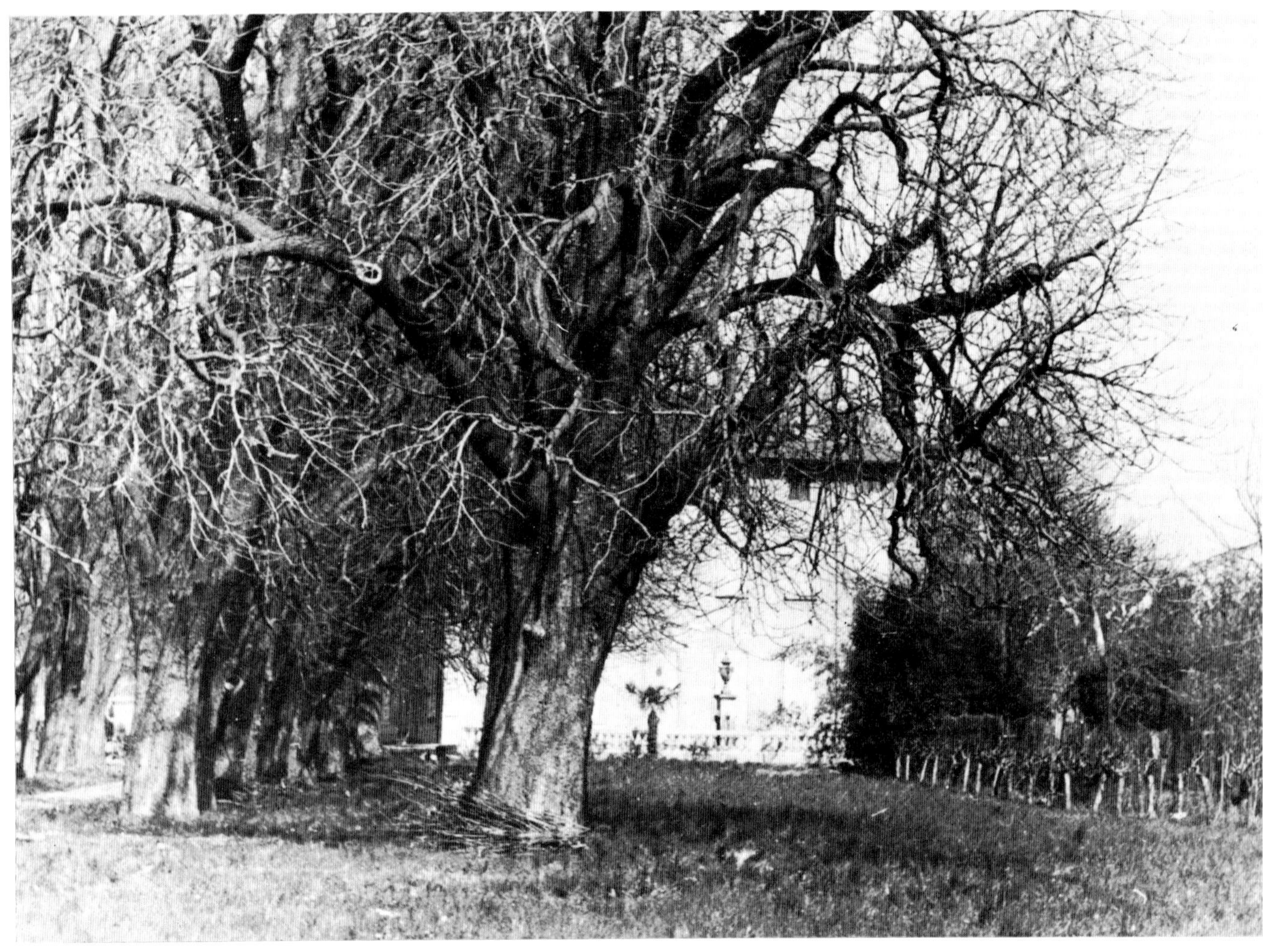

ABOVE The Jas de Bouffan, with its chestnut trees.
OPPOSITE Paul Cézanne: *The Jas de Bouffan*, 1867–9 (Tate Gallery, London).
Cézanne made a series of studies in the grounds of the Jas de Bouffan, selecting such subjects as the superb avenue of chestnut trees, a cluster of isolated pines, and intertwined plane tree branches.

and he did indeed stay there on many occasions, in 1882, 1884, 1885 and more particularly 1887, the year in which he painted *L'Estaque and the Gulf of Marseilles* from the top of one of the hills in the suburbs of Marseilles. The deep blue sea appears almost to have set like a jelly between the village of L'Estaque in the foreground of the composition and a mass of low mountains in the background. In this painting colour predominates over shapes, and seems to have weighed down the original subject, which has nothing of the Impressionist shimmer that Monet or Renoir would have lent it. Cézanne had already drifted away from Impressionism and was searching for a much more complex image of the world concealed by the apparent reality of visual conventions: the less obvious but more authentic reality of the mind.

Nearer to the Jas de Bouffan, the old village of Gardanne with its pyramid of houses clinging to the rock wall for protection against the vengeful Mistral wind was a perfect subject for Cézanne. During a stay there in 1886

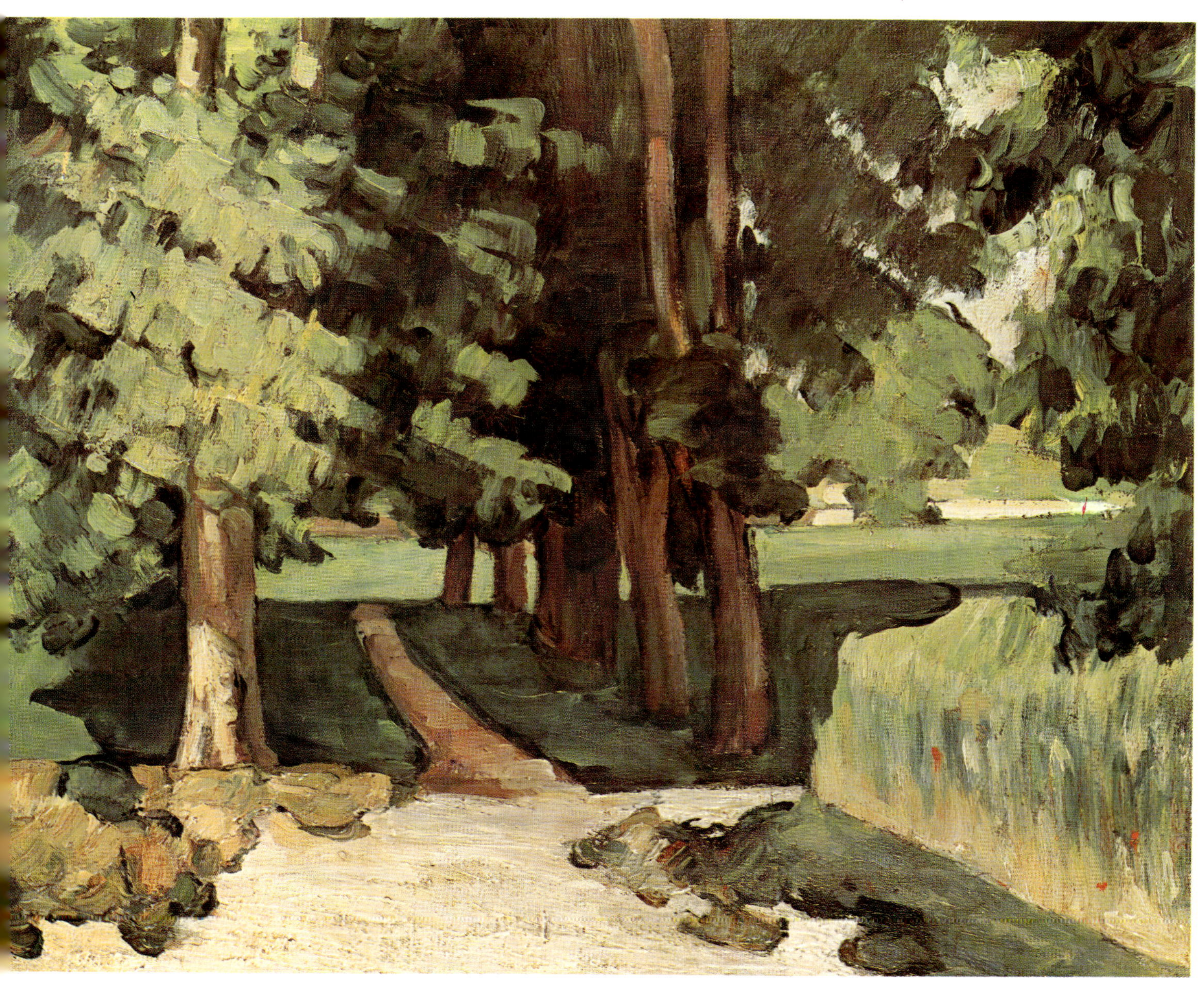

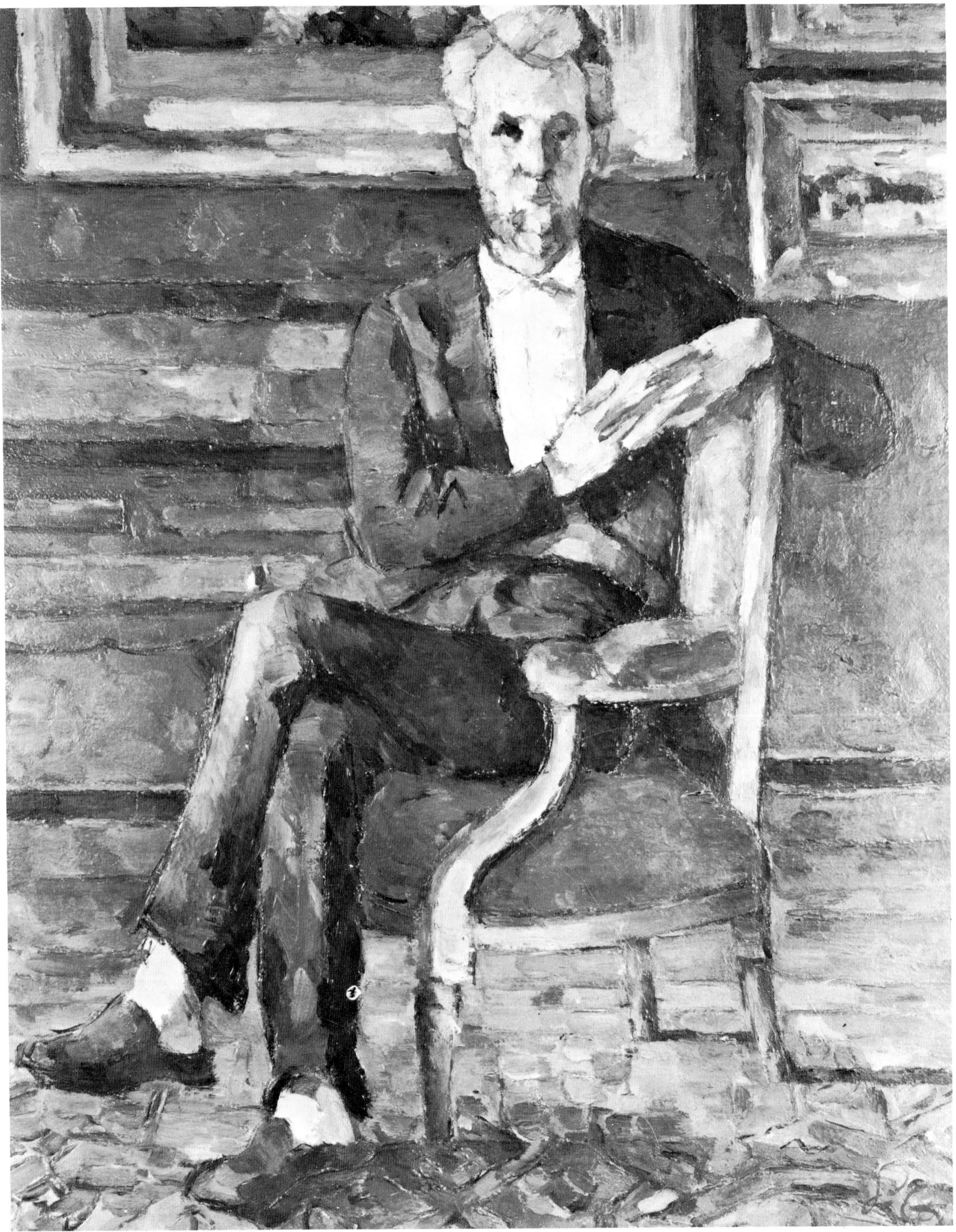

with Hortense and Paul, he was sent a copy of Zola's latest work, *L'Oeuvre*. The novel, which had been serialized for several months in *Gil Blas*, caused consternation in Impressionist circles. The central character, Claude Lantier, a painter of genius who failed miserably in expressing himself, was unfortunately all too recognizable as Cézanne. Every page contained allusions to childhood memories – which still so influenced Cézanne that they seemed to have impeded his development as a man and as an artist. The dreams, impulses and enthusiasms shared with Zola had been exposed and traduced by the author's unforgivable lack of sensitivity and artistic understanding. Cézanne was determined not to give any hint of how deeply hurt he was by such a betrayal. He acknowledged receipt of the book in a curt, impersonal note to the author. The two were never to meet again. When he broke off with Zola, Cézanne escaped from the overpowering childish emotions that still enslaved him.

On 28 April 1886, Cézanne married Hortense at the town hall of Aix-en-Provence. A tall, burly forty-seven-year-old, he had a bushy beard, a very prominent forehead, and a bald pate bordered by rather long, still dark hair. Cézanne's inquisitive, anxious and very intense eyes gave him a certain youthfulness, while his overall expression was benign. His wife was thirty-six; she had regular features, and her expression remains curiously frozen in all Cézanne's portraits of her except one, *Madame Cézanne in the Conservatory*, where she looks almost pleasant. Cézanne, who never finished this portrait, was unable to remove all traces of spontaneity from it, thus leaving us with the only lifelike image of Hortense.

Six months after his son's marriage, Louis-Auguste Cézanne died at the age of eighty-eight, leaving the sum of 400,000 francs to each of his children. Paul Cézanne, who had never managed to earn a cent in his life, was full of admiration and went round saying: 'My father was a genius, he's left me with an income of 25,000 francs!'

Although little in Cézanne's life had apparently changed, his sensuality became less frenzied, and he channelled all his energies in one direction: painting. The result was a long succession of masterpieces which he had been mulling over for more than twenty years in a constant state of self-doubt, anguish and despair.

Cézanne worked in and around Paris when he stayed with Hortense and Paul in the flat he had rented for them; otherwise, he tended to spend most of his time at the Jas de Bouffan with his ageing mother and his sister Marie, a bigoted and fussy spinster who ruled his material existence with a rod of iron inherited from her father. Cézanne worked feverishly, turning out still lifes, portraits (of his wife, his son, Chocquet and himself), and countless landscapes around the Jas de Bouffan and at L'Estaque. While exploring the

Paul Cézanne: *Victor Chocquet*, 1879–82 (Columbus Gallery of Fine Arts, Ohio). Cézanne painted several portraits of Victor Chocquet, who admired him intensely.

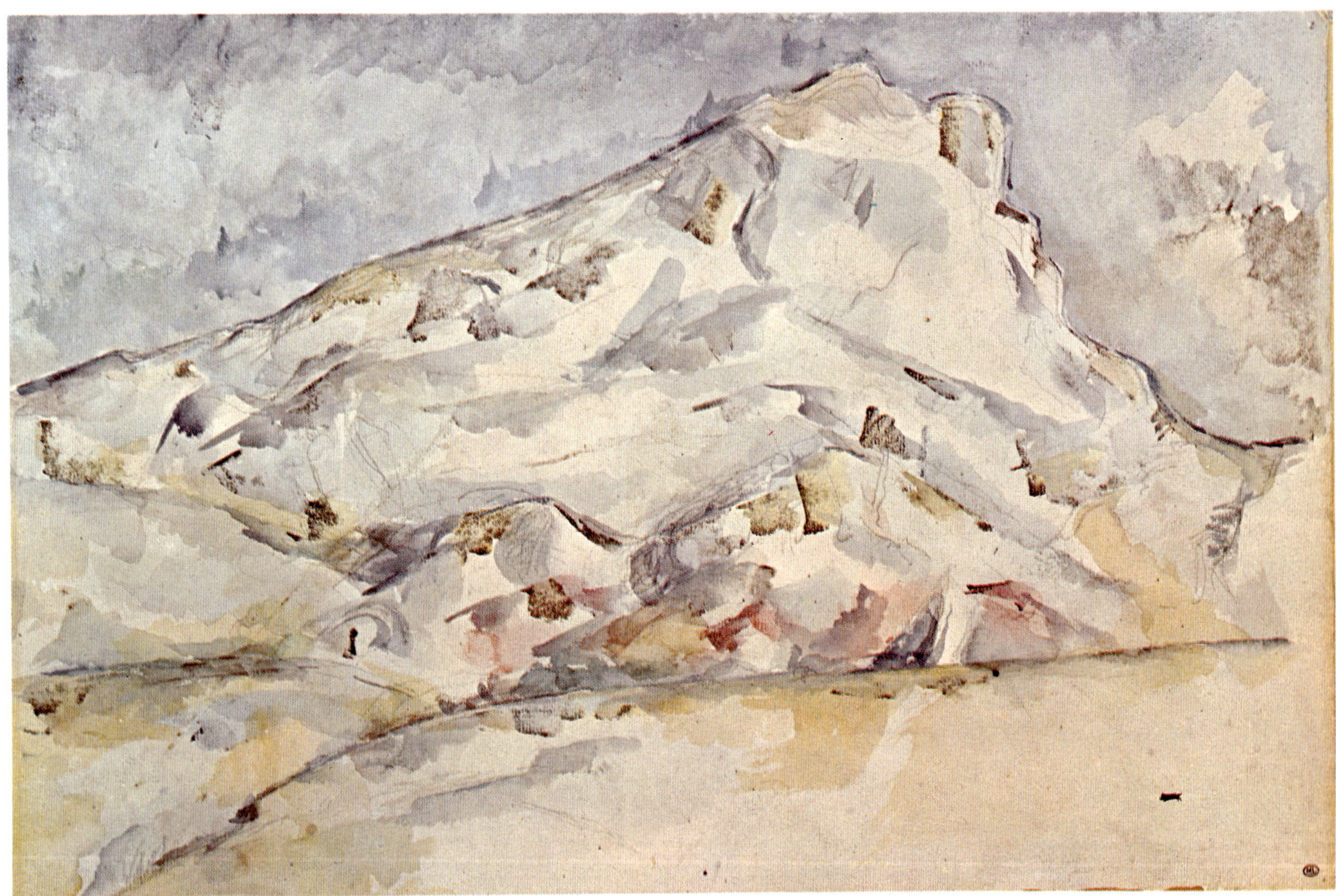

plain around Gardanne, he came across a landscape of hills following each other like a series of breakers up to the Mont de Cengle, behind which rose the Montagne Sainte-Victoire. Steeped in history and legend, the ever-changing yet immutable Montagne Sainte-Victoire, which had already appeared in several of his landscapes, gradually became one of Cézanne's favourite subjects. From Beaurecueil, a small village near Aix, he portrayed it as a low-lying mass; on other occasions, he made it look tall and steep, overlooking the valleys of Bellevue or Montbriand, or else sitting serenely on the far side of a vast plain, framed by a large pine tree.

By five or six in the morning Cézanne would be out painting in the open air. He worked slowly, for as he told the young Symbolist painter Emile Bernard: 'Nature presents itself to me as something very complex.' No less than a hundred working sessions were necessary to complete a single still life. Often, too, he would contemplate a landscape for hours before daring to put brush to canvas, for 'every stroke must contain air, light, composition, character, outline, and style.' He used to observe nature – spy on it, even – in order to catch it unawares, so to speak, every time it was lent a different appearance by a combination of light and space. The exceptionally good

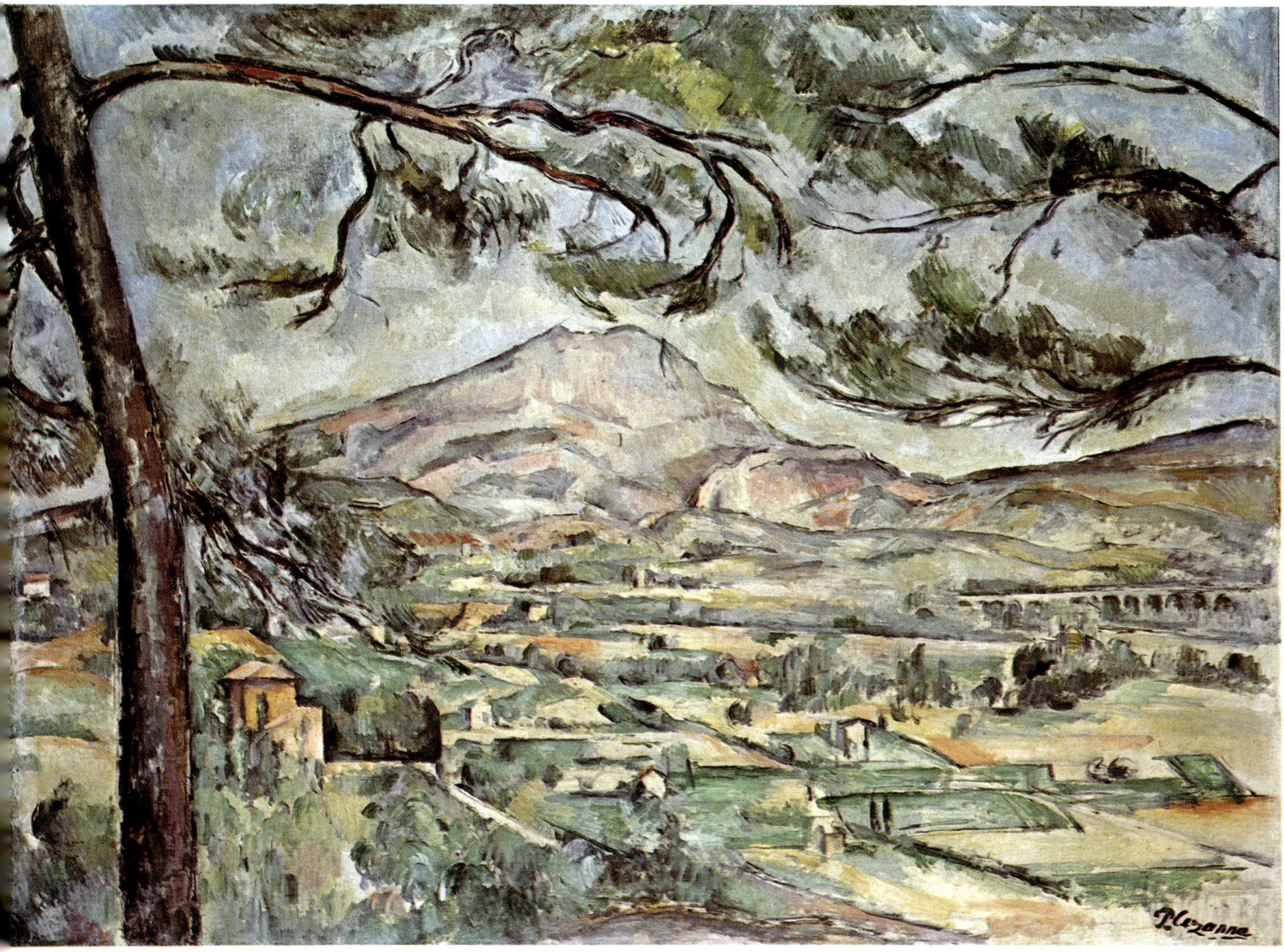

Perhaps Cézanne's most famous subject is the enigmatic Montagne Sainte-Victoire which dominates the landscape around Aix-en-Provence. Cézanne depicted the mountain from every side, in different lights, in different media, and at different times in his working life.

OPPOSITE Paul Cézanne: *Montagne Sainte-Victoire*, watercolour, *c.* 1900 (Musée du Louvre, Paris). A free, sparse watercolour sketch.

ABOVE Paul Cézanne: *Montagne Sainte-Victoire*, *c.* 1886–8 (Courtauld Institute Galleries, London). One of the several versions of the mountain framed by the branches of a pine tree.

BELOW Photograph of Montagne Sainte-Victoire.

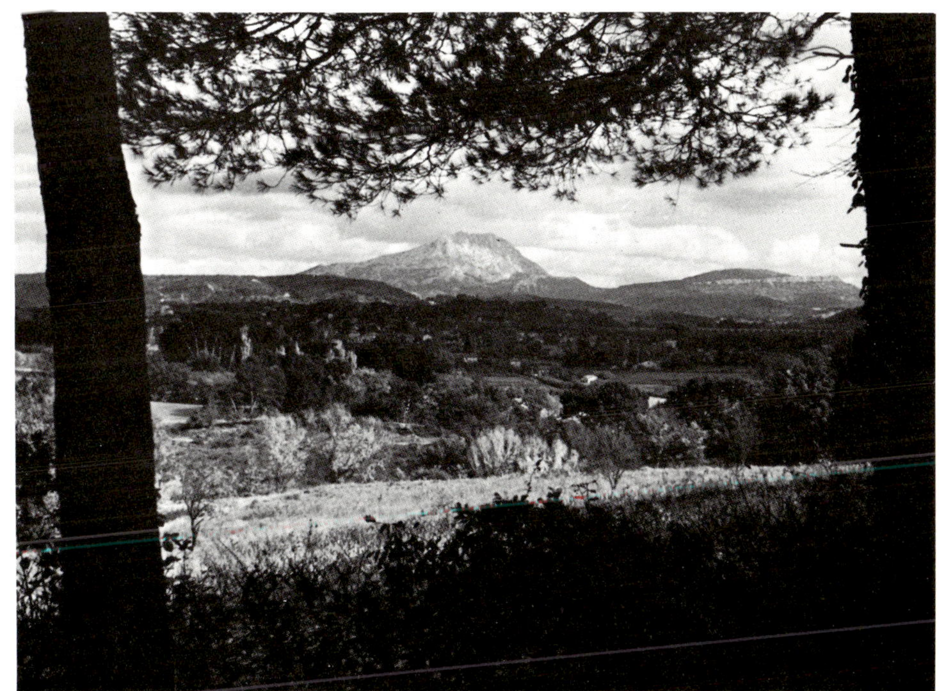

Two photographs of Montagne Sainte-Victoire, showing it from different angles.

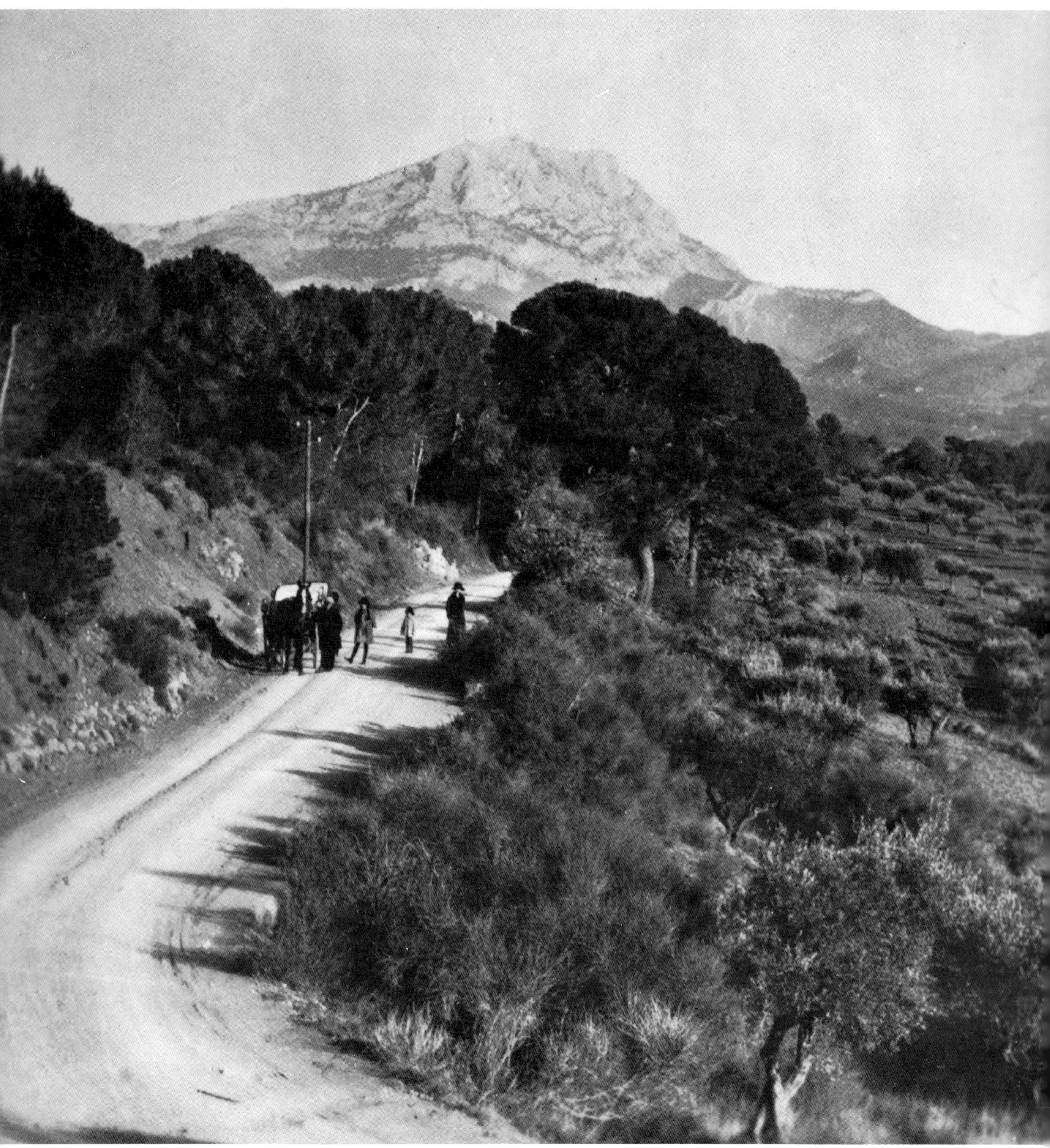

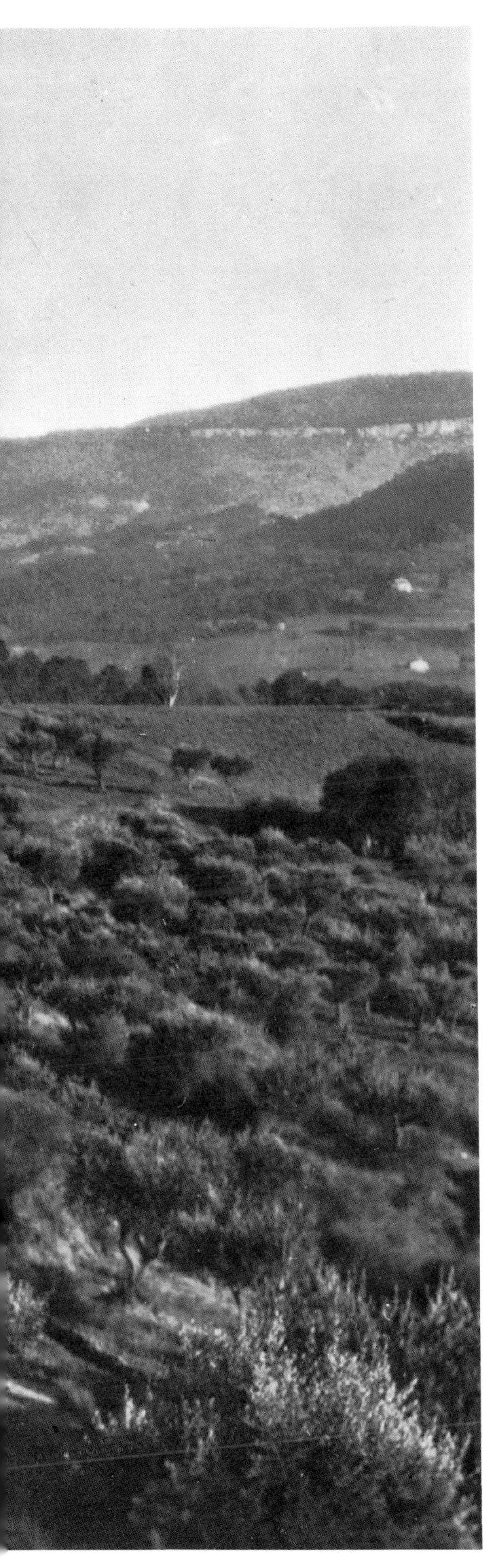

light in the South of France enabled Cézanne to return again and again to the same spot and paint for hours on end.

Although he was almost immobile when engrossed in painting, sometimes he would fly into a furious rage when he felt that he had failed – stabbing holes in his canvas and throwing it by the wayside. Cézanne's personality was still a very complex combination of pride and modesty: he could be alternately patient or hot-headed, self-confident or dogged by self-doubt. And yet while he was toiling away in the harsh light of the Provençal sun his name was beginning to become the talk of the capital.

Even though he himself had become a Pointillist, Pissarro still admired Cézanne as keenly as ever, and urged his friends to go and see his work at the shop run by Père Tanguy, their mutual friend and dealer in artist's colours and materials. Julien Tanguy owned many paintings which Cézanne had given him in exchange for a few tubes of colour or some canvases. According to a contemporary description, he was 'a short, thick-set elderly man with a grizzled beard', who, when asked, willingly showed his collection 'with all the affection of a mother for her beloved children'. The young Symbolist painters, to whom Paul Gauguin had succeeded in communicating his admiration for the greatness and 'mystical' nature of Cézanne's pictures, flocked to see them at Père Tanguy's little shop on the Rue Clauzel in Montmartre.

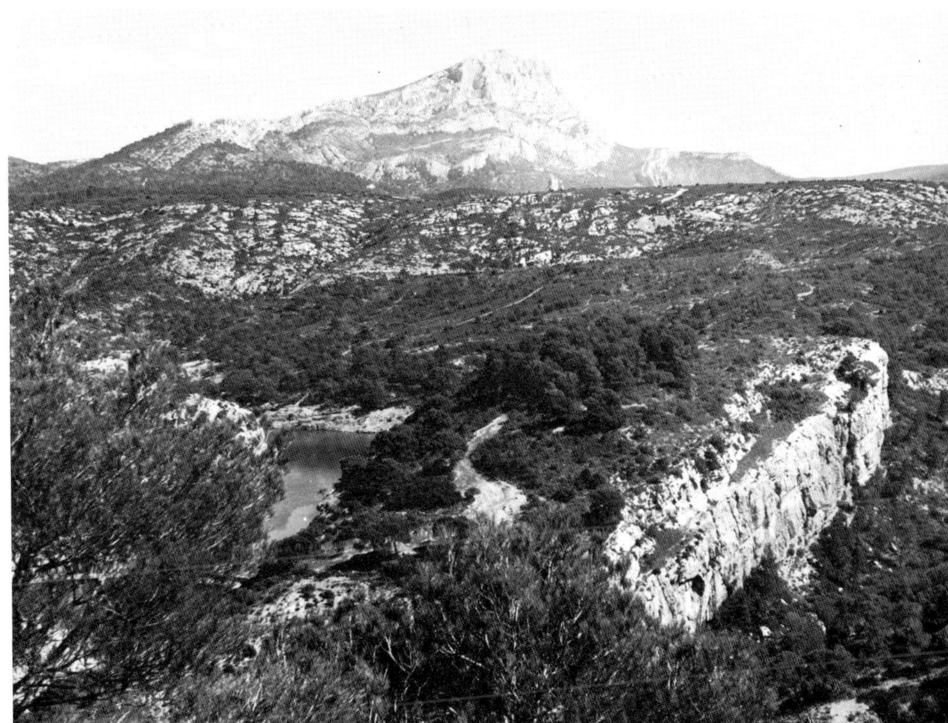

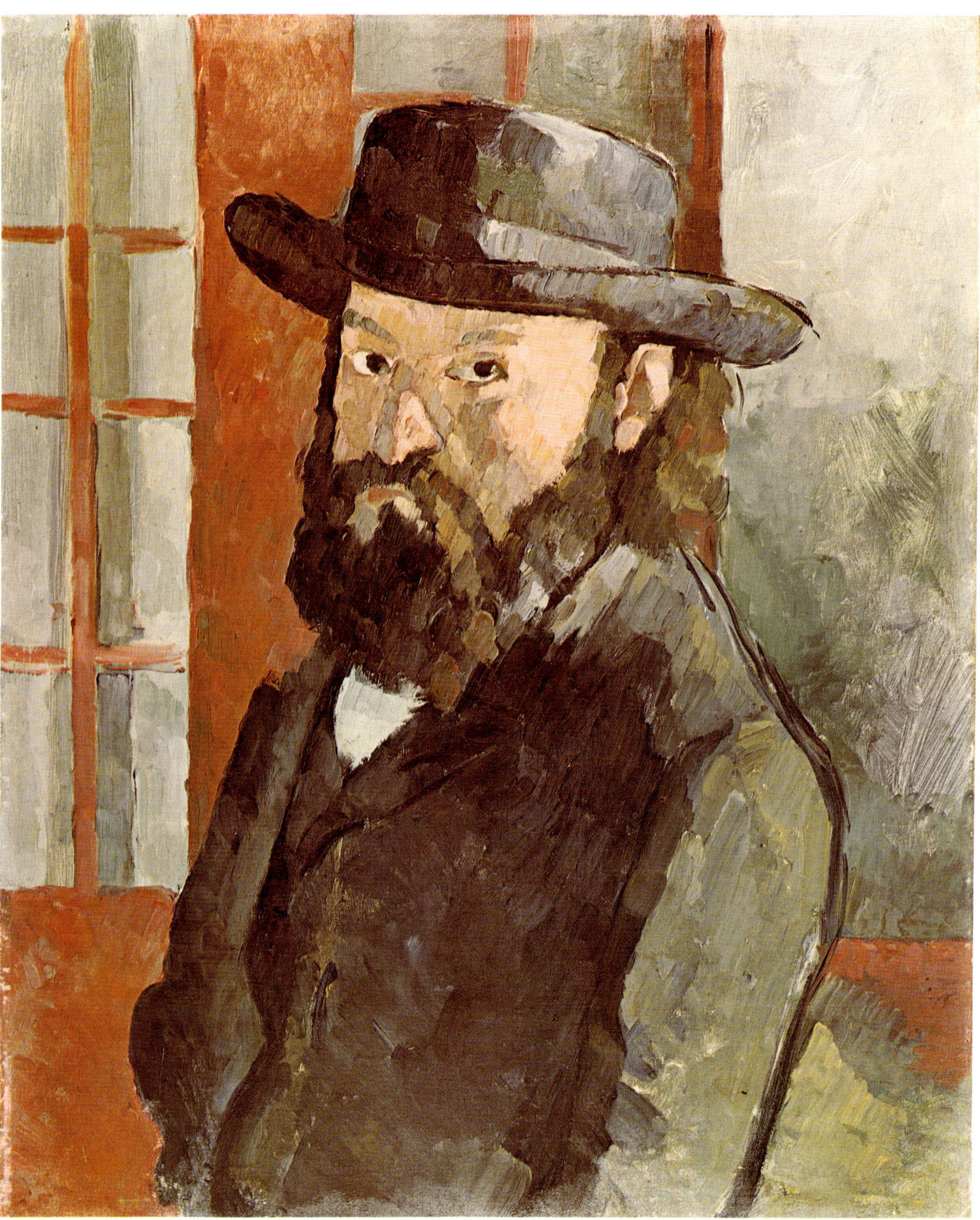

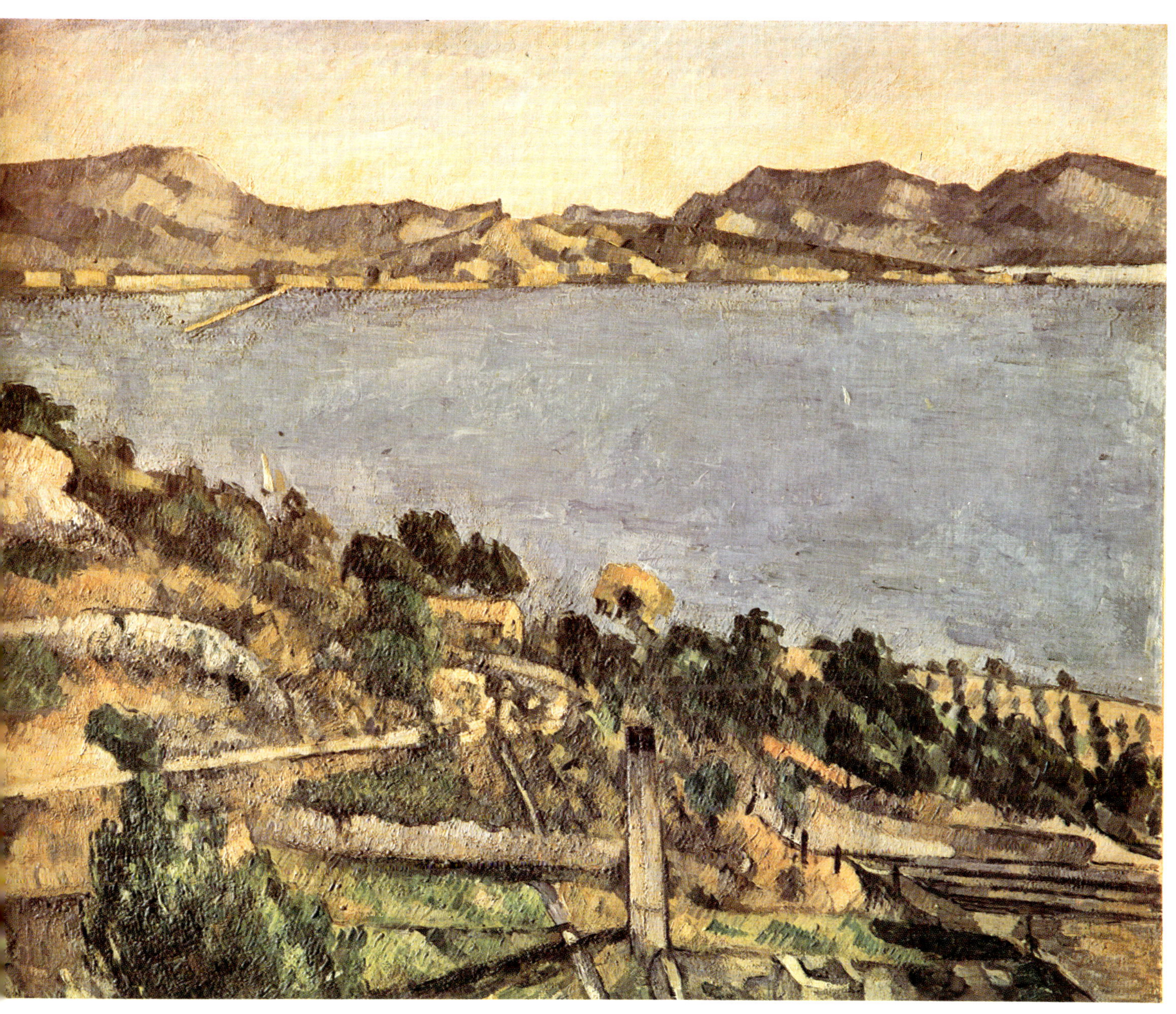

OPPOSITE Paul Cézanne: *Self-Portrait with a Hat*, 1879–82 (Kunstmuseum, Berne). Throughout his career, Cezanne painted many self portraits, scrutinizing his face as though trying to seize some elusive truth.
ABOVE Paul Cézanne: *L'Estaque*, *c.* 1882–5 (Musée du Louvre, Paris). 'There are many views here, but none of them makes a proper motif. Even so, if one goes up into the hills at sunset, there is a fine panoramic view of Marseilles and the islands, which in the evening are shrouded in some very decorative light effects' – Cézanne, 1882.

In the delightful town of Moret-sur-Loing, where he settled in 1882, Sisley found motifs ideally suited to his outstanding qualities as a colourist.
BELOW Alfred Sisley: *The Church at Moret*, 1893 (Musée des Beaux-Arts, Rouen).

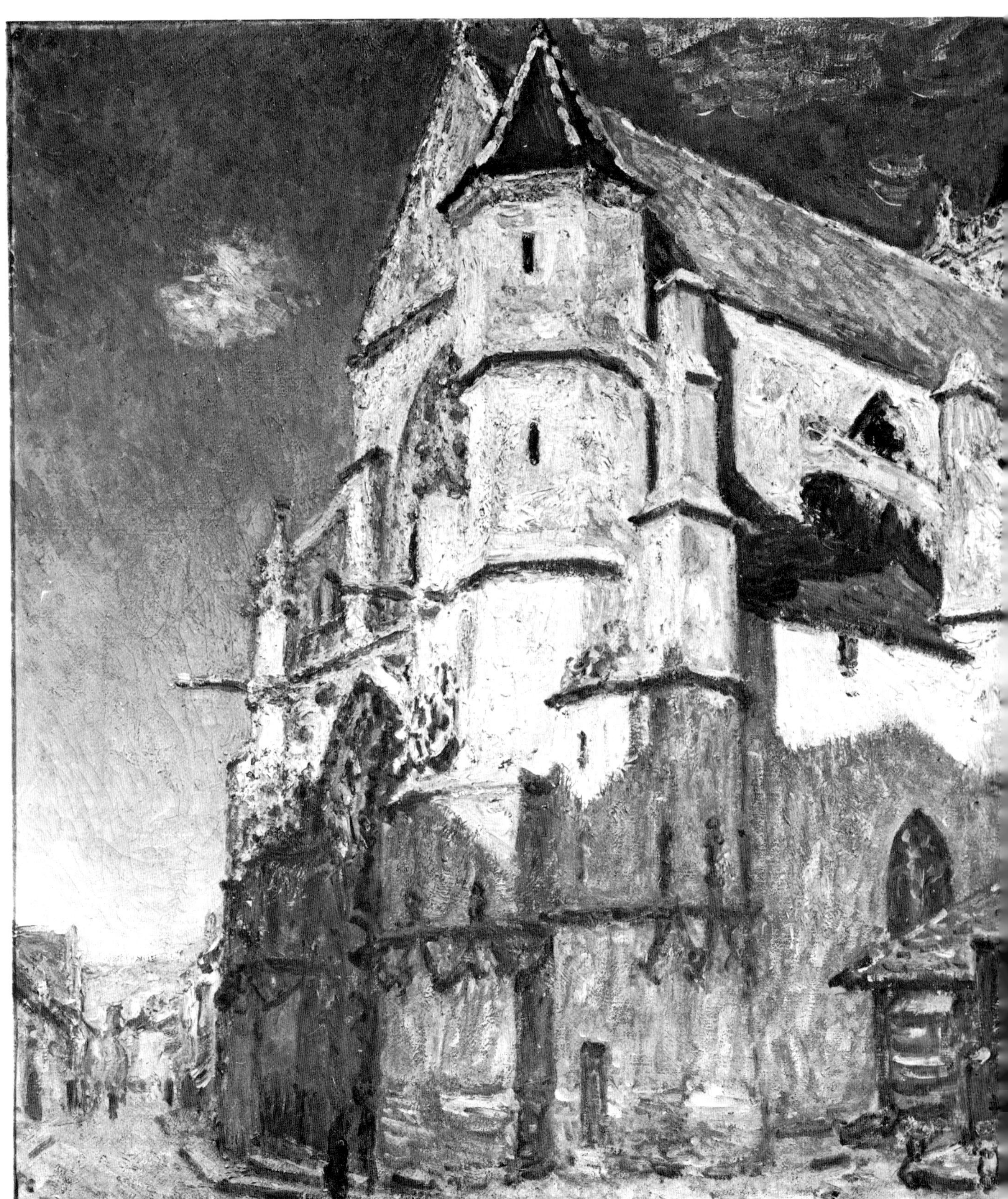

9 Fruition and Solitude

The End of an Era

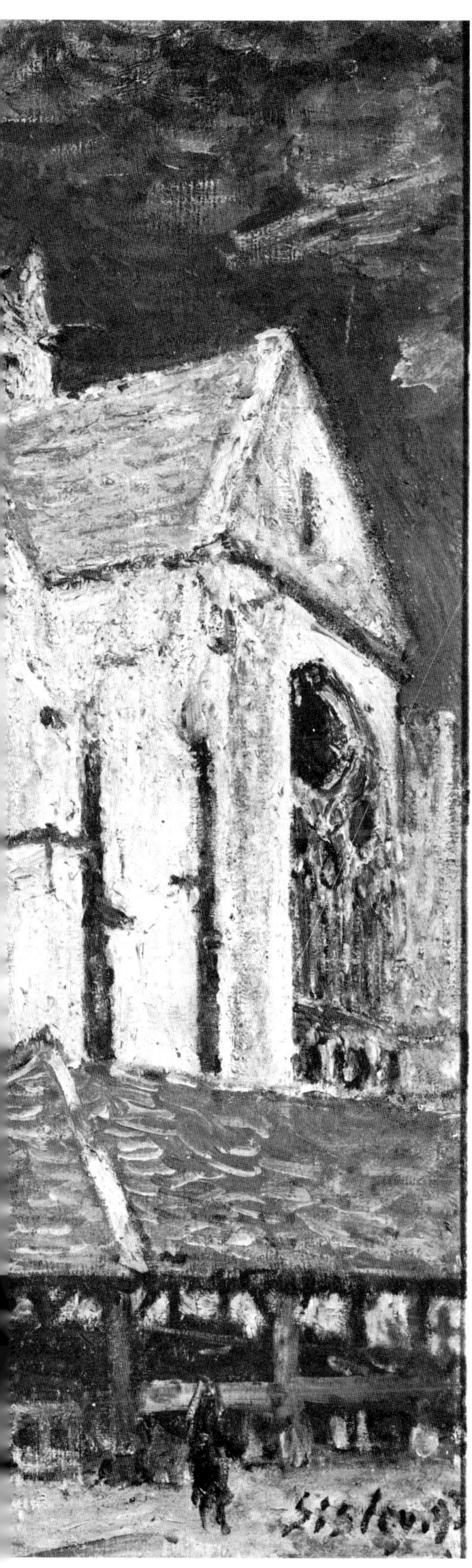

The changes that separate the beginning of the Impressionist movement from its end were so far-reaching that, at the close of their lives, the Impressionists themselves felt that a new, modern and generally uncongenial world was opening up around them.

Even within the group, radical changes had not been long in coming. The circumstances which had brought the young artists together in 1874 were doomed to disappear by the very weight of their obsolete traditionalism. The artists reacted in various ways to the altered situation. The fact remains that the only original Impressionists to take part in the group's eighth and last show, in 1886, were Pissarro, Degas and Berthe Morisot. Monet, Renoir and Sisley had stopped exhibiting in protest against the presence of Pissarro's young friends – Gauguin and Pointillists such as Signac and Seurat. The works of both Monet and Sisley were shown by Georges Petit, the most serious competitor of Durand-Ruel, who handled Renoir's paintings. New dealers had followed in the footsteps of the pioneering Durand-Ruel, and the Impressionists were also able to offer their work to Ambroise Vollard, Goupil or Bernheim-Jeune. Moreover, an avant-garde group called 'Les Vingt' had been formed in Belgium which took it upon itself to publicize works by French and foreign independent painters, and at various times exhibited Renoir, Monet, Sisley and Cézanne.

Lastly, the government of the Third Republic completely gave up its prerogative to elect members of the jury of the annual artists' exhibition and the newly-formed Société des Artistes Français, which replaced the Salon, proved infinitely more liberal than its predecessor. By some miracle, the Impressionists eventually mustered enough support in official circles to get the collection of their works bequeathed to the State by Gustave Caillebotte in 1894 accepted three years later. Thus, despite fierce opposition from the painters of the Institut, Pissarro, Cézanne, Renoir, Monet, Sisley, Degas and Manet found their way on to the walls of the Musée du Luxembourg. However, the celebrated official artist Gérôme, when showing the President of the Republic round the World Exhibition of 1900, came to a halt before the door of the Impressionists' gallery and issued this solemn warning: 'Go no further, Monsieur le Président. This is a disgrace to France.'

But attacks on the Impressionists were beginning to run out of steam: the bourgeoisie showed greater tolerance of artistic revolutions, which were relatively harmless compared with the nascent rebelliousness of the working classes. The general public gradually adjusted to the Impressionist vision of the world, and the number of collectors grew. All the painters except Sisley began to rise in public esteem; as a result they became fairly well-to-do and could forget the financial problems that had harassed them in the past.

Sisley was unfortunately not endowed with the instinct for survival that enabled Degas, for instance, who also suffered a reverse of fortune, to find a

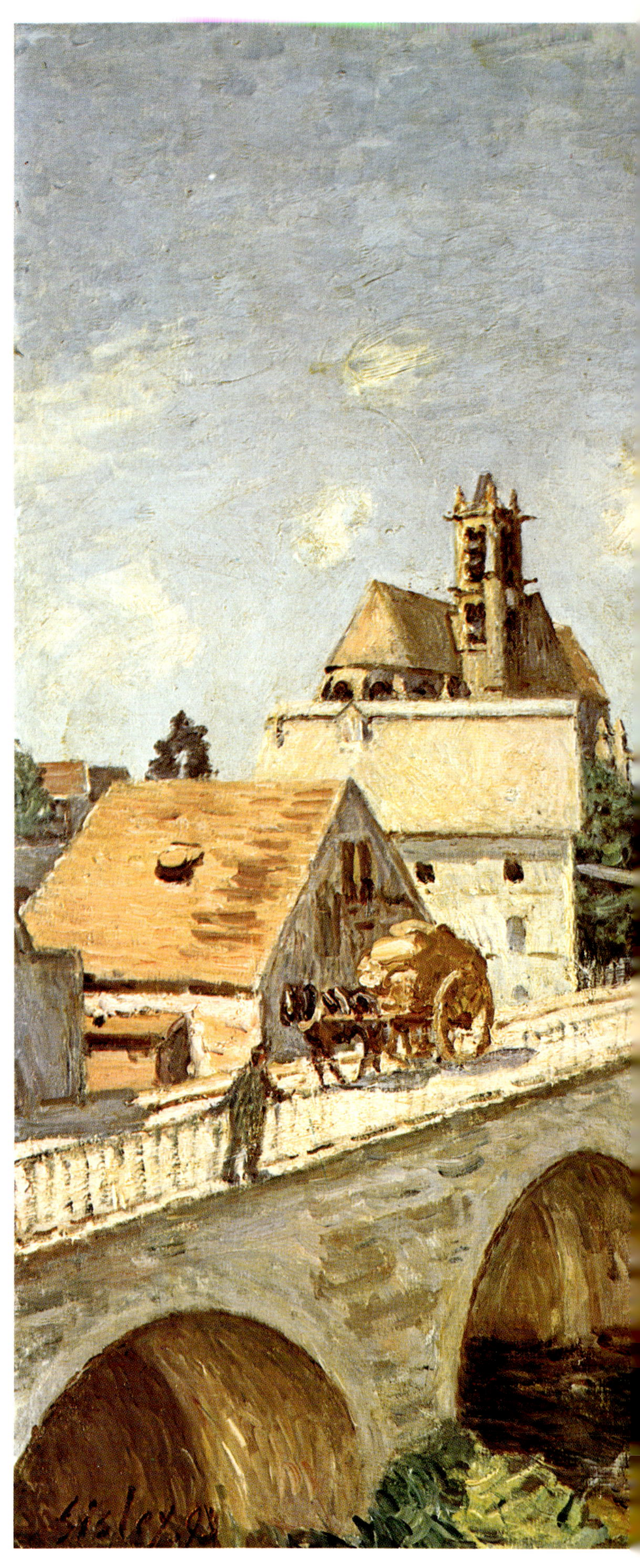

Alfred Sisley: *The Bridge at Moret*, 1893 (Musée du Louvre, Paris – Jeu de Paume).

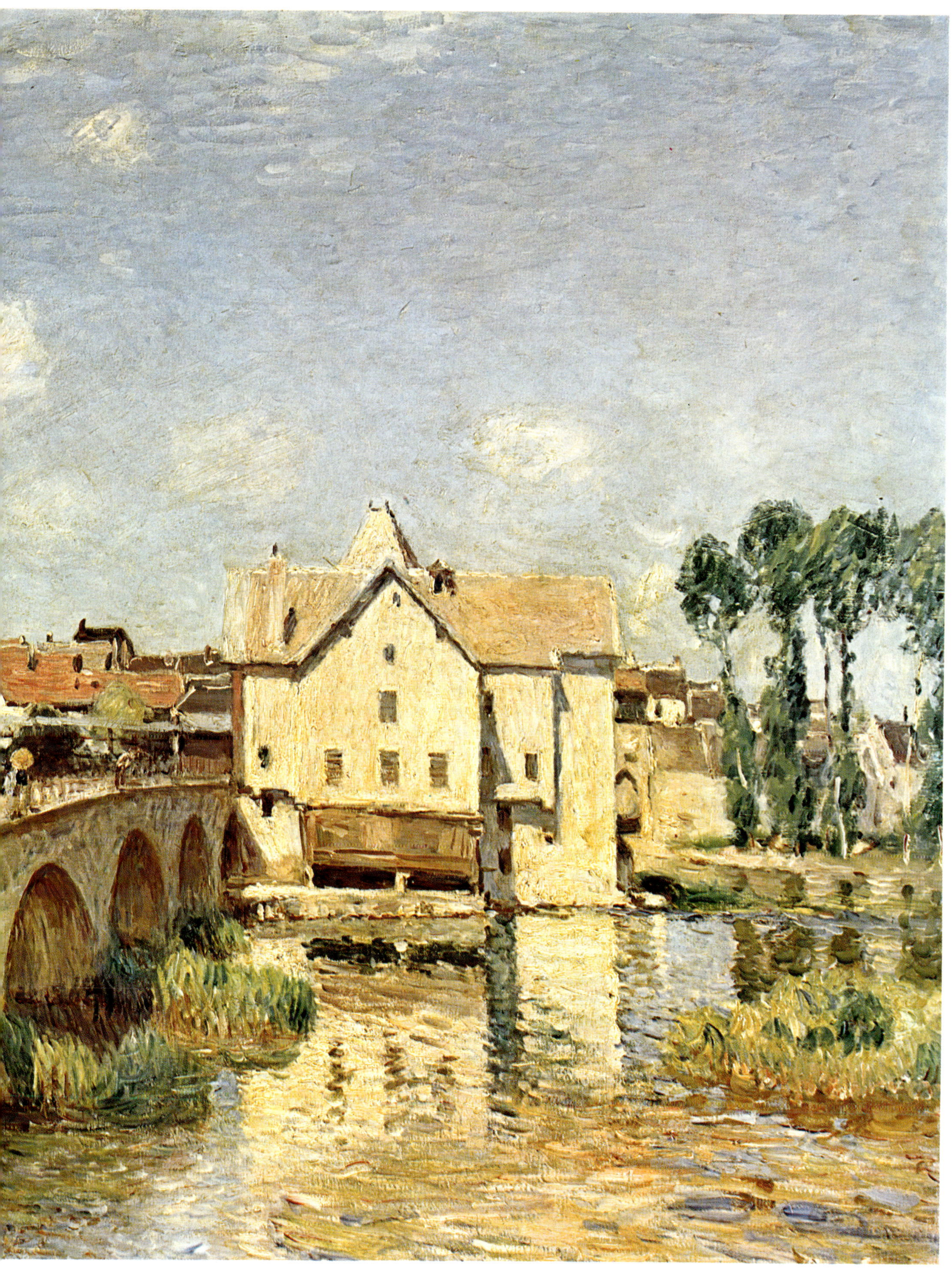

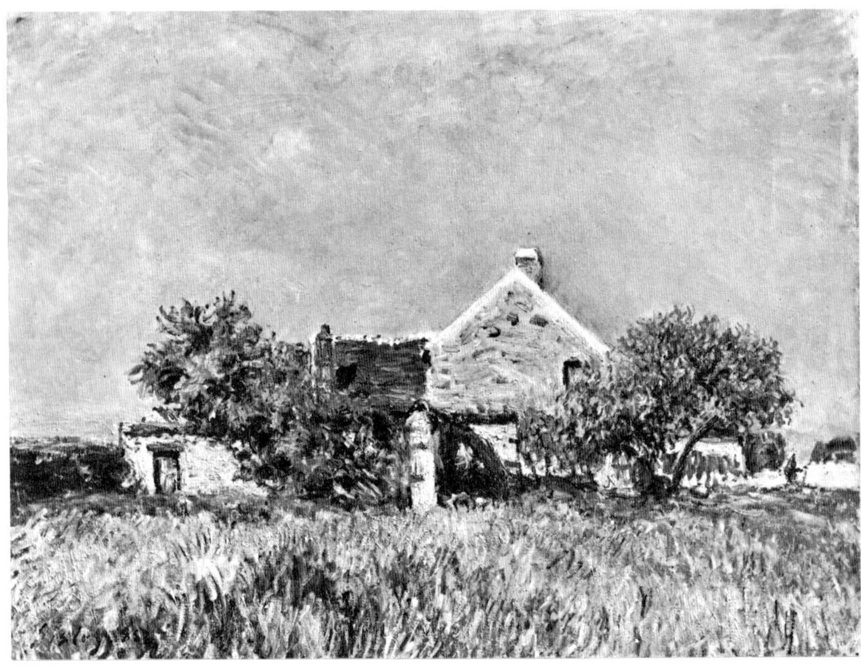

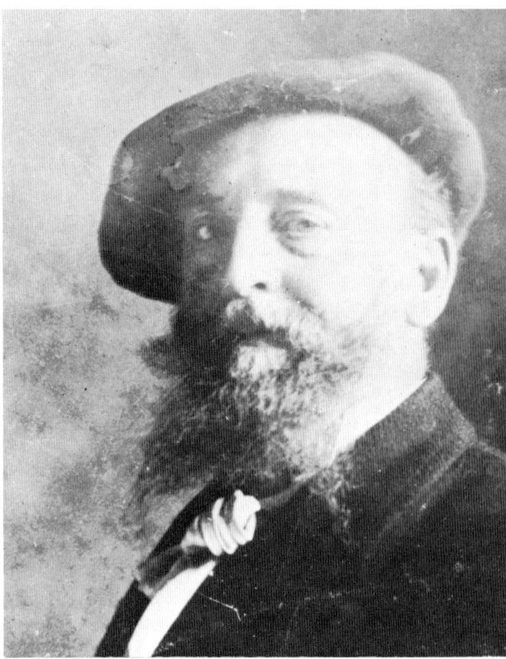

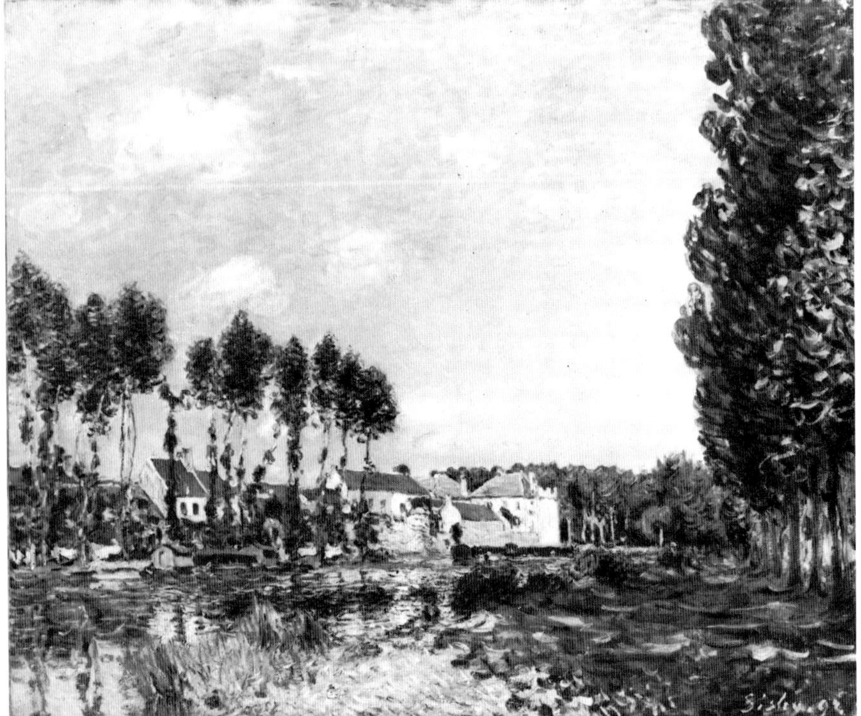

Sisley's ill health and lack of means at the end of his life restricted his world to Moret and its immediate environs.
ABOVE LEFT Alfred Sisley: *Cottage at Les Sablons*, 1885 (Private Collection).
ABOVE Photograph of Sisley in 1895.
BELOW LEFT Alfred Sisley: *The Banks of the Loing, Moret*, 1892 (Musée du Louvre, Paris – Jeu de Paume).
OPPOSITE ABOVE Moret-sur-Loing, showing the fine flying-buttressed church.
OPPOSITE CENTRE Moret in 1889, with women doing their washing in a backwater of the Loing.
OPPOSITE BELOW Sisley's house at Moret.

way of winning through. Nor did he possess the startling, healthy aggressiveness that Monet used to such good effect. He remained poor all his life, morally and physically prostrate, unappreciated, and bitterly resigned to the fact that 'never in his lifetime would a ray of glory ever shine on [his] art.' And whereas most of his friends had met with success or achieved a small reputation by the end of their lives, Sisley's last years were desperately sad.

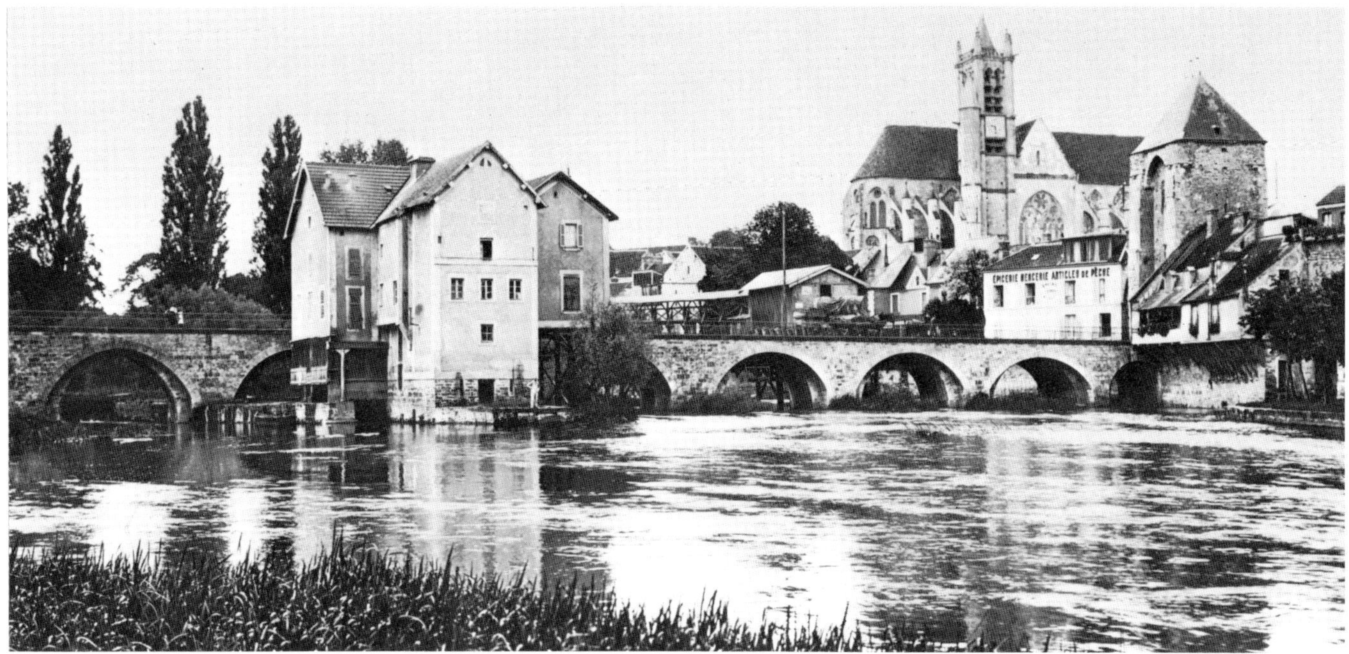

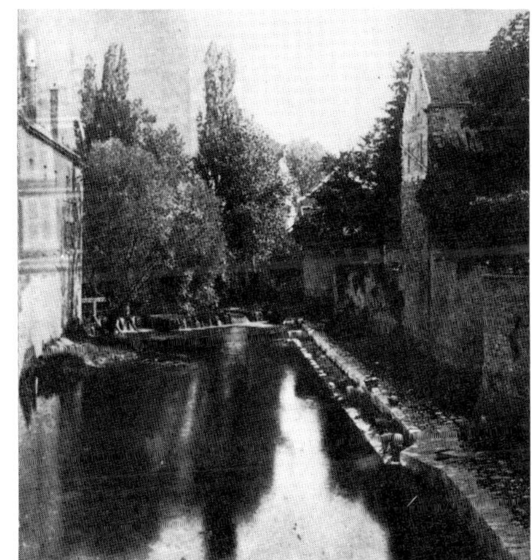

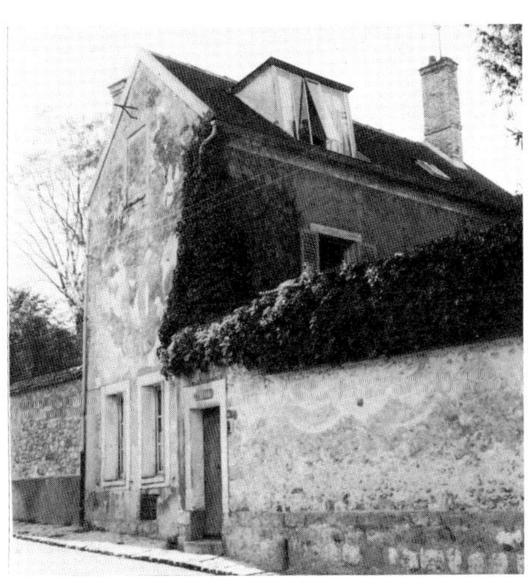

He suffered from rheumatism and facial paralysis, which he had contracted from working long hours outside in all weathers in the damp region of Moret. No wonder, then, that the man Renoir had referred to as the 'gentle, affectionate Sisley' became cantankerous and dissatisfied. He clutched eagerly at the slightest token of sympathy, and would then revert without any apparent reason to the attitude of deep mistrust that had become his second nature.

From time to time, however, the sense of humour which had made him such pleasant company in his youth would dispel Sisley's peevishness. On 2 March 1895, for instance, he wittily apologized in a letter to Georges Charpentier that he would be unable to attend the Humorists' Banquet: 'Do not expect me for the dinner of the *Pris de Rhum* ('Tipsy with Rum', a pun on Prix de Rome) . . . In spite of the pleasure it would give me to join you, it is virtually impossible for me to take part; I live too Loing (a pun on *loin*, 'far away').'

Such flashes of good humour became increasingly rare. Sisley fell out with Durand-Ruel and signed a contract with Georges Petit, who in 1897 organized the painter's last exhibition. Yet again, it was a failure. In December 1898, Sisley wrote to Dr Viau, who was treating him for cancer of the throat: 'I can no longer put up a fight, I have no energy left. I am scarcely able to get out of my bed so it can be made.' A few days later he asked for Monet, who came to his bedside from Giverny. And on 29 January 1899, only just after he had reached his sixtieth year, Alfred Sisley, the most English of the French Impressionists (he had retained British nationality), died at Moret-sur-Loing, on the edge of the forest of Fontainebleau.

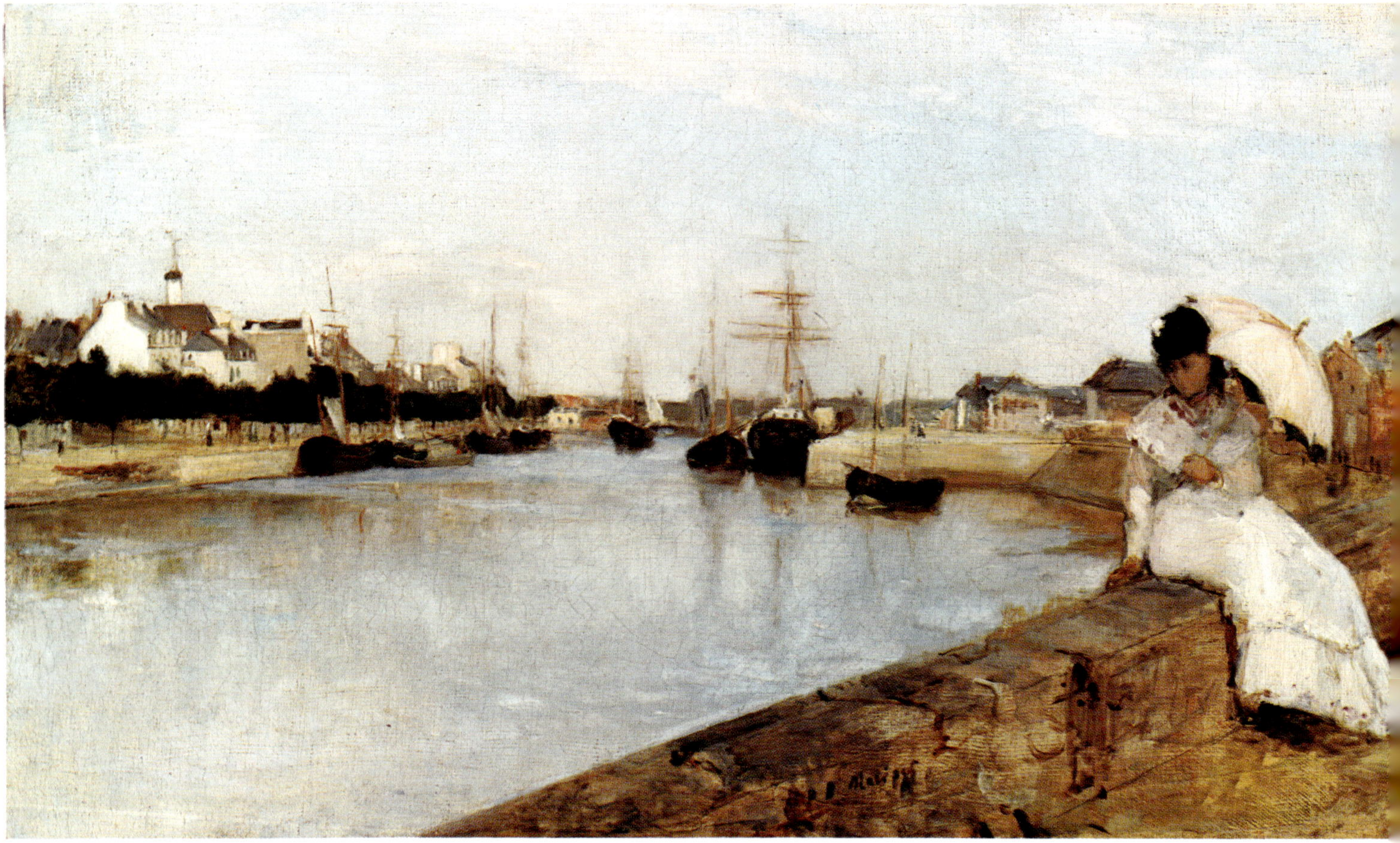

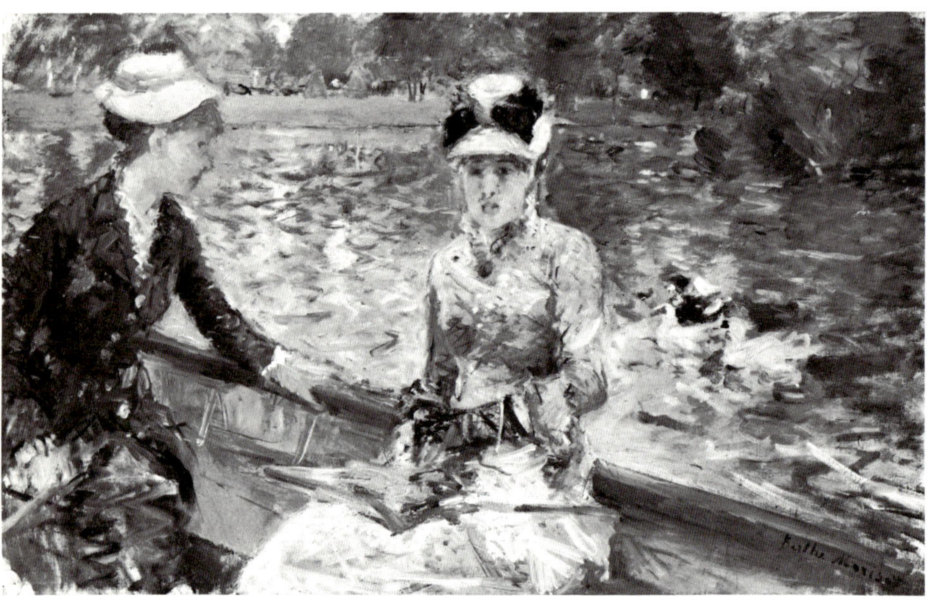

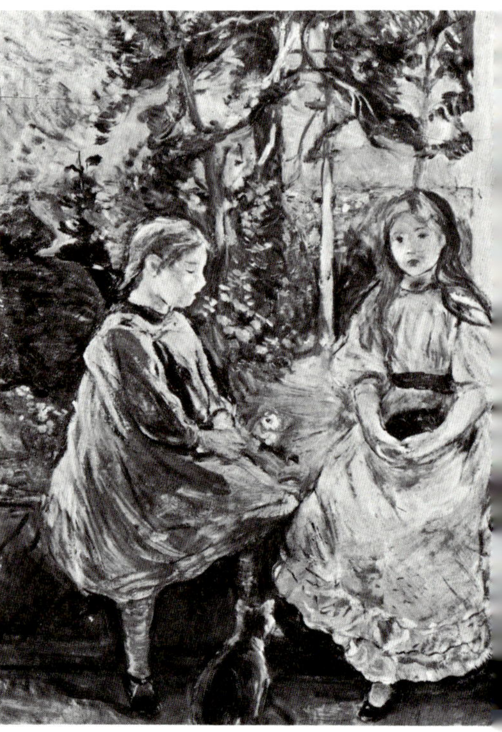

Berthe Morisot was not represented in Caillebotte's collection. True, she was of independent means, and was probably prevented by the fact she was a woman from being accepted as a fully-fledged Impressionist. Luckily Mallarmé, who was a close friend and active admirer of Morisot, managed to get one of her canvases accepted by the Musée du Luxembourg before she died in 1895.

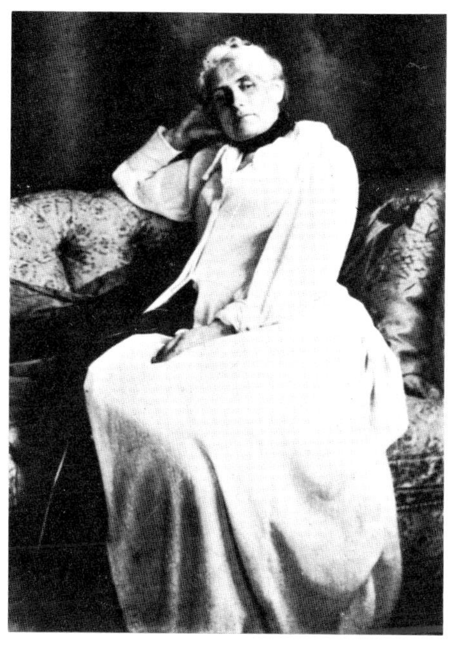

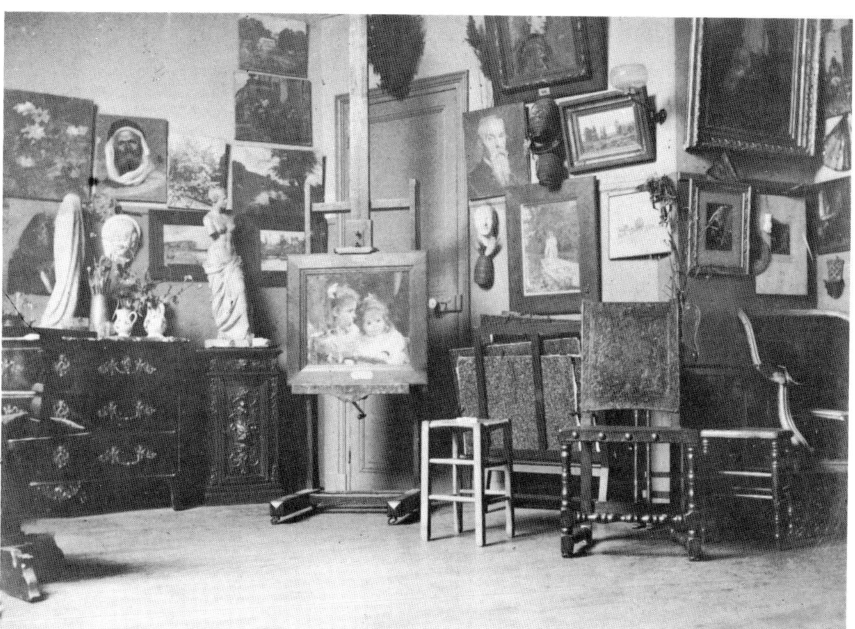

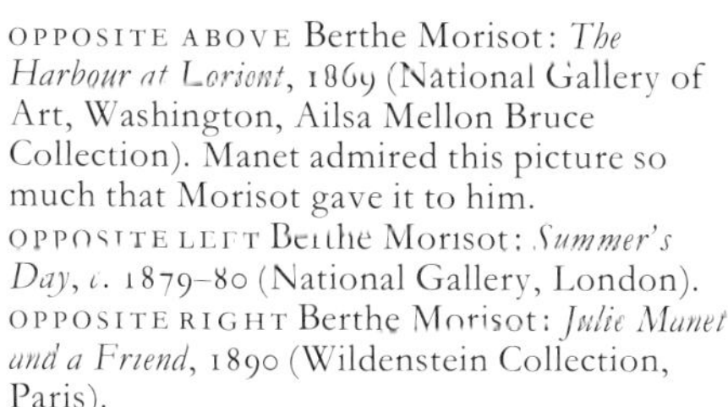

OPPOSITE ABOVE Berthe Morisot: *The Harbour at Lorient*, 1869 (National Gallery of Art, Washington, Ailsa Mellon Bruce Collection). Manet admired this picture so much that Morisot gave it to him.
OPPOSITE LEFT Berthe Morisot: *Summer's Day*, c. 1879–80 (National Gallery, London).
OPPOSITE RIGHT Berthe Morisot: *Julie Manet and a Friend*, 1890 (Wildenstein Collection, Paris).
ABOVE Berthe Morisot a few years before her death.
ABOVE RIGHT Berthe Morisot's studio.
RIGHT Berthe Morisot at work in her studio.

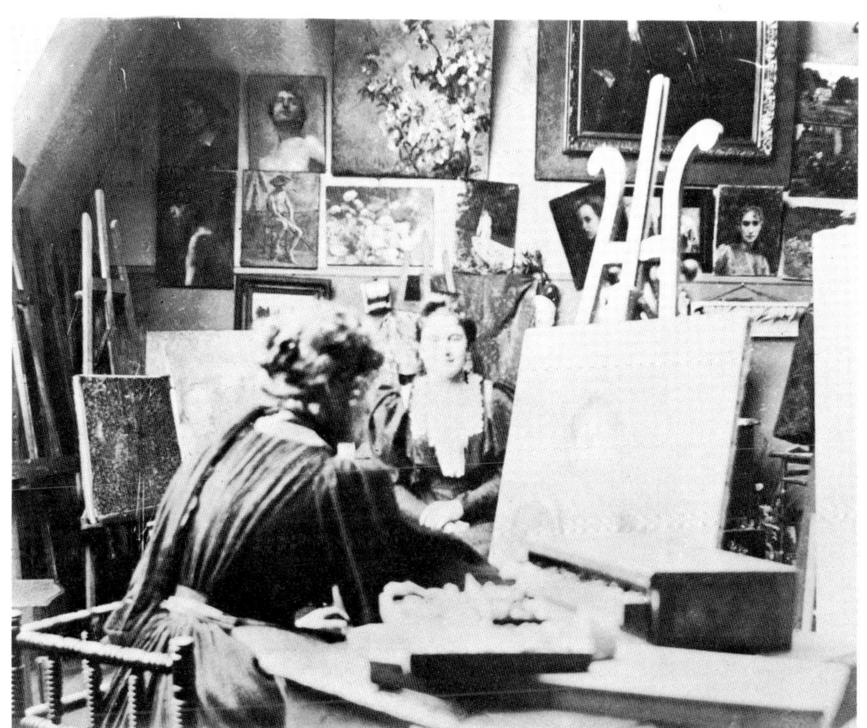

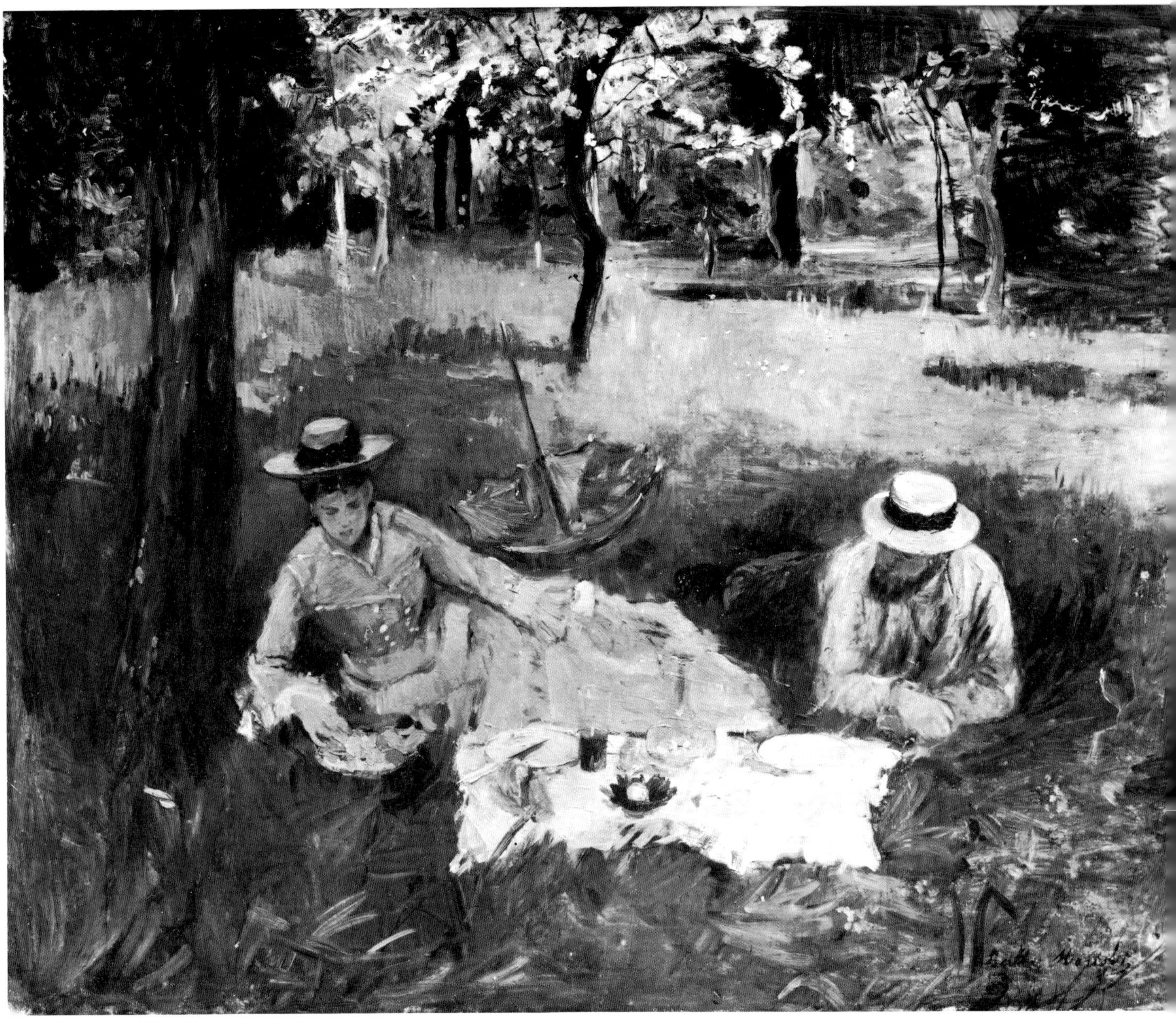

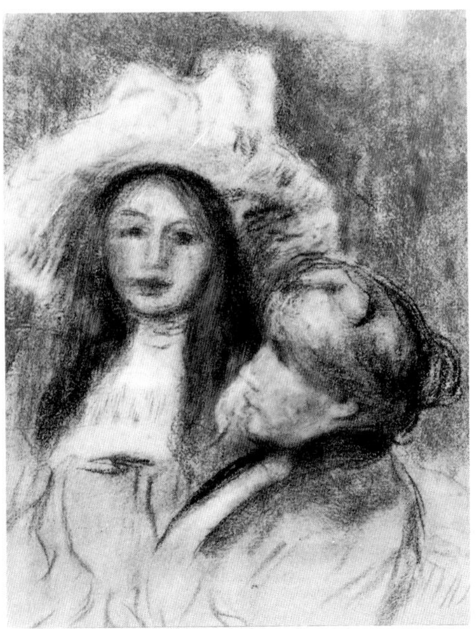

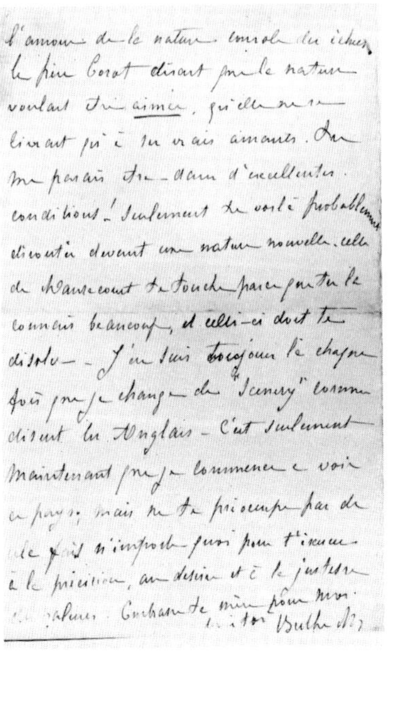

l'amour de la nature console des échecs, le père Corot disant que la nature voulant être aimée, qu'elle ne se livrait qu'à ses vrais amants. Tu me parais être dans d'excellentes conditions! Seulement te voilà probablement déroutée devant une nature nouvelle, celle de Mauvecourt te touche parce que tu la connais beaucoup, et celle-ci doit te désoler – J'en suis toujours là chaque fois que je change de "scenery" comme disent les Anglais – C'est seulement maintenant que je commence à voir ce pays; mais ne te préoccupe pas de ce [illegible] pour t'exercer à la précision, au dessin et à la justesse des valeurs. Embrasse ta mère pour moi. ta tante Berthe M.

ABOVE Berthe Morisot: *Le Déjeuner sur l'Herbe*, 1875 (Private Collection).
FAR LEFT Auguste Renoir: *Berthe Morisot and Her Daughter*, 1894, pastel (Petit Palais, Paris).
LEFT Letter from the artist to her niece.
OPPOSITE Berthe Morisot: *Woman Powdering Herself*, 1877 (Musée du Louvre, Paris).

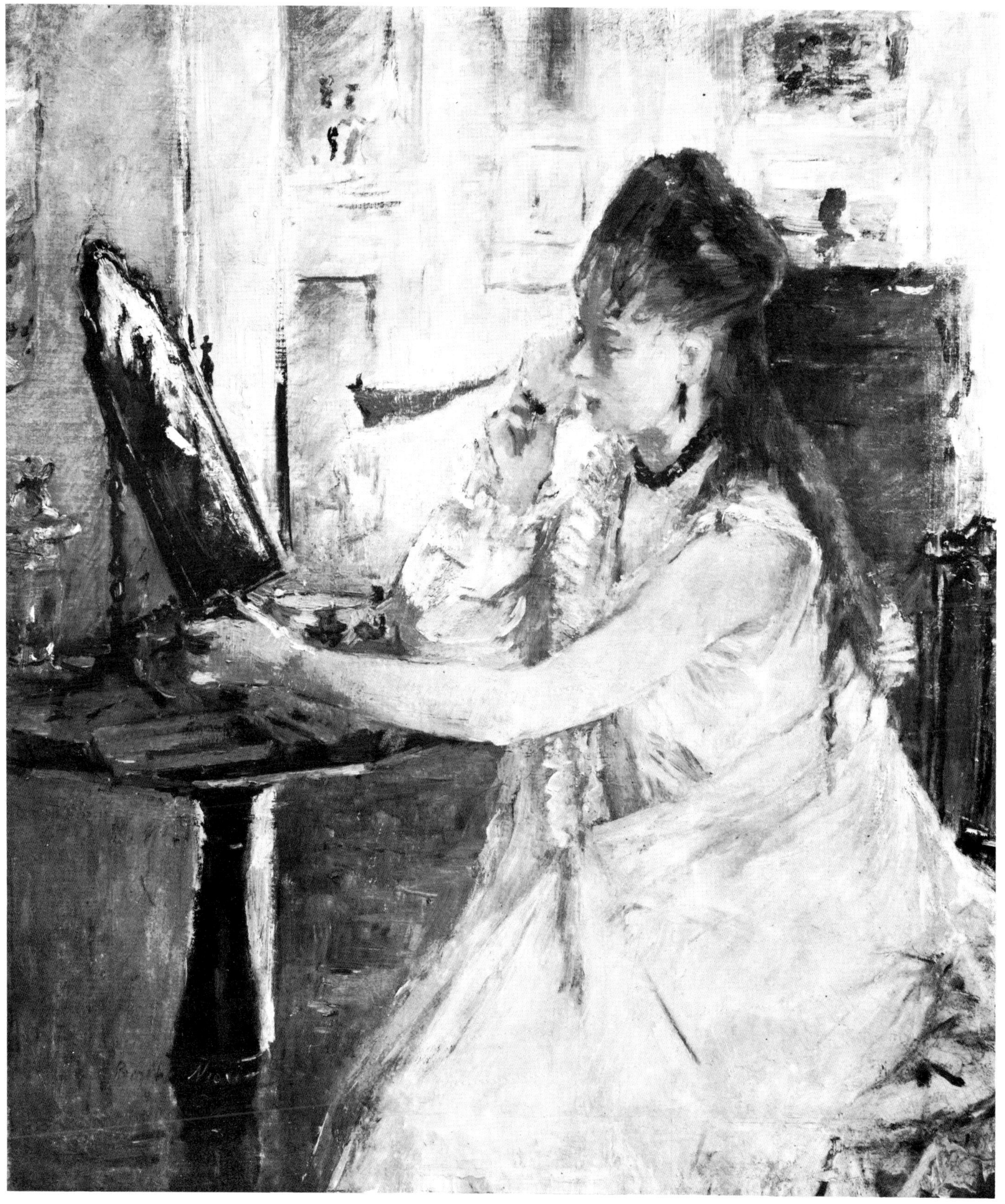

Pissarro's long life enabled him to enjoy to the full the fruits of his indomitable courage. In 1896, after his artistic vision had been enriched by a brief sortie into Pointillism, he began a notable series of paintings of the Rue Saint-Lazare, Boulevard Montmartre, Avenue de l'Opéra and Place du Théâtre-Français in Paris. He was sixty-six at the time. Prevented from working in the open air by an eye complaint, he would rent a room or a flat overlooking his chosen subject. Although forced to walk countless times back and forth between the window of his vantage point and his easel, he was so happy at still being able to paint that physical fatigue meant nothing to him.

Pissarro divided his time between work on such subjects in Paris and his family at their house in Eragny. In the fine studio that he had fitted out there,

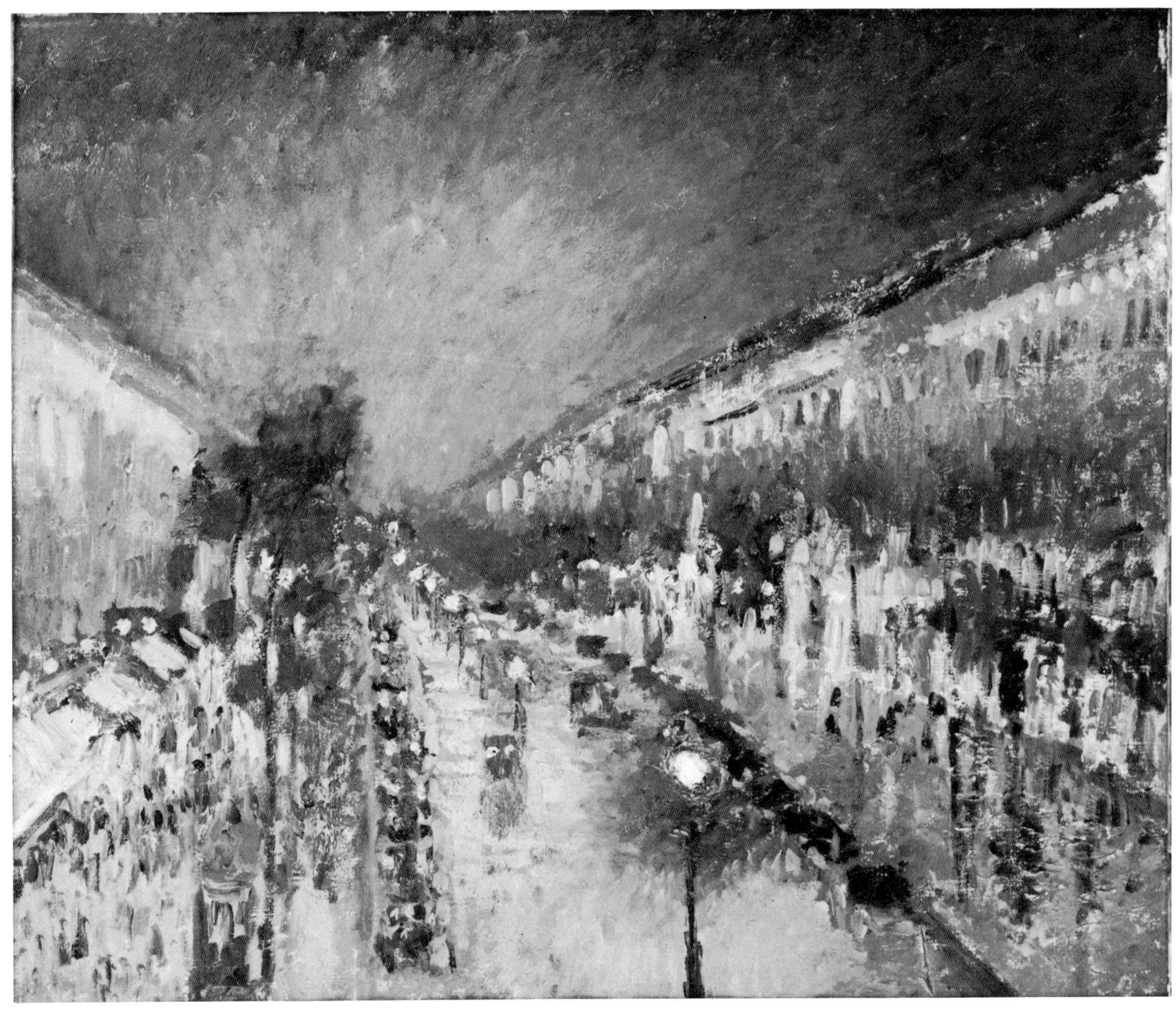

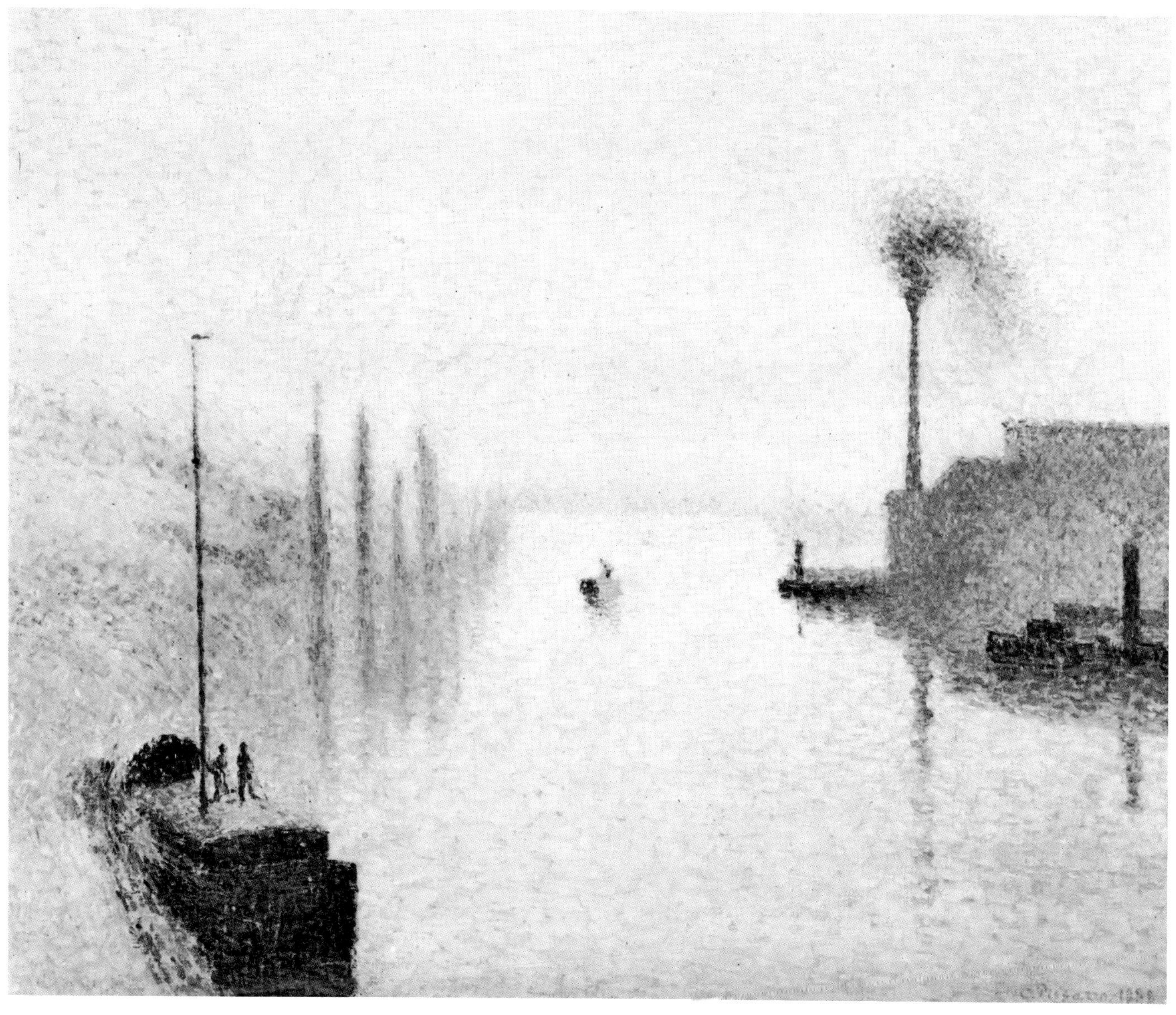

OPPOSITE Camille Pissarro: *Boulevard Montmartre – Effect of Rain*, c. 1897 (National Gallery, London).
ABOVE Camille Pissarro: *Ile Lacroix, Rouen – Effect of Fog*, 1888 (Philadelphia Museum of Art, John G. Johnson Collection).

he worked on drawings, engravings and lithographs, for he had become closely interested in the graphic arts. Durand-Ruel still exhibited his works, and even found enough buyers to enable Pissarro to repay the sum he had borrowed from Monet to buy his house.

Pissarro had become a house-owner in order to guarantee the future of his wife and children. But this did not change his political opinions, which had always been anarchist. During his difficult period as a Pointillist, he took an active part in the campaign against social injustice waged by the anarchist leader Jean Grave, kept up a close correspondence with him, and even, although far from well-off, regularly sent him money and pictures which could be sold. Pissarro contributed illustrations to two anarchist organs, *La Plume* and *Père Peinard*, the latter of which was written mostly in slang and had among its subscribers such literary figures as Mallarmé, Daudet, Anatole France and Huysmans. In 1894, Pissarro had no alternative but to take temporary refuge in Belgium to avoid the fate of his friend the Pointillist painter Frédéric Luce and the brilliant young critic Félix Fénéon, both of whom had been arrested.

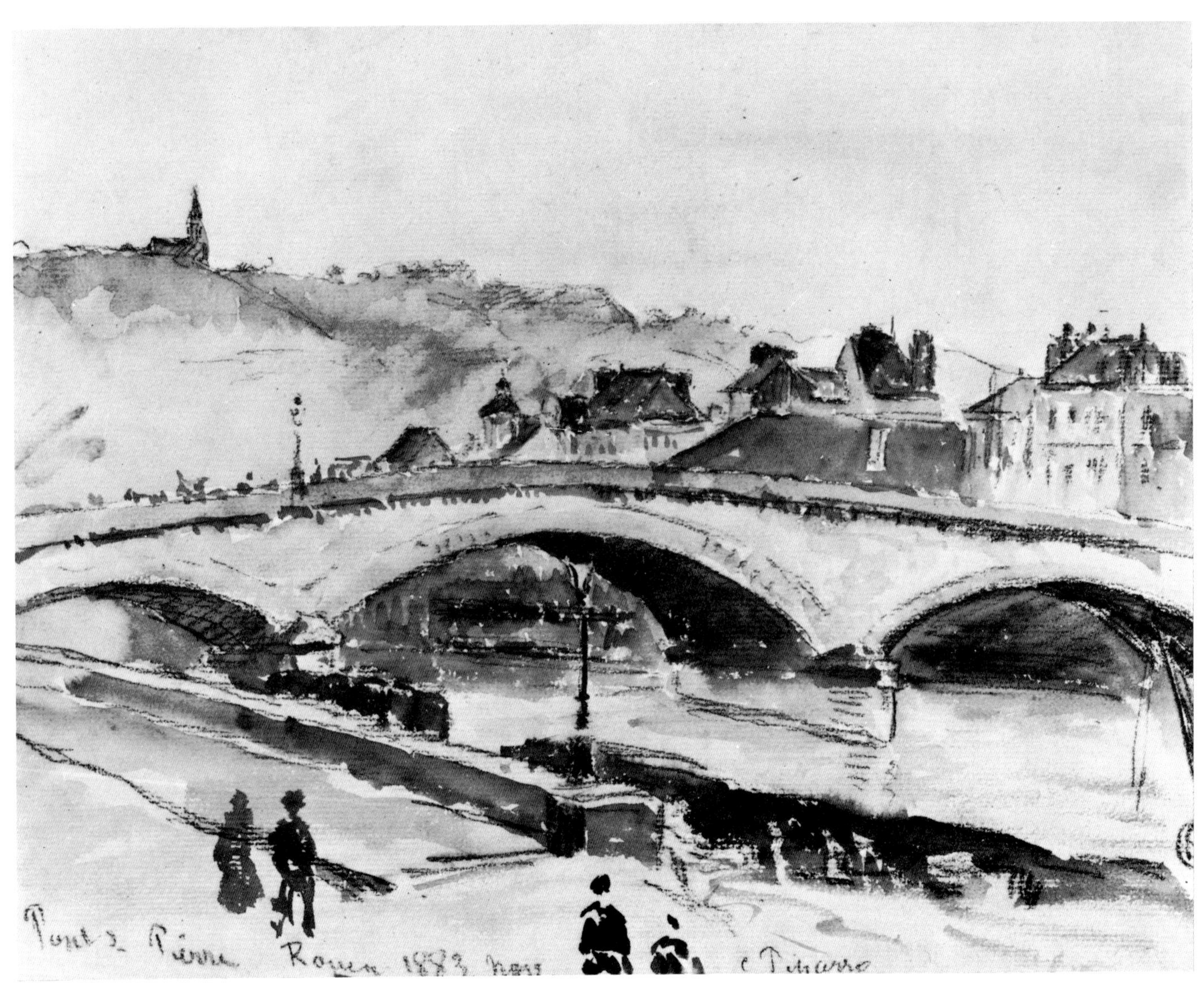

Camille Pissarro made frequent and fruitful visits to the capital of Normandy.
ABOVE Camille Pissarro: *Pont St Pierre, Rouen*, watercolour, 1883 (Galerie Robert Schmit, Paris).
OPPOSITE ABOVE Camille Pissarro: *The Great Bridge at Rouen*, 1896 (Museum of Art, Carnegie Institute, Pittsburgh, Penn.).
OPPOSITE BELOW The Pont St Pierre, Rouen, with the statue of Corneille in the middle distance.

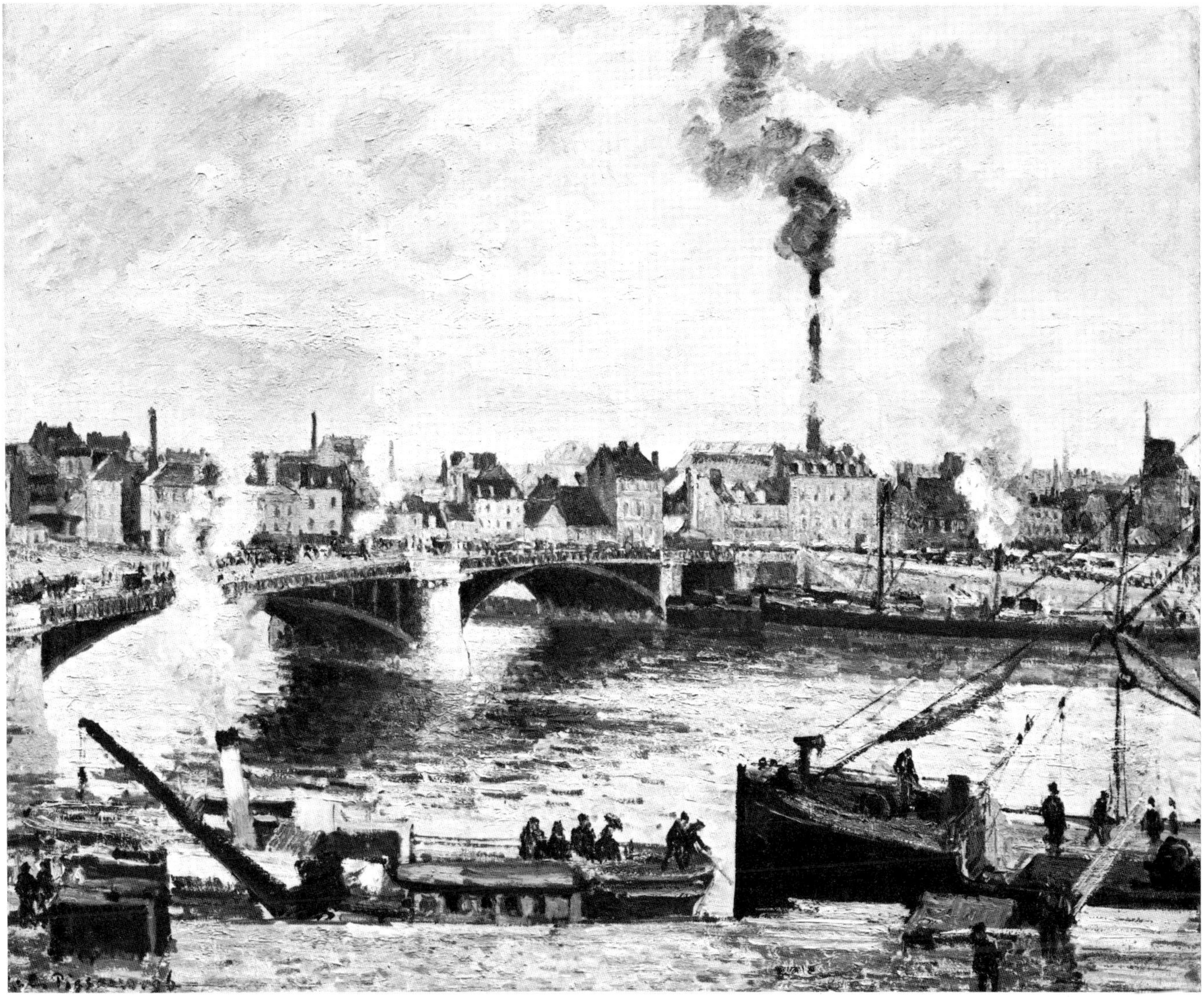

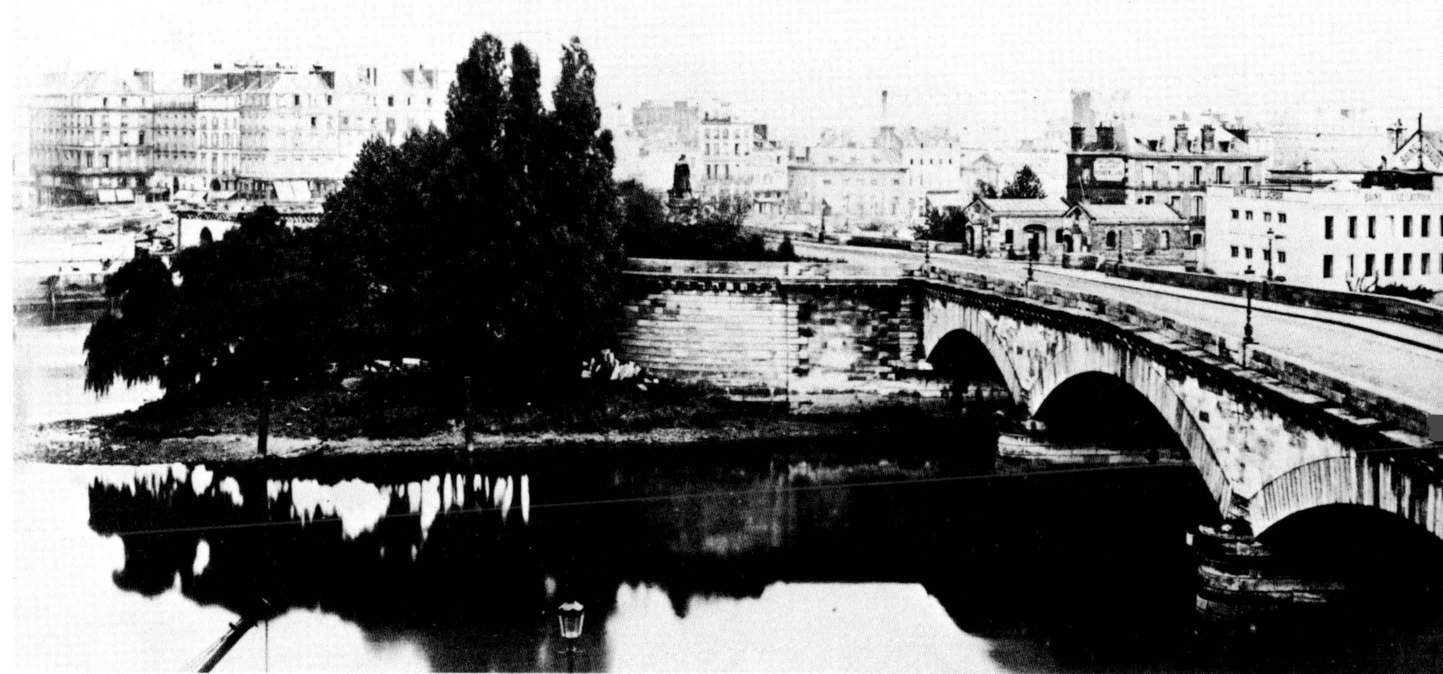

Pissarro made no bones about his anarchist sympathies, and the cautious Renoir, who hated politics, was so scared that he was reluctant to go on show with him. With his noble patriarchal appearance, the elderly Pissarro was occasionally placed in preposterous situations by his extremist beliefs. Pascal Forthuny, who later became a writer, tells the following story: while doing his military service in Rouen, he spotted Pissarro in the street and asked him whether he could visit his studio and look at his paintings. Next day, the young man knocked on Pissarro's door and announced loudly: 'An Impressionist officer here!' He was indeed accompanied by an officer, who, going through the motions he thought indispensable, did his best to admire the painter's work. He picked up *Bridge at Rouen, Effect of Fog*, taking care not to stain his gloves, held it to the light, put it back on its easel, and then, with all the seriousness in the world, admitted that it left him cold: 'No, I'm afraid I can't yet be enough of an anarchist!' he admitted. The cunning Forthuny, who knew the officer to have anarchist leanings, had engineered the meeting with Pissarro in the hope of avoiding too many fatigues and reprimands in the course of his military service.

Towards the end of his life, Pissarro at last enjoyed some degree of financial security (in 1901 one of his paintings was auctioned for 10,000 francs), and was able to do a lot of travelling, in England, where his son had settled, and Belgium, as well as France. He visited Lyons, Mâcon and Troyes, where his wife came from, and returned again and again to the Normandy coast he so adored. It was in Le Havre that Pissarro produced his last paintings during the summer of 1903, before dying from an abscess of the prostate gland, which his doctor had attempted to cure by homeopathy.

BELOW Camile Pissarro: *Three Sketches of Working and Peasant Life*, c. 1890 (Musée du Louvre, Paris).
OPPOSITE Camille Pissarro: *Self-Portrait*, 1903 (Tate Gallery, London).

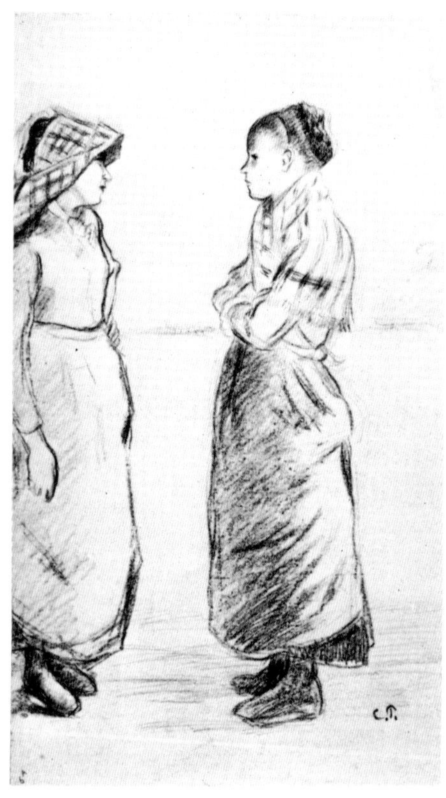

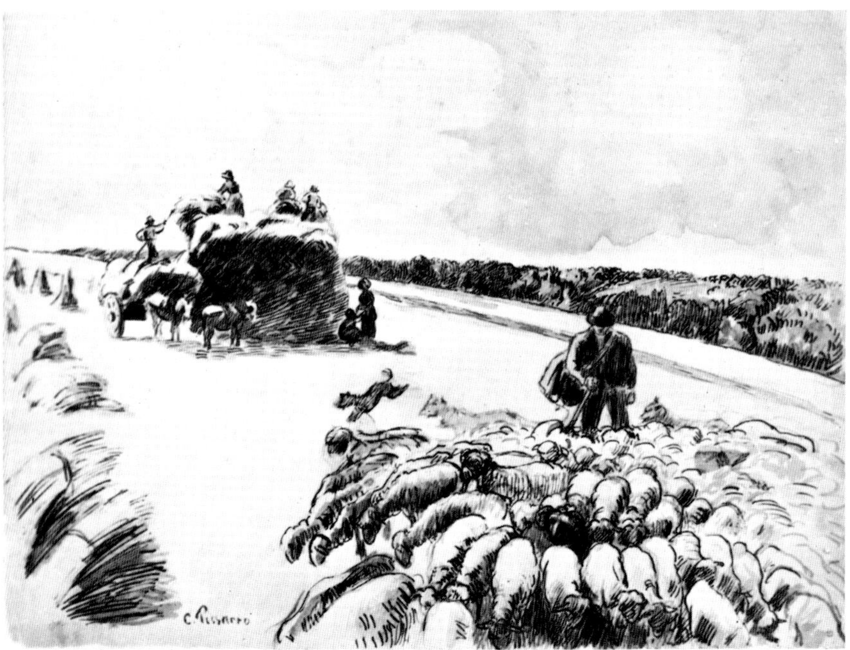

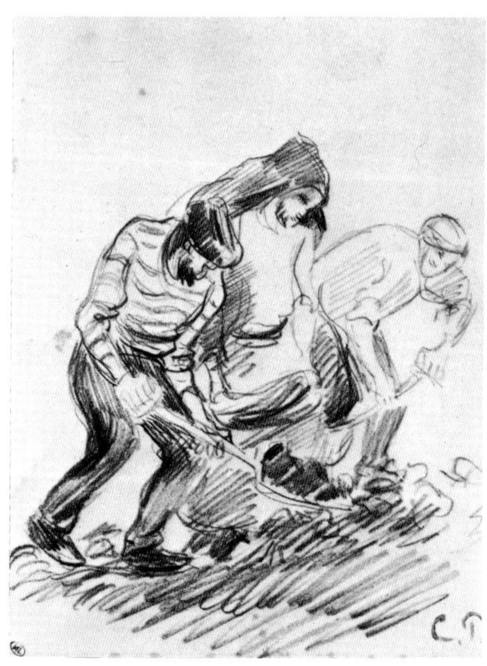

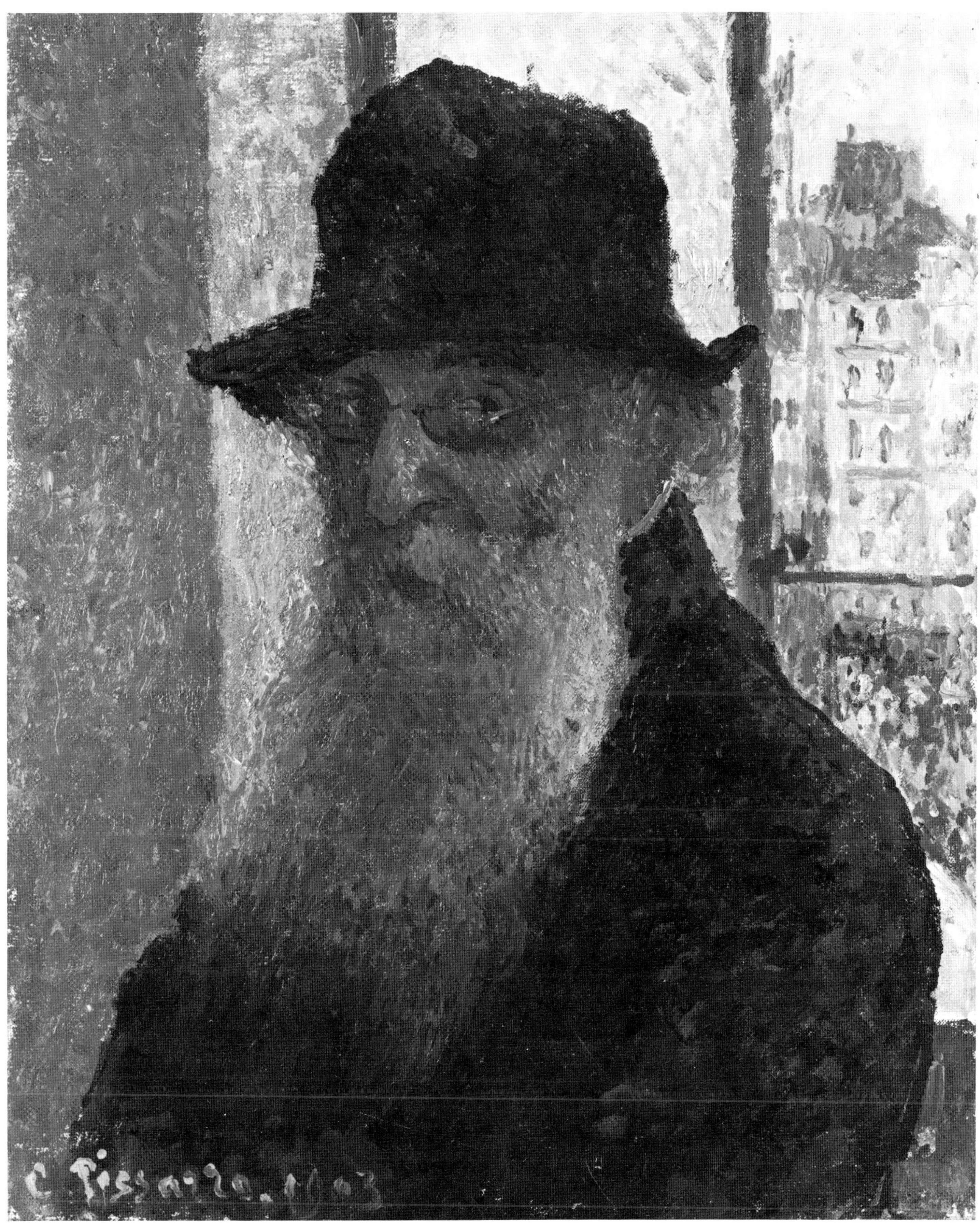
C. Pissarro. 1903

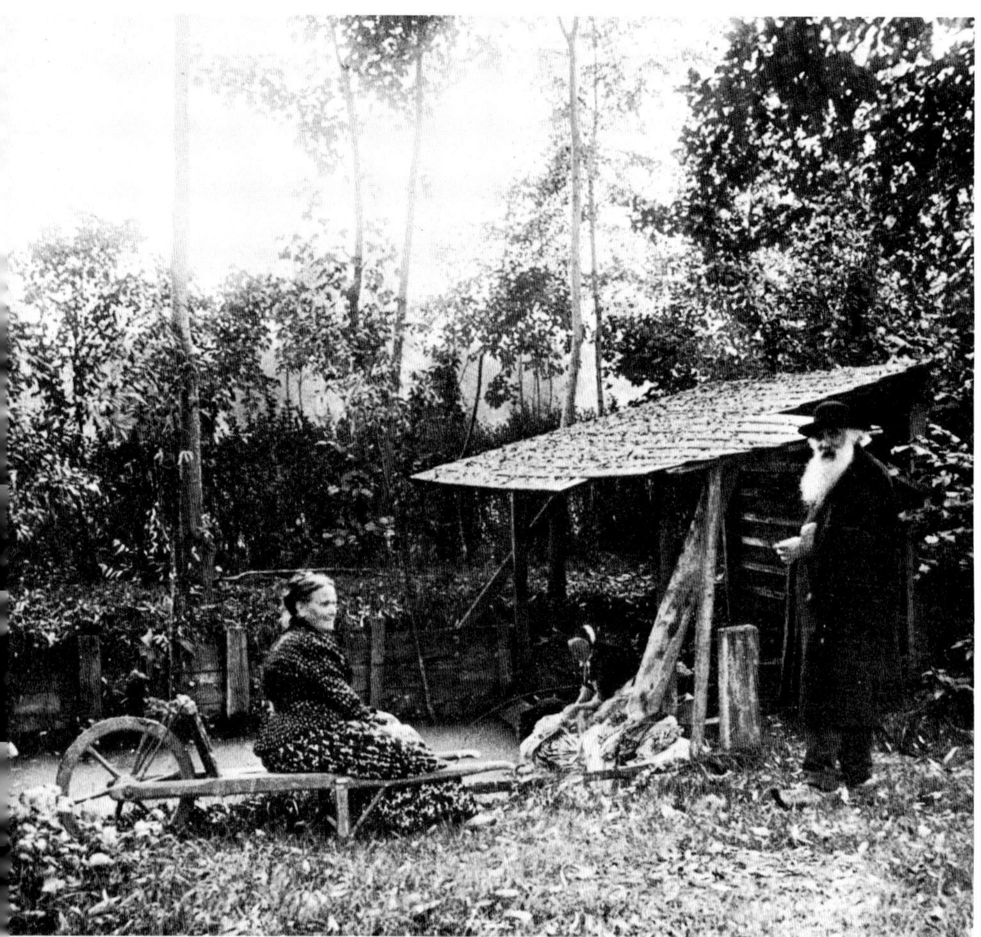

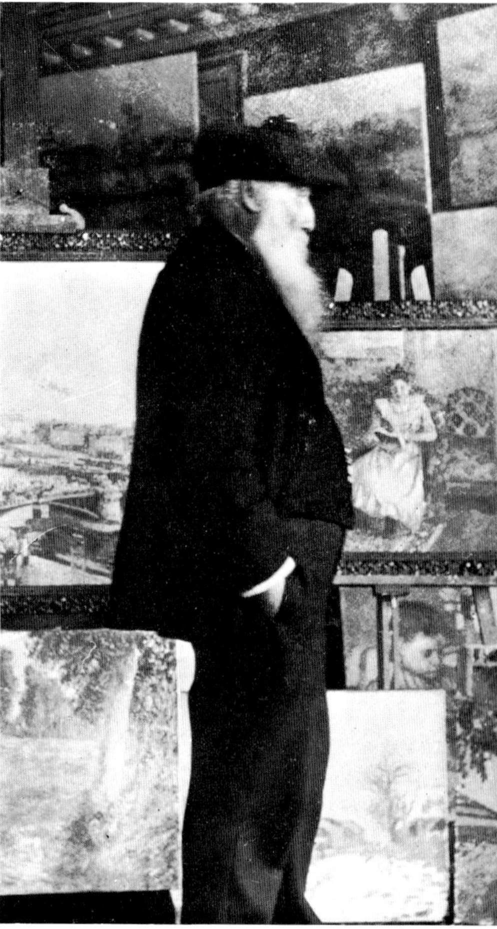

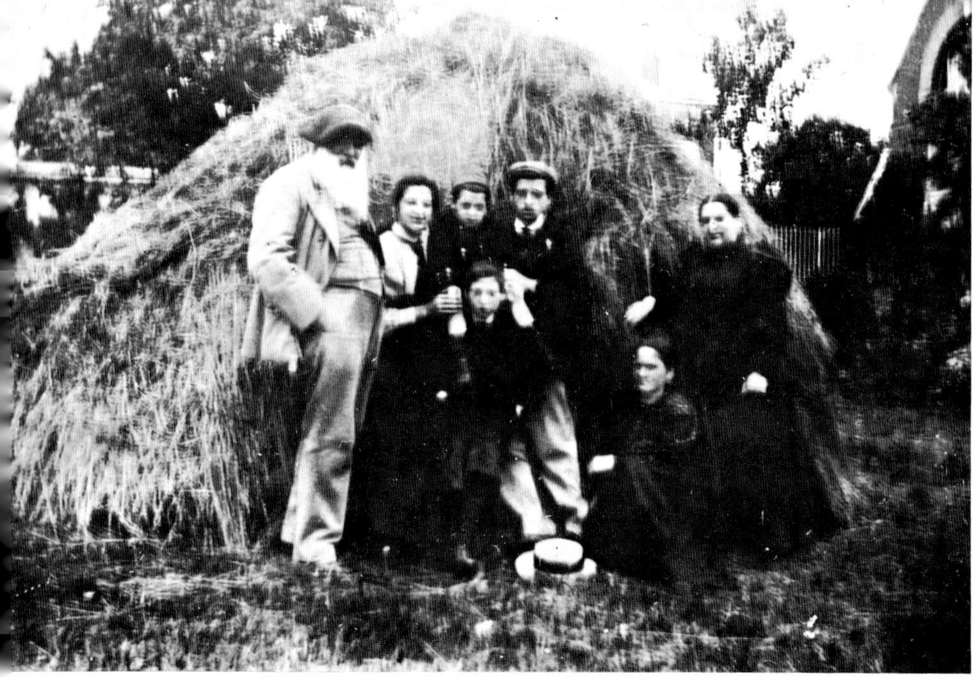

ABOVE LEFT Pissarro and his wife at a washhouse in the garden at Eragny.
ABOVE Pissarro in his studio.
LEFT Pissarro, Jeanne, Paul-Emile, Rodo, Alice Isaacson and Julie Pissarro posed by a haystack.
OPPOSITE Photographs of Pissarro including (ABOVE LEFT) with his daughter Jeanne, and (LEFT) with his son Lucien.

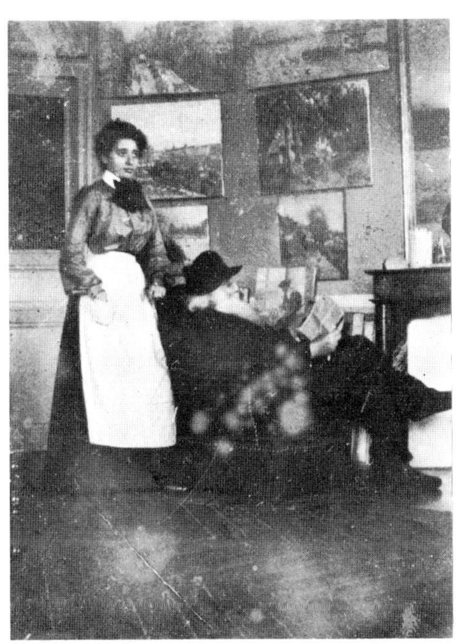

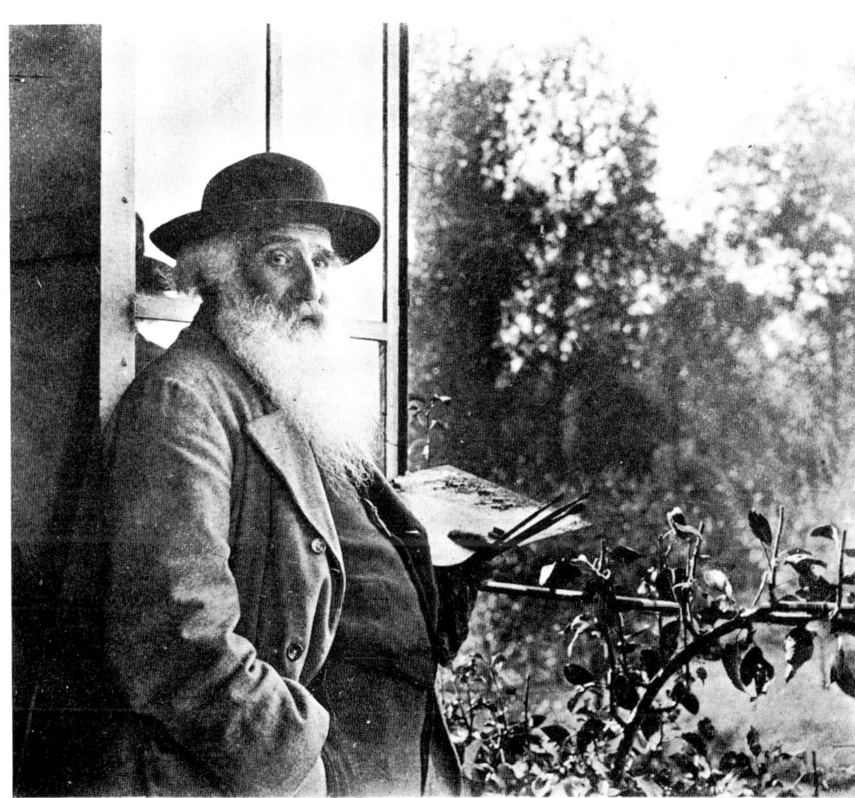

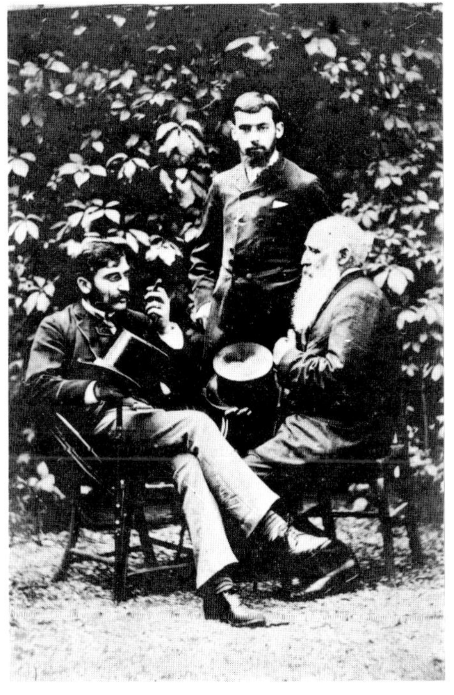

For ten years, through a miraculous feat of will-power, Degas fought a brave battle against failing eyesight and old age. In the loneliness of his studio, uncertain of his movements, he would occasionally pick up his paintbrushes and turn out a portrait. Using charcoal or pastels, which were less tiring on the eyes, he returned to subjects whose contours he knew almost by heart. But above all he devoted more and more of his time to modelling – the art of the blind *par excellence*. And with noisy displays of bad temper, he fought off intruders, journalists, and the trappings of success.

An old friend, the Irish writer George Moore, found himself barred from the studio as soon as he mentioned that he was going to write an article. When Stéphane Mallarmé came to tell Degas that he had approached a friend with a view to getting the government to buy one of his pictures, the artist flew off the handle. In the poet's words, 'he paced up and down his studio like a lion, and easels seemed to take to the air as he touched them.' Every token of official recognition irked Degas, because in his view there was something disgraceful about being well-known to people who did not understand you. He therefore refused to let his works be put on show in a special room during the Paris World's Fair, in 1889.

Yet Degas did see a few young painters. He gave useful advice to his friend Henri Rouart's son Ernest, who wanted to become a painter. He corrected the drawings of Suzanne Valadon, a young woman of great beauty who was Puvis de Chavannes' regular model and also sat for Renoir. Degas allowed a young poet he had met at the Rouarts', Paul Valéry, to visit him. But such youthful admirers were no substitute for the old friends whom Degas was gradually losing. The Dreyfus Affair brought out a vehement antisemitism in him, and caused him to fall out with Ludovic Halévy and Pissarro, both of whom were Jewish. Little by little, the society he adored was giving way to the modern world – a world that in Degas' view was becoming poorer in talent and originality. 'Education, what a crime!' he was fond of exclaiming. 'Look at the Bretons: they cross themselves and they work hard. Take away their faith, and they turn into slackers! What a crime! Art for the people? How dismal! Beauty is a mystery . . .'

During his last days, Degas would leave his studio at dusk and walk down to the Rue Laffite, stopping to look in the windows of the great dealers of the period, such as Bernheim, Durand-Ruel and Ambroise Vollard. Then he would continue on his way, back up to Montmartre, wrapped in a dark overcoat that made his bowed figure melt into the darkness. 'My legs are still in working order,' he would repeat with a satisfied air, 'and I'm getting some sleep, plenty of it even . . . eight to ten hours a night . . . Sleep, and my legs – I've still got those.'

When his house in the Rue Victor-Massé was demolished in 1912, he reluctantly moved to a flat that Suzanne Valadon had found him on the Boulevard de Clichy. But he never really found the necessary energy to settle properly in his new home: his canvases, his boxes, all his belongings remained piled against the walls unpacked. Nor had they moved when finally sadness, old age and loneliness got the better of Edgar Degas, and one November day in 1917, when he was eighty-three, his weary eyes remained closed for ever.

Renoir was the first of the Impressionists to achieve some degree of material security with his paintings. In 1899 *La Grenouillère* fetched a record sum of 20,000 francs. In 1901 his talent was rewarded with the Légion d'Honneur: with a good dose of naive modesty, Renoir felt he had to apologize to Monet for accepting the honour. But life was also unkind to him: the rheumatism

Auguste Renoir: study for *The Bathers*, *c.* 1887 (courtesy of the Art Institute of Chicago). Suzanne Valadon posed for the final version of this work.

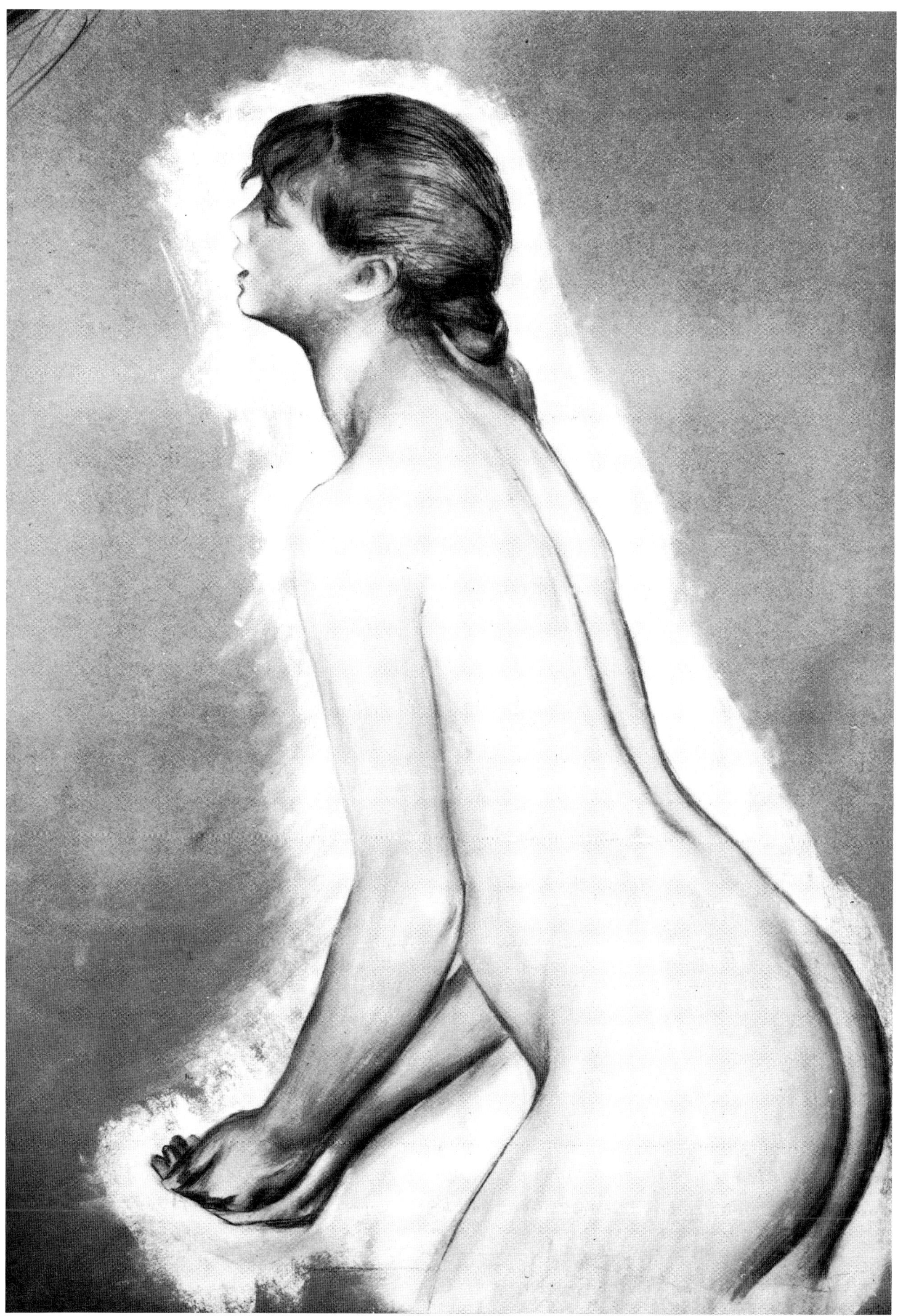

from which he was beginning to suffer was later to cause him immense anguish by deforming and paralyzing his limbs.

But a unique combination of innate optimism and will-power enabled Renoir, whom Cézanne had once charged with being 'a bit of a cissy', to endure a physical purgatory for twenty years while still continuing to paint. As he had to spend an increasing amount of his time on the Côte d'Azur for health reasons, he bought Les Collettes, an estate covered with century-old olive trees and cork oaks, perched on a rock at the foot of the village of Cagnes. In the rambling house he had built there, Renoir, who was the subject of constant care and attention from his wife Aline, worked at his paintings surrounded by his high-spirited, playful children, Jean, Claude (who was known as 'Coco') and Pierre, and amidst the comings and goings of

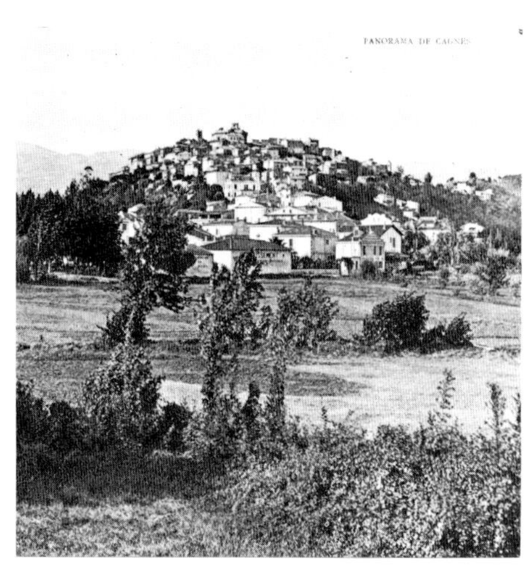

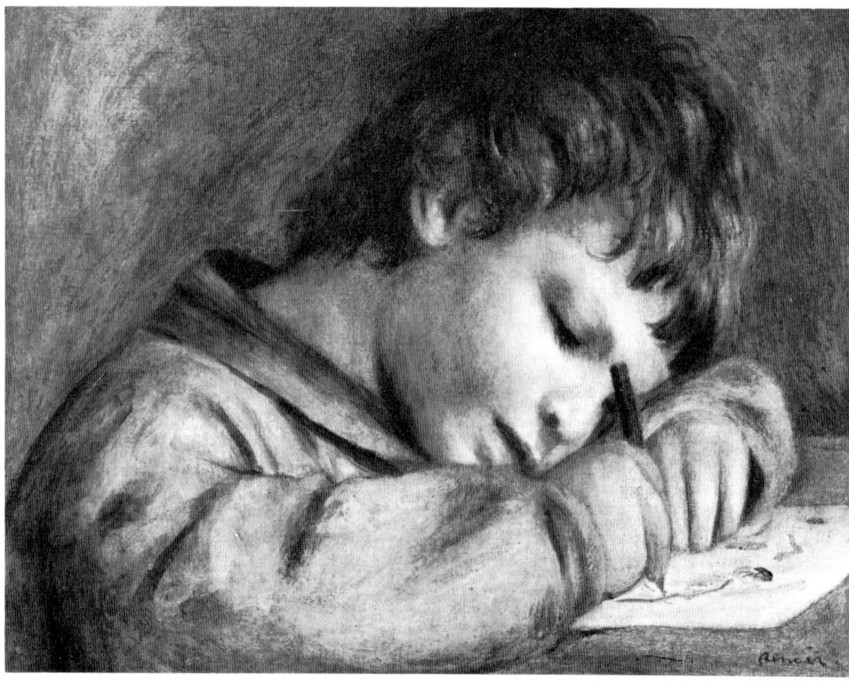

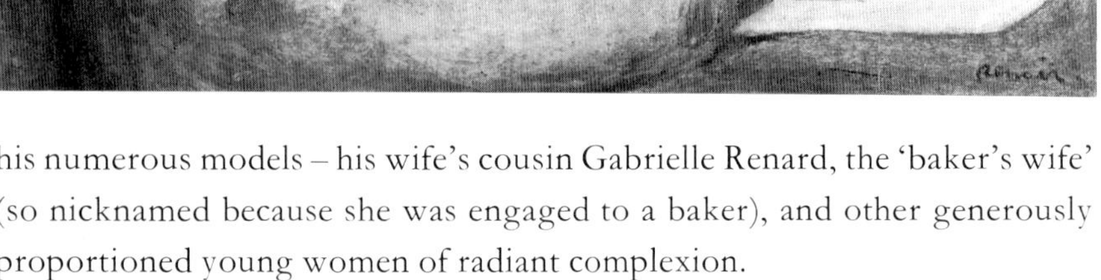

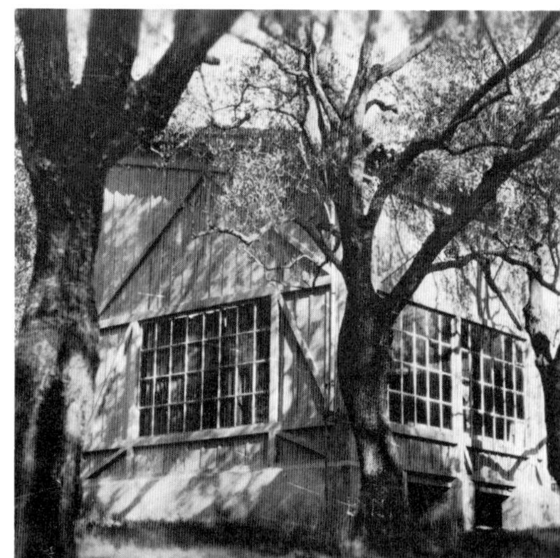

Renoir, forced to spend his winters in the south because of his rheumatism, decided in 1905 to buy Les Collettes, an estate at the foot of the hill-top village of Cagnes (TOP).
ABOVE Renoir's house at Les Collettes.
LEFT Auguste Renoir: *Coco Drawing*, 1905 (Durand-Ruel Collection, Paris).
OPPOSITE Auguste Renoir: *The Washerwomen*, 1886–9, (Baltimore Museum of Art, Maryland, Cone Collection).

his numerous models – his wife's cousin Gabrielle Renard, the 'baker's wife' (so nicknamed because she was engaged to a baker), and other generously proportioned young women of radiant complexion.

While his health permitted, Renoir would spend a few weeks in Paris at the end of the summer, before going to Essoyes, where Aline was born, to enjoy the splendours of autumn in the Burgundy countryside. When the villagers returned from working in the vineyards, they would stop for a chat with Renoir, who just before midday used to take the air in the courtyard of his little house: together they regretted the felling of trees to supply the newly established sawmill, and deplored the first signs of the modern era, about which Renoir felt so deeply pessimistic.

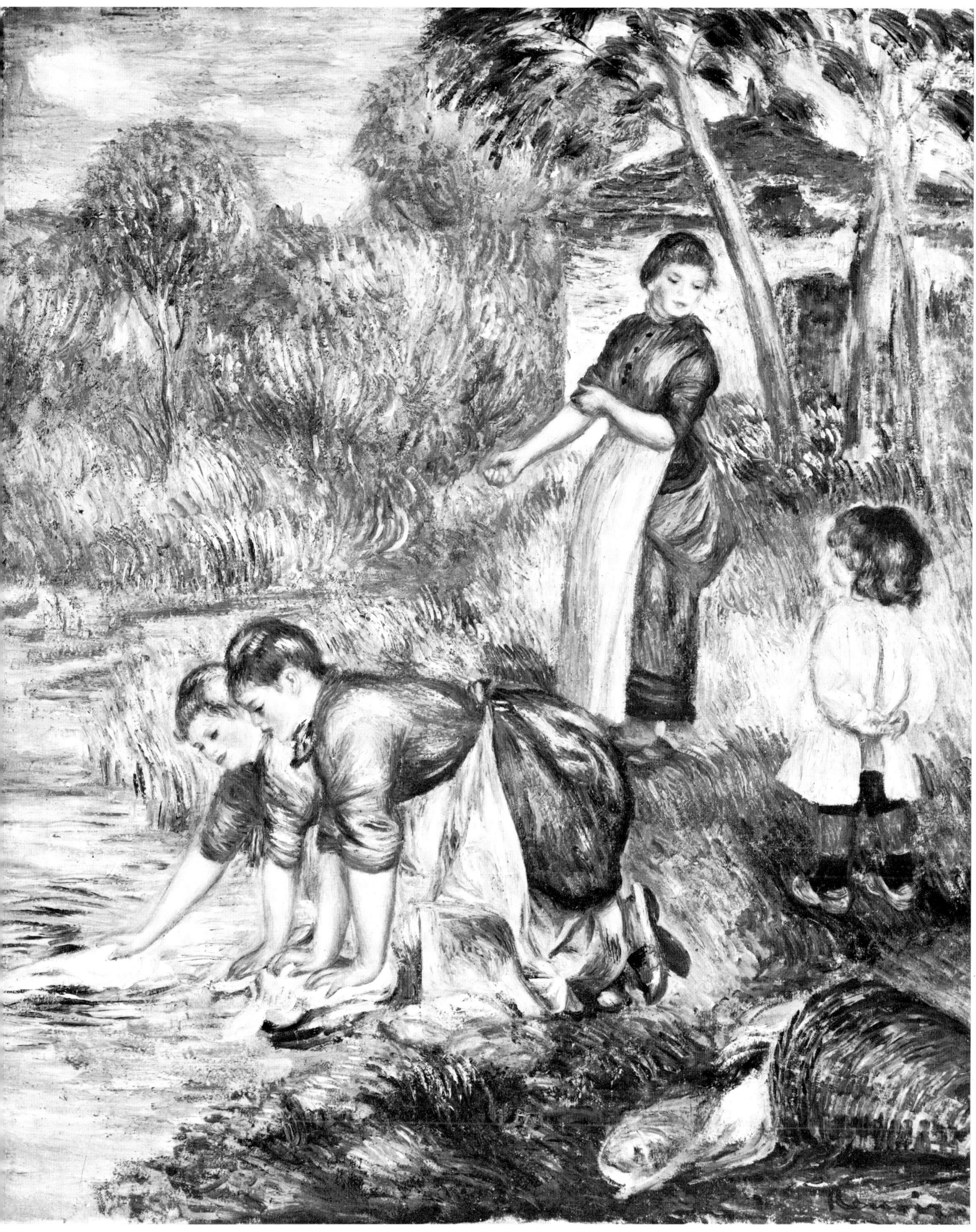

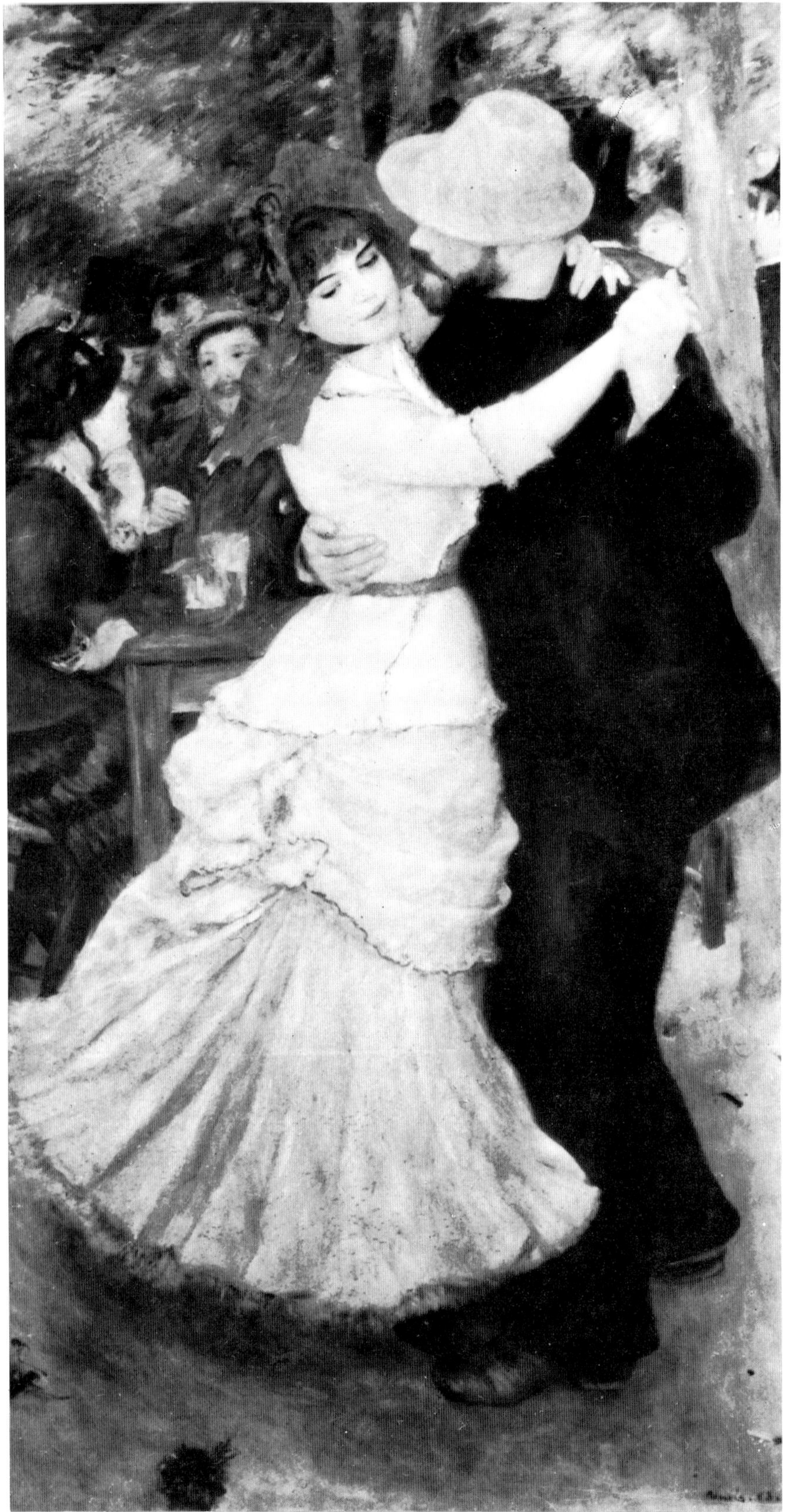

In Burgundy, as in the South of France, Renoir would go out into the open to catch the slightest shaft of sunlight. He also loved to be visited by friends, for although his body was as thin and as gnarled as an old vine he had lost nothing of his lust for life and his quick-wittedness. He was frequented by young artists such as Albert André and Aristide Maillol, the sculptor,

LEFT August Renoir: *The Dance at Bougival*, 1883 (Museum of Fine Arts, Boston). Suzanne Valadon and Renoir's brother posed for this painting.
OPPOSITE Auguste Renoir: *The Harvest*, watercolour sketch, *c.* 1883–6 (Musée du Louvre, Paris).

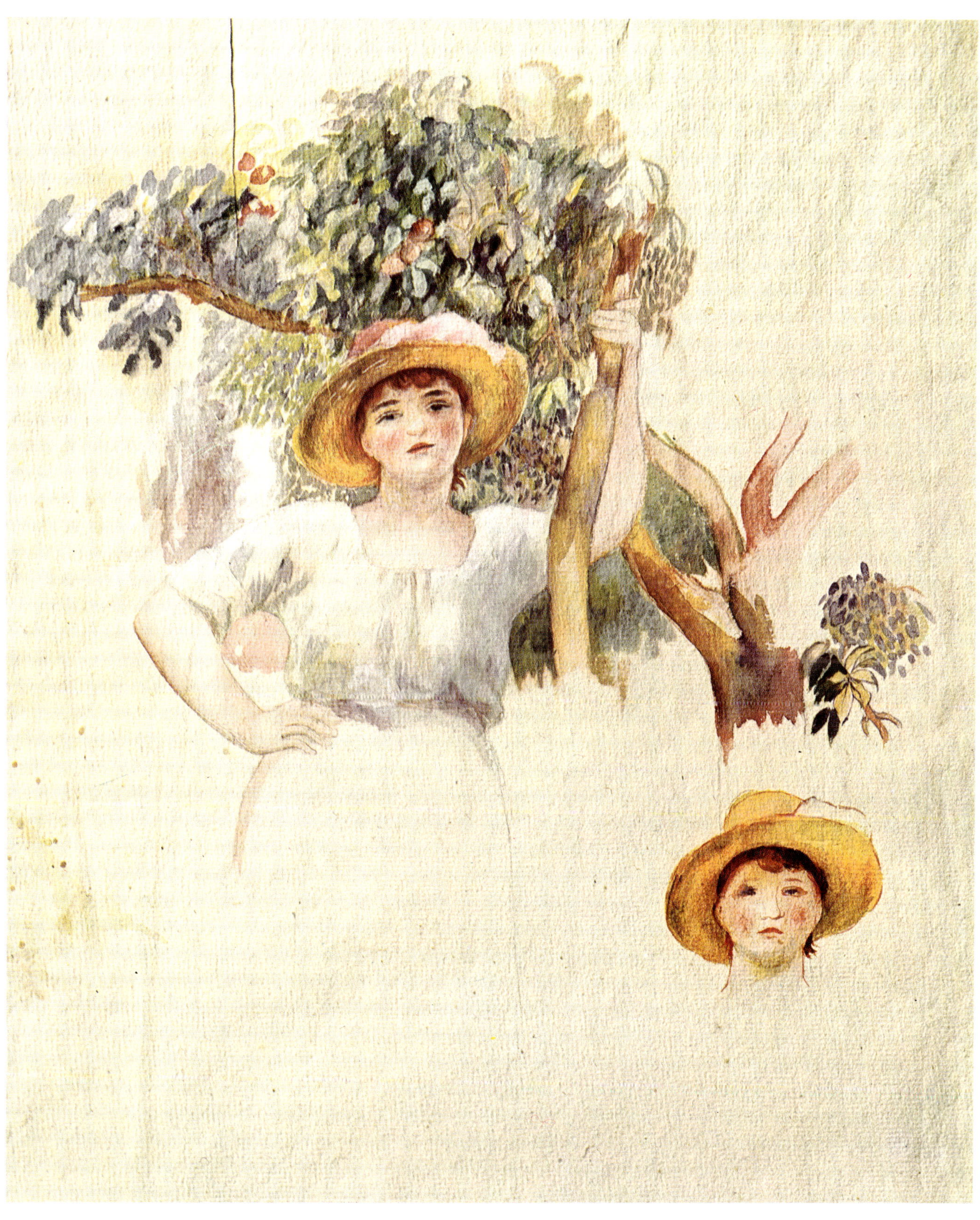

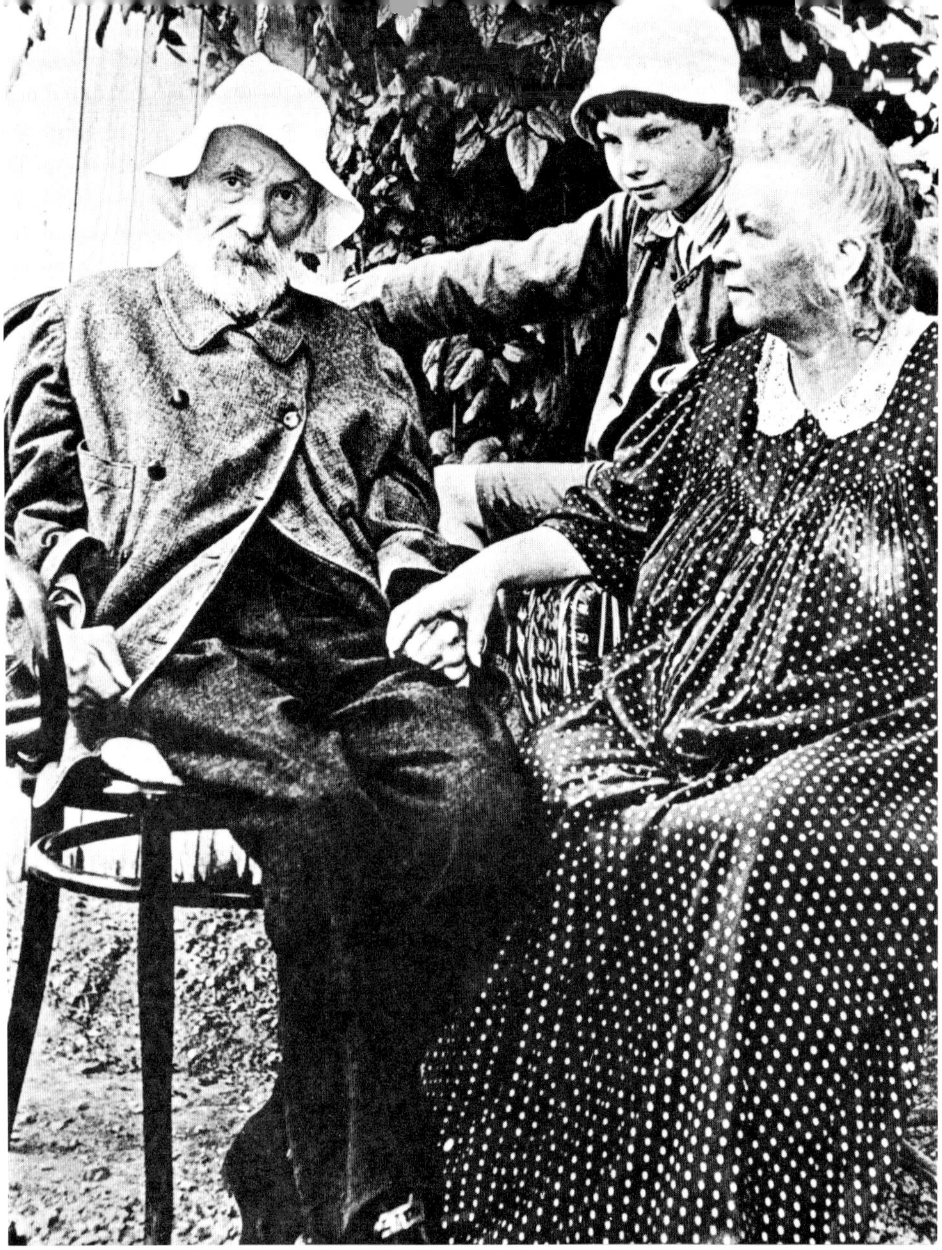

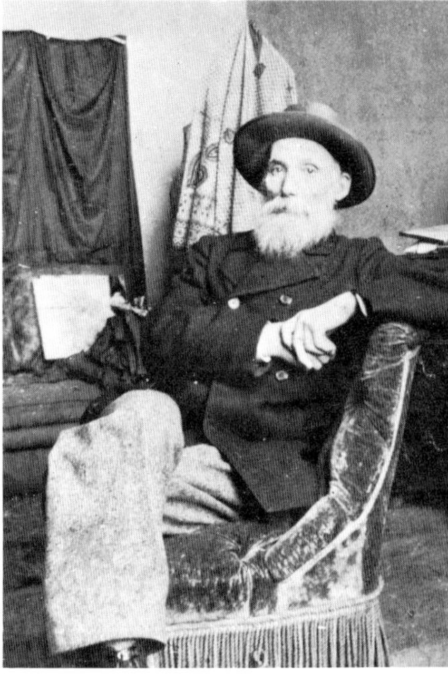

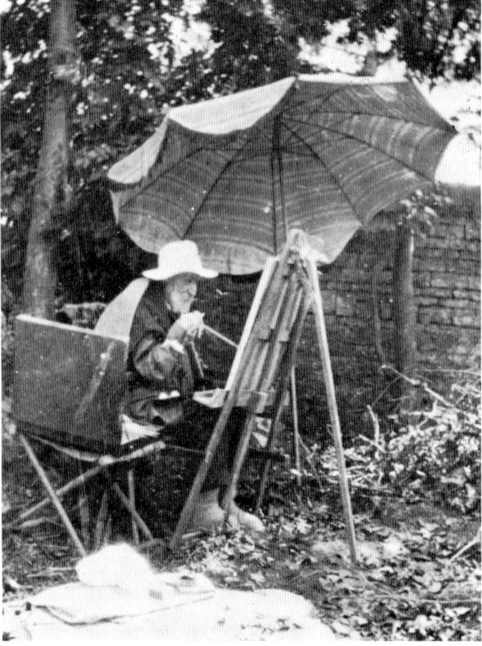

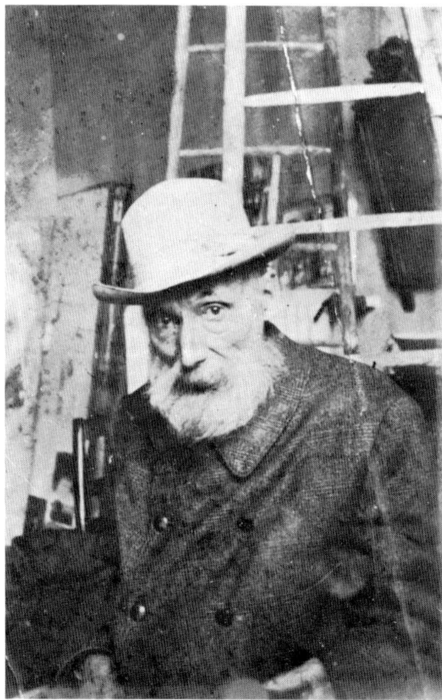

ABOVE LEFT Renoir, Madame Renoir and Coco at Essoyes, 1909.
ABOVE Renoir at Fontainebleau, 1901.
LEFT and FAR LEFT Renoir continued painting until the end of his life in spite of the rheumatism which had crippled his hands.

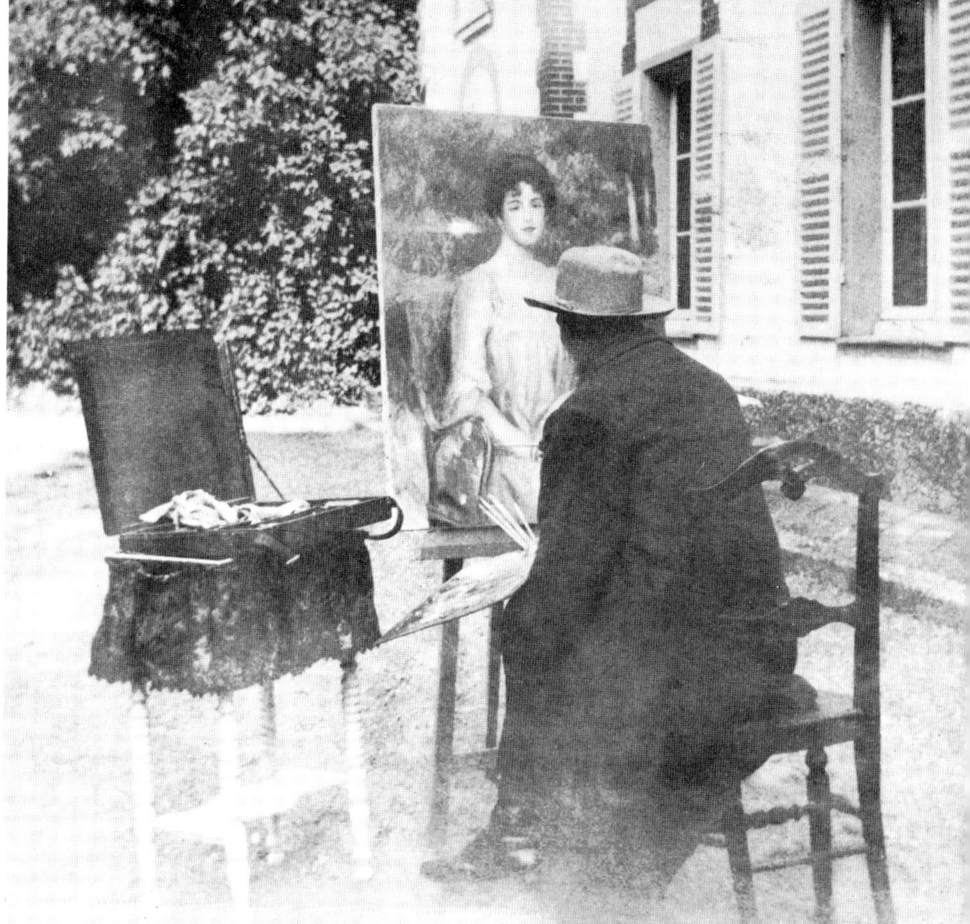

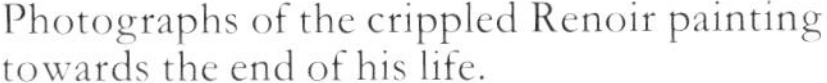

Photographs of the crippled Renoir painting towards the end of his life.

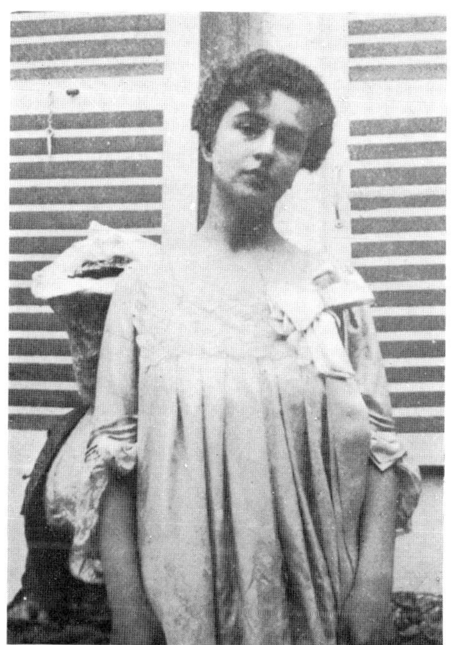

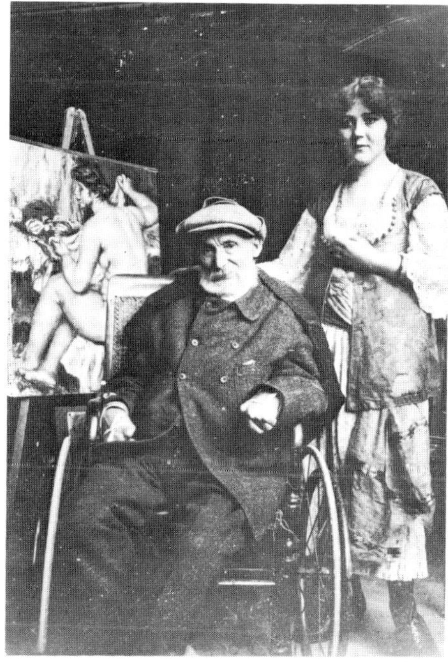

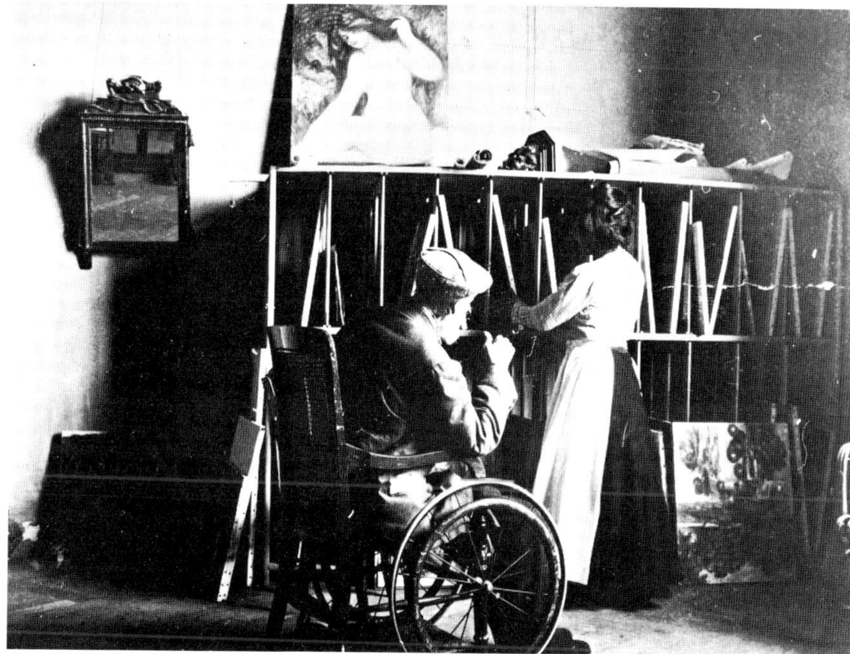

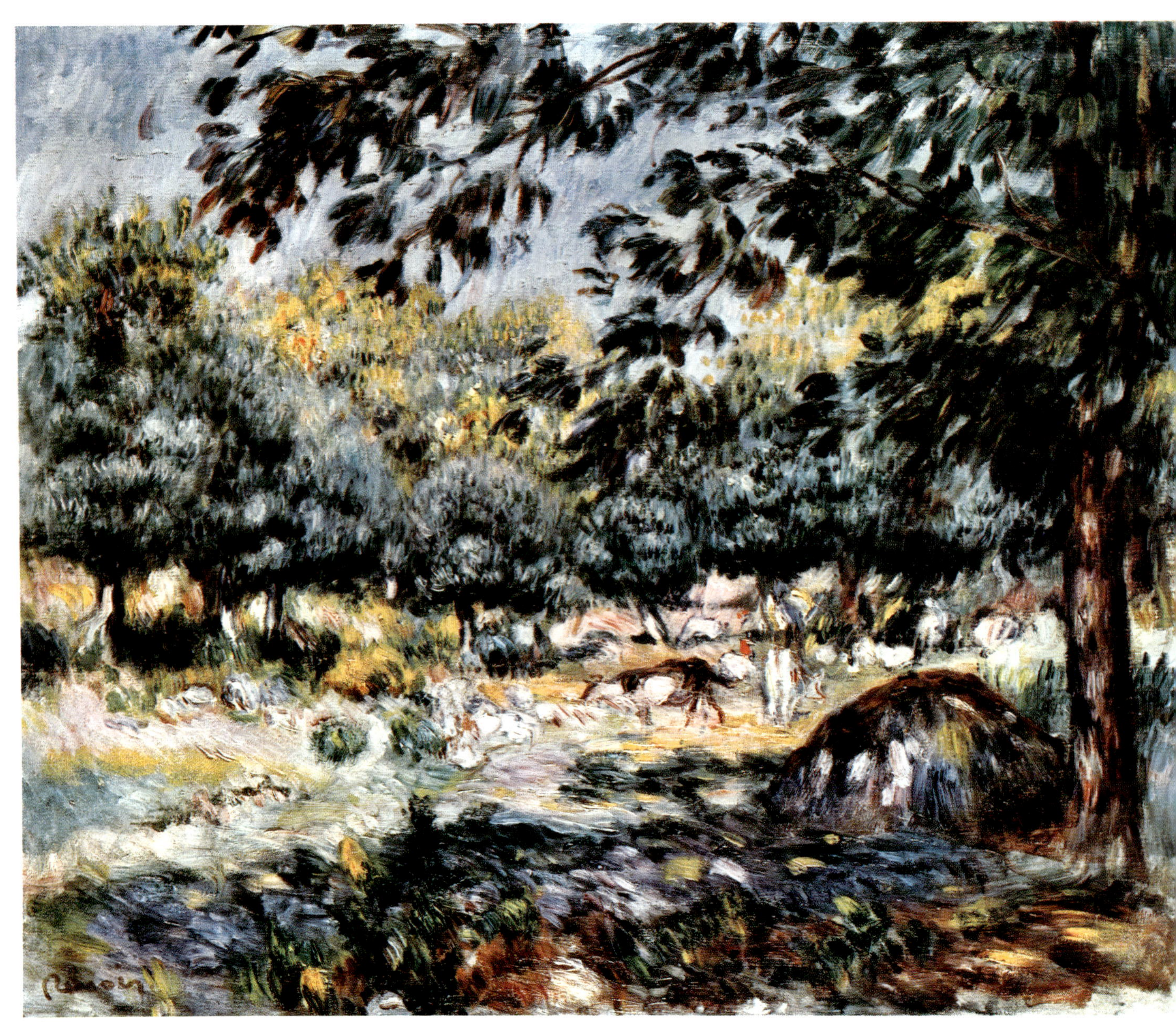

ABOVE Auguste Renoir: *Trees and Cattle*, *c.* 1892 (Private Collection).
OPPOSITE Auguste Renoir: *Portrait of Ambroise Vollard*, 1908 (Courtauld Institute Galleries, London).

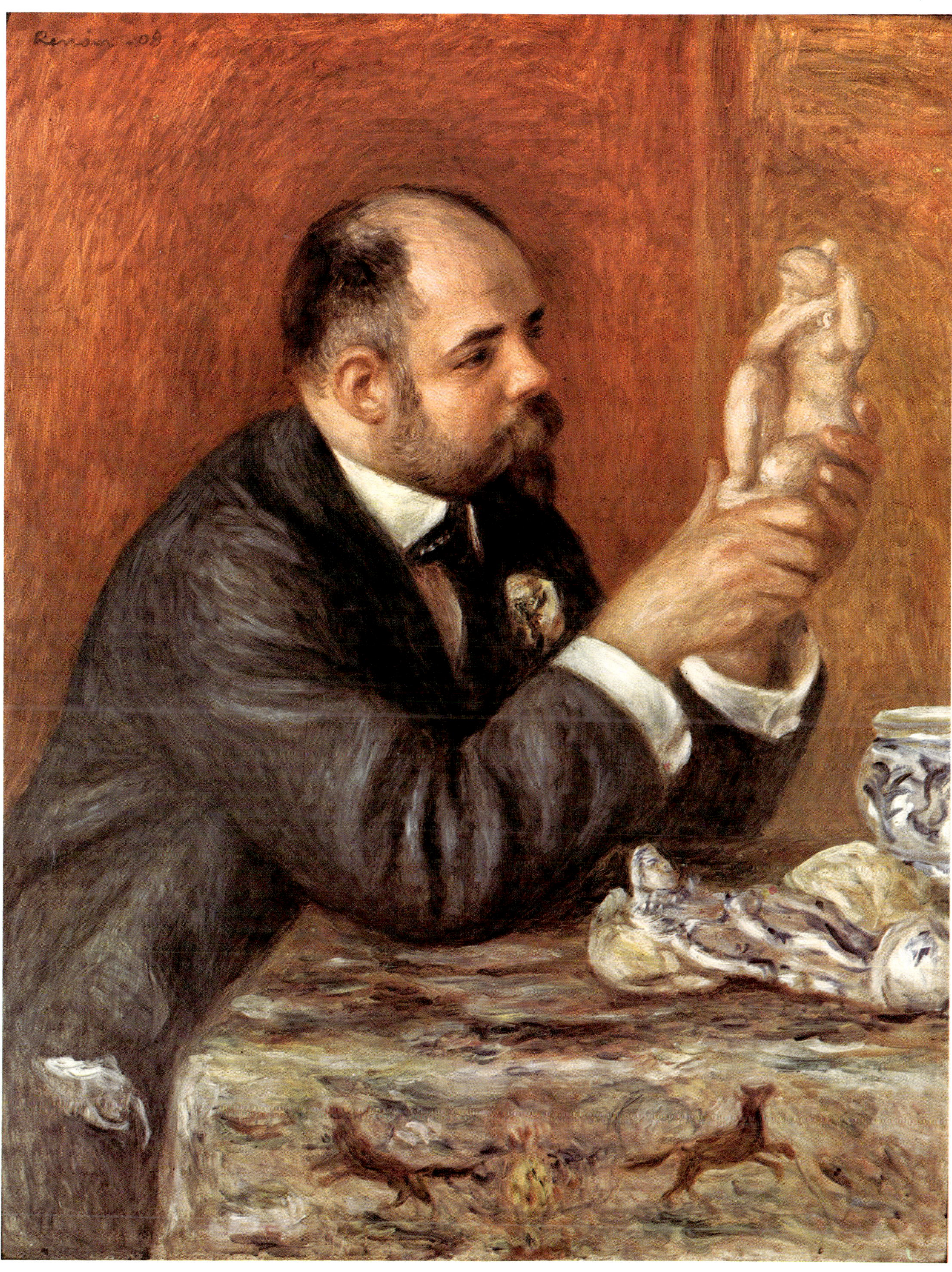

who kept Renoir away from his easel for a whole week during the summer of 1905 while he worked on a bust of him.

But soon Renoir was completely immobilized by his illness, and had to be carried by stretcher up to his studio on the first floor of Les Collettes. His brushes were prepared for him and placed on his lap so that he could pick them up easily: then, leaning awkwardly forward to his canvas, Renoir would become totally engrossed in the act of painting, in order to forget the grief, loneliness and worry that the death of his wife and the call-up of his sons were causing him.

In December 1919, as he lay dying, Renoir still asked for the things that had meant most to him all his life: his palette and his brushes.

Renoir at Fontainebleau, 1901.

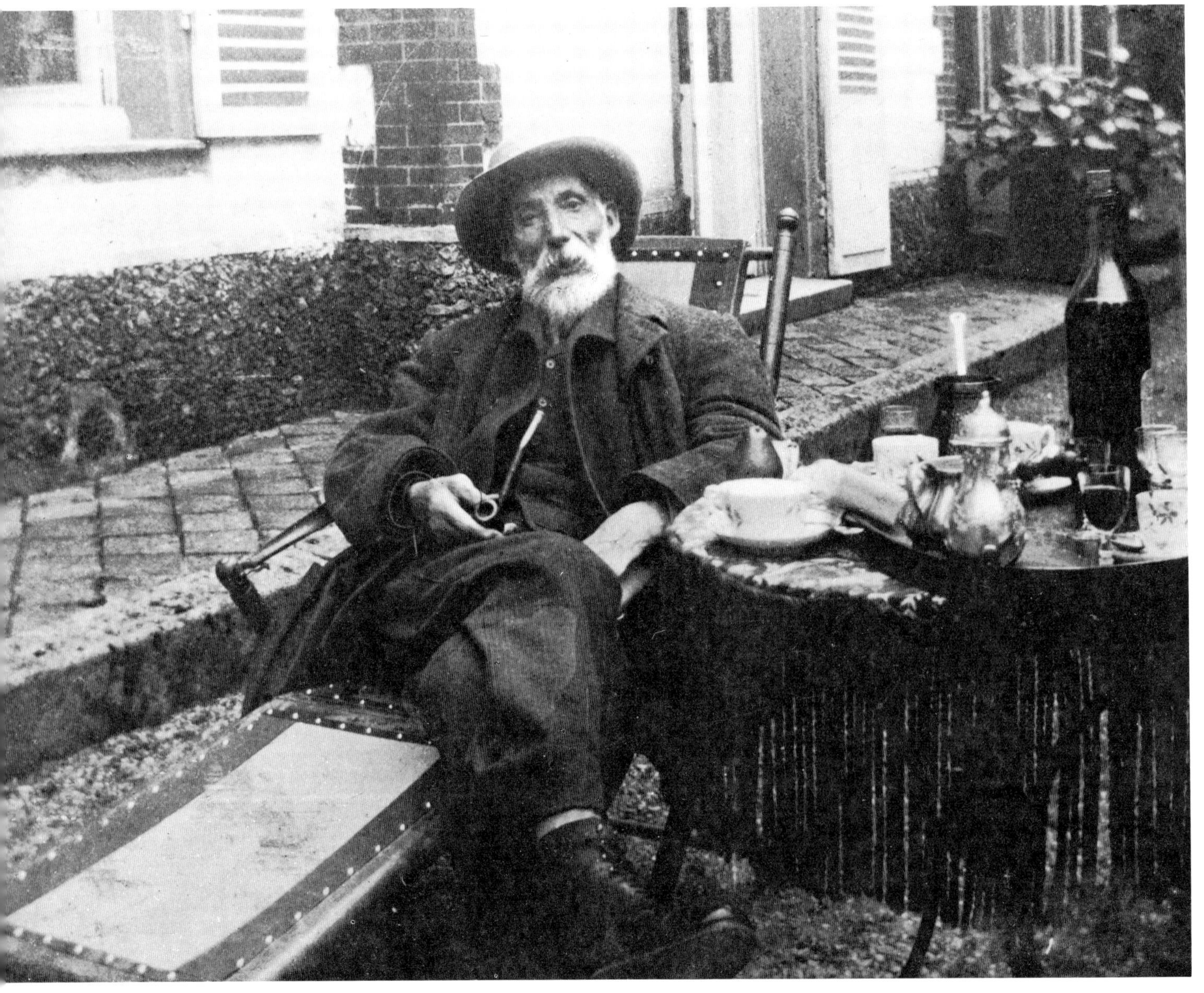

Cézanne's name occasionally began to appear in 1886 in the small avant-garde reviews in which new writers, poets and artists championed the latest aesthetic canons. Consequently in 1889 he was invited along with Sisley and Vincent van Gogh to exhibit in Brussels with the Belgian group 'Les Vingt', whose chief aim was to give avant-garde art greater notoriety. Cézanne, 'faced with the pleasure of finding [himself] in such good company', broke his resolution never to go on show again, and sent *La Maison du Pendu*, which he borrowed for the occasion from Victor Chocquet. The fact that his painting was scarcely mentioned in reviews of the exhibition is a perfect illustration of Cézanne's predicament: although the subject of wild admiration by a small group of cognoscenti, he was totally unknown to the general public.

When mention was actually made of him, it was often couched in the past tense: as the critic Arsène Alexandre put it: 'It is far from certain whether, like Homer or Shakespeare, Cézanne has really existed.' The mystery shrouding him was almost complete when in 1894 Tanguy's collection was dispersed by auction after his death, and there was no longer anywhere in Paris where a Cézanne could be seen. In 1895, Ambroise Vollard, who had recently arrived in Paris from Mauritius, opened a gallery at 39 Rue Laffite in an attempt to fill the gap left by Tanguy's death: on Pissarro's advice, he organized the first solo exhibition of Cézanne's works.

Vollard's gallery was so small that he was able to put on show only a few of the 150 paintings Cézanne had given him. But in the atmosphere of intellectual effervescence that Paris was experiencing at the time the event caused a considerable stir. The longest-standing members of the Impressionist group, such as Monet, Renoir, Degas and of course Pissarro, and young artists with an appetite for new visual experiences, took the gallery by storm on the day of the opening. 'It's really amazing,' Camille Pissarro wrote to his son Lucien, 'there are still lifes, landscapes of tremendous authority, and some very strange bathers. Visitors are bewildered – they don't get the point at all. But [Cézanne] has all the subtlety, truth and classicism of a really first-class painter, it's quite amazing.'

True, the public either snubbed or jeered at Cézanne. 'You're not going to force me to look at stuff like that – I won an art prize at school!' exclaimed a young woman angrily to her escort as they stood in front of Vollard's gallery. As for the critics, those who were not yet used to the new art were annoyed at their own inability to understand the paintings, and noisily deplored 'the nightmarish sight of such atrocities . . . which go beyond the bounds of what may legally be considered to be a joke in bad taste.' But it has been too often forgotten that others, such as Monet's friend Gustave Geffroy, produced admirative judgments of great insight. Geffroy wrote in *Le Journal*: '[Cézanne] is a painter of great veracity, both ardent and ingenuous, severe

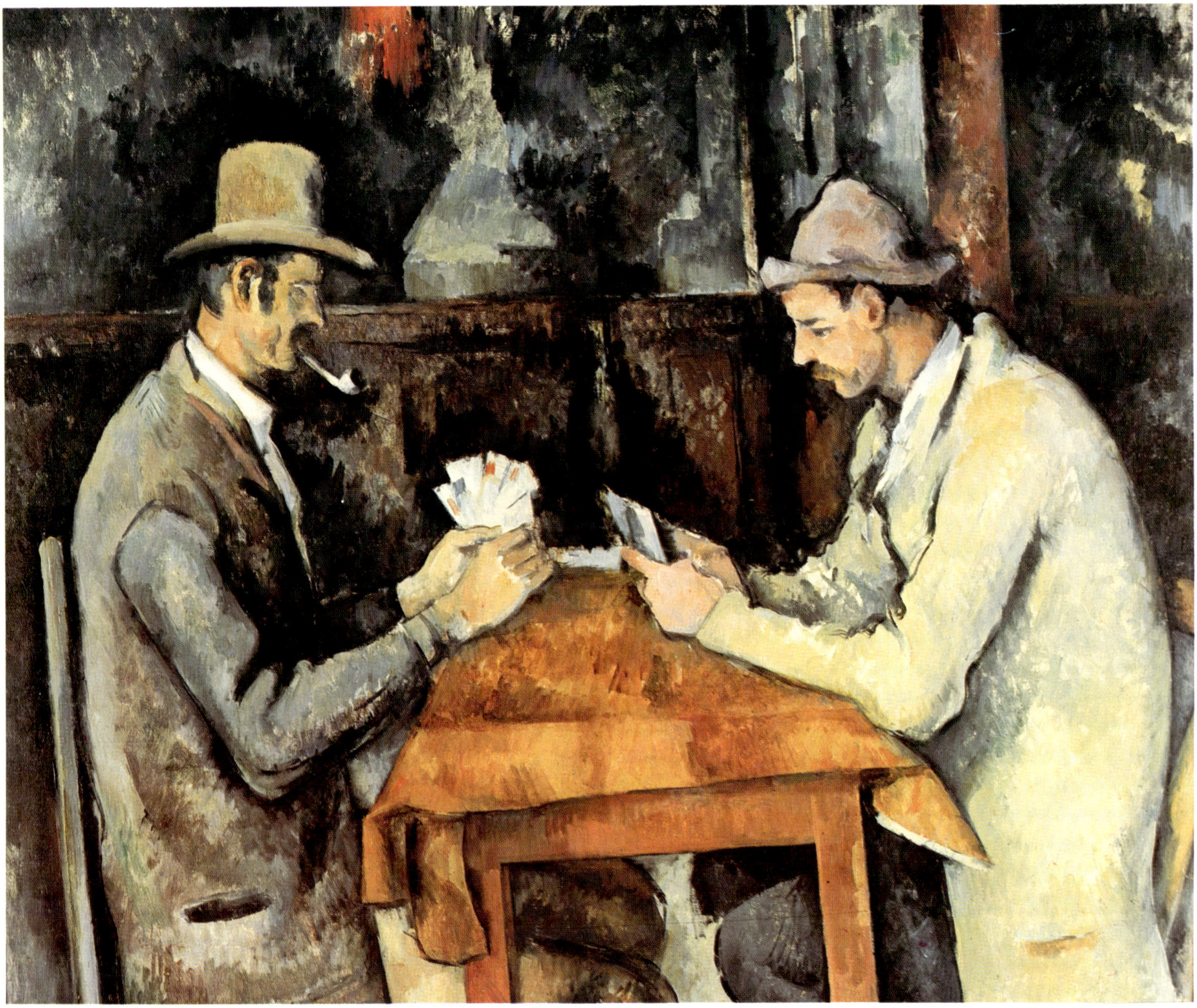

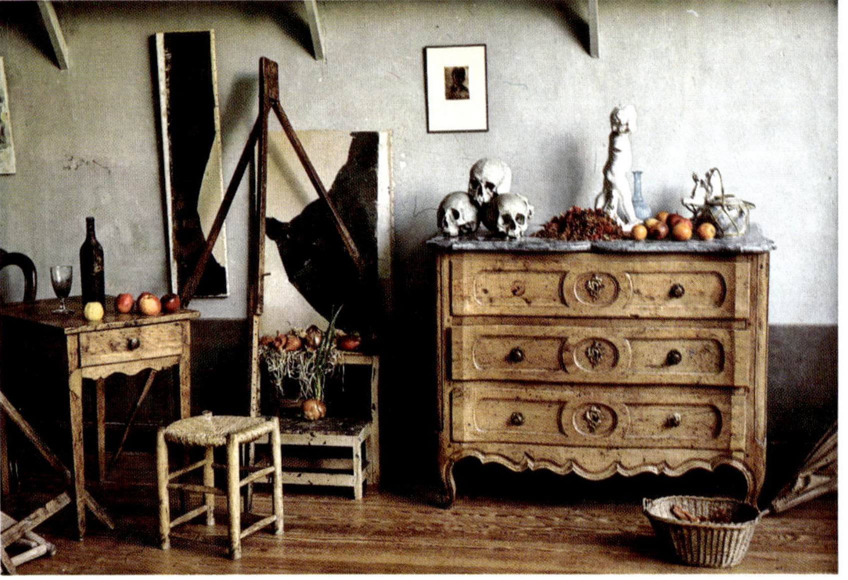

ABOVE Paul Cézanne: *The Card Players*, *c.* 1892 (Courtauld Institute Galleries, London). One of the five versions of card players that Cézanne painted at Aix in the early 1890s.
LEFT Cézanne's studio at Aix-en-Provence, which is now open to the public.
OPPOSITE ABOVE Paul Cézanne: *View of the Château Noir*, *c.* 1898 (Oskar Reinhart Collection, Winterthur).

OPPOSITE LEFT The well in the Château Noir.
OPPOSITE RIGHT Paul Cézanne: *Rocks at Bibémus*, watercolour, *c.* 1900 (Mattioli Collection, Milan).

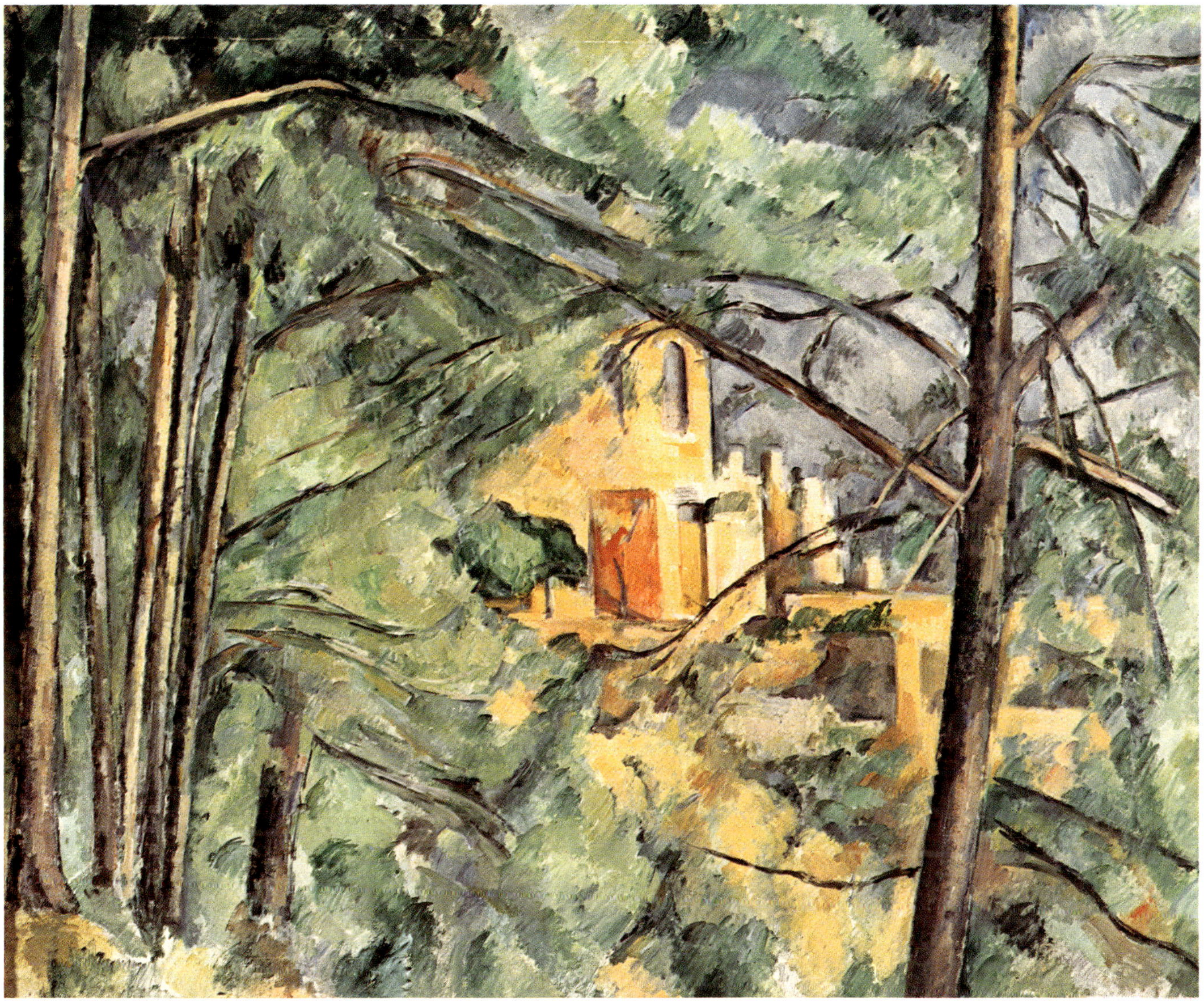

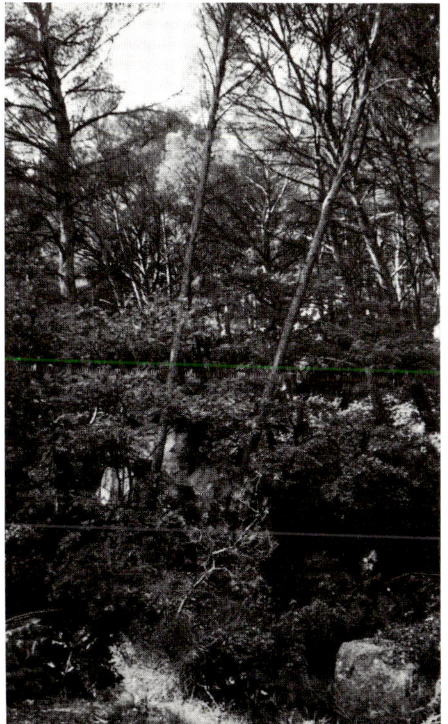

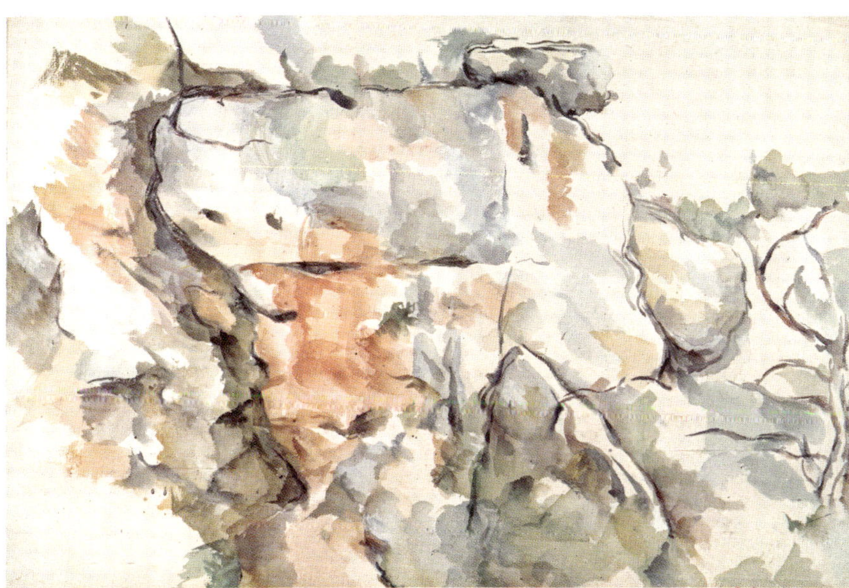

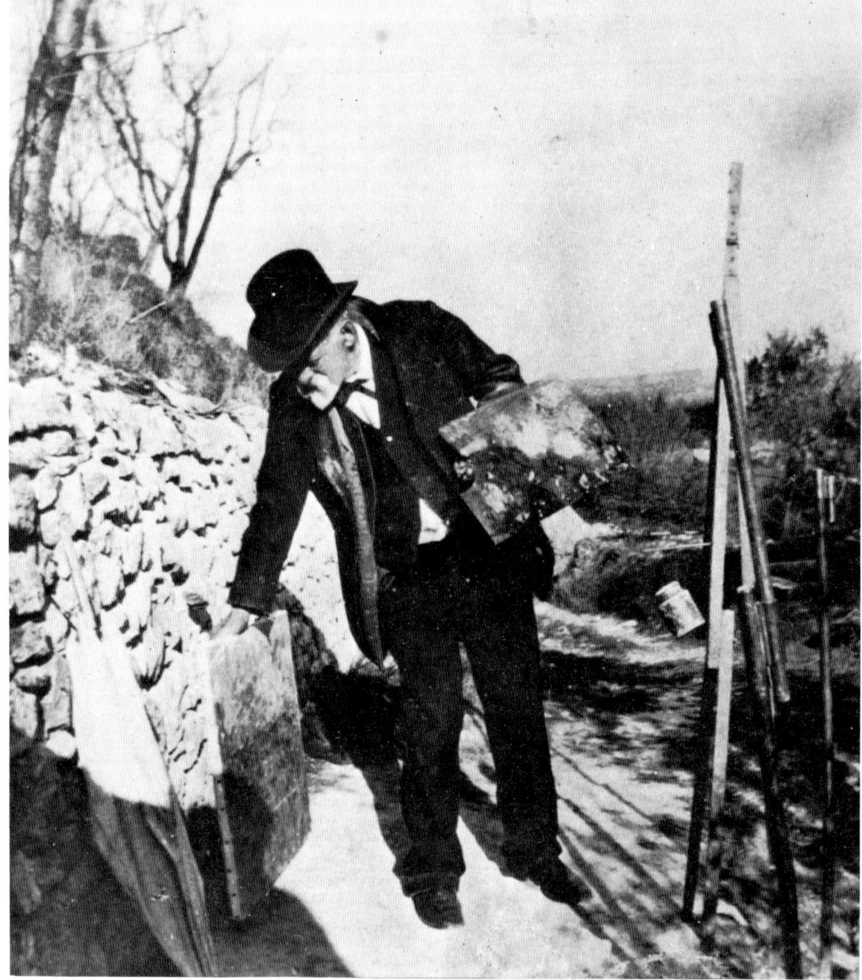

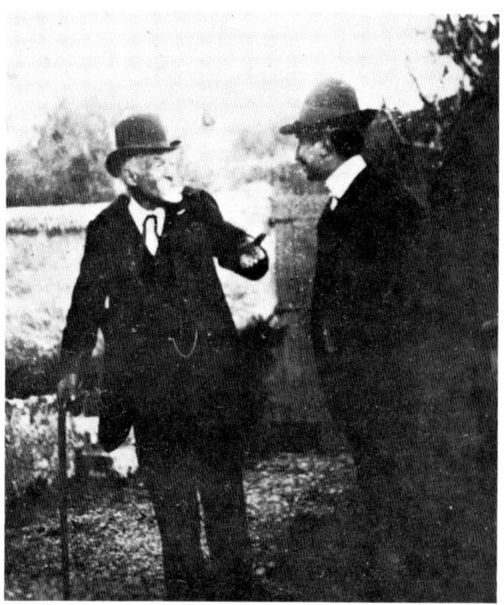

ABOVE LEFT Cézanne painting in the countryside near Aix-en-Provence, 1904.
ABOVE Cézanne with the famous dealer, Bernheim.
OPPOSITE ABOVE LEFT Cézanne's studio at Chemin des Lauves.
OPPOSITE ABOVE RIGHT Paul Cézanne: *Mardi Gras Sketches*, 1888 (Musée du Louvre, Paris).
OPPOSITE RIGHT Paul Cézanne: *Still Life with Water Jug*, 1892–3 (Tate Gallery, London).

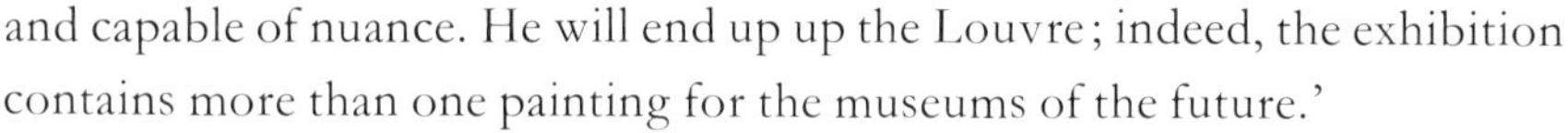

and capable of nuance. He will end up up the Louvre; indeed, the exhibition contains more than one painting for the museums of the future.'

Cézanne, of course, did not show his face during the exhibition. But news of his success filtered down to Aix-en-Provence and reached the ears of his fellow-citizens – which was the last thing in the world he wanted. Their unremitting hostility towards his tight-fisted banker father had been transferred to the painter son – a long-haired bohemian 'of few words'. But when Les Amis des Arts, an association of artists in Aix, invited him to go on show with some of the favourite painters of the region, Cézanne dared not refuse, and entered *Cornfield* and *Sainte-Victoire*. The reactions of the Aixois were pathetically crass and sarcastic, and seemed to affect the painter much more deeply that the praise he had earned in Paris. 'I curse people like X and other jokers like him,' he wrote to his friend, the young Provencal poet Joachim Gasquet, 'who just in order to earn a fast 50 francs from their newspapers wrote articles drawing me to the attention of the public.'

Cézanne's already difficult temperament was not made any more manageable by diabetes, from which he had been suffering for several years: it made him moodier and more irritable than ever. His hypersensitivity turned him into a timorous misanthrope who felt truly at ease only with his family or when alone. Safely ensconced at the Jas de Bouffan, where his aged mother was gradually approaching death and his sister had set herself up as the embittered guardian of his material wellbeing and moral salvation, Cézanne was able to 'work without bothering about anybody in order to become strong', which was the aim he had set himself.

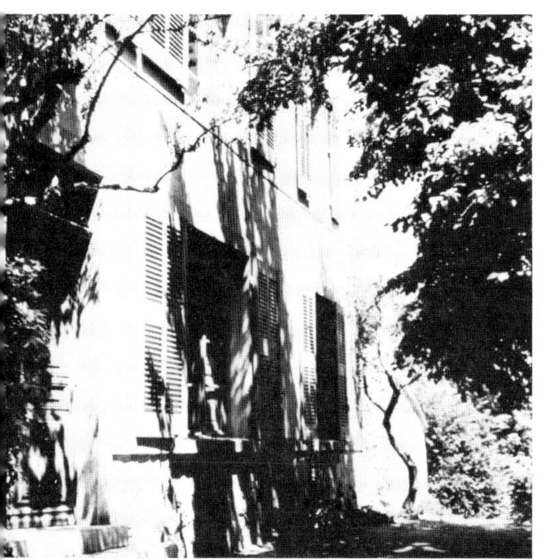

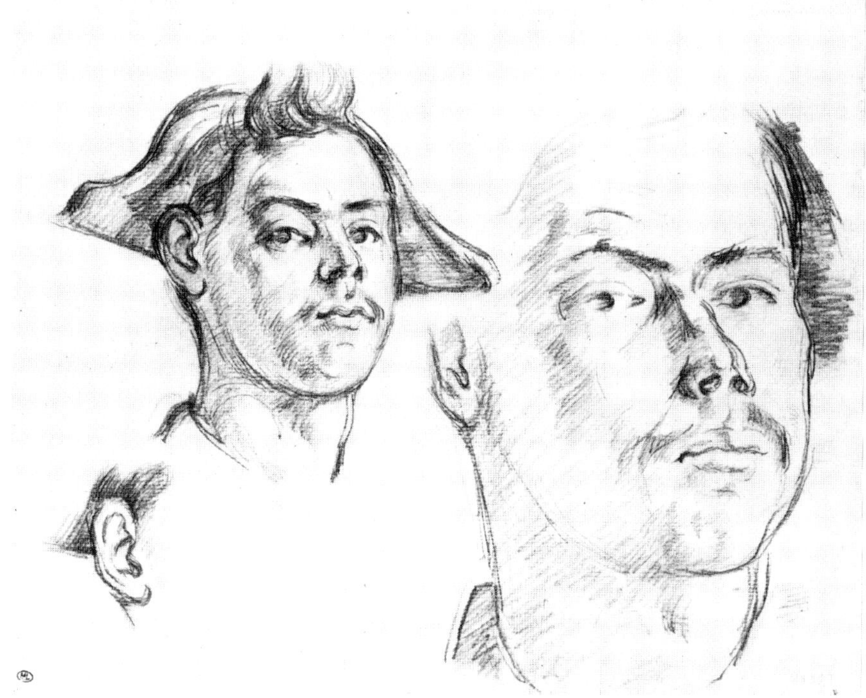

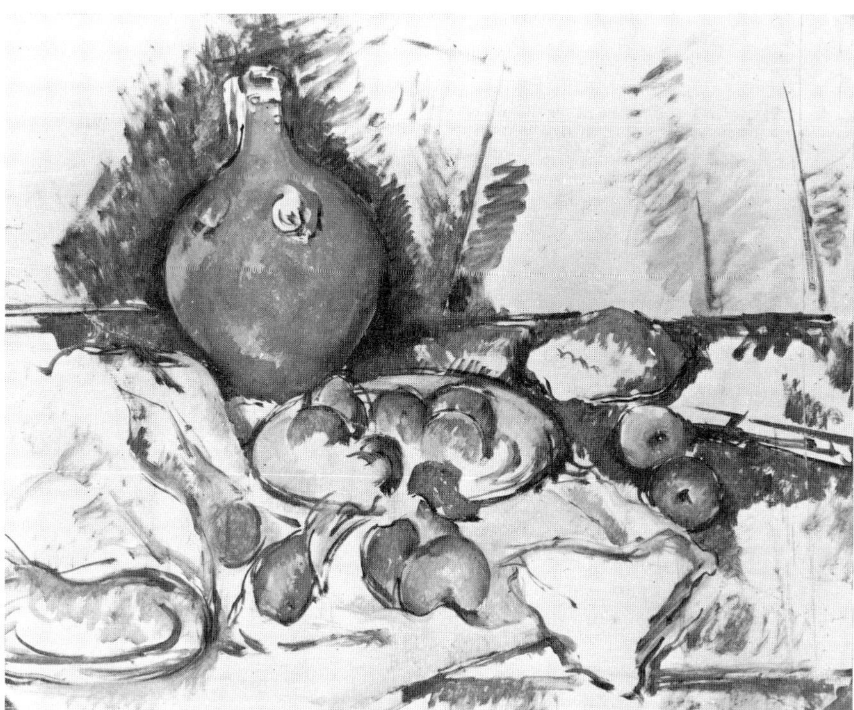

In his withdrawal from the world, Cézanne soon found sufficient psychological equilibrium to tackle enthusiastically a theme that was new to him, though a great favourite of the old masters: card players, illustrated in the Musée d'Aix by *The Card Players*, a painting attributed to Louis Le Nain. Having severed almost all connections with his fellow painters,

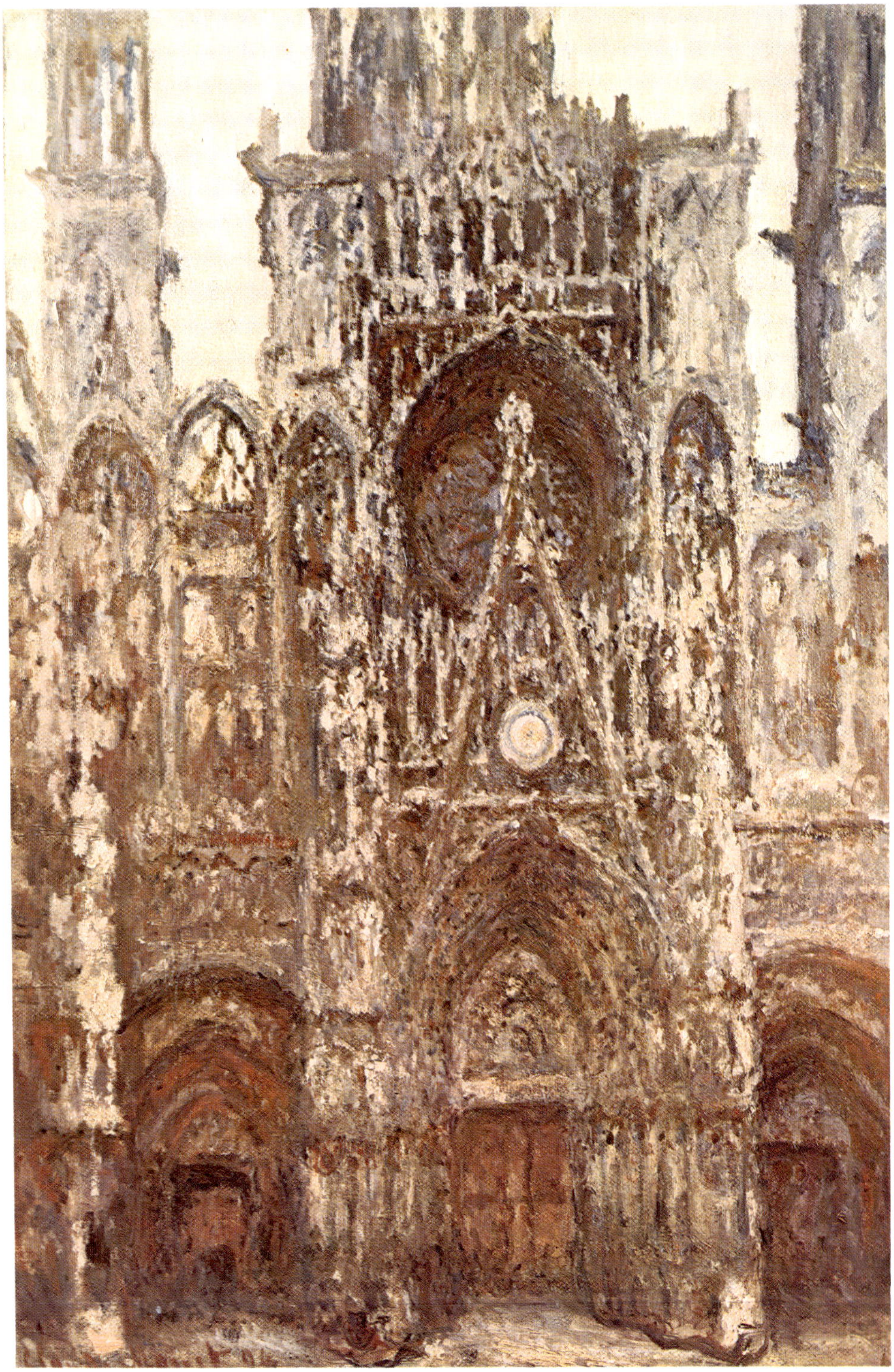

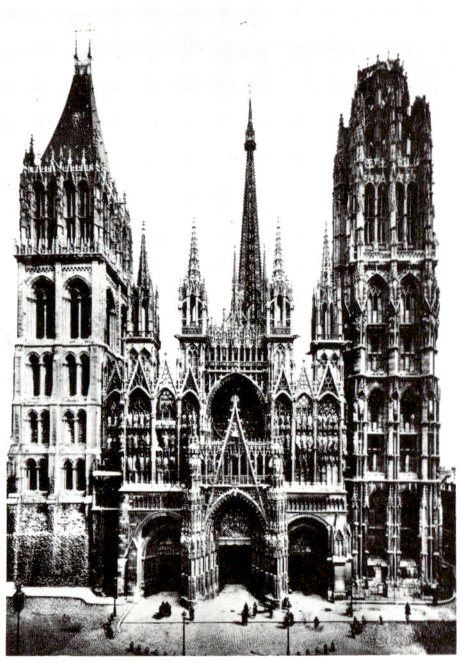

LEFT Claude Monet: *Rouen Cathedral*, *c.* 1894 (Musée du Louvre, Paris).
ABOVE The Cathedral in the 1890s.
OPPOSITE Claude Monet: *Rouen Cathedral*, 1890 (Musée du Louvre, Paris – Jeu de Paume).

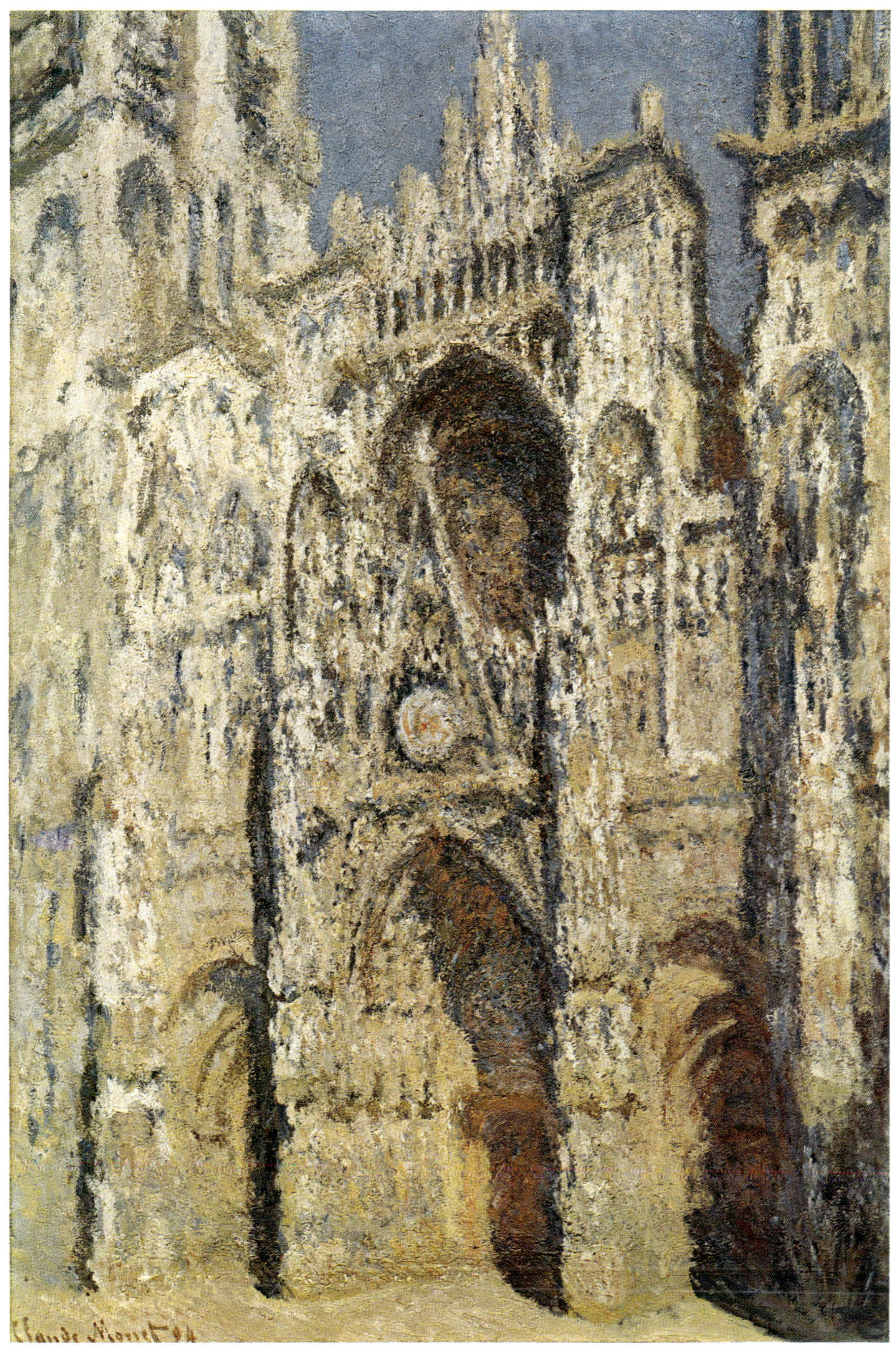
Claude Monet 94

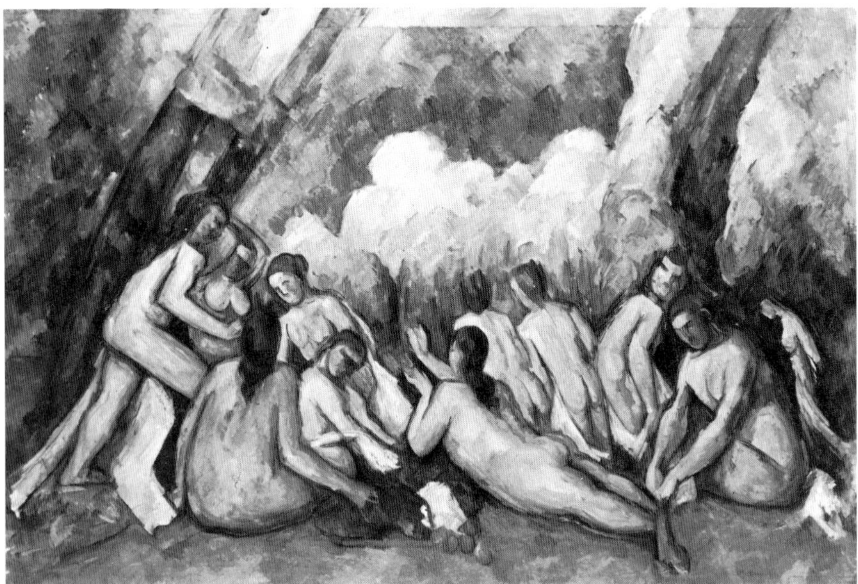

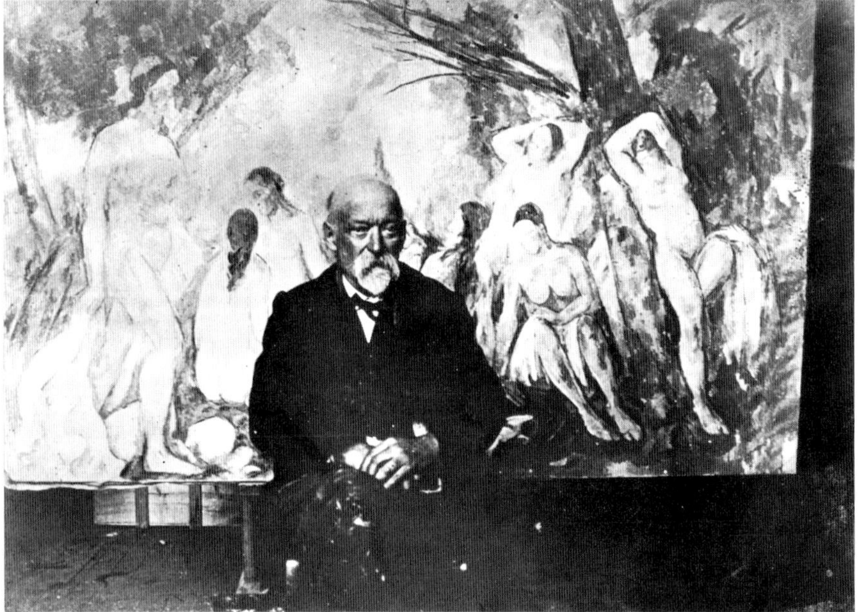

ABOVE LEFT Paul Cézanne: *Les Grandes Baigneuses*, *c.* 1903 (National Gallery, London). LEFT Cézanne photographed sitting in front of one of his series of paintings of bathers.

Cézanne had begun to identify himself with the farm labourers at the Jas de Bouffan – simple, straightforward men, and hard workers like himself, who were just the models he needed for the new theme he had undertaken. He produced a greater number of studies, watercolours and drawings in preparation for the five masterpieces in his series. First five, then four figures feature in the first compositions, which Cézanne simplified and whittled down until he had obtained the desired result in the last small canvases. There, two men sit facing each other with all the concentration of the painter himself: those two silent, thoughtful figures – the victor and the vanquished, or rather, as they are playing cards, the winner and the loser – confront each other in a final *tête-à-tête*, almost as though they represented the two sides of the artist's character. These hieratic paintings, charged with visual beauty, are truly classical in their simplicity.

After the series of card players, Cézanne seems to have exhausted the visual possibilities of the Jas de Bouffan. He returned to one of his favourite subjects, which gradually became obsessive: the Montagne Sainte-Victoire, the mountain overlooking the whole area of Aix-en-Provence. Cézanne approached it from every angle: he went two or three kilometres from the Jas de Bouffan to the plateau of Entremont, north of Aix, where the Celts founded a colony in the third century AD. Cézanne also went to Pinchinats, to Beaurecueil, to Montbriand, the estate where his sister Rose and his brother-in-law Conil lived, and up on to the wonderfully wild pine-capped hills round the village of Vauvenargues.

In the autumn of 1897, Cézanne's mother died at the age of eighty-three. Two years later he and his sisters decided to put an end to the joint ownership which bound them together, and sold the Jas de Bouffan. It was a terrible experience for Cézanne, who, because Hortense and Paul spent most of their time in Paris, was virtually living the life of a lonely bachelor. From then on, he occupied a small flat at 23 Rue Boulegon, in the centre of the craftsmen's quarter in Aix. He took possession of the second floor of a finely proportioned building, and set up his studio in the loft, which was ice-cold in winter and stiflingly hot in summer. But Cézanne did not mind so long as he could live the life of 'a monk like Fra Angelico, so as to be able, when one's existence has been sorted out once and for all, to paint from dawn to dusk.'

Cézanne would rise at daybreak, and by six o'clock he was in front of his easel in the open air or in his studio. The only time he changed this schedule was on Sundays, when he went to high mass, 'to get a slice of the Middle Ages' as he put it. Indeed, he went so far as to say, not without a tinge of irony, that what kept him going were 'mass and shower-baths'.

At Château-Noir, an estate he found on the road to Le Tholonet, some five kilometres outside Aix, Cézanne discovered fresh subjects in the chaotic profusion of twisted pines, gnarled olive trees and massive rocks, and the château itself, partly destroyed by a fire. There was not a soul to be seen there, since the château was completely overrun by the anarchy of nature, and Cézanne was consequently encouraged to follow the whims of his inspiration more freely and more lyrically than before. He produced some watercolours of quite extraordinary transparency, and a number of oil paintings where an effect of intense luminosity is vividly rendered by a riot of yellows, blues, oranges and greens.

With the coming of old age and ill health, Cézanne's once sturdy legs now began to fail him. Soon, to avoid exerting himself too much, he was forced to hire the services of a coachman, who would pick him up every day at 2 pm

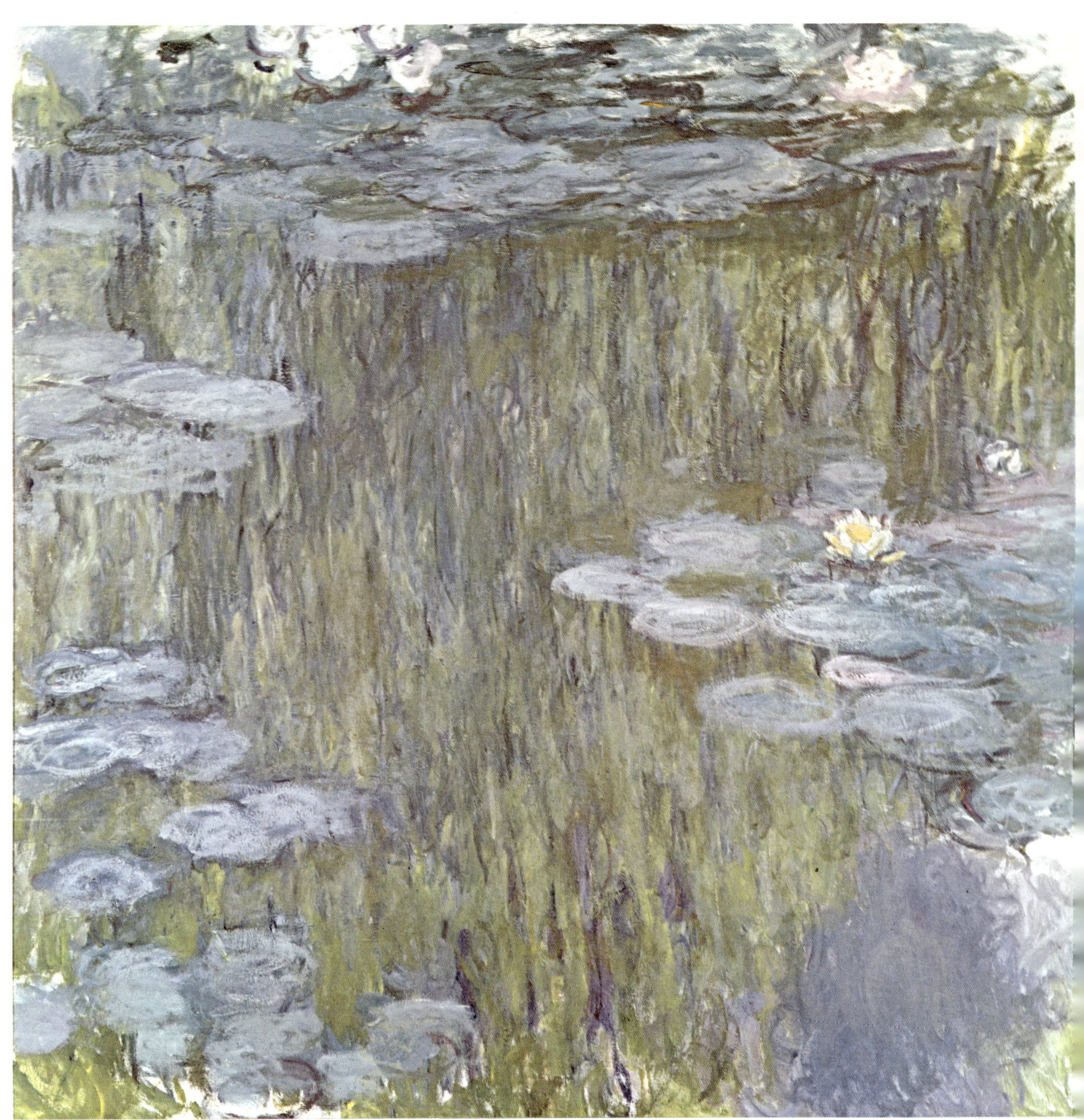

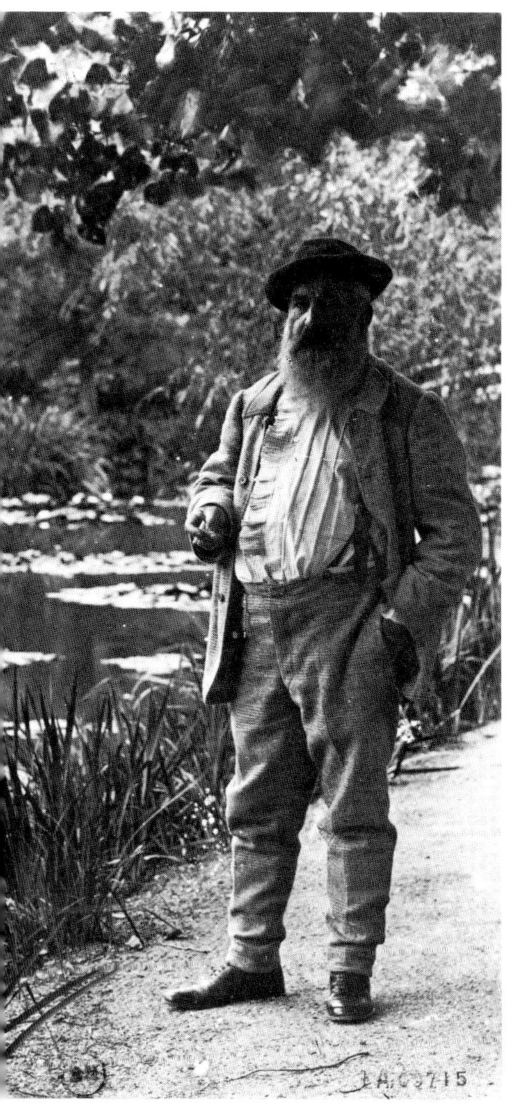

OPPOSITE Claude Monet: *Water Lilies at Giverny*, 1918 (Private Collection, Basle). ABOVE Monet beside a water lily pool.

and drive him to the spot where he wished to paint. As he found it increasingly difficult to clamber up the several flights of stairs leading to his studio and because he wanted to do some large-scale paintings, Cézanne decided to have a studio specially built for him to the north of Aix, on the Chemin des Lauves. He directed an architect to build a simple and practical house. The ground floor would be split up into two rooms separated by a corridor, and the whole of the first floor would be taken up by a spacious studio which, lit by a tall bay window facing north, would enable him to execute the huge compositions he had been planning for some time. Its two large windows overlooked a garden and gave him a striking view of the roofs of the town and the spire of Saint-Sauveur Cathedral, set against the distant mountain range of L'Etoile and Le Pilon du Roi.

So it was that Cézanne was able to continue 'the fanciful pursuit of art' in the remote retreat he had designed for himself. But art-lovers were beginning to take a keen interest in him. Vollard had held several further exhibitions of his work, and in 1897 two of Cézanne's pictures were hung in the Musée du Luxembourg as part of the Caillebotte collection. In 1899, two still lifes and a landscape shown at the Salon des Indépendants caused a sensation among art students; and in 1900, thanks to Roger Marx, an inspector in the Beaux-Arts, and a fervent admirer of the Impressionists in general and of Cézanne in particular, three Cézannes were shown at the Petit Palais on the occasion of the centenary of French Art.

But while he was becoming famous in Paris and even sought after in Aix – much to the surprise of most of his fellow-townsmen – Cézanne continued to work away in the solitude of his studio. He was painting a portrait of Vallier, his gardener, and the series of *Les Grandes Baigneuses*, as well as several luminous *Natures Mortes*.

Nervous tension, however, was taking its toll: Cézanne was in poor health, depressed, tetchy, and terribly lonely. 'I am old and ill, and I have promised myself that I will die at my easel,' he wrote to Emile Bernard. On 15 October 1906, while painting on the dusty road that ran from his studio into the woods, Cézanne was caught in a storm and lost consciousness. He was transported to his flat on the Rue Boulegon on a laundryman's cart, and died on 22 October 1906, without having seen his wife and son again.

For many years Monet had to fight against overwhelming material and moral difficulties. He was sorely tried in 1879 by the long-drawn-out illness of Camille, which led to her death at Vétheuil, the little village on the banks of the Seine where, as Monet put it, he had 'yet again pitched camp.'

There, Monet's life became closely involved with that of the enthusiastic collector of Impressionist works Ernest Hoschedé, and his wife. Hoschedé, who had inherited a large drapery business from his father, had gone

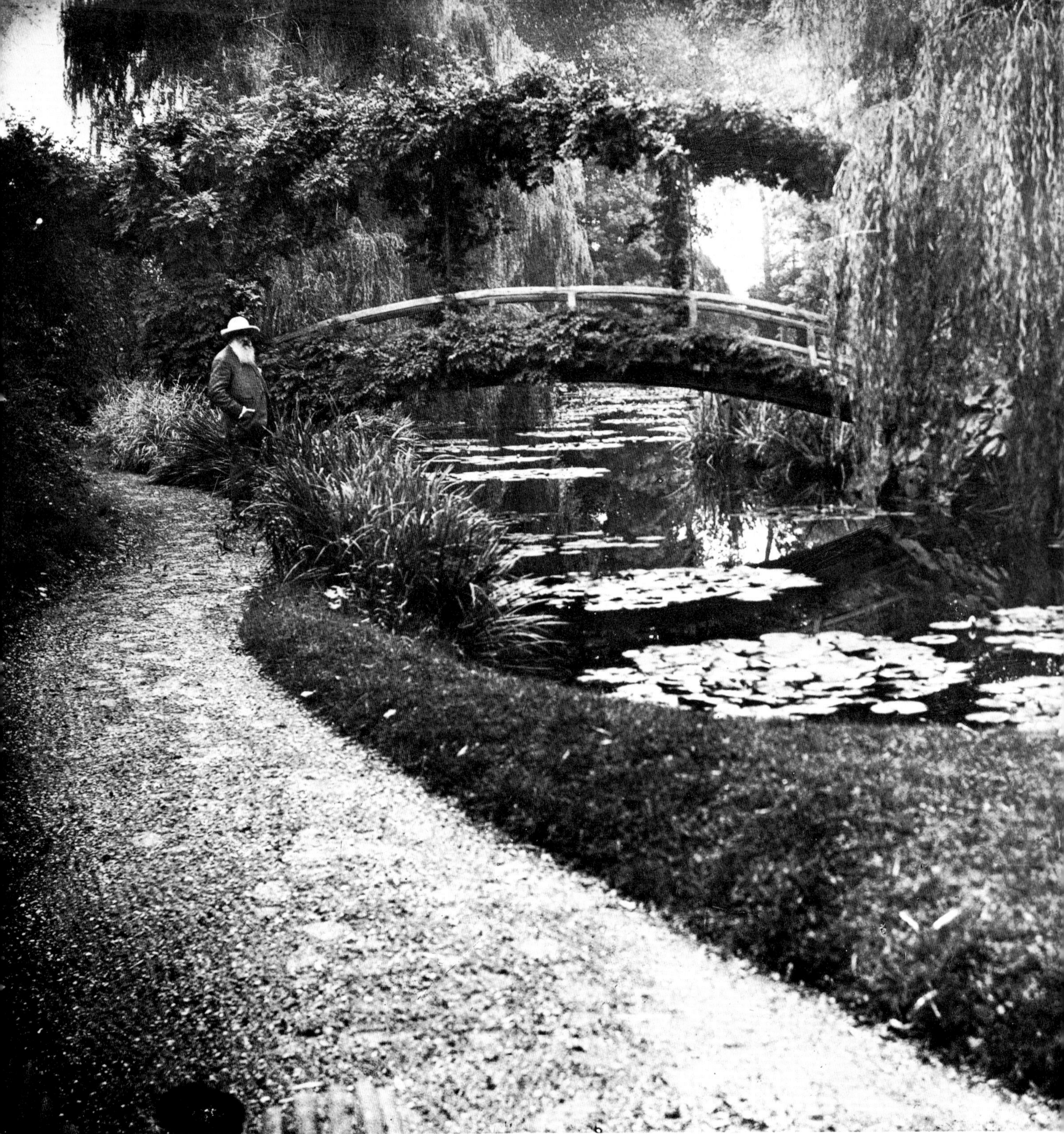

bankrupt for the second time and was fighting off a pack of creditors, while his wife Alice, who had taken refuge in Vétheuil with their children, helped to make Camille's last moments easier and took charge of her children Jean and Michel, who was scarcely eighteen months old.

As always when he had his back to the wall, Monet drew on every ounce of his fighting instinct. With an obstinacy, cunning, courage and will to win out that precluded any pointless scruples of conscience, he borrowed money,

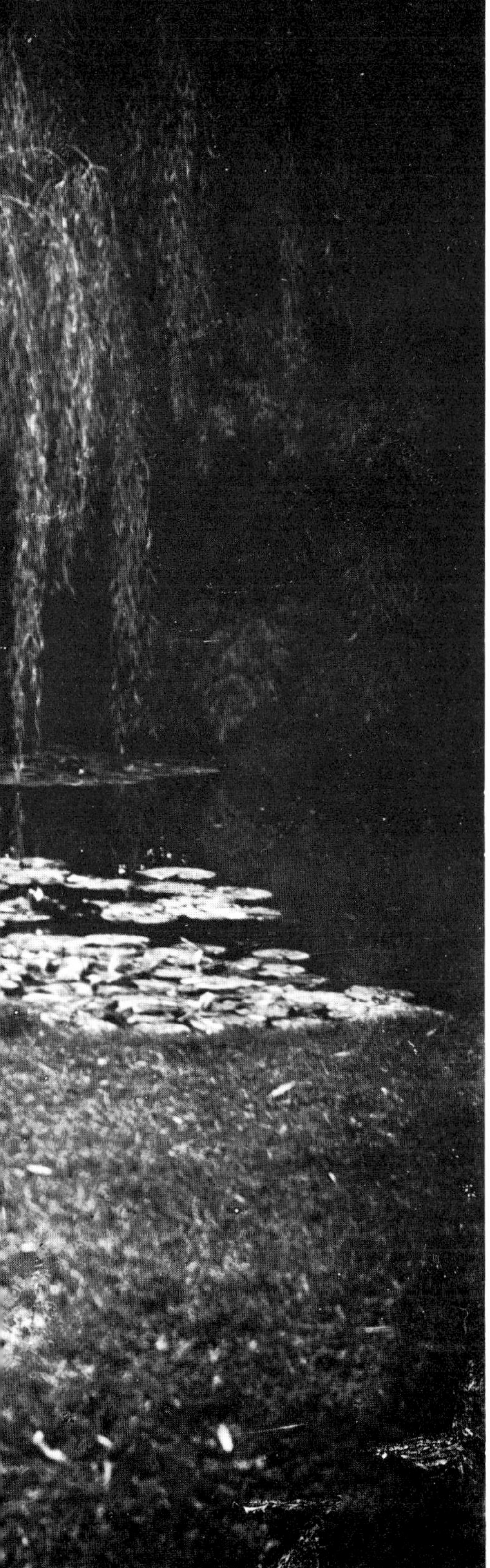

hunted down collectors, struck hard bargains, sold his pictures, dropped Durand-Ruel in favour of Georges Petit, and then later returned to him. And all the while Monet managed to keep painting.

At Vétheuil, then at Poissy, where the Monet/Hoschedé ménage had moved in precarious circumstances, Monet produced countless studies of the ever-changing River Seine – in spate, full of drift-ice, or else sparkling cheerfully in the summer sun. These mobile subjects necessitated a fluent technique that could easily be adapted to the capricious aspects of nature that so attracted his interest. Thus his style varied: often the backgrounds are smooth, but the drift-ice, for instance, is rendered by narrow white rectangles with a greenish, bluish or yellowish tinge, while dashes of light pigment mark the waves as they reflect the snow-laden sky.

In 1883, Monet at last found in Giverny the pastoral setting and large, unpretentious house he had been looking for. This village in the Seine

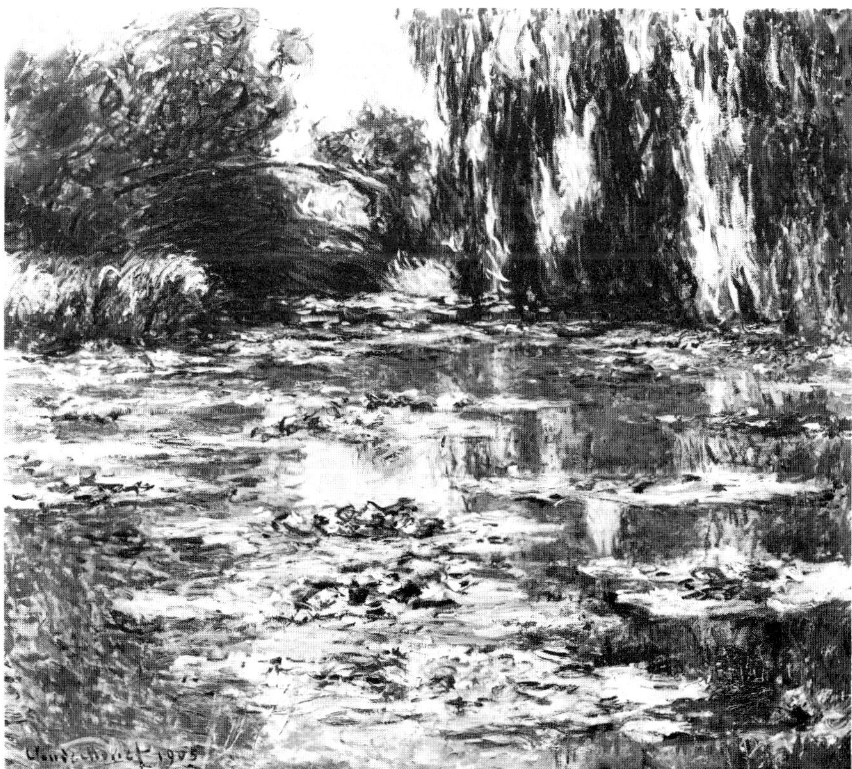

ABOVE Monet beside the bridge at Giverny. RIGHT Claude Monet: *Water Lilies*, 1905 (Musée du Louvre, Paris).

valley, set amidst meadows and cornfields on the banks of the River Epte (a small tributary of the Seine) bristled with subjects that he was to turn into unforgettable masterpieces.

In 1892, Monet married Alice Hoschedé (now a widow), and at last experienced fame and its attendant financial security. His last exhibitions, at the Petit and Durand-Ruel galleries in 1889 and 1891, which included his *Rouen Cathedral*, *Haystack* and *Poplars* series of paintings, were tremendously

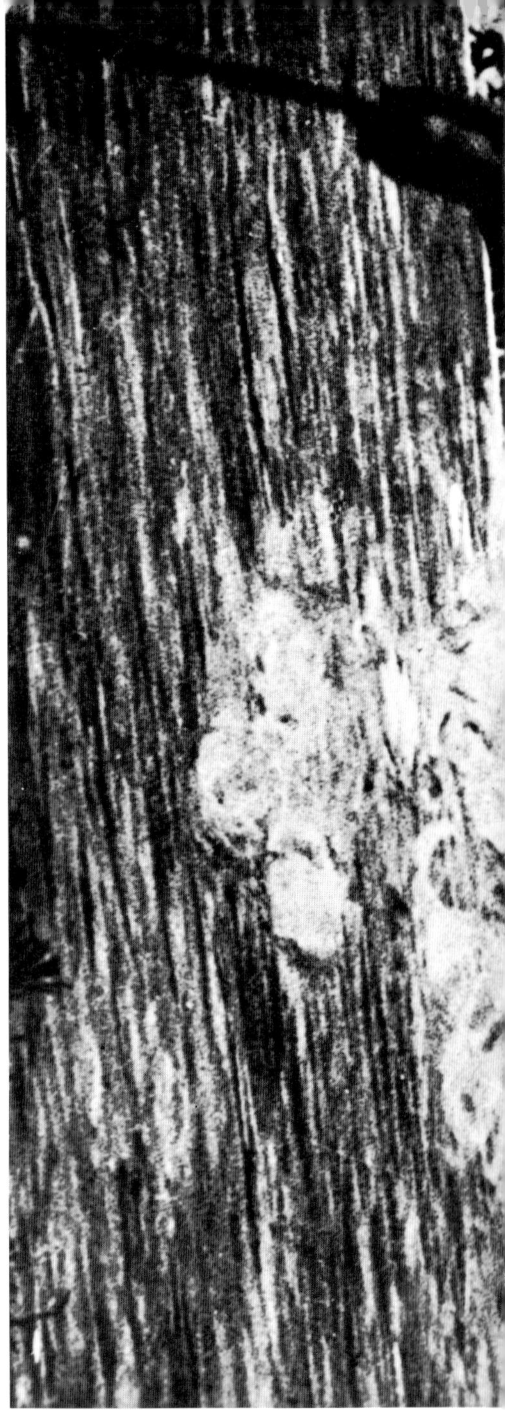

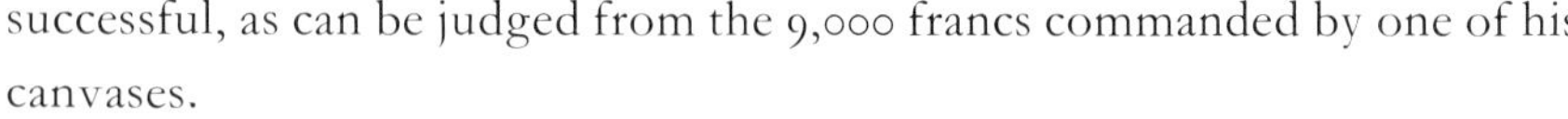

successful, as can be judged from the 9,000 francs commanded by one of his canvases.

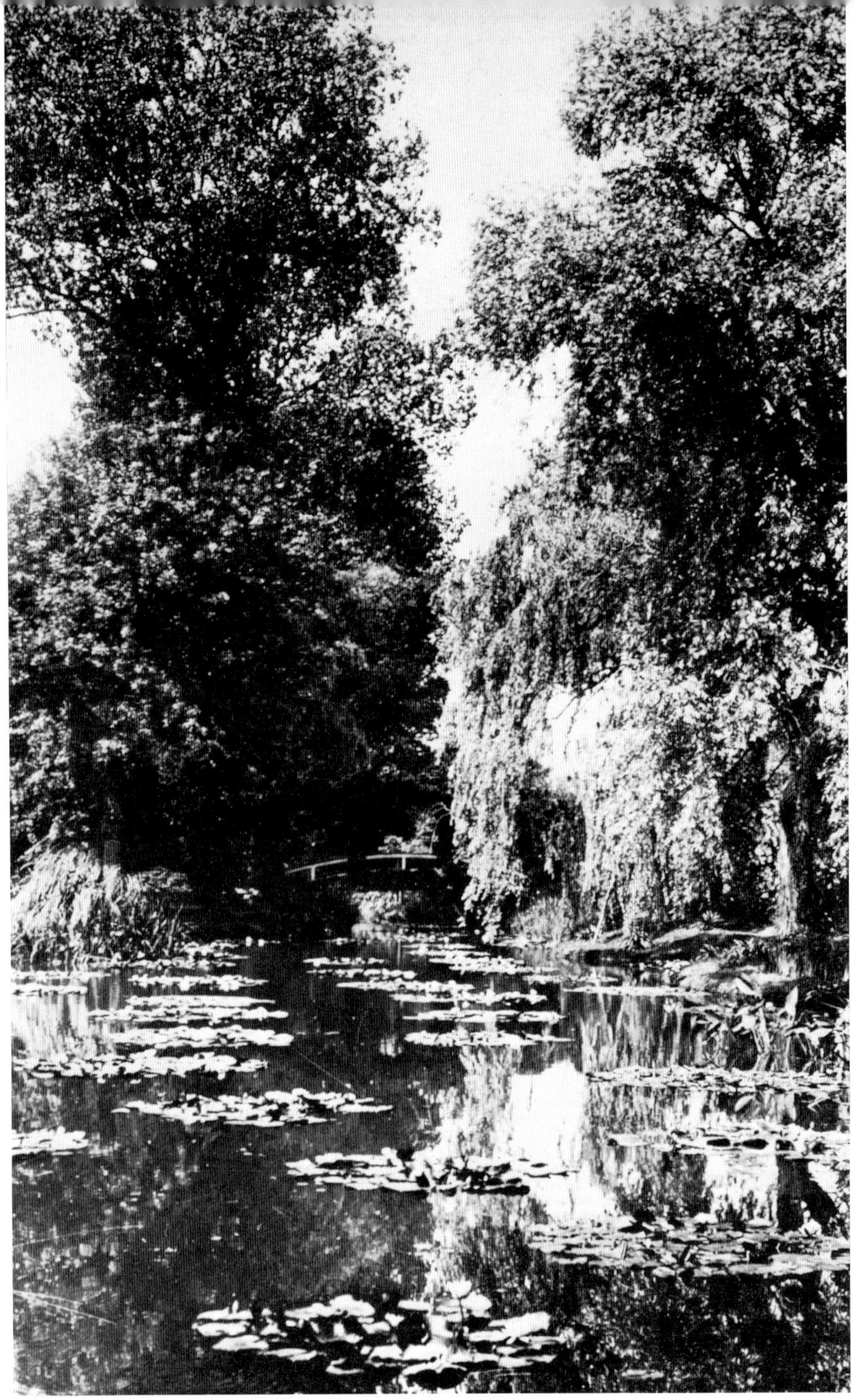

Monet was at last in a position to yield to the impulses of his rich and sensual nature, so often frustrated up to then. For his own pleasure, he literally constructed – such was the attention and single-mindedness he applied to the task – a garden whose subtle design and superb colours in summer and autumn excited the admiration of his guests. He succeeded in diverting a little arm of the River Epte and creating a pond that was soon covered with water lilies and kingcups. Having surrounded his Japanese garden with bamboo, weeping willows, poplars and other exotic plants, Monet made the resulting riot of different colours one of the recurrent subjects of the huge canvases he was still producing, in spite of the eye illness from which he suffered.

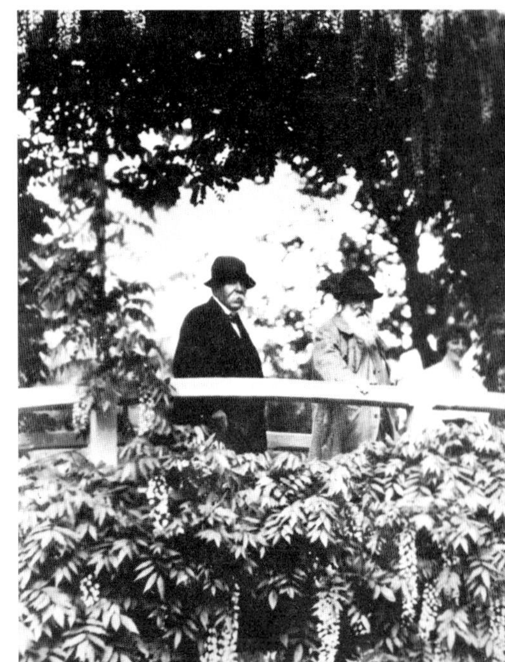

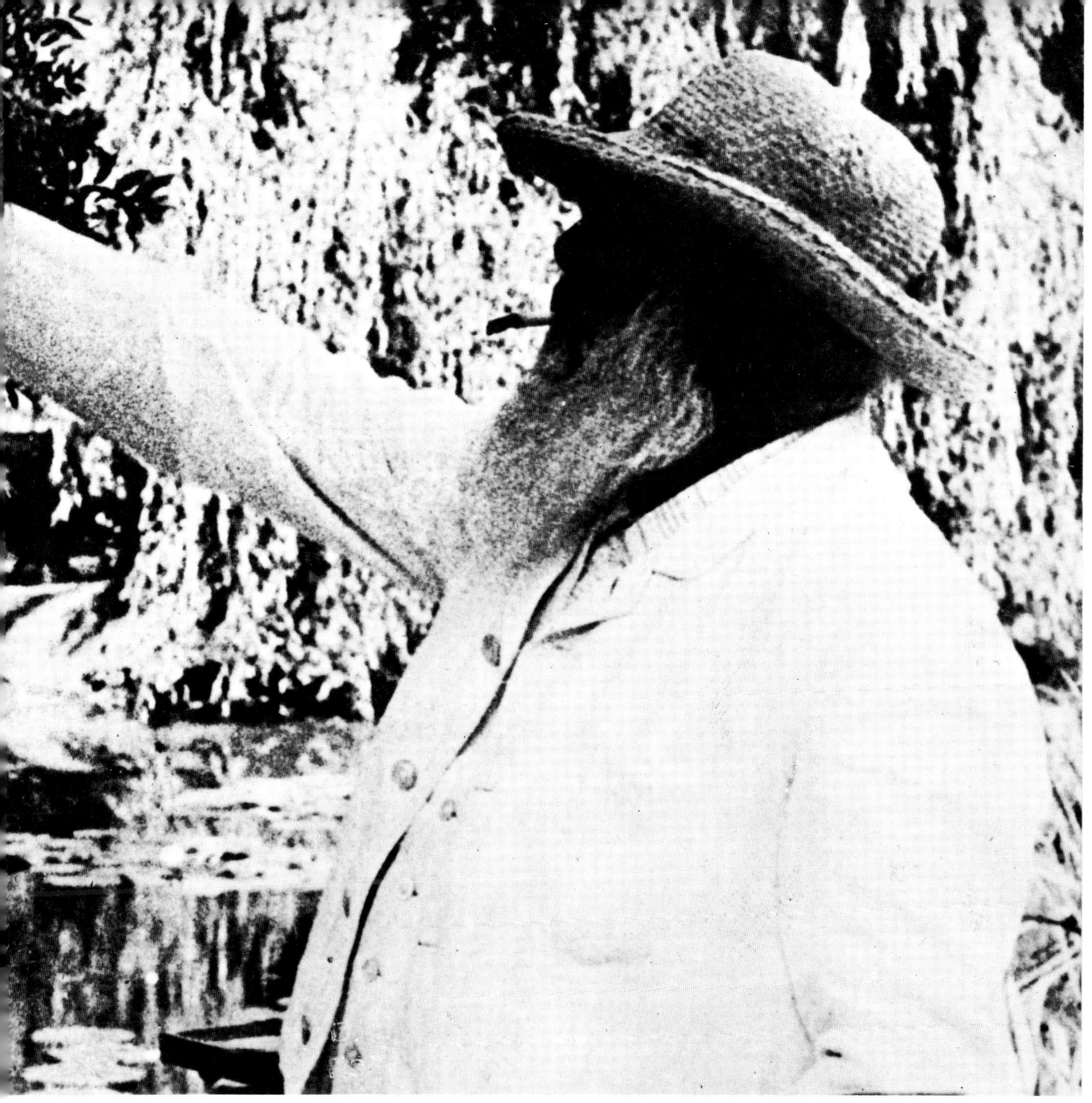

OPPOSITE Life at Giverny. The garden (ABOVE) with Monet and his friends on the bridge (BELOW).
ABOVE Monet painting in his garden.

The numerous friends and admirers who were frequent guests at the house were provided with the added pleasure of Madame Monet's delicious, refined and copious cuisine. Among those who came to admire Monet's 'own' corner of nature and his paintings were President Georges Clémenceau (whom Monet had met when he first arrived in Paris), the critics Geffroy and Mirbeau, Stéphane Mallarmé, Rodin, Renoir, Degas and the unsociable Cézanne (who, overawed by the celebrity of his fellow guests and possibly affected by the wines, found himself on the verge of tears).

And yet painting never ceased to be the very keystone of Monet's life and preoccupations. The pictures of his garden and the series of water lilies, in which Monet destroys form with colour, mean that, like Cézanne, (though for very different reasons), he can justifiably be described as one of the precursors of modern art.

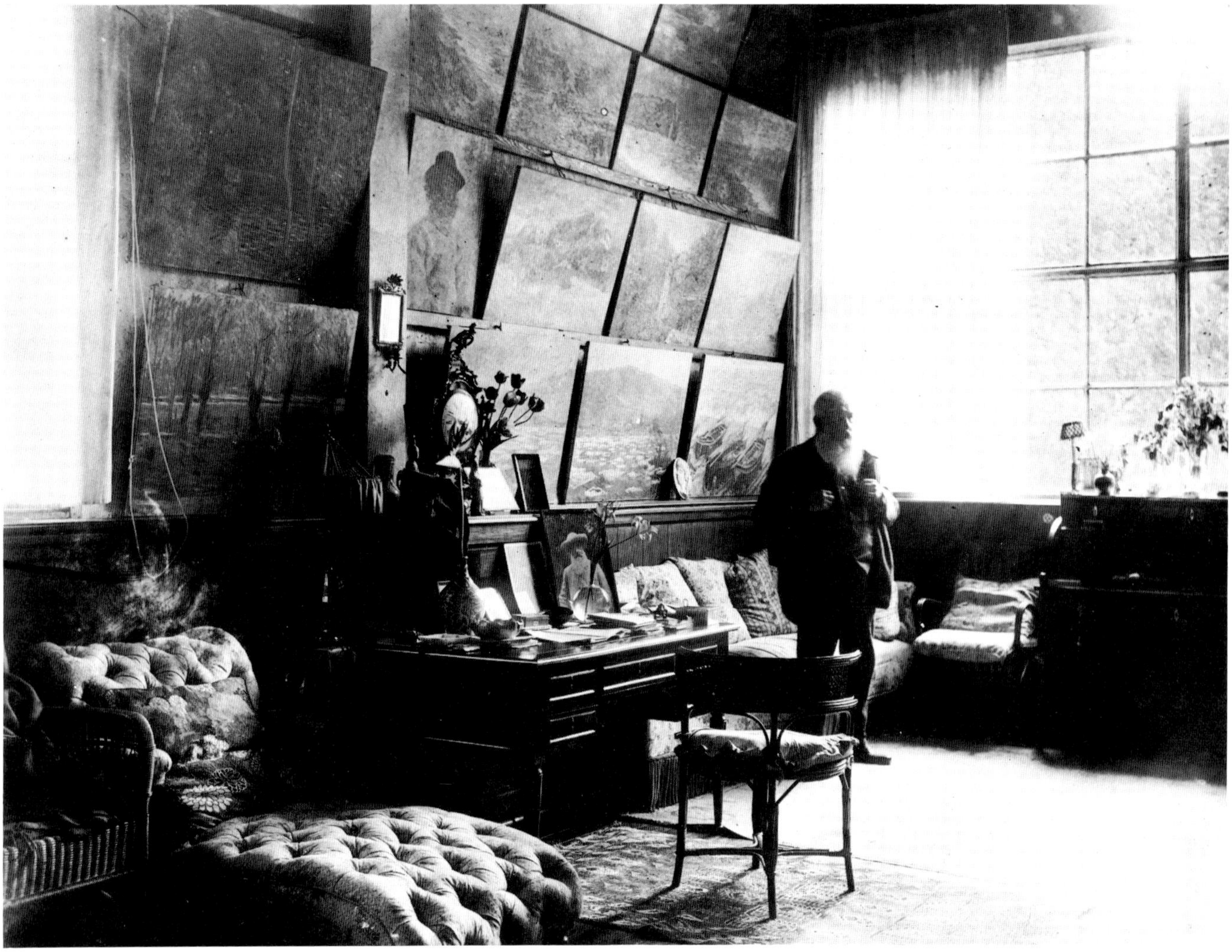

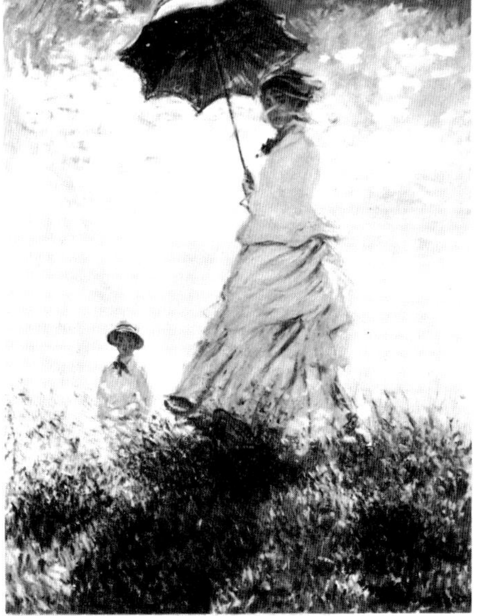

ABOVE Monet in his studio.
LEFT Claude Monet: *The Walk – Woman with a Parasol*, 1875 (Mr and Mrs Paul Mellon Collection, New York). Monet returned to this theme several times. One of two similar paintings made of Germaine Hoschedé can be seen in the photograph of his dressing-room (OPPOSITE).

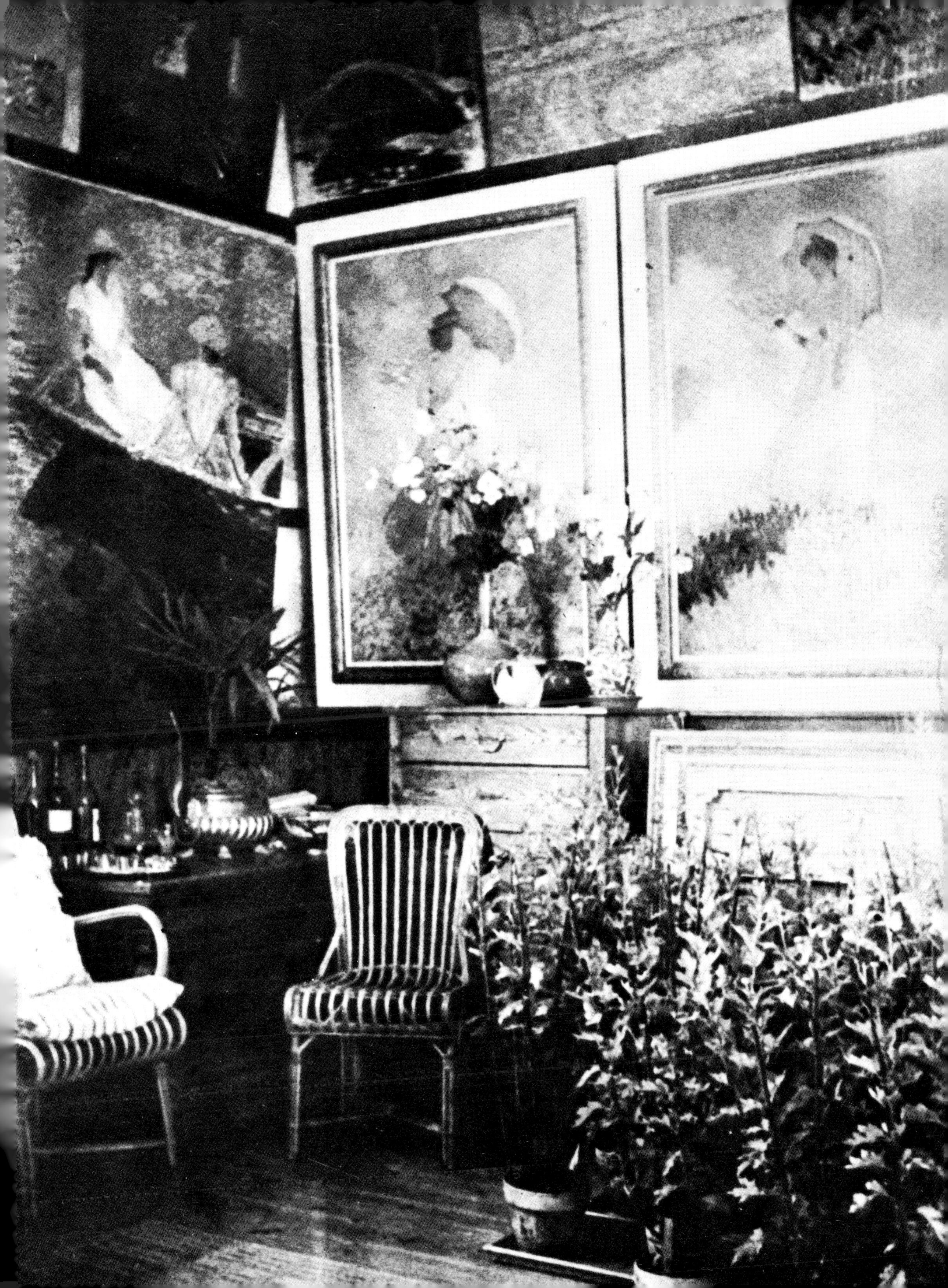

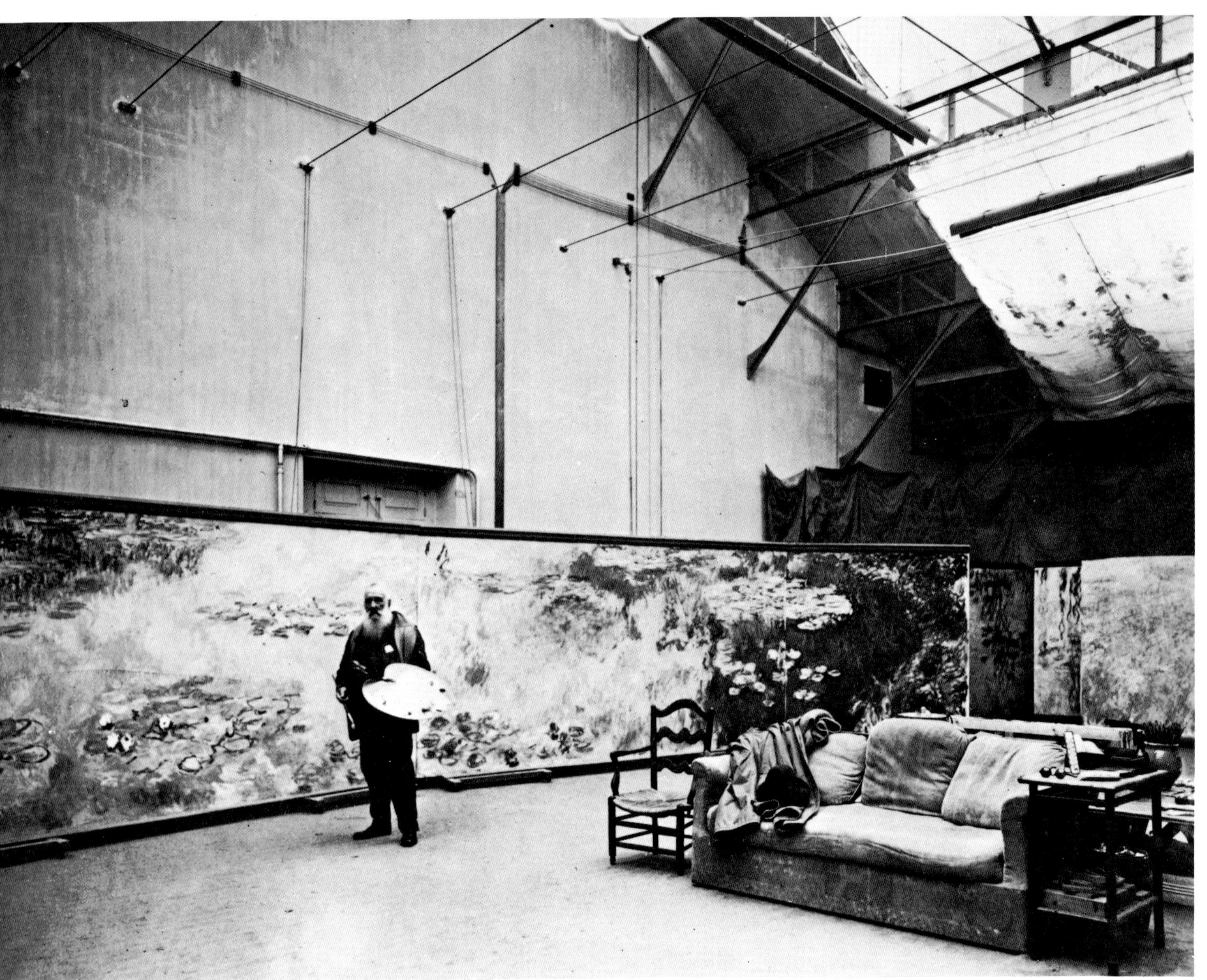

ABOVE Monet painting the Orangerie version of the water lilies, in the studio he had built for this series of large paintings.

While Pissarro, Cézanne, Renoir, Monet and Degas were at work on their last masterpieces, the very world that they had set out to celebrate had begun to disappear. As the century turned, they found that they were old men who had survived into an increasingly alien epoch. And with the First World War, of course, their world became little more than a memory, gilded by works whose skill and inventiveness are matched only by a love of life.

Select Bibliography

GENERAL

Bazin, G. *Impressionist Painting in the Louvre*. London, 1958.

Blanche, J.-E. *Essais et Portraits*. Paris, 1912.

Blanche, J.-E. *Propos de Peintre, de David à Degas*. Paris, 1919.

Champa, K. S. *Studies in Early Impressionism*. New Haven, Conn., 1973.

De Forges, M.-T. *Barbizon et l'école de Barbizon*. Paris, 1971.

Dictionary of Impressionism. London, 1973.

Dewhurst, W. *Impressionist Painting, Its Genesis and Development*. London, 1904.

Duret, T. *Histoire des peintres impressionnistes*. Paris, 1906.

Francastel, P. *L'impressionnisme : les origines de la peinture moderne de Monet à Gauguin*. Paris, 1937.

Gaunt, W. *The Impressionists*. London, 1970.

Gautier, T. 'Salon', *Le Moniteur Universel*, 3 July 1961.

Geffroy, G. *Histoire de l'impressionnisme*. Paris, 1894.

Halévy, D. *Pays parisien*. Paris, 1932.

Huyghe, R. *Formes*, Nov. 1931.

Huyghe, R. 'L'impressionnisme et la pensée de son temps'. *Prométhée*, Feb. 1939.

Lecomte, G. *L'art impressionniste d'après la collection privée de Durand-Ruel*. Paris, 1892.

Leymarie, J. *The Graphic Works of the Impressionists*. London, 1972.

Leymarie, J. *Impressionism*. Geneva, 1955.

Mirbeau, O. *Des artistes*. Paris, 1924.

Moore, G. *Confessions of a Young Man*. London, 1888.

Moore, G. *Impressions and Opinions*. London, 1891.

Moore, G. *Modern Painting*. London, 1893.

Pool, P. *Impressionism*. London, 1967.

Rewald, J. *The History of Impressionism*. 4th edition. London, 1973.

Roskill, M. *Van Gogh, Gauguin and the Impressionist Circle*. London, 1970.

Taylor, B. *The Impressionists and Their World*. London, 1959.

Zola, E. *Mes Haines*. Paris, 1928.

Zola, E. *Salons*; recueillis, annotés et présentés par F.W.J. Hemmings et R.J. Niess. Geneva, 1959.

FRÉDÉRIC BAZILLE

Daulte, F. *Frédéric Bazille et son temps*. Geneva, 1952.

Poulain, G. *Bazille et ses amis*. Paris, 1932.

PAUL CÉZANNE

Badt, K. *The Art of Paul Cézanne*. London, 1965.

Cézanne, P. *Letters*. Oxford, 1946.

Dunlop, *Complete Paintings of Cézanne*. London, 1972.

Lindsay, J. *Cézanne, His Life and Art*. London, 1969.

Rewald, J. *The Ordeal of Paul Cezanne*. London, 1950.

Venturi, L. *Les Archives de l'Impressionisme*. Paris–New York, 1939.

Vollard, A. *Paul Cézanne, His Life and Art*. New York, 1926.

EDGAR DEGAS

Boggs, J. S. *Portraits by Degas*. Berkeley, 1962.

Bouret, J. *Degas*. London, 1965.

Degas, H.G.E. *Letters*. Oxford, 1947.

Halévy, D. *Degas parle*. Paris, 1960.

Lemoisne, P.A. *Degas et son oeuvre*. 4 vols. Paris, 1947.

Valéry, P. *Degas, danse, dessin*. Paris, 1936.

EDOUARD MANET

Bataille, G. *Manet*. Geneva, 1955.

Hamilton, G. H. *Manet and His Critics*. New York, 1969.

Mallarmé, S. 'The Impressionists and Edouard Manet'. *Art Monthly Review*, 1877.

Perruchot, H. *Manet*. London, 1962.

Richardson, J. *Edouard Manet: Paintings and Drawings*. London, 1958.

Rouart, D. and Wildenstein, D. *Catalogue raisonné de l'oeuvre de Manet*. 2 vols. Lausanne, 1975.

Sandblad, N. G. *Manet: Three Studies in Artistic Conception*. Lund, 1954.

CLAUDE MONET

Clemenceau, G. *Claude Monet, Les Nymphéas*. Paris, 1928.

Clemenceau, G. *Claude Monet: Cinquante ans d'amitié*. Paris, 1965.

Geffroy, G. *Claude Monet, sa vie, son temps, son oeuvre*. Paris, 1922.

Cogniat, R. *Monet and His World*. London, 1966.

Isaacson, J. *Monet: Le déjeuner sur l'herbe*. London, 1972.

Seitz, W.C. *Monet*. London, 1960.

Wildenstein, D. *Monet, sa vie et oeuvre*, vol. 1. Lausanne, 1974.

BERTHE MORISOT

Angoulevent, M. *Berthe Morisot*. Paris, 1933.

Morisot, B. *Correspondence*; edited by D. Rouart. London, 1957.

Moskowitz, I. *Berthe Morisot*. New York, 1960.

Wildenstein & Co. *Berthe Morisot: Loan Exhibition of Paintings*. London, 1961.

CAMILLE PISSARRO

Lecomte, G. *Camille Pissarro*. Paris, 1922.

Marlborough Fine Art. *Pissarro in England*. London, 1968.

Pissarro, C. *Letters to His Son*; edited by J. Rewald, London, 1943.

Pissarro, L. R. and Venturi, L., *Camille Pissarro, son art, son oeuvre*. 2 vols. Paris, 1939.

PIERRE AUGUSTE RENOIR

Daulte, F. *Renoir*. London, 1973.

Fosca, F. *Renoir, his life and work*. London, 1969

Gaunt, W. *Renoir*. London, 1952.

Rouart, D. *Renoir*. Geneva, 1954.

Perruchot, H. *La vie de Renoir*. Paris, 1964.

ALFRED SISLEY

Daulte, F. *Alfred Sisley: catalogue raisonné de l'oeuvre peint*. Lausanne, 1959.

Gachet, P. *Lettres Impressionistes au Dr Gachet et à Murer*. Paris, 1957.

Acknowledgments

The author and publisher would like to thank the following museums, collections and private individuals by whose kind permission the illustrations are reproduced. Numbers are page numbers. Sources without parentheses indicate the owners of paintings and photographs; those within parentheses refer to illustration sources only.

7 Catalogue frontispiece. (Weidenfeld and Nicolson Archives, London.)
8 Phot: Napoleon III. Sirot Collection, Paris.
9 Cartoon. (Weidenfeld and Nicolson Archives, London.)
10–11 Manet: *Le Déjeuner sur l'Herbe.* Musée du Louvre, Paris (Bulloz, Paris).
12 Phot: Pissarro and his wife. Roger-Viollet Collection, Paris.
14 Phot: Courbet. Bibliothèque Nationale, Paris.
15 Phot: Corot. Sirot Collection, Paris.
16 Degas: *Portrait of Manet.* Denis Rouart Collection, Paris (Bulloz, Paris).
17 above Phot: Manet, Bibliothèque Nationale, Paris.
17 below Phot: Degas. Bibliothèque Nationale, Paris.
18 Phot: Cézanne. Atelier Cézanne, Aix-en-Provence (Robert Ratcliffe, London).
19 Phot: Zola. Sirot Collection, Paris.
20 Phot: Sisley. Durand-Ruel Collection, Paris.
21 Renoir: *Portrait of Claude Monet.* Mr and Mrs Paul Mellon Collection, New York.
22 above left Caricature. Bibliothèque Nationale, Paris.
22 above centre Caricature detail. Bibliothèque Nationale, Paris.
22 above right Monet: *Caricature from Panthéon Nadar.* Private Collection, Paris (Photo Routhier).
22 below Phot: Monet. Private Collection.
23 left Caricature of Nadar. Bibliothèque Nationale, Paris.
23 right Phot: Exhibition. Musée Kodak-Pathé, Vincennes.
24 above Boudin: *At the Saint-Siméon Farm.* Galerie Robert Schmit, Paris.
24 below Phot: Berthe Morisot. Denis Rouart Collection, Paris.
25 Manet: *Portrait of Berthe Morisot.* Denis Rouart Collection, Paris (Fabbri, Milan).
26 Renoir: *Portrait of Bazille.* Musée du Louvre, Paris (Bulloz, Paris).
27 Phot: Bazille. Bibliothèque Nationale, Paris.
28 Courbet: *Portrait of Alfred Bruyas.* Musée de la Ville, Montpellier.
29 above Phot: Paul Durand-Ruel. Durand-Ruel Collection, Paris.
29 below left Phot: Goncourt brothers. Caisse National des Monuments Historiques, Paris.
29 below right Phot: Baudelaire. Sirot Collection, Paris.
30 Phot: Renoir, Bibliothèque Nationale, Paris.
31 Bazille: *Portrait of Renoir.* Musée National des Beaux-Arts, Algiers (Bulloz, Paris).
32–3 Monet: *Le Déjeuner sur l'Herbe,* fragment. Musée du Louvre, Paris (Fabbri, Milan).
34 left Phot: Fontainebleau. Sirot Collection, Paris.
34 above Phot: Elephant rock. Sirot Collection, Paris.
34 below Phot: Weeping rock. Sirot Collection, Paris.
35 Phot: Barbizon. Sirot Collection, Paris.
36–7 Monet: *The Bas-Bréau Road.* Musée du Louvre, Paris.
37 Sisley: *Garde-Champêtre in the Forest of Fontainebleau.* Private Collection, Switzerland (Smeets Offset, Weert).
40 Bazille: *Monet after His Accident at the Inn in Chailly.* Musée du Louvre, Paris (Smeets Offset, Weert).
41 Renoir: *At the Inn of Mother Anthony, Marlotte.* Nationalmuseum, Stockholm.
42 Phot: Carrefour de l'épine. Sirot Collection, Paris.
43 Cartoon. Private Collection, Paris.
46 Phot: Fontainebleau. Sirot Collection, Paris.
47 Monet: *The Road from Chailly to Fontainebleau.* Private Collection, Paris (Giraudon, Paris).
48 Monet: *Le Déjeuner sur l'Herbe* (study). Pushkin Museum, Moscow (Wildenstein, Paris).
51 Sisley: *Village Street in Marlotte.* Albright-Knox Art Gallery, Buffalo.
52 Sisley: *The Avenue of Chestnut Trees.* Petit Palais, Paris (Bulloz, Paris).
53 Renoir: *Portrait of Alfred Sisley and His Wife.* Wallraf-Richartz Museum, Cologne (Bulloz, Paris).
54 Monet: *L'Hôtel des Roches Noires, Trouville.* Musée du Louvre, Paris (Giraudon, Paris).
56 below Phot: Berneval-sur-Mer. Sirot Collection, Paris.
56 top Phot: Le Havre. Sirot Collection, Paris.
57 Monet: *Honfleur Ferry* (detail). Walter Johr Collection, St Gall (Smeets Offset, Weert).
58 Phot: Honfleur. Sirot Collection, Paris.
59 top Phot: La Lieutenance, Honfleur. Sirot Collection, Paris.
59 below Phot: Chapelle Notre-Dame-de-Grâce. Sirot Collection, Paris.
60–1 Degas: *At the Seaside.* National Gallery, London.
63 top Manet: *The Battle of the Kearsarge and the Alabama.* Philadelphia Museum of Art, John G. Johnson Collection.
63 below Phot: Crew of *Kearsarge.* Musée de la Marine, Paris.
64 top Monet: *The Terrace at Sainte-Adresse.* Metropolitan Museum of Art, New York (Giraudon, Paris).
64 below Monet: *Impression, Sunrise.* Musée Marmottan, Paris (Bulloz, Paris).
67 Morisot: *The Green Parasol.* Cleveland Museum of Art, Ohio (Bulloz, Paris).
68 above Renoir: *View of the Seacoast near Wargemont.* Metropolitan Museum of Art, New York – Julia Emmons Bequest.
68 below Renoir: *Portrait of Marthe Bérard.* Sao Paolo Museum (Bulloz, Paris).
69 Renoir: *Madame Charpentier and Her Children.* Metropolitan Musuem of Art, New York (Fabbri, Milan).
70 Phot: Wargemont. Courtesy François d'Ault.
72 Phot: Trouville. Sirot Collection, Paris.
73 Monet: *Beached Boats.* Private Collection (Marlborough Fine Art, London.)
74 above Phot: Seascape. Sirot Collection, Paris.
74 below Phot: Etretat. Sirot Collection, Paris
75 Phot: Rocks at Etretat. Sirot Collection, Paris.
78 below (and detail above) Le Poitevin: *Bathing at Etretat.* Musée de Troyes.
79 Manet: *The Croquet Party.* Private Collection.
81 Manet: *On the Beach.* Musée du Louvre, Paris (Giraudon, Paris).
82 Renoir: *Victor Chocquet.* Fogg Art Museum, Harvard University, Cambridge, Mass. – Grenville L. Winthrop Bequest.
85 Pissarro: *Place de la République, Rouen.* (Durand-Ruel, Paris.)
87 Pissarro: *The Roofs of Old Rouen.* Toledo Museum of Art, Ohio (Durand-Ruel, Paris).
90–1 Monet: *The River.* Courtesy of the Art Institute of Chicago – Mrs Potter Palmer Collection.
92–3 Phot: Poissy. Sirot Collection, Paris.
95 left Phot: Château de Monte-Cristo. Private Collection.
96 above Monet: *The Bridge at Bougival.* Currier Gallery of Art, Manchester, New Hampshire (Bulloz, Paris).
96 below Phot: Bougival (Sirot Collection, Paris).
97 Morisot: *Quay at Bougival.* National Gallery, Oslo.
99 Phot: The Seine at Chatou. Roger-Viollet, Paris.
100–1 Pissarro: *Outskirts of a Village.* Musée du Louvre, Paris – Jeu de Paume (Marlborough Fine Art, London).
101 Pissarro: *The Seine at Marly.* Private Collection (Marlborough Fine Art, London.)
103 Pissarro: *The Road from Versailles to Louveciennes.* Bührle Collection, Zurich (Bulloz, Paris).
104–5 Monet: *La Grenouillère.* Metropolitan Museum of Art, New York – H.O. Havemeyer Collection.
106 Sisley: *Flood at Port-Marly.* Musée du Louvre, Paris (Bulloz, Paris).
107 Phot: The Machine, Port-Marly. Sirot Collection.
108 above Renoir: *The Seine at Argenteuil.* Portland Art Museum, Oregon (Fabbri, Milan),
108 below Monet: *Argenteuil.* Musée de l'Orangerie, Paris (Smeets Offset, Weert).
109 Monet: *The Artist's Garden at Argenteuil.* Wildenstein Collection, Paris (Smeets Offset, Weert).
110 Phot: Berthe, Eugène and Julie Manet. Musée de l'Ile de France.
111 Morisot: *Eugène Manet and His Daughter at Bougival.* Private Collection (Giraudon, Paris).
112 Renoir: *Le Déjeuner des Canotiers.* Phillips Collection, Washington.
113 left Phot: Hôtel Fournaise, Chatou. Sirot Collection, Paris.
113 right Phot: Hôtel Fournaise, Chatou, from road. Sirot Collection, Paris.
115 Monet: *Regatta at Argenteuil.* Musée du Louvre, Paris – Jeu de Paume (Smeets Offset, Weert).
117 Monet: *The Wooden Bridge at Argenteuil.* (Christie, Manson & Woods, London.)
118–19 Monet: *Camille in the Garden with Jean and Her Maid.* Bührle Collection, Zurich (Marlborough Fine Art, London.)
120–1 Monet: *Basin at Argenteuil.* Musée du Louvre, Paris (Bulloz, Paris).
121 below Monet: *The Bridge at Argenteuil.* Musée du Louvre, Paris – Jeu de Paume (Bulloz, Paris).
122 Manet: *Monet Working on His Boat in Argenteuil.* Neue Pinakothek, Munich (Bulloz, Paris).
123 Manet: *Argenteuil.* Musée des Beaux-Arts, Tournai (Bulloz, Paris).
124 left Monet: *The Artist's House at Argenteuil.* Courtesy of the Art Institute of Chicago.
124 right Phot: Monet's house. R. Walter Collection, Paris.
125 Renoir: *Monet Painting in His Garden.* Wadsworth Atheneum, Hartford, Conn.
126 top Monet: *Breakfast.* Musée du Louvre – Jeu de Paume (Smeets Offset, Weert).
126 below Caillebotte: *Self-Portrait.* Musée du Louvre – Jeu de Paume.
127 Monet: *The Railway Bridge at Argenteuil.* Musée du Louvre, Paris.
128 Phot: Cézanne. Atelier Cézanne, Aix-en-Provence (Robert Ratcliffe, London).
130–1 Morisot: *The Butterfly Hunt.* Musée du Louvre, Paris (Fabbri, Milan).
132 Morisot: *The Recorder Players.* Private Collection.
133 Morisot: *View from La Blottière, Mézy.* Private Collection.
134 Phot: Pontoise. Jean Hecquet Collection, Paris.
135 Pissarro: *View of Pontoise, Quai du Pothuis.* Kunsthalle, Mannheim (Fabbri, Milan).
136 Pissarro: *The River Oise near Pontoise.* Sterling and Francine Clark Art Institute, Williamstown, Mass.
137 Phot: River Oise. Jean Hecquet Collection, Paris.
138 above Phot: Pontoise. Jean Hecquet Collection, Paris.
138 below Phot: L'Hermitage, Pontoise. Jean Hecquet Collection, Paris.
139 Pissarro: *Le Chemin de l'Hermitage.* Wildenstein, New York (Bulloz, Paris).
141 Pissarro: *Market Shoppers in Pontoise.* Musée du Louvre, Paris.

142 above Pissarro: *Pontoise Market.* Private Collection (Sotheby & Co., London).
142 below Phot: Market day, Pontoise. Sirot Collection, Paris.
143 Pissarro: *The Pork Butcher.* Tate Gallery, London.
144 Phot: Water-mill. Jean Hecquet Collection, Paris.
145 Cézanne: *The Mill on the Couleuvre at Pontoise.* Staatliche Museen, East Berlin (Cooper-Bridgeman Library, London).
146 Manzana Pissarro: *An Impressionist Picnic.* Courtesy André Watteau, Paris.
147 Cézanne: *Pissarro on His Way to Work.* Musée du Louvre, Paris (Giraudon, Paris).
148 Morisot: *The Cherry Tree.* Denis Rouart Collection, Paris.
149 Pissarro: *The Road to Rouen, Pontoise.* Private Collection (Marlborough Fine Art, London.)
150 Phot: Auvers-sur-Oise. Sirot Collection, Paris.
150–1 Cézanne: *View of Auvers.* Courtesy of the Art Institute of Chicago (Bulloz, Paris).
152–3 Cézanne: *Le Château de Médan.* City Art Gallery, Glasgow – Burrell Collection (Fabbri, Milan).
154 Phot: Zola. Musée Kodak-Pathé, Vincennes.
155 Phot: Médan. Musée Kodak-Pathé, Vincennes.
156 Cézanne: *The House of Dr Gachet.* Musée du Louvre, Paris.
157 Cézanne: *La Maison du Pendu.* Musée du Louvre, Paris.
158 Pissarro: *Portrait of Gauguin;* Gauguin: *Portrait of Pissarro.* Musée du Louvre, Paris (Giraudin, Paris).
160 above Pissarro: *View of Pontoise.* Private Collection (Marlborough Fine Art, London.)
160 below Pissarro: *Woman in an Orchard.* Musée du Louvre, Paris – Jeu de Paume.
161 Pissarro: *Woman Guarding a Grazing Cow.* Private Collection (Marlborough Fine Art, London.)
162–3 Pissarro: *The Orchard.* Musée du Louvre, Paris (Giraudon, Paris).
164 Degas: *Ludovic Halévy at the Opera.* D. Halévy Collection, Paris (Bulloz, Paris).
167 above Degas: *The Foyer de la Danse at the Rue Le Peletier Opera.* Musée du Louvre, Paris (Fabbri, Milan).
167 below Degas: *Rehearsal for a Ballet.* Metropolitan Museum of Art, New York – H.O. Havemeyer Collection (Fabbri, Milan).
168–9 Manet: *Rue Mosnier with Flags.* Goldschmidt Collection, Chicago (Bulloz, Paris).
171 Degas: *The Collector of Prints.* Metropolitan Museum of Art, New York – H.O. Havemeyer Collection.
172 Manet: *Chez le Père Lathuille.* Musée des Beaux-Arts, Tournai (Bulloz, Paris).
173 Manet: *Café-Concert.* Private Collection (Giraudon, Paris).
174 Degas: *Absinthe.* Musée du Louvre, Paris – Jeu de Paume.
175 above Manet: *A Café on the Place du Palais-Royal.* City Art Gallery, Glasgow – Burrell Collection (Fabbri, Milan).
175 below Manet: *Bar at the Folies-Bergère.* Courtauld Institute of Art Galleries, London (Fabbri, Milan).
176 Manet: *La Servante de Bocks.* Musée du Louvre, Paris (Fabbri, Milan).
177 Degas: *Miss La La at the Cirque Fernando.* National Gallery, London.
178 Renoir: *La Loge.* Courtauld Institute of Art Galleries, London.
179 Degas: *Singer with a Glove.* Fogg Art Museum, Harvard University, Cambridge, Mass. (Fabbri, Milan).
180 above Monet: *Boulevard des Capucines.* Gallery of Art, Kansas City, Missouri – William Rockhill Nelson Collection.
180 below Phot: Pont des Arts. Société Française de Photographie.
181 Monet: *Rue Montorgueil, Paris, 30 June 1878.* Musée des Beaux-Arts, Rouen (Fabbri, Milan).
182 Manet: *Nana.* Kunsthalle, Hamburg.
183 Degas: *Jockey.* Private Collection, Zurich (Smeets Offset, Weert).
184–5 Degas: *At the Races, in Front of the Stands.* Musée du Louvre, Paris – Jeu de Paume (Bulloz, Paris).
186 *Manet: Racecourse near Paris.* Courtesy of the Art Institute of Chicago – Mrs Potter Palmer Collection.
187 above Degas: *Study of a Racehorse in Full Gallop.* Galerie Robert Schmit, Paris.
187 below Degas: *Carriage at the Races.* Courtesy of the Museum of Fine Arts, Boston – Arthur Gordon Tomkins Fund.
188 Manet: *The Gare St-Lazare* National Gallery, Washington (Smeets Offset, Weert).
189 Monet: *The Gare St-Lazare.* Musée du Louvre, Paris (Fabbri, Milan).
190 above Phot: Montmartre windmill. Sirot Collection, Paris.
190 below Phot: Gardens. Private Collection.
191 Pissarro: *The Tuileries.* Private Collection.
192 Monet: *View of the Tuileries.* Musée Marmottan, Paris (Smeets Offset, Weert).
193 Renoir: *Les Tuileries.* Private Collection.
194 Degas: *Portrait of Edmond Duranty.* City Art Gallery, Glasgow (Cooper-Bridgeman Library, London).
195 Manet: *Portrait of Stéphane Mallarmé.* Musée du Louvre, Paris – Jeu de Paume (Fabbri, Milan).
196 Degas: *The Morning Bath,* Courtesy of the Art Institute of Chicago (Smeets Offset, Weert).
197 Degas: *The Pedicure.* Musée du Louvre, Paris – Jeu de Paume.
198–9 Degas: *Portrait of the Bellelli Family.* Musée du Louvre, Paris (Bulloz, Paris).
200 left Phot: Degas at window. Bibliothèque Nationale, Paris.
200 centre Phot: Degas. Bibliothèque Nationale, Paris.
200 below Phot: Degas. Bibliothèque Nationale, Paris.
201 left Phot: Degas. Bibliothèque Nationale, Paris.
201 right Phot: Degas. Bibliothèque Nationale, Paris.
202–3 Degas: *The Cotton Office at New Orleans.* Musée Municipal, Pau.
204 left Phot: The Halévys. Bibliothèque Nationale, Paris.
204 right Phot: Ludovic Halévy. Sirot Collection, Paris.
205 Degas: *Degas and Valernes.* Musée du Louvre, Paris (Bulloz, Paris).
206 Degas: *Trying Hats at the Milliner's.* Gompel Collection (Bulloz, Paris).
207 Degas: *At the Milliner's.* Metropolitan Museum of Art, New York – H.O. Havemeyer Collection.
208 Degas: *Café in the Boulevard Montmartre.* Musée du Louvre, Paris (Bulloz, Paris).
209 Degas: *The Conversation.* Private Collection, USA (Acquavella Galleries, Inc.).
210 above Phot: Degas' niece. Bibliothèque Nationale, Paris.
210 left Phot: Degas. Bibliothèque Nationale, Paris.
211 above left Phot: Mme Howland. Bibliothèque Nationale, Paris.
211 above right Phot: Mlle Degas. Bibliothèque Nationale, Paris.
211 centre Phot: Mlle Degas. Bibliothèque Nationale, Paris.
211 below left Phot: Degas. Bibliothèque Nationale, Paris.
211 below right Phot: Caricature. Bibliothèque Nationale, Paris.
212 above left Degas: *Dancer with a Raised Arm.* Private Collection, Paris.
212 above right Phot: Dancer. Bibliothèque Nationale, Paris.
212 below Degas: *Seated Dancer.* Musée du Louvre, Paris.
213 Degas: *Dancers* Private Collection (Marlborough Fine Art, London.)
214 above Degas: *After the Bath – Woman Drying Herself.* M. Lutjous Collection (Giraudon, Paris).
214 below Degas: *The Tub.* Hill-Stead Museum, Farmington, Conn.
215 Degas: *Woman Ironing.* Private Collection (Marlborough Fine Art, London.)
216 Phot: Degas. Bibliothèque Nationale, Paris.
217 left Phot: Degas and friend. Bibliothèque Nationale, Paris (Roger-Viollet, Paris).
217 right Phot: Map. Bibliothèque Nationale, Paris (Roger-Viollet, Paris).
218 Cézanne: *The Village of Gardanne.* Courtesy of the Brooklyn Museum, New York – Ella C. Woodward and A.T. White Funds.
219 right Phot: Gardanne. Sirot Collection, Paris.
220 Phot: Aix-en-Provence. Bibliothèque Nationale, Paris.
221 Cézanne: *The Jas de Bouffan.* Private Collection (Marlborough Fine Art, London).
222 Cézanne: *L'Estaque and the Gulf of Marseilles.* Philadelphia Museum of Art.
223 above Cézanne: *The House and Garden of the Jas de Bouffan.* National Gallery, Prague.
224 Phot: The Jas de Bouffan J.R. Collection.
225 Cézanne: *The Jas de Bouffan.* Tate Gallery, London (Marlborough Fine Art, London.)
226 Cézanne: *Victor Chocquet.* Columbus Gallery of Fine Arts, Ohio.
228 Cézanne: *Montagne Ste-Victoire.* Musée du Louvre, Paris.
229 above Cézanne: *Montagne Ste-Victoire.* Courtauld Institute of Art Galleries, London.
229 below Phot: Montagne Ste-Victoire. Robert Ratcliffe, London.
230 Phot: Montagne Ste-Victoire. Bibliothèque Nationale, Paris.
231 Phot: Montagne Ste-Victoire. Robert Ratcliffe, London.
232 Cézanne: *Self-Portrait with a Hat.* Kunstmuseum, Berne (Fabbri, Milan).
233 Cézanne: *L'Estaque.* Musée du Louvre, Paris (Fabbri, Milan).
234–5 Sisley: *The Church at Moret.* Musée des Beaux-Arts, Rouen (Giraudon, Paris).
236–7 Sisley: *The Bridge at Moret.* Musée du Louvre, Paris – Jeu de Paume.
238 above left Sisley: *Cottage at Les Sablons.* (Private Collection).
238 above right Phot: Sisley. Sirot Collection, Paris..
238 below Sisley: *The Banks of the Loing, Moret.* Musée du Louvre, Paris – Jeu de Paume.
239 above Phot: Moret. Sirot Collection, Paris.
239 centre Phot: Women washing clothes. Sirot Collection, Paris.
239 below Phot: Sisley's house. Roger-Viollet, Paris.
240 above Morisot: *The Harbour at Lorient.* National Gallery of Art, Washington – Ailsa Mellon Bruce Collection.
240 below left Morisot: *Summer's Day.* National Gallery, London.
240 below right Morisot: *Julie Manet and a Friend.* Wildenstein, Paris.
241 above left Phot: Morisot. Denis Rouart Collection, Paris.
241 above right Phot: Morisot's studio. Sirot Collection, Paris.
241 below Phot: Morisot's studio. Sirot Collection, Paris.
242 above Morisot: *Le Déjeuner sur l'Herbe.* Private Collection (Bulloz, Paris).
242 below left Renoir: *Berthe Morisot and Her Daughter.* Petit Palais, Paris (Bulloz, Paris).
242 below right Phot: Letter. Denis Rouart Collection, Paris.
243 Morisot: *Woman Powdering Herself.* Musee du Louvre, Paris (Bulloz, Paris).
244 Pissarro: *Boulevard Montmartre – Effect of Rain.* National Gallery, London.
245 Pissarro: *Ile Lacroix, Rouen – Effect of Fog.* Philadelphia Museum of Art – John G. Johnson Collection (Fabbri, Milan).
246 Pissarro: *Pont St Pierre, Rouen.* Galerie Robert Schmit, Paris.

247 above Pissarro: *The Great Bridge at Rouen.* Museum of Art, Carnegie Institute, Pittsburgh, Penn.
247 below Phot: Pont St Pierre, Rouen. Sirot Collection, Paris.
248 above Pissarro: *Two Peasant Women.* Musée du Louvre, Paris.
248 left Pissarro: *Driving Sheep.* Musée du Louvre, Paris.
248 right Pissarro: *Labourers.* Musée du Louvre, Paris.
249 Pissarro: *Self-Portrait.* Tate Gallery, London.
250 above left Phot: Pissarro and wife. Private Collection, France.
250 above right Phot: Pissarro. Pissarro Family Collection.
250 below Phot: Pissarro and family. Pissarro Family Collection.
251 above left Phot: Pissarro and daughter. Pissarro Family Collection.
251 below left Phot: Pissarro and son. Pissarro Family Collection.
251 below right Phot: Pissarro. Pissarro Family Collection.
253 Renoir: *The Bathers* (study). Courtesy of the Art Institute of Chicago (Bulloz, Paris).
254 left Renoir: *Coco Drawing.* Durand-Ruel Collection, Paris.
254 top Phot: Cagnes-sur-Mer. Private Collection.
254 centre Phot: Renoir's studio. Durand-Ruel Collection, Paris.
255 Renoir: *The Washerwomen.* Baltimore Museum of Art – Cone Collection.
256 Renoir: *The Dance at Bougival.* Museum of Fine Arts, Boston (Fabbri, Milan).
257 Renoir: *The Harvest.* Musée du Louvre, Paris (Fabbri, Milan).
258 above left Phot: Renoir, Mme Renoir and Coco. (From *Renoir My Father* by Jean Renoir, Collins, 1962.)
258 above right Phot: Renoir at Fontainebleau. Sirot Collection, Paris.
258 below left Phot: Renoir painting. Durand-Ruel Collection, Paris.
258 below right Phot: Renoir. Durand-Ruel Collection, Paris.
259 above left Phot: Renoir's model. Sirot Collection, Paris.
259 above right Phot: Renoir painting. Sirot Collection, Paris.
259 below left Phot: Renoir. Durand-Ruel Collection, Paris.
259 below right Phot: Renoir. René Dazy Collection, Paris.
260 Renoir: *Trees and Cattle.* Private Collection (Cooper-Bridgeman Library, London).
261 Renoir: *Portrait of Ambroise Vollard.* Courtauld Institute of Art Galleries, London.
262 Phot: Renoir at Fontainebleau. Sirot Collection, Paris.
264 above Cézanne: *The Card Players.* Courtauld Institute of Art Galleries, London.
264 below Phot: Cézanne's studio. Courtesy of the Atelier Cézanne, Aix-en-Provence (Robert Ratcliffe, London).
265 above Cézanne: *View of the Château Noir.* Oskar Reinhart Collection, Winterthur.
265 below left Phot: well. Robert Ratcliffe, London.
265 below right Cézanne: *Rocks at Bibémus.* Mattioli Collection, Milan (Fabbri, Milan).
266 left Phot: Cézanne painting. Sirot Collection, Paris.
266 right Phot: Cézanne and Bernheim. Durand-Ruel Collection, Paris.
267 above left Phot: Cézanne's studio. J.R. Collection.
267 above right Cézanne: *Mardi Gras Sketches.* Musée du Louvre, Paris.
267 below Cézanne: *Still Life with Water Jug.* Tate Gallery, London.
268 left Monet: *Rouen Cathedral.* Musée du Louvre, Paris (Giraudon, Paris).
268 right Phot: Rouen Cathedral. Roger-Viollet, Paris.
269 Monet: *Rouen Cathedral.* Musée du Louvre, Paris – Jeu de Paume (Giraudon, Paris).
270 above Cézanne: *Les Grandes Baigneuses.* National Gallery, London.
270 below Phot: Cézanne with *Les Grandes Baigneuses.* Sirot Collection, Paris.
272 Monet: *Water Lilies at Giverny.* Private Collection, Basle (Smeets Offset, Weert).
273 Phot: Monet by pool. Bibliothèque Nationale, Paris.
274 Phot: Monet by bridge. Roger-Viollet, Paris.
275 Monet: *Water Lilies.* Musée du Louvre, Paris (Service de Documentation Photographique).
276 above Phot: Giverny. Roger-Viollet, Paris.
276 below Phot: Monet on bridge at Giverny. Kuroki Family Collection.
277 Phot: Monet painting at Giverny. Bibliothèque Nationale, Paris.
278 above Phot: Monet in studio. Roger-Viollet, Paris.
278 below Monet: *The Walk – Woman with a Parasol.* Durand-Ruel Collection, Paris.
279 Phot: Monet in drawing-room. Courtesy of the Estate of Lilla Cabot Perry.
280 Phot: Monet in studio. Durand-Ruel Collection, Paris.

The publisher has taken all possible care to trace and acknowledge the ownership of all the illustrations. If by chance we have made an incorrect attribution we apologise most sincerely and will be happy to correct the entry in any future reprint, provided that we receive notification.

Paintings researched by Enid Gordon.
Photographs researched by Robert Gordon.
Picture editor Julia Brown.
Cartography by Tony Garrett.

Index

Page numbers in *italic* indicate illustrations and their captions.